Solutions Manual
Nile R. Leach

Operations Management
Strategy & Analysis

Fourth Edition

Krajewski/Ritzman

Solutions Manual
Nile R. Leach

Operations Management
Strategy & Analysis

Fourth Edition

Krajewski/Ritzman

▲▼ **ADDISON-WESLEY PUBLISHING COMPANY**

Reading, Massachusetts • Menlo Park, California • New York
Don Mills, Ontario • Wokingham, England • Amsterdam • Bonn
Sydney • Singapore • Tokyo • Madrid • San Juan • Milan • Paris

ISBN 0-201-60719-0
10 9 8 7 6 5 4 3 2 1 VG 98979695

Preface

This *Solutions Manual* is one of three ancillary publications prepared exclusively for instructors using **Operations Management: Strategy and Analysis,** 4th edition. The other publications are:

Instructor's Manual
Sample course outlines, general teaching notes for each chapter of the text, detailed lecture outlines, case notes to all the cases found in the main text, and a formula review section.

Transparency Masters
The transparency masters feature key exhibits, diagrams, and problems from the book. Many of these are new visuals that do not appear in the text and are designed to complement the lecture notes found in the Instructor's Manual.

Acetates
A set of over 100 four-color overhead acetates of key exhibits from the text are available to adopters.

Test bank and Computerized Test bank
Containing close to 2000 items, the test bank has been carefully coded according to level of difficulty, and every effort has beenmade to include a balance of conceptual and technique-oriented questions. New to this version are 4-5 short answer questions, and 1-2 essay questions per chapter that will further test the student's conceptual understanding of the material and their critical thinking skills. The computerized test bank allows instructors to custom-design their examinations, and is available in both IBM PC and Macintosh versions.

Two additional ancillary publications are available for sale to students.

Study Guide
Detailed chapter notes, self-testing questions, additional review problems, and solutions for all chapters and supplements. The Study Guide is also coordinated with the lecture notes in the Instructors' Manual and the Transparency Masters.

Computer Models for Operations Management
A collection of analytical software models designed to support operations management decisions, example problems and mini-cases designed to enhance learning.

This manual provides complete answers to all end-of-chapter study questions and problems. The study question answers are typically four or five sentences, enough to fully answer the questions without introducing new material. The problem solutions are worked out in detail.

My thanks go to those who have carefully prepared previous editions of the Solutions Manual. Some of this work has been reused or updated from earlier editions, and it was nice to have an accurate foundation to build upon. Thank you Sharen Pflughoeft of Colorado State University, for conscientiously performing a thorough check of the solutions. I also want to acknowledge the authors and the many faculty reviewers, for their support and inputs along the way. Thank you to Julia Berrisford and Kate Morgan of Addison-Wesley for the opportunity to do this work, for coordinating this project, and for guidance, patience and support.

Nile R. Leach

Table of Contents

Solutions Manual
Nile R. Leach

Operations Management
Strategy & Analysis

Fourth Edition

Krajewski/Ritzman

Chapter 1

Operations as a Competitive Weapon

Study Questions

1. A possible list of inputs and outputs for these firms follows.

Firm	Inputs	Outputs
Hotel	Patrons Clerks Buildings Capital	Rested patron
Public warehouse	Customer merchandise Employees Equipment Building	Stored merchandise, available when needed
Paper mill	Wood, chemicals Employees Plant	Paper products
Newspaper company	Paper, ink, chemicals Employees Machines	Newspapers
Supermarket	Food Clerks, manager Customers Building Capital	Satisfied customers
Home office of bank	Management Building Money Computers	Efficient branch offices Satisfied investors

2. This question asks the student to characterize a firm, or some portion of it, in terms of the chapter's framework. Students might relate to a firm where they worked, make a phone call to a new firm, or even visit a facility in the area.

3. The distinctions between manufacturing and service organizations include the nature of the product, inventories, customer contact, response time, markets, facility size, capital intensity, and quality measurement. Comparisons can be found in Figure 1.2. As for organizations that do not fit the pattern shown in Figure 1.2, the U.S. Postal Service is a service organization that fits many of the characteristics of a manufacturer, except that its output cannot be inventoried (for an extended period) and short response times are desirable. Another example is a milk producer who deals in local markets, cannot inventory the product for extended periods, and has a perishable product.

4. Employment shifts to the service sector are explained more by lagging productivity in the service sector than by reduced demand for goods. In terms of real dollars, consumer demand for goods is more than three times what it was in 1940. Because of rapid productivity improvements in manufacturing, goods are now produced by a smaller proportion of the work force. On the other hand, lagging productivity in the service sector requires proportionally more workers to

fulfill demand for services. The trend of increased jobs in the service sector is expected to continue, but the rate of change will likely decrease. Productivity in services will gradually increase due to improved technology, better job design, and computerization. Jobs in manufacturing are likely to continue to diminish as a percentage of the total number of jobs. However, the actual number of manufacturing jobs will probably remain about constant. U.S. manufacturers are showing an increased will and ability to compete in world markets, and many jobs vulnerable to automation and computerization have already disappeared.

5. Figure 1.4a suggests a downward trend in U.S. productivity *increases* over the last few decades. Such trends cannot continue if current standards of living are to be maintained. Many reasons have been offered for the downward trend of productivity. Increased government regulations, lagging investment, changing work-force composition and attitudes, and high wage rates have been suggested as obstacles to increased productivity. However, the responsibility for productivity gains ultimately lies with the managers and employees at individual organizations. Productivity in the manufacturing sector is rebounding, but progress in the service sector has been spotty.

6. Operations managers are responsible for managing the lion's share of the resources in an organization. Productivity improvements in operations will have a large impact on the performance of the organization.

7. Operations managers must have many skills, ranging from decision-making processes to interpersonal behavior, and a background in diverse areas such as international business and business law. Disciplines such as quantitative methods, organizational behavior, general management, management information systems, economics, international business, business ethics, and law all contribute to the field of operations management.

8. This study question is intended to prepare students for the first discussion question. It is possible to reach a consensus that the goal of all for-profit organizations is to make money. However, where individuals would draw the lines for responsibility varies widely.

9. Cross-functional coordination reduces the elapsed time required for some functions which have traditionally been performed sequentially. Many companies report that a cross-functional team approach to identifying a market, designing the product, finding qualified suppliers, manufacturing, and distribution will get the product to the customer sooner than if those activities are performed in isolation.

10. This question is intended to show the effects on other functions of a seemingly insignificant marketing decision. Some of the considerations associated with the green paint option follow.

   - Product design: resist deterioration in sunlight, protect metal from corrosion, bonding and coverage of primer and clear paint coats, application techniques.
   - Purchasing: locate/qualify supplier, price/delivery of green paint, effect on volume, price of green and black paint at various volumes
   - Industrial engineering: setup time and procedure to switch paint colors.
   - Operations: scheduling green and black cars, coordinate paint materials handling, storage
   - Quality: performance and acceptance standards for green paint, defective application
   - Manufacturing engineering: specify techniques, equipment for switching and applying green paint,
   - Finance: investment in new equipment, green paint inventory
   - Human resources: train workers to switch paint color, apply green paint
   - Accounting: inventories, costs of green paint inventory, setup charges
   - Distribution: inventories of black and green cars, inventories of green paint for repairs

- Sales and service: inform customers of option availability, train service employees to repair damaged green cars, distribute inventory of green paint for repairs

11. Surface-mount technology has resulted in faster, smaller and more reliable electronic products. Purchasing must find suppliers that are competent in this technology. Solderless connections improve the environment by removing the need to control vapor from melted solder. Quality is improved by a better design and more reliable assembly process. Operations must learn the new technology and update the production process and facility. Some assembly workers may be displaced. Marketing will have the opportunity to sell a better product at a lower price. In the event that a surface-mounted component is defective, service personnel must be trained in how or whether to attempt the repair.

12. Western State University.
    - Advisers will need to learn how to use the new system.
    - Bookstores will have better information for ordering texts.
    - Peak work load for clerical staff during registration should be reduced.
    - Department chairs might use current enrollment as basis for adding needed sections.
    - Better information about course availability tends to increase utilization. Instructors will teach fewer classes in which the number of students is far below enrollment limits.
    - Management information system development, refinement, and new applications for available information will require more computer systems personnel and expertise.
    - Students will need to learn how to use the new system. Immediate feedback on enrollment and total cost (tuition, fees and books) might affect individual class enrollment decisions and permit better coordination of work and class schedules.

13. The types of decisions relating to the **design** of a production system deal with operations design, process design, new technologies, job design, capacity, location, and layout. These design decisions have an enduring effect: The results are not easily changed once they are implemented. Design decisions answer questions such as the following:
    - What inputs and processes are best for the products and services being produced?
    - How much specialization is desired in each job and department?
    - How should each job be designed to balance productivity and quality of work life?
    - How much capacity is needed?
    - How much capacity slack should be included?
    - Where should the facilities be located and whom should they be near: customers, suppliers, or employers?
    - How should multiple facilities be organized: by product, geography, or type of customer?
    - What physical arrangement is desired?
    - Is openness or privacy to be emphasized?

Decisions relating to the **operation** of a production system are concerned with inventory and output plans as well as output control. Choices regarding materials management, production and staffing plans, master production scheduling, inventory control systems, and scheduling are all part of deciding how to operate a production system. These decisions have a shorter time horizon, and choices can be changed somewhat more easily than can design choices. Specific questions related to operations include the following:
- Should inventory, scheduling, purchasing, and distribution be centralized or decentralized?
- How much inventory is needed, and where will it be kept?
- How should suppliers be selected?
- How frequently should new orders be placed?

- What size should orders be?
- What decision support system should be used?
- What output and inventory levels are best?
- Should there be overtime? A stable work force?
- What output levels are desired for individual products or services?
- How is it best to cushion shocks from last-minute rushes or supplier stockouts?
- What customers have priority?
- What shift schedule is best?

14. Linking decisions means that plans, policies, and actions within operations must all be focused in the same direction and be mutually supportive if organizational goals are to be met. Individual decisions may make sense on their own, but collectively they may not add up to the best result.

Discussion Questions

1. Refer to Study Question #8. Some responsibilities generally supported will include responsibilities to stockholders, to customers, to the environment, to provide safe working conditions, and to pay taxes. More debatable are responsibilities to provide medical care, maternity leave, child care, retirement, minimum wages and responsibilities to the community other than paying taxes.

2. The problems of unions faced with international competition is mentioned in the Caterpillar video. As this is written, NAFTA and GATT are in the news. It is hoped that some of the issues will still be remembered at the time this is published. Will lifting trade barriers expose American workers to competition from workers in undeveloped economies? Or will increased opportunity to compete result in more exports and more jobs? With decreased tariffs will multinationals move operations elsewhere to escape unions and environmental regulations? It is hoped that students will recognize that effective operations management is the key to favorable outcomes.

Problems

1. **Boehring University.**
   a. Productivity has decreased slightly compared to Solved Problem 1 (productivity = 1.00). Value of output:

   $$60 \frac{\text{students}}{\text{class}} \times 3 \frac{\text{credit - hours}}{\text{student}} \times \left(\frac{\$100 \text{ tuition} + \$100 \text{ state support}}{\text{credit - hour}} \right) = \$36,000 \Big/ \text{class}$$

   Value of input: labor + material + overhead

   $$\frac{\$4000 + \left(\dfrac{\$20}{\text{student}} \times 60 \text{ students} \right) + \$31,000}{\text{class}} = \$36,200 \Big/ \text{class}$$

   Productivity ratio:

   $$\text{Productivity} = \frac{\text{Output}}{\text{Input}} = \frac{\$36,000}{\$36,200} = 0.994$$

b. Labor productivity has increased about 5% compared to Solved Problem 1.

Value of output is the same as in part a: $36,000/class

Labor-hours of input:

$$16\frac{\text{hours}}{\text{week}} \times 16\frac{\text{weeks}}{\text{class}} = 256 \frac{\text{hours}}{\text{class}}$$

Productivity ratio:

$$\text{Labor Productivity} = \frac{\text{Output}}{\text{Labor Input}} = \frac{\$36,000}{256 \text{ hours}} = \$140.63 /\text{hour}$$

The $192 season ticket price is not used in this calculation. It is a "red herring."

2. **Natalie Attired.**

   a. Labor productivity

   Value of output is:

$$\left(8 \text{ defectives} \times \$90 /\text{defective}\right) + \left(120 \text{ garments} \times \$200 /\text{garment}\right) = \$24,720$$

   Labor-hours of input is given: 360 hours

$$\text{Labor Productivity} = \frac{\text{Output}}{\text{Labor Input}} = \frac{\$24,720}{360 \text{ hours}} = \$68.67 /\text{hour}$$

   b. Value of output increased by ($24,720 – $20,680)   = $4,040.

   Cost of materials decreased by (132 – 128) x $70   = $ 280.

   Total value of improvements   = $4,320.

   Under the terms of gain sharing, half ($2,160) is available for sharing. The workers worked a total of 360 hours, so on an hourly basis the quality bonus is:

$$\frac{\$2160}{360 \text{ hours}} = \frac{\$6.00}{\text{hour}}$$

3. **Suds and Duds Laundry.**

   Output per person does not vary much whether it is Sud, Dud or Jud working. Productivity declines when all three are present. Perhaps there isn't enough work to keep three persons occupied, or perhaps there is not enough work space or equipment to accommodate three workers.

Week	Number of Workers	Input (Labor-hours)	Output (Shirts)	Output/Input Ratio:
1	2	24	68	2.83 shirts/hour
2	2	46	130	2.83 shirts/hour
3	3	62	152	2.45 shirts/hour
4	3	51	125	2.45 shirts/hour
5	2	45	131	2.91 shirts/hour

4. Compact disc players.

Value of Output: $200

Value of Input: Labor + Materials + Overhead

$$\text{Productivity} = \frac{\text{Output}}{\text{Input}} = \frac{\$200}{\$15 + \$60 + \$30} = 1.905$$

5% productivity improvement => 1.905 x 1.05 = 2.000

Given productivity = 2.000, and the value of output = $200,
we solve for the cost of inputs:

$$\text{Productivity} = \frac{\text{Output}}{\text{Input}} = \frac{\$200}{\text{Input}} = 2.00$$

$$\text{Input} = \frac{\$200}{2.00} = \$100$$

The cost of inputs must decrease by ($105 − $100) = $5.

a. A $5 reduction in material costs is $5/$60 = 8.33%

b. A $5 reduction in labor costs is $5/$15 = 33.33%

c. A $5 reduction in overhead costs is $5/$30 = 16.67%

5. Big Black Bird Company.

The Big Black Bird Company problem is based on a product made by Raven Industries. None of the numbers are representative of actual costs or volume.

a. Productivity

<u>Original situation</u>:

Value of output:

$$(2500 \text{ uniforms} \times \$200) = \$500,000$$

Value of input:

$$(2500 \text{ uniforms} \times \$120) = \$300,000$$

Productivity ratio:

$$\text{Productivity} = \frac{\text{Output}}{\text{Input}} = \frac{\$500,000}{\$300,000} = 1.67$$

<u>Overtime situation</u>:

Value of output:

$$(4000 \text{ uniforms} \times \$200) = \$800,000$$

Value of input:

$$(4000 \text{ uniforms} \times \$144) = \$576,000$$

Productivity ratio:

$$\text{Productivity} = \frac{\text{Output}}{\text{Input}} = \frac{\$800,000}{\$576,000} = 1.39$$

Productivity decreases by:

$$\frac{1.67 - 1.38}{1.67} \times 100\% = 17.37\%$$

b. Labor productivity

Original situation:
Value of output (from part a) is: $500,000
Labor-hours of input:
(70 x 40 hours) + (30 x 40 hours) = 4000 hours
Labor productivity = $500,000/4000 hours = $125/hour

Overtime situation:
Value of output (from part a) is: $800,000
Labor-hours of input:
(70 x 72 hours) + (30 x 72 hours) = 7200 hours
Labor productivity = $800,000/7200 hours = $111/hour

Labor productivity decreases by:

$$\frac{125-111}{125} \times 100\% = 11.2\%$$

c. Gross Profits

Original situation: $500,000 – $300,000 = $200,000
Overtime situation: $800,000 – $576,000 = $224,000

Weekly profits increased.

Note: Wartime situations typically decrease productivity, and increase profitability.

Chapter 2

Operations Strategy

Study Questions

1. The following questions answered by mission statements are listed in the text:
   - What business are we in? What should it be ten years from now?
   - Who are our customers? or clients?
   - What are our basic beliefs?
   - What are our key performance objectives by which to monitor success?

2. When a mission is too narrow the firm may miss promising growth opportunities. If new products are not continually introduced the firm will decline when their product reaches the end of its life cycle (such as a firm specializing in the manufacture of slide rules).

3. Environmental scanning, adjusting to environmental change, and identifying distinctive competencies are all part and parcel of corporate strategy. Finding the "threats" to the organization is a necessary first step to corporate strategy, which involves plans for coping with environmental change. Identifying distinctive competencies provides a basis for formulating effective strategies.

4. One way collaborative efforts, joint ventures and licensing agreements can be distinguished is in the different ways the firms are motivated to work together. In a collaborative effort the organizations bring to the table complimentary strengths (distinctive competencies) which make it possible to produce goods or services that the organizations could not provide individually. Joint ventures are motivated by tariffs that limit access to markets. A foreign firm having the technical ability to produce, will form a joint venture with a domestic firm having a developed distribution system. Trade agreements foster licensing of technology. When countries agree to honor each others copyrights and patents, one firm may obtain a license to use technology from another firm having ownership rights. For example, Dolby noise-reduction technology is licensed by electronics firms located in countries having trade agreements with the United States.

5. Mass production is demonstrated by the Model T; high volume, no customization, and competition on the basis of low cost. Mass customization uses computers, robotics and telecommunication to bring the efficiencies of mass production to markets as small as a single customer. Flexible automation attains economies of scale by producing small quantities of a large variety of customized products. Mass customization competes on the basis of cost, high-performance design, development speed, and customization.

6. The following table shows customer benefit packages.

Product or Service	Facilitating Resources	Core Services	Peripheral Services
Insurance Policy	Agent Computers Office equipment	Coverage Dividends	Reduced anxiety Claims service
Airline trip	Airplane Airport Attendants	Transportation to another location	Less weary Baggage handling Car parking/rental
Dental work	Dentist Chair Drill	Cavity repaired Tooth pulled	Better smile Anesthesia Insurance billing

7. The following table compares competitive priorities.

Business	Time	Other Priorities
Air-package delivery	Fast delivery time	Volume flexibility
Passenger Airline	On-time delivery	Low cost operations, Consistent quality
Airplane Manufacturer	Development Speed	High-performance design, Customization

8. Being able to reduce lead times gives a firm an important competitive advantage, given that customers value quick delivery. Honda's ability to introduce many motorcycle models quickly, Motorola's quick introduction of its MicroTac phone, and Atlas Door's ability to compress delivery times are three good examples. Time reductions resulted in higher market share and profit margins.

9. To prepare for a peak period of business, campus bookstores will increase the inventory of text books on the shelves, extend operating hours, schedule extra staff, and shift office staff to provide more direct customer services. Competitive priorities are fast delivery (facilitated by stocking textbooks) and volume flexibility (facilitated by opening additional checkout lanes).

10. Competitive priorities
    a. *McDonald's*. A fast-food service with strengths in offering consistent quality, low price, and fast delivery time.
    b. *McDonnel-Douglas*. A manufacturer of aerospace and defense products generally in a job-shop environment. McDonnel-Douglas competes on the basis of development speed, high-performance design, and customization.
    c. *Old MacDonald's*. Farms generally produce commodities, which compete on the basis of low cost operations and consistent quality.

11. Positioning strategies for businesses that work with paper.
    a. *Resume preparation*. **Process focus.** A job-shop providing a custom tangible product which requires high-performance design and on-time delivery.
    b. *Photocopy shop*. **Intermediate Strategy.** A job-shop with dominant lines providing standard products in moderate volume, with options such as collation, and binding. Competes on the basis of consistent quality and fast delivery time.
    c. *Paper mill*. **Product focus.** Produces a commodity, which competes on the basis of low cost operations and consistent quality.
    d. *Regional personal-check printer*. **Intermediate to Product focus.** High volume production, flow lines with standard options, assembles to order.
    e. Recycling center. **Product focus.** High volume production of several commodities, dominant flowlines with a few optional processes.

Process focus
x---Resume preparation

Intermediate Strategy
x---Photocopy Shop

Product focus
Recycling Center ---x   **Check printing ---x**   **Paper Mill ---x**

12. Positioning strategies of businesses that involve aluminum or microwaves.

   a. *Rockets.* Low volume, high priced customized products with competitive priorities on high-performance design. A **process focus.**

   b. *Subcontractor to aerospace.* A job shop with low to moderate volume. **Intermediate strategy.**

   c. *Aluminum refinery.* A commodity produced with a capital intensive flow line system and competing on low cost operations. A **product focus.**

   d. *Microwave oven manufacturer.* High-volume, standardized products with competitive priorities of consistent quality and low cost. A **product focus.**

Process focus
x---**Space launch vehicles**
x---**Microwave towers**
Intermediate Strategy
x---**Aerospace subcontractor**
Product focus
Microwave manufacturer ---x
Radar Detector ---x
Aluminum refinery ---x

   e. *Communications tower builder.* Low-volume, custom product designed for a specific location and assembled as a project. A **process focus.**

   f. *Radar detector manufacturer.* High-volume, standardized product competing on cost and consistent quality. A **product focus.**

13. Positioning strategies of businesses that work with utilities or with education.

   a. *Electricity generation.* A capital-intensive, high-volume service. Produces a commodity with low cost operations. A **product focus.**

   b. *Builder of power plants.* A one-of-a-kind project. **Process focus.**

   c. *Power plant designer.* A one-of-a-kind service arranged by discipline. **Process focus.**

   d. *Bookstore.* A moderate-volume standard service arranged by process (receiving area, checkout area, shelf area with departments) combined with single-unit book ordering. An **intermediate strategy.**

Process focus
x---**Power plant construction**
x---**Power plant design**
x---**Power plant construction**
Intermediate Strategy
x---**Savings and Loan**
x---**Bookstore**
Product focus
Electric Utility ---x

   e. *College campus.* Jumbled flows, facilities dedicated to purpose (chemistry, music, P.E., classroom, administration), produces custom products and competes on the basis of high-performance design. Low cost operations are debatable. A **process focus.**

   f. *Savings and loan branch office.* Moderate volume, combines standardized deposit and checking services and customized loan services. Competes on consistent quality. Arranged according to activity (loan department, safe-deposit box, tellers). An **intermediate strategy.**

14. Customized, low-volume products:

    a. Large work-in-process (WIP) inventories are needed to buffer operations from the uncertainties and jumbled flows so that resources can be utilized more effectively. Manufacturing lead time is proportional to (WIP). This makes it difficult to provide short customer delivery times. Low costs are difficult to achieve when the skills and resources needed vary considerably with customized products. With low volume, per-unit product design costs are high.

    b. High capital intensity is unlikely because large outlays of capital typically can be justified only with high volumes.

15. Product focus:

    a. Forward planning is more feasible because the products are standardized and demands are more predictable. The rewards are also greater because high capacity utilization is a top concern and can be improved by planning further into the future.

    b. The same items are purchased repeatedly and in high volumes. This justifies the effort required to negotiate long-term contracts with suppliers. The more predictable usage rates also allow the firms to give their suppliers more advance notice of their supply needs.

    c. Line flows make it unnecessary to decouple operations with large amounts of work-in-process inventory. An emphasis on low cost also argues against such excesses. With standard products, it is possible to push WIP through to finished goods, where (it is hoped) it will be sold.

16. The concept of life cycles demonstrates that sales of any product or service will eventually diminish. To ensure the long-run profitability of the firm, new products or services must be planned to replace the existing ones.

17. Sealtight Company.

    a. Product A is in the later maturity stage. Annual sales are substantial but are starting to erode. Price increases are negligible, and unit profit margins are decreasing. The net result is declining profits. Product B is experiencing rapid growth in sales and high unit profit margin, representative of the growth stage.

    b. Low cost would be a higher competitive priority for product A because sales are leveling out and price competition may be intensive.

18. Singh DeCajon.

    a. The June and Ozzie Stone Show is in decline. Sales and profit margin are dropping quickly. Dysfunctional Family Matters is in growth to maturity. Sales and profit margins are rapidly increasing. This may occur after the first season and the show has proven to be a hit. Negotiated contracts for subsequent seasons then dramatically increase in price.

    b. Low cost is a higher competitive priority for the Stones. Since these are reruns, the only significant costs are for rights. Old shows may have extended lives in late-night time slots if the rights are cheap enough. One reason the movie *It's a Wonderful Life* has become a Christmastime tradition is that the rights were allowed to expire. It's a TV freebie.

19. If a firm decides to **enter and exit early**, the operations function should have volume flexibility and be able to produce a wide variety of low-volume products or services. If a firm decides to **enter and exit late**, the firm likely will compete on high volume and low cost, typical of a **product focus**. The **enter-early-and-exit-late** strategy requires that the firm be able to make the transition from a low-volume, flexible producer to a high-volume, low-cost producer.

20. A customer-driven operations strategy is guided by customers' needs and competitors' abilities. Marketing analyzes customers and competitors, then identifies customer needs and strategies that offer competitive advantages. That information is used to determine competitive priorities. Operations then designs processes and systems having the capabilities and strengths needed to match competitive priorities.

21. LFKHS needs more volume flexibility. The ability to change staffing levels to match daily workload requirements is a priority. Chaparral, on the other hand, seeks to maximize the utilization of its capital-intensive facility, making volume flexibility of less concern. LFKHS closely monitors its hospital census and patient acuity. Overtime is the alternative of choice to handle short-time surges. An employee's work schedule therefore is not very predictable. To handle seasonal peaks and unexpected demand surges, the hospital census is less than 70 percent for most of the year, giving it a lower facility utilization than at most other organizations.

22. Customer contact is most needed at LFKHS. It is so intensive that patients must be located on site to receive their customized services. Inventories at LFKHS are for medical and surgical supplies, which are raw materials. There is no finished goods inventory as at Chaparral, which carries a substantial finished goods inventory at the mill for a variety of standard items. LFKHS has no finished goods inventory because it is a service organization. However, even if it were a manufacturer, there would be little finished goods inventory because of the extensive amount of customization.

Discussion Questions

1. The sign implies that the decision to go to the abandoned mine, once made, cannot be easily reversed. Product and service planning and competitive priorities are some of the most strategic decisions made by a firm. Therefore these decisions must be made with care. For example, investing large amounts of resources in a venture that is supposed to produce products or services with long life cycles is not compatible with competitive priorities that emphasize customization.

2. Broadened missions usually result from perceived threats or opportunities. These are often accompanied by mergers designed to obtain strengths and capabilities needed to compete in a new arena. Some issues associated with narrowed missions are described below (Discussion Question 3).

3. Firms that are narrowing their missions usually have entered a business in which they have no distinctive competencies. This could result from misguided strategy, as when AT&T went into the highly competitive personal computer business with high overhead and a work force left over from their monopoly era. At other times this happens through mergers of firms which have some similar interests and some divisions which just tag along as part of the deal. Subsequent sales of divisions that don't fit the surviving firm's mission result in additional reorganizations. Very broad missions sometimes make it difficult for stock analysts to assess the value of the firm. By splitting the businesses into segments having similar characteristics, full value is realized by stockholders.

4. It is hoped that this question will broaden horizons if students recognize the impact of international business on their local economy. My most recent information indicates that Pacific-Rim countries enjoy the fastest growing economies.

5. Technology Management. To identify a market segment, we need to determine answers to questions such as: Which colleges and departments within colleges currently offer the subject? What do instructors desire in the way of textbook support? Is there a trend toward Technology Management courses? Are there other Technology Management texts? Some needs assessment can be accomplished by survey, but response rate may be low. A high-investment strategy would be to ask or hire instructors to review and critique a list of topics, then an outline, then a draft. The core

benefit is education about the subject in the form of a textbook. Peripheral services include instructor support in the form of ancillary publications.

6. Escher's Fish and Fowl. It is usually not possible to excel in all eight competitive priorities simultaneously. Mediocrity is a predictable result.

7. The fast food restaurant making hamburgers to stock is recognizable as McDonalds. Service-clerk duties include taking customer orders, filling entire orders from stock, and collecting payment. Short product shelf lives require close finished-goods inventory management. When a trademark sandwich is ordered without the special sauce, customers are asked to "Please step aside". Meanwhile, materials committed to a similar sandwich in stock (but with sauce) may expire and have to be thrown away. McDonalds handles volume flexibility by opening and closing service lanes.

   An alternative operation is Wendy's, which assembles hamburgers to order. When materials are held at the stage just before final assembly, they can be used to complete a wide variety of different sandwiches. Since no finished-goods stock exists, when customers say "hold the sauce" there is no delay or waste of materials. Service clerks specialize. One clerk takes orders and payment. Others fill portions of the order. Orders are processed in single-file. Throughput is normally restricted by transactions at the cash register. At busy times, throughput is increased by splitting the bottleneck operation. One clerk takes customer orders, another receives payment. The Wendy's operation has some characteristics of assembly lines and a product focus. Therefore, the impact of new menu items on the production operations must be carefully considered.

8. Grandmother's Chicken.
   a. Kathryn Shoemaker's strategic plans include the following:
      - Product and service plans: Should the new location offer a new mix?
      - Competitive priorities: If the product mix and service mix are different at the new location, the thrust could be on low volumes and high quality.
      - Positioning strategy: Again, depending on the competitive priorities and a new location, the process could be product-focused or process-focused.
      - Quality management: Should the goal be reliability or top-of-the-line quality?
      - Process design: What processes will be needed to make chicken dinners in the addition?
      - New technologies: Is it time to automate? Is this why there is a problem in service times.
      - Capacity: How large should the addition or new facility be?
      - Location: Should we locate in Uniontown or expand in Middlesburg?
   b. Attitudes toward nutrition could change the demand for fried chicken. Competitors such as Boston Chicken may be planning to move to Uniontown or even Middlesburg. There may be a trend toward demands for ever-faster service, which can not be supported by the processes specified in the "unique recipe". The economy of Uniontown might not be supportive of restaurant services. Shoemaker should also consider the availability of key resources, such as servers, whole chickens, spices, and cooking oil. Will Uniontown labor organize?
   c. The possible distinctive competencies at Grandmother's Chicken Restaurant include the "unique recipe", the homey atmosphere, and friendly, prompt service.

9. Russell's Pharmacy probably should not move to Large Island.
   a. Russell's strategic plans should include the following:
      - Product and service plans: Should new services be offered?
      - Competitive priorities: How could Russell respond to price competition in Large Island?
      - Quality management: Will accurate prescriptions justify higher prices?
      - Capacity: How large would the Large Island facility be?
      - Location: Should Russell move to Large Island?

b. Environmental factors include a declining and aging population in River City, and strong price competition in larger markets. An aging population indicates increased demand for prescription drugs. Russell might consider offering in-home services needed by older clients.

c. Russell's distinctive competency is knowing his customers and their health histories, and accurate, if occasionally slow or costly service. If he moves to Large Island, he would not know his customers, who would be less forgiving of slow or costly service.

10. Wild West, is recognizable as U S WEST, but many other "baby bells" are in a similar position.

a. Strategic plans include reducing overhead, re-engineering operations, and investing in new technologies to meet competition. The "do nothing" option of remaining a local monopoly telephone company is not viable because of competition from cable systems and wireless systems which are capable of business and personal communication. If the mission is too broad, Wild West should do as U S WEST did, and sell its financial services and commercial real-estate businesses. Those businesses do not match their distinctive competencies.

b. One environmental issue is whether communication, like health care, will be viewed as a "right" and therefore should be free. A significant portion of Wild West's business is governed by regulatory agencies. Customer service in their core business is essential to maintaining a favorable regulatory environment. Other business opportunities, such as manufacturing and providing information services, are prohibited by the same court order that formed the "baby bells" from AT&T.

c. Wild West's distinctive competency is in connecting people (or machines) for the purpose of communication. A weakness is high overhead inherited from the era of telecommunication monopoly.

11. An order qualifier is a "must have" feature. Without this feature, the item does not receive further consideration. An order qualifier for a college might be that it not be located in the student's home town or that classes not begin before noon. For a bicycle, it might be that the gearshift components are made in Japan.

12. The air-powered hand tool might be recognized as Ingersoll-Rand. Concurrent engineering involving customers, marketing, design engineers, purchasing and manufacturing is credited with producing a superior product while reducing development time from 4 years to 18 months. Hurdles to overcome involve moving the design engineers from plush air-conditioned, quiet offices out to the hot, noisy manufacturing area so that communication will occur and the design can be manufactured. Similar moves are required of marketing and purchasing. I-R encountered initial reluctance to these moves, followed by acceptance and endorsement by the participants.

Supplement A

Decision Making

Study Questions

1. Break-even analysis applied to *product screening* — Design studies result in a rough idea of the relationship between volume and total production costs. This could be plotted as the total cost line on a break-even chart. Market tests result in a rough idea of price and volume relationship for the product. Price times volume would generate a revenue line (or curve, if price varies with volume). Inspection of the chart would then show whether any price-volume combination would generate a profit. If profit is possible, the product survives the break-even screen.

   Break-even analysis applied to *alternative processes* — Alternative processes result in different relationships between volume and total production costs. Break-even charts show which process is favored as volume changes. We could also use this concept in product screening, where the total revenue curve is the result of multiplying price times volume, and the total cost line is replaced by a curve, or piecewise linear curve showing the lowest process cost at each volume.

   Break-even analysis applied to *facility location* — Location alternatives are associated with fixed costs and variable costs in a similar manner to that when comparing alternative processes. Comparing locations is analogous to comparing processes.

2. Newlywed apartment location. The preference matrix indicated the best location of those considered, based on the given criteria . This points out that 1) not all locations are considered by this technique, 2) the criteria may not be complete, and 3) both quantitative and qualitative factors should be considered in making decisions.

3. The slope of the total revenue line is the price per unit. The slope of the total cost line is the cost per unit. When the difference between the price and cost is small, the difference between the slope of the total revenue and total cost line is small. The two lines will be near each other over a large range of volume. If costs are slightly underestimated, an expected profit could turn into a loss. On the other hand, since the total revenue and total cost lines do not converge or diverge rapidly with small changes in volume, the analysis is less sensitive to volume forecast errors.

4. This question is intended to focus thought on characteristics of environments which encourage risk taking. Discussion may invovle judgement about the risks and rewards presented in a situation. Business students often cite job opportunities as the basis for their choice of college major. That could be an indication of a pessimistic, maximin, or risk-avoiding approach to decision making.

5. The stadium will only be built once. The law-of-averages approach of the expected value may not be an appropriate criterion for evaluating this decision tree. If there is a large potential for second-guessing, and if the penalty for overbuilding is severe, a maximin, wait-and-see decision criteria may be used to avoid risk. The stadium may be built for 42,000, while an option for future expansion to 50,000 seats is included in the design. Based on the Rockies league leading attendance during their first two seasons at Denver's Mile-High Football Stadium the option to expand Coors Field from 42,000 to 50,000 seats was implemented during initial construction.

6. No. The expert's forecast will still be wrong. No matter how qualified, when it comes to forecasting, no one has perfect information.

Problems

1. Williams Products.

   a. Break-even quantity (Q) = Fixed costs / (Unit price – Unit variable costs)

   $$Q = \frac{F}{p-c} = \frac{\$46{,}500}{\$17/\text{unit} - \$5/\text{unit}} = 3875 \text{ units}$$

   The graphic approach is shown on the following illustration. Two lines must be drawn:

   Revenue: $= \$17Q$

   Total cost: $= \$46{,}500 + \$5Q$

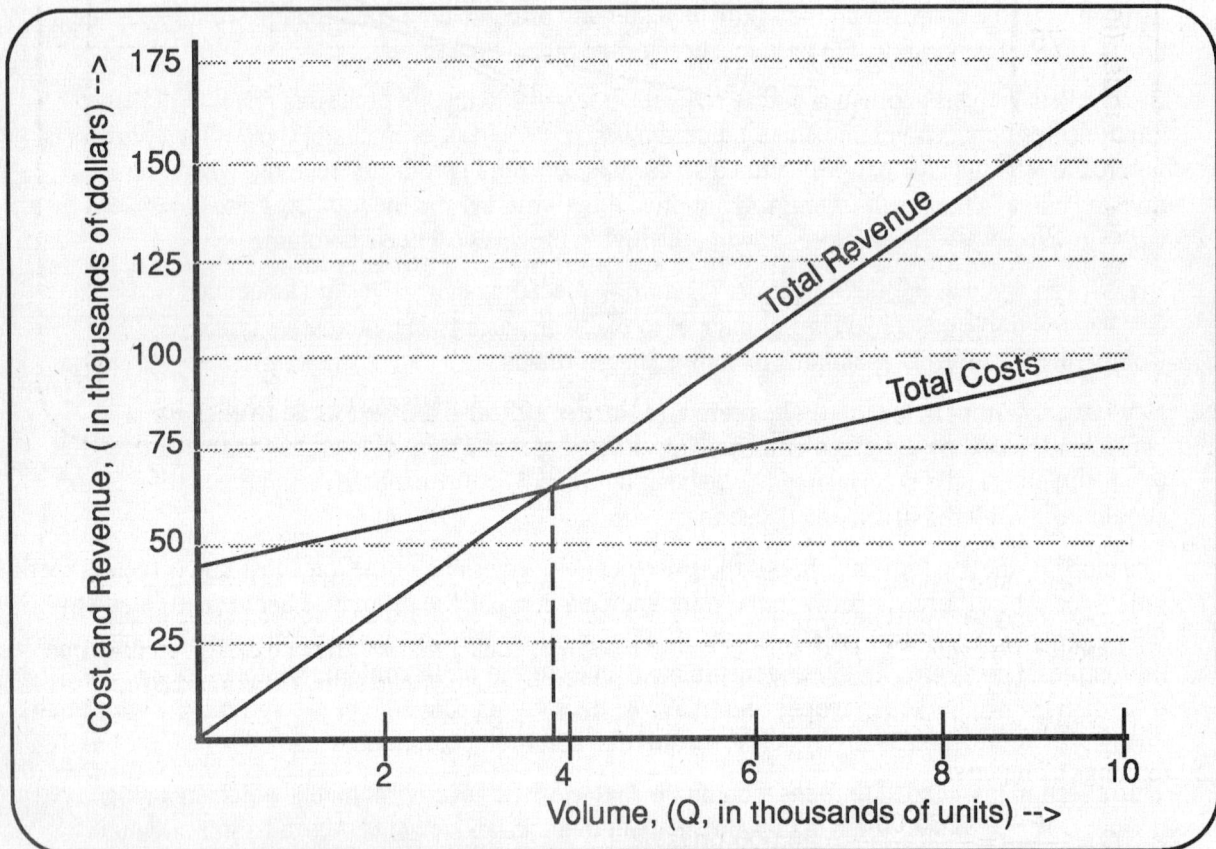

   b. Profit = Revenue – Total cost

      = $Qp - (F + Qc)$

      = $8{,}000(\$12.50) - [\$46{,}500 + 8{,}000(\$5)]$

      = $\$100{,}000 - \$86{,}500$

      = $\$13{,}500$

   c. Profit = Revenue – Total cost

      = $Qp - (F + Qc)$

      = $10{,}000(\$11.50) - [\$46{,}500 + 10{,}000(\$5)]$

      = $\$115{,}000 - \$92{,}500$

      = $\$18{,}500$

   Therefore the strategy of using a price of $11.50 will result in a greater contribution to profits.

   A graphic approach to solving parts b and c is shown on the next illustration.

Break-Even Analysis: Graphical Solution for Williams Products, (b & c)

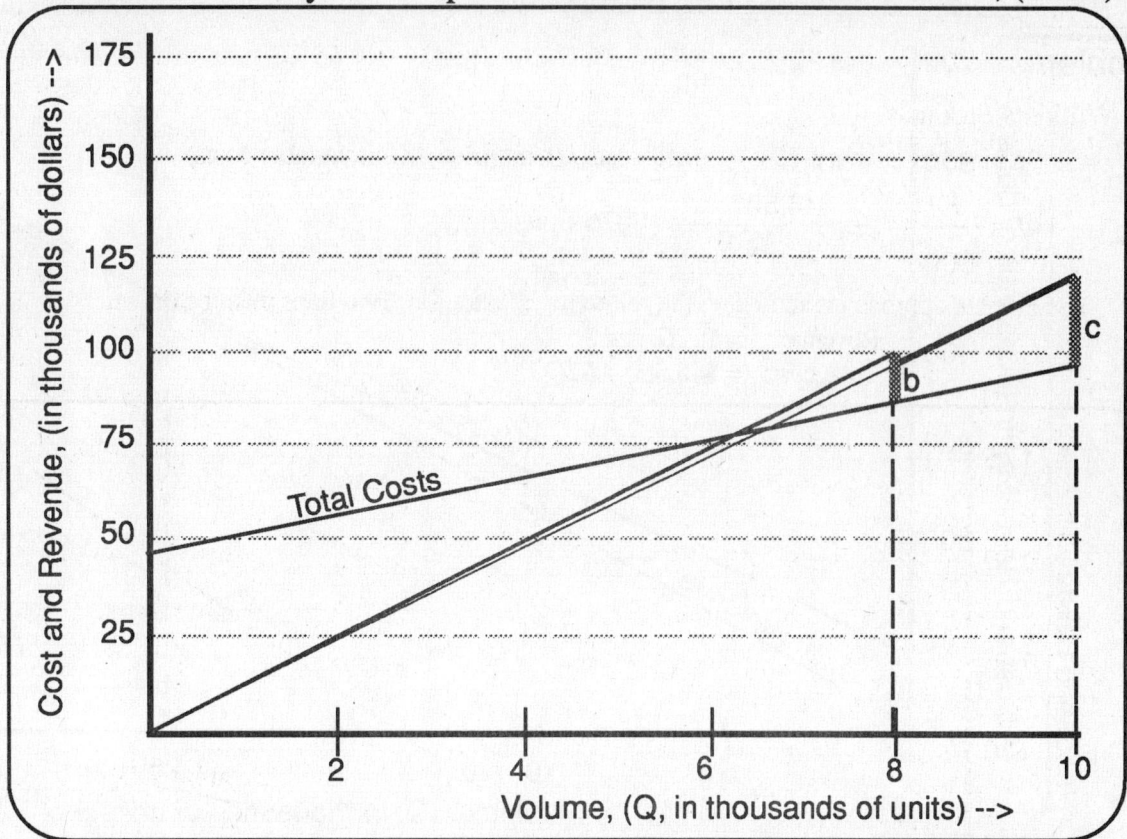

d. Williams must consider whether she will follow a strategy to **enter early and exit late** or to **enter early and exit early** because she is getting involved in the introduction stage of the product life cycle. She must also consider how this product fits within her existing product line from the perspective of required technologies and distribution channels. Other marketing, operations, and financial criteria must also be considered.

2. Jennings Company.

a. $Q = \dfrac{F}{p-c} = \dfrac{\$80,000}{\$22 - \$18} = 20,000$ units

The graphic approach is shown on the next page. The two lines are :

Revenue: $= \$22Q$
Total Cost: $= \$80,000 + \$18Q$

b. Alternative 1: Sales increase by 30 percent, to 22,750 units.

Profit $= Qp - (F + Qc)$
$= 22,750(\$22) - [\$80,000 + 22,750(\$18)]$
$= \$11,000$

Alternative 2: Cost reduction to 85 percent results in \$15.30 unit costs.

Profit $= Qp - (F + Qc)$
$= 17,500(\$22) - [\$80,000 + 17,500(\$15.30)]$
$= \$37,250$

Therefore the cost reduction leads to higher profits in this example.

Break-Even Analysis: Graphical Solution for Jennings Company

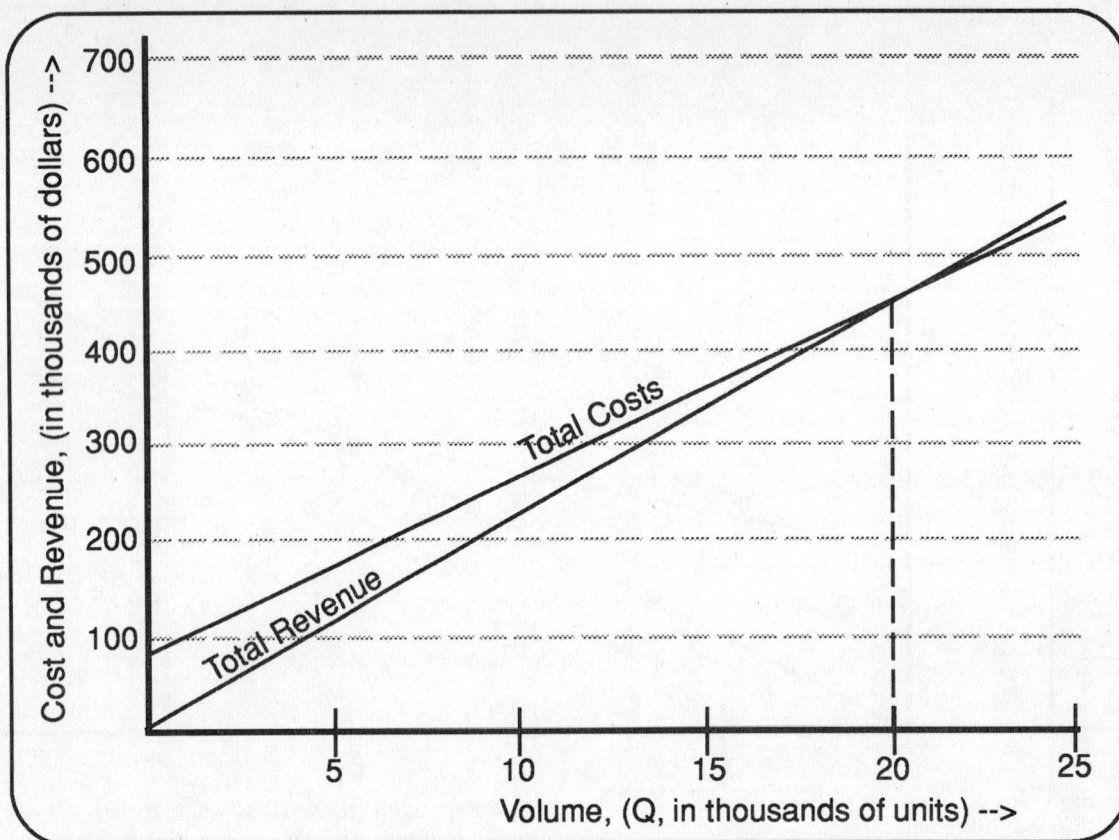

c. Initial unit profit margin is $4.00 ($22 – $18)

  Alternative 1 : ($22 – $18) = $4.00. The percentage change in profit margin is zero.

  Alternative 2 : ($22 – $15.30) = $6.70. The percentage change is

$$($6.70 – $4) / $4 = \ 67.5 \text{ percent.}$$

3. Interactive television service.

$$Q = \frac{F}{p-c}$$

$$F = Q(p-c)$$

$$F = 10,000(\$12 - \$7)$$

$$F = \$50,000 \text{ available to cover annual fixed costs}$$

4. Brook trout.

$$Q = \frac{F}{p - c}$$

$$p - c = \frac{F}{Q}$$

$$p = \frac{F}{Q} + c$$

$$p = \frac{\$10,600}{800} + \$6.70$$

$$p = \$19.95$$

5. Goliath Manufacturing.

a.
$$\begin{aligned} \text{Total cost} &= \text{Fixed cost} + \text{Variable cost} \\ TC &= F + CQ \\ TC \text{ (first process)} &= \$205,000 + \$650Q \\ TC \text{ (second process)} &= \$145,000 + \$800Q \end{aligned}$$

At the break-even quantity,

$$\begin{aligned} \$205,000 + \$650Q &= \$145,000 + \$800Q \\ \$150Q &= \$60,000 \\ Q &= 400 \text{ units} \end{aligned}$$

Beyond 400 units the first process becomes more attractive.

b. At $Q = 500$ units

$$\begin{aligned} TC \text{ (first process)} &= \$205,000 + \$650(500) = \$530,000 \\ TC \text{ (second process)} &= \$145,000 + \$800(500) = \$545,000 \end{aligned}$$

The difference in total cost $= \$545,000 - \$530,000 = \$15,000$

6. News clipping service.

a. $$Q = \frac{F_m - F_a}{c_a - c_m} = \frac{\$400,000 - \$1,300,000}{\$2.25 - \$6.20} = 227,848 \text{ clippings}$$

b. Profit = Total Revenue − Total Cost

Current (manual) situation:

$$= (225,000 \times \$8.00) - [\$400,000 + (225,000 \times \$6.20)]$$

Profit = \$5,000

Modernization:

$$= (900,000 \times \$4.00) - [\$1,300,000 + (900,000 \times \$2.25)]$$

Profit = \$275,000

The clipping service should be modernized.

c. $$Q = \frac{F}{p - c} = \frac{\$1,300,00}{\$4.00 - \$2.25} = 742,857 \text{ clippings}$$

7. Hahn Manufacturing.

a. Total cost of buying 750 units from the supplier:

$$TC_b = (\$1,500/\text{unit})(750 \text{ units}) = \$1,125,000$$

Total cost of making 750 units in-house:

$$TC_m = (\$1,100/\text{unit} + \$300/\text{unit})(750 \text{ units}) + \$40,000 = \$1,090,000$$

Therefore Hahn should make the components in-house, saving $35,000 per year.

b. At the break-even quantity, the total cost of the two alternatives will be equal:

$$\$1,500Q = \$40,000 + \$1,400Q$$
$$100Q = \$40,000$$
$$Q = 400 \text{ units}$$

c. If the decision is to "buy," Hahn may get a quantity discount from the supplier (we would be ordering 750 per year instead of the current 150 per year). Just a $50 per unit quantity discount would make the "buy" alternative more attractive than the "make" alternative. Because the component is a key item, Hahn should check the reliability of the supplier and of their own processes. Reliability may argue for the "make" decision.

8. Rent or buy concrete pump.

a. Comparing the total annual cost of buying the pump (process 1) to the total annual cost of renting (process 2), and solving for Q (the number of pours per year), we get

$$F_1 + c_1 Q = F_2 + c_2 Q$$
$$(\$8,800 + \$2,000) + (\$35 \times 8)Q = (0) + (\$125 \times 8)Q$$
$$\$720 Q = \$10,800$$
$$Q = 15 \text{ pours}$$

The break-even quantity is only 15 pours.

b. The company should buy, because the 40-pour forecast is above the break-even quantity.

Buy cost: $(\$8,800 + \$2,000) + (\$35 \times 8)(40) = \$22,000$

Rent cost: $(\$125)(8)(40) = \$40,000$

The difference in annual costs is $18,000.

9. This problem is a thinly disguised portrayal of an actual situation faced by Tri-State G&T Association, Inc. of Thornton, Colorado, and which is common to many other REA Utilities. However the costs, prices and demands stated in the problem are fiction.

a.

$$Q = \frac{F}{p - c}$$

$$p = \frac{F}{Q} + c = \frac{\$82,500,000}{1,000,000} + \$25 = \$107.5 \text{ per MWH}$$

b. Profit (or loss) = Total Revenue – Total Cost

= [(1,000,000 x 95%)($107.5)] – [$82,500,00 + (1,000,000 x 95%)($25)]

= $102,125,000 – $106,250,000

Loss = ($4,125,000)

In order to break even the price would have to be raised to (107.5 + 4.125 = $111.625), assuming even more conservation would not occur at this higher price.

Tri-County G&T:
■■■■ Problem 9
● ● ● ● Problem 11

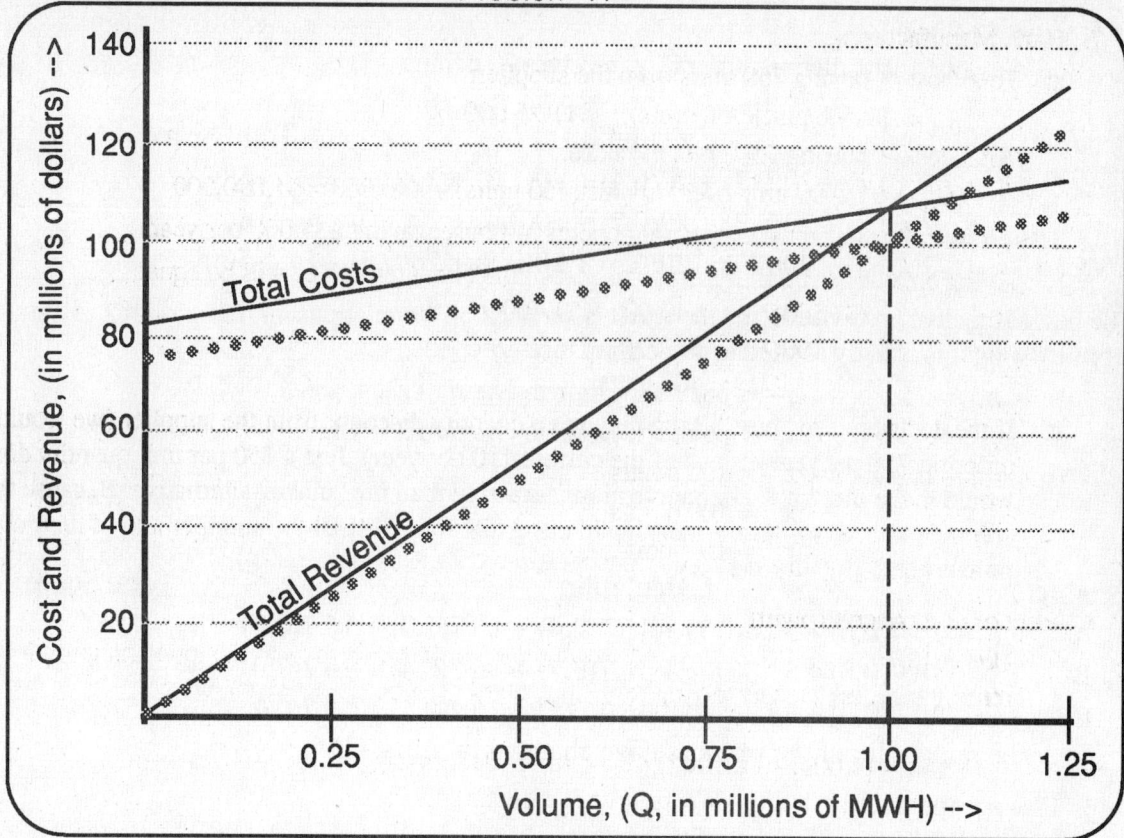

Cost and Revenue, (in millions of dollars) -->

140

120

100

Total Costs

80

60

40

Total Revenue

20

0.25   0.50   0.75   1.00   1.25

Volume, (Q, in millions of MWH) -->

10. Earthquake ... Build or Buy. This problem is related to problem 9.

Build: $F_1 + Qc_1 = \$10,000,000 + (150,000 \text{ MWH} \times \$35) = \$15,250,000$

Buy: $F_2 + Qc_2 = \quad \$0 \quad + (150,000 \text{ MWH} \times \$75) = \$11,250,000$

It would be less costly for Boulder to buy power from Tri-County. Note that Boulder enjoys a lower price ($75) than Tri-County charges its own REA customers ($107.50).

11. Tri-County G&T continued. This problem builds on problems 9 and 10 to show that Tri-County's REA customers also benefit from the bargain arrangement with Boulder.

Contribution from sales to Boulder $= Q(p - c)$
$= 150,000 (\$75 - \$25)$
$= \$7,500,000$

Remaining fixed costs to cover $= \$82,500,000 - \$7,500,000 = \$75,000,000$

$$Q = \frac{F}{p - c}$$

$$p = \frac{F}{Q} + c = \frac{\$75,000,000}{1,000,000} + \$25 = \$100 \text{ per MWH}$$

Note that selling power to Boulder at a reduced price also reduces the price to the REA customers. However, it may be difficult to persuade REA's that selling electricity to city slickers below "cost" also benefits rural customers.

12. Forsite Company.

    a. Say that each criterion (arbitrarily) receives 20 points:

Product	Calculation		Total Score
A	$20(0.6) + 20(0.7) + 20(0.4) + 20(1.0) + 20(0.2)$	=	58
B	$20(0.8) + 20(0.3) + 20(0.7) + 20(0.4) + 20(1.0)$	=	64
C	$20(0.3) + 20(0.9) + 20(0.5) + 20(0.6) + 20(0.5)$	=	56

The best alternative is service B and the worst is service C. This relationship holds as long as any arbitrary weight is equally applied to all performance criteria.

    b. Let

$$x = \text{point allocation to criteria 1, 3, 4, and 5}$$
$$2x = \text{point allocation to criterion 2 (ROI)}$$
$$x + 2x + x + x + x = 100 \text{ points}$$
$$6x = 100 \text{ points}$$
$$x = 16.7 \text{ points}$$

Product	Calculation		Total Score
A	$16.7(0.6) + 33.3(0.7) + 16.7(0.4) + 16.7(1.0) + 16.7(0.2)$	=	60.0
B	$16.7(0.8) + 33.3(0.3) + 16.7(0.7) + 16.7(0.4) + 16.7(1.0)$	=	58.4
C	$16.7(0.3) + 33.3(0.9) + 16.7(0.5) + 16.7(0.6) + 16.7(0.2)$	=	57.7

       The rank order of the services have changed to A, B, C.

13. Five new products.

    a. Let:

$$x = \text{point allocation to criteria 2 and 3}$$
$$5x = \text{point allocation to criterion 1}$$
$$3x = \text{point allocation to criterion 4}$$
$$5x + x + x + 3x = 100 \text{ points}$$
$$10x = 100 \text{ points}$$
$$x = 10 \text{ points}$$

Product	Calculation		Total Score
A	$50(8) + 10(3) + 10(7) + 30(7)$	=	710
B	$50(7) + 10(8) + 10(5) + 30(6)$	=	660
C	$50(3) + 10(4) + 10(7) + 30(9)$	=	530
D	$50(6) + 10(7) + 10(6) + 30(1)$	=	460
E	$50(8) + 10(7) + 10(2) + 30(6)$	=	670

    b. The threshold is $0.7[10(50 + 10 + 10 + 30)]$ = 700

    c. Because product A is the only product that has a score greater than 700, it is the only product that should be introduced.

14. Schlemiel, et al.

    a. The solution is shown in the table on the next page. The preference matrix indicates that with the given criteria and weights, Milwaukee is the better of the two locations.

    b. If the analyst, (Shirley LaVerne) places equal weights on the criteria, the two locations will be tied.

Location Factors	Factor Weight	Location Milwaukee	Points	Location Boulder	Points
Construction costs	10	8	80	5	50
Utilities available	10	7	70	7	70
Business services	20	4	80	7	140
Real estate cost	30	7	210	4	120
Quality of life	10	4	40	8	80
Transportation	20	7	140	6	120
Total		37	620	37	580

15. B & K Construction.

   a. Maximin — Do Nothing ... $250,000

   b. Maximax — Hire ... $625,000

   c. Laplace — Do Nothing ... $275,000

Alternative	Weighted Payoff
Hire	0.5 (−$250,000) + 0.5 ($625,000) = $187,500
Subcontract	0.5 ($100,000) + 0.5 ($415,000) = $257,500
Do Nothing	0.5 ($250,000) + 0.5 ($300,000) = $275,000

   d. Minimax regret — Subcontract ... $150,000

Regrets ($000)

Alternative	Low Demand	High Demand	Maximum Regret
Hire	250 − (−250) = 500	625 − 625 = 0	$500,000
Subcontract	250 − 100 = 150	625 − 415 = 110	$150,000
Do Nothing	250 − 250 = 0	625 − 300 = 325	$325,000

16. Fletcher, Cooper, and Wainwright under uncertainty.

The following calculations show the payoffs for each policy - product combination

Policy	Product — Arrows
Land, no treaty	9,000,000($0.15) − [$60,000 + (9,000,000 x $0.05)] = $ 840,000
Land, with treaty	5,000,000($0.15) − [$60,000 + (5,000,000 x $0.05)] = $ 440,000
Sea	2,500,000($0.15) − [$60,000 + (2,500,000 x $0.05)] = $ 190,000

Policy	Product — Barrels
Land, no treaty	300,000($3.00) − [$80,000 + (300,000 x $1.50)] = $ 370,000
Land, with treaty	200,000($3.00) − [$80,000 + (200,000 x $1.50)] = $ **220,000**
Sea	500,000($3.00) − [$80,000 + (500,000 x $1.50)] = $ 670,000

Policy	Product — Conestoga Wagons
Land, no treaty	5,000 ($75.00) − [$100,000 + (5,000 x $50.00)] = $ 25,000
Land, with treaty	50,000($75.00) − [$100,000 + (50,000 x $50.00)] = **$1,150,000**
Sea	3,000 ($75.00) − [$100,000 + (3,000 x $50.00)] = $ −25,000

   a. Maximin — $220,000 ... Cooper, a pessimist, would make barrels.

   b. Maximax — $1,150,000 ... Wainwright, an optimist, would make wagons.

   c. Laplace — Fletcher, a realist, would make arrows.

Alternative	Weighted Payoff
Arrows	1/3 ($840,000) + 1/3 ($440,000) + 1/3 ($190,000) = $490,000
Barrels	1/3 ($370,000) + 1/3 ($220,000) + 1/3 ($670,000) = $420,000
Conestoga	1/3 ($25,000) + 1/3 ($1,150,000) + 1/3 ($−25,000) = $383,333

17. Fletcher, Cooper and Wainwright under risk.

   a. Expected Value

   Arrows   [0.5 ($840,000) + 0.3 ($440,000) + 0.2 ($190,000)] = $590,000

   Barrels   [0.5 ($370,000) + 0.3 ($220,000) + 0.2 ($670,000)] = $385,000

   Conestogas [0.5 ($25,000) + 0.3 ($1,150,000) + 0.2 ($–25,000)] = $352,500

   The decision tree is shown in the following illustration.

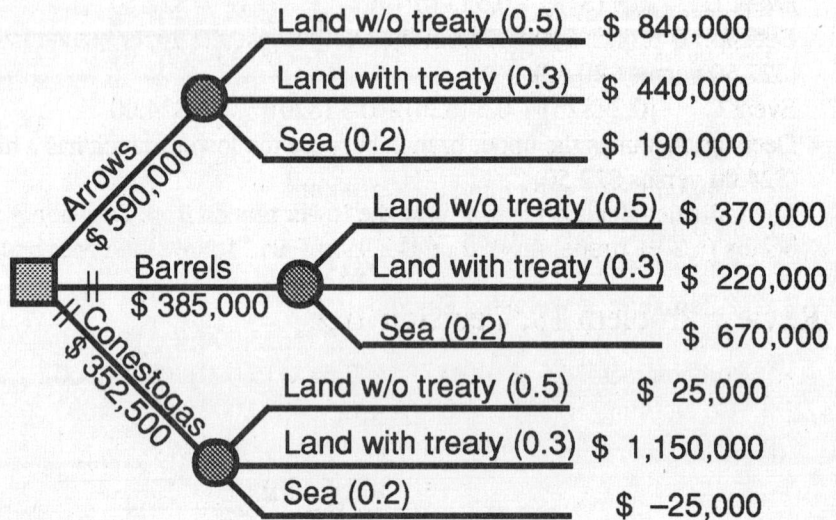

   b. Value of perfect information.

Policy	Best Payoff
Land—no treaty	$840,000
Land—with treaty	$1,150,000
Sea	$670,000

$$EV_{perfect} = \left[(0.5 \times \$840,000) + (0.3 \times \$1,150,000) + (0.2 \times \$670,000)\right]$$
$$= \$899,000$$

$$EV_{imperfect} = \left[(0.5 \times \$840,000) + (0.3 \times \$440,000) + (0.2 \times \$190,000)\right]$$
$$= \$590,000$$

The value of perfect information is $899,000 – $590,000 = $309,000

18. Decision Tree.

Choose Alternative 2, expected value = $24.00.

The decision tree is shown below. Working from right to left the expected value of

Event G   [0.6 ($20) + 0.4 ($30)]   = $24.00

Decision F prunes Event G from the tree because the upper branch has a higher expected value ($25 versus $24).

Event E   [0.4 ($20) + 0.3 ($18) + 0.3 ($24)]   = $20.60

Event D   [0.5 ($15) + 0.5 ($30)]   = $22.50

Decision B prunes Event E from the tree because the upper branch has a higher expected value ($22.50 versus $20.60).

Event C   [0.2 ($25) + 0.5 ($26) + 0.3 ($20)]   = $24.00

Decision A prunes the upper branch because the lower branch has a higher expected value ($24.00 versus $22.50).

The indicated decision is to follow the lower branch from Decision A. If the top branch of Event C occurs (a 20% probability), then Decision F will follow the upper branch.

Review Problem 18, Decision Tree

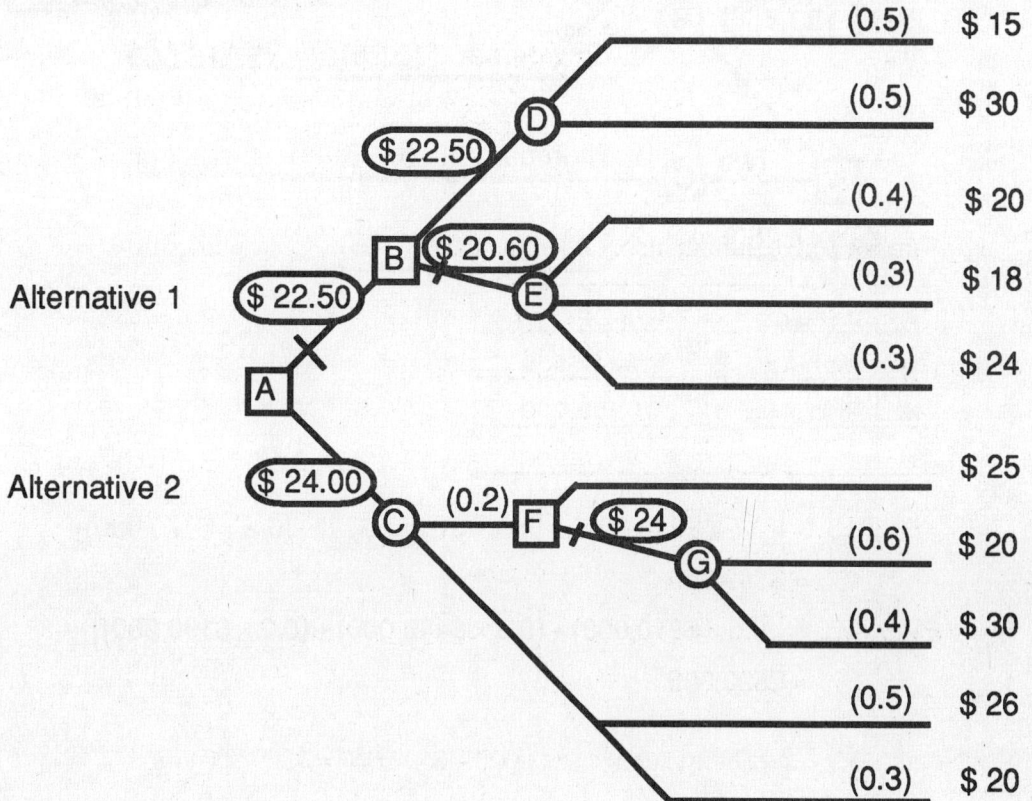

19. One machine or two. The decision tree is shown on the the next page. Working from right to left: Decision D is to subcontract because the upper branch has the highest expected value.

Event B   [0.75 ($140,000) + 0.25 ($115,000)]   = $133,750

Event C   [0.75 ($165,000) + 0.25 ($ 94,000)]   = $147,250

Decision A prunes Event B from the tree because the lower branch has a higher expected value. The indicated decision is purchase two machines now.

Review Problem 19, Decision Tree

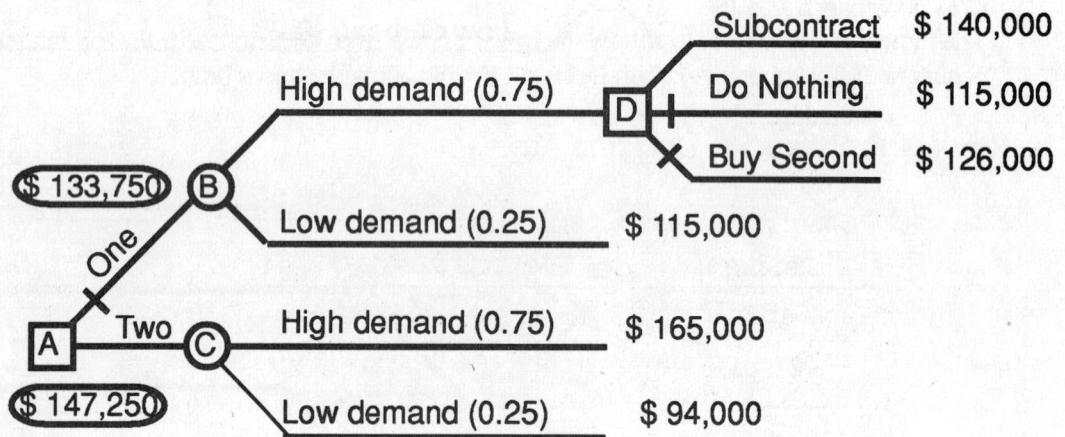

20. Small, medium, or large facility. The decision tree is shown below. Working from right to left: Decisions E, F and G are pruned according to highest payoff. Then the expected values are:

Event B   [0.35 ($220,000) + 0.40 ($125,000) − 0.25 ($60,000)] = $112,000
Event C   [0.35 ($150,000) + 0.40 ($140,000) − 0.25 ($25,000)] = $102,250
Event D   [0.35 ($125,000) + 0.40 ($ 75,000) + 0.25 ($18,000)] = $ 78,250

Decision A prunes Events C and D from the tree because the upper branch has the highest expected value. The indicated decision is to build the large facility now.

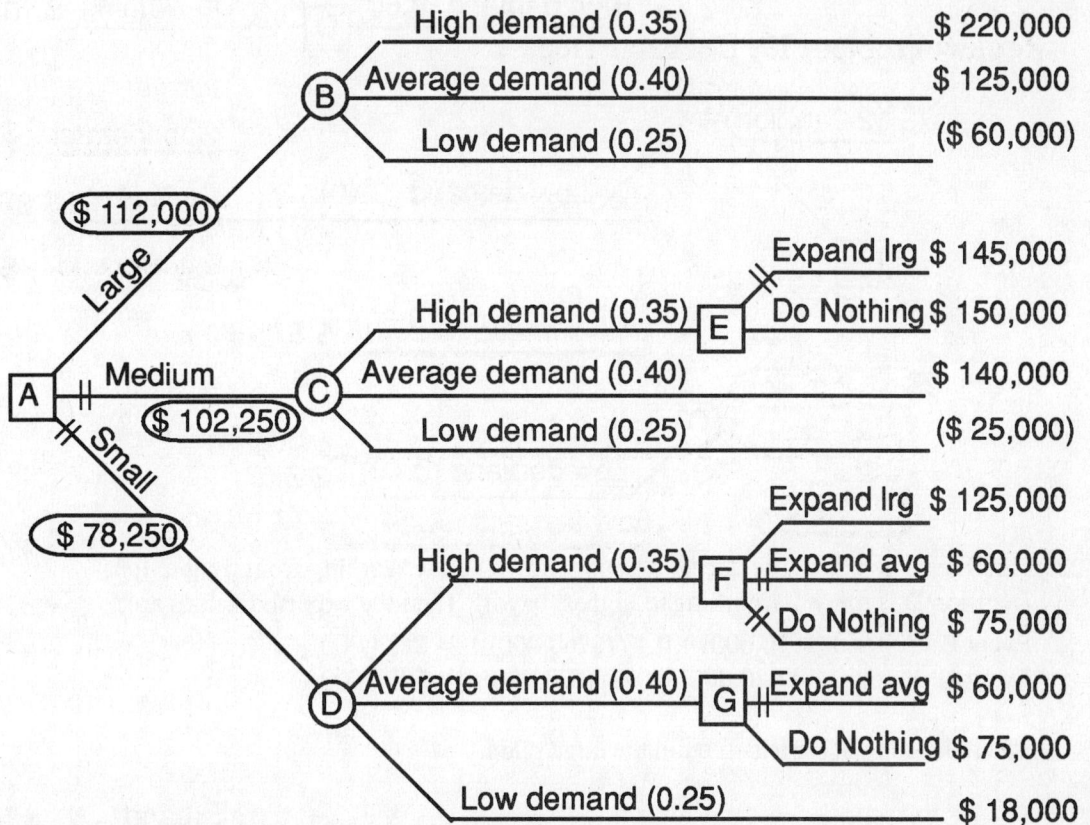

21. Small or large plant. The decision tree is shown below. Working from right to left: Decision D is pruned according to highest payoff. Then the expected values are:

Event B   [0.60 ($15,000,000) + 0.40 ($8,000,000)]   = $12,200,000
Event C   [0.60 ($17,000,000) + 0.40 ($5,000,000)]   = $12,200,000

Decision A is tied between building the small or large plant. Other criteria, such as maximin, minimax, or minimax regret may be used to make this decision.

Payoffs are in Millions of Dollars

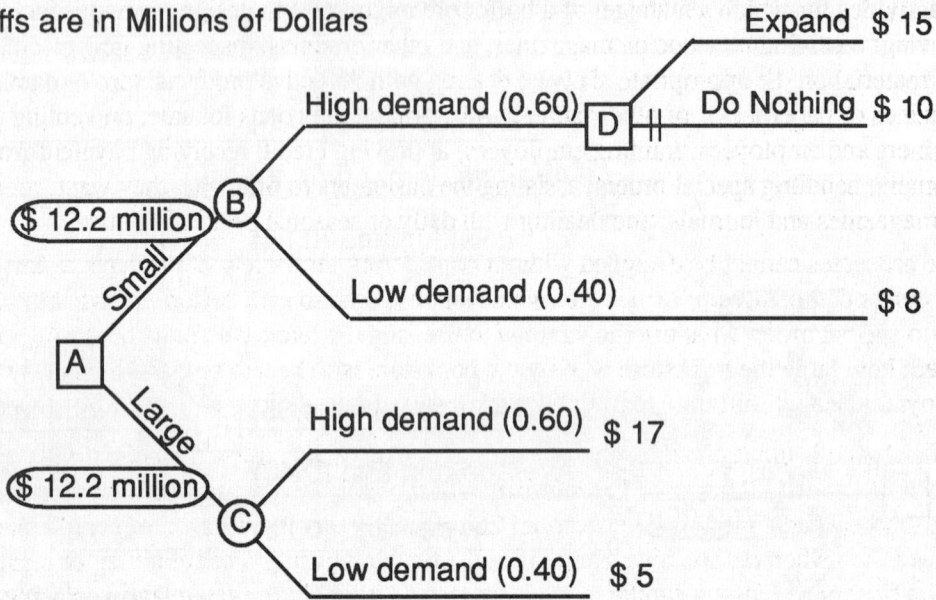

22. Small or large plant. The decision tree is shown below. Working from right to left: Decision D is pruned according to highest payoff. Then the expected values are:

Event B   [0.60 ($950,000) + 0.40 ($760,000)] = $874,000
Event C   [0.60 ($1,520,000) − 0.40 ($20,000)] = $904,000

The indicated decision is to build the large plant.

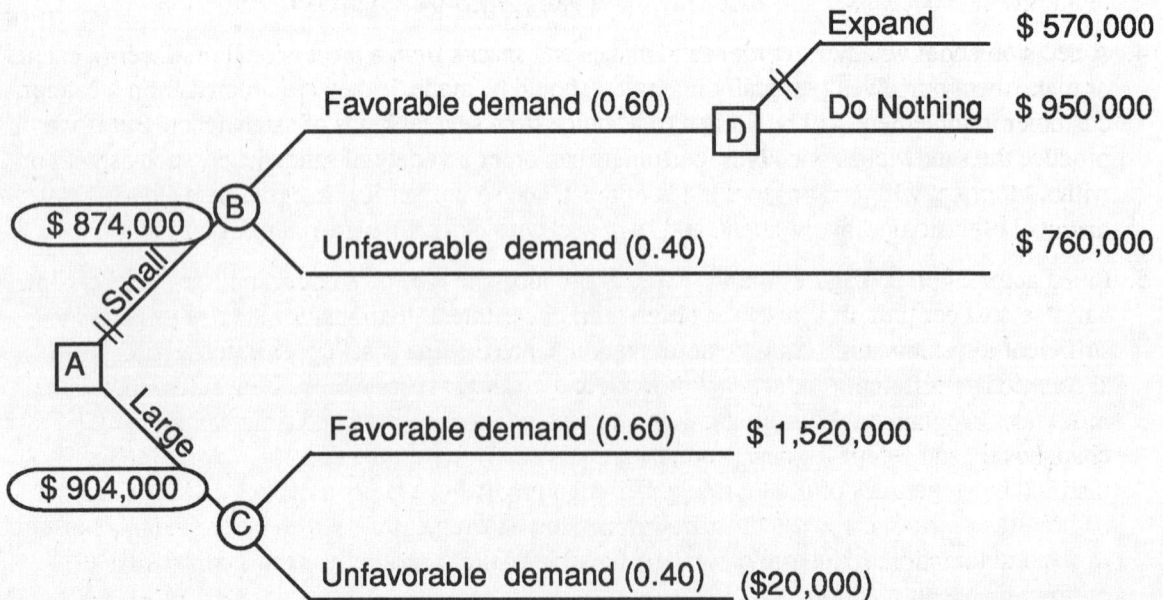

Chapter 3

Process Management

Study Questions

1. The activities for which a manager of a bookstore might need to design processes include the following: receiving new books, magazines, and other products; inspecting new receipts; placing good material on the appropriate shelves; dealing with defective products, torn or damaged magazines or paperbacks, or other faulty goods; pricing the goods for sale; preventing theft by customers and employees; training employees; approving credit; receiving payment from customers; handling special orders; assisting the customers to find what they want; returning out-of-date magazines and journals; and dealing with daily or seasonal peaks in demand.

   These processes cannot be designed without considering the variety of products to carry; what the bookstore's competitive priorities are (what response time to give customers, what to stock and what to special order, what pricing strategy to use, and the like); where the bookstore is to be located; how large the bookstore is; how the bookstore is to be laid out; and the background and employment status (full time, part time, temporary) of the employees.

2. When demand is unpredictable, an organization is likely to choose volume flexibility as its competitive priority. Therefore the company will probably have a process-focused production system rather than a product-focused one. Consequently the desired level of capital intensity should be lower than when production volume is high enough to justify a commitment of resources to one product or service. Higher capital intensity means a larger break-even quantity, placing the firm in a very risky position in the face of highly unpredictable demands. Also, the vertical integration level should be low to assure the flexibility of resource utilization.

3. Compared to a retail store, a mail order company need not display merchandise, maintain a pleasant-looking shop, provide dressing rooms for customers, or have close customer contact with salespersons. This lower customer involvement provides opportunities to automate the warehouse and computerize the order-entry process. Consequently mail order companies are more automated. Neither business is likely to integrate vertically. Resource flexibility is likely to be higher in the retail business because of the added merchandising functions it must perform.

4. A decision about whether to order sandwiches and snacks from a professional producer (a caterer) or make them ourselves (vertically integrate) should be made. If they are ordered from a caterer, customer involvement will be limited to a choice from several kinds of sandwiches. But if we produce the sandwiches ourselves, customers can order a variety of sandwiches, such as with or without tomato, with one or more kinds of meat, and so on. Vertical integration is closely related to the level of customer involvement, and such decisions can have a great impact on success.

5. Fixed automation configures the flow line to produce one type of product and achieves very low variable cost per unit, thus justifying high initial investment if volume for the one product is sufficient to achieve high equipment utilization. Once the line is set up, changeovers to accommodate different products are difficult and costly. In other words, fixed automation is inflexible. Programmable automation, in contrast, utilizes programmable machines so that changeovers and setups for new products are less costly. Investment in flexible automation is justified by economies of scale achieved through producing a large variety of custom products having low break-even costs. Chemical processing and automobile plants before 1980 are examples of fixed automation; industrial robots and Flexible Manufacturing Systems are examples of programmable automation.

6. The problem is not with the techniques themselves but with how they are applied. In the past, labor savings were the mainstay for justifying automation projects. Because labor is a shrinking component of total costs, further reductions in labor are unlikely to outweigh the cost of more automation. Thus managers must look at the full range of benefits, such as quality, customer service, inventories, delivery times, and resource flexibility. These benefits should be estimated and considered as part of (or in addition to) the financial analysis. Expected costs and benefits of a new technology should be compared to the costs and benefits of using the existing technology to the best of the existing technology's capability. If a company is not doing the best it can with what it already has, they can not expect to gain the full benefits attributed to a new technology. In addition, the new technology may not appear so attractive when compared to making effective use of existing technology.

7. From the university's point of view, the registration process is likely to include the following steps:
    * Prepare a list of courses, times, and places of their meetings
    * Prepare a list of potential registrants (currently enrolled students and newly admitted ones)
    * Prepare registration materials for all potential students
    * Arrange for potential registrants to receive registration materials (either by mail or in person)
    * Arrange for advisers to be available
    * Receive proposed schedules from the registering students
    * Match proposed schedules with courses and sections available and approve or disapprove the schedule. Also substitute another schedule for disapproved ones
    * Return schedules to the students along with bills for tuition and fees
    * Receive payments for tuition and fees from the students
    * Process requests for changes to the students' schedules, which may involve repeating some or all of the steps preceding

    Suggestions for change in the process depend on the processes now used. Suggestions include the following:
    * Computerized parts of the process not now computerized
    * The ability to accomplish several steps by mail or phone rather than in person
    * Longer hours of availability for advisers
    * Ability to reserve space in specific sections of courses by on-line computer terminals
    * Central (or decentralized) location for advisers
    * More (or fewer) advisers available
    * Automatic inclusion of grants and scholarships in the bill
    * Ability to use a bank card to pay the bill
    * Ability to pay the bill in installments
    * An easier way to execute desired changes in a student's schedule

8. This question is intended to relate theory to a situation within the students' experiences. Creating flow diagrams and process charts, and answering what, when, who, where, how long, and how questions are helpful in understanding existing processes. However process improvements only derive from asking why. It seems that students, or unhappy customers, are often better at asking the why questions needed to challenge ineffective processes than are those who are employed in the ineffective processes.

9. Serving your own lunch involves the production of one unit: one pizza pie, one bowl of salad, and one glass of beverage. Also, you serve only one type of product. In contrast, a pizza parlor produces various kinds of products: pepperoni pizza or Italian sausage, Coke or Sprite, a salad bar, and so on. Production volume is also higher. Therefore all inputs are in larger volumes, and more variety must be allowed for; so inventory is held at the pizza parlor. Also, the parlor may be able to produce at lower unit cost due to economies of scale.

   Basically, both processes use the same inputs: dough, cheese, pizza toppings, beverages, vegetables, and the same kind of baking procedure. At the pizza parlor, in addition to processes for preparing and serving the food, a process must be designed for taking customers' orders and for receiving payment from customers. At home the preparer, server, and consumer are likely to be the same person. At a pizza parlor, the preparer and server may be two different people and the consumers are certain to be different people.

10. Window sales in this case will require a flexible work force or working part time during the peak demand periods. Bakery personnel may have to change their daily routine to satisfy the demands for doughnuts early in the day. Also, workers will need to respond quickly to customer orders to avoid long lines of cars. Extra storage, bags, cups, napkins, and the like will now be needed. Customers will now have to verbalize their orders, whereas the usual bakery arrangement allowed the customer to "shop" more for the "perfect" doughnut.

11. The custom cake line is process focused with little capital intensity, making volume flexibility relatively easy to achieve. Leveling output to get full equipment utilization is not necessary because the investment in the individual work stations is low. Producing cakes to inventory in the earlier months to help meet peak demand in December is not reasonable anyway, unless refrigeration is possible and the cakes are not customized to individual customer order. The best strategy is to use as much overtime as possible in December, increasing the utilization of the skilled work force on the custom cake line. Another likely choice would be cross training workers normally stationed at other operations in King Soopers, so that they can help out during the peak season. The one disadvantage is the amount of training required. If these two options do not provide enough extra capacity, then hiring part timers or seasonal workers during December should be considered. The big disadvantage of this option is the amount of training required. Particular attention should be paid to hiring people on a seasonal basis who would be available in subsequent years.

12. The change allows some product variety but moves away from one-of-a-kind products. Customization becomes less of a competitive priority, with more emphasis given to cost and short delivery times. Higher-volume production of standard products will become more the norm, with more capital intensity and less resource flexibility. The cake line will take on more of the attributes of the pastry line or even the bread line.

Discussion Questions

1. Pollution control technology. The approach described in this question has actually been proposed in the regulatory arena, but I do not know the outcome. The discussion is expected to focus on these issues: 1) whether utilities ought to be able to buy the right to pollute, 2) fairness of making no improvement in the local environment while lowering average pollution for the nation, 3) universal requirement to install the new technology (the technology is so expensive, great resistance to universal enforcement could result in defeating the regulation), and 4) the broad "reduced regulation versus big government" debate.

2. This question was inspired by a similar situation faced by Ontario Hydro-Electric. Today electricity is a commodity, which competes on the basis of low-cost operations and reliability. If the environmental protection equipment is installed, HEC must either absorb the costs as a loss (immediate bankruptcy) or attempt to pass on the costs to customers and see further erosion of their market (eventual bankruptcy). HEC would probably decide to delay investment in environmental protection equipment for as long as possible. Some discussion may focus on the issue of whether customers, as users of both electricity and the environment, are better served by competition (lower cost of electricity), or by regulated monopolies (better environment).

3. This situation is a disguised version of events reported in a newspaper article. Chip's actions, when exposed, caused great loss of good will for his employer. Security tends to decrease over time. Employees may not recognize the competitive value of information they hold, or may tire of the nuisances associated with maintaining security. Repeated training and checking of security procedures are necessary.

4. Students from other countries may have experiences to relate here. NAFTA may reduce the tendency to move dirty work to other countries to avoid stringent environmental regulations. However, even small differences in regulations can have a large effect. Within the United States a large amount of electric generation capacity is located in the desert just outside the reach of California's more stringent pollution standards.

Problems

1. Referendum 13.

   Flow diagram for yard sign assembly:

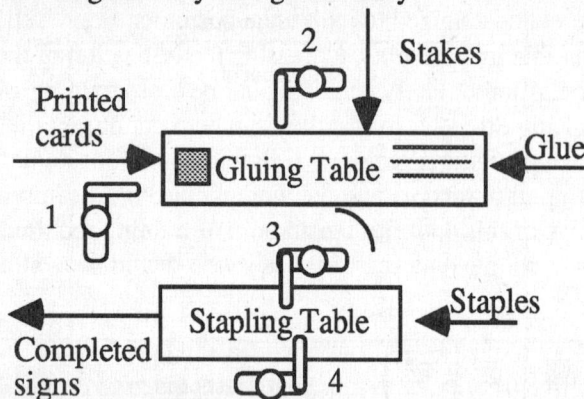

Human resource requirements:

   One of many possible arrangements is to create several cells with four workers in each cell.

   Worker 1 is a materials handler, bringing printed cards and stakes (say in stacks or bundles of 25) to the gluing table, and taking completed signs (again in bundles of 25) to the shipping area.

   Worker 2 glues printed cards to the stakes. Worker 2 is also responsible for keeping the area supplied with glue, staples, pizza and beer.

   Worker 3 is also a materials handler, transferring glued signs in small quantities (a transfer batch) to the stapling table.

   While worker 3 holds the material in place, Worker 4 staples the card to the stake to hold them while the glue dries. Worker 4 also inspects the staples, drives loose ones home with a hammer, and stacks completed signs in bundles of 25 for Worker 1 to take away.

Accounting for interruptions, material shortages, and chaos, each cell will complete about eight signs per minute, or about two signs per worker-minute. 10,000 signs would require about 5,000 worker-minutes, or 83.33 worker-hours. In order to accomplish this work within three hours (maximum attention span of college students) 83.33/3 = 27.78 or about 28 student volunteers are required to staff 7 cells.

Material requirements (for 7 cells of 4 workers each) are:

10,000	printed cards
10,000	stakes
32,000	staples (16 boxes of 2,000 each)
28	12-ounce bottles of wood glue
4	cases beer
10	pizzas

Equipment requirements

14	tables
7	staple guns
7	hammers (to set staples)

Process chart

Process: YARD SIGN ASM (bundles of 25)	Summary			
	Activity	Number of Steps	Time	Distance
Subject charted: VOLUNTEER	Operation ●	2	6.2	—
Beginning: MATERIAL TO TABLE	Transport ➡	4	4.0	155
Ending: COMPLETED SIGNS REMOVED	Inspect ■	1	1.0	—
	Delay ❭	1	1.0	—
	Store ▼	2	1.0	—

Step No.	Time (min)	Distance (ft)	●	➡	■	❭	▼	Step Description
1	0.5	50		✗				25 Printed cards to gluing table
2	0.5	50		✗				25 Stakes to gluing table
3	3.2		✗					Glue 25 cards to 25 stakes
4	2.5	5		✗				Transfer individually to stapling
5	1.0					✗		Hold in position for stapling
6	3.0		✗					Insert three staples per sign
7	1.0				✗			Inspect staples and sign
8	1.0						✗	Stack signs into bundles of 25
9	0.5	50		✗				Carry signs to shipping area
10							✗	Store signs until distributed

2. King Soopers. A tour of the King Soopers bakery is provided in the video.

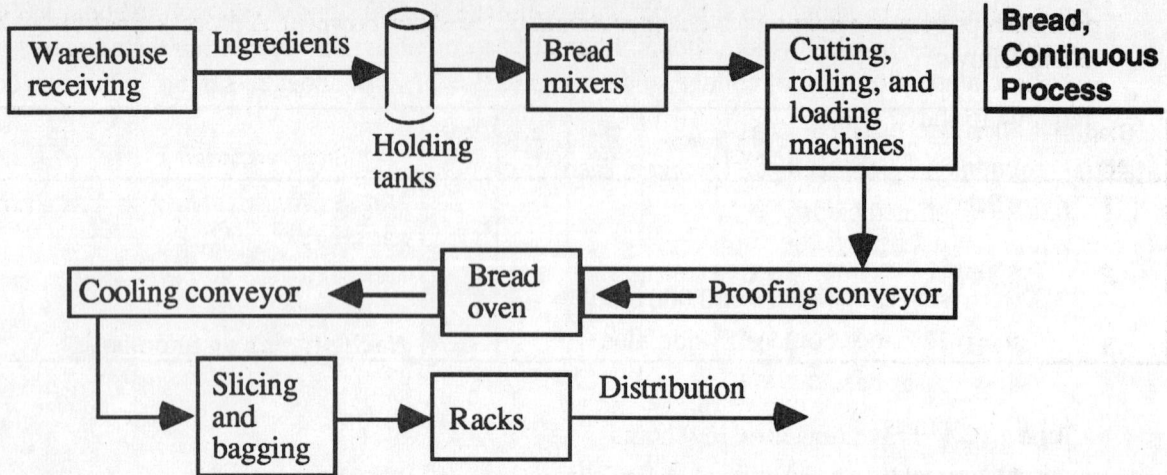

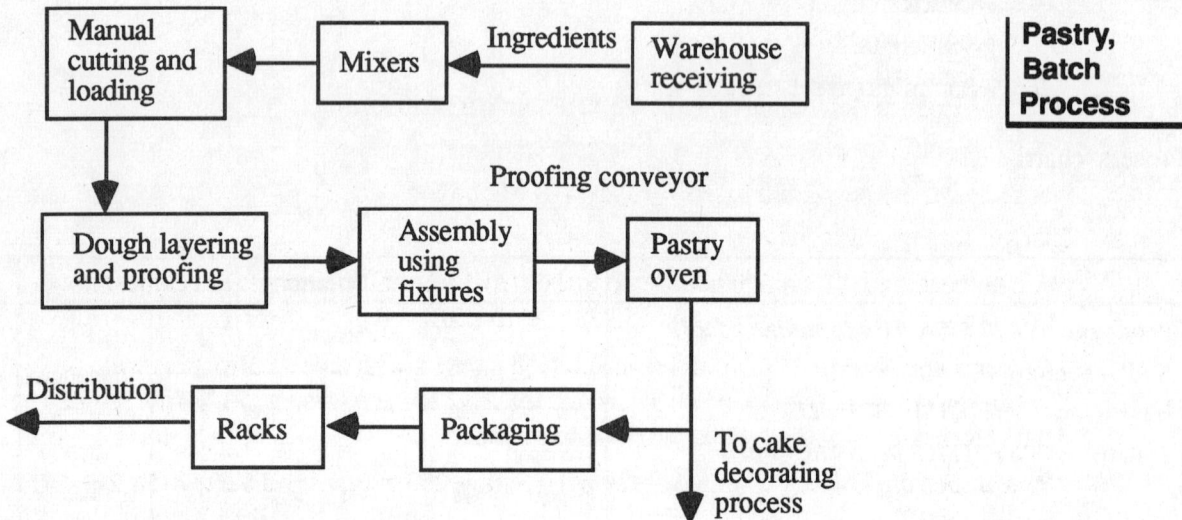

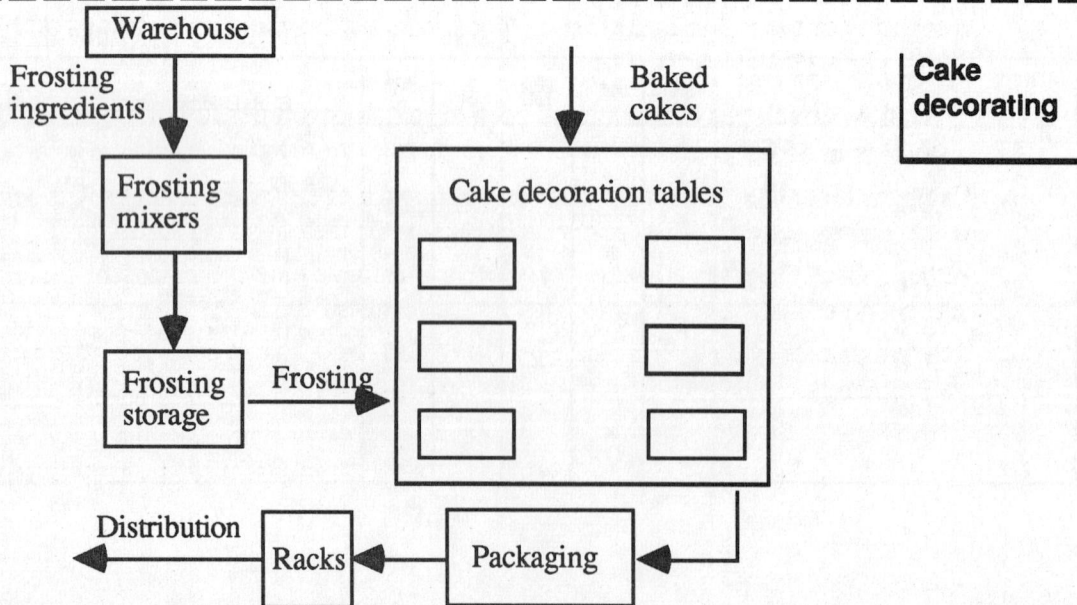

Bread, Continuous Process

Warehouse receiving → Ingredients → Holding tanks → Bread mixers → Cutting, rolling, and loading machines → Proofing conveyor → Bread oven → Cooling conveyor → Slicing and bagging → Racks → Distribution

Pastry, Batch Process

Warehouse receiving → Ingredients → Mixers → Manual cutting and loading → Dough layering and proofing → Assembly using fixtures → Proofing conveyor → Pastry oven → Packaging → Racks → Distribution

To cake decorating process

Cake decorating

Warehouse → Frosting ingredients → Frosting mixers → Frosting storage → Frosting → Cake decoration tables

Baked cakes → Cake decoration tables → Packaging → Racks → Distribution

3. The solution to this problem depends on the particular time estimates the student uses. The relationships between the process changes should be the same, however. A process chart for 2000 letters follows.

Step No.	Time (min.)	Distance (ft)	●	→	■	◗	▼	Step Description ✍
1	400*		X					*Match proper letters to addressed envelopes*
2	534†		X					*Fold letters, stuff and seal envelopes*
3	200‡		X					*Place stamps on envelopes*

Total   1134 minutes or 18.9 hours

    *12 seconds to process one letter x 2000 letters = 400 minutes

    † 7 seconds to fold one letter
       6 seconds to stuff into envelope
       <u>3 seconds to seal the envelope</u>
     16 seconds to process one letter x 2000 letters = 534 minutes

    ‡ 6 seconds per stamp x 2000 stamps = 200 minutes

    The cost to process 2000 letters = ($8/hr)(18.9 hr) = $151.20.

a. Changes that would reduce the time and cost of the process:

    A letterhead with "Dear Alumnus" will make step 1 (matching letters to envelopes) not necessary, saving 400 minutes and $53.33 [$8(400/60)].

    With mailing labels, step 1 involves matching the letters with labels rather than with addressed envelopes, but now we must stick the label to the envelope. We do everything we did before plus some extra. The time would increase.

    Prestamped envelopes will eliminate step 3 and save 200 minutes and $26.67 [$8(200/60)].

    If envelopes are to be stamped by a postage meter, it will take, say, 10 minutes, assuming the capacity of the meter is 200 letters per minute. This results in a savings of 190 minutes and $25.33 [$8(190 / 60)].

    Window envelopes eliminate the need to match envelopes to letters, resulting in a savings of $53.33.

b. Using the letter with "Dear Alumnus" may reduce the effectiveness of the project because it would be less personal. This concern goes also for the use of mailing labels.

c. Although including a preaddressed envelope will increase time and cost of the process, alumni may be more likely to contribute if they have an envelope available to them.

d. Relative costs of plain versus windowed envelopes, preaddressed envelopes, letterhead, and mailing labels.

4. a. The gas station in part (b) has a more efficient flow from the perspective of the customer because traffic moves in only one direction through the system.

   b. The gas station in part (a) creates the possibility for a random direction of flow, thereby causing occasional conflicts at the gas pumps.

   c. At the gas station in part (b) a customer could pay from the car. However, this practice could be a source of congestion at peak periods.

5. a. The summary of the process chart should appear as follows:

Summary			
Activity	Number of Steps	Time	Distance
Operation ●	6	1.70	—
Transport ➡	6	0.80	31
Inspect ■	1	0.25	—
Delay ◗	1	0.50	—
Store ▼	0	—	—

   b. Each cycle of making a single-scoop ice cream cone takes $1.70 + 0.80 + 0.25 + 0.50 = 3.25$ minutes. The total labor cost is ($10/hr)[(3.25 min/cone)/60 min](10 cones/hr)

   (10 hr/day)(363 day/yr) = $19,662.50.

   c. To make this operation more efficient, we can eliminate delay and reduce traveling by having precleaned scoops available. The improved process chart is shown in below:

Process:	MAKING ONE SINGLE-SCOOP ICE-CREAM CONE		Summary			
Subject charted:	SERVER AT COUNTER		Activity	Number of Steps	Time	Distance
Beginning:	WALK TO CONE STORAGE AREA		Operation ●	5	1.65	—
Ending:	GIVE SERVER OR CUSTOMER THE CONE		Transport ➡	4	0.45	15
			Inspect ■	1	0.25	—
			Delay ◗	0		—
			Store ▼	0		—

Step No.	Time (min.)	Distance (ft)	●	➡	■	◗	▼	Step Description	✍
1	0.20	5		x				WALK TO CONE STORAGE AREA	
2	0.05		x					REMOVE EMPTY CONE	
3	0.10	5		x				WALK TO SCOOPS-STORAGE AREA	
4	0.05		x					REMOVE SCOOP	
5	0.10	2.5		x				WALK TO FLAVOR ORDERED	
6	0.75		x					SCOOP ICE-CREAM FROM CONTAINER	
7	0.75		x					PLACE ICE CREAM IN CONE	
8	0.25				x			CHECK FOR STABILITY	
9	0.05	2.5		x				WALK TO ORDER PLACEMENT AREA	
10	0.05		x					GIVE SERVER OR CUSTOMER THE CONE	

   The cycle time is reduced to $1.65 + 0.45 + 0.25$, or 2.35 minutes. The total labor cost is ($10/hr)[(2.35 min/cone)/60 min](10 cones/hr)(10 hr/day)(363 day/yr) = $14,217.50.

   Therefore, the annual labor saving is $19,662.50 − $14,217.50 = $5,445.00.

6. Grading Homework Steps:
   1. Check each paper to identify the author of the homework, then mark each paper with section number and graduate status.
   2. Sort by section and graduate status
   3. Correct and grade papers
   4. Alphabetize by section
   5. Record grades
   6. Return homework to appropriate instructor

7. DMV. The process chart appears at the top of the next page.

Many students will suggest that the "unkempt man" be tossed out on his ear and the "uniformed person" be fired. However, this may be difficult to accomplish in a public building/civil-service environment, and is not a permanent solution.

The root cause of this problem is that the tax assessment clerks' time is being wasted by an inefficient waiting line process. Whenever the customer arrival rate exceeds the service rate, a waiting line will form. While the clerk is waiting for phantom customers, service rate declines, and waiting lines become even longer. More disgusted customers leave the waiting area (renege). More of the clerks' time is wasted and this spiraling process continues until a market is generated for the "unkempt man". He creates an informal priority system to replace the inefficient formal system. The "unkempt man" sells low ticket numbers to knowledgeable customers (car dealers) who are unwilling to wait four hours for service through the formal waiting line system. By collecting the discarded tickets from the floor near the ticket dispenser, the "unkempt man" is not providing a public service. He is protecting his market.

This process can be improved by arranging the waiting area to work like the "batter's circle and batter's box" in baseball. Customer's who have reneged would be replaced before the clerks' time is wasted. Service rates would increase, waiting lines would decrease, there would be no market for the "unkempt man" to exploit, and he would move on to other endeavors. Kickbacks to the "uniformed person" would cease. Civil-service disciplinary actions would be unnecessary. Customers would be better served.

Typical of many service situations, the customer's anger is misguided. It is directed to the last person in the process (the license clerk), who has done nothing wrong. The customer pays for this misguided anger. While taking the one minute to abuse the license clerk, a bus approaches. Blinded by rage, the taxpayer drives his new car into the path of the oncoming bus, and the car is totaled. Now the customer will have to start the process again!

Eplogue.
It is almost sad how little exaggeration was used in creating this problem. When this location of the DMV closed, the local news announcer referred to it as "the city's most popular place to wait in line". This DMV process has since been replaced by an automated one-stop, one-transaction process. Just today I visited the new DMV, and completed the entire process in five minutes.

8. Oil Change.
   a. Each oil changing cycle takes $16.5 + 5.5 + 5.0 + 0.7 + 0.3 = 28$ minutes. The total labor cost is ($17/hr)[(28min/service)/(60 min/hr)](2 services/hr * 10 hrs/day * 350 days/yr) = $55,533.33.
   b. ($17/hr) * (2.7 minutes saved per service/60 min/hr) (2 services/hr * 10 hrs/day * 350 days/yr) = $5,355.00 saved per year.

Review Problem 7, Process Chart

Process: *Automobile license*								Summary		
Subject charted: *Customer*					Activity		Number of Steps	Time	Distance	
Beginning: *Customer arrives*					Operation ●		5	9	—	
Ending: *Customer leaves*					Transport ➡		6	—	265	
					Inspect ■		1	—	—	
					Delay ◗		4	351	—	
					Store ▼		1	—	—	

Step No.	Time (min.)	Distance (ft)	●	➡	■	◗	▼	Step Description	✍
1	—		x					*Take a number*	
2	—	50		x				*Walk to waiting area*	
3	240					x		*Wait for service*	
4	—				x			*Number is called and checked*	
5	—	60		x				*Walk to clerk*	
6	4		x					*Calculate/pay city sales taxes*	
7		80		x				*Walk to property tax area*	
8	—		x					*Take a number*	
9	100					x		*Wait for service*	
10		25		x				*Walk to clerk*	
11	2		x					*Calculate/pay property taxes*	
12	—	50		x				*Walk to license area*	
13	10					x		*Wait for service*	
14	3		x					*Calculate/pay license fee*	
15	1					x		*Abuse license clerk*	
16	—	?		x				*Walk to car in parking lot*	
17	—						x	*Crash with bus, return to step 1*	

9. Dr. Gulakowicz

Fixed cost, $F = \$105,000$

Revenue per patient, $p = \$1925$

Variable cost per unit, $c = \$250$

Break-even volume, $V = \dfrac{F}{p-c} = \dfrac{\$105,000}{\$1925 - \$250} = 62.69$ or 63 patients

10. Two manufacturing processes.

$F_1 + c_1 V = F_2 + c_2 V$

$\$50,000 + \$400V = \$200,000 + \$150V$

$(\$400 - \$150)V = (\$200,000 - \$50,000)$

$V = \dfrac{\$150,000}{\$250} = 600$ units

Supplement B

Computer-Integrated Manufacturing

Study Questions

1. Computer-integrated manufacturing (CIM) is an umbrella term for the total integration of product design and engineering, process planning, and manufacturing by means of computer systems. CAD, NC equipment, robots, AGVs, AS/RS, and FMS are elements of CIM. So are computerized systems for production and inventory control. Managers should investigate CIM carefully. However, to conclude that all firms should opt for each element is not valid. The appropriate degree of computer integration is situational.

2. By using a CAD system, the following advantages can be expected:

   Old designs can be accessed and modified quickly, thereby saving development time.

   Several views of a part from different dimensions can be shown to the analyst.

   Tests of strength and stress can be done by the computer without building prototypes.

   Several alternative designs can be tested and analyzed quickly.

3. Both NC machines and industrial robots can be programmed to repeat a sequence of instructions. Different from traditional automation, in which changeovers are difficult and costly, NC machines and robots can be adjusted to new processes quickly and easily by changing their programs.

4. A labor shortage, or any shortage of an input resource, tends to increase its cost. The productivity ratio (and therefore the standard of living) would tend to decline. One way Just-in-Time manufacturing methods maintain flexibility is by avoiding the use of fixed automation. JIT is relatively labor intensive. Japanese business successes due to Just-in-Time manufacturing techniques, in combination with labor intensive manufacturing, absorbed the entire traditional work force. The labor shortage has stimulated cultural changes to increase the number of women and older workers included in the Japanese work force.

5. Moving, packaging, and storing are known as materials-handling processes. Because materials handling takes time and costs money but adds no value to the product, any needless handling should be eliminated. Materials handling in a product-focused facility is more repetitious, structured, and automatic because materials literally flow along fixed paths. The flow of materials in a process-focused facility is very jumbled and unstructured. Jobs are unlikely to follow the same path.

6. Flexible automation is computer-controlled equipment that can be reprogrammed to handle new products and operations. The AGV and AS/RS are computer controlled and flexible. An AGV's flexibility comes from the ability to route it along many different paths, depending on current conditions and the location of transportation blockages. An AS/RS is flexible where newly arriving material entering the system is stored. Optical sensors confirm that materials will fit a location.

7. Three key components of an FMS:

   1. Several work stations controlled by a computer
   2. A computer-controlled transport system
   3. Loading and unloading stations

   The FMS is flexible particularly because setup times for machines in such a system can be very short due to automatic tool interchange capabilities. That is, tools can be switched quickly to enable machines to perform a different process. Also, because of the computerized materials-handling process, the routing of jobs through the system can be flexible.

8. Visualizing the required motion is simplified if it is assumed that the welding robot can travel along the assembly line at the same speed as the automobile. However, long tranverses are not a strength of robots. Robots must know with precision where they are, and where the work is located. With the possible exception of "roll", every degree of movement shown in Fig. B.1 plus the ability to traverse would be required to make these welds on a moving target. Since the cost of robots increases with the number of degrees of movement, these welding robots must be very costly.

9. Connecting the exotic metal, razor-thin walls of tubing found in today's $2,000 bicycle frames is a challenge for the best of human welders. Further design advances may require the exclusive use of welding robots, or moving to silver soldering or chemical bonding techniques. Bicycle frame welds can be accomplished using roll, pitch, yaw and elbow extention movements. Moving to the next weld on the same frame would require either the fixture to move or the robot to have shoulder swivil and arm sweep cabability. Reprogramming is required when the frame size changes.

10. Tasks which are repetitive, time-consuming, dangerous, the source of quality defects or requiring no creativity tend to be good candidates for automation. These tasks are more likely to be found in manufacturing than in services. The relative ease of implementing automation in manufacturing is one reason productivity has increased faster in that sector of the economy.

Discussion Questions

1. Questions such as this one put the student in the center of a dilemma. Sometimes a firm has a clear ethical choice, but it runs counter to the firm's short-term financial interests or jeopardizes the manager's job. In other cases, there is not even a clear-cut choice on ethical grounds. The larger the gray area, the better the class discussion.

   As for this particular question some argue that if Fiat hadn't automated, its market share would have dropped to the point that it could not retain even 72,000 employees. The automation improved worker productivity, reduced costs, and ushered in a period of high profits. The automation also responded to opposition by trade unions to traditional and stressful assembly line work. Retaining the 72,000 jobs and enhancing the quality of the remaining jobs can be offered as ethical defenses to the automation at Fiat. On the other hand, cutting so many jobs in the Turin region certainly had a human cost. A responsible and ethical employer will try to avoid such layoffs and, when cutbacks are necessary, make the transition as easy as possible for the employees affected. Transfers to other facilities, retraining, or retirement packages are all possibilities.

2. High volume, standardized production tends to be produced in flow shops. Repetitive work requires little training. World class competition makes it difficult to justify high salaries for specialized, work. The fixed automation typically found in flow shops cannot be used to respond to demand for new products. Flow shops are economically inflexible. The majority of the U. S. economy is in the service sector. Services are bought with discretionary income. If the U. S. attempted to compete on the basis of low cost labor, discretionary income would decline and the U.S. economy would collapse. Reich saw that flexible manufacturing systems (FMS) offer an opportunity for high paying jobs while manufacturing customized products in low volume (the opposite of high volume, standardized production). However, FMS is costly. In this article Reich criticized a trend of the 1980's to invest in mergers and acquistions for short-term quick returns rather than investing to revitalize manufacturing. Mergers and acquistions tend to decrease economic flexibility.

Chapter 4

Total Quality Management

Study Questions

1. Christmas tree lights. Customer-driven definitions of quality include:
   - (i) conformance to specifications; mean time between failure
   - (ii) value: the number of seasons the light string can be safely used for the price, performance relative to advertising
   - (iii) fitness for use: suitable for outdoor use, cool bulbs to reduce fire danger
   - (iv) support: the warranty associated with the product and brand name reputation. Since repairs are not economically justifiable, customers expect hassle-free replacement.
   - (v) psychologoical impressions; the visible appearance of the product and packaging

2. Income-tax preparation. In the case of IRS rules, the specifications are stated as law and stated explicitly (but often not clearly for the average taxpayer). Consequently, conformance to the law is one definition of quality. The company may also have standards on promptness. The consumer's perception of quality would include: the perceptions of courtesy and expertise of the tax preparer or service contact, the impression that all legal deductions have been taken, the extent of the warranty the tax preparer gives on the service rendered, and the amount of help that has been given to improve the client's tax status in subsequent years.

3. Few professor's will have the time to examine every available textbook alternative. A snappy cover can bring a favorable psychological impression so that the text receives further consideration, but the adoption decision is rooted in subject matter content. Fitness for use, support in the form of ancillary publications are important considerations. Since the prices of most popular texts are similar, value is not a significant factor in this decision.

4. Marketing is in the best position to learn of external customers' expectations and perceptions of quality. Marketing is responsible for bringing that information into the organization, and this may affect product specifications. Marketing can also influence external customers' expectations regarding value, fitness for use, support after the sale, and psychological impressions. It is important that these expectations match the specified performance of the product.

5. Poor quality can be expensive for companies because of appraisal costs, internal failure costs, and external failure costs. Internal failure costs increase as scrap and rework increase because the company must use extra resources just to get the same level of output. External failure costs due to warranty work or litigation increase as quality decreases. These costs can be very large. Finally, as quality improves, there is less need to create quality checkpoints and search for causes of poor quality. Appraisal costs can be reduced. When *all* of the costs of poor quality are considered, it is likely that total costs will be lower when quality improves. Customers will pay more for high quality. Therefore, not only is quality free, it is profitable.

6. In addition to specifying clear quality standards and goals, a manager can (i) develop an environment conducive to employee involvement and teamwork, (ii) provide on-the-job training programs, (iii) tie awards and monetary incentives directly to quality improvement, and (iv) provide resources for quality circles.

7. Product design. Design changes can either add or remove sources of defects. Evolutionary design changes and simplification tend to remove defects, while revolutionary changes tend to increase them. On the other hand, occasional revolutionary changes are required to avoid obsolescence. Improved designs often require process changes. For example, new designs for electronic products require surface mount technology in manufacturing circuit boards, which in turn improves product reliabilty. Concurrent engineering is a way to bring all of the functions involved in product development together.

8. Looking at the formula for reliability, the more components which are required for the system to function, the lower the system reliability. When a design is simplified, potential sources of failure are removed.

9. Several problems may be present. Suppliers may be unaware of the importance of specific raw material characteristics to the product design. Another problem could be unrealistically tight specifications. Finally, the problem might be a purchasing department willing to accept substandard materials in favor of reduced prices.

   Correcting this situation may require the cooperation of the purchasing department, engineering, and top management. Buyers are typically rated on money saved. If quality is to be emphasized, the buyer needs the cooperation of top management so that the buyer's evaluation is based on some reasonable measure of quality *and* cost.

   If the suppliers need information on how to provide better parts, the cooperation of top management is needed as a liaison between purchasing and the other departments as well as the supplying companies. Suggestions would include (i) involving suppliers in the design of the product, (ii) performing a process capability study, and (iii) providing quality-incentive contracts to suppliers.

10. ISO 9000 costs include a lengthy and time consuming certification process. Certification indicates to customers that suppliers can provide documentation to support their quality claims. Certification is in some situations becoming an "order qualifier" in that certification is a prerequisite for further consideration.

11. Deming. This would indeed require a revolution. Some changes are outlined below.
    - Allow more time for supervisors (instructors) to work with the employees (students).
    - Drive out fear. Witness the condition of students during final's week.
    - Break down barriers between departments. (!!)
    - Avoid management by the numbers. Tests would be given to determine who needs help, but <u>not</u> used for performance evaluations, which pit people against each other and acts as a hurdle to building teams.

    (If your school bears any resemblance to the above, I'd like to send you my résumé.)

12. Under TQM, quality is a responsibility that must be shared by all employees in an organization, especially those who actually make a product. All personnel share the view that quality control is an end in itself. Errors should be caught and corrected at the source. Top management must be directly involved.

    As for implementing these ideas in the United States, the potential certainly exists and some plants are employing much of the essence of TQM. In many cases, however, significant management and employee attitude changes are necessary. For example, the resistance to basing an individual's pay on group performance is similar to that encountered when assigning the same grade to all students who participated (or failed to participate) in a group project.

13. If this problem is worked as a group exercise additional strengths of the cause-and-effect diagram become apparent. This techneque focuses the efforts of the group and organizes the investigation into categories. When it comes time to analyze potential sources of the problem, it is efficient to assign individuals or subcommittees to follow up all potential sources appearing in one category. A very brief version of the cause-and-effect diagram follows:

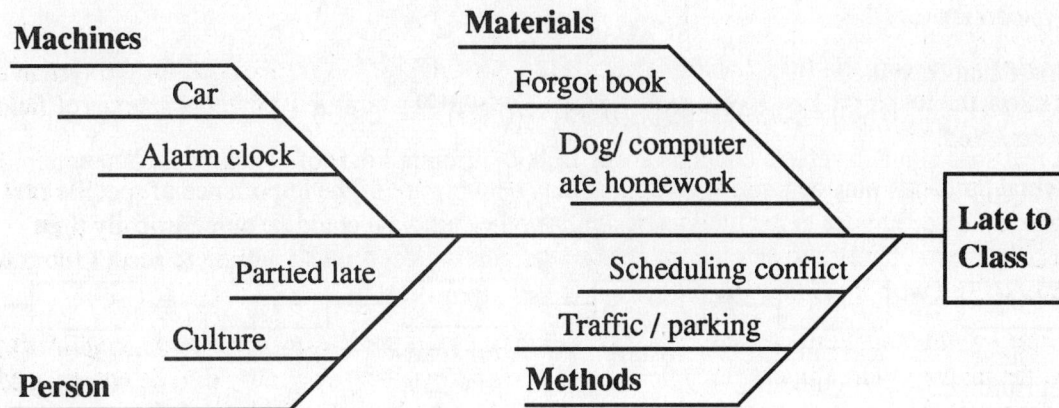

Problems

1. Contented Airlines.

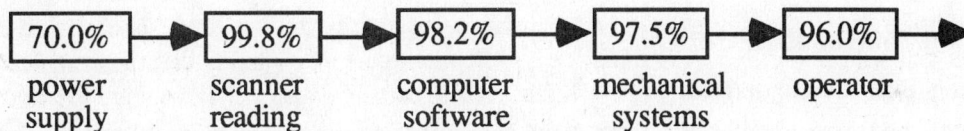

a. $r_s = (r_1)(r_2)(r_3)(r_4)(r_5)$
   $= 0.700 \times 0.998 \times 0.982 \times 0.975 \times 0.960$
   $= 0.642$

b. $r_s = (r_1)(r_2)(r_3)(r_4)(r_5)$
   $= 0.999 \times 0.998 \times 0.982 \times 0.975 \times 0.960$
   $= 0.916$

c. Computer software and operators are subsystems that hold potential for significant improvement. Software glitches are difficult to find. However the corrections tend to be at least semi-permanent in nature. Training will reduce operator error, but for this solution to be permanent, an ongoing training program is required. If the software becomes glitch-free and the operators achieve 98% reliability, the system reliability objective can be met.

2. Semiconductor.

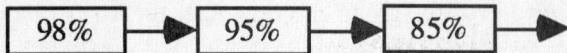

$$\boxed{98\%} \rightarrow \boxed{95\%} \rightarrow \boxed{85\%} \rightarrow$$

$$r_s = (r_1)(r_2)(r_3)$$
$$= 0.98 \times 0.95 \times 0.85$$
$$= 0.791$$

3. Space launch vehicle.

$$r_s = (r_1)(r_2)\ldots(r_{100}) = (0.99)(0.99)\ldots(0.99) = (0.99)^{100} = 0.366$$

A real space launch vehicle contains about 15,000 different kinds of components. The reliability of each component must be very high.

4. Confucius Unversity.

$$\boxed{95\%} \rightarrow \boxed{94\%} \rightarrow \boxed{99\%} \rightarrow \boxed{96\%} \rightarrow \boxed{99\%} \rightarrow \boxed{97\%} \rightarrow$$

| course registration | room assignment | roster | misread schedule | schedule | class cancelled |

The probability a student will successfully enroll for one course is:

$$r_s = (r_1)(r_2)(r_3)(r_4)(r_5)(r_6)$$
$$= 0.95 \times 0.94 \times 0.99 \times 0.96 \times 0.99 \times 0.97$$
$$= 0.815$$

The probability a student will successful enroll for all five courses is:

$$(0.815)^5 = 0.3596 \text{ or about } 36\%.$$

5. a. Checkers Pizza Pareto diagram

   Although the frequency of partly eaten pizza is low, it is a serious quality problem because it is deliberate rather than accidental. It is likely to cause extreme loss of good will. A common root cause of many of these problems could be miscommunication between the customer and the order taker, between the order taker and production and between production and distribution.

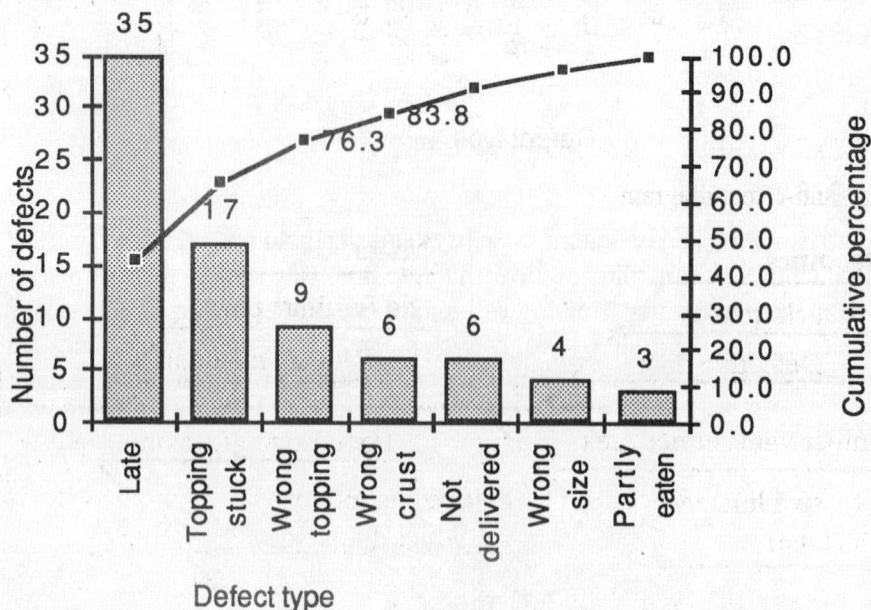

b. Cause-and-effect diagram

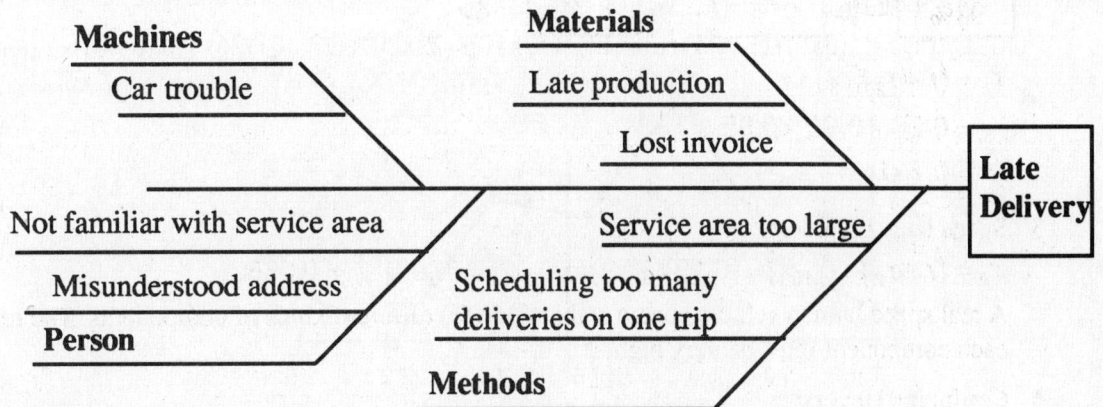

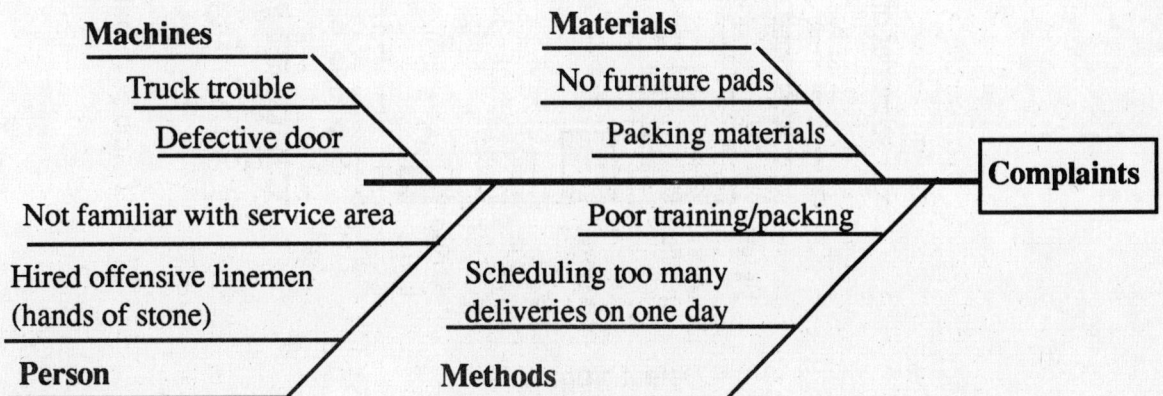

Machines
Car trouble

Materials
Late production
Lost invoice

Not familiar with service area

Misunderstood address

Person

Service area too large

Scheduling too many
deliveries on one trip

Methods

Late Delivery

6. Skosch, Smidgeon, and Tadd (short moves).

a. The tally sheet given in the problem is essentially a horizontal bar chart. To create a Pareto diagram, the categories are arranged in order of decreasing frequency.

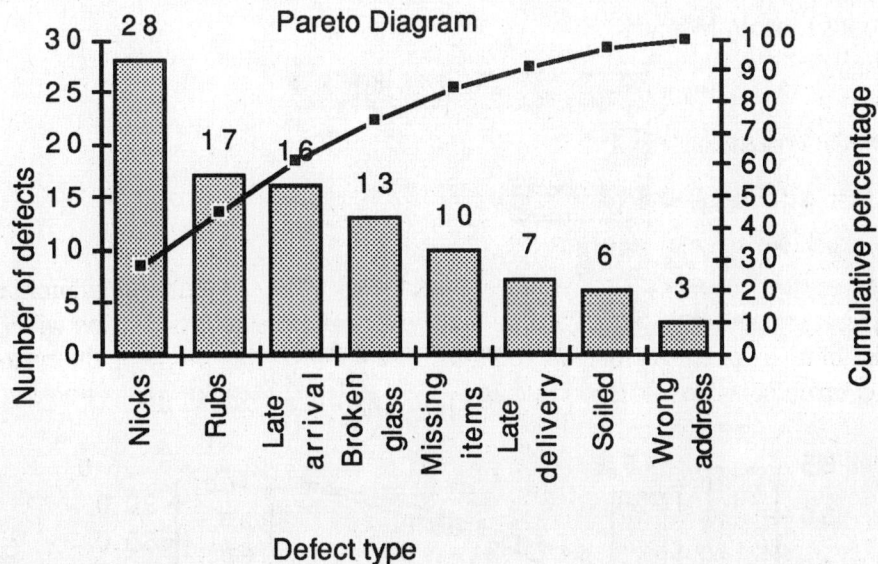

Pareto Diagram

Number of defects: Nicks 28, Rubs 17, Late arrival 16, Broken glass 13, Missing items 10, Late delivery 7, Soiled 6, Wrong address 3

Defect type

b. Cause-and-effect diagram

Machines
Truck trouble
Defective door

Materials
No furniture pads
Packing materials

Not familiar with service area

Hired offensive linemen
(hands of stone)

Person

Poor training/packing

Scheduling too many
deliveries on one day

Methods

Complaints

7. Golden Valley Bank.
   a. histogram
      average = [(5x8)+(12x11)+(38x14)+(19x17)+(22x20)+(23x0)+(26x8)]/104 =16.1 hours

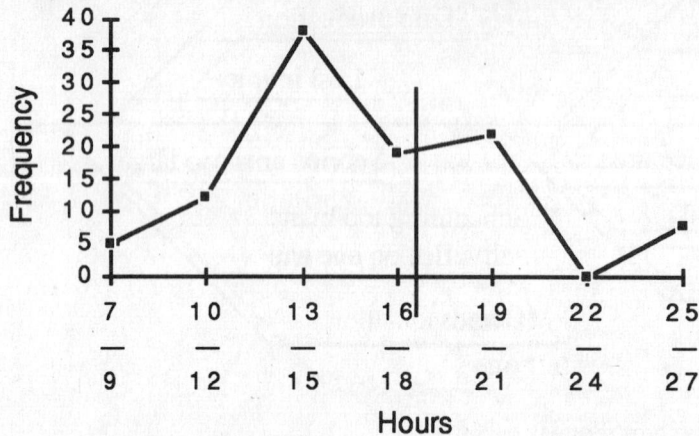

   b. Golden Valley's average time is 16.1 hours or about two business days. However 30 of 104 customers waited longer than two days. Titus should first investigate the eight applications that required 25 — 27 hours to find causes of long delays.

8. North Woods Lincoln-Mercury.
   a. bar chart

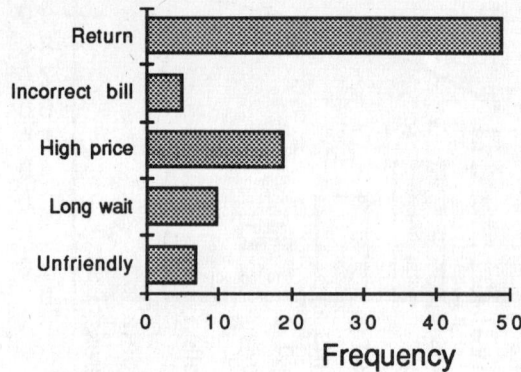

   Pareto diagram

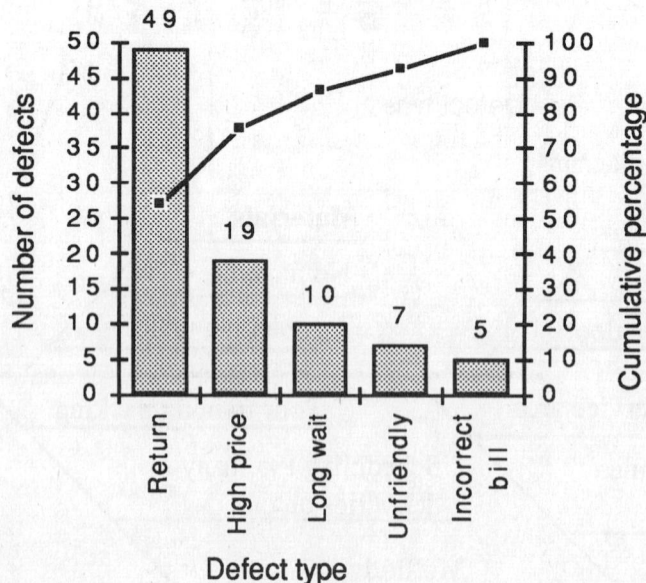

b. Cause-and-effect diagram

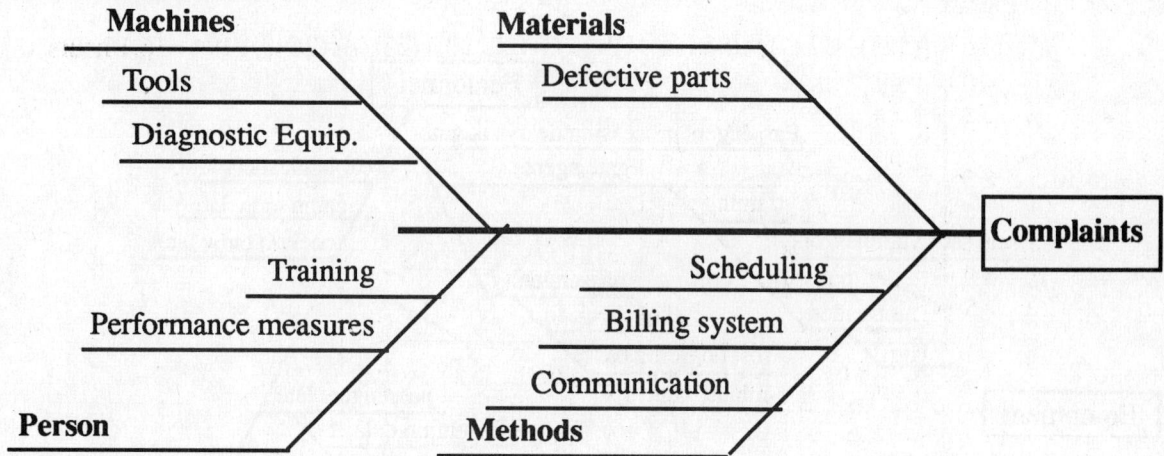

9. Wellington Fiber Board.
   a. scatter diagram
   b. as the production run size increases, the percent defective decreases.

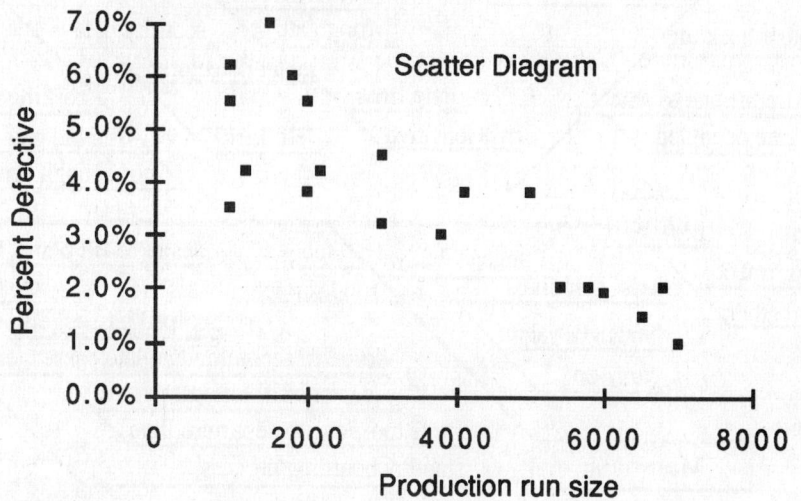

10. a. The Lucky Star restaurant line graph.
    b. The incidence of complaints increased during the summer when college students were not employed.

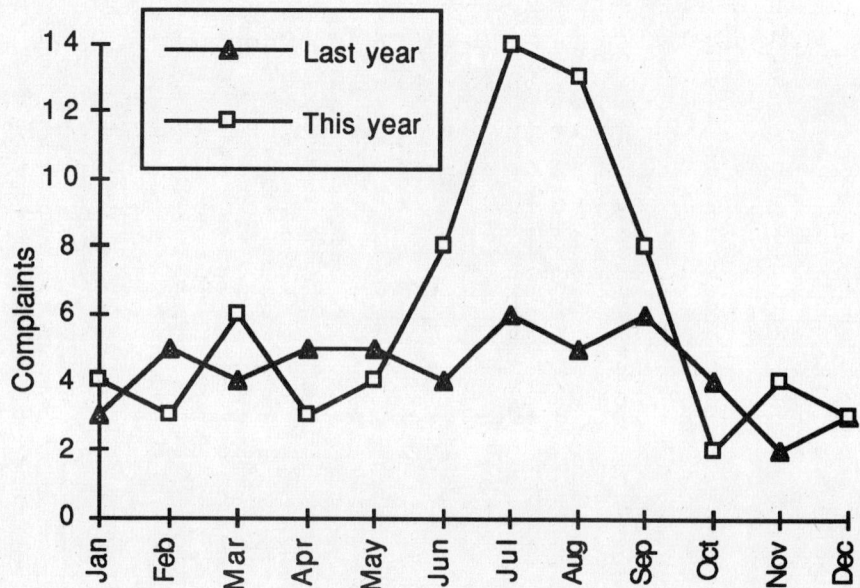

11. Checker Board Airlines. One of many possible cause-and-effect diagrams follows.

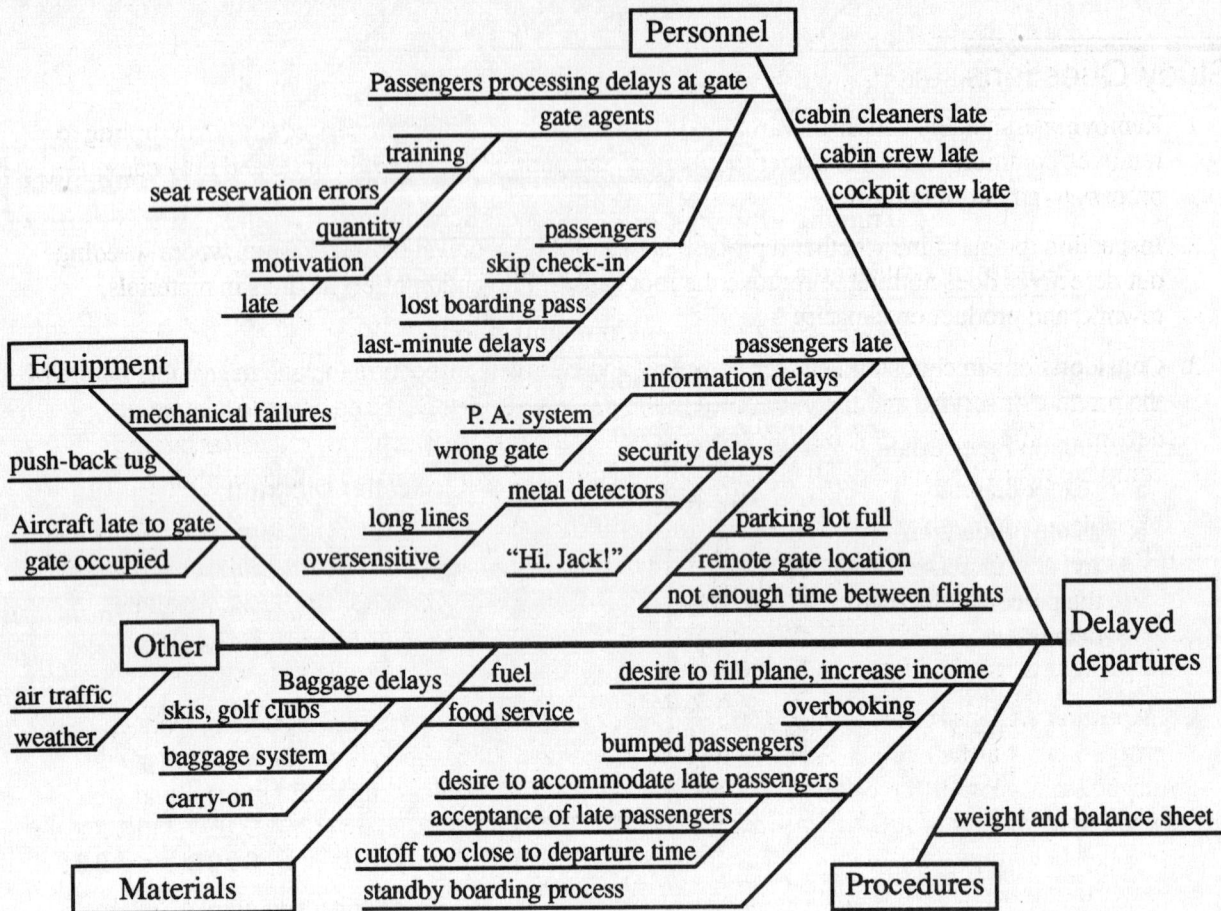

```
                                    ┌───────────┐
                                    │ Personnel │
                                    └───────────┘
        Passengers processing delays at gate
                      gate agents              cabin cleaners late
              training                         cabin crew late
     seat reservation errors                  cockpit crew late
            quantity          passengers
            motivation        skip check-in
            late              lost boarding pass
                              last-minute delays    passengers late
 ┌───────────┐                                 information delays
 │ Equipment │                    P. A. system
 └───────────┘                    wrong gate    security delays
        mechanical failures                metal detectors
 push-back tug                                     parking lot full
                           long lines             remote gate location
 Aircraft late to gate     oversensitive  "Hi. Jack!"  not enough time between flights
 gate occupied
                                                          ┌───────────┐
 ┌───────┐                                                │  Delayed  │
 │ Other │                                                │ departures│
 └───────┘                                                └───────────┘
 air traffic    Baggage delays    fuel    desire to fill plane, increase income
 weather    skis, golf clubs    food service        overbooking
            baggage system           bumped passengers
            carry-on        desire to accommodate late passengers
                            acceptance of late passengers
                            cutoff too close to departure time    weight and balance sheet
 ┌───────────┐              standby boarding process    ┌────────────┐
 │ Materials │                                          │ Procedures │
 └───────────┘                                          └────────────┘
```

Chapter 5

Statistical Process Control

Study Questions

1. Removing assignable causes of variation is important to obtaining process control. Attempting to remove "common" causes is sometimes called "tampering" because it is futile and may cause a process to go out of control.

2. Inspection to determine whether a process is in control is a preventative measure, where weeding out defectives does nothing to remove the root causes. Prevention offers savings in materials, rework, and production capacity.

3. Considerations in choosing between sampling and complete inspection include the critical nature of the product or service and the variability of the process. Typically, the decision to sample is determined by the cost of sampling versus the cost of passing a defective product (assuming complete inspection catches all defects). Destructive testing, of course, requires sampling.

   Variable measurements are used when the specification is measurable on a continuous scale (such as grams or inches) and when the results of the measures are used to correct or adjust the process. Knowing whether the process is too high or too low and by how much is desirable. Attribute measures are used when measurements are too complex to be of value or when the quality characteristic can be identified as conforming to specifications on a simple yes-no basis.

4. Inspection stations can be located at three stages of the process: purchased materials, work-in-process, and finished goods. An obvious factor regarding the number, if not the location, of inspection stations is the extent of success the company has had dealing with suppliers and instituting "quality programs" in-house. Fishbone charts can be used to put inspection stations at the points where important quality characteristics should be checked. Quality also should be checked just prior to the steps that involve costly operations. The cost of checking the materials should be balanced against the cost of passing defects.

5. The purpose of the upper and lower control limits is to detect abnormal variation in the process. These control limits establish a boundary for normal variation. If a sample measure is found to be outside a control limit, we say that the process is out of control and should be investigated for an assignable cause. The control-limit approach views variations within the control limits as having no consequence. Taguchi views any variation from the center as having some cost.

6. The central line, the control limit spread, the sample size, and the frequency of inspection are all parameters that must be specified for control charts. However, sample size, control limits, and the frequency of inspection are interrelated decisions. Sample sizes affect the control limits, and for a given sample size a given choice of k affects the probability of detecting shifts or searching for causes when none exist. Also, taking large samples frequently affords the best protection, but this practice is often too costly. Therefore, the parameters must be adjusted together to provide the best overall protection.

7. Hours of useful life is a continuous variable controlled by $\bar{x}$-charts and R-charts. Format failures would be controlled by p-charts, and number of bad sectors require c-charts.

8. x-charts indicate whether the process center has drifted, and R-charts indicate whether the process variability has increased. Either of these is an indication of assignable causes of variation.

9. Narrower control limits are more likely to detect process changes, but are also more likely to indicate an assignable cause of variation when none exists.

10. A process can be in statistical control and still produce bad products if the process or machine on which the product is produced is incapable of meeting design specifications. Statistical control is obtained when all assignable causes of variation are eliminated. If after achieving statistical control it is determined that the process or machine is producing products that fall out of the design specification range, it must be concluded that the process is incapable and will produce bad products. In other words, the process capability ratio is less than one.

11. Products are designed to perform satisfactorily when components are manufactured to certain tolerance limits. When process variability is reduced, the process capability ratio increases. There is less chance of making a product that does not conform to specifications (design tolerances).

12. When the process capability ratio is less than one, the process will create defectives no matter how many adjustments we make to keep the process mean centered on the nominal value of the design specifications. In this case, the process capability ratio of 1.5 means the tolerance range (upper specification – lower specification) is 1.5 times greater than the range of actual process outputs (6 sigma s). As long as this process is centered and in control, it will not produce defective parts. The process capability index indicates whether a process distribution is sufficiently centered on the nominal value of the design specifications. A process capability index below one means that the process distribution center is too close to one of the tolerance limits. When both the process capability ratio and the process capability index are 1.5, it means that the process is capable.

13. Pareto diagrams can be used to determine which problems should receive priority. The cause-and-effect diagram can be used to identify potential causes, and relate causes to effects. The plan-do-check-act cycle can be used to organize the search for the root causes of problems.

Problems

1. Quayle Potatoe Chips.

   $\bar{x} = 385$ grams, $n = 7$, $\bar{R} = 13$ grams

   From Table 5.1,

   $A_2 = 0.419$, $D_3 = 0.076$, $D_4 = 1.924$

   $UCL_R = D_4\bar{R} = 1.924(13 \text{ grams}) = 25.012 \text{ grams}$

   $LCL_R = D_3\bar{R} = 0.076(13 \text{ grams}) = 0.988 \text{ grams}$

   $UCL_{\bar{x}} = \bar{\bar{x}} + A_2\bar{R} = 385 \text{ grams} + 0.419(13 \text{ grams}) = 390.447 \text{ grams}$

   $LCL_{\bar{x}} = \bar{\bar{x}} - A_2\bar{R} = 385 \text{ grams} - 0.419(13 \text{ grams}) = 379.553 \text{ grams}$

2. Clinton Pharmaceuticals.

   $\bar{x} = 150$ milliliters, $n = 4$, $\bar{R} = 7$ ml

   From Table 5.1,

   $A_2 = 0.729$, $D_3 = 0.0$, $D_4 = 2.282$

$$UCL_R = D_4\overline{R} = 2.282(7 \text{ ml}) = 15.974 \text{ ml}$$

$$LCL_R = D_3\overline{R} = 0.0(7 \text{ ml}) = 0.0 \text{ ml}$$

$$UCL_{\overline{x}} = \overline{\overline{x}} + A_2\overline{R} = 150 \text{ ml} + 0.729(7 \text{ ml}) = 155.103 \text{ milliliters}$$

$$LCL_{\overline{x}} = \overline{\overline{x}} - A_2\overline{R} = 150 \text{ ml} - 0.729(7 \text{ ml}) = 144.897 \text{ milliliters}$$

3. Ross' Garage.

$$\overline{p} = 0.10, \; n = 100, \; z = 2$$

$$\sigma_p = \sqrt{\overline{p}(1-\overline{p})/n} = \sqrt{0.10(0.90)/100} = 0.03$$

$$UCL_{\overline{p}} = \overline{p} + z\sigma_p = 0.10 + 2(0.03) = 0.16$$

$$LCL_{\overline{p}} = \overline{p} - z\sigma_p = 0.10 - 2(0.03) = 0.04$$

At 15 of 100, the number of returns for service are above average, but this one observation by itself does not indicate that the process is out of control.

4. Canine Gourmet Company.

$$\overline{\overline{x}} = 43.5 \text{ grams}, \; n = 8, \; \overline{R} = 10 \text{ grams}$$

a. From Table 5.1

$$A_2 = 0.373, \; D_3 = 0.136, \; D_4 = 1.864$$

$$UCL_R = D_4\overline{R} = 1.864(10 \text{ grams}) = 18.64 \text{ grams}$$

$$LCL_R = D_3\overline{R} = 0.136(10 \text{ grams}) = 1.360 \text{ grams}$$

$$UCL_{\overline{x}} = \overline{\overline{x}} + A_2\overline{R} = 43.5 \text{ grams} + 0.373(10 \text{ grams}) = 47.23 \text{ grams}$$

$$LCL_{\overline{x}} = \overline{\overline{x}} - A_2\overline{R} = 43.5 \text{ grams} - 0.373(10 \text{ grams}) = 39.77 \text{ grams}$$

b. The range is in control, but the process average is out of control (sample 5). We should look for assignable causes.

5. Marlin Company.

	Bottle					
Sample	1	2	3	4	$\overline{x}$	R
1	.604	.612	.588	.600	.601	.024
2	.597	.601	.607	.603	.602	.010
3	.581	.570	.585	.592	.582	.022
4	.620	.605	.595	.588	.602	.032
5	.590	.614	.608	.604	.604	.024
6	.585	.583	.617	.579	.591	.038
					$\overline{\overline{x}} = 0.597$	$\overline{R} = 0.025$

$$\overline{\overline{x}} = 0.597", \ n = 4, \ \overline{R} = 0.025"$$

From Table 5.1,

$$A_2 = 0.729, \ D_3 = 0.0, \ D_4 = 2.282$$

$$UCL_R = D_4\overline{R} = 2.282(0.025") = 0.057"$$

$$LCL_R = D_3\overline{R} = 0.0(0.025") = 0.0"$$

$$UCL_{\overline{x}} = \overline{\overline{x}} + A_2\overline{R} = 0.597" + 0.729(0.025") = 0.615"$$

$$LCL_{\overline{x}} = \overline{\overline{x}} - A_2\overline{R} = 0.597" - 0.729(0.025") = 0.579"$$

b. Process capability ratio:

$$C_p = \frac{\text{Upper specification} - \text{Lower specification}}{6\sigma}$$

$$= \frac{0.650 - 0.550}{6(0.012)} = \frac{0.100}{0.072} = 1.39$$

As long as the process average is centered, this process is capable.

Process capability index:

$$C_{pk} = \text{minimum of} \ \frac{x - \text{Lower specification}}{3\sigma}, \ \frac{\text{Upper specification} - x}{3\sigma}$$

$$\frac{0.597 - 0.550}{3(0.012)} = \underline{1.306}, \ \frac{0.650 - 0.597}{3(0.012)} = 1.472$$

The process average is centered okay.

6. We initially assume the historical grand average is adequate for the central line of the chart:

Year	Student 1	2	3	4	5	6	7	8	9	10	Average
1	63	57	92	87	70	61	75	58	63	71	69.7
2	90	77	59	88	48	83	63	94	72	70	74.4
3	67	81	93	55	71	71	86	98	60	90	77.2
4	62	67	78	61	89	93	71	59	93	84	75.7
5	85	88	77	69	58	90	97	72	64	60	76.0
6	60	57	79	83	64	94	86	64	92	74	75.3
7	94	85	56	77	89	72	71	61	92	97	79.4
8	97	86	83	88	65	87	76	84	81	71	81.8
9	94	90	76	88	65	93	86	87	94	63	83.6
10	88	91	71	89	97	79	93	87	69	85	84.9
											$\overline{\overline{x}} = 77.8$

The average for the process, $\bar{\bar{x}} = 77.8$ and the standard deviation of the entire historical data is 13.

$$\sigma_{\bar{x}} = \frac{\sigma}{\sqrt{n}} = \frac{13}{\sqrt{10}} = 4.1$$

$$UCL_{\bar{x}} = \bar{\bar{x}} + z\sigma_{\bar{x}} = 77.8 + (2 \times 4.1) = 86.0$$

$$LCL_{\bar{x}} = \bar{\bar{x}} - z\sigma_{\bar{x}} = 77.8 - (2 \times 4.1) = 69.6$$

Although the process is in control, the last four observations are all above the average and exhibit an ever-increasing trend. Mega-Byte should explore for causes of corruption, such as instructor performance measures which give incentives for improved test scores. It is (remotely) possible that students are getting brighter, or are becoming more highly motivated. Perhaps admissions standards have been raised. It is (also remotely) possible that teaching methods have improved. The point shown here is: the process must be stable while data are collected for setting control limits.

7. Emerald Dormer.

a. $\bar{p} = 0.15$, $z = 2$

$$\sigma_p = \sqrt{\bar{p}(1-\bar{p})/n} = \sqrt{0.15(0.85)/100} = 0.0357$$

$$UCL_{\bar{p}} = \bar{p} + z\sigma_p = 0.15 + 2(0.0357) = 0.2214$$

$$LCL_{\bar{p}} = \bar{p} - z\sigma_p = 0.15 - 2(0.0357) = 0.0786$$

b. Any sample proportions in excess of 0.2214 are considered "rejects."

Week	Number of surveys having score < 75	Proportion
March 1	12	0.120
March 8	18	0.180
March 15	26	0.260
March 22	6	0.060
March 29	21	0.210

March 15, a week when service was particularly bad, was followed by a week of exceptional service. Was there a special effort to improve service following a particularly bad week? Were the results of managements' exhortations for improved service short lived? (a common occurrence) Assuming the trail is not now too cold, it would be worth investigating the circumstances of those two weeks. We should find the root-causes of poor service and permanently correct the problems.

8. Stosh Motor Company.

a. $\bar{p} = 0.015$, $z = 3$, $n = 250$

$$\sigma_p = \sqrt{\bar{p}(1-\bar{p})/n} = \sqrt{0.015(0.985)/250} = 0.0077$$

$$UCL_{\bar{p}} = \bar{p} + z\sigma_p = 0.015 + 3(0.0077) = 0.038$$

$$LCL_{\bar{p}} = \bar{p} - z\sigma_p = 0.015 - 3(0.0077) = -0.008 \quad \text{(adjusted to zero)}$$

b.

Sample	Number of Bad Bolts	Proportion
1	2	.008
2	8	.032
3	6	.024
4	10	$\boxed{.040}$
5	1	.004

Sample 4 is out of control. We should check for assignable causes.

9. IRS. This one is tricky.

$n = 20$, $\bar{p} = 0.70$

The average proportion of correct responses for the 20 observations is 0.758.

$$\sigma_p = \sqrt{\bar{p}(1-\bar{p})/n} = \sqrt{0.70(0.30)/20} = 0.1025$$
$$UCL_{\bar{p}} = \bar{p} + z\sigma_p = 0.70 + 2(0.1025) = 0.905$$
$$LCL_{\bar{p}} = \bar{p} - z\sigma_p = 0.70 - 2(0.1025) = 0.495$$

The higher test score average falls within these rather wide control limits. Therefore the slight improvement might be the result of common variation rather than improved training. In order to make effective use of the p-chart, the sample size ought to be increased to around 200. On the other hand, if we redesign the study so that test scores are treated as a continuous variable, a sample size of 20 would be sufficient to make effective use of x-charts and R-charts.

10. Travel Agency. Since we can not estimate how many errors were <u>not</u> made, we use a c-chart.

a. $\bar{c} = 7$

$$\sigma_c = \sqrt{\bar{c}} = \sqrt{7} = 2.646$$
$$UCL_c = \bar{c} + z\sigma_c = 7 + (2 \times 2.646) = 12.29$$
$$LCL_c = \bar{c} - z\sigma_c = 7 - (2 \times 2.646) = 1.71$$

b. The number of defectives exceeds the upper control limit. Therefore, the process is probably out of control.

11. Sam's Taylor Shop.

a. $$\bar{c} = \frac{(9+3+6+11+3+12+0+4+7+5)}{10} = 6$$

$$\sigma_c = \sqrt{\bar{c}} = \sqrt{6} = 2.45$$
$$UCL_c = \bar{c} + z\sigma_c = 6 + (3 \times 2.45) = 13.35$$
$$LCL_c = \bar{c} - z\sigma_c = 6 - (3 \times 2.45) = -1.35 \qquad \text{(adjusted to zero)}$$

b. The number of defectives is close to, but does not exceed the upper control limit. Therefore, the process is assumed to be in control.

12. **Big Black Bird.**

a.
$$\bar{c} = \frac{(7+9+14+11+3+12+8+4+7+6)}{10} = 8.1$$

$$\sigma_c = \sqrt{\bar{c}} = \sqrt{8.1} = 2.846$$

$$UCL_c = \bar{c} + z\sigma_c = 8.1 + (3 \times 2.846) = 16.64$$

$$LCL_c = \bar{c} - z\sigma_c = 8.1 - (3 \times 2.846) = -0.438 \qquad \text{(adjusted to zero)}$$

b. The lower control limit is adjusted to zero because the number of dimples can not be negative. (A negative dimple would be a bump!) In this observation, the 15 defectives is above average, but below the upper control limit. On the basis of this one observation, we can not say that this process is out of control.

13. **Happy Soda, Inc.**

| | Observation | | | | | |
Sample	1	2	3	4	$\bar{x}$	R
1	12.00	11.97	12.10	12.08	12.0375	0.13
2	11.91	11.94	12.10	11.96	11.9775	0.19
3	11.89	12.02	11.97	11.99	11.9675	0.13
4	12.10	12.09	12.05	11.95	12.0475	0.15
5	12.08	11.92	12.12	12.05	12.0425	0.20
6	11.94	11.98	12.06	12.08	12.015	0.14
7	12.09	12.00	12.00	12.03	12.03	0.09
8	12.01	12.04	11.99	11.95	11.9975	0.09
9	12.00	11.96	11.97	12.03	11.99	0.07
10	11.82	11.86	12.09	12.18	11.9875	0.36
11	11.91	11.99	12.05	12.10	12.0125	0.19
12	12.01	12.00	12.06	11.97	12.01	0.09
13	11.98	11.99	12.06	12.03	12.015	0.08
14	12.02	12.00	12.05	11.95	12.005	0.10
15	12.00	12.05	12.01	11.97	12.0075	0.08
					12.0095	0.13933

$\bar{\bar{x}} = 12.0095$ ounces, $n = 4$, $\bar{R} = 13.933$ ounces

From Table 5.1,

$A_2 = 0.729$, $D_3 = 0.0$, $D_4 = 2.282$

$$UCL_R = D_4\bar{R} = 2.282(0.13933) = 0.31795 \text{ ounces}$$

$$LCL_R = D_3\bar{R} = 0.0(13.933) = 0.0 \text{ ounces}$$

$$UCL_{\bar{x}} = \bar{\bar{x}} + A_2\bar{R} = 12.0095 + 0.729(0.31795) = 12.2413 \text{ ounces}$$

$$LCL_{\bar{x}} = \bar{\bar{x}} - A_2\bar{R} = 12.0095 - 0.729(0.31795) = 11.7777 \text{ ounces}$$

Happy Soda, Inc. (continued)

a. The range for the tenth sample is out of control.

b. Process capability ratio:

$$C_p = \frac{\text{Upper specification } - \text{ Lower specification}}{6\sigma}$$

$$= \frac{12.1 - 11.9}{6(0.0668777)} = \frac{0.200}{0.4012662} = 0.4984222$$

This process is not capable. It will produce too many bottles outside of the allowable tolerances.

14. Pony-Express Burger Corral.

The average number of defects per order is:

$$\bar{c} = \frac{(211)}{100} = 2.11$$

$$\sigma_c = \sqrt{\bar{c}} = \sqrt{2.11} = 1.453$$

$$UCL_c = \bar{c} + z\sigma_c = 2.11 + (2 \times 1.453) = 5.016$$

$$LCL_c = \bar{c} - z\sigma_c = 2.11 - (2 \times 1.453) = 0.0$$

Four defects were present in the quality scout's order: 1) mustard, 2) condiment packets, 3) napkins, and 4) lid. The numbers work out so that this process appears to be in control, (4 < 5). However, when a customer says to hold the ketchup and mustard and "three handfuls of ketchup and mustard packets" are delivered, it is clear that there is an assignable cause. SPC assumes that assignable causes of variation have been removed *before* data is collected to set the control limits. In this case, Pony-Express has never established control of the order-filling process.

Defect	Frequency
Incomplete, shorted order	15
Unordered items dispensed	4
Wrong product dispensed	14
Wrong toppings	27
Wrong size drink	12
Drink lid not sealed	17
No drinking straw with soft drink order	8
No napkins	18
Far too many condiment packets	62
No salt with sandwich or fries order	10
Wrong change	7
Other	17
Total	211

15. *Today*. Since we don't know how many customers did not complain, we can not calculate a proportion of defective service. The number of defectives is an integer, so we might consider *c*-charts. However, it is reasonable to treat the number of complaints as a continuous variable.

Week	Sun.	Mon.	Tue.	Wed.	Thur.	Fri.	Sat.	Avg.	Range
1	127	163	201	175	111	150	158	155.0	90
2	199	189	136	154	119	107	153	151.0	92
3	120	145	106	165	183	151	124	142.0	77
4	182	105	139	159	163	141	161	150.0	77
5	139	186	188	164	116	175	159	161.0	72
								151.8	81.6

a. $\bar{\bar{x}} = 151.8$, $\bar{R} = 81.6$, $n = 7$

From Table 5.1:
$A_2 = 0.419$, $D_3 = 0.076$, $D_4 = 1.924$

$UCL_R = D_4\bar{R} = 1.924(81.6) = 157$

$LCL_R = D_3\bar{R} = 0.076(81.6) = 6.2$

$UCL_{\bar{x}} = \bar{\bar{x}} + A_2\bar{R} = 151.8 + 0.419(81.6) = 186.0$

$LCL_{\bar{x}} = \bar{\bar{x}} - A_2\bar{R} = 151.8 - 0.419(81.6) = 117.6$

b.

Week	Sun.	Mon.	Tue.	Wed.	Thur.	Fri.	Sat.	Avg.	Range
6	101	138	229	194	211	155	183	173	128

On the basis of this one sample, the process is not out of control.

16. Webster Chemical Company.

Sample	Tube Number								Avg.	Range
	1	2	3	4	5	6	7	8		
1	7.98	8.34	8.02	7.94	8.44	7.68	7.81	8.11	8.040	0.76
2	8.33	8.22	8.08	8.51	8.41	8.28	8.09	8.16	8.260	0.43
3	7.89	7.77	7.91	8.04	8.00	7.89	7.93	8.09	7.940	0.32
4	8.24	8.18	7.83	8.05	7.90	8.16	7.97	8.07	8.050	0.41
5	7.87	8.13	7.92	7.99	8.10	7.81	8.14	7.88	7.980	0.33
6	8.13	8.14	8.11	8.13	8.14	8.12	8.13	8.14	8.130	0.03
									8.067	0.38

Webster Chemical Company (continued)

a. $\bar{\bar{x}} = 8.00$, $\bar{R} = 0.38$, $n = 8$

From Table 5.1:

$A_2 = 0.373$, $D_3 = 0.136$, $D_4 = 1.864$

$$UCL_R = D_4\bar{R} = 1.864(0.38) = 0.708$$

$$LCL_R = D_3\bar{R} = 0.136(0.38) = 0.052$$

$$UCL_{\bar{x}} = \bar{\bar{x}} + A_2\bar{R} = 8.0 + 0.373(0.38) = 8.142$$

$$LCL_{\bar{x}} = \bar{\bar{x}} - A_2\bar{R} = 8.0 - 0.373(0.38) = 7.858$$

Referring to the table on the previous page, the range for the first observation is above the upper control limit and the range for the sixth observation is below the lower control limit.

b. Deleting the sixth observation and recalculating the control limits, the ranges then fall within the control limits.

Sample	Tube Number								Avg.	Range
	1	2	3	4	5	6	7	8	Avg.	Range
1	7.98	8.34	8.02	7.94	8.44	7.68	7.81	8.11	8.040	0.76
2	8.33	8.22	8.08	8.51	8.41	8.28	8.09	8.16	8.260	0.43
3	7.89	7.77	7.91	8.04	8.00	7.89	7.93	8.09	7.940	0.32
4	8.24	8.18	7.83	8.05	7.90	8.16	7.97	8.07	8.050	0.41
5	7.87	8.13	7.92	7.99	8.10	7.81	8.14	7.88	7.980	0.33
									8.054	0.45

$$\bar{R} = \frac{(0.76 + 0.43 + 0.32 + 0.41 + 0.33)}{5} = 0.45$$

$$UCL_R = D_4\bar{R} = 1.864(0.45) = 0.839$$

$$LCL_R = D_3\bar{R} = 0.136(0.45) = 0.061$$

$$UCL_{\bar{x}} = \bar{\bar{x}} + A_2\bar{R} = 8.0 + 0.373(0.45) = 8.168$$

$$LCL_{\bar{x}} = \bar{\bar{x}} - A_2\bar{R} = 8.0 - 0.373(0.45) = 7.832$$

The ranges, including the range for the first sample are all in control, but now the process average for the second sample falls outside of the revised control limits. We should look for assignable causes that would make the sample average become too high.

17. Webster, p-chart.

$$n = 144, \quad \bar{p} = \frac{72}{20(144)} = 0.025$$

$$\sigma_p = \sqrt{\bar{p}(1-\bar{p})/n} = \sqrt{0.025(0.975)/144} = 0.013$$

$$UCL_{\bar{p}} = \bar{p} + z\sigma_p = 0.025 + 3(0.013) = 0.064$$

$$LCL_{\bar{p}} = \bar{p} - z\sigma_p = 0.025 - 3(0.013) = -0.014, \text{ adjusted to zero}$$

The highest proportion of defectives occurs in sample #10, but is still within the control limits.
$p = 9/144 = 0.0625$
The process is in control.

18. Webster, c-chart.

$$\bar{c} = \frac{(6+5+0+4+6+4+1+6+5+0+9+2)}{12} = 4$$

$$\sigma_c = \sqrt{\bar{c}} = \sqrt{4} = 2$$

$$UCL_c = \bar{c} + z\sigma_c = 4 + (2 \times 2) = 8$$

$$LCL_c = \bar{c} - z\sigma_c = 4 - (2 \times 2) = 0$$

The eleventh tube has too many lumps (9), so the process is probably out of control.

19. Webster, process capability.

Process capability ratio:

$$C_p = \frac{\text{Upper specification} - \text{Lower specification}}{6\sigma} = \frac{8.6 - 7.4}{6(0.192)} = 1.0417$$

Process capability index:

$$C_{pk} = \text{minimum of} \quad \frac{x - \text{Lower specification}}{3\sigma}, \quad \frac{\text{Upper specification} - x}{3\sigma}$$

$$= \frac{8.054 - 7.400}{3(0.192)} = 1.135, \quad \frac{8.600 - 8.054}{3(0.192)} = 0.948$$

$$C_{pk} = 0.948$$

The process is not capable. Defectives will be produced even when the process is in control.

20. This problem uses an alternative approach (to Table 5.1) for setting control limits.

$$\bar{\bar{x}} = 8.0, \quad \sigma = 0.192, \quad n = 8$$

$$\sigma_{\bar{x}} = \frac{\sigma}{\sqrt{n}} = \frac{0.192}{\sqrt{8}} = 0.0679$$

$$UCL_{\bar{x}} = \bar{\bar{x}} + 3\sigma = 8.0 + 3(0.0679) = 8.204$$

$$LCL_{\bar{x}} = \bar{\bar{x}} - 3\sigma = 8.0 - 3(0.0679) = 7.796$$

Advanced Problems

21. Canine Gourmet.

The standard deviation of the <u>packet population</u> is 3.52 grams. The packaging process is essentially a sampling process from that population, with a sample size of 8. The standard deviation of that sample mean is:

$$\sigma_{\bar{x}} = \frac{\sigma}{\sqrt{n}} = \frac{3.52}{\sqrt{8}} = 1.2445$$

The packaging process capability ratio:

$$C_p = \frac{\text{Upper specification} - \text{Lower specification}}{6\sigma} = \frac{360 - 336}{6(1.2445)} = 3.214$$

The process capability ratio *does* meet the target of 1.33. If the student directly uses 3.52 grams for sigma, they would be led to believe the process is not capable. ($C_p = 1.136$) The point of this exercise is to show the averaging effect of the packaging process. This trick is sometimes used when a process is not capable. For example, if a process can not reliably produce a length within tolerances, the product is redesigned to require the assembly of several parts adding up to that length. Variability within the parts tends to cancel out, so the assembly of those parts is more likely to fall within the specified tolerances. In this case, if the treats are themselves large lumps, the weight in each packet will vary significantly depending on how many lumps happened to fall into the packet. Use of the package of eight tends to average out the variation present in the individual packets.

The process capability index:

$$C_{pk} = \text{minimum of} \quad \frac{X - \text{Lower specification}}{3\sigma}, \quad \frac{\text{Upper specification} - x}{3\sigma}$$

$$= \frac{(43 \times 8) - 336}{3(1.2445)} = 2.143, \quad \frac{360 - (43 \times 8)}{3(1.2445)} = 4.286$$

22. Mansfield Machinery Company. (measurements in thousandths of inches)

a. With $n = 4$, $\bar{R} = 2.0$, $\bar{\bar{x}} = 15$ the parameters of the x-chart are:

$$UCL_{\bar{x}} = \bar{\bar{x}} + A_2\bar{R} = 15 + 0.729(2) = 16.46$$

$$LCL_{\bar{x}} = \bar{\bar{x}} - A_2\bar{R} = 15 - 0.729(2) = 13.54$$

Sample	Minutes	$\bar{x}$
1	1– 4	15.75
2	9–12	15.00
3	17–20	13.75
4	25–28	14.75
5	33–36	15.50
6	41–44	16.25
7	49–52	14.75
8	57–60	16.00
9	65–68	14.00
10	73–76	16.75*

* Out-of-control points are observed in the tenth sample. The process would be stopped at the 76th minute.

b. With $n = 8$, $\overline{R} = 2.0$, $\overline{\overline{x}} = 15$ the parameters of the x-chart are:

$$UCL_{\overline{x}} = \overline{\overline{x}} + A_2\overline{R} = 15 + 0.373(2) = 15.746$$

$$LCL_{\overline{x}} = \overline{\overline{x}} - A_2\overline{R} = 15 - 0.373(2) = 14.254$$

Sample	Minutes	$\overline{x}$
1	1– 8	15.625
2	13–20	14.875
3	25–32	15.375
4	37–44	16.250* Out of control

i. We would stop the process at the end of minute 44.

ii. Taking larger samples on a frequent sampling interval will catch process average shifts more quickly than taking smaller samples.

23. Mansfield Machinery Company, continued.

a. From Problem 21a, $UCL_{\overline{x}} = 16.46$ and $LCL_{\overline{x}} = 13.54$.

Sample	Minutes	$\overline{x}$
1	1– 4	15.75
2	13–16	16.00
3	25–28	14.75
4	37–40	16.25
5	49–52	14.75
6	61–64	16.50 * Out of control

We would stop the process at the end of minute 64.

b. From Problem 21b, $UCL_{\overline{x}} = 15.75$ and $LCL_{\overline{x}} = 14.25$.

Sample	Minutes	$\overline{x}$
1	1– 8	15.63
2	17–24	14.75
3	33–40	15.88 * Out of control

We would stop the process at the end of minute 40.

c. Larger sample sizes resulted in faster detection of changes in the process average; however, the cost of inspection may be greater than for taking smaller sample sizes. The real trade-off is the cost of inspection versus the cost of not detecting the shift in the process average.

24. Northern Pines Brewery.

From data in Table 5.4, assuming 3 sigma control limits

$$\overline{p} = \frac{225}{30(250)} = 0.03$$

$$UCL_p = \overline{p} + 3\sigma_p = 0.03 + 3\sqrt{\frac{0.03(0.97)}{250}} = 0.062$$

$$LCL_p = \overline{p} - 3\sigma_p = 0.03 - 3\sqrt{\frac{0.03(0.97)}{250}} = -0.002 \quad \text{(adjusted to zero)}$$

All samples fall within the control limits, but samples 11, 12, 13, 14, and 15 have an upward run and samples 21, 22, 23, 24, and 25 have a downward run. Because runs of 5 or more usually indicate nonrandom behavior, we should investigate. We would like to avoid whatever was done when samples 11–15 were taken and to repeat what was done during samples 21–25.

25. Red Baron Airlines.

$$\bar{p} = \frac{195}{30(300)} = 0.0217$$

$$UCL_p = \bar{p} + 3\sigma_p = 0.0217 + 3\sqrt{\frac{0.0217(0.9783)}{300}} = 0.047$$

$$LCL_p = \bar{p} - 3\sigma_p = 0.217 - 3\sqrt{\frac{0.0217(0.9783)}{300}} = -0.004 \qquad \text{(adjusted to zero)}$$

Sample	Proportion Defective	Sample	Proportion Defective
1	0.010	16	0.017
2	0.027	17	0.013
3	0.017	18	0.030
4	0.037	19	0.043
5	0.023	20	0.013
6	0.007	21	0.040
7	0.040	22	0.033
8	0.030	23	0.020
9	0.003	24	0.007
10	0.027	25	0.003
11	0.010	26	0.027
12	0.017	27	0.013
13	0.023	28	0.017
14	0.030	29	0.027
15	0.040	30	0.007

The data indicate that all samples were within the control limits. Management should determine what occurred during samples 11–15 (an upward run) and samples 21–25 (a downward run) to determine the cause of the nonrandom behavior.

Supplement C

Acceptance Sampling

Problems

1. Alpha is the producer's risk. To find alpha, p is set equal to the acceptable quality level $(AQL = 0.5\%)$. Then $np = (180 \times 0.005) = 0.90$. From Appendix 4 where $c = 3$, $P(x \le c) = 0.987$. Alpha $= (1 - 0.987) = 0.013$, or 1.3%.

   Beta is the consumer's risk. To find beta, p is set equal to the lot tolerance proportion defective. $(LTPD = 4\%)$. Then $np = (180 \times 0.04) = 7.2$. From Appendix 4 where $c = 3$, $P(x \le c) = 0.072$. Beta $= 0.072$, or 7.2%.

2. a. A variety of sampling plans will satisfy the requirements. One such plan is $n = 280$, $c = 6$.

   To find alpha:

   $np = (280 \times 0.01) = 2.8$. Then $P(x \le c) = 0.976$ and Alpha $= (1 - 0.976) = 0.024$, or 2.4%.

   To find beta, $np = (280 \times 0.04) = 11.2$. Then $P(x \le c) = 0.071$ and Beta $= 0.071$, or 7.1%.

   b. The maximum value of the AOQ over various possible values of the proportion defective is 0.0122. The $AOQL$ is therefore 1.22 percent defective when the lot proportion defective is 0.02.

$$AOQ = \frac{p(P_a)(N-n)}{N}$$

Proportion Defective (p)	np	P_a	$(N - n / N)$	AOQ
0.000	0.0	1.000	0.907	0.0000
0.005	1.4	0.999	0.907	0.0045
0.010	2.8	0.976	0.907	0.0089
0.015	4.2	0.867	0.907	0.0118
0.020	5.6	0.670	0.907	**0.0122**
0.025	7.0	0.450	0.907	0.0102
0.030	8.4	0.267	0.907	0.0073
0.035	9.8	0.143	0.907	0.0045
0.040	11.2	0.071	0.907	0.0026

Average Outgoing Quality, AOQ

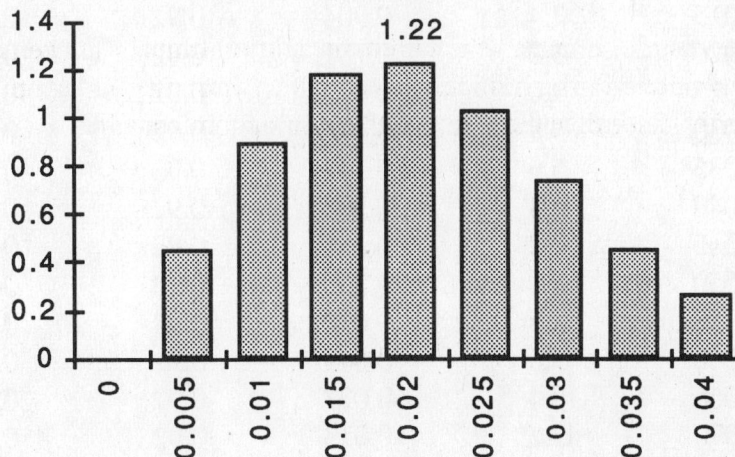

c. The OC curve is:

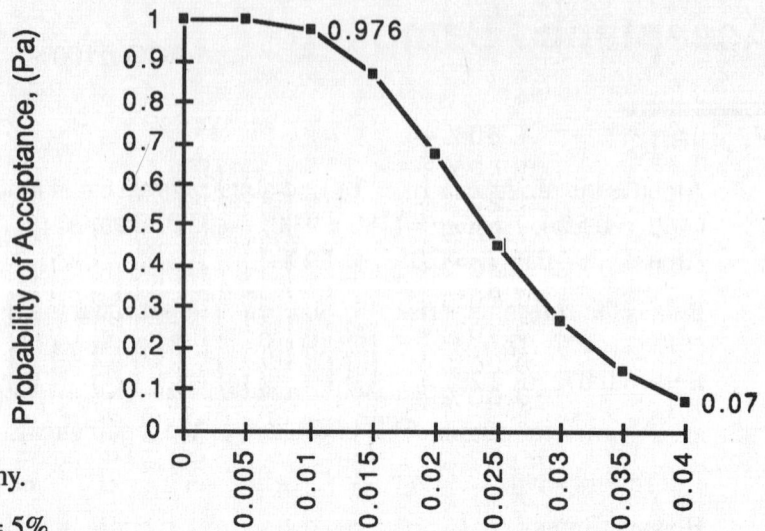

3. Lustre-Potion Shampoo Company.

   AQL = 10/1000, or 1%, LTPD = 5%

   a. Again, a variety of sampling plans will satisfy the requirements. One plan is $n = 160$, $c = 4$.

   To find alpha:
   $np = (160 \times 0.01) = 1.6$. Then $P(x \le c) = 0.976$ and Alpha $= (1 - 0.976) = 0.024$, or 2.4%.

   To find beta, $np = (160 \times 0.05) = 8.0$. Then $P(x \le c) = 0.100$ and Beta $= 0.100$, or 10.0%.

   b. $np = (160)(0.03) = 4.80$

   From Appendix 4, $Pa = 0.476$. There is a 47.6 percent probability that a shipment with 3 percent defectives will be rejected.

   c. The maximum value of the *AOQ* over various possible values of the proportion defective is 0.0145. The *AOQL* is 1.45 percent defective when the lot proportion defective is 0.025.

   $$AOQ = \frac{p(P_a)(N-n)}{N}$$

Proportion Defective (p)	np	P_a	$(N-n/N)$	AOQ
0.000	0.0	1.000	0.92	0.0000
0.005	0.8	0.999	0.92	0.0046
0.010	1.6	0.976	0.92	0.0090
0.015	2.4	0.904	0.92	0.0125
0.020	3.2	0.781	0.92	0.0144
0.025	4.0	0.629	0.92	**0.0145**
0.030	4.8	0.476	0.92	0.0131
0.035	5.6	0.342	0.92	0.0110
0.040	6.4	0.235	0.92	0.0086
0.045	7.2	0.156	0.92	0.0065
0.050	8.0	0.100	0.92	0.0046
0.055	8.8	0.070	0.92	0.0035
0.060	9.6	0.049	0.92	0.0027
0.065	10.4	0.023	0.92	0.0014
0.070	11.2	0.013	0.92	0.0008

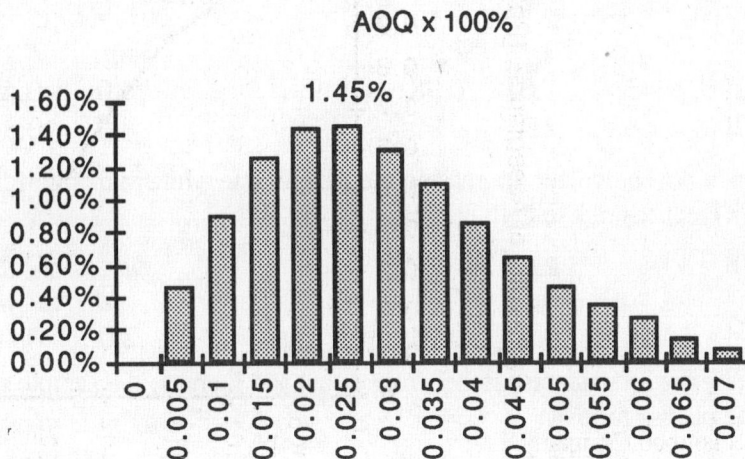

AOQ x 100%

4. Hospital Supply.

   a. $p = 0.0020$, $n = 400$

      $np = (400)(0.0020) = 0.8$

      From Appendix 4: when $c = 2$, $P_a = 0.953$,

      Therefore the producer's risk is $(1 - 0.953) = 0.047$, or 4.7%.

   b. $np = (400)(0.0025) = 1.0$

      From Appendix 4: $P_a = 0.920$.

      Therefore, there is an 8 percent (100% – 92%) probability that a shipment with a proportion defective equal to 0.025% will be returned.

   c. If alpha is required to be less than 5%, $P_a \geq 0.95$ (100% – 5%). Given $np = (400 \times 0.025) = 1.0$, then, from Appendix 4, when $c = 2$, $P_a = 0.920$, when $c = 3$, $P_a = 0.981$. c should have been set equal to 3.

      At $np = 0.8$ and $c = 3$, $P_a = 0.991$ and the producer's risk is $1 - 0.991 = 0.009$.

5. Electronic components

   $np = 2000(40 / 10000) = 8.0$

   Use Appendix. At $np = 8.0$ and $c = 4$, $P_a = 0.100$ and beta, the consumer's risk is $= 0.10$.

   If the AQL $= 10/10000 = 0.001$

   $np = 2000(0.001) = 2.0$

   At $np = 2.0$ and $c = 4$, $P_a = 0.947$ and alpha, the producer's risk is $= 0.053$. Increasing the sample would reduce the risk to both parties. Note that at high quality levels, the required sample size is very large and approaches the lot size.

6. We can make a comparison by computing the producer's and the consumer's risk for each plan using the Poisson chart in Appendix 4.

Plan		$p = $ AQL = 1%			$p = $ LTPD = 4%		
		np	P_a	α	np	P_a	β
1	$n = 100, c = 3$	1.0	0.981	1.9%	4.0	0.433	43.3%
2	$n = 200, c = 6$	2.0	0.995	0.5%	8.0	0.313	31.3%

The two plans are not equivalent. Increasing the sample size while maintaining the same acceptance proportions (c/n) reduces risk to both parties.

7. a. $n = 40, c = 1$

	$p = $ AQL = 1%			$p = $ LTPD = 5%		
	np	P_a	α	np	P_a	β
	0.4	0.938	6.2%	2.0	0.406	40.6%

b. If we increase the acceptance number from 1 to 4 and increase the sample size to 160, we can improve the plan as follows:

$n = 160, c = 4$

	$p = $ AQL = 1%			$p = $ LTPD = 5%		
	np	P_a	α	np	P_a	β
	1.6	0.976	2.4%	8.0	0.100	10.0%

c.

Proportion Defective (p)	Old Plan $n = 40, c = 1$				New Plan $n = 160, c = 4$			
	$(N-n/N)$	np	P_a	AOQ	$(N-n/N)$	np	P_a	AOQ
0.01	0.96	0.4	0.938	0.0090	0.84	1.6	0.976	0.0082
0.02	0.96	0.8	0.809	0.0155	0.84	3.2	0.781	0.0131
0.03	0.96	1.2	0.663	0.0191	0.84	4.8	0.476	0.0120
0.04	0.96	1.6	0.525	0.0202	0.84	6.4	0.235	0.0079
0.05	0.96	2.0	0.406	0.0195	0.84	8.0	0.100	0.0042
0.06	0.96	2.4	0.308	0.0177	0.84	9.6	0.038	0.0019
0.07	0.96	2.8	0.231	0.0155	0.84	11.2	0.013	0.0008

The *AOQL* is 2.02 percent for the old plan and 1.31 percent for the new plan.

8. $p = $ AQL = 0.020, $n = 200$

   $np = (200)(0.020) = 4.0$

   From Appendix 4: when $c \geq 8$, $P_a \geq 0.95$, and alpha $\leq 5\%$.

   $p = $ LTPD = 0.080, $n = 200$

   $np = (200)(0.080) = 16.0$

   From Appendix 4: when $c \leq 9$, $P_a \leq 0.05$, and beta $\leq 5\%$.

   Therefore, when $n = 100$ and $8 \leq c \leq 9$, alpha and beta will <u>both</u> be less than 5%.

9. $p = $ AQL = 0.020, $c = 5$

   In Appendix 4, follow the $c = 5$ column down to 0.951, read to the left to find $np = 2.6$.
   $np = (n)(0.020) = 2.6$
   Therefore, $n = 130$

   $p = $ LTPD = 0.080, $c = 5$, $n = 130$

   From Appendix 4, follow the $c = 5$ column down to 0.951, read to the left to find $np = 2.6$.
   $np = (130)(0.080) = 10.4$, $P_a = 0.053$, and Beta = 5.3%
   Therefore, $n = 130$

10. In Appendix 4, in the $c = 11$ column, the value 0.100 is in the row where $np = 16.6$.
    Given p = LTPD = 8%, $np = 16.6$,
    $n (0.08) = 16.6$
    $n = 207.5$ or 208

11. A variety of sampling plans will satisfy the requirements.

    To find the ranges of n, select a value for c and solve for n.

    Example: if $c = 4$, then

    Producer's risk

    AQL = 0.1%, $p = 0.001$

    $\alpha = 1 - Pa \le 5\%$, therefore Pa $\ge 95\%$

    Follow column where $c = 4$ down to where Pa = 0.956.

    $np \le 1.9$ and therefore n ≤ 1900

    Consumer's risk

    LTPD = 0.5%, $p = 0.005$

    $\beta = Pa \le 10\%$, therefore Pa $\ge 90\%$

    Follow column where $c = 4$ down to where Pa = 0.100.

    $np \le 8.0$ and therefore n ≥ 1600

    Therefore, when $c = 4$, any plan with $1600 \le n \le 1900$ will satisfy the requirements.

    One such plan is $n = 1600$, $c = 4$.
    To find alpha:
        $np = (1600 \times 0.001) = 1.6$. Then $P(x \le c) = 0.976$ and Alpha $= (1 - 0.976) = 0.024$, or 2.4%.
    To find beta: $np = (1600 \times 0.005) = 8.0$. Then $P(x \le c) = 0.100$ and Beta $= 0.100$, or 10.0%.

12. This problem is similar to Review Problem 11. It is intended to show that as the desired quality
    level increases from percent defective to parts per million defective, the required sample size
    increases in direct proportion. At some point, either 100% inspection or an entirely different
    approach (such statistical process control) is required to achieve the desired quality assurance.
    One plan is $n = 16000$, $c = 4$.
    To find alpha:
        $np = (16000 \times 0.0001) = 1.6$. Then $P(x \le c) = 0.976$ and Alpha $= (1 - 0.976) = 0.024$, or 2.4%.
    To find beta: $np = (16000 \times 0.0005) = 8.0$. Then $P(x \le c) = 0.100$ and Beta $= 0.100$, or 10.0%.

13. a. $AOQL = 0.002982$, $n = 508$, $c = 5$.
    b. i.   When N is increased to 2000, $AOQL = 0.004515$, $n = 508$, $c = 5$.
        ii. When AQL is increased to 0.008, $AOQL = 0.000441$, $n = 948$, $c = 12$.
        iii. When LTPD is increased to 0.06, $AOQL = 0.012518$, $n = 99$, $c = 2$.

    c. i.   Increasing N raises the $AOQL$ because the sample is a smaller proportion of the total lot.
             When we accept the lot, only the defects in the sample are replaced; consequently, a greater
             proportion of defects gets passed.

        ii. Increasing AQL reduces the $AOQL$ because it causes a great increase in the sample size. All
             defects found in the sample are replaced, even if the lot is accepted. The sample size
             increases because the plan must be more discriminating now that the AQL and LTPD are
             closer in value.

        iii. Increasing LTPD serves to increase the $AOQL$. The sample size is smaller, and in effect we
             are saying that we will accept worse quality with the same probabilities.

14. a. $AOQL = 0.00263$, $n = 399$, $c = 3$.
    b. i. When N is increased to 2000,
            $AOQL = 0.003501$, $n = 399$, $c = 3$.
        ii. When AQL is increased to 0.003,
            $AOQL = 0.002773$, $n = 461$, $c = 4$.
        iii. When LTPD is increased to 0.04,
            $AOQL = 0.00524$, $n = 207$, $c = 2$.
    c. i. Increasing N raises the $AOQL$ because the sample is a smaller proportion of the total lot. When we accept the lot, only the defects in the sample are replaced; consequently, a greater proportion of defects gets passed.
        ii. Increasing AQL reduces the $AOQL$ because it causes a great increase in the sample size. All defects found in the sample are replaced, even if the lot is accepted. The sample size increases because the plan must be more discriminating now that the AQL and the LTPD are closer in value.
        iii. Increasing the LTPD serves to increase the $AOQL$. The sample size is smaller, and in effect we are saying that we will accept worse quality with the same probabilities.

15. Breakthrough Technologies.
    a. With a sampling plan where $c = 5$, $n = 120$
        When AOQ $= 0.02$, $np = 2.4$, and $\alpha = 3.6\%$.
        When LTPD $= 0.08$, $np = 9.6$, and $\beta = 8.4\%$.
    b. OC Curve

Proportion Defective (p)	np	P_a
0.000	0.0	1.000
0.010	1.2	0.998
0.020	2.4	**0.964**
0.030	3.6	0.844
0.040	4.8	0.651
0.050	6.0	0.446
0.060	7.2	0.276
0.070	8.4	0.157
0.080	9.6	**0.084**
0.090	10.8	0.042
0.100	12.0	0.020

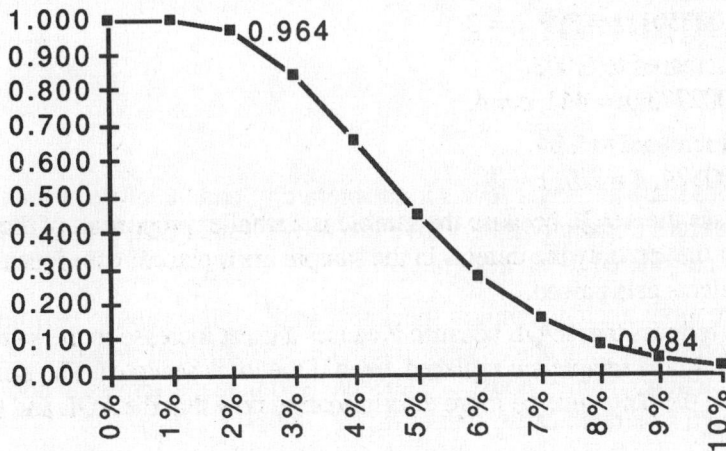

c. When the lot is 4% defective, $p = 0.04$, $np = 5.2$, Pa = 58.1%

   When the lot is 6% defective, $p = 0.06$, $np = 7.8$, Pa = 21.0%

d. AOQL with $n = 120$ and $N = 1000$

Proportion Defective (p)	np	P_a	$(N - n / N)$	AOQ
0.000	0.0	1.000	0.88	0.0000
0.010	1.2	0.998	0.88	0.0088
0.020	2.4	0.964	0.88	0.0170
0.030	3.6	0.844	0.88	0.0223
0.040	4.8	0.651	0.88	**0.0229**
0.050	6.0	0.446	0.88	0.0196
0.060	7.2	0.276	0.88	0.0146
0.070	8.4	0.157	0.88	0.0097
0.080	9.6	0.084	0.88	0.0059
0.090	10.8	0.042	0.88	0.0033
0.100	12.0	0.020	0.88	0.0018

AOQL with $n = 120$ and $N = 2000$

Proportion Defective (p)	np	P_a	$(N - n / N)$	AOQ
0.000	0.0	1.000	0.94	0.0000
0.010	1.2	0.998	0.94	0.0094
0.020	2.4	0.964	0.94	0.0181
0.030	3.6	0.844	0.94	0.0238
0.040	4.8	0.651	0.94	**0.0245**
0.050	6.0	0.446	0.94	0.0210
0.060	7.2	0.276	0.94	0.0156
0.070	8.4	0.157	0.94	0.0103
0.080	9.6	0.084	0.94	0.0063
0.090	10.8	0.042	0.94	0.0036
0.100	12.0	0.020	0.94	0.0019

Chapter 6

Workforce Management

Study Questions

1. In horizontal organizations there are fewer levels in the hierarchy, and therefore promotions from one level to another occur less frequently. Alternative incentives (other than promotion and advancement) should be considered in job design.

2. Vertical organizations are more likely to employ specialists in disciplines and to perform functions sequentially with little communication across department lines. Horizontal organizations employ generalists to perform functions simultaneously. "The idea is to manage across functional areas as opposed to managing down a hierarchical structure."

3. Seven key elements of horizontal organizations:

   - Organization around the process
   - Flat organizational hierarchy
   - Team management
   - Customer driven performance measures
   - Rewards for team performance
   - Supplier and customer contact
   - Training programs for all employees

4. Scientific management focuses on the engineering or technical aspects of work and ignores the behavioral and social aspects of work.

5. The arguments for narrowly defined jobs include:

   - Less training time required to learn specialized methods
   - An increase of output due to the faster work pace
   - Lower wage rates because education and skill requirements are lower

   The arguments against narrowly defined jobs include:

   - Adverse behavioral consequences; poor morale, high turnover and absenteeism, lower quality because of boredom
   - Increased requirement for management coordination of a large number of narrow jobs
   - Employees receiving narrow training are less likely to be able to fill in for absent coworkers

6. Horizontal job enlargement entails increasing the number of tasks assigned to an employee, whereas vertical job enrichment entails increasing the tasks and responsibilities of the worker. In the first case, a worker may learn several different operations of a given process. In the second case, the employee may not only learn these different operations but may also be responsible for determining when maintenance must be performed on the machines processing these operations or for inspecting the output of these operations. Job enlargement can help in overcoming many of the arguments against narrowly defined jobs (boredom, poor quality, work imbalance, and the like) without significantly hampering the operation.

7. An assembly line worker has the opportunity to perfect a given skill or skills. However, the assembly line worker lacks the opportunity to interact with other workers or to control the pace or type of work. The law office secretary may have the opportunity to control and vary her workload and interact with other employees. Both the assembly line worker and law office secretary may lack the opportunity to advance to a better position or to show initiative.

8. A labor standard (grade for the course) is the time required for a trained worker (student) to perform a given task (get to the goal line) using a prescribed work method (running) with normal effort and skill. The key word here is **normal**. It is likely that only world-class sprinters will ever pass the course with this standard. Normal effort should be the pace that we would expect most students to achieve in running 50 yards—it certainly should be more than 5 seconds. Besides, sprinting is not related to passing an operations management course—or is it?

9. Italian Maiden Pizza Company. Time standards might be developed for the new product in one of three ways: study a similar process at other companies making the same product (unlikely to do this); use expert judgment based on historical data to arrive at a standard; or use predetermined time standards.

10. Time studies are not as precise as they appear. The observer can make errors in recording the data or in starting and stopping the watch properly. In addition, after all the base times have been recorded, someone must arrive at a performance rating and an allowance factor. Both of these measures require considerable judgment, which detracts from objectivity.

11. In this example it is likely that some elements require about the same amount of time each time a new contract is started, while others depend upon the dimensions of the job. For example, you could use the historical averages of the normal times for the elements "consultation with the customer to get the specifications" and "drawing the plans" because these elements would probably not vary much from contract to contract. The other three activities—"digging the foundation," "building the forms," and "laying the concrete"—would likely be a function of the width, length, and depth of the patio floor. Equations for estimating the times for these elements could be developed.

12. With reference to the formula for sample size in a work sampling study:

$$n = \frac{z^2 \hat{p}(1-\hat{p})}{e^2}$$

for a proportion of 0.28, a precision of 0.05, and a confidence interval of 95%:

$$n = \frac{(1.96)^2(0.28)(1-0.28)}{(0.05)^2} = 309.8 \text{ or } 310 \text{ observations}$$

a precision of 0.01 at the same confidence interval would require:

$$n = \frac{(1.96)^2(0.28)(1-0.28)}{(0.01)^2} = 7744.7 \text{ or } 7745 \text{ observations}$$

Obviously there is a considerable difference in the required sample size for the greater precision. Is it worth it? The cost of sampling must be weighed against the cost of making a poor decision based on a wrong estimate. If for example, the microcomputers can be justified by a 10% savings in employees' time, there is no need to show with precision that the current proportion of time spent on this activity is between 27% and 29%. 95% confidence that the actual proportion of time spent manually completing forms is somewhere between 23% and 32% (28% ± 5%), would be sufficient to make the decision. On the other hand, if a 25% reduction in labor is required to justify the investment, and the investment is substantial, the more comprehensive study may be appropriate.

Problems

1. A worker.
   a. Normal time per cycle = (Average observed time)(Rating factor)
      The average observed time is: 50 minutes/10 parts
      = 5.0 min/part
      The normal time per cycle is then:

      $$NT = \bar{t}(F)(RF) = 5.0(1)(0.95) = 4.75 \text{ min / part}$$

   b. Standard time = Normal time (1.0 + allowance):

      $$ST = NTC\,(1.0 + A)$$
      $$= 4.75\,(1.0 + 0.20)$$
      $$= 5.70 \text{ min/part}$$

2. Swifty Car Lube.
   a. Normal time per cycle = (Average observed time)(Rating factor)
      The average observed time is: 178 minutes/20 oil changes
      = 8.9 min/change

      $$NT = 8.9\,(1.10) = 9.79 \text{ min/change}$$

   b. $ST = 9.79\,(1.10) = 10.77$ min/change

3. Bill's fast-food restaurant

Work

Element	1	2	3	4	5	$\bar{t}$	RF	F	NT
1	0.45	0.41	0.50	0.48	0.36	0.44	0.9	1	0.396
2	0.85	0.81	0.77	0.89	0.83	0.83	1.2	1	0.996
3	0.60	0.55	0.59	0.58	0.63	0.59	1.2	1	0.708
4	0.31	0.24	0.27	0.26	0.32	0.28	1.0	1	0.280

Normal time per cycle (*NTC*), in minutes per burger   = 2.380

Standard time = Normal time per cycle (1.0 + allowance)

$$ST = NTC\,(1.0 + A)$$
$$= 2.380\,(1.0 + 0.15)$$
$$= 2.737 \text{ min/unit}$$

Employees needed = 300 (2.737) / 190

= 4.322 or 5 employees (The employees will have some slack time.)

4. Bill's fast-food restaurant, continued.

a. Work element 3, select time.

$$\bar{t} = \frac{0.45 + 0.31 + 0.50 + 0.48 + 0.39 + 0.31 + 0.44 + 0.29 + 0.33 + 0.40}{10} = 0.390$$

Revised normal time: 0.390 (1) (1.2) = 0.468

b. Revised normal time per cycle.

Work Element	NT
1	0.396
2	0.996
3'	0.468
4	0.280

Normal time per cycle, (NTC)   = 2.140 min/burger

Revised standard time per cycle.

$ST = NTC (1.0 + A)$

$\quad = 2.140 (1.0 + 0.15)$

$\quad = 2.461$ min/burger

c. Sample size for work element 3, — 98% confident to be within ± 13 %.

$$\sigma = \sqrt{\frac{\sum(t_i - \bar{t})}{n-1}} = \sqrt{\frac{\sum(t_i - 0.468)}{9}} = 0.077$$

$$n = \left[\left(\frac{z}{p}\right)\left(\frac{\sigma}{\bar{t}}\right)\right]^2 = \left[\left(\frac{2.33}{0.13}\right)\left(\frac{0.077}{0.468}\right)\right]^2 = 8.7$$

$n = 9$, therefore enough observations have been already made.

d. Number of employees required when 3rd work element is inflated by 13%.

Standard time (3rd work element time is increased by 13%)

ST = NTC x 1.15 = [0.396 + 0.996 + (1.13x0.468) + 0.280] (1.15) = 2.53

Employees needed   = 300 (2.53) / 190

$\qquad\qquad\qquad$ = 3.996 = or 4 employees (There would be almost no slack time.)

There is often little or no trust between management and labor. In such an environment, the suspicious cook will not tell management about his improved method. He would be concerned that a co-worker would be fired and those remaining would have to work harder.

5. Black Sheep Wool Company.

To get the normal time for this job we must first determine the observed time for each work element for each cycle. This is found by subtracting successive continuous clock readings. The table below contains the data needed to compute the normal time per cycle.

Work Element	1	2	3	4	5	6	7	8	9	10	11	12	$\bar{t}$	F	RF	NT
1 fill	0.20	0.22	0.24	0.18	0.20	0.21	0.22	0.19	0.24	0.18	0.19	0.25	0.21	1.00	1.2	0.252
2 sew	0.40	0.38	0.37	0.41	0.41	0.40	0.36	0.37	0.41	0.42	0.39	0.36	0.39	1.00	0.8	0.312
3 transport	—	—	0.82	—	—	0.84	—	—	0.73	—	—	0.85	0.81	0.33	1.1	0.294

Normal time per cycle (NTC) = 0.858 min/unit

6. Thicket Bros.

Work Element	Observed cycle number						F	RF
	1 Left side	2 Right side	3 Left side	4 Right side	5 Left side	6 Right side		
1. Wait for car lift	2.9	—	69.0	—	155.6	—	0.5	1.0
2. Remove lugs	6.2	24.3	72.6	91.0	159.6	176.8	1	0.9
3. Switch tires	12.6	31.4	79.4	98.3	165.8	183.2	1	1.2
4. Tighten lugs	16.7	35.2	82.9	103.2	169.3	187.4	1	0.8
5. Move to right side	20.5	—	87.2	—	172.5	—	0.5	1.2
6. Clear away for drop	—	37.3	—	105.9	—	189.4	0.5	0.9
Prepare for next drill	—	65.8	—	153.0	—	—	na	na

The following table shows the elapsed times for each of the observations, the average time and normal time for each work element, and the normal time for the (left plus right side) cycle. The time between pit stops is not relevant to the study.

Work Element	Observed cycle number						$\bar{t}$	F	RF	NT
	1 Left side	2 Right side	3 Left side	4 Right side	5 Left side	6 Right side				
1. Wait for car lift	2.9	—	3.2	—	2.6	—	2.9	0.5	1.0	1.45
2. Remove lugs	3.3	3.8	3.6	3.8	4.0	4.3	3.8	1	0.9	3.42
3. Switch tires	6.4	7.1	6.8	7.3	6.2	6.4	6.7	1	1.2	8.04
4. Tighten lugs	4.1	3.8	3.5	4.9	3.5	4.2	4.0	1	0.8	3.20
5. Move to right side	3.8	—	4.3	—	3.2	—	3.7667	0.5	1.2	2.26
6. Clear away for drop	—	2.1	—	2.7	—	2.0	2.6667	0.5	0.9	1.02
Prepare for next drill	—	28.5	—	47.1	—	—	na	na	NTC=	19.39

a. The normal time for changing four tires is 19.39 seconds. (A bit slow for a pit stop. Apparently the Thicket Bros. still need some improvement in order to compete with the Woods Bros.)

b. $\sigma = \sqrt{\dfrac{\sum(t_i - \bar{t})}{n-1}} = \sqrt{\dfrac{\sum(t_i - 6.7)}{5}} = 0.438$

$n = \left[\left(\dfrac{z}{p}\right)\left(\dfrac{\sigma}{\bar{t}}\right)\right]^2 = \left[\left(\dfrac{1.96}{0.05}\right)\left(\dfrac{0.438}{6.7}\right)\right]^2 = 6.57$ or 7 observations

As 6 observations are already taken, only one more observation is needed.

7. Cellular telephone assembly. 95% confident work element 1 is within ± 3%.

Work Element	Observation								$\bar{t}$	F	RF	NT
	1	2	3	4	5	6	7	8				
1. Assemble unit	0.78	0.70	0.75	0.80	0.79	0.82	0.81	0.80	0.7812	1.0	1.2	0.9375
2. Insert batteries	0.20	0.21	0.16	0.19	0.23	0.25	0.24	0.26	0.2175	1.0	1.0	0.2175
3. Test	0.61	0.60	0.55	0.57	0.63	0.61	0.62	0.60	0.5988	1.0	0.9	0.5389
4. Package	0.41	0.36	0.45	0.37	0.39	0.40	0.43	0.44	0.4063	1.0	1.1	0.4469

$$\sigma = \sqrt{\frac{\sum(t_i - \bar{t})}{n-1}} = \sqrt{\frac{\sum(t_i - 0.7812)}{7}} = 0.0391$$

$$n = \left[\left(\frac{z}{p}\right)\left(\frac{\sigma}{\bar{t}}\right)\right]^2 = \left[\left(\frac{1.96}{0.03}\right)\left(\frac{0.0391}{0.7812}\right)\right]^2 = 10.69 \text{ or } 11 \text{ observations}$$

$(11 - 8) = 3$ more observations are required.

8. Coffee cup packaging.

   a. The select times, average times, and normal times for each work element are shown in the following table.

Operation: COFFEE CUP PACKAGING		Date 1/23		Operator: B. LARSON		Clock no: 43-6205									
Element Description		Observations										$\bar{t}$	F	RF	NT
		1	2	3	4	5	6	7	8	9	10				
1. Get two cartons	t	0.48	—	0.46	—	0.54	—	0.49	—	0.51	—	0.496			0.2604
	r	0.48		4.85		9.14		13.53		17.83			0.5	1.05	
2. Put liner into carton	t	0.11	0.13	0.09	0.10	0.11	0.13	0.08	0.12	0.10	0.09	0.106			0.1007
	r	0.59	2.56	4.94	6.82	9.25	11.23	13.61	15.50	17.93	19.83		1.0	0.95	
3. Place cups into carton	t	0.74	0.68	0.71	0.69	0.73	0.70	0.68	0.74	0.71	0.72	0.710			0.7810
	r	1.33	3.24	5.65	7.51	9.98	11.93	14.29	16.24	18.64	20.55		1.0	1.10	
4. Seal carton, set aside	t	1.10	1.15	1.07	1.09	1.12	1.11	1.09	1.08	1.10	1.13	1.104			0.9936
	r	2.43	4.39	6.72	8.60	11.10	13.04	15.38	17.32	19.74	21.68		1.0	0.90	

NTC = 0.2604 + 0.1007 + 0,7810 + 0.9936 = 2.1357

ST = 1.15 (2.1357) = 2.456

Coffe cup packaging, continued.

b. Because of the relatively high ratio $(\sigma/\bar{t})$ for the second work element, it requires more observations than do the other work elements.

Element Description	s	$\bar{t}$	$s/\bar{t}$
1. Get two cartons	0.0305	0.496	0.0615
2. Put liner into carton	0.0171	0.106	**0.1613**
3. Place cups into carton	0.0226	0.710	0.0318
4. Seal carton, set aside	0.0241	1.104	0.0219

$$n = \left(\frac{z\sigma}{p\bar{t}}\right)^2 = \left(\frac{1.96 \times 0.0171}{0.05 \times 0.106}\right)^2 = 39.99 \text{ or } 40 \text{ observations}$$

Work elements 1, 3, and 4 require 6, 2 and 1 observations, respectively.

c. Doubling the precision interval reduces the required number of observations by a factor of four. The number of observations required for 10% precision is 10. We have already made enough observations for 95% confidence with a 10% precision interval.

9. Package delivery service. The preliminary work sample provides an estimate for the proportion of time spent outside of the truck.

$$\hat{p} = \frac{15+29+10+18+24+11+13}{127+186+114+125+157+148+143} = \frac{120}{1000} = 0.12$$

$$n = \frac{z^2\hat{p}(1-\hat{p})}{e^2} = \frac{(1.96)^2(0.12)(1-0.12)}{(0.02)^2} = 1014.2 \text{ or } 1015 \text{ observations}$$

Only 15 more observations are required. A recent newspaper article titled "The UPS Rings Twice", noted that UPS customer's value personal contact. Therefore, drivers' time spent outside of the truck while waiting for customers to answer the door is not necessarily wasted time.

10. Eye contact.

a. $$n = \frac{z^2\hat{p}(1-\hat{p})}{e^2} = \frac{(1.65)^2(0.40)(1-0.40)}{(0.03)^2} = 726 \text{ observations}$$

b. The available time for the study is 29 x 75 minutes = 2175 minutes. The graduate assistant should make an observation on the average of once every (2175/726) = 2.996 or 3 minutes. In order to obtain representative data, is important to randomly vary the elapsed time between observations. Observations should not be made at 3 minute intervals.

11. Graft City Mayoral Election.

    a. Calculation of normal and standard times

Graft City					Form # 13-4927-R364			Public Works Department			James (Jimmy) Johnson, Director		
Operation: *YARD SIGN ASSEMBLY*					Date *9/27*			Observer: *JERIMIAH (JERRY) JOHNSON*					
Element Description	**Observations**										$\bar{t}$	*F*	*RF*	*NT*
	1	2	3	4	5	6	7	8	9	10				
1. Get stake *t*	8	9	6	10	10	5	8	9	6	9	8.00			8.40
and sign *r*	*8*	*39*	*70*	*107*	*293*	*332*	*358*	*405*	*433*	*463*		*1.0*	*1.05*	
2. Put glue *t*	6	7	5	5	9	4	7	5	3	4	5.50			4.40
onto stake *r*	*14*	*46*	*75*	*112*	*302*	*336*	*365*	*410*	*436*	*467*		*1.0*	*0.8*	
3. Place sign, *t*	11	14	15	—*	17	11	22	11	13	22	15.11			13.60
four staples *r*	*25*	*60*	*90*	*277*	*319*	*347*	*387*	*421*	*449*	*489*		*1.0*	*0.9*	
4. Check asm., *t*	5	4	7	6	8	3	9	6	5	5	5.80			6.96
set aside *r*	*30*	*64*	*97*	*283*	*327*	*350*	*396*	*427*	*454*	*494*		*1.0*	*1.2*	

$$\text{NTC} = 8.40 + 4.40 + 13.60 + 6.96 = 33.36$$
$$\text{ST} = (1.25 \times 33.36) = 41.70$$

    b. The second work element has the highest ratio of $\sigma/\bar{t}$ so it will require the most observations.

Element Description	*s*	$\bar{t}$	$s/\bar{t}$
1. Get stake and sign	1.7638	8.00	0.2205
2. Put glue onto stake	1.7795	5.50	**0.3235**
3. Place sign, four staples	4.4001	15.11	0.2912
4. Check asm., set aside	1.8135	5.80	0.3127

$$n = \left(\frac{z\sigma}{p\bar{t}}\right)^2 = \left[\frac{(2.58)(0.3235)}{(0.05)(5.5)}\right]^2 = 9.21 \text{ or } 10 \text{ observations}$$

No addtional observations are required.

12. Evergreen Life Insurance Company. The preliminary work sample provides an estimate for the proportion of time data entry operator is idle.

$$\hat{p} = \frac{2+3+3+4+1+3+6}{13+15+14+16+14+16+12} = \frac{22}{100} = 0.22$$

$$n = \frac{z^2\hat{p}(1-\hat{p})}{e^2} = \frac{(1.96)^2(0.22)(1-0.22)}{(0.05)^2} = 263.7 \text{ or } 264 \text{ observations}$$

$(264 - 100) = 164$ more observations are required.

13. Twin Fork Post Office. (Assuming 95% confidence interval)

a. Special stamp sales.

$$\hat{p} = \frac{4}{100} = 0.04$$

$$n = \frac{z^2 \hat{p}(1-\hat{p})}{e^2} = \frac{(1.96)^2(0.04)(0.96)}{(0.05)^2} = 59 \text{ observations}$$

T-shirts.

$$\hat{p} = \frac{5}{100} = 0.05$$

$$n = \frac{z^2 \hat{p}(1-\hat{p})}{e^2} = \frac{(1.96)^2(0.05)(0.95)}{(0.05)^2} = 73 \text{ observations}$$

Passports.

$$\hat{p} = \frac{3}{100} = 0.03$$

$$n = \frac{z^2 \hat{p}(1-\hat{p})}{e^2} = \frac{(1.96)^2(0.03)(0.97)}{(0.05)^2} = 44.7 \text{ or } 45 \text{ observations}$$

The sample size is adequate for special stamp sets, T-shirts, and passports because the sample size of 100 is greater than the sample size requirements . The clerks spend 69 percent of their time selling postage, 11 percent dealing with priority mail, 4 percent selling special stamp sets, 5 percent selling T-shirts, 3 percent helping customers with passport applications, and 8 percent of their time doing other things.

b. If a special stamp machine is purchased, payback would take approximately

$$\frac{\$3500}{(0.04)(3)(\$25,000/yr)} = 1.16 \text{ years}$$

at the current demand rate. Management must assess the future demand of special stamp sales before purchasing. If demand is expected to remain constant or to increase, the purchase should be made. In addition, management must determine whether purchasers of special stamp sets would actually use the machine or if they prefer personal contact with a clerk.

14. Bank encoding department.

   a. Proportion of time spent cleaning $= \hat{p} = \dfrac{15}{100} = 0.15$

   Estimated annual net saving $= 0.75(0.15)(\$24,000)(25)$
   $$= \$67,500$$

   b. 95 percent confidence interval (CI):

   $$CI = \hat{p} \pm z\sigma_p = \hat{p} \pm z\left(\sqrt{\dfrac{\hat{p}(1-\hat{p})}{n}}\right)$$

   $$= 0.15 \pm 1.96\sqrt{\dfrac{0.15(0.85)}{100}}$$

   $$= 0.15 \pm 0.07$$

   $$0.08 \le CI \le 0.22$$

   If P turns out to be 0.08, the annual savings would be reduced to \$36,000. If the payback at 0.08 is unacceptable, we should take a larger sample to be more sure of the estimate.

Advanced Problems

15. Lamps "R" Us

Observation

Element	1	2	3	4	5	6	7	8	9	10	F	RF	$\bar{t}$	NT
1	1.27	1.27	1.24	1.25	1.20	1.26	1.24	1.27	1.26	1.24	1	1.05	1.25	1.3125
2	2.10	2.09	2.18	2.17	2.09	2.08	2.15	2.18	2.14	2.12	1	0.95	2.13	2.0235
3	0.60	0.59	0.64	0.67	0.65	0.68	0.61	0.62	0.64	0.60	1	1.05	0.63	0.6615
4	0.39	0.42	0.32	0.40	0.34	0.36	0.37	0.38	0.40	0.32	1	0.90	0.37	0.3330
5	0.51	0.53	0.45	0.44	0.47	0.49	0.45	0.50	0.46	0.50	1	0.95	0.48	0.4560
6	0.26		0.29		0.30		0.27		0.28		0.5	1.00	0.28	0.1400
7	0.86	0.91	0.89	0.86	0.84	0.85	0.91	0.88	0.86	0.84	1	1.10	0.87	0.9570
8	1.19	1.18	1.20	1.16	1.21	1.15	1.16	1.20	1.18	1.17	1	1.00	1.18	1.1800

NTC = 7.0635

ST = NTC (1 + A) = 7.0635 (1.15) = 8.123 minutes per unit.

Output = (480 minutes/day)/8.123 minutes/unit = 59.09 or 59 units per day

Supplement D

Learning Curves

Study Questions

1. In Chapter 2, Fig. 2.5 shows that firms position themselves along a diagonal that starts with low volumes in the upper left corner and high volumes in the lower right corner. Those firms in the lower right corner compete on low price and high volume. Consider a firm just entering a new market. Initially volumes are low and prices high to cover start-up costs. As the learning curve takes hold, and volumes increase, the firm slides down the diagonal of Fig. 2.5 toward the high-volume, low-price position. Indeed, the competitive strategy may be to price the product aggressively to take advantage of the volume increases and move down the learning curve ahead of competitors.

2. An 80 percent learning curve would produce a lower number of direct labor hours per unit because each time cumulative production is doubled, the direct labor per unit is reduced by 20 percent. This reduction is only 10 percent for the 90 percent curve.

3. Simple tasks require little learning. After the first few repetitions, just about all that can be learned, has been learned. The time required for the simple task is then determined by physical rather than mental ability.

4. The learning effect of automation resembles more of a step function than it does the exponential decay characteristic of the traditional learning curve. When automation is implemented, the learning curve usually takes a brief spike upwards due to disruption and required training. That is soon followed by a steep drop, which then just as suddenly levels off. With few exceptions, such as some computer chess programs, machines do not learn. Learning is a human characteristic. When automation replaces human effort to the extent that production becomes machine paced, learning stops altogether. A characteristic of just-in-time systems is for continuous improvement. Automation that would result in machine-paced lines is delayed until all learning has been accomplished.

5. Implementing changes disrupts the learning effect. Continuous disruption due to continuous design changes would defeat all learning.

6. This is related to Study Question 1. Low prices can speed market development and market penetration. Production response to high demand quickly moves costs down the learning curve. The company has an advantage in competing on the basis of low-cost operations. The investment hurdle for competition to enter this market is now too high. Aggressive early pricing then pays off over the long term. The risk of this strategy is that low initial profit margins result in long payback periods. However, with short product life cycles, there is increased financial risk.

   The traditional approach (high initial profit margin), is accompanied by high market risk. This strategy is vulnerable to low cost competition. High profit margins may justify the investment required for a product focus. That done, a competitor could move in and quickly become the low cost producer.

Problems

1. Mass Balance Company.

   a. $b = \log r / \log 2$
   $$= \log (0.80) / \log 2$$
   $$= -0.321928$$

   $k_n = k_1 n^b$
   $k_3 = 60(3)^{-0.321928}$
   $k_3 = 42.126$

   b. $k_n = k_1 n^b$
   $k_{40} = 60(40)^{-0.321928}$
   $$= 18.30 \text{ hr}$$

   c. Estimated total time for 40 units, From Table D.1, conversion factor = 0.42984
   40 units (0.42984 x 60 hr/unit) = 1031.616 hr

   d. Estimated total time for 30 units, From Table D.1, conversion factor = 0.46733
   30 units (0.46733 x 60 hr/unit) = 841.194 hr

   The last ten units (#31 - #40) require (1031.616 – 841.194) = 190.422 hours.

2. Cambridge Instruments.

   $b = \log r / \log 2$
   $b = \log 0.93 / \log 2 = -0.1047$

   $k_n = k_1 n^b$
   $k_5 = 85(5)^{-0.1047}$
   $$= 71.82 \text{ hr}$$

   $k_{10} = 85(10)^{-0.1047}$
   $$= 66.79 \text{ hr}$$

   $k_{15} = 85(15)^{-0.1047}$
   $$= 64.02 \text{ hr}$$

   $k_{30} = 85(30)^{-0.1047}$
   $$= 59.53 \text{ hr}$$

3. The first unit required 30 hours. $k_1 = 30$. We can use Table D.1 and straight-line interpolation to get the cumulative average time factor for a 90% learning curve. The straight-line interpolation process is demonstrated in the solution to Problem 6, part a.

		(1)	(2)	k_1 x (1) x (2)		
	Units	Cumulative	Cumulative	Cumulative	Total	Total
Week	Scheduled	Production	Avg. Factor	Total Hr	Hr/Wk	Employees/Wk
1	20	20	0.73039	438	438	11
2	65	85	0.60083	1532	1094	28
3	100	185	0.53627	2976	1444	37
4	140	325	0.49241	4801	1825	**46**
5	120	445	0.46901	6261	1460	37

The production schedule is not feasible because the number of employees needed in week 4 exceeds the maximum of 40 by 6 workers.

To obtain a feasible schedule we can produce some of the requirements in week 4 earlier, say in week 2 or 3. Such a change may result in excess inventory cost if the customer does not accept early shipment. Furthermore, the production schedule of other products may be affected by this alternative.

One possible production schedule is:

Week	Units Scheduled	(1) Cumulative Production	(2) Cumulative Avg. Factor	k_1 x (1) x (2) Cumulative Total Hr	Total Hr/Wk	Total Employees/Wk
1	20	20	0.73039	438	438	11
2	85	105	0.58216	1834	1396	35
3	100	205	0.52771	3245	1411	36
4	120	325	0.49241	4801	1556	**39**
5	120	445	0.46901	6261	1460	37

By shifting 20 units from week 4 to weeks 2 and 3, we obtain a feasible schedule.

4. Texas Toothpick. $k_1 = 8.69$,

   a. From Table D.1, 80 percent learning curve, n = 13, cumulative average factor = 0.58960.

   8.69 x 13 x 0.58960 = 66.6 hours

   b. Week of Friday the thirteenth.

Week	Units Scheduled	(1) Cumulative Production	(2) Cumulative Avg. Factor	k_1 x (1) x (2) Cumulative Total Hr	Total Hr/Wk
Oct. 2 - 6	8	8	0.66824	46.46	
Oct. 9 - 13	19	27	0.48167	113.01	66.6

   c. Week before Halloween.

Week	Units Scheduled	(1) Cumulative Production	(2) Cumulative Avg. Factor	k_1 x (1) x (2) Cumulative Total Hr	Total Hr/Wk
Oct. 2 - 6	8	8	0.66824	46.4	
Oct. 9 - 13	19	27	0.48167	113.0	66.6
Oct. 16 - 20	10	37	0.43976	141.3	28.3
Oct. 23 - 27	27	64	0.37382	207.9	66.6

Since Freddie and Jason have 80 hours of capacity, they should be able to meet this schedule.

5. Bovine Products Company. We know the time required for the sixteenth unit, and need to use a 90% learning curve work backwards to estimate the time for the 1st unit.

   $b = \log r / \log 2$

   $b = \log 0.90 / \log 2 = -0.152$

   $k_n = k_1 n^b$

   $k_1 = k_n n^b = 15 (16)^{-0.152} = 9.8415$

	Units Scheduled	(1) Cumulative Production	(2) Cumulative Avg. Factor	k_1 x (1) x (2) Cumulative Total Hr	Hours/ Order
First order	16	16	0.75249	118.49	118.49
Second order	48	64	0.62043	390.78	272.29

6. $k_1 = \$3500$

  a. Using straight-line interpolation, the 80 percent learning curve conversion factor for $n = 100$ is computed as follows:

  From Table D.1, 80 percent

  When $n = 64$, conversion factor = 0.37382

  When $n = 128$, conversion factor = 0.30269

  0.07113

  $(128 - 100)/(128 - 64) = 0.4375$

  $0.4375 \times 0.07113 = 0.03112$

  When $n = 128$, conversion factor = 0.30269

  When $n = 100$, interpolated factor = 0.33381

  Estimated total labor cost = $100 \times 0.33381 \times \$3500 = \$116,833.50$

  b. $\$1200/\$3500 = 0.34286$

  From Table D.1, 80 percent

  When $n = 64$, conversion factor = 0.37382

  When $n = 128$, conversion factor = 0.30269

  0.07113

  When $n = 64$, conversion factor = 0.37382

  When $n = ???$, conversion factor = 0.34286

  0.03096

  $0.03096/0.07113 = 0.4353$

  $(0.4353)/(128 - 64) = 27.86$

  $n = 64 + 27.86 = 91.86$ or about 92

  In other words, when $n = 92$, interpolated conversion factor = $0.34270 \approx 0.34286$

  Estimated total labor cost = $92 \times 0.34270 \times \$3500 = \$110,349$ or $\$1199.45$ each.

  The company will break even on labor cost at approximately the 92nd unit.

Advanced Problems

7. Powerwest Inc.

  a. Direct hours for the thirteenth unit

  $$k_n = k_1 n^b$$

  $$b = \frac{\log r}{\log 2} = \frac{\log(0.9)}{\log 2} = \frac{-0.04576}{0.30103} = -0.152$$

  $$k_{13} = 30,000(13)^{-0.152}$$

  $$k_{13} = 20,314 \text{ hours}$$

  b. Total hours for 30 units. From Table D.1, 90% learning curve, conversion factor for average number of hours per unit = 0.69090

  $30,000(0.69090)(30) = 621,810$ hours

c. By inspection the maximum number of employees will occur sometime during the first four months. Because of the learning effect, production following April can not possibly exceed the hours required for April. For example, the four units in August require about 9,500 fewer hours than do the four units in April.

Month	Units Scheduled	(1) Cumulative Production	(2) Cumulative Avg. Factor	k_1 x (1) x (2) Cumulative Total Hr	Hours/ Month
January	2	2	0.95000	57,000	57,000
February	3	5	0.86784	130,176	73,176
March	2	7	0.83496	175,342	45,166
April	4	11	0.78991	260,670	85,328
May	3	14			
June	2	16			
July	2	18	0.74080	400,032	
August	4	22	0.72102	475,873	75,841
September	3	25			
October	3	28			
November	1	29			
December	1	30			

The maximum number of employees is 85,328/200 = 426.64 or 427 employees

d. If the learning curve is changed to 0.85, we can not use Table D.1 to find the cumulative average factor. We have used a spreadsheet to generate the cumulative average factor for a learning rate of 85%.

Learning Rate	85%	
b=	-0.2344653	Cumulative
n	kn	Average Factor
1	1.00000	1.00000
2	0.85000	0.92500
3	0.77291	0.87430
4	0.72250	0.83635
5	0.68567	0.80622
6	0.65698	0.78134
7	0.63366	0.76025
8	0.61413	0.74198
9	0.59740	0.72592
10	0.58282	0.71161
11	0.56994	0.69873
12	0.55843	0.68704

Month	Units Scheduled	(1) Cumulative Production	(2) Cumulative Avg. Factor	k_1 x (1) x (2) Cumulative Total Hr	Hours/ Month
January	2	2	0.92500	55,500	55,500
February	3	5	0.80622	120,933	65,433
March	2	7	0.76025	159,653	38,720
April	4	11	0.69873	230,581	70,928

The maximum number of employees is 70,928/200 = 354.64 or 355 employees

8. Really Big Six Corporation.

Cost to buy = $1500 x 1000 = $1,500,000.

Materials cost to make = $400 x 1000 = $400,000.

From Table S6.1, 90 percent learning curve conversion factor for $n = 1000$, = 0.41217

Total labor cost = 0.41217 x 1000 desks x 100 hours x $25/hour = $1,030,425.

Estimated total cost of labor and materials = $1,030,425 + $400,000 = $1,430,425

It would be slightly less costly to make the desks.

9. When the learning curve is 80 percent

$b = \log r / \log 2$

$b = \log 0.80 / \log 2 = -0.322$

$k_n = k_1 n^b$

$k_{n+1} = k_1 (n+1)^b$

We seek the point at which the difference between k_n and k_{n+1} is 0.5%.

$$\frac{k_1 n^b - k_1(n+1)^b}{k_1 n^b} = 0.005$$

$$\frac{n^b - (n+1)^b}{n^b} = 0.005$$

$$n^b - (n+1)^b = 0.005 n^b$$

$$0.995 n^b = (n+1)^b$$

$$0.995 n^{-0.322} = (n+1)^{-0.322}$$

$$0.995^{-3.10559} n^1 = (n+1)^1$$

$$1.0156887 n = n + 1$$

$$0.0156887 n = 1$$

$$n = \frac{1}{0.0156887}$$

$$n = 63.74 \text{ or } \approx 64$$

Check:

Say $k_1 = 1000$ hours, $n = 64$, and learning curve is 80 percent.

$k_n = k_1 n^b$

$k_{64} = 1000 (64)^{-0.322} = 262.06$ hours

$k_{65} = 1000 (65)^{-0.322} = 260.76$ hours

$(262.06 - 260.76)/260.76 = 0.004985 \approx 0.5\%$

10. Compton Company.

a.

$$k_n = k_1(n)^b$$

$$24 = 46(10)^b$$

$$\frac{24}{46} = (10)^b$$

$$\log_{10}\left(\frac{24}{46}\right) = \log_{10}(10)^b$$

$$\log_{10}\left(\frac{24}{46}\right) = b = \left(\frac{\log(r)}{\log(2)}\right) = -0.2825466$$

$$\log_{10}\left(\frac{24}{46}\right)\log(2) = \log(r)$$

$$-0.085055 = \log(r)$$

$$r = 0.8221385 \text{ or } 82.21385\%$$

b. Given $k_1 = 46$ hours and the estimated learning curve rate from part a,

$$k_{80} = (46)(80)^{(-0.28252466)}$$

$$k_{80} = 13.338 \text{ hours}$$

11. Hand-To-Mouth Company. Poor cash management is the number one cause of bankruptcy. The following spreadsheet shows the calculation of cash flow. HTM must not take this order unless they are assured they can obtain a loan to cover the cash shortages occurring in weeks 8 - 10.

Week	Beginning Cash	Del. Units	Cum. Contr. Units	Cum. Avg. Hours Table 7.4	100 Labor Hours	Cum. Labor Hours	$20 Labor Costs	$400 Material Costs	$1,500 Cash Recd.	Ending Cash Balance
1	$200,000	2	2	0.95000	190	190	$3,800	$800		$195,400
2	$195,400	4	6	0.85013	320	510	$6,402	$1,600		$187,398
3	$187,398	8	14	0.76580	562	1072	$11,241	$3,200	$3,000	$175,958
4	$175,958	12	26	0.70472	760	1832	$15,203	$4,800	$6,000	$161,955
5	$161,955	14	40	0.66357	822	2654	$16,440	$5,600	$12,000	$151,914
6	$151,914	24	64	0.62043	1316	3971	$26,329	$9,600	$18,000	$133,985
7	$133,985	64	128	0.56069	3206	7177	$64,122	$25,600	$21,000	$65,263
8	$65,263	128	256	0.50586	5773	12950	$115,464	$51,200	$36,000	($65,400)
9	($65,400)	128	384	0.48090	5517	18467	$110,331	$51,200	$96,000	($130,931)
10	($130,931)	128	512	0.45594	4878	23344	$97,551	$51,200	$192,000	($87,683)
11	($87,683)	88	600	0.44519	3367	26711	$67,345	$35,200	$192,000	$1,772
12	$1,772	100	700	0.43496	3736	30447	$74,716	$40,000	$192,000	$79,056
13	$79,056	100	800	0.42629	3656	34103	$73,120	$40,000	$132,000	$97,936
14	$97,936	100	900	0.41878	3587	37690	$71,740	$40,000	$150,000	$136,196
15	$136,196	100	1000	0.41217	3527	41217	$70,536	$40,000	$150,000	$175,660
16	$175,660								$150,000	$325,660
17	$325,660								$150,000	$475,660

Chapter 7

Capacity Planning

Study Questions

1. Several factors make capacity planning a challenge. Some relate to our ability (or inability) to foretell the future. For example, capacity decisions depend on uncertain future events such as changes in long-term demand levels or product mix, new governmental regulations, tax law changes on investment incentives, and the manner in which costs will change with the scale of operations. Other factors relate to the importance of the decision and the visibility it places on those who must make it. Mistakes in this area could permanently damage an organization and/or a career.

2. Alternative ways of responding to capacity gaps include various expansion and short-term options. Expansion options include the expansionist strategy, the wait-and-see strategy, or the follow-the-leader strategy. Short-term capacity options include leasing, overtime, extra shifts, hiring temporary workers, subcontracting, postponing maintenance, and allowing back orders or stockouts.

3. Capacity for a drive-in window at a bank can be measured by the **maximum** number of customers (or cars) per hour. The complication with using this measure is the definition of *maximum* because capacity can be temporarily increased with overtime or extra clerks. Also, a change in the mix of services requested could change the average service time per customer, which in turn will affect the number of customers processed per hour.

   Because a toy company produces a wide variety of products, a measure such as the maximum number of available employee hours per day (or month) makes sense. If the product mix changes or new automation is introduced, however, the relationship between the maximum number of employee hours and output capability will change.

4. Forecasts of demand, productivity, and effects of competition and technological changes and time standard estimates are useful in capacity planning.

5. The effective capacity of the system is limited by the bottleneck operation, H, to 18 units per day. If operation A produces 24 units per day, a large WIP inventory will build in front of operation H, but throughput will still be limited to 18 units per day.

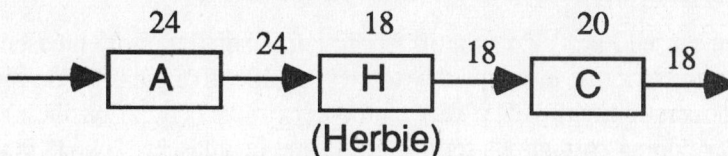

With overtime, the daily capacities are:

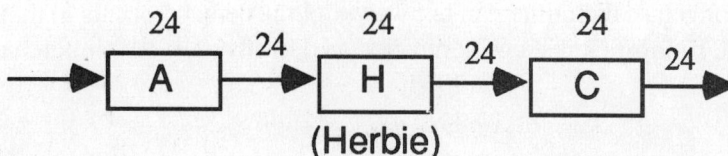

We would expect the throughput to increase to 24 units per day. However, the output increased to only 21 units per day. Possible causes include 1) fatigue from overtime, 2) material shortages, and 3) the loss of throughput that always occurs when variable operations are closely linked. The output rates are *average rates*, meaning that at any particular time the production rate at one of the operations could be less than the 24 units per day rate and cause a temporary bottleneck. When the operations are closely linked, (no WIP) throughput is always determined by the (momentary) weakest link. The system can not take advantage of favorable conditions at one operation unless those favorable conditions occur simultaneously at all operations. The upshot of all this is that the average throughput of closely linked operations will almost always be less than would be expected from just looking at average capacities. For a thorough discussion of bottlenecks, see *The Goal*, by Eli Goldratt.

6. When demand for the drink is large enough, there are several ways that economies of scale would benefit the boy. First, he can save on raw material costs. For example, one 32-ounce box of lemonade mix costs less than four 8-ounce boxes. Also, he could get a price break by buying ice in bulk. Second, the cost of larger ice-boxes can be spread over more units (sales), keeping the cost per sale low.

7. If the business grows very large, diseconomies could set in. For example, hiring others to help could result in a more complicated managerial processes, and sales and payroll taxes. If the boy added more lemonade stands, coordinating material and staff requirements could be a problem. It is also possible that the boy introduced different products to maintain volume, thereby causing production scheduling and inventory control problems.

8. The primary economies of scale concern spreading the instructor's salary over a larger class, and filling classrooms to capacity (and then some). Diseconomies occur when additional help is required to review homework, administer tests, and coordinate schedules of students and assistants. Growth eventually requires larger classrooms or lecture halls. If we view the product as learning, there is a possibility that there are diminishing returns on the amount of learning that occurs as class size increases. Symptoms of diseconomies of scale setting in are decreased job satisfaction for instructors and unmotivated, dissatisfied students.

9. As the shift from a process focus towards a product focus occurs, the product tends to become standardized, and the volume increases. Economies of scale derive from quantity discounts for materials, learning curve labor savings, spreading engineering, distribution and overhead costs over a larger volume. Steel, oil, paper and beer are commodities, which compete on the basis of low-cost operations. Economies of scale in large facilities tend to reduce per-unit costs.

10. Diseconomies of scale may have caused Pac Tel to spin off Air Touch. A smaller, more focused business may be able plan better and to move more quickly to meet competitive pressures in the cellular business. Subsequent cooperation with U S WEST (and others in the cellular business) created economies of scale in developing contiguous service areas, and in amassing "clout" in the bidding war for radio frequency spectrum in major markets needed for the future personal communication services market.

11. The wait-and-see strategy is not an option for electric utilities because there are few short-term options. Utilities can not increase electricity production through the use of overtime. Building new capacity may take a decade or longer, so the utility can not wait until the demand occurs to think about how to serve that demand. Unless planned and contracted well in advance, power purchases from other utilities are too costly.

12. The wait-and-see strategy risks reduced market share because demand not served, or served at the higher cost of short-term options such as overtime, is vulnerable to competition. One risk of expansion is that the investment may be made in a technology quickly becomes obsolete and noncompetitive. Those who waited could later invest in the new technology, and use it to an advantage over the expansionist.

13. The utility with the larger facility needs a larger capacity cushion to protect against the possible loss of the use of a large facility.

14. One-stage expansion resembles the expansionist strategy. Two-stage expansion is more like the wait-and-see strategy because expansion involves small, frequent jumps and because capacity actually falls short in year 3.

    Qualitatively, the wait-and-see strategy gives Kathryn more time to gauge demand. If her forecasts are wrong, she has a chance to adjust her plans before investing in a major expansion. The restaurant's "homey" image might be lost with a capacity much beyond the dining room's current size. Perhaps she should consider opening a second restaurant on the other side of town, rather than continuing to expand the first one. The two-stage alternative fits this possibility better.

15. In order to increase the seating capacity of an airplane, it must be shown that the increased number of passengers can be safely evacuated in the event of an emergency. During the required demonstration of emergency evacuation procedures in this case, several injuries occurred. Other facility changes include increased requirement for gate area seating and for luggage handling.

Problems

1. Pete's Garage and Manhole Cover Recycling Center.
   a. regular hours of operations per week = [(5*11)+(5)] = 60 hours
      effective capacity = (60 hours x 60 min/hour)/40 min/alignment) = 90 alignments/week
      peak hours of operations per week (during March) = [(5*14)+(10)] = 80 hours
      peak capacity = (80 hours x 60 min/hour)/(40 min/alignment) = 120 alignments/week
   b. 100 alignments per week is
      (100/90) * 100% = 111.1% of effective capacity
      (100/120) * 100% = 83.3% of peak capacity

2. Sterling Motors.
   a. Order taking
      regular hours of order taking per week = 5 * 10 = 50 hours
      effective capacity = (6 telephone lines)(50 hours x 60 min/hour)/(3 min/line) = 6000 lines/week
      Stock picking
      regular hours of stock picking per week = 5 * 8 = 40 hours
      effective capacity = (8 workers)(40 hours x 60 min/hour)/(5 min/line) = 3840 lines/week
   b. peak hours of stock picking per week = 6 * 10 = 60 hours
      peak capacity = (8 workers)(60 hours x 60 min/hour)/(5 min/line) = 5760 lines/week
   c. 5000 lines per week is
      (5000/3840) * 100% = 130.2% of effective capacity
      (5000/5760) * 100% = 86.8% of peak capacity

3. Dahlia Medical Center.

Labor room capacity = 20 rooms * 3 days * 24 hours/day = 1440 hours

Labor room utilization = (65 babies * 24 hours/baby)/(1440 hours) = 108.33%

Combination labor-delivery room capacity = 16 rooms * 3 days * 24 hours/day = 1152 hours

Combination labor-delivery room utilization = (45 babies * 24 hours/baby)/(1152 hours) = 93.75%

Delivery room capacity = 2 rooms * 3 days * 24 hours/day = 144 hours

Delivery room utilization = (65 babies * 1 hours/baby)/(144 hours) = 45.14%

The labor rooms have the highest utilization.

4. Clip Joint.

peak hours of hair cutting per week = 6 * 9 = 54 hours

effective capacity = (3 chairs)(54 hours x 60 min/hour) = 9720 min/week

Before semester break:

$$\text{Utilization} = \frac{100 \text{ military haircuts}\left(1 \ ^{min}\!/_{haircut}\right) + 450 \text{ other haircuts}\left(20 \ ^{min}\!/_{haircut}\right)}{9720\left(^{min}\!/_{week}\right)}$$

$$= \frac{9100}{9720}(100\%) = 93.62\%$$

Before graduation:

$$\text{Utilization} = \frac{800 \text{ military haircuts}\left(1 \ ^{min}\!/_{haircut}\right) + 400 \text{ other haircuts}\left(20 \ ^{min}\!/_{haircut}\right)}{9720\left(^{min}\!/_{week}\right)}$$

$$= \frac{8800}{9720}(100\%) = 90.53\%$$

Although the number of haircuts is lower, utilization is higher before the semester break.

5. Automobile brake supplier.

a. The total machine hour requirements (R) for all three demand forecasts:

Component	Pessimistic Forecast		Expected Forecast		Optimistic Forecast	
	Process Time	Setup Time	Process Time	Setup Time	Process Time	Setup Time
A	750	250.0	900	300.0	1250	416.7
B	2000	562.5	2600	731.3	3400	956.3
C	850	1161.7	1250	1708.3	2000	2733.3
	3600 +	1974.2	4750 +	2739.6	6650 +	4106.3
R		5574.2		7489.6		10,756.3

The number of hours (H) provided per machine is:

H = (2 shifts/day x 8 hours/shift x 5 days/week x 52 weeks/year)(1.0 − 0.2) = 3328

The capacity requirements for three forecasts are:

Pessimistic: M = 5574.2 / 3328 = 1.67 or 2 machines

Expected: M = 7489.6 / 3328 = 2.25 or 3 machines

Optimistic: M = 10756.3 / 3328 = 3.23 or 4 machines

b. The current capacity is sufficient for the pessimistic and expected forecasts. However, there is a gap of one machine for the optimistic forecast. The gap drops to zero when the 20 percent increase from short-term options is included.

3 machines x 3328 hours/machine x 1.2 = 11981 hrs. This is greater than 10,756 hrs. required.

6. Up, Up and Away.

    Summing up the machine hour requirements for two products, we get:

    R = $[30,000(0.30) + (30,000 / 20)(3)] + [12,000(1.0) + (12,000 / 70)(4)]$
          =   26,186 hours

    The number of hours provided per machine is:

    H =   (2 shifts/day x 8 hours/shift x 200 days/year)(1 – 0.25)
          =   2,400 hours / machine

    The capacity requirement is:

    M = R/H = 26,186 / 2,400 = 10.91 or 11 machines

    The capacity gap is (11 – 4.0) = 7 machines. Seven more machines must be purchased if short-term options are not allowed.

7. Summing up the machine hour requirements for both bikes:

    R = $[2,000(0.5) + (2,000 / 100)(1.0)] + [15,000(2 / 3) + (15,000 / 100)(1.0)]$
          =   11,170 hours

    The number of hours (H) provided per work station is :

    H =   (8 hours/day x 5 days/week x 50 weeks/year)(1.0 – 0.2)
          =   1,600 hours

    The capacity requirement is:

    M = R/H = 11,170 / 1,600 = 6.98 or 7 work stations

    Trak will require 7 work stations.

8. Bank 21.

    Machine hour requirements and hours per machine are:

    R =   (400,000 x 1.2 x 12 x 0.25 min) / (60 minutes/hour)
          =   24,000

    H = (2 shifts/day x 8 hours/shift x 260 days/year)(1.0 – 0.20)

          =   3,328

    The capacity requirement is:

    M = R/H = 24,000 / 3,328 = 7.21 or 8 machines.

9. Worchester Athletic Club.
   Present capacity = 500 members
   Annual membership fee = $40/month * 12 months/year = $480
   Incremental membership fees = (Forecasted membership – Present capacity) * $480

Year	Membership Forecast	Membership Above Present Capacity	Incremental Membership Fees	Incremental Rent	Net Cash Flow
1	450	0	0	$45,000	($45,000)
2	480	0	0	$45,000	($45,000)
3	510	10	$4,800	$45,000	($40,200)
4	515	15	$7,200	$45,000	($37,800)
5	530	30	$14,400	$45,000	($30,600)
6	550	50	$24,000	$45,000	($21,000)
7	600	100	$48,000	$45,000	3,000

Worchester should wait at least five years before expanding or aggressively recruit new membership. The current rate of growth is too low to justify expansion at this time.

10. The French Prints of Arabelle. The solution is based on the assumption that sales vary in direct proportion to floor area.

    a. The last column in the table shows quarterly before-tax cash flows. The first year's $16,000 loss is followed by a $1,000 loss in the second year.

    b. The third year looks better. However, the $15,500 gain just about covers the first year's loss. Considering the time value of money would further discourage this expansion.

Year	Quarter	Sales, ($ per s f)	30% of Sales x 1000 sf	Incremental Quarterly Rent	Incremental Salaries	Incremental Revenue minus costs
1	1	$ 90.00	$27,000	$27,500	$12,000	($12,500)
	2	$ 60.00	$18,000	$27,500	$ 8,000	($17,500)
	3	$110.00	$33,000	$27,500	$12,000	($6,500)
	4	$240.00	$72,000	$27,500	$24,000	$20,500
2	1	$ 99.00	$29,700	$27,500	$12,000	($9,800)
	2	$ 66.00	$19,800	$27,500	$ 8,000	($15,700)
	3	$121.00	$36,300	$27,500	$12,000	($3,200)
	4	$264.00	$79,200	$27,500	$24,000	$27,700
3	1	$ 108.90	$32,670	$27,500	$12,000	($6,830)
	2	$ 72.60	$21,780	$27,500	$ 8,000	($13,720)
	3	$133.10	$39,930	$27,500	$12,000	$430
	4	$290.40	$87,120	$27,500	$24,000	$35,620

11. Magic World.

a. The table shows incremental before-tax cash flows

Year	Projected attendance	Incremental attendance (with expansion)	Admission Price	Incremental revenue (with expansion)	Investment and operating costs	Cash flow
0					$500,000	($500,000)
1	30,000	6,000	$30	$180,000	$100,000	$80,000
2	34,000	6,800	$30	$204,000	$100,000	$104,000
3	36,250	7,250	$32	$232,000	$100,000	$132,000
4	38,500	7,700	$32	$246,400	$100,000	$146,400
5	41,000	8,200	$32	$262,400	$100,000	$162,400

b. Payback occurs during the 5th year. At the end of 4 years, all but $37,600 of the initial investment has be recovered. $37,600/162,400 = 0.23. Payback occurs at about 4.23 years.

12. Rex Saul drugstore. After two years, Rex will have little to show for this expansion. Continued growth and price increases may make expansion attractive after that. However, yet another expansion might have to be considered for the fourth year.

Year	Quarter	Prescriptions per quarter	Incremental Prescriptions	Price * 35%	Incremental Revenue	Incremental Salary	Incremental Cash Flow
1	1	5400	400	$7.70	$3,080	$12,000	($8,920)
	2	6600	1600	$7.00	$11,200	$12,000	($800)
	3	3600	0	$8.40	$0	$12,000	($12,000)
	4	6300	1300	$10.50	$13,650	$12,000	$1,650
2	1	6300	1300	$11.20	$14,560	$12,600	$1,960
	2	7700*	2500	$10.50	$26,250	$12,600	$13,650
	3	4200	0	$11.90	$0	$12,600	($12,600)
	4	7350	2350	$14.00	$32,900	$12,600	$20,300

* Exceeds capacity of three pharmacists @ 2,500 each

13. Roche Brothers.

a. Expand to 700,000 capacity now.

Year	Customers	Incremental customers	2% of sales	Incremental revenue	Incremental costs & rent	Incremental cash flow
0					$200,000	($200,000)
1	560,000	60,000	$1.00	$60,000	$120,000	($60,000)
2	600,000	100,000	$1.06	$106,000	$120,000	($14,000)
3	685,000	185,000	$1.12	$207,200	$120,000	$87,200
4	700,000	200,000	$1.20	$240,000	$120,000	$120,000
5	715,000*	200,000	$1.28	$256,000	$120,000	$136,000

b. Expand to 700,000 capacity, end of year 2.

Year	Customers	Incremental customers	2% of sales	Incremental revenue	Incremental costs & rent	Incremental cash flow
0						
1	560,000	0	$1.00	$0		
2	600,000	0	$1.06	$0	$240,000	($240,000)
3	685,000	185,000	$1.12	$207,200	$144,000	$63,200
4	700,000	200,000	$1.20	$240,000	$144,000	$96,000
5	715,000*	200,000	$1.28	$256,000	$144,000	$112,000

14. Mel, Danny, and Arnold.

Robot Model	Arnold		Mel and Danny		Lot Size (units/lot)	Annual Demand Forecast
	Processing (hr/unit)	Setup (hr/unit)	Processing (hr/unit)	Setup (hr/unit)		
Maverick	5	3.0	4	2.0	6	144
Angel	2	4.0	1.5	2.0	8	320
Terminator	4	5.0	3	3.0	10	400

a. Dividing the work to equalize the number of units.

Arnold: Mel and Danny:

72 Mavericks $\longrightarrow \left(\dfrac{72}{6}\right)3 + (72 \times 5) = 396$ 72 Mavericks $\longrightarrow \left(\dfrac{72}{6}\right)2 + (72 \times 4) = 312$

160 Angels $\longrightarrow \left(\dfrac{160}{8}\right)4 + (160 \times 2) = 400$ 160 Angels $\longrightarrow \left(\dfrac{160}{8}\right)2 + (160 \times 1.5) = 280$

200 Terminators $\longrightarrow \left(\dfrac{200}{10}\right)5 + (200 \times 4) = 900$ 200 Terminators $\longrightarrow \left(\dfrac{200}{10}\right)3 + (200 \times 3) = 660$

Utilization = (1696 + 1252)/ 4000 hours = 73.7%

b. Dividing the work to equalize work hours.

Arnold:

66 Mavericks $\longrightarrow \left(\dfrac{66}{6}\right)3 + (66 \times 5) = 363$

128 Angels $\longrightarrow \left(\dfrac{128}{8}\right)4 + (128 \times 2) = 320$

170 Terminators $\longrightarrow \left(\dfrac{170}{10}\right)5 + (170 \times 4) = 765$

Mel and Danny:

78 Mavericks $\longrightarrow \left(\dfrac{78}{6}\right)2 + (78 \times 4) = 338$

192 Angels $\longrightarrow \left(\dfrac{192}{8}\right)2 + (192 \times 1.5) = 336$

230 Terminators $\longrightarrow \left(\dfrac{230}{10}\right)3 + (230 \times 3) = 759$

Utilization = (1448 + 1433)/ 4000 hours = 72.0%

Equalizing the work according to standard hours results in a lower utilization (and a higher capacity) than results from equalizing the number of units produced.

15. Truck-Tuff.

500 liners per day x $20 = $10,000 per day

$8,000,000/$10,000 per day = 800 days

a. Payback occurs in less than 4 years.

b. Say 4 years = (365 + 365 + 365 + 366) = 1461 days.

$8,000,000/1461 days = $5475.70/day

$5,475.70/day ÷ $20/liner = 273.79 liners/day + 2.000 liners/day = 2,273.79 liners/day

16. Grandmother's Chicken.

Alternative 1: Expand both kitchen and dining area now to 130,000 capacity, cost $336,000.

Year	Projected Demand (meals/year)	Projected Capacity (meals/year)	Calculation of Incremental Cash Flow Compared to Base Case 80,000 meals/year	Cash Inflow (outflow)
0	80,000	130,000		($336,000)
1	90,000	130,000	80,000 meals ($2.20 − $2.00) = + 90,000 − 80,000 = 10,000 meals ($2.20 / meal) =	$16,000 + $22,000 $38,000
2	100,000	130,000	80,000 meals ($2.20 − $2.00) = 100,000 − 80,000 = 20,000 meals ($2.20 / meal) =	$16,000 + $44,000 $60,000
3	110,000	130,000	80,000 meals ($2.20 − $2.00) = 110,000 − 80,000 = 30,000 meals ($2.20 / meal) =	$16,000 + $66,000 $82,000
4	120,000	130,000	80,000 meals ($2.20 − $2.00) = 120,000 − 80,000 = 40,000 meals ($2.20 / meal) =	$16,000 + $88,000 $104,000
5	130,000	130,000	80,000 meals ($2.20 − $2.00) = 130,000 − 80,000 = 50,000 meals ($2.20 / meal) =	$16,000 + $110,000 $126,000

Alternative 2: Expand only kitchen now to 105,000 capacity, cost $220,000. At end of Year 3 expand kitchen and dining to 130,000 capacity, cost $224,000.

Year	Projected Demand (meals/year)	Projected Capacity (meals/year)	Calculation of Incremental Cash Flow Compared to Base Case 80,000 meals/year		Cash Inflow (outflow)
0	80,000	105,000		Investment	($220,000)
1	90,000	105,000	80,000 meals ($2.20 − $2.00) = + 90,000 − 80,000 = 10,000 meals ($2.20 / meal) =		$16,000 + $22,000 $38,000
2	100,000	105,000	80,000 meals ($2.20 − $2.00) = 100,000 − 80,000 = 20,000 meals ($2.20 / meal) =		$16,000 + $44,000 $60,000
3	110,000	105,000	80,000 meals ($2.20 − $2.00) = 105,000 − 80,000 = 25,000 meals ($2.20 / meal) = Investment =		$16,000 $55,000 ($204,000) ($133,000)
4	120,000	130,000	80,000 meals ($2.20 − $2.00) = 120,000 − 80,000 = 40,000 meals ($2.20 / meal) =		$16,000 + $88,000 $104,000
5	130,000	130,000	80,000 meals ($2.20 − $2.00) = 130,000 − 80,000 = 50,000 meals ($2.20 / meal) =		$16,000 + $110,000 $126,000

Quantitatively, the new technology turns out to be best, introduced with a one- stage expansion.

17. Acme Steel Fabricators.
   a. Decision tree

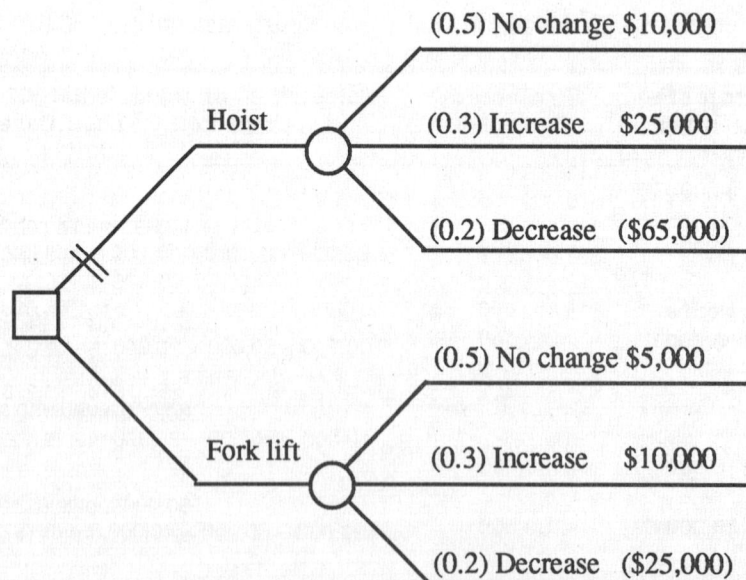

   b. Expected Value of Hoist   =   [(0.5 * $10,000) + (0.3 * $25,000) − (0.2 * $65,000)] = − $500

   Expected Value of Fork lift = [(0.5 * $ 5,000) + (0.3 * $10,000) − (0.2 * $25,000)] = + $500

18. Dintell Corporation. Assuming a five-year life.
    Decision tree:

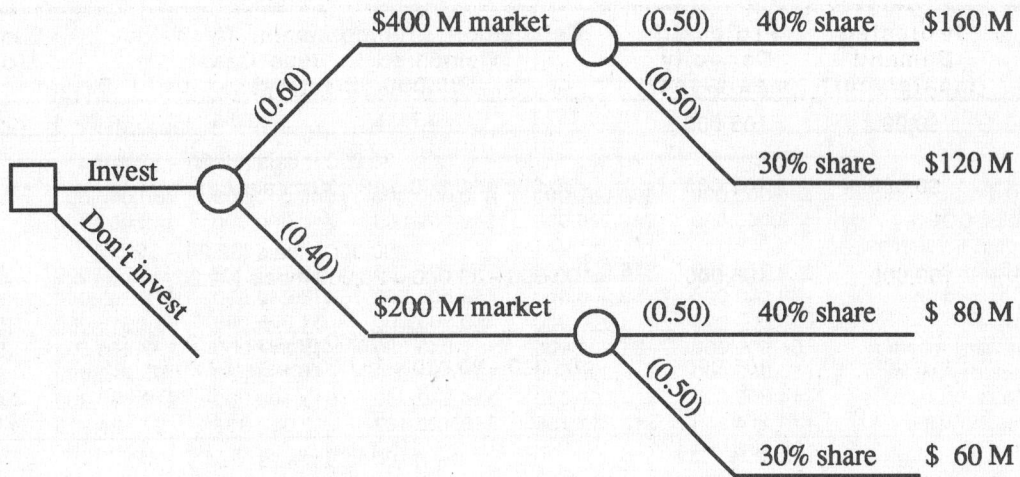

```
                                        $400 M market    (0.50)   40% share   $160 M
                                   (0.60)            O
                                                       (0.50)
                                                                   30% share   $120 M
        [ ]──── Invest ────O
             Don't invest       (0.40)
                                        $200 M market    (0.50)   40% share   $ 80 M
                                                    O
                                                       (0.50)
                                                                   30% share   $ 60 M
```

Expected Sales = {(0.6)[(0.5)($160 M)+(0.5)($120 M)]} + {(0.4)[(0.5)($80 M)+(0.5)($60 M)]}
                = $112,000,000 per year

Gross Profit   = Sales – COGS = $112,000,000 – (70% x $112,000,000)
                = $33,600,000

Initial Information						
Initial Investment	$50,000,000					
Tax Rate	0.40					
Discount Rate	0.12					
MACRS Depreciation	0.2000	0.3200	0.1920	0.1152	0.1142	0.0576
Present Value Factor	0.8929	0.7972	0.7118	0.6355	0.5674	0.5066

	Year					
	1	2	3	4	5	6
Expected Sales	$112,000,000	$112,000,000	$112,000,000	$112,000,000	$112,000,000	$0
Expenses: COGS = 70%	$78,400,000	$78,400,000	$78,400,000	$78,400,000	$78,400,000	$0
Depreciation Shelter	$10,000,000	$16,000,000	$9,600,000	$5,760,000	$5,710,000	$2,880,000
Pre-tax income	$23,600,000	$17,600,000	$24,000,000	$27,840,000	$27,890,000	($2,880,000)
Taxes	$9,440,000	$7,040,000	$9,600,000	$11,136,000	$11,156,000	($1,152,000)
Net operating income	$14,160,000	$10,560,000	$14,400,000	$16,704,000	$16,734,000	($1,728,000)
Add back depreciation	$10,000,000	$16,000,000	$9,600,000	$5,760,000	$5,710,000	$2,880,000
Total Cash Flow	$24,160,000	$26,560,000	$24,000,000	$22,464,000	$22,444,000	$1,152,000
Net Present Value	$21,571,429	$21,173,469	$17,082,726	$14,276,278	$12,735,328	$583,639
Sum of NPV	$37,422,869					

a. Dintell should make the investment. The NPT is positive. Even in the worst case as shown below (Sales = $60 M), the NPV remains positive.

Initial Information						
Initial Investment	$50,000,000					
Tax Rate	0.40					
Discount Rate	0.12					
MACRS Depreciation	0.2000	0.3200	0.1920	0.1152	0.1142	0.0576
Present Value Factor	0.8929	0.7972	0.7118	0.6355	0.5674	0.5066
	Year					
	1	2	3	4	5	6
Expected Sales	$60,000,000	$60,000,000	$60,000,000	$60,000,000	$60,000,000	$0
Expenses: COGS = 70%	$42,000,000	$42,000,000	$42,000,000	$42,000,000	$42,000,000	$0
Expenses: Investment						
Depreciation Shelter	$10,000,000	$16,000,000	$9,600,000	$5,760,000	$5,710,000	$2,880,000
Pre-tax income	$8,000,000	$2,000,000	$8,400,000	$12,240,000	$12,290,000	($2,880,000)
Taxes	$3,200,000	$800,000	$3,360,000	$4,896,000	$4,916,000	($1,152,000)
Net operating income	$4,800,000	$1,200,000	$5,040,000	$7,344,000	$7,374,000	($1,728,000)
Add back depreciation	$10,000,000	$16,000,000	$9,600,000	$5,760,000	$5,710,000	$2,880,000
Total Cash Flow	$14,800,000	$17,200,000	$14,640,000	$13,104,000	$13,084,000	$1,152,000
Net Present Value	$13,214,286	$13,711,735	$10,420,463	$8,327,829	$7,424,213	$583,639
Sum of NPV	$3,682,164					

b. The decision remains the same. Greater expected payoffs favor making the investment.

c. A decrease in the discount rate will have no effect on the decision. The following spreadsheet shows that even at a discount rate = 12% + 15% = 27%, the NPV remains positive.

Initial Information						
Initial Investment	$50,000,000					
Tax Rate	0.40					
Discount Rate	0.27					
MACRS Depreciation	0.2000	0.3200	0.1920	0.1152	0.1142	0.0576
Present Value Factor	0.7874	0.6200	0.4882	0.3844	0.3027	0.2383
	Year					
	1	2	3	4	5	6
Expected Sales	$112,000,000	$112,000,000	$112,000,000	$112,000,000	$112,000,000	$0
Expenses: COGS = 70%	$78,400,000	$78,400,000	$78,400,000	$78,400,000	$78,400,000	$0
Depreciation Shelter	$10,000,000	$16,000,000	$9,600,000	$5,760,000	$5,710,000	$2,880,000
Pre-tax income	$23,600,000	$17,600,000	$24,000,000	$27,840,000	$27,890,000	($2,880,000)
Taxes	$9,440,000	$7,040,000	$9,600,000	$11,136,000	$11,156,000	($1,152,000)
Net operating income	$14,160,000	$10,560,000	$14,400,000	$16,704,000	$16,734,000	($1,728,000)
Add back depreciation	$10,000,000	$16,000,000	$9,600,000	$5,760,000	$5,710,000	$2,880,000
Total Cash Flow	$24,160,000	$26,560,000	$24,000,000	$22,464,000	$22,444,000	$1,152,000
Net Present Value	$19,023,622	$16,467,233	$11,716,559	$8,635,196	$6,793,313	$274,556
Sum of NPV	$12,910,479					

d. If we consider an additional investment of $10,000,000 in the third year, depreciation would greatly complicate the calculations, but would not change the answer. Perhaps the easiest approach would be to generate another section of the spread sheet showing just the effect on total cash flow of depreciating $10,000,000 over the remaining three years of life. Then use that information to adjust the total cash flow. The NPV will remain positive.

Initial Investment	$50,000,000						
Third year investment	$10,000,000						
Tax Rate	0.40						
Discount Rate	0.12						
MACRS Depreciation				0.3333	0.4445	0.1481	0.0741
Present Value Factor		0.8929	0.7972	0.7118	0.6355	0.5674	0.5066
		Year					
		1	2	3	4	5	6
Depreciation Shelter				$3,333,000	$4,445,000	$1,481,000	$741,000
Pre-tax income (loss)				($3,333,000)	($4,445,000)	($1,481,000)	($741,000)
Taxes				($1,333,200)	($1,778,000)	($592,400)	($296,400)
Net operating income				($1,999,800)	($2,667,000)	($888,600)	($444,600)
Add back depreciation				$3,333,000	$4,445,000	$1,481,000	$741,000
Adjustment to cash flow				($8,666,800)	$1,778,000	$592,400	$296,400
Previous Cash Flow		$24,160,000	$26,560,000	$24,000,000	$22,464,000	$22,444,000	$1,152,000
Total Cash Flow		$24,160,000	$26,560,000	$15,333,200	$24,242,000	$23,036,400	$1,448,400
Net Present Value		$21,571,429	$21,173,469	$10,913,869	$15,406,229	$13,071,472	$733,805
Sum of NPV		$22,870,273					

Supplement E

Waiting Lines

Study Questions

1. Waiting lines occur whenever the instantaneous customer arrival rate exceeds the current service rate. In this situation the doorway is the server, the students are the customers, and the service is access to or egress from the lecture hall. If the service rate is 30 students per minute, then 1800 students could be served per hour, which exactly matches the traffic required for hourly lectures in the 900-seat hall. However, if the hall is designed so that the door capacity matches the seating capacity, a dangerous level of congestion would occur at the class change time. The students would spend 30 minutes filing into the hall. Then in order to clear the hall for the next class, they must immediately begin to leave. (Perhaps this explains the arrival and departure pattern observed during lectures?) This study question intends to demonstrate that as the customer arrival rate becomes more widely distributed around the mean, the service capacity must exceed the arrival rate by ever greater amounts.

2. Better customer service results when:

   a. The pool of customers is finite. When a customer is in the waiting line, the chances of a new arrival diminishes.

   b. When the service time is constant, waiting lines are generally about half of what they are when service time varies according to the exponential distribution. Waiting lines grow rapidly when higher than average arrivals occur simultaneously with lower than average service rate. When service time is constant, service rate is never below average.

   c. Service is better when there is only one waiting line. With multiple waiting lines, a customer requiring vastly greater than average service time blocks service to the customer immediately behind him (usually me). When there is only one waiting line, the next customer is served by the first available of several servers. This effect is demonstrated in the video.

   d. The multiple-server model with twice the arrivals and twice the service capacity will provide better service than the single-server model. As the number of servers increases, variations in service time at individual service stations tend to cancel each other, and approximate a constant service rate. When service rate is constant, waiting lines are shorter (see part b above).

3. A customer that balks, never actually joins the waiting line. The term is also used when a mule refuses to attempt an impossible or stupid task requested by its owner. When a customer that has spent some time in the waiting line leaves before getting service, they are said to have reneged. The term is also used in card games when a card is played and then taken back into the hand.

   Multiple channels provide the same service in parallel. Multiple phases provide different services in series.

4. First-come, first-served (FCFS) is the most common priority rule in services. Services are provided in the presence of the customer. FCFS tends to equalize waiting time, and so is perceived as being fair. However, FCFS does not perform well when priorities other than arrival time are important. Manufacturing is not done in the presence of the customer. Other priorities, such as equipment utilization, due date, and set up considerations may dictate doing the work in an order that is different than the order in which it arrived.

5. The Poisson distribution is the inverse of the exponential distribution much like service rates are the inverse of service times. For example, a Poisson distributed service rate with a mean of 3 customers per hour produces an exponentially distributed service time with a mean of 1/3 hour per customer.

6. In the single-server model when $n = 1$

$$P_n = (1-\rho)\rho^n$$
$$P_1 = (1-\rho)\rho^1$$

where

$$\rho = \frac{\lambda}{\mu}$$

The following table shows the probability of one customer in the system as ρ varies from 0 to 1 in increments of 0.1.

$\rho = \lambda/\mu$	0	0.1	0.2	0.3	0.4	0.5	0.6	0.7	0.8	0.9	1.0
$P_1 = (1-\rho)\rho^1$	0.00	0.09	0.16	0.21	0.24	0.25	0.24	0.21	0.16	0.09	0.00

As the arrival rate increases, the probability of there being one customer in the system increases. Then as the arrival rate exceeds one half of the service rate, the probability of there being one customer in the system decreases. The decrease is explained by increased probability of there being more than one customer in the system.

Problems

1. Howard, Smith and Parke.

   a. Single-server model, average utilization rate

   $$\rho = \frac{\lambda}{\mu} = \frac{4}{5} = 0.8 \text{ or } 80\% \text{ utilization}$$

   b. The probability of four or fewer documents in the system is 0.6723 as shown below. Therefore, the probability of more than four documents in the system is $1 - 0.6723 = 0.3277$.

   $$P_n = (1-\rho)(\rho)^n$$
   $$P_4 = (1-0.8)(0.8)^4 = 0.0819$$
   $$P_3 = (1-0.8)(0.8)^3 = 0.1024$$
   $$P_2 = (1-0.8)(0.8)^2 = 0.1280$$
   $$P_1 = (1-0.8)(0.8)^1 = 0.1600$$
   $$P_0 = (1-0.8)(0.8)^0 = \underline{0.2000}$$
   $$= 0.6723$$

c. The average number of documents waiting to be typed,

$$L_q = \rho L = \left(\frac{\lambda}{\mu}\right)\left(\frac{\lambda}{\mu-\lambda}\right) = \left(\frac{4}{5}\right)\left(\frac{4}{5-4}\right) = 3.2 \text{ documents}$$

d. The average waiting time for documents in the waiting line,

$$W_q = \rho W = \left(\frac{\lambda}{\mu}\right)\left(\frac{1}{\mu-\lambda}\right) = \left(\frac{4}{5}\right)\left(\frac{1}{5-4}\right) = 0.8 \text{ hours}$$

2. Clara (Mayberry Telephone). Single-server model

The average arrival rate is 120 calls per hour.

The average service *time* is 20 seconds per call.

The average service rate is (1 call / 20 seconds) (60 sec/min)(60 min/hr) = 180 calls per hour

$$\rho = \frac{\lambda}{\mu} = \frac{120}{180} = 0.667$$

a   The probability of three or more calls in the system (waiting plus talking to Clara) is one minus the probability of two or less calls in the system.

$$P_n = (1-\rho)(\rho)^n$$
$$P_2 = (1-0.667)(0.667)^2 = 0.1481$$
$$P_1 = (1-0.667)(0.667)^1 = 0.2222$$
$$P_0 = (1-0.667)(0.667)^0 = \underline{0.3333}$$
$$= 0.7036$$

$1 - 0.7036 = 0.2964.$

b. The average time for callers waiting for Clara to answer,

$$W_q = \rho W = \left(\frac{\lambda}{\mu}\right)\left(\frac{1}{\mu-\lambda}\right) = \left(\frac{120}{180}\right)\left(\frac{1}{180-120}\right) = 0.1111 \text{ hours or 400 seconds}$$

c. The average number of calls waiting to be answered,

$$L_q = \rho L = \left(\frac{\lambda}{\mu}\right)\left(\frac{\lambda}{\mu-\lambda}\right) = \left(\frac{120}{180}\right)\left(\frac{120}{180-120}\right) = 1.333 \text{ calls}$$

3. Moore, Akin, and Payne (dental clinic). Multiple-server model

$$s = 3, \lambda = 5, \mu = 2 \quad \rho = \frac{\lambda}{s\mu} = \frac{5}{3(2)} = 0.8333$$

a. Probability of no patients, $P_0 =$

$$P_0 = \left[\sum_{n=0}^{s-1} \frac{(\lambda/\mu)^n}{n!} + \frac{(\lambda/\mu)^s}{s!} \left(\frac{1}{1-\rho} \right) \right]^{-1} = \left[\sum_{n=0}^{2} \frac{(5/2)^n}{n!} + \frac{(5/2)^3}{3!} \left(\frac{1}{1-\frac{5}{6}} \right) \right]^{-1}$$

$$= \left\{ \left[\frac{(5/2)^0}{0!} + \frac{(5/2)^1}{1!} + \frac{(5/2)^2}{2!} \right] + \left[\frac{(5/2)^3}{3!} \left(\frac{1}{1-\frac{5}{6}} \right) \right] \right\}^{-1}$$

$$= \left\{ [1 + 2.5 + 3.125] + [2.604(6)] \right\}^{-1}$$

$$= \frac{1}{(6.625) + (15.625)} = 0.04494$$

b. The probability of 6 or more customers in the clinic is

$P_0 = 0.04494$ (from part a)

$s = 3$

for $n < s$

$$P_n = \frac{\left(\frac{\lambda}{\mu}\right)^n}{n!} P_0$$

$$P_1 = \frac{\left(\frac{5}{2}\right)^1}{1!} (0.04494) = 0.11235$$

$$P_2 = \frac{\left(\frac{5}{2}\right)^2}{2!} (0.04494) = 0.14044$$

for $n \geq s$

$$P_n = \frac{\left(\frac{\lambda}{\mu}\right)^n}{s! s^{n-s}} P_0$$

$$P_3 = \frac{\left(\frac{5}{2}\right)^3}{3! 3^0} (0.04494) = 0.11703$$

$$P_4 = \frac{\left(\frac{5}{2}\right)^4}{3! 3^1} (0.04494) = 0.09753$$

$$P_5 = \frac{\left(\frac{5}{2}\right)^5}{3! 3^2} (0.04494) = 0.08127$$

$$1 - (P_0 + P_1 + P_2 + P_3 + P_4 + P_5) =$$
$$1 - (0.04494 + 0.11235 + 0.14044 + 0.11703 + 0.09753 + 0.08127) = 0.40644$$

c. The average number of patients waiting in the lobby, $L_q =$

$$L_q = \frac{P_0 \left(\frac{\lambda}{\mu}\right)^s \rho}{s!(1-\rho)^2} = \frac{0.04494 \left(\frac{5}{2}\right)^3 \left(\frac{5}{6}\right)}{3! \left(1-\frac{5}{6}\right)^2} = \frac{0.58516}{\frac{1}{6}} = 3.5109$$

d. The average time spent in the clinic, $W =$

$$w = w_q + \frac{1}{\mu} = \frac{L_q}{\lambda} + \frac{1}{\mu} = \frac{3.5109}{5} + \frac{1}{2} = 1.2022 \text{ hours}$$

4. Floyd's Barber Shop.

Multiple-server model, $s = 3$, $\lambda = 9$, $\mu = 4$ $\rho = \dfrac{\lambda}{s\mu} = \dfrac{9}{3(4)} = 0.75$

a. The probability that the shop will be empty is

$$P_0 = \left[\sum_{n=0}^{s-1} \frac{(\lambda/\mu)^n}{n!} + \frac{(\lambda/\mu)^s}{s!}\left(\frac{1}{1-\rho}\right)\right]^{-1} = \left[\sum_{n=0}^{2} \frac{(9/4)^n}{n!} + \frac{(9/4)^3}{3!}\left(\frac{1}{1-0.75}\right)\right]^{-1}$$

$$= \left\{\left[\frac{(9/4)^0}{0!} + \frac{(9/4)^1}{1!} + \frac{(9/4)^2}{2!}\right] + \left[\frac{(9/4)^3}{3!}\left(\frac{1}{1-0.75}\right)\right]\right\}^{-1}$$

$$= \left\{[1 + 2.25 + 2.53125] + [1.8984(4)]\right\}^{-1}$$

$$= \frac{1}{(5.78125) + (7.59375)} = 0.07477$$

b. The probability of 5 or more customers in the shop is equal to 1 minus the probability of 4 or less customers in the shop.

$P_0 = 0.07477$ (from part a)

$s = 3$

for $n < s$
$$P_n = \frac{\left(\frac{\lambda}{\mu}\right)^n}{n!} P_0$$

$$P_1 = \frac{\left(\frac{9}{4}\right)^1}{1!}(0.07477) = 0.16823$$

$$P_2 = \frac{\left(\frac{9}{4}\right)^2}{2!}(0.07477) = 0.18926$$

for $n \geq s$
$$P_n = \frac{\left(\frac{\lambda}{\mu}\right)^n}{s!s^{n-s}} P_0$$

$$P_3 = \frac{\left(\frac{9}{4}\right)^3}{3!3^0}(0.07477) = 0.14195$$

$$P_4 = \frac{\left(\frac{9}{4}\right)^4}{3!3^1}(0.07477) = 0.10646$$

$$1 - (P_0 + P_1 + P_2 + P_3 + P_4) =$$
$$1 - (0.07477 + 0.16823 + 0.18926 + 0.14195 + 0.10646) = 0.31933$$

c. The average number of customers waiting for haircuts, $L_q =$

$$L_q = \frac{P_0\left(\frac{\lambda}{\mu}\right)^s \rho}{s!(1-\rho)^2} = \frac{0.07477\left(\frac{9}{4}\right)^3\left(\frac{9}{12}\right)}{3!\left(1-\frac{9}{12}\right)^2} = \frac{0.63876}{0.375} = 1.7034$$

d. The average time spent waiting for service, $W_q =$

$$w_q = \frac{L_q}{\lambda} = \frac{1.7034}{9} = 0.189 \text{ hours or about } 11.3 \text{ minutes}$$

5. More Floyd's Barbershop. (with 4 chairs)

$$s = 4, \lambda = 9, \mu = 4,$$

$$\rho = \frac{\lambda}{s\mu} = \frac{9}{4(4)} = 0.5625$$

$$P_0 = \left[\sum_{n=0}^{s-1} \frac{(\lambda/\mu)^n}{n!} + \frac{(\lambda/\mu)^s}{s!} \left(\frac{1}{1-\rho} \right) \right]^{-1} = \left[\sum_{n=0}^{3} \frac{(9/4)^n}{n!} + \frac{(9/4)^4}{4!} \left(\frac{1}{1-0.5625} \right) \right]^{-1}$$

$$= \left\{ \left[\frac{(9/4)^0}{0!} + \frac{(9/4)^1}{1!} + \frac{(9/4)^2}{2!} + \frac{(9/4)^3}{3!} \right] + \left[\frac{(9/4)^4}{4!} \left(\frac{1}{1-0.5625} \right) \right] \right\}^{-1}$$

$$= \left\{ [1 + 2.25 + 2.53125 + 1.89844] + [1.06787(2.28571)] \right\}^{-1}$$

$$P_0 = \frac{1}{(7.6797) + (2.4408)} = 0.09881$$

$$L_q = \frac{P_0 \left(\frac{\lambda}{\mu} \right)^s \rho}{s!(1-\rho)^2} = \frac{0.09881 (9/4)^4 (9/16)}{4!(1 - 9/16)^2}$$

$$L_q = \frac{1.42447}{4.59375} = 0.31$$

$$W_q = \frac{L_q}{\lambda} = \frac{0.31}{9}$$

$W_q = 0.0345$ hours or about 2.07 minutes

Therefore, this expansion would reduce the wait time below five minutes.

6. KRAN radio. Single-server model

$$\mu = \frac{60 \text{ min / hr}}{10 \text{ min / call}} = 6 \text{ calls / hr}$$

$$\lambda = \frac{60 \text{ min / hr}}{25 \text{ min / call}} = 2.4 \text{ calls / hr}$$

$$\rho = \frac{\lambda}{\mu} = \frac{2.4}{6} = 0.4$$

A caller will not recieve a busy signal when there are zero, one or two callers in the system. Therefore, the probability of receiving a busy signal is one minus the probability of two or fewer callers in the system.

$$P_n = (1 - \rho)(\rho)^n$$

$$P_2 = (1 - 0.4)(0.4)^2 = 0.096$$

$$P_1 = (1 - 0.4)(0.4)^1 = 0.240$$

$$P_0 = (1 - 0.4)(0.4)^0 = \underline{0.600}$$

$$= 0.936$$

$1 - 0.936 = 0.064$ Niles' callers will get busy signals 6.4% of the time.

7. Ace Job Shop. Single-server model.

   With the junior attendant, the average number of idle machinists, L

   $$L = \frac{\lambda}{\mu - \lambda} = \frac{8}{10 - 8} = 4$$

   Average hourly idle machinist cost = $18(L) = $18 (4) = $72
   With the senior attendant, average number of idle machinists, L

   $$L = \frac{\lambda}{\mu - \lambda} = \frac{8}{12 - 8} = 2$$

   Average hourly cost of idle machinists drops to = $18(L) = $18 (2) = $36

   Adding the attendant pay gives a total cost of $77 per hour ($72 + $5) for the junior attendant and $45 per hour ($36 + $9) for the senior attendant. The best choice is the senior attendant.

8. Hasty Burgers. Single-server model, $\lambda = 20$

   a. Find μ resulting in $L = 4$.

   $$L = \frac{\lambda}{\mu - \lambda}$$

   $$4 = \frac{20}{\mu - 20}$$

   $$4\mu - 80 = 20$$

   $$4\mu = 100$$

   $$\mu = 25$$

   The required service rate is 25 customers per hour.

   b. Find the probability that *more than* four customers are in the system. This is one minus the probability of four or fewer customers in the system.

   First we calculate average utilization of the drive-in window

   $$\rho = \frac{\lambda}{\mu} = \frac{20}{25} = 0.8$$

   The probability that more than 4 customers are in line and being served is:

   $$P = 1 - (P_0 + P_1 + P_2 + P_3 + P_4)$$

   where

   $$P_n = (1 - \rho)(\rho)^n$$

   $$P = 1 - \left\{ \left[(1-\rho)(\rho)^0 \right] + \left[(1-\rho)(\rho)^1 \right] + \left[(1-\rho)(\rho)^2 \right] + \left[(1-\rho)(\rho)^3 \right] + \left[(1-\rho)(\rho)^4 \right] \right\}$$

   $$P = 1 - \left\{ (1-\rho) \left[(\rho)^0 + (\rho)^1 + (\rho)^2 + (\rho)^3 + (\rho)^4 \right] \right\}$$

   when $\rho = 0.8$

   $$P = 1 - \left\{ (0.2)[1 + 0.8 + 0.64 + 0.512 + 0.4096] \right\}$$

   $$P = 0.3277$$

   Consequently, there is about a 33 percent chance of more than 4 customers in the system.

c. Find the average time in line

$$W_q = \rho W = \rho\left(\frac{1}{\mu - \lambda}\right)$$

$$= 0.8\left(\frac{1}{25-20}\right)$$

$W_q = 0.16$ hours or 9.6 minutes

Ten minutes borders on being unbearable, particularly in the atmosphere of exhaust fumes. Keep in mind that this is an **average** and some people must wait longer.

Advanced Problems

9. Pinball Wizard. Multiple-server model. In this analysis we determine the expected total labor and machine failure costs for the existing complement of three employees and then compare it to larger maintenance complements until costs begin to rise.

Three maintenance people:

$$s = 3, \lambda = 0.333, \mu = 0.125,$$

Average utilization

$$\rho = \frac{\lambda}{s\mu} = \frac{0.333}{3(0.125)} = 0.888$$

Probability of an empty system

$$P_0 = \left[\sum_{n=0}^{s-1}\frac{(\lambda/\mu)^n}{n!} + \frac{(\lambda/\mu)^s}{s!}\left(\frac{1}{1-\rho}\right)\right]^{-1} = \left[\sum_{n=0}^{2}\frac{(0.333/0.125)^n}{n!} + \frac{(0.333/0.125)^3}{3!}\left(\frac{1}{1-0.888}\right)\right]^{-1}$$

$$= \left\{\left[\frac{(0.333/0.125)^0}{0!} + \frac{(0.333/0.125)^1}{1!} + \frac{(0.333/0.125)^2}{2!}\right] + \left[\frac{(0.333/0.125)^3}{3!}\left(\frac{1}{1-0.888}\right)\right]\right\}^{-1}$$

$$= \left\{[1 + 2.664 + 3.548] + [3.151(9)]\right\}^{-1}$$

$$P_0 = \frac{1}{(7.212)+(28.359)} = 0.02811$$

Number of machines in waiting line

$$L_q = \frac{P_0\left(\lambda/\mu\right)^s \rho}{s!(1-\rho)^2} = \frac{0.028\left(0.333/0.125\right)^3(0.888)}{3!(1-0.888)^2}$$

$$L_q = \frac{0.4719}{0.0753} = 6.267$$

The time waiting in line

$$W_q = \frac{L_q}{\lambda} = \frac{6.267}{0.333} = 18.82$$

Total time in system

$$W = W_q + \frac{1}{\mu}$$

$$= 18.82 + \frac{1}{0.125}$$

$$= 26.82$$

Total machines in system

$$L = \lambda W = 0.333(26.82)$$

$$L = 8.93$$

The total expected hourly costs for the current crew size of three employees is:

Labor:	3($8 per hour)	$ 24.00
Machine downtime:	8.93($10 per hour)	89.30
	TOTAL	$113.30

Four maintenance people:

Average utilization

$$\rho = \frac{\lambda}{s\mu} = \frac{0.333}{4(0.125)} = 0.667$$

Probability of an empty system

$$P_0 = \left[\sum_{n=0}^{s-1} \frac{(\lambda/\mu)^n}{n!} + \frac{(\lambda/\mu)^s}{s!}\left(\frac{1}{1-\rho}\right)\right]^{-1} = \left[\sum_{n=0}^{3} \frac{(0.333/0.125)^n}{n!} + \frac{(0.333/0.125)^4}{4!}\left(\frac{1}{1-0.666}\right)\right]^{-1}$$

$$= \left\{\left[\frac{(2.67)^0}{0!} + \frac{(2.67)^1}{1!} + \frac{(2.67)^2}{2!} + \frac{(2.67)^3}{3!}\right] + \left[\frac{(2.67)^4}{4!}\left(\frac{1}{1-0.666}\right)\right]\right\}^{-1}$$

$$= \left\{[1 + 2.667 + 3.556 + 3.160] + [2.107(3)]\right\}^{-1}$$

$$P_0 = \frac{1}{(10.383) + (6.321)} = 0.0599$$

Number of machines in waiting line

$$L_q = \frac{P_0\left(\frac{\lambda}{\mu}\right)^s \rho}{s!(1-\rho)^2} = \frac{0.0599(2.667)^4(0.667)}{4!(1-0.667)^2}$$

$$L_q = \frac{1.941}{2.677} = 0.758$$

The time waiting in line

$$W_q = \frac{L_q}{\lambda} = \frac{0.758}{0.333} = 2.277$$

Total time in system

$$W = W_q + \frac{1}{\mu}$$

$$= 2.277 + \frac{1}{0.125}$$

$$= 10.277$$

Total machines in system

$$L = \lambda W = 0.333(10.277)$$

$$L = 3.422$$

The total expected hourly costs for the crew size of four employees is:

Labor:	4($8 per hour)	$ 32.00
Machine downtime:	3.422($10 per hour)	34.22
	TOTAL	$66.22

Five maintenance people

Average utilization

$$\rho = \frac{\lambda}{s\mu} = \frac{0.333}{5(0.125)} = 0.5328$$

Probability of an empty system

$$P_0 = \left[\sum_{n=0}^{s-1} \frac{(\lambda/\mu)^n}{n!} + \frac{(\lambda/\mu)^s}{s!}\left(\frac{1}{1-\rho}\right) \right]^{-1} = \left[\sum_{n=0}^{3} \frac{(0.333/0.125)^n}{n!} + \frac{(0.333/0.125)^4}{5!}\left(\frac{1}{1-0.5328}\right) \right]^{-1}$$

$$= \left\{ \left[\frac{(2.67)^0}{0!} + \frac{(2.67)^1}{1!} + \frac{(2.67)^2}{2!} + \frac{(2.67)^3}{3!} + \frac{(2.67)^4}{4!} \right] + \left[\frac{(2.67)^5}{5!}\left(\frac{1}{0.4672}\right) \right] \right\}^{-1}$$

$$= \left\{ [1 + 2.667 + 3.556 + 3.160 + 2.107] + [1.124(2.14)] \right\}^{-1}$$

$$P_0 = \frac{1}{(12.490) + (2.405)} = 0.067$$

Number of machines in waiting line

$$L_q = \frac{P_0\left(\lambda/\mu\right)^s \rho}{s!(1-\rho)^2} = \frac{0.067(2.67)^5(0.5328)}{5!(1-0.5328)^2}$$

$$L_q = \frac{4.814}{26.193} = 0.184$$

The time waiting in line

$$W_q = \frac{L_q}{\lambda} = \frac{0.184}{0.333} = 0.553$$

Total time in system

$$W = W_q + \frac{1}{\mu}$$

$$= 0.553 + \frac{1}{0.125}$$

$$= 8.553$$

Total machines in system

$$L = \lambda W = 0.333(8.553)$$

$$L = 2.848$$

The total expected hourly costs for the crew size of five employees is:

Labor: 4($8 per hour)	$ 40.00
Machine downtime: 2.848($10 per hour)	28.48
TOTAL	$68.48

This total is higher than that for employing four maintenance people. Therefore the manager of the Pinball Palace should add only one more maintenance person.

10. Benton University, Finite Source Model

   a.   To calculate the utilization in a finite source waiting line situation, we must first compute the probability that the maintenance person will have no customers.

$$P_0 = \left[\sum_{n=0}^{N} \frac{N!}{(N-n)!} \left(\frac{\lambda}{\mu} \right)^n \right]^{-1}$$

$$= \left\{ 1 + \left[\frac{5!}{(5-1)!} \left(\frac{0.4}{2.5} \right)^1 \right] + \left[\frac{5!}{(5-2)!} \left(\frac{0.4}{2.5} \right)^2 \right] + \left[\frac{5!}{(5-3)!} \left(\frac{0.4}{2.5} \right)^3 \right] + \left[\frac{5!}{(5-4)!} \left(\frac{0.4}{2.5} \right)^4 \right] + \left[\frac{5!}{(5-5)!} \left(\frac{0.4}{2.5} \right)^5 \right] \right\}^{-1}$$

$$= \{ 1 + 0.8 + 0.512 + 0.246 + 0.079 + 0.013 \}^{-1}$$

$$P_0 = \frac{1}{2.65} = 0.3774$$

$$\rho = 1 - P_0 = 1 - 0.3774 = 0.6226$$

   b.   Copy machines in repair system

$$L = N - \frac{\mu}{\lambda}(1 - P_0)$$

$$= 5 - \left[\frac{2.5}{0.4}(1 - 0.3774) \right]$$

$$= 5 - 3.891$$

$$= 1.109$$

   c.   Time spent in repair system

$$W = L\left[(N - L)\lambda \right]^{-1}$$

$$= \frac{1.109}{\left[(5 - 1.109)0.4 \right]}$$

$$= 0.712 \text{ days}$$

$$= 5.7 \text{ hours, assuming an 8-hour day}$$

11. Bryant Manufacturing.

a. To calculate the utilization in a finite source queuing situation, we must first compute the probability that the repair person will have no customers.

$$N = 6, \lambda = 0.25, \mu = 2$$

$$P_0 = \left[\sum_{n=0}^{N} \frac{N!}{(N-n)!} \left(\frac{\lambda}{\mu} \right)^n \right]^{-1}$$

$$= \left\{ \left[\frac{6!}{(6-0)!} \left(\frac{0.25}{2} \right)^0 \right] + \left[\frac{6!}{(6-1)!} \left(\frac{0.25}{2} \right)^1 \right] + \left[\frac{6!}{(6-2)!} \left(\frac{0.25}{2} \right)^2 \right] + \left[\frac{6!}{(6-3)!} \left(\frac{0.25}{2} \right)^3 \right] \right.$$
$$\left. + \left[\frac{6!}{(6-4)!} \left(\frac{0.25}{2} \right)^4 \right] + \left[\frac{6!}{(6-5)!} \left(\frac{0.25}{2} \right)^5 \right] + \left[\frac{6!}{(6-6)!} \left(\frac{0.25}{2} \right)^6 \right] \right\}^{-1}$$

$$= \{1 + 0.75 + 0.469 + 0.234 + 0.088 + 0.022 + 0.003\}^{-1}$$

$$P_0 = \frac{1}{2.566} = 0.3897$$

$$\rho = 1 - P_0 = 1 - 0.3897 = 0.6103$$

b. Machines in repair system

$$L = N - \frac{\mu}{\lambda}(1 - P_0)$$

$$= 6 - \left[\frac{2}{0.25}(1 - 0.3897) \right]$$

$$= 6 - 4.8824$$

$$= 1.1176$$

c. Waiting time in system

$$W = L \left[(N - L)\lambda \right]^{-1}$$

$$= \frac{1.1176}{(6 - 1.1176)0.25}$$

$$= 0.9156 \text{ days or } 7.32 \text{ hours (assuming an 8-hour day)}$$

Supplement F

Simulation

Problems

1. Eagle Dry Cleaners

    a. NGNC = Number of garments needing cleaning

    MNGD = Maximum number of garments that could be dry cleaned

Day	RN	New Garments	Queue at Start of Day	NGNC	RN	MNGD	Actual Garments Cleaned	Queue at End of Day
1	49	70	0	70	77	80	70	0
2	27	60	0	60	53	70	60	0
3	65	80	0	80	08	60	60	20
4	83	80	20	100	12	60	60	40
5	04	50	40	90	82	80	80	10
6	58	70	10	80	44	70	70	10
7	53	70	10	80	83	80	80	0
8	57	70	0	70	72	80	70	0
9	32	60	0	60	53	70	60	0
10	60	70	0	70	79	80	70	0
11	79	80	0	80	30	70	70	10
12	41	70	10	80	48	70	70	10
13	97	90	10	100	86	80	80	20
14	30	60	20	80	25	60	60	20
15	80	80	20	100	73	80	80	20
						Total		**160**

The average daily number of garments held overnight is 160/15 = 10.67 garments.

    b. The expansion reduces the number of garments held overnight from 15 to 10.67 (calculated as 160/15), saving $108.25 [$25(4.33)] per day. The saving exceeds the $100 expansion cost, making expansion a good idea.

2. Precision Manufacturing Company. The following Table A simulates the arrival of 10 batches over a 60 minute horizon. With a different choice of random numbers, the results will vary. Random numbers from row 1 of the random number table were used with the probability distribution to simulate the number of units in each batch. Random numbers from the second and third rows were similarly used to establish setup times and processing times, respectively. Resulting assignments for setup and processing times for each machine are also shown.

    Table B determines the work requirements of each machine, based on the job arrivals and times selected in Table A. The totals are very similar, with NC machine 1 being slightly more productive. The totals of 2646 seconds and 2680 seconds are considerably less than the capacity of 3600 seconds for the 60-minute horizon. Capacity is more than sufficient for either machine.

processing times

	...es (min)		Processing Times (sec)		
Ba...	...ine	Machine 2	RN	Machine 1	Machine 2
		3	50	7	5
		5	63	8	5
		5	95	9	7
		2	49	7	5
		3	68	8	5
		3	11	6	3
8		3	40	7	4
9		4	93	9	7
10		5	61	8	5
		2	48	7	5

Tabl...

Batc...				Machine 2 Requirements (sec)		
				Setup	Processing	Total
1				180	70	250
2				300	40	340
3		162	462	300	126	426
4	60	126	186	120	90	210
5	120	48	168	180	30	210
6	120	48	168	180	24	204
7	120	42	162	180	24	204
8	240	72	312	240	56	296
9	300	144	444	300	90	390
10	120	42	162	120	30	150
	Totals	**2646**				**2680**

The small sample size of just 10 batches may cause us some estimation errors. Another approach is to work with the expected values of the five probability distributions. They can be computed as

Number of jobs	= 10.3 units every 6 minutes
Machine 1 setup	= 3.0 minutes/batch
Machine 2 setup	= 3.4 minutes/batch
Machine 1 processing	= 7.15 seconds/job
Machine 2 processing	= 4.70 seconds/job

Using these expected values to estimate the work requirements for each machine for a 60-minute horizon, we get

Machine 1: 10[3.0 min(60 sec/min) + 10.3 units(7.15 sec/job)] = 2536 seconds
Machine 2: 10[3.4min(60 sec/min) + 10.3 units(4.70 sec/job)] = 2524 seconds

These numbers suggest that a much longer simulation would show that machine 2 is the slightly better choice. Its shorter processing times more than compensate for the longer setup times, given the sizes of batches that arrive. Smaller batches favor machine 1.

3. Since either machine has plenty of capacity, and continuing to assume equal operation and maintenance costs, we should purchase the lower price machine. In other words, the decision should not favor the machine with higher capacity. Capacity in excess of that needed has no value. Greater capacity merely results in more idle time.

4. Omega University.

   a. Preliminary estimates or utilization and proportion of unanswered calls:

      arrival rate: 90 calls per hour x 60% forwarded to office = 54 calls/hour
      answering service rate: 60 minutes/hour / 1 minute/call = 60 calls per hour
      estimated utilization = 54/60 = 90%

      Of 90 calls, we would expect (40%x90 =) 36 to be answered by the professors. 54 would be forwarded, and since the clerk has some idle time, we might expect the lion's share of those calls to be answered as well. Surely only a few calls would go unanswered.

   b. Simulation. A table showing the simulation is on the next page.

      During the 60 minutes, 82 calls were placed. Of those, 68 were answered. Even though this simulation is for an hour when fewer than the expected average of 90 calls were received, 14 calls or 14/82 = 17% went unanswered by anyone.

   c. Professors answered 34 calls (41%) and 48 (59%) were forwarded to the department office. Of the 48 forwarded calls, only 34 calls (or 71%) were answered by the clerk. The clerk was idle 26 of 60 minutes. Utilization was only 34/60 = 57%, not the estimated 90%.

      The simulation shows that even though the clerk has lots of idle time, calls were being missed because they do not arrive at a steady pace.

5. Voice mail-boxes. The office assistant is currently spending 57% of his time answering the telephone. Assuming that time saved could be productively used elsewhere,

   Labor savings = $2,000/month x 57% x 50% = $570/month.
   Voice mail cost = $20/month x 32 telephones = $640/month.

   The voice mail-box system would increase costs but would also increase customer satisfaction. If the present call forwarding system is missing about 15 calls per hour, the additional $70 per month cost of the voice mail-box system could easily be justified (roughly 3¢ per missed call).

6. Capitol City Shuttle.

   a. Average hourly revenue.

Hour	Queue at Start of Hour	RN	New Arrivals	Total People Needing Service	People Shuttled	Queue at End of Hour
1	0	87	13	13	12	1
2	1	44	11	12	12	0
3	0	29	11	11	11	0
4	0	02	10	10	10	0
5	0	97	15	15	12	3
6	3	20	11	14	12	2
7	2	71	12	14	12	2
8	2	15	10	12	12	0
				TOTAL	93	

   The bus shuttled a total of 93 people. However, 8 of these had to wait and therefore paid reduced prices. Therefore, we took 85 at $10.00 apiece and 8 at $8.50 apiece for a total of $918 over an 8-hour period. The average hourly income is $114.75.

   b. The bus carried 93 people in 8 trips. Its capacity was 96 people [8(12)]. Consequently, the average utilization was 93 / 96 = 97 percent.

Time	RN	No. of calls made	RN	1st call forward? (Yes/No)	RN	2nd call forward? (Yes/No)	RN	3rd call forward? (Yes/No)	RN	4th call forward? (Yes/No)	No. of calls not answered	√ asst idle
10:00	68	2	30	Yes	54	Yes					1	
10:01	76	2	36	Yes	32	Yes					1	
10:02	68	2	04	Yes	07	Yes					1	
10:03	98	4	08	Yes	21	Yes	28	Yes	79	No	2	
10:04	25	1	77	No							0	√
10:05	51	1	23	Yes							0	
10:06	67	2	22	Yes	27	Yes					1	
10:07	80	2	87	No	06	Yes					0	
10:08	03	0									0	√
10:09	03	0									0	√
10:10	33	1	78	No							0	√
10:11	32	1	40	Yes							0	
10:12	56	2	92	No	61	No					0	√
10:13	39	1	05	Yes							0	
10:14	93	3	43	Yes	54	Yes	30	Yes			2	
10:15	33	1	26	Yes							0	
10:16	33	1	83	No							0	√
10:17	62	2	60	No	25	Yes					0	
10:18	12	0									0	√
10:19	30	1	96	No							0	√
10:20	83	3	48	Yes	23	Yes	11	Yes			2	
10:21	09	0									0	√
10:22	92	3	66	No	21	Yes	76	No			0	
10:23	31	1	19	Yes							0	
10:24	51	1	75	No							0	√
10:25	15	0									0	√
10:26	27	1	52	Yes							0	
10:27	58	2	94	No	45	Yes					0	
10:28	74	2	72	No	19	Yes					0	
10:29	20	0									0	√
10:30	64	2	71	No	39	Yes					0	
10:31	04	0									0	√
10:32	75	2	01	Yes	05	Yes					1	
10:33	45	1	58	Yes							0	
10:34	15	0									0	
10:35	66	2	94	No	60	No					0	√
10:36	61	2	72	No	99	No					0	√
10:37	32	1	90	No							0	√
10:38	73	2	14	Yes	25	Yes					1	
10:39	52	1	20	Yes							0	
10:40	86	3	89	No	97	No	63	No			0	√
10:41	65	2	99	No	89	No					0	√
10:42	36	1	54	Yes							0	
10:43	19	0									0	√
10:44	07	0									0	√
10:45	56	2	04	Yes	52	Yes					1	
10:46	01	0									0	√
10:47	14	0									0	√
10:48	55	1	49	Yes							0	
10:49	23	1	62	No							0	√
10:50	59	2	61	No	21	Yes					0	
10:51	49	1	64	No							0	√
10:52	36	1	45	Yes							0	
10:53	26	1	20	Yes							0	
10:54	26	1	46	Yes							0	
10:55	41	1	78	No							0	√
10:56	79	2	73	No	45	Yes					0	
10:57	87	3	47	Yes	77	No	89	No			0	
10:58	99	4	78	No	08	Yes	21	Yes	61	No	1	
10:59	24	1	15	Yes							0	

7. Swift Airlines.

a.

Day	RN	New Arrivals	Previous Day's Queue	Total Needing Service	Aircraft Overhauled	End of Day Queue
1	24	1	0	1	1	0
2	05	1	0	1	1	0
3	19	1	0	1	1	0
4	53	2	0	2	2	0
5	20	1	0	1	1	0
6	80	3	0	3	2	1
7	58	2	1	3	2	1
8	32	1	1	2	2	0
9	93	3	0	3	2	1
10	77	3	1	4	2	2

b. The maximum number of aircraft held overnight was 2 on day 10.

8. A machine center.

a. Two random numbers could be used for each client — one for demand and one for processing time. Once this has been done for all four clients, it is possible to compute the value of R for the year just simulated. The result is one observation for constructing a frequency chart or probability distribution.

b. For the first year simulated:

RN	Event
78	A's demand is 4200 units (in 70–99 range)
10	A's processing time is 10 hours/unit (in 0–34 range)
62	B's demand is 800 units (in 30–79 range)
72	B's processing time is 90 hours/unit (in 25–74 range)
11	C's demand is 3000 units (in 10–59 range)
28	C's processing time is 15 hours/unit (in 25–84 range)
16	D's demand is 600 units (in 0–39 range)
99	D's processing time is 80 hours/unit (in 95–99 range)

Then for the first year:

$R = 4200(10) + 800(90) + 3000(15) + 600(80)$
$= 207,000$ hours.

Chapter 8

Location

Study Questions

1. Factors that have expanded the range of possible locations for an organization include improved transportation and communication technology and more open financial systems. Transportation infrastructure and communication technology reduce the need for facilities to have close proximity. Open financial systems make it easier to locate where capital, material and human resources are cheapest.

2. International activity is particularly evident in Mexico's maquiladoras, the European Community, East Europe, and the former Soviet Union, Japan, and East Asia. It is also evident in the globalization of services. The term "electronic immigration" has been used to describe a future in which it will be common for information services to be produced in one country and consumed in another, while using communication technology to cross borders.

3. Differences in language, politics, norms and customs create problems for managers of international production. Unfamiliar labor laws, tax laws, regulatory requirements, and cultural differences must be addressed. Another issue is determining the proportion of production that should be transplanted overseas and the extent to which the foreign environment will accept new techniques. Finally, having multiple plants raises the question of how much control the home office should retain.

4. The ethical issue stems from the employer's responsibility to provide good work opportunities to its current work force. Growth of the maquiladoras often means lost jobs elsewhere, painful restructuring in certain industries, downward pressure on U.S. wages, diminishing organized labor, and an uneven impact (Texas is less hurt than Michigan). Companies must deal with these issues. For example, Dianna Forster is an unemployed mother because Jerrold Electronics closed its Kansas City, Missouri, plant in favor of a plant in Matamoros, Mexico (see "Is Free Trade with Mexico Good or Bad for the U.S.?" *Business Week*, November 12, 1990, pp. 112-113).

The other side of the coin is that such relocations often are necessary to avoid being driven out of the business by low-wage competition and to maintain a world-class competitive position. Workers at Packard Electric Division of General Motors feel that job erosion in Warren, Ohio, has been slowed because the assembly work for electrical systems has already been moved to Mexico, allowing Ohio workers to concentrate on building the switches and couplings that go into the systems. Packard gets access to cheaper labor and a growing export market. There are also advantages to Mexico's economy. The 2.5 to 3 million Mexicans depending on maquiladora paychecks might otherwise be moving north of the border as illegal immigrants.

5. **Favorable labor climate** — textiles, furniture, consumer electronics.

   Proximity to markets — paper, plastic pipe, cars, heavy metals, and food processing.

   Quality of life — high technology and research firms.

   Proximity to suppliers and resources — paper mills, food processors, and cement manufacturers.

   Proximity to company's other facilities — feeder plants and certain product lines in computer manufacturing industry.

6. The usually dominant location factor in the service industry is the proximity to markets, which is related to revenues. One complication is predicting the impact of present competitor locations on revenues, let alone new openings made after the location decision. Locating near the competition sometimes helps sales; in other cases, the opposite occurs.

7. Building another plant has the advantages of not having to rely solely on the production from one plant, escaping from unproductive labor, modernizing with new technology, and reducing transportation costs.

8. Firms choosing to relocate rather than expand on the present site are usually small, cramped for space, and needing to change production processes (for example from a process focus to a product focus.) Other possible advantages include reduced transportation costs, temporarily escaping poor management-labor relations, and government economic development and tax incentives.

9. The "rust belt" city has made long-term investments to build roads and utilities to support the auto manufacturer. It has expanded schools and developed residential and commercial property to accommodate the manufacturer's employees and their families. Leaving the rust belt city leaves the city with these long-term obligations with no means to pay for them. When General Motors closed a large facility in a small community, the results were so devastating that the community sued GM for damages. Sorry, in the years of delay through the courts, I never learned of the outcome.

10. This is similar to question number nine. However baseball fans that were not sympathetic to the "rust belt" city in Study Question 9 may suddenly switch sides at the prospect of their own ox being gored. The city has made the same sort of long-term investments in the stadium, roads, zoning and planning to the benefit of the baseball team (an entertainment service) as they would have for the manufacturer. The same obligations apply.

11. Preference matrix —when qualitative factors which cannot be evaluated in dollar terms are important to the location decision.

    Break-even — when the manager wishes to define the ranges over which each alternative is best while comparing different location alternatives on the basis of quantitative factors that can be expressed in terms of total cost.

    Transportation method — when the manager wishes to consider multiple-facility locations to find the location resulting in the best shipping pattern for the system.

    Heuristics — when the manager desires to find a good, but not necessarily the best location, and needs an efficient approach to identify a good location.

    Simulation — to evaluate the effect of changing variables on different location alternatives by trial and error.

12. Even though euclidean or rectilinear distances may not be exactly correct in measuring distance in a location analysis, they provide a consistent means to measure **relative** distances so that one alternative may be compared to another. That is, if location A is actually 5 miles from location B, and location C is actually 3 miles from location B, we know that location C is 2 miles closer to location B than is location A. If we use euclidean or rectilinear distance measures, we will still conclude that C is closer to B than A. This is important because we can use mathematical approaches to location analysis based on these measures. In practice, using a measure such as euclidean or rectilinear distances will result in an incorrect comparison of alternatives only in exceptional cases.

13. The full-grid search is less efficient because it evaluates more points than a patterned search. However, it provides more information because it provides the costs of locations around the lowest

cost location. Due to qualitative considerations the best location may not be where the load-distance score is minimized. The patterned search only evaluates a subset of the potential locations and therefore provides less information.

14. A multiple-facility location problem breaks down into several single-facility location problems as soon as decisions are made on work allocation and capacity. Such is the case when the number of new facilities has already been decided (perhaps through the budgetary process) and the geographical market area can be determined a priori for each new facility.

15. If management makes the work allocation decision, the manual method **begins** with the allocation and capacity decisions and **ends** with the location decision. If customers make the allocation choice by deciding at which location to get service, the sequence is reversed. Location decisions are made first, followed by allocation and capacity choices.

16. In general, computer models are needed because of the complexity of the location problem in many practical applications. The complexities include: thousands of demand centers; hundreds of potential sites; several manufacturing plants; multiple product lines; varying transportation rates; fixed and variable operating costs; and varying inventory policies. Specifically, heuristics find a solution to the problem but do not guarantee optimality; simulation adds great realism to the details of the problem but is essentially a trial-and-error process; and optimization prescribes the best solution given the assumptions but typically is limited to simplified problem statements because problem size limits its ability to arrive at a solution.

17. The transportation method finds the optimal allocation pattern, given a particular combination of location-capacity choices. The analyst must propose different combinations, which may or may not include the optimal one. In this sense, an optimization procedure is being used as part of a larger heuristic procedure, with no guarantee of finding the optimal solution.

Problems

1. Preference matrix location for A, B, C, or D.

Location Factor	Factor Weight	Factor Score for Each Location							
		A		B		C		D	
1. Labor Climate	5	5	25	4	20	3	15	5	25
2. Quality of Life	30	2	60	3	90	5	150	1	30
3. Transportation system	5	3	15	4	20	3	15	5	25
4. Proximity to markets	25	5	125	3	75	4	100	4	100
5. Proximity to materials	5	3	15	2	10	3	15	5	25
6. Taxes	15	2	30	5	75	5	75	4	60
7. Utilities	15	5	75	4	60	2	30	1	15
Total	100		345		350		400		350

Location C, with 400 points.

2. John and Marcia Darling.

Location Factor	Factor Weight	Factor Score for Each Location							
		A		B		C		D	
1. Rent	25	3	75	1	25	2	50	5	125
2. Quality of Life	20	2	40	5	100	5	100	4	80
3. Schools	5	3	15	5	25	3	15	1	5
4. Proximity to work	10	5	50	3	30	4	40	3	30
5. Proximity to recreation	15	4	60	4	60	5	75	2	30
6. Neighborhood Security	15	2	30	4	60	4	60	4	60
7. Utilities	10	4	40	2	20	3	30	5	50
Total	100		310		320		370		380

Location D, the in-laws' downstairs apartment is indicated by the highest score. This points out a criticism of the technique: the Darlings did not include or give weight to a relevant factor.

3. Knoxville or Dayton locations.

Knoxville —

$200(25,000) - [$1,800,000 + ($60 x 25,000)] = $5,000,000 - $3,300,000 = $1,700,000

Dayton —

$200(30,000) - [$2,400,000 + ($85 x 30,000)] = $6,000,000 - $4,950,000 = $1,050,000

Dayton has a $1,700,000 profit at a volume of about 36,000 units per year.

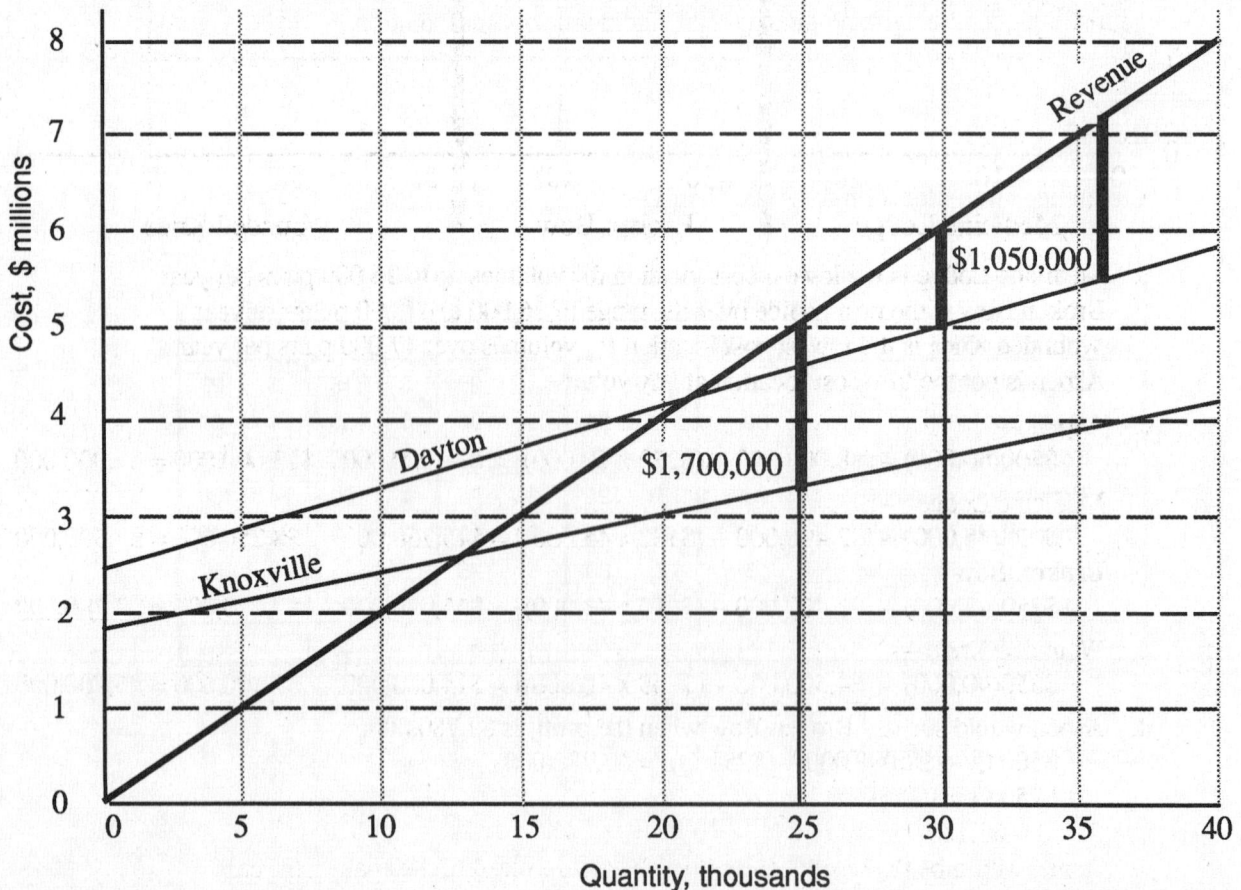

4. Fall-Line, Inc.

a. Plot of total costs (in $ millions) versus volume (in thousands)

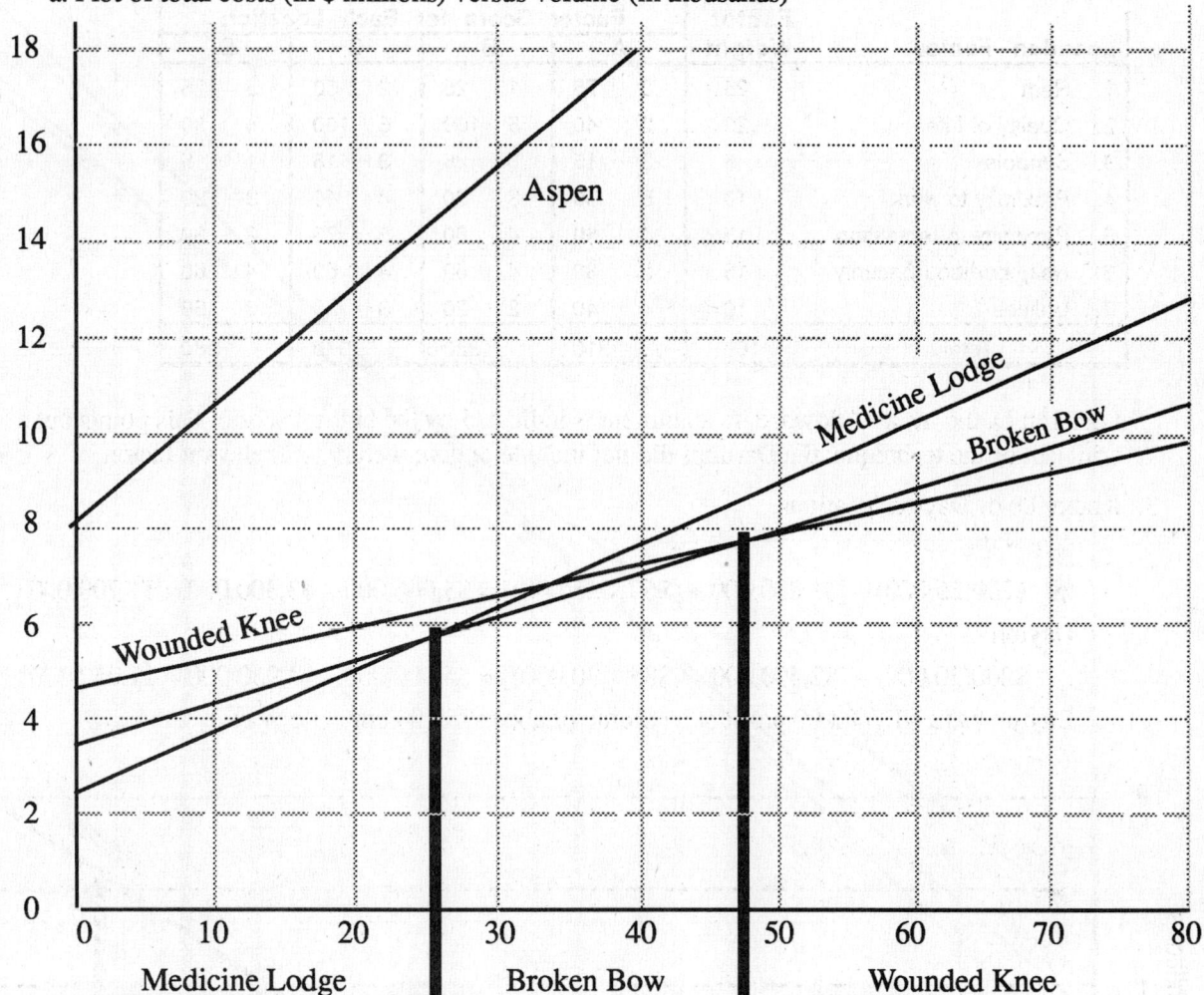

b. Medicine Lodge is the lowest cost location for volumes up to 26,000 pairs per year.
   Broken Bow is the best choice over the range of 26,000 to 47,000 pairs per year.
   Wounded Knee is the lowest cost location for volumes over 47,000 pairs per year.
   Aspen is not the low-cost location at any volume.

c. Aspen —
   $500(60,000) − [$8,000,000 + ($250 x 60,000)] = $30,000,000 − $23,000,000 = $7,000,000
   Medicine Lodge —
   $350(45,000) − [$2,400,000 + ($130 x 45,000)] = $15,750,000 − $8,250,000 = $7,500,000
   Broken Bow —
   $350(43,000) − [$3,400,000 + ($ 90 x 43,000)] = $15,050,000 − $7,270,000 = **$7,780,000**
   Wounded Knee —
   $350(40,000) − [$4,500,000 + ($ 65 x 40,000)] = $14,000,000 − $7,100,000 = $6,900,000

d. Aspen would surpass Broken Bow when the profit is $7,780,000.
   $500 Q − [$8,000,000 + ($250 Q)] = $7,780,000
   $250 Q = 15,780,00
   Q = 63,120
   Aspen would be the best location if sales would exceed 63,120 pairs per year.

5. Wiebe Trucking, Inc.

    a. Plot of total costs (in $millions) versus volume (in thousands)

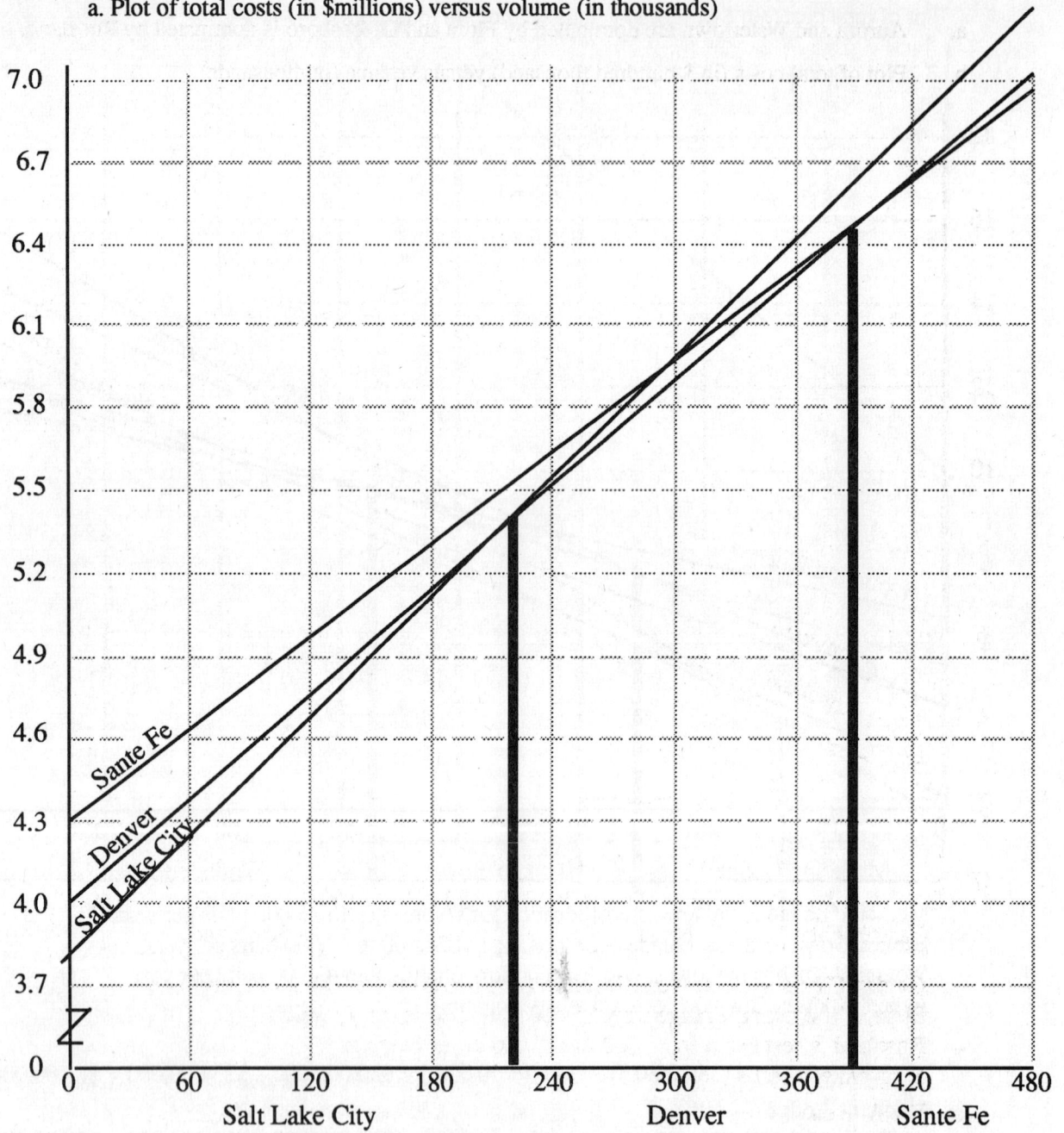

    b.   For the range of 450,000 to 600,000 shipments per year, Sante Fe is the best location.

6. Hot House Roses.

a.   Aurora and Watertown are dominated by Flora and Greensboro is dominated by Roseland.

b.   Plot of total costs (in $ hundred thousand) versus volume (in thousands)

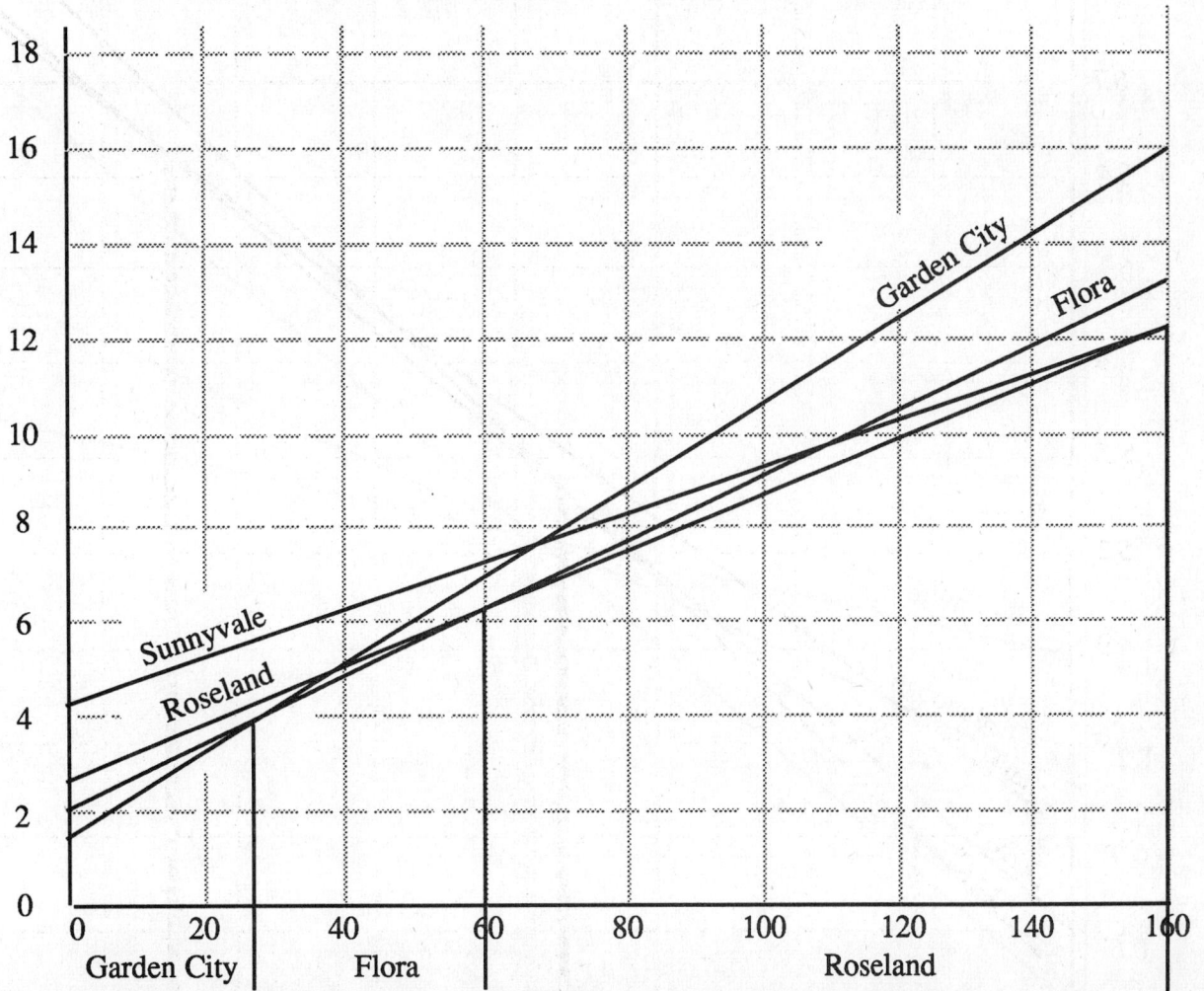

Garden City is the lowest cost location from 0 to about 25,000 dozen per year.
Flora is best over the range from 25,000 to 60,000 dozen per year.
Roseland is best between 60,000 to 160,000 dozen per year.
Sunnyvale is best at volumes over 160,000 dozen per year.

c.   Break-even
Garden City — Flora
$150,000 + 9\,Q = 200,000 + 7\,Q$
$2\,Q = 50,000$
$Q = 25,000$
Flora — Roseland
$200,000 + 7\,Q = 260,000 + 6\,Q$
$Q = 60,000$
Roseland — Sunnyvale
$260,000 + 6\,Q = 420,000 + 5\,Q$
$Q = 160,000$

7. Ethel and Earl Griese.
   a. Plot of total costs (in $millions) versus volume (in units)

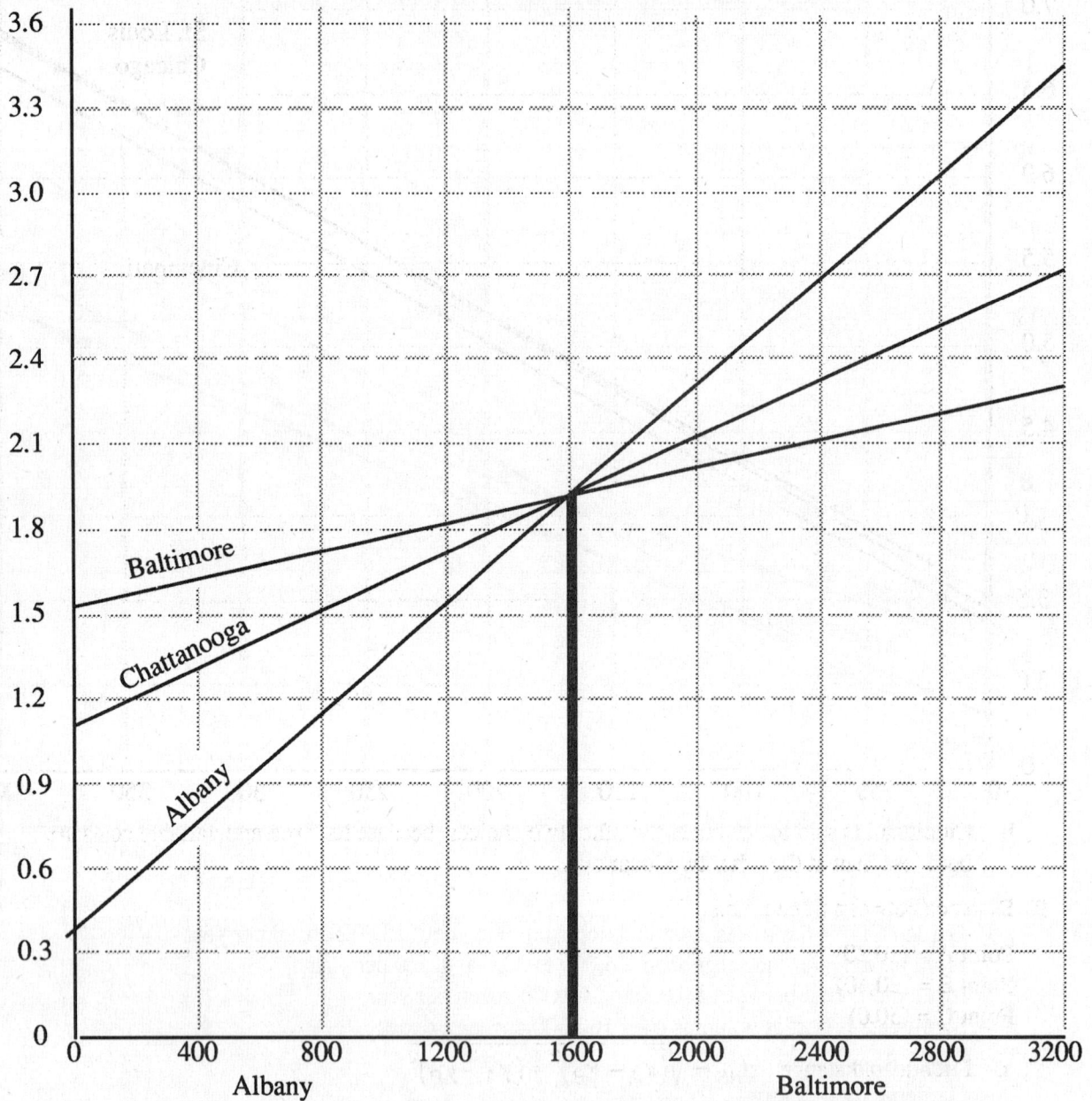

Albany is the best location below 1600 units, and Baltimore is better above than volume.

   b. Break-even
      Albany — Baltimore
      $350,000 + 980 Q = 1,500,500 + 240 Q$
      $740 Q = 1,150,500$
      $Q = 1,555$
      Total cost = $1,500,500 + 240 (1,555) = \$1,873,700$
      Chattanooga cost @ 1,555 = $\$1,100,000 + 500(1555) = \$1,877,500$ therefore Chattanooga is never the low-cost location.

8. Excel Foods.
   a. The narrow difference between the slopes makes the plot difficult to do accurately.

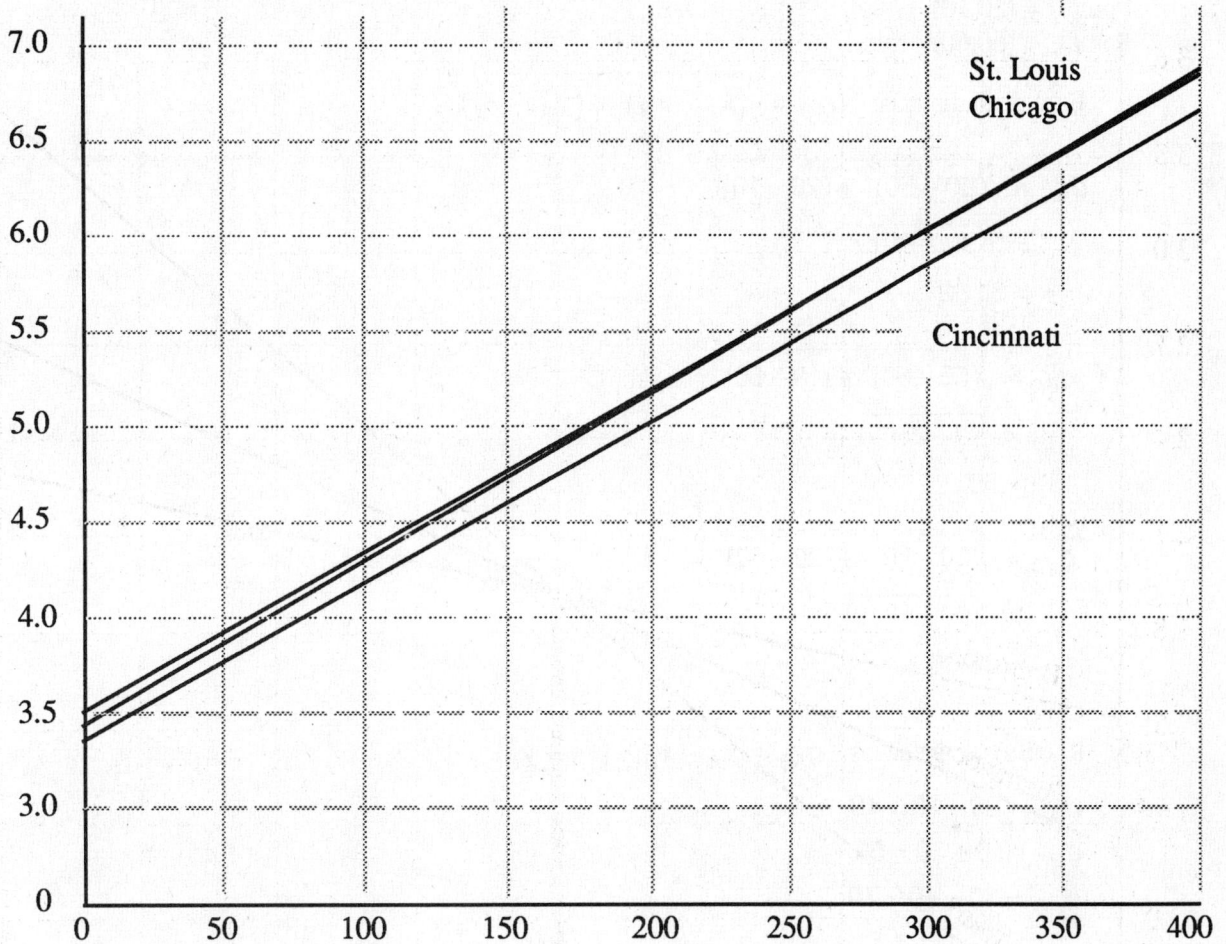

   b. Cincinnati is said to dominate the other two choices, because its fixed and variable costs are both less than at the other two locations.

9. Distance between three points.

   Point A = (10,20)
   Point B = (20,40)
   Point C = (50,0)

   a. Euclidean distance $d_{AB} = \sqrt{(x_A - x_B)^2 + (y_A - y_B)^2}$

$$d_{AB} = \sqrt{(10-20)^2 + (20-40)^2} \qquad d_{BC} = \sqrt{(20-50)^2 + (40-0)^2} \qquad d_{AC} = \sqrt{(10-50)^2 + (20-0)^2}$$

$$= \sqrt{(100+400)} \qquad\qquad = \sqrt{(900+1600)} \qquad\qquad = \sqrt{(1600+400)}$$

$$= 22.36 \qquad\qquad\qquad = 50 \qquad\qquad\qquad = 44.72$$

   b. Recilinear distances $d_{AB} = |x_A - x_B| + |y_A - y_B|$

$$d_{AB} = 10 + 20 = 30$$
$$d_{BC} = 30 + 40 = 70$$
$$d_{AC} = 40 + 20 = 60$$

10. Distance between three points.

Point A = (20,20)
Point B = (50,10)
Point C = (50,60)

a. Euclidean distance $d_{AB} = \sqrt{(x_A - x_B)^2 + (y_A - y_B)^2}$

$$d_{AB} = \sqrt{(20-50)^2 + (20-10)^2}$$
$$= \sqrt{(900+100)}$$
$$= 31.62$$

$$d_{BC} = \sqrt{(50-50)^2 + (10-60)^2}$$
$$= \sqrt{(0+2500)}$$
$$= 50$$

$$d_{AC} = \sqrt{(20-50)^2 + (20-60)^2}$$
$$= \sqrt{(900+400)}$$
$$= 36.06$$

b. Rectilinear distances $d_{AB} = |x_A - x_B| + |y_A - y_B|$

$$d_{AB} = 30 + 10 = 40$$
$$d_{BC} = 0 + 50 = 50$$
$$d_{AC} = 30 + 40 = 70$$

11. Centura High School

$$x^* = \frac{\sum_i l_i x_i}{\sum_i l_i} \quad \text{and} \quad y^* = \frac{\sum_i l_i y_i}{\sum_i l_i}$$

$$x^* = \frac{(228 \times 0) + (737 \times 5.2) + (356 \times 9)}{(228 + 737 + 356)}$$

$$x^* = \frac{7036.4}{1321} = 5.33$$

$$y^* = \frac{(228 \times 5.0) + (737 \times 0.0) + (356 \times 9.0)}{(228 + 737 + 356)}$$

$$y^* = \frac{4344}{1321} = 3.29$$

This location would place the school in the river!

12. Val's Pizza.

   Point A location (1.00,1.75), demand = 4000
   Point B location (3.75,2.00), demand = 1000
   Point C location (4.75,2.25), demand = 1000
   Point D location (5.00,0.00), demand = 1000
   Point E location (0.75,0.50), demand =   500

   a.
$$x^* = \frac{\sum_i l_i x_i}{\sum_i l_i} \quad \text{and} \quad y^* = \frac{\sum_i l_i y_i}{\sum_i l_i}$$

$$x^* = \frac{(4000 \times 1.00)+(1000 \times 3.75)+(1000 \times 4.75)+(1000 \times 5.00)+(500 \times 0.75)}{(4000+1000+1000+1000+500)}$$

$$x^* = \frac{17,875}{7500} = 2.38$$

$$y^* = \frac{(4000 \times 1.75)+(1000 \times 2.00)+(1000 \times 2.25)+(1000 \times 0.00)+(500 \times 0.50)}{(4000+1000+1000+1000+500)}$$

$$y^* = \frac{11500}{7500} = 1.53$$

   Val's should start looking for locations at about 30th and "O" streets.

   b. Rectilinear load-distance score. Assuming Val's location at (2.5, 1.5).

Location	Load	Distance	ld score
Point A	4000	1.75	7000
Point B	1000	1.75	1750
Point C	1000	3.00	3000
Point D	1000	4.00	4000
Point E	500	2.75	1375
			17,250

   c. Rectilinear distance from Vals (at 2.5, 1.5) to the farthest point D (5.0, 0.0) is 4 miles. At two minutes per mile, the travel time is 8 minutes.

13. Improvement on Figure 8.4. Locating at (7.0, 2.5) yields the lowest of all locations tried so far.

Location	Load	@ (6.5, 2.0)	ld	@ (7.0, 2.5)	ld	@ (7.0, 1.5)	ld
Point A (2.5, 4.5)	2	4.0+2.5=6.5	13	4.5+2.0=6.5	13	4.5+3.0=7.5	15
Point B (2.5, 2.5)	5	4.0+0.5=4.5	22.5	4.5+0.0=4.5	22.5	4.5+1.0=5.5	27.5
Point C (5.5, 4.5)	10	1.0+2.5=3.5	35	1.5+2.0=3.5	35	1.5+3.0=4.5	45
Point D (5.0, 2.0)	7	1.5+0.0=1.5	10.5	2.0+0.5=2.5	17.5	2.0+0.5=2.5	17.5
Point E (8.0, 5.0)	10	1.5+3.0=4.5	45	1.0+2.5=3.5	35	1.0+3.5=4.5	45
Point F (7.0, 2.0)	20	0.5+0.0=0.5	10	0.0+0.5=0.5	10	0.0+0.5=0.5	10
Point G (9.0, 2.5)	14	2.5+0.5=3.0	42	2.0+0.0=2.0	28	2.0+1.0=3.0	42
			178.0		161.0		202.0

14. In Solved Problem 3, the center of gravity is at (12.4, 9.2) and the load-distance score is 2662.4. Moving one unit of distance to the North reduces the load-distance score to 2483.8, an improvement of about 7%.

Customer Locations	Tons Shipped	xy-loc	Load- distance to N (12.4, 10.2)	Load-distance to E (13.4, 9.2)	Load-distance to S (12.4, 8.2)	Load-distance to W (11.4, 9.2)
Three Rivers, Mich.	5,000	(7,13)	5(5.4+2.8)= 41.0	5(6.4+3.8)= 51.0	5(5.4+4.8)= 51.0	5(4.4+3.8)= 41.0
Fort Wayne, In.	92,000	(8,12)	92(4.4+1.8)=570.4	92(5.4+2.8)=754.4	92(4.4+3.8)=754.4	92(3.4+2.8)=570.4
Columbus, Ohio	70,000	(11,10)	70(1.4+0.2)=112.0	70(2.4+0.8)=224.0	70(1.4+1.8)= 224.0	70(0.4+0.8)= 84.0
Ashland, Ky.	35,000	(11, 7)	35(1.4+3.2)=161.0	35(2.4+2.2)=161.0	35(1.4+1.2)= 91.0	35(0.4+2.2)= 91.0
Kingsport, Tenn.	9,000	(12, 4)	9(0.4+6.2)= 59.4	9(1.4+5.2)= 59.4	9(0.4+4.2)= 41.4	9(0.6+5.2)= 52.2
Akron, Ohio	227,000	(13,11)	227(0.6+0.8)=317.8	227(0.4+1.8)=499.4	227(0.6+2.8)=771.8	227(1.6+1.8)=771.8
Wheeling, W.V.	16,000	(14,10)	16(1.6+0.2)= 28.8	16(0.6+0.8)= 22.4	16(1.6+1.8)= 54.4	16(2.6+0.8)= 54.4
Roanoke, Va.	153,000	(15, 5)	153(2.6+5.2)=1193.4	153(1.6+4.2)=887.4	153(2.6+3.2)=887.4	153(3.6+4.2)=1193.4
			Total = 2483.8	Total = 2659.0	Total = 2875.4	Total = 2858.2

15. Davis, California Post Office.

a. Center of Gravity
$$x^* = \frac{\sum_i l_i x_i}{\sum_i l_i} \quad \text{and} \quad y^* = \frac{\sum_i l_i y_i}{\sum_i l_i}$$

$$x^* = \frac{(6\times2)+(3\times6)+(3\times8)+(3\times13)+(2\times15)+(7\times6)+(5\times18)+(3\times10)}{(6+3+3+3+2+7+5+3)}$$

$$x^* = \frac{285}{32} = 8.9$$

$$y^* = \frac{(6\times8)+(3\times1)+(3\times5)+(3\times3)+(2\times10)+(7\times14)+(5\times1)+(3\times3)}{(6+3+3+3+2+7+5+3)}$$

$$y^* = \frac{207}{32} = 6.5$$

b. Load distance scores

Mail Source Point	Round Trips per Day (l)	xy-Coord	Load-distance to M: (10,3)	Load-distance to CG: (8.9,6.5)
1	6	(2,8)	6(8+5) = 78	6(6.9+1.5)=50.4
2	3	(6,1)	3(4+2) = 18	3(2.9+5.5)=25.2
3	3	(8,5)	3(2+2) = 12	3(0.9+1.5)= 7.2
4	3	(13,3)	3(3+0) = 9	3(4.1+3.5)=22.8
5	2	(15,10)	2(5+7) = 24	2(6.1+3.5)=19.2
6	7	(6,14)	7(4+11) =105	7(2.9+7.5)=72.8
7	5	(18,1)	5(8+2) = 50	5(9.1+5.5)=73.0
M	3	(10,3)	3(0+0) = 0	3(1.1+3.5)=13.8
			Total = 296	Total = 284.4

16. Paramount

a. Euclidean distance $d_{AB} = \sqrt{(x_A - x_B)^2 + (y_A - y_B)^2}$

$$d_{AB} = \sqrt{(100 - 400)^2 + (200 - 100)^2}$$
$$= \sqrt{(90,000 + 10,000)}$$
$$d_{AB} = 316.2$$

$$d_{BC} = \sqrt{(400 - 100)^2 + (100 - 100)^2}$$
$$= \sqrt{(90,000)}$$
$$d_{BC} = 300$$

$$d_{AC} = \sqrt{(100 - 100)^2 + (200 - 100)^2}$$
$$= \sqrt{(10,000)}$$
$$d_{AC} = 100$$

Location A

— A	4000($3)(0)	=	$	0
— B	3000($1)(316.2)	=	$	948,600
— C	4000($3)(100)	=		$1,200,000
				$2,148,600

Location B

— A	4000($3)(316.2)	=	$3,794,400
— B	3000($1)(0)	=	$ 0
— C	4000($3)(300)	=	$3,600,000
			$7,394,400

Location C

— A	4000($3)(100)	=	$1,200,000
— B	3000($1)(300)	=	$ 900,000
— C	4000($3)(0)	=	$ 0
			$2,100,000 <--- lowest transportation cost

b. Rectilinear distance $d_{AB} = |x_A - x_B| + |y_A - y_B|$

$$d_{AB} = |100 - 400| + |200 - 100|$$
$$d_{AB} = 400$$
$$d_{BC} = |400 - 100| + |100 - 100|$$
$$d_{BC} = 300$$
$$d_{AC} = |100 - 100| + |200 - 100|$$
$$d_{AC} = 100$$

Location A

—	A	4000($3)(0)	=	$ 0
—	B	3000($1)(400)	=	$1,200,000
—	C	4000($3)(100)	=	$1,200,000
				$2,400,000

Location B

—	A	4000($3)(400)	=	$4,800,000
—	B	3000($1)(0)	=	$ 0
—	C	4000($3)(300)	=	$3,600,000
				$8,400,000

Location C

—	A	4000($3)(100)	=	$1,200,000
—	B	3000($1)(300)	=	$ 900,000
—	C	4000($3)(0)	=	$ 0
				$2,100,000

$2,100,000 <--- Location C is again indicated

c.   Center of Gravity (133.33, 144.44)

$$x^* = \frac{\sum_i l_i x_i}{\sum_i l_i} \quad \text{and} \quad y^* = \frac{\sum_i l_i y_i}{\sum_i l_i}$$

$$x^* = \frac{(100 \times \$12,000) + (400 \times \$3,000) + (100 \times \$12,000)}{(27,000)}$$

$$x^* = \frac{3,600,000}{27,000} = 133.33$$

$$y^* = \frac{(200 \times \$12,000) + (100 \times \$3,000) + (100 \times \$12,000)}{(27,000)}$$

$$y^* = \frac{3,900,000}{27,000} = 144.44$$

17. Personal computer manufacturer

From port at Los Angeles:

To Chicago:	$0.0017/mile	1,800 miles	=	$3.06/unit
To Atlanta:	$0.0017/mile	2,600 miles	=	$4.42/unit
To New York:	$0.0017/mile	3,200 miles	=	$5.44/unit

From port at San Francisco:

To Chicago:	$0.0020/mile	1,700 miles	=	$3.40/unit
To Atlanta:	$0.0020/mile	2,800 miles	=	$5.60/unit
To New York:	$0.0020/mile	3,000 miles	=	$6.00/unit

Now we use the load-distance method to evaluate each port, where $ld = l_i d_i$

Cost of port at Los Angeles:
$3.06(10,000) + $4.42(7,500) + $5.44(12,500) = **$131,750**

Cost of port at San Francisco:
$3.40(10,000) + $5.60(7,500) + $6.00(12,500) = **$151,000**

Therefore the more cost effective city is Los Angeles.

18. Two medical facilities.

    a. The solution can be found using the following procedure. We calculate (see table below) the distance from each census tract to each of the candidate locations (C and G). For example, A and C are 3 miles apart ($2.5 - 5.5 + 4.5 - 4.5$).

        The results show that a facility at C would serve A through E, leaving F and G to be served by a facility at G.

Census Tract	Coordinate x	y	Population l (000)	Distance to C	G	Nearest Facility
A	2.5	4.5	2	3	8.5	C
B	2.5	2.5	5	5	6.5	C
C	5.5	4.5	10	0	5.5	C
D	5	2	7	3	4.5	C
E	8	5	10	3	3.5	C
F	7	2	20	3	2.5	G
G	9	2.5	14	4	0	G

        Measuring capacity as the population served, we calculate C's capacity as $(2 + 5 + 10 + 7 + 10)$ = 34 and G's capacity as $(20 + 14) = 34$. The capacities well balanced.

    b. We find the total ld score by multiplying the loads by the distances to the nearest facility:
$ld = 2(3) + 5(5) + 10(0) + 7(3) + 10(3) + 20(2.5) + 14(0) = 132$

19. Reconsider #18.

    a. The following analysis is for locating the facilities at D and G.

Census Tract	Coordinate x	y	Population l (000)	Distance to D	G	Nearest Facility
A	2.5	4.5	2	5	8.5	D
B	2.5	2.5	5	3	6.5	D
C	5.5	4.5	10	3	5.5	D
D	5	2	7	0	4.5	D
E	8	5	10	6	3.5	G
F	7	2	20	2	2.5	D
G	9	2.5	14	4.5	0	G

$ld = 2(5) + 5(3) + 10(3) + 7(0) + 10(3.5) + 20(2) + 14(0) = 130$

        The l-d score for locating the facilities in D and G is 130, beating the previous score of 132.

    b. The facility at location D serves population centers A, B, C, D, and F. The total population to be served by this facility is 44,000 (2,000 + 5,000 + 10,000 + 7,000 + 20,000). Similarly, the facility at location G serves population centers E and G and only needs the capacity to serve 24,000 people (10,000 + 14,000).

20. A different option

    a. The centers of gravity are (4.5, 3.4) for facility 1 and (7.9, 2.8) for facility 2, after rounding to the nearest tenth unit of distance.

Facility 1

$$x^* = \frac{2(2.5) + 5(2.5) + 10(5.5) + 7(5.0)}{2 + 5 + 10 + 7} = 4.5$$

$$y^* = \frac{2(4.5) + 5(2.5) + 10(4.5) + 7(2.0)}{2 + 5 + 10 + 7} = 3.4$$

Facility 2

$$x^* = \frac{10(8.0) + 20(7.0) + 14(9.0)}{10 + 20 + 14} = 7.9$$

$$y^* = \frac{10(5.0) + 20(2.0) + 14(2.5)}{10 + 20 + 14} = 2.8$$

    b. Measuring capacity as the population served, we calculate facility 1's capacity as (2 + 5 + 10 + 7) = 24. Facility 2's capacity is much larger at 44 (or 10 + 20 + 14). The capacities are not well balanced with this solution. If this is a particular concern, we can redivide the market and repeat the process until we obtain an acceptable solution.

    c. The load-distance score for the two facilities is 131.6.

$$ld = [2(2.0 + 1.1) + 5(2.0 + 0.9) + 10(1.0 + 1.1) + 7(0.5 + 1.4)] + [10(0.1 + 2.2) + 20(0.9 + 0.8) + 14(1.1 + 0.3)] = 131.6$$

21. Two facilities to serve two groups of demand points.

    a. Grid map.

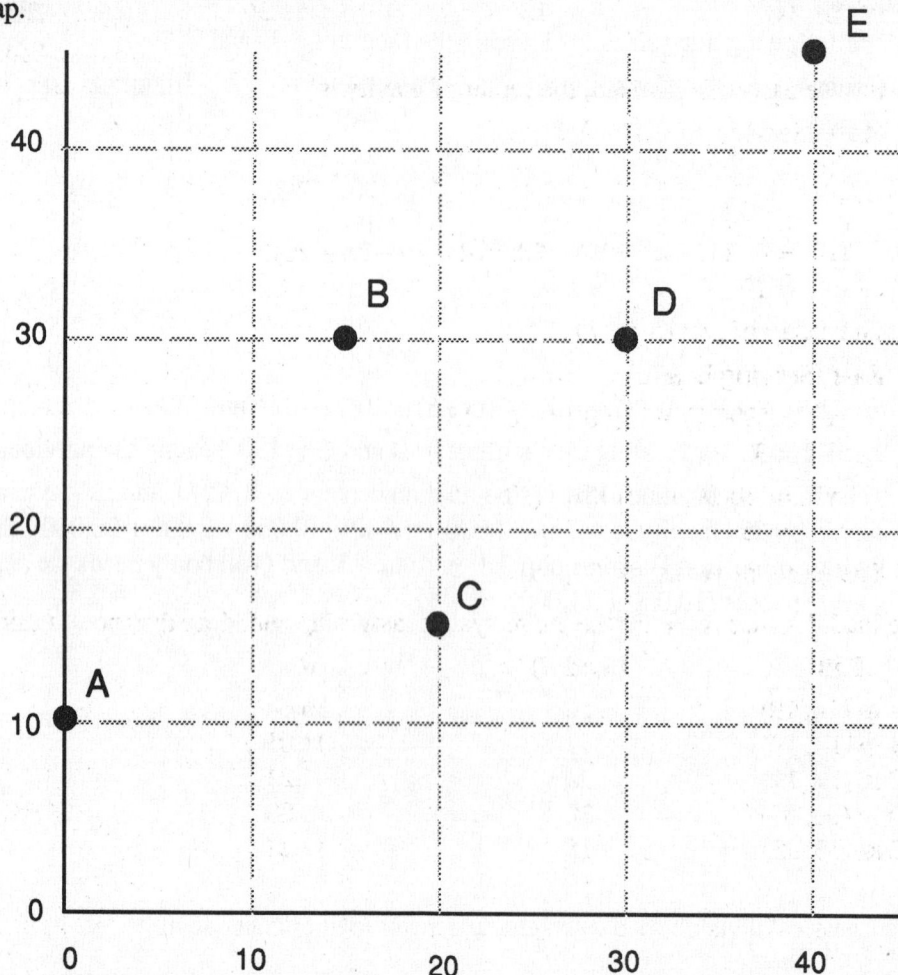

b. For the north-south division, the center of gravity is:

North (Serving B, D, & E)

x^* = [15(15) + 30(30) + 15(40)] / (15 + 30 + 15)
   = 28.75 or 29

y^* = [15(30) + 30(30) + 15(45)] / (15 + 30 + 15)
   = 33.75 or 34

The center of gravity is (29, 34).

South (Serving A & C)

x^* = [10(0) + 20(20)] / (10 + 20)
   = 13.33 or 13

y^* = [10(10) + 20(15)] / (10 + 20)
   = 13.33 or 13

The center of gravity is at about (13, 13).

The load-distance score, assuming euclidean distance, is calculated in the following table.

Pair	Load (_l_)	_d_	_ld_
A to (13, 13)	10	13.34	133.4
B to (29, 34)	15	14.56	218.4
C to (13, 13)	20	7.28	145.6
D to (29, 34)	30	4.12	123.6
E to (29, 34)	15	15.56	233.4
			854.4

c. For the east-west division, the center of gravity is:

West (Serving A, B, & C)

x^* = [10(0) + 15(15) + 20(20)] / (10 + 15 + 20)
   = 13.89 or 14

y^* = [10(10) + 15(30) + 20(15)] / (10 + 15 + 20)
   = 19

The center of gravity is (14, 19).

East (Serving D & E)

x^* = [30(30) + 15(40)] / (30 + 15)
   = 33

y^* = [30(30) + 15(45)] / (30 + 15)
   = 35

The center of gravity is (33, 35).

The load-distance score for the entire system, assuming euclidean distance, is calculated in the table

Pair	Load (_l_)	_d_	_ld_
A to (14, 19)	10	16.64	166.4
B to (14, 19)	15	11.05	165.75
C to (14, 19)	20	7.21	144.2
D to (33, 35)	30	5.83	174.9
E to (33, 35)	15	12.21	183.15
			834.4

The east-west division (part c) results in a lower load-distance score.

22. PG Oil Company

   a. The load-distance score for locating facilities at locations C and H is calculated by multiplying the distance to a population center's assigned facility by the population density and summing over all population centers. Based on proximity, population centers C, D, and E would select the facility at C and all the rest would select the facility at H. The load-distance score is:

$$ld = 55(5) + 45(0) + 0(10) + 30(20) + 5(20) + 25(0) + 40(4) + 0(20)$$
$$= \mathbf{1135}$$

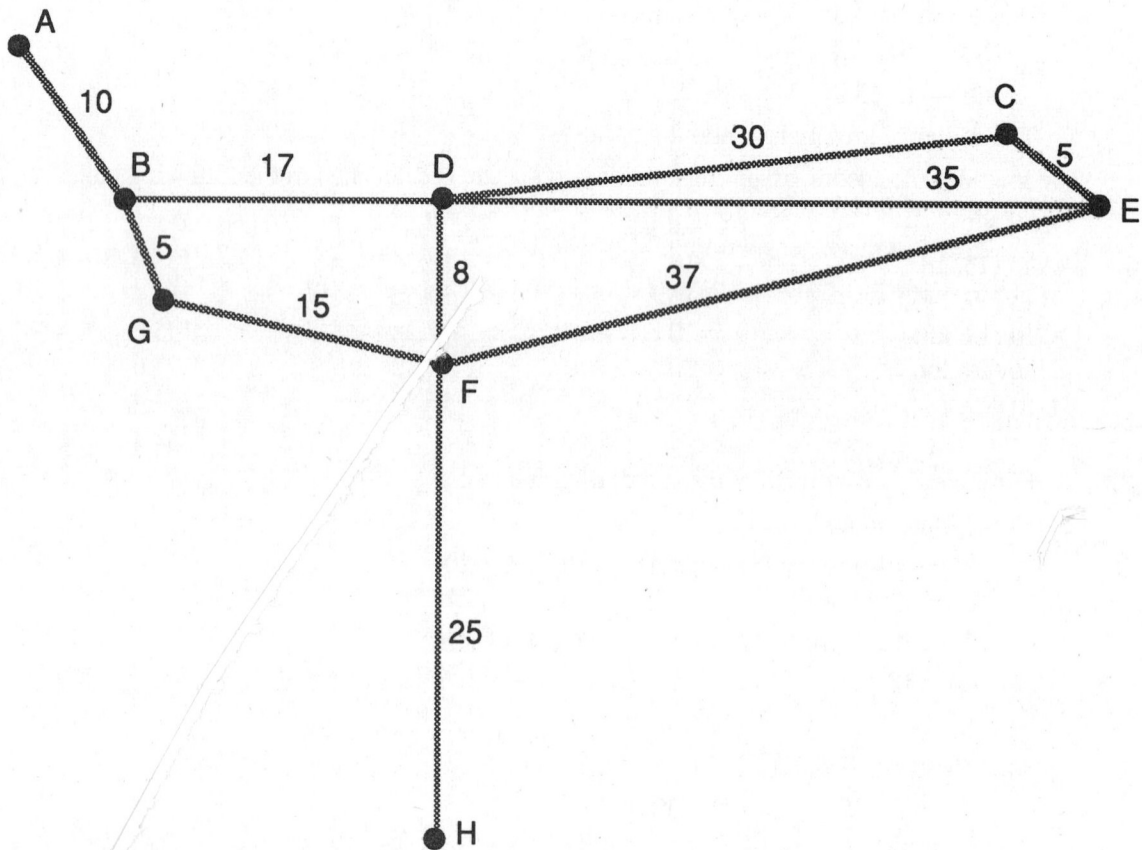

   b. A solution that is better than the one in part (a) is to locate facilities at C and F. Facility C still gets population centers C and E, while the new facility at F gets all the others. The load-distance score is:

$$ld = 30(5) + 20(0) + 0(10) + 8(20) + 5(20) + 0(0) + 15(4) + 25(20)$$
$$= \mathbf{970}$$

23. Cross-median technique

a. Median = $l_i / 2 = 68 / 2 = 34$

b.
Location	x-Coordinate	l_i
A	2.5	2
B	2.5	7
D	5.0	14
C	5.5	24
F	7.0	44>34

The optimal location has 7 as its x-coordinate.

c.
Location	y-Coordinate	l_i
D	2	7
F	2	27
B	2.5	32
G	2.5	46>34

The optimal location has 2.5 as its y-coordinate.

d. The load-distance score for optimal location (7, 2.5):

$$2(6.5) + 5(4.5) + 10(3.5) + 7(2.5) + 10(3.5) + 20(0.5) + 14(2) = 161$$

The optimal solution has a load-distance score of 161, whereas the best one found in Example 8.3, for location (7.2), was 168.

24. Immediate Access Health Care, Inc.

a. Center of gravity (1.561, 1.933)

$$x^* = \frac{\sum_i l_i x_i}{\sum_i l_i} \quad \text{and} \quad y^* = \frac{\sum_i l_i y_i}{\sum_i l_i}$$

$$x^* = \frac{(0.5 \times 20) + (0.5 \times 15) + (0.5 \times 22) + (0.5 \times 12)}{(180)}$$

$$+ \frac{(1.5 \times 9) + (1.5 \times 4) + (1.5 \times 11) + (1.5 \times 7)}{(180)}$$

$$+ \frac{(2.5 \times 18) + (2.5 \times 25) + (2.5 \times 20) + (2.5 \times 17)}{(180)}$$

$$x^* = \frac{281}{180} = 1.561$$

$$y^* = \frac{(0.5 \times 20) + (1.5 \times 15) + (2.5 \times 22) + (3.5 \times 12)}{(180)}$$

$$+ \frac{(0.5 \times 9) + (1.5 \times 4) + (2.5 \times 11) + (3.5 \times 7)}{(180)}$$

$$+ \frac{(0.5 \times 18) + (1.5 \times 25) + (2.5 \times 20) + (3.5 \times 17)}{(180)}$$

$$y^* = \frac{348}{180} = 1.933$$

Immediate Access Health Care, Inc. continued

b. Euclidean minimized *ld* score.

CMOM locates the optimal location very close to the centroid (probably within rounding distance) at (1.60, 1.93), with a load-distance score = 243.5.

c. Rectilinear minimized *ld* score.

CMOM locates the optimal location at (1.50, 1.61), with a load-distance score = 321.29.

d. Since ambulances generally travel on a rectilinear grid of streets, locate the facility to minimize rectilinear distances. On the other hand, if the facility will be served by helicopter ambulance, recommend the location indicated by minimizing the Euclidean distance.

e. Minimized ld score with Zone 11 load doubled to 40.

Euclidean — Again, CMOM locates the optimal location very close to the centroid, but the centroid has moved. The minimum load-distance score of 277.72 occurs at (1.47, 1.75).

Rectilinear — CMOM locates the optimal location at (1.50, 1.64), with a load-distance score = 362.07.

25. Pelican Company.

a. Initial tableau.

Wholesaler	Distribution Center				Capacity
	A	B	C	D	
1	1.7	1.6	1.6	1.6	60
2	1.5	1.8	1.6	1.7	80
3	1.8	1.5	1.8	1.6	50
Requirements	50	40	60	40	190 / 190

b. The sum of requirements equals the sum of demands, so no dummy plant or warehouse is needed. The capacity is fully utilized and the demand is fully satisfied. The following shows the optimal solution, where the quantities are in thousands of gallons.

Wholesaler	Distribution Center				Capacity
	A	B	C	D	
1	1.7	1.6	1.6 30	1.6 30	60
2	1.5 50	1.8	1.6 30	1.7	80
3	1.8	1.5 40	1.8	1.6 10	50
Requirements	50	40	60	40	190 / 190

Total cost of the above solution is

(30 x 1.6) + (30 x 1.6) + (50 x 1.5) + (30 x 1.6) + (40 x 1.5) + (10 x 1.6) = $295 (000)

26. Acme Company.

a. The optimal solution is shown below. The sum of the production in each row equals the capacity for each factory. The sum of shipments in each column equals the demand for each warehouse. All capacities have been exhausted and all demands can be met with this solution.

| Factory | Shipping Cost ($/case) to Warehouse | | | | | Capacity |
	W1	W2	W3	W4	W5	
F1	$1 / 60,000	$3 / 20,000	$4	$5	$6	80,000
F2	$2	$2	$1 / 50,000	$4 / 10,000	$5	60,000
F3	$1	$5	$1	$3 / 20,000	$1 / 40,000	60,000
F4	$5	$2 / 50,000	$4	$5	$4	50,000
Demand	60,000	70,000	50,000	30,000	40,000	250,000

b. The total transporation costs are

$[(60,000 \times \$1) + (20,000 \times \$3) + (50,000 \times \$1) + (10,000 \times \$4) + (20,000 \times \$3) + (40,000 \times \$1) + (50,000 \times \$2)] = \$410,000$

27. Summit Company

a. The optimal tableau is shown below. No dummy sources or destinations are required to balance supply with demand.

| Warehouse | Shipping Cost ($/case) to Retail | | | | | Capacity |
	R1	R2	R3	R4	R5	
W1	$4	$3 / 20,000	$1 / 40,000	$5	$6	60,000
W2	$2 / 20,000	$2 / 10,000	$3	$4	$5	30,000
W3	$1	$5	$1	$3 / 10,000	$2 / 40,000	50,000
Demand	20,000	30,000	40,000	10,000	40,000	140,000

b. Total cost = ($3 x 20,000) + ($1 x 40,000) + ($2 x 20,000) + ($2 x 10,000)+

($3 x 10,000) + ($2 x 40,000) = $270,000

28. JavaMart International.

a. Optimal solution for existing system.

Total cost = ($0.50 x 1,500) + ($0.90 x 500) + ($0.45 x 750) + ($1.15 x 1,500) + ($0.80 x 500) + ($1.00 x 750) = $4,412.50

Plant	Wholesale Outlet					Dummy	Capacity
	W1	W2	W3	W4	W5		
P1	$0.50 1,500	$0.75	$0.90 500	$1.10	$1.25		2,000
P2	$0.80	$0.45 750	$1.15 1,500	$0.80 500	$1.00 750	500	4,000
Demand	1,500	750	2,000	500	750	500	6,000

b. Optimal solution for three-plant system.

Total cost = ($0.50 x 1,500) + ($0.90 x 500) + ($0.45 x 750) + ($0.90 x 1,500) + ($0.55 x 500) + ($0.65 x 750) = $3,650.00

Transportation costs are reduced by ($4,412.50 – $3,650.00) = $762.50

Production costs are reduced by $0.50 x 2,750 = $1,375.00

Total costs are reduced by $2,137.50

Plant	Wholesale Outlet					Dummy	Capacity
	W1	W2	W3	W4	W5		
P1	$0.50 1,500	$0.75	$0.90 500	$1.10	$1.25		2,000
P2	$0.80	$0.45 750	$1.15	$0.80	$1.00	3,250	4,000
P3	$1.10	$0.75	$0.90 1,500	$0.55 500	$0.65 750	2,250	5,000
Demand	1,500	750	2,000	500	750	5,500	6,000

c. If Plant 1 is closed, the total costs are:

Total cost = ($0.80 x 1,500) + ($0.45 x 750) + ($0.90 x 2,000) + ($0.55 x 500) + ($0.65 x 750) = $4,100.00

Plant	Wholesale Outlet					Dummy	Capacity
	W1	W2	W3	W4	W5		
P2	$0.80 1,500	$0.45 750	$1.15	$0.80	$1.00	1,750	4,000
P3	$1.10	$0.75	$0.90 2,000	$0.55 500	$0.65 750	1,750	5,000
Demand	1,500	750	2,000	500	750	3,500	9,000

c. continued.

If Plant 2 is closed, the total costs are:

Total cost = ($0.50 x 1,500) + ($0.75 x 250) + ($0.75 x 250) + ($0.90 x 2,000) +
              + ($0.55 x 500) + ($0.65 x 750) = $3,875.00

Plant	Wholesale Outlet					Dummy	Capacity
	W1	W2	W3	W4	W5		
P1	$0.50	$0.75	$0.90	$1.10	$1.25		2,000
	1,500	500					
P3	$1.10	$0.75	$0.90	$0.55	$0.65		5,000
		250	2,000	500	750	2,250	
Demand	1,500	750	2,000	500	750	5,500	6,000

Since the production costs are the same at Plant 1 and Plant 2, on the basis of lower transportation costs, it would be better to close Plant 2.

d. If Plant 1 is closed and demand increases at Wholesale Outlets #2 and #4:

Total cost = ($0.80 x 1,500) + ($0.45 x 1,750) + ($0.90 x 2,000) + ($0.55 x 1,500) +
              ($0.65 x 750) = $5,100.00

Plant	Wholesale Outlet					Dummy	Capacity
	W1	W2	W3	W4	W5		
P2	$0.80	$0.45	$1.15	$0.80	$1.00		4,000
	1,500	1,750				750	
P3	$1.10	$0.75	$0.90	$0.55	$0.65		5,000
			2,000	1,500	750	750	
Demand	1,500	1,750	2,000	1,500	750	1,500	9,000

If Plant 2 is closed there would not be enough capacity to meet the demand increases at Wholesale Outlets #2 and #4.

Supplement G

Transportation Method of Linear Programming

Study Questions

1. The extra effort associated with using the more complex methods of finding an initial solution usually is rewarded by reduced computation required to find the optimal solution. In the examples used in this supplement, the initial solution obtained by the Vogel's approximation method (VAM) often is within one iteration of the optimal solution.

2. When existing sources have greater capacity than required to meet existing demand, an artificial or "dummy" demand column is added to absorb the excess capacity. The added column represents unused capacity.

3. In a minimization problem when we calculate the loop for a nonallocated cell, a negative result indicates the solution can be improved by selecting the nonallocated cell as an entering route.

4. There would be one column for each of the 12 months of demand in the planning horizon, plus one column for unused capacity and one rim column to display the total capacity of each source — a total of 14 columns. There would be three rows (regular time, overtime, subcontracted) to represent capacity for each of the twelve months = 36, plus one row for initial inventory and one rim row for monthly demand—a total of 38 rows. The number of cells is 14 x 38 = 532 cells.

Problems

1. Puuci, Inc. initial solution (using NW corner method).

Factory	Shipping Cost to Distribution Centers ($/collar)					Capacity
	Baustin	Vegas	Nawlns	New Yawk	Dummy	
Chihuahua	$8 4,000	$5 6,000	$4 2,000	$9	$0	12,000
Saint Bernard	$4	$6	$3 1,000	$3 6,000	$0	7,000
Yorkshire	$2	$8	$6	$1 2,000	$0 2,000	4,000
Demand	4,000	6,000	3,000	8,000	2,000	23,000

$m + n - 1 = 7$

	Shipping Cost to Distribution Centers ($/collar)					
Factory	Baustin	Vegas	Nawlns	New Yawk	Dummy	**Capacity**
Chihuahua	$8 *	$5 *	$4 *	$9	$0	12,000
Saint Bernard	$4	$6	$3 *	$3 *	$0	7,000
Yorkshire	$2	$8	$6	$1 *	$0 *	4,000
Demand	4,000	6,000	3,000	8,000	2,000	23,000

First Iteration:

Chihuahua — New Yawk	$+9 -4 +3 -3 = +5$
Chihuahua —Dummy	$+0 -4 +3 -3 +1 -0 = -3$
Saint Bernard — Baustin	$+4 - 3 + 1 -8 = -3$
Saint Bernard — Vegas	$+6 -3 +4 -5 = +2$
Saint Bernard — Dummy	$+0 -3 +1 -0 = -2$
Yorkshire — Baustin	$+2 -1 +3 -3 +4 -8 = -3$
Yorkshire — Vegas	$+8 -1 +3 -3 +4 -5 = +6$
Yorkshire — Nawlins	$+6 -1 +3 -3 = +5$

	Shipping Cost to Distribution Centers ($/collar)					
Factory	Baustin	Vegas	Nawlns	New Yawk	Dummy	**Capacity**
Chihuahua	$8 / 3,000	$5 / 6,000	$4 / 3,000	$9	$0	12,000
Saint Bernard	$4 / 1,000	$6	$3	$3 / 6,000	$0	7,000
Yorkshire	$2	$8	$6	$1 / 2,000	$0 / 2,000	4,000
Demand	4,000	6,000	3,000	8,000	2,000	23,000

Second Iteration:

Chihuahua — New Yawk	$+9 -8 +4 -3 = +2$
Chihuahua —Dummy	$+0 -8 +4 -3 +1 -0 = -6$
Saint Bernard — Vegas	$+6 -5 +8 -4 = +5$
Saint Bernard — Nawlns	$+3 -4 +8 -4 = +3$
Saint Bernard — Dummy	$+0 -3 +1 -0 = -2$
Yorkshire — Baustin	$+2 -1 +3 -4 = 0$
Yorkshire — Vegas	$+8 -1 +3 -4 +8 -5 = +9$

| Factory | Shipping Cost to Distribution Centers ($/collar) | | | | | Capacity |
	Baustin	Vegas	Nawlns	New Yawk	Dummy	
Chihuahua	$8 — 1,000	$5 — 6,000	$4 — 3,000	$9	$0 — 2000	12,000
Saint Bernard	$4 — 3,000	$6	$3	$3 — 4,000	$0	7,000
Yorkshire	$2	$8	$6	$1 — 4,000	$0	4,000
Demand	4,000	6,000	3,000	8,000	2,000	23,000

Third (optimal) Iteration:

Chihuahua — New Yawk	$+9 -8 +4 -3 = +2$
Saint Bernard — Vegas	$+6 -5 +8 -4 = +5$
Saint Bernard — Nawlns	$+3 -4 +8 -4 = +3$
Saint Bernard — Dummy	$+0 -4 +8 -0 = +4$
Yorkshire — Baustin	$+2 -1 +3 -4 = 0$
Yorkshire — Vegas	$+8 -1 +3 -4 +8 -5 = +9$
Yorkshire — Nawlns	$+6 -1 +3 -4 +8 -4 = +8$

Since all of these are positive or zero, bringing in any other route will not improve the solution. This is optimal solution. This was a lot of work! From here forward, Vogel's approximation method (VAM) will be used to find better initial solutions. Of course the easiest way is to use linear programming software to find the solution. The following CMOM output displays an alternative optimal (equal cost) solution.

Review Problem1.   CMOM Output for the Pucci Problem

CMOM — Location Analysis
Minimization
Data Entered

Number of Columns   :   5
Number of Rows   :   4

Model

	Baust	Vegas	Nawln	NYawk	DUM	CAP
Chihu	8	5	4	9	0	12000
St. B	4	6	3	3	0	7000
Yorks	2	8	6	1	0	4000
DMD	4000	6000	3000	8000	2000	23000

CMOM — Location Analysis
Minimization
Solution

	Baust	Vegas	Nawln	NYawk	DUM	CAP
Chihu	1000	6000	3000	0	2000	12000
St. B	0	0	0	7000	0	7000
Yorks	3000	0	0	1000	0	4000
REQ	4000	6000	3000	8000	2000	23000

Total Payoff   :   78000

	Shipping Cost ($/case) to Warehouse						
Factory	W1	W2	W3	W4	W5	Dummy	Capacity
F1	$1 / 45,000	$3 / 5,000	$3	$5	$6	$0	50,000
F2	$2	$2 / 25,000	$1 / 30,000	$4 / 5,000	$5	$0 / 20,000	80,000
F3	$1	$5	$1	$3 / 30,000	$1 / 50,000	$0	80,000
F4	$5	$2	$4	$5	$4	$0 / 40,000	40,000
Demand	45,000	30,000	30,000	35,000	50,000	60,000	250,000

	Shipping Cost ($/case) to Warehouse						
Factory	W1	W2	W3	W4	W5	Dummy	Capacity
F1	$1 *	$3 *	$3	$5	$6	$0	50,000
F2	$2	$2 *	$1 *	$4 *	$5	$0 *	80,000
F3	$1	$5	$1	$3 *	$1 *	$0	80,000
F4	$5	$2	$4	$5	$4	$0 *	40,000
Demand	45,000	30,000	30,000	35,000	50,000	60,000	250,000

First Iteration:

F1 — W3	$+3 -1 +2 -3 = +1$
F1 — W4	$+5 -4 +2 -3 = +0$
F1 — W5	$+6 -1 +3 -4 +2 -3 = +3$
F1 — Dum	$+0 -0 +2 -3 = -1$
F2 — W1	$+2 -1 +3 -2 = +2$
F2 — W5	$+5 -1 +3 -4 = +3$
F3 — W1	$+1 -1 +3 -2 +4 -3 = +2$
F3 — W2	$+5 -2 +4 -3 = +4$
F3 — Dum	$+0 -0 +4 -3 = +1$
F4 — W1	$+5 -0 +0 -2 +3 -1 = +5$
F4 — W2	$+2 -0 +0 -2 = +0$
F4 — W3	$+4 -0 +0 -1 = +3$
F4 — W4	$+5 -0 +0 -4 = +1$
F5 — W5	$+4 -0 +0 -4 +3 -1 = +2$

(F1 — Dum $+0 -0 +2 -3 = -1$ is boxed)

Factory	Shipping Cost ($/case) to Warehouse					Dummy	Capacity
	W1	W2	W3	W4	W5		
F1	$1	$3	$3	$5	$6	$0	50,000
	45,000					5,000	
F2	$2	$2	$1	$4	$5	$0	80,000
		30,000	30,000	5,000		15,000	
F3	$1	$5	$1	$3	$1	$0	80,000
				30,000	50,000		
F4	$5	$2	$4	$5	$4	$0	40,000
						40,000	
Demand	45,000	30,000	30,000	35,000	50,000	60,000	250,000

Second Iteration: (optimal)

F1 — W2   +3 –2 +0 –0 = +1
F1 — W3   +3 –1 +0 –0 = +2
F1 — W4   +5 –4 +0 –0 = +1
F1 — W5   +6 –1 +5 –4 +0 –0 = +4
F2 — W1   +2 –1 +0 –0 = +1
F2 — W5   +5 –1 +3 –4 = +3
F3 — W1   +1 –1 +0 –0 +4 –3 = +1

F3 — W2   +5 –2 +4 –3 = +4
F3 — W3   +1 –1 +4 –3 = +1
F3 — Dum +0 –0 +4 –3 = +1
F4 — W1   +5 –0 +0 –1 = +4
F4 — W2   +2 –0 +0 –2 = +0
F4 — W3   +4 –0 +0 –1 = +3
F4 — W4   +5 –0 +0 –4 = +1
F5 — W5   +4 –0 +0 –4 +3 –1 = +2

Total cost = ($45,000 + $60,000 + $30,000 + $20,000 + $90,000 + $50,000) = $295,000
CMOM finds an alternative optimal solution.

Review Problem2.   CMOM Output for the Original Ajax International Problem

CMOM — Location Analysis
Data Entered

Number of Columns   :   6
Number of Rows   :   4

Model

	W1	W2	W3	W4	W5	DUMMY	CAP
F1	1	3	3	5	6	0	50
F2	2	2	1	4	5	0	80
F3	1	5	1	3	1	0	80
F4	5	2	4	5	4	0	40
REQ	45	30	30	35	50	60	250

CMOM — Location Analysis
Minimization Solution

	W1	W2	W3	W4	W5	DUMMY	CAP
F1	45	0	0	0	0	5	50
F2	0	25	30	5	0	20	80
F3	0	0	0	30	50	0	80
F4	0	5	0	0	0	35	40
REQ	45	30	30	35	50	60	250

Total Payoff   :   295

3. Consider Ajax further. Initial Solution

Factory	Shipping Cost ($/case) to Warehouse						Capacity
	W1	W2	W3	W4	W5	Dummy	
F1	$1	$3	$3	$5	$6	$0	50,000
	45,000				5,000		
F2	$2	$2	$1	$4	$5	$0	80,000
		30,000	35,000		15,000		
F4	$5	$2	$4	$5	$4	$0	90,000
		30,000			30,000	30,000	
Demand	45,000	30,000	30,000	35,000	50,000	30,000	220,000

First Iteration:
F1 — W2 +3 –6 +4 –2 = –1
F1 — W3 +3 –6 +5 –1 = +1
F1 — W4 +5 –6 +5 –4 = +0
F1 — Dum +0 –0 +4 –6 = –2
F2 — W1 +2 –1 +6 –5 = +2
F2 — W2 +2 –5 +4 –2 = –1
F2 — Dum +0 –0 +4 –5 = –1
F4 — W1 +5 –1 +6 –4 = +6
F4 — W3 +4 –1 +5 –4 = +4
F4 — W4 +5 –0 +0 –4 = +1

Factory	Shipping Cost ($/case) to Warehouse						Capacity
	W1	W2	W3	W4	W5	Dummy	
F1	$1	$3	$3	$5	$6	$0	50,000
	45,000					5,000	
F2	$2	$2	$1	$4	$5	$0	80,000
			30,000	35,000	15,000		
F4	$5	$2	$4	$5	$4	$0	90,000
		30,000			35,000	25,000	
Demand	45,000	30,000	30,000	35,000	50,000	30,000	220,000

Second Iteration:
F1 — W2 +3 –0 +0 –2 = +1
F1 — W3 +3 –0 +0 –4 +5 –1 = +3
F1 — W4 +5 –0 +0 –4 +5 –4 = +2
F1 — W5 +6 –0 +0 –4 = +2
F2 — W1 +2 –1 +0 –0 +4 –5 = +0
F2 — W2 +2 –5 +4 –2 = –1
F2 — Dum +0 –0 +4 –5 = –1
F4 — W1 +5 –1 +0 –0 = +4
F4 — W3 +4 –1 +5 –4 = +4
F4 — W4 +5 –0 +0 –4 = +1

	Shipping Cost ($/case) to Warehouse						
Factory	**W1**	**W2**	**W3**	**W4**	**W5**	**Dummy**	**Capacity**
F1	$1 45,000	$3	$3	$5	$6	$0 5,000	50,000
F2	$2	$2 15,000	$1 30,000	$4 35,000	$5	$0	80,000
F4	$5	$2 15,000	$4	$5	$4 50,000	$0 25,000	90,000
Demand	45,000	30,000	30,000	35,000	50,000	30,000	220,000

Third Iteration: (Optimal)
F1 — W2   +3 –0 +0 –2 = +1
F1 — W3   +3 –0 +0 –2 +2 –1 = +2
F1 — W4   +5 –0 +0 –2 +2 –4 = +1
F1 — W5   +6 –0 +0 –4 = +2
F2 — W1   +2 –1 +0 –0 +2 –2 = +1
F2 — W5   +5 –2 +2 –4 = +1
F2 — Dum +0 –0 +2 –2 = +0
F4 — W1   +5 –1 +0 –0 = +4
F4 — W3   +4 –1 +2 –2 = +3
F4 — W4   +5 –4 +2 –2 = +1

Total cost, revised problem = $45,000 + $30,000 + $30,000 + $30,000 +$140,000 + $200,000 = $475,000

Total cost, original problem 2 = $295,000

The logistics manager should receive a budget increase of ($475,000 – $295,000) = $180,000 for increased transportation costs. By shifting the shipping pattern, the increase in costs is less than the $210,000 requested.

Review Problem 3.   CMOM Output for Revised Ajax International Problem

CMOM — Location Analysis
Minimization
Data Entered

Number of Columns   :   6
Number of Rows   :   3

Model

	W1	W2	W3	W4	W5	DUMMY	CAP
F1	1	3	3	5	6	0	50
F2	2	2	1	4	5	0	80
F4	5	2	4	5	4	0	90
REQ	45	30	30	35	50	30	220

CMOM — Location Analysis
Minimization
Solution

	W1	W2	W3	W4	W5	DUMMY	CAP
F1	45	0	0	0	0	5	50
F2	0	15	30	35	0	0	80
F4	0	15	0	0	50	25	90
REQ	45	30	30	35	50	30	220

Total Payoff   :   475

4. Giant Farmer Company. Initial Solution (VAM)

Supplier	Shipping cost to Distribution Centers ($/ case)				Capacity (x100)
	Miami	Denver	Lincoln	Jackson	
Chicago	$7	$2 — 90	$4 — 10	$5	100
Houston	$3	$1	$5 — 35	$2 — 40	75
Atlanta	$2 — 70	$10	$8	$3 — 10	80
Demand (x100)	70	90	45	50	255

First Iteration:

Chicago — Miami	$+7 -4 +5 -2 +3 -2 = +7$
Chicago — Jackson	$+5 -2 +5 -4 = +4$
Houston — Miami	$+3 -2 +3 -2 = +2$
Houston — Denver	$+1 -2 +4 -5 = -2$
Atlanta — Denver	$+10 -2 +4 -5 +2 -3 = +6$
Atlanta — Lincoln	$+8 -5 +2 -3 = +2$

Supplier	Shipping cost to Distribution Centers ($/case)				Capacity (x100)
	Miami	Denver	Lincoln	Jackson	
Chicago	$7	$2 — 55	$4 — 45	$5	100
Houston	$3	$1 — 35	$5	$2 — 40	75
Atlanta	$2 — 70	$10	$8	$3 — 10	80
Demand (x100)	70	90	45	50	255

Second (optimal) Iteration:

Chicago — Miami	$+7 -2 +1 -2 +3 -2 = +5$
Chicago — Jackson	$+5 -2 +1 -2 = +2$
Houston — Miami	$+3 -2 +3 -2 = +2$
Houston — Lincoln	$+5 -1 +2 -4 = +2$
Atlanta — Denver	$+10 -3 +2 -1 = +8$
Atlanta — Lincoln	$+8 -3 +2 -1 +2 -4 = +4$

Review Problem 4. CMOM Output for Giant Farmer with Atlanta Plant

CMOM — Location Analysis
Data Entered

Number of Columns   :   4
Number of Rows   :   3

Model

	MIAMI	DENVE	LINCO	JACKS	CAP
CHICA	7	2	4	5	100
HOUST	3	1	5	2	75
ATLAN	2	10	8	3	80
REQ	70	90	45	50	255

CMOM — Location Analysis
Minimization
Solution

	MIAMI	DENVE	LINCO	JACKS	CAP
CHICA	0	55	45	0	100
HOUST	0	35	0	40	75
ATLAN	70	0	0	10	80
REQ	70	90	45	50	255

Total Payoff   :   575

CMOM Output for Giant Farmer with Memphis Plant

CMOM — Location Analysis
Data Entered

Number of Columns   :   4
Number of Rows   :   3

Model

	MIAMI	DENVE	LINCO	JACKS	CAP
CHICA	7	2	4	5	100
HOUST	3	1	5	2	75
MEMPH	3	11	6	5	80
REQ	70	90	45	50	255

CMOM — Location Analysis
Minimization
Solution

	MIAMI	DENVE	LINCO	JACKS	CAP
CHICA	0	65	35	0	100
HOUST	0	25	0	50	75
MEMPH	70	0	10	0	80
REQ	70	90	45	50	255

Total Payoff   :   665

The total costs are $57,500 and $66,500 because of the scaling (times 100) of shipping quantities. Total shipping costs are higher with the Memphis location.

5. Bright Paint Company. The given initial solution is degenerate.

Supplier	Shipping cost to Bright Plant ($/100 cans)					Capacity (x100)
	A	B	C	D	Dummy	
S1	$54	$48 200	$50 ε	$46 200	$0	400
S2	$52 300	$50	$54	$48	$0	300
S3	$46 ε	$48	$50 100	$52	$0 100	200
Demand (x100)	300	200	100	200	100	900

First Iteration:

S1 — A	+54 −46 +50 −50	= +8
S1 — Dum	+0 −50 +50 −0	= +0
S2 — B	+50 −48 +50 −50 +46 −52	= −4
S2 — C	+54 −52 +46 −50	= −2
S2 — D	+48 −52 +46 −50 +50 −46	= -4
S2 — Dum	+0 −52 +46 −0	= −6
S3 — B	+48 −48 +50 −50	= +0
S3 — D	+52 −50 +50 −46	= +6

Supplier	Shipping cost to Bright Plant ($/100 cans)					Capacity (x100)
	A	B	C	D	Dummy	
S1	$54	$48 200	$50 ε	$46 200	$0	400
S2	$52 200	$50	$54	$48	$0 100	300
S3	$46 100	$48	$50 100	$52	$0	200
Demand (x100)	300	200	100	200	100	900

Second Iteration:

S1 — A	+54 −46 +50 −50	= +8
S1 — Dum	+0 −0 +52 −46 +50 −50	= +6
S2 — B	+50 −52 +46 −50 +50 −48	= −4
S2 — C	+54 −52 +46 −50	= −2
S2 — D	+48 −52 +46 −50 +50 −46	= −4
S3 — B	+48 −48 +50 −50	= +0
S3 — D	+52 −50 +50 −46	= +6
S3 — Dum	+0 −0 +52 −46	= +6

Supplier	Shipping cost to Bright Plant ($/100 cans) A	B	C	D	Dummy	Capacity (x100)
S1	$54	$48 \ 200	$50 \ 100	$46 \ 100	$0	400
S2	$52 \ 100	$50	$54	$48 \ 100	$0 \ 100	300
S3	$46 \ 200	$48	$50	$52	$0	200
Demand (x100)	300	200	100	200	100	900

Third (optimal) Iteration:

S1 — A	$+54 -46 +48 -52 = +4$
S1 — Dum	$+0 -0 +48 -46 = +2$
S2 — B	$+50 -48 +46 -48 = +0$
S2 — C	$+54 -48 +46 -50 = +4$
S3 — B	$+48 -48 +50 -50 = +0$
S3 — D	$+52 -50 +50 -46 = +6$
S3 — Dum	$+0 -0 +52 -46 = +6$

The original plan costs

$(300 \times 52) + (200 \times 48) + (100 \times 50) + (200 \times 46) = \$39,400$

The optimal plan costs

$(100 \times 52) + (200 \times 46) + (200 \times 48) + (100 \times 50) +$
$\qquad (100 \times 46) + (100 \times 48) = \$38,400$

The optimal plan saves $1000

Review Problem 5.   CMOM Output for Bright Paint Company

CMOM — Location Analysis
Data Entered

Number of Columns	:	5	
Number of Rows	:	3	

Model

	A	B	C	D	DUMMY	CAP
S1	54	48	50	46	0	400
S2	52	50	54	48	0	300
S3	46	48	50	52	0	200
REQ	300	200	100	200	100	900

CMOM — Location Analysis
Minimization
Solution

	A	B	C	D	DUMMY	CAP
S1	0	200	100	100	0	400
S2	100	0	0	100	100	300
S3	200	0	0	0	0	200
REQ	300	200	100	200	100	900

Total Payoff :   38400

Review Problem 6. CMOM Output for the Chambers Corporation

a. Alternative 1 (Portland)

CMOM — Location Analysis
Minimization
Data Entered

Number of Columns   :   4
Number of Rows   :   3

			Model		
	AT	CO	LA	SE	CAP
BALT	35	20	85	75	6000
MILW	55	15	70	65	6000
PORT	85	60	30	10	6000
DMD	5000	3000	6000	4000	18000

CMOM — Location Analysis
Minimization
Solution

	AT	CO	LA	SE	CAP
BALT	5000	1000	0	0	6000
MILW	0	2000	4000	0	6000
PORT	0	0	2000	4000	6000
DMD	5000	3000	6000	4000	18000

Total Payoff   :   6050.00

b. Alternative 2 (San Antonio)

CMOM — Location Analysis
Data Entered

Number of Columns   :   4
Number of Rows   :   3

			Model		
	AT	CO	LA	SE	CAP
BALT	35	20	85	75	6000
MILW	55	15	70	65	6000
SANT	55	40	40	55	6000
DMD	5000	3000	6000	4000	18000

CMOM — Location Analysis
Minimization
Solution

	AT	CO	LA	SE	CAP
BALT	5000	1000	0	0	6000
MILW	0	2000	0	4000	6000
SANT	0	0	6000	0	6000
DMD	5000	3000	6000	4000	18000

Total Payoff: 7250.00

c. Alternative 3 (Portland and San Antonio)

CMOM — Location Analysis
Minimization
Data Entered

Number of Columns   :   4
Number of Rows   :   4

Model

	AT	CO	LA	SE	CAP
BALT	35	20	85	75	6000
MILW	55	15	70	65	6000
PORT	85	60	30	10	3000
SANT	55	40	40	55	3000
DMD	5000	3000	6000	4000	18000

CMOM — Location Analysis
Minimization
Solution

	AT	CO	LA	SE	CAP
BALT	5000	1000	0	0	6000
MILW	0	2000	3000	1000	6000
PORT	0	0	0	3000	3000
SANT	0	0	3000	0	3000
DMD	5000	3000	6000	4000	18000

Total Payoff :   6500.00

7. The tableau method described in the production planning chapter offers a greatly simplified solution procedure for production planning problems.

Source of Product	Demand				Unused Capacity	Capacity (barrels)
	First Quarter	Second Quarter	Third Quarter	Fourth Quarter		
Initial Inventory	$0.00 — 100	$1.50	$3.00	$4.50	$4.50	100
First Quarter Regular Time	$10.00 — 400	$11.50	$13.00 — 200	$14.50 — 300	$6.00	900
First Quarter Overtime	$12.00	$13.50	$15.00	$16.50	$0.00 — 300	300
Second Quarter Regular Time	$99	$10.00 — 900	$11.50	$13.00	$6.00	900
Second Quarter Overtime	$99	$12.00	$13.50	$15.00 — 150	$0.00 — 150	300
Third Quarter Regular Time	$99	$99	$10.00 — 800	$11.50	$6.00	800
Third Quarter Overtime	$99	$99	$12.00 — 200	$13.50	$0.00	200
Fourth Quarter Regular Time	$99	$99	$99	$10.00 — 600	$6.00	600
Fourth Quarter Overtime	$99	$99	$99	$12.00 — 150	$0.00	150
Demand (barrels)	500	900	1200	1200	450	4250

The minimum cost production plan is: $40,400.

Produce 900 barrels during regular time in the first quarter. 500 barrels will be carried into inventory.

Produce 900 barrels during regular time in the second quarter, and 150 barrels during overtime. 500 barrels from the first remain in inventory (but the stock should be rotated) and 150 barrels from overtime production are added to inventory (total = 650 barrels).

Produce 800 barrels during regular time in the second quarter, and 200 barrels during overtime. 200 barrels are withdrawn from inventory.

Produce 600 barrels during regular time in the second quarter, and 150 barrels during overtime. The remainder of inventory is consumed.

CMOM finds an alternative optimal solution.

Review Problem 7. CMOM Output for Production Planning Problem

CMOM — Location Analysis
Minimization
Data Entered

Number of Columns : 5
Number of Rows : 9

	Model					
	Q1	Q2	Q3	Q4	UNUSED	CAP
IINV	0.0	1.5	3.0	4.5	4.5	100
Q1RT	10.0	11.5	13.0	14.5	6.0	900
Q1OT	12.0	13.5	15.0	16.5	0.0	300
Q2RT	99	10	11.5	13.0	6.0	900
Q2OT	99	12	13.5	14.5	0.0	300
Q3RT	99	99	10.0	11.5	6.0	800
Q3OT	99	99	12.0	13.5	0.0	200
Q4RT	99	99	99	10.0	6.0	600
Q4OT	99	99	99	12.0	0.0	150
DMD	500	900	1200	1200	450	4250

CMOM — Location Analysis
Minimization
Solution

	Q1	Q2	Q3	Q4	UNUSED	CAP
IINV	100	0	0	0	0	100
Q1RT	400	0	400	100	0	900
Q1OT	0	0	0	0	300	300
Q2RT	0	900	0	0	0	900
Q2OT	0	0	0	150	150	300
Q3RT	0	0	800	0	0	800
Q3OT	0	0	0	200	0	200
Q4RT	0	0	0	600	0	600
Q4OT	0	0	0	150	0	150
DMD	500	900	1200	1200	450	4250

Total Payoff : 40400

8. The tableau method has difficulty finding the optimal solution when there is a cost associated with unused capacity. The subcontracting option reduces production costs to $39,325, but this does not take into account the ($6 x 500) $3,000 cost for unused regular time in the first quarter. The CMOM output on the next page shows the true optimal solution.

Source of Product	Demand				Unused Capacity	Capacity (barrels)
	First Quarter	Second Quarter	Third Quarter	Fourth Quarter		
Initial Inventory	$0.00 / 100	$1.50	$3.00	$4.50	$4.50	100
First Quarter Regular Time	$10.00 / 400	$11.50	$13.00	$14.50	$6.00 / 500	900
First Quarter Overtime	$12.00	$13.50	$15.00	$16.50	$0.00 / 300	300
First Quarter Subcontract	$12.50	$14.00	$15.50	$17.00	$0.00 / 500	500
Second Quarter Regular Time	$99	$10.00 / 900	$11.50	$13.00	$6.00	900
Second Quarter Overtime	$99	$12.00	$13.50	$15.00	$0.00 / 300	300
Second Quarter Subcontract	$99	$12.50	$14.00	$15.50	$0.00 / 500	500
Third Quarter Regular Time	$99	$99	$10.00 / 800	$11.50	$6.00	800
Third Quarter Overtime	$99	$99	$12.00 / 200	$13.50	$0.00	200
Third Quarter Subcontract	$99	$99	$12.50 / 200	$14.00	$0.00 / 300	500
Fourth Quarter Regular Time	$99	$99	$99	$10.00 / 600	$6.00	600
Fourth Quarter Overtime	$99	$99	$99	$12.00 / 150	$0.00	150
Fourth Quarter Subcontract	$99	$99	$99	$12.50 / 450	$0.00 / 50	500
Demand (barrels)	500	900	1200	1200	2450	6250

CMOM finds the true optimal solution.

Review Problem 8. CMOM Output for Production Planning Problem with Subcontracting

CMOM — Location Analysis
Minimization
Data Entered

Number of Columns : 5
Number of Rows : 13

| | | | Model | | |
	Q1	Q2	Q3	Q4	UNUSED	CAP
IINV	0.0	1.5	3.0	4.5	4.5	100
Q1RT	10.0	11.5	13.0	14.5	6.0	900
Q1OT	12.0	13.5	15.0	16.5	0.0	300
Q1SC	12.5	14.0	15.5	17.0	0.0	500
Q2RT	99	10.0	11.5	13.0	6.0	900
Q2OT	99	12.0	13.5	15.0	0.0	300
Q2SC	99	12.5	14.0	15.5	0.0	500
Q3RT	99	99	10.0	11.5	6.0	800
Q3OT	99	99	12.0	13.5	0.0	200
Q3SC	99	99	12.5	14.0	0.0	500
Q4RT	99	99	99	10.0	6.0	600
Q4OT	99	99	99	12.0	0.0	150
Q4SC	99	99	99	12.5	0.0	500
DMD	500	900	1200	1200	2450	6250

CMOM — Location Analysis
Minimization
Solution

	Q1	Q2	Q3	Q4	UNUSED	CAP
IINV	100	0	0	0	0	100
Q1RT	400	0	400	100	0	900
Q1OT	0	0	0	0	300	300
Q1SC	0	0	0	0	500	500
Q2RT	0	900	0	0	0	900
Q2OT	0	0	0	0	300	300
Q2SC	0	0	0	0	500	300
Q3RT	0	0	800	0	0	800
Q3OT	0	0	0	0	200	200
Q3SC	0	0	0	0	500	500
Q4RT	0	0	0	600	0	600
Q4OT	0	0	0	150	0	150
Q4SC	0	0	0	350	150	500
DMD	500	900	1200	1200	2450	6250

Total Payoff : 39825

Chapter 9

Layout

Study Questions

1. The most strategic choice to be made is the layout type. The layout patterns (process, product, hybrid, or fixed-position layout) should match the positioning strategy (process-focused or product-focused).

   Because the layout design must be related to the positioning strategy of the firm (process or product focus), it could be argued that layout design is related to every decision area in the text. Given that it must be consistent with the positioning strategy, it is perhaps most closely connected to the design decisions and the capacity decisions. The type of equipment, degree of capital intensity, degree of work-force flexibility, size of capacity cushion, and the specialization of the work force all play a role in designing the appropriate layout.

2. A process layout clusters the resources performing similar functions into one center so that many different products can be processed intermittently at the same work stations. A product layout arranges resources around the product's routing, rather than share them across many products. An example of a process layout is a laundromat where all washing machines are grouped together, separate from the dryers. An automatic car wash is an example of a product line.

3. A U-shaped assembly line
   - Facilitates the flow of materials and information — receiving, inspection, and shipping occur on the same end (open part of the U) of the line.
   - Increases the efficient utilization of labor — a worker in a U-shaped assembly line has more options for tasks to be assigned, possibly achieving a more efficient assembly line balance.

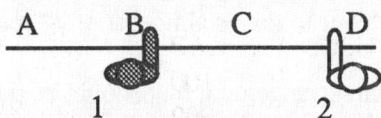

If Worker 1 is idle, assignment options include A and C

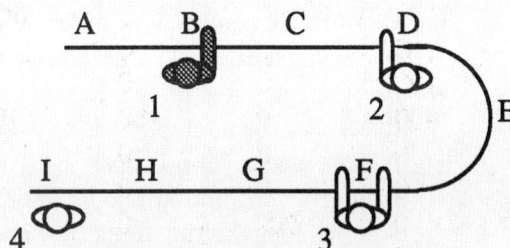

If Worker 1 is idle, assignment options include A, C, G, and H.

   - Improves communication. Worker 1 can communicate with all workers, not just worker 2.

4. Layout performance measures.
   a. Airport — customer convenience, requirements for materials handling, capital investment
   b. For a bank layout, important criteria would include customer convenience, atmosphere, sales (loan applications), communication, and capital investment.
   c. Classroom — flexibility, communication
   d. Product Design — comunication with production, work environment
   e. For a law firm, important criteria would include capital investment, communication, flexibility, atmosphere, organizational structure, and employee attitudes.

f. Metal fabricator — important criteria would include capital investment, materials handling, flexibility, labor productivity, ease of maintenance, work environment, and employee attitudes.

g. For a parking lot, important criteria would include capital investment, material handling (flow of cars), and safety.

h. Human resources —proximity to entrance, privacy of communications.

5. OWMM can be applied when volumes are not sufficient to keep several workers busy on one operation. By setting up a smaller line that keeps just one person busy, the benefits of repeatability can still be achieved. The GT concept considers parts that have design or processing similarities or both. Parts with similarities are combined into part families, and machines are grouped into cells containing the machines necessary to process the parts in a family in an efficient line flow. The common purpose of these systems is to achieve the benefit of repeatability even when production volumes are not high. They differ in scale (OWMM is usually of a smaller scale than the GT).

6. Office arrangement.

a. Some of the types of information that we might want to gather in developing a new layout are:
   - What are the space requirements?
   - What space is available?
   - How important is it for various centers to be close to one another?
   - Are there any areas that cannot or should not be moved?
   - How many centers are needed?
   - Should new centers be created?
   - How many people should be in each center?
   - What is the type of work done in each center?
   - What are the levels of employees (such as clerical, professional, or supervisory) needed in each center?
   - What is the rate of interaction between current centers within the department and with other centers outside the department?
   - What is the interaction (communication) with those outside the organization?
   - Do different centers have different needs (the answer to this is almost surely "yes") for internal and external communication?
   - Are there any real dissatisfactions with the present arrangement that should be overcome (or at least the attempt made to overcome) with the new layout?
   - Is there a need for privacy?
   - Is there a need for more joint conference areas?
   - Are there regulations about how many square feet must be allocated to a person?
   - Is individual status to be considered? (That is, do the center supervisors have or need any way to separate or distinguish themselves from the employees they supervise?)
   - Does there need to be access for the physically handicapped (employees and/or clients)?
   - Is there equipment to be considered, such as word processors, micro-computers, data entry terminals, printers, bookkeeping equipment?
   - How many flexible barriers, and how much furniture is available?
   - Where are the telephone lines located, and how many are there?
   - Where are the electrical outlets, and what are the needs for these?
   - What is the budget for this move?
   - What is the time frame in which it must be accomplished?

After we recover from thinking about what needs to be done, and find out the answers to the last two questions, then we will start to gather the rest of the information. Some sources for the rest of the data needed are:

- Blueprints of the building
- Physical inventory of equipment
- Powers of the director's own observation
- Talking to supervisors of the present centers about their needs for communication, privacy, equipment access, meeting space, and storage
- Surveying employees for their opinions on what they like best about the present arrangement, what they like least, and what they might change if they were in charge
- Analyzing historical evidence, if it exists, to determine interdepartmental and external departmental frequencies of communication. If there is no "hard-evidence," then managerial judgment should be applied to determine this.
- Advice from the legal department or some other department on regulations relating to health, safety, and space requirements

b. All of this information, much of which is qualitative, will need managerial judgment to analyze. A computer model can be used to generate possible layout designs. This means that everything that can be quantified should be quantified, and weights assigned to various requirements in order to rank them.

c. It is hard to know how much employee involvement to recommend because this is really a reflection of individual management style. When people are going to have less space than they presently have, they are probably not going to be happy about it at first. One recommendation is that employees should be involved to the extent that the need for the move is explained to them. This could be couched in terms of spreading the workload: There will be more employees to do the work. If indeed this is not the case, and extra duties will indeed accompany the extra employees, then perhaps a sense of the increased importance of the department as a whole could be projected. The cooperation of all employees should be enlisted. Department employees should probably be told of the move, its reasons, and the probable impact on them, as soon as we have something truthful to tell them. This will probably stimulate the "rumor mill," but not nearly so much as if the employees are told nothing. If this company always seeks the opinions of its employees, then this decision is not the time to stop doing so. In fact, employee input in the form of a formal but short survey, as suggested in part (a), might uncover some overlooked items. At a bare minimum, the supervisors of the present centers, and the supervisors of the newly aligned centers (if they are different), should surely be consulted.

7. In a "top quality" department store, atmosphere and customer convenience seemed to be the most important criteria. The "image" of the store has considerable impact on its attractiveness, and the layout helps to reinforce the feeling of quality.

   In a "discount" store, capital investment is the most important criterion. In one such store, stock is arranged on standard shelving, and the customers record the stock numbers of the items they want. A clerk at a centrally located checkout counter records the requests, checks for inventory availability, and receives payment from the customer. Finally, the customer goes to a pickup area where the merchandise from the warehouse attached to the store is located. All of this is done to keep costs low.

8. Sitting in the same seat each time can be explained several ways. The front rows provide the proximity to the instructor and blackboard, allowing better communication visually and verbally. The back rows, which tend to have more empty seats, provide privacy so that you can concentrate better without being distracted by the movements of neighboring classmates. They also provide anonymity for those who don't want to communicate with the instructor or make a quick escape. Staying in the seat initially chosen, whether it be in the front or back, seems to relate to a need for "turf", familiarity or privacy, and sometimes, social interaction.

9. This circularity can be real. If two departments are close together prior to a layout revision, the interactions between them tend to be stronger than if the departments were some distance apart. Since layouts are usually designed to fit current work activities and interaction patterns, many features of the current layout could be perpetuated.

10. Before solving a line-balancing problem, one needs to know the following:
   - What are the tasks?
   - How long does each task take?
   - What is the precedence (the order in which the tasks must be done) among the tasks?
   - What is the desired output rate from the line?

11. There are many examples possible. Examples of relative location considerations are to locate purchasing near product design to facilitate communication and to isolate engineering from the reception area to prevent engineers from talking to salespersons. Absolute location considerations include locating shipping and receiving near the shipping dock, placing air compressors on foundations designed to isolate vibrations, providing the art department with a northern exposure for good light, or locating the executive offices for a view of the mountains.

12. If the output rate desired from a line is 20 units per hour, a frequently selected cycle time would be 180 seconds [(60 min/20 units)(60 seconds/min)]. However, management might want to consider a cycle time other than 180 seconds for the following reasons:

   There might be individual tasks that take longer than 3 minutes. This would force a cycle time of longer than 180 seconds, or would require two work stations doing the same task, where each one takes every other unit to work on.

   If there is very little slack at some of the work stations and quite a bit at others, management might want to rebalance with duplicate work stations where each worker does more tasks, but not so many that efficiency drops.

   The maximum efficiency possible from the line might be improved. Overtime, shorter shifts, and inventory can be used to keep production in line with demand, even when the cycle time is different from 180 seconds.

13. With the production rate of 192 units, the cycle time is 150 seconds and the balanced assembly line is very efficient (96%). When the production rate increases to 198 units, the cycle time decreases to 145.5 seconds. The same assembly line balance now has an efficiency of 99%. If the production rate increases to 200 units, the cycle time decreases to 144 seconds. The line would have to be rebalanced, requiring at least six workers (two assigned to task H to prevent a bottleneck). The line-balance efficiency would drop to 80%.

14. High specialization can make workers on the line bored and dissatisfied with the job itself. Machine paced lines are stressful. Workers must sometimes choose between doing the work correctly or failing to keep up with the pace of the assembly line. Job enlargement, by increasing the cycle time and assigning more work elements to a work station, sometimes reduces dissatisfaction. Also, worker groups can be more involved in various decisions such as job assignment, rotation, and other aspects of layout design. These changes do not guarantee higher satisfaction or productivity. Individuals react differently to approaches such as these. If employees would rather not have to think about their work, job enrichment may be detrimental to productivity.

15. Yes, but it requires ingenuity and a cultural change. The pull system of material flow associated with Just-in-Time production offers the possibility of simultaneously reducing stress, inventory and space requirements.

Problems

1. Baker Machine Company

Department Pair	Closeness Rating (l_{ij})	Current Plan Distance (d_{ij})	$l_{ij}d_{ij}$	Proposed Plan Distance (d_{ij})	$l_{ij}d_{ij}$
1-2	10	3	30	3	30
1-4	15	2	30	2	30
1-6	45	2	90	1	45
2-5	45	2	90	1	45
3-4	25	1	25	1	25
3-6	50	3	150	2	100
4-5	35	1	35	2	70
4-6	20	2	40	1	20
		$ld =$	490	$ld =$	365

The difference is (490 – 365 =) 125, which implies a 26 percent [(490 – 365) / 490] improvement.

2. Baker Machine Block Plan. A good plan would locate the following department pairs close together: 3-6, 1-6, 2-5, 4-5, and 3-4. The following layout satisfies these requirements and leaves department 3 unmoved.

3	4	5
6	1	2

The load-distance score is 265 [10(1) + 15(1) + 45(1) + 45(1) + 25(1) + 50(1) + 35(1) + 20(2)].

3. A good layout would locate the following pairs of analysts close together: B-D, C-E, and A-C. Furthermore, analysts A and D would get locations 4 and 3, respectively. Fortunately, the following layout has all of these features.

1-C	2-E	3-D
4-A	5-F	6-B

Its ld score is [6(1) + 12(1) + 2(2) + 7(1) + 4(2)] =37.

4. Insurance company department.
   a. Offices A and F should be located most closely, all other factors being equal.
   b. The ld scores for the current plan are shown in the following table.

Department	Closeness Rating	Distance (d_{ij})	$l_{ij}d_{ij}$
A–F	140	1	140
C–F	130	1	130
C–E	130	2	260
B–E	95	1	95
E–F	95	1	95
A–C	75	2	150
A–B	10	3	30
D–E	10	1	10
		$ld =$	910

c. The layout appears to be reasonably good, with most department pairs with high l_{ij} values being only one unit of distance apart. The main exceptions involve department C, because C-E and A-C are both pairings that are two units of distance apart. One possible switch is departments C and D. Department C would be closer to both A and E (but further away from F).

Due to the large number of possible switches, the only way to be sure which switch is best is to evaluate each one, as done below.

Switch	Change in *ld* Score		
A-B	$1(140) + 1(95) - 1(75)$	=	160
A-C	$-2(10)$	=	**-20**
A-D	$1(140) + 1(75) - 1(10) + 1(10)$	=	215
A-E	$2(95) - 2(10)$	=	170
A-F	$1(130) + 1(95) - 1(75) - 1(10)$	=	140
B-C	$1(130) - 1(130) + 1(95) + 1(75) - 1(10)$	=	160
B-D	$-1(10)$	=	**-10**
B-E	$-1(130) + 1(95) - 1(10) + 1(10)$	=	**-35**
B-F	$2(140) - 2(10)$	=	260
C-D	$1(130) - 1(130) - 1(75) + 1(10)$	=	**-65**
C-E	$2(10)$	=	20
C-F	$1(140) - 1(130) + 1(95) - 1(75)$	=	30
D-E	$1(130) + 1(95) + 1(95)$	=	320
D-F	$2(130)$	=	260
E-F	$1(140) + 1(130) - 1(130) + 1(95) + 1(10)$	=	245

The above calculations show that four department exchanges would reduce the *ld* score, and the switching of departments C and D leads to the biggest improvement.

5. Four departments.

a. The load-distance score is 84, as calculated in the left side of the following table.

Department Pair	Closeness Rating (l_{ij})	Current Plan		Proposed Plan	
		Distance (d_{ij})	$l_{ij}d_{ij}$	Distance (d_{ij})	$l_{ij}d_{ij}$
A-B	12	1	12	1	12
A-C	10	1	10	2	20
A-D	8	2	16	1	8
B-C	20	2	40	1	20
B-D	6	1	6	2	12
			$ld = 84$		$ld = 72$

b. A better layout is one that switches departments C and D, as shown by the following block plan. The calculations on the right side of the above table show that its load-distance score drops to 72.

A	B
D	C

6. Department of Philosophy

    a. The following heuristic process was used to construct the block diagram shown below. The faculty member pairing with the highest number of contacts is B and D, which suggests B gets assigned to office 5. Putting E at office 4 responds to the frequent contacts between C and E. Member F gets assigned to office 3, the only one left.

    b. The load-distance score is calculated below to be 45. Only two of the least frequent contacts between C and D is not matched with the minimum distance of one unit.

Faculty Pair	Rating (l_{ij})	Distance (d_{ij})	$l_{ij}d_{ij}$
B–D	12	1	12
B–F	10	1	10
C–E	7	1	7
A–C	4	1	4
D–F	4	2	8
C–D	2	2	4
			$ld = 45$

1-A	2-C
3-F	4-E
5-B	6-D

7. Office of Budget Management. This problem is related to Study Question 6.

    a. The following four section pairs have a closeness rating of 5 or more: 1-4(10), 3-8(6), 4-6(5), and 5-6(8). A block plan that allows all of these pairings to share a common boundary, with section 2 in the northeast corner, is shown below (many different solutions are possible here):

    Sections with shared boundaries, and their closeness ratings, are:

Shared Boundaries	Score
1-2	3
1-4	10
1-6	2
1-7	2
2-3	0
2-5	0
2-6	2
2-7	2
3-8	6
4-6	5
4-7	3
5-6	8
5-8	0
Total	43

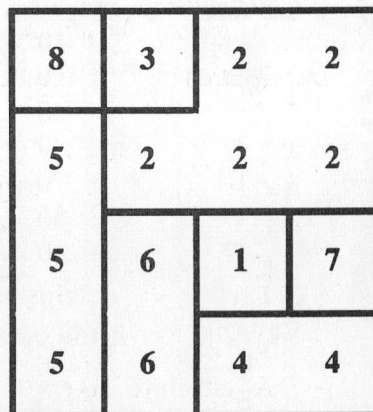

8	3	2	2
5	2	2	2
5	6	1	7
5	6	4	4

    b. Among the behavioral issues that need to be addressed in this project are:
    - designing the "atmosphere" so that employees feel like working
    - balancing the privacy and proximity needs
    - providing station designs that are appropriate for the position in the organization
    - determining the amount of employee involvement
    - dealing with possible adverse reaction to relocations and space reductions

8. Begin by computing the ratio of trips to block spaces for each department. Then, ranking the departments by their ratios (shown in parentheses), we get G(220), B(180), C(130), A(125), E(100), F(95), and D(80). Entering the departments in this sequence, the best layout, as constrained by contiguous space requirement, is shown at right.

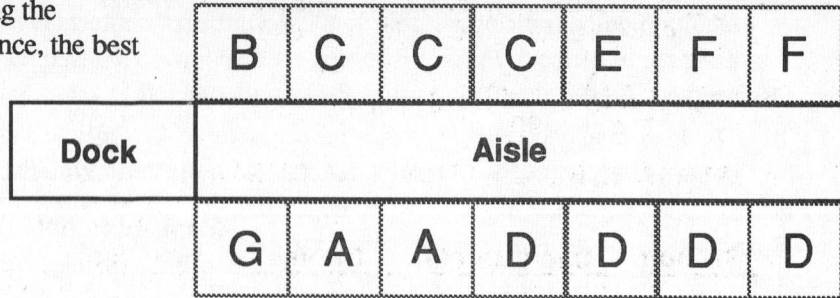

B	C	C	C	E	F	F

Dock	Aisle					

G	A	A	D	D	D	D

9. Begin by computing the ratio of trips to block spaces for each department. Then, ranking the departments by their ratios (shown in parentheses), we get E(300), B(240), G(140), D(115), A(110), C(90), and F(60). Entering the departments in this sequence, the best layout is shown at right.

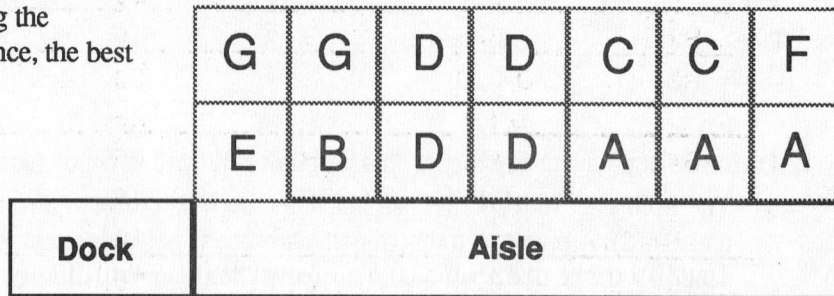

G	G	D	D	C	C	F

E	B	D	D	A	A	A

Dock	Aisle					

10. Big Reaper. We will assign the part categories with the greatest number of trips per section to those storage sections closest to the assembly line. This assignment minimizes the load-distance measure (number of trips times distance).

Part Category	Trips per Day	Sections Needed	Trips per Section	Priority	Sections Assigned
A	80	1	80	3	4
B	140	2	70	4	5,6
C	60	1	60	5	7
D	240	4	60	6	8,9,10,11
E	320	2	160	1	1,2
F	150	1	150	2	3
G	60	1	60	7	12

Part Category	Trips per Section	Section Assigned	Distance	Trips x Distance
E	160	1	60	9,600
E	160	2	80	12,800
F	150	3	90	13,500
A	80	4	110	8,800
B	70	5	140	9,800
B	70	6	160	11,200
C	60	7	190	11,400
D	60	8	230	13,800
D	60	9	300	18,000
D	60	10	305	18,300
D	60	11	320	19,200
G	60	12	360	21,600
				168,000

11. Assembly-line balancing. Longest work element rule to produce 40 units per hour.

a. $$c = \frac{1}{r} = \frac{1 \text{ hour}}{40 \text{ units}} = \frac{3600 \text{ sec}}{40 \text{ units}} = 90 \frac{\text{sec}}{\text{unit}}$$

b. $$TM = \left(\frac{\sum t}{c}\right) = \frac{415}{90} = 4.611 \text{ or } 5$$

c. $S1 = \{A, C, E\}, S2 = \{B\}, S3 = \{G, D\}, S4 = \{H, F, I\}, S5 = \{J, K\}$

Station	Candidate(s)	Choice	Work Element time (sec)	Cumulative time (sec)	Idle time (c=90sec)
S1	A	A	40	40	50
	C	C	30	30	70
	E	E	20	90	0
S2	B	B	80	80	10
S3	D, F, G	G	60	60	30
	D, F, I	D	25	85	5
S4	F, H, I	H	45	45	45
	F, I	F	15	60	30
	I	I	10	70	20
S5	J	J	75	75	15
	K	K	15	90	0

d.

$$\text{Efficiency (\%)} = \frac{(\sum t)}{nc}(100\%) = \frac{415}{5(90)} = 92.2\%$$

$$\begin{aligned}\text{Balance delay (\%)} &= 100\% - \text{Efficiency} \\ &= 100\% - 92.2\% \\ &= 7.8\%\end{aligned}$$

12. A company.

  a. Before calculating the theoretical minimum number of stations, we find the cycle time as:

$$c = \frac{3600 \text{ sec/hr}}{60 \text{ sec/unit}} = 60 \text{ sec/unit}$$

Then we find

$$TM = \left(\frac{\Sigma t}{c}\right) = \frac{274}{60} = 4.56 \text{ or } 5$$

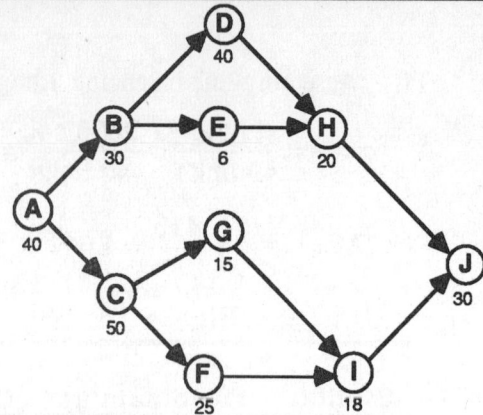

(Network diagram: A(40) → B(30), A → C(50); B → D(40), B → E(6); D → H(20), E → H(20); C → G(15), C → F(25); G → I(18), F → I(18); H → J(30), I → J(30))

  b. Task assignments using longest work-element time rule:

Station	Candidates	Assignment	Cumulative Time	Idle Time (c = 60)
S1	A	A	40	20
S2	B, C	C	50	10
S3	B, F, G	B	30	30
	E, F, G	F	55	5
S4	D, E, G	D	40	20
	E, G	G	55	5
S5	E, I	I	18	42
	E	E	24	36
	H	H	44	16
S6	J	J	30	30

Six work stations are required.

  c. Largest number of followers. The number of followers for each work element are:

Work Element	Number of Followers	Work Element	Number of Followers
A	9	F	2
B	4	G	2
C	4	H	1
D	2	I	1
E	2	J	0

Task assignments using largest number of followers rule:

Station	Candidates	Assignment	Cumulative Time	Idle Time (c = 60)
S1	A	A	40	20
S2	B, C (tie)	C	50	10
S3	B, F, G	B	30	30
	E, F, G (tie)	F	55	5
S4	D, E, G (tie)	D	40	20
	E, G	G	55	5
S5	E, I	E	6	54
	H, I (tie)	H	26	34
	I	I	44	16
S6	J	J	30	30

d. Efficiency with 5 work stations:

$$\text{Efficiency} = \left(\frac{\Sigma t}{c}\right)(100\%) = \frac{274}{5(60)}(100\%) = 91.33\%$$

13. Illinois Appliance Company.

a. Exhibit 10.2 shows the precedence diagram. We must first determine the cycle time, expressed in seconds because the work element times are also in seconds.

$$\begin{aligned} r &= 480 \text{ units/day} / (8 \text{ hours/shift } 2 \text{ shifts/day}) \\ &= 30 \text{ units per hour} \\ c &= (1/30)(3600) = 120 \text{ sec/unit} \end{aligned}$$

The sum of the work element times (t) is 450 seconds.

$$TM = \left(\frac{\Sigma t}{c}\right) = \frac{450}{120} = 3.75 \text{ or } 4$$

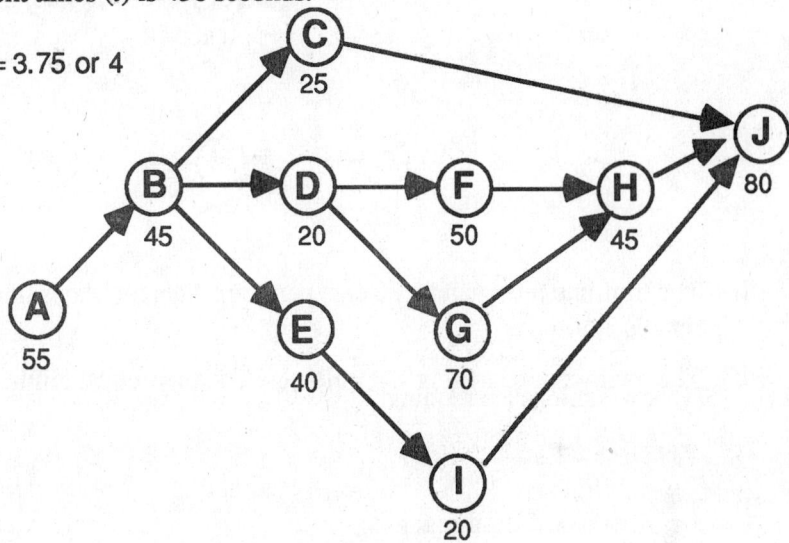

b. Solution using longest work-element time rule: S2 = {G, F}

Station	Candidates	Choice	Cumulative Time	Idle Time ($c = 120$)
S1	A	A	55	65
	B	B	100	20
	D	D	120	0
S2	C, E, F, G	G	70	50
	C, E, F	F	120	0
S3	C, E, H	H	45	75
	C, E	E	85	35
	C, I	C	110	10
S4	I	I	20	100
	J	J	80	20

The second work station would be assigned elements G and F, and be fully utilized.

14. Trim line at PW.

    a. Precedence diagram for PW.

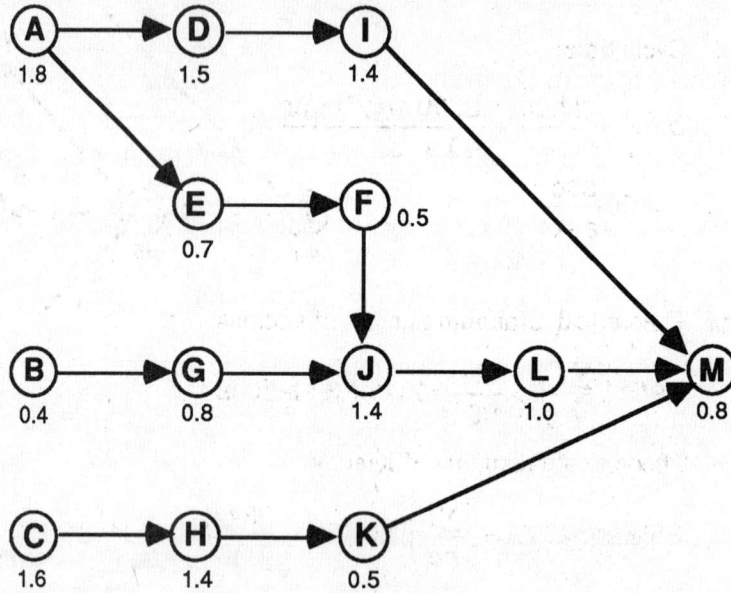

    b. The trim line must handle 20 cars per hour. This translates into 3 minutes per car. Thus the cycle time is 3 minutes.

    c. The total work content is 13.8 minutes. The theoretical minimum number of stations is:

$$TM = \left(\frac{\sum t}{c}\right) = \frac{13.8}{3}$$

    = 4.6 or 5 stations

    d. Using the precedence diagram as a guide, packing each station as close as possible to the cycle time and considering the two zoning constraints, the following solution results:

Station	Work Elements Assigned	Total Content	Station Slack
S1	A, B, E	2.9	0.1
S2	C, F, G	2.9	0.1
S3	D, H	2.9	0.1
S4	I, J	2.8	0.2
S5	K, L, M	2.3	0.7

    e. Efficiency = [(13.8) / ((5)(3)]100 = 92%

15. Air Conditioners

a. Precedence Diagram for Air Conditioners

F 35
C 25
H 40
A 20   B 55   D 40   G 14
E 5

b. Cycle time:

$$c = \frac{1}{r} = \frac{1 \text{ hour} \times 3600 \text{ sec} / \text{hour}}{40 \text{ a-c}}$$

$$= 90 \frac{\text{sec}}{\text{a-c}}$$

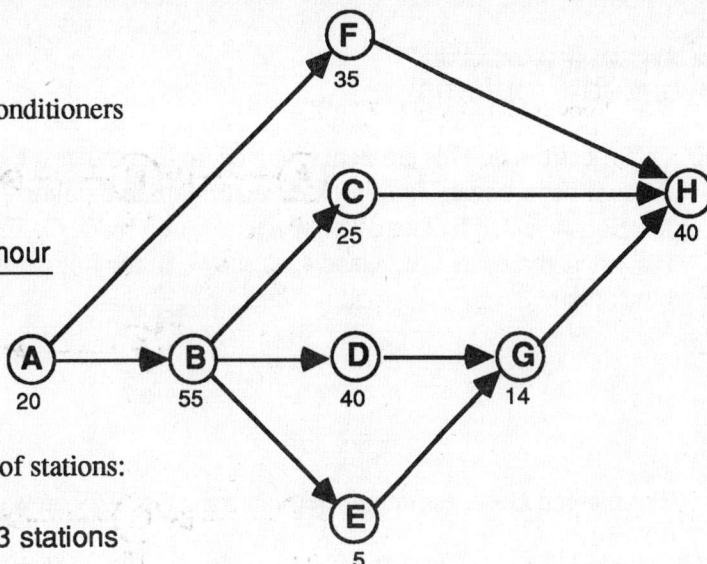

c. Theoretical minimum number of stations:

$$TM = \left(\frac{\Sigma t}{c}\right) = \frac{234}{90} = 2.6 \text{ or } 3 \text{ stations}$$

Theoretical maximum efficiency:

$$\text{Efficiency (\%)} = \left(\frac{\Sigma t}{nc}\right)(100\%) = \frac{234}{(3)90}(100\%) = 86.7\%$$

d. Assembly line assignments, using longest work element rule:

Station	Candidates	Choice	Cumulative Time	Idle Time ($c = 90$)
S1	A	A	20	70
	B, F	B	75	15
	E	E	80	10
S2	C, D, F	D	40	50
	C, F, G	F	75	15
	G	G	89	1
S3	C	C	25	65
	H	H	65	25

Only three stations (the theoretical minimum) are needed, so the line's efficiency is equal to the theoretical maximum efficiency of 86.7%.

e. No improvement is possible in terms of efficiency. It is possible, however, to get better balance between stations and relieve some of the pressure on work station S2. If work element 7 is transferred from S2 to S3, station idle times are better balanced (15 for S2 and 11 for S3). A cycle time of 80 seconds would increase efficiency to 97.5%.

Advanced Problems

16. CCI Electronics. This problem involves finding the best location for four departments, limiting their placement to the four locations vacated by them. The spaces vacated by D, G, K, and L are designated as 1, 2, 3, and 4, as shown in the following block plan.

1	H	B	2
F	I	J	A
C	3	E	4

The merged closeness ratings derived from Fig. 9.29 are shown below for each department:

Department	A	B	C	D	E	F	G	H	I	J	K	L
A	✖	...	...	...	...	...	...	...	...	90	...	80
B	–	✖	...	...	...	...	30	...	50	70	...	...
C	–	–	✖	...	...	120	...	...	70	...	80	60
D	–	–	–	✖	120	...	...	...	...	...	...	...
E	–	–	–	–	✖	...	...	...	40	...	90	...
F	–	–	–	–	–	✖	120	...	...	...	...	...
G	–	–	–	–	–	–	✖	40	50	...	...	...
H	–	–	–	–	–	–	–	✖	80	...	...	...
I	–	–	–	–	–	–	–	–	✖	...	60	...
J	–	–	–	–	–	–	–	–	–	✖	...	...
K	–	–	–	–	–	–	–	–	–	–	✖	...
L	–	–	–	–	–	–	–	–	–	–	–	✖

Many reasonable solutions are possible using trial and error. The best possible solution is shown below. It is found by formulating the problem as a linear assignment problem and solving it using the revised assignment algorithm. Since neither this formulation nor the algorithm is covered in the text, you may not have been able to find a solution quite as good.

L	H	B	K
F	I	J	A
C	D	E	G

(Current Layout)

G	H	B	L
F	I	J	A
C	K	E	D

(Revised Layout)

Load-Distance Scores

Department Pair	Merged Closeness Rating (l)	Current Layout (d)	ld	Revised Layout (d)	(ld)
A–J	90	1	90	1	90
A–L	80	4	320	1	80
B–G	30	3	90	2	60
B–I	50	2	100	2	100
B–J	70	1	70	1	70
C–F	120	1	120	1	120
C–I	70	2	140	2	140
C–K	80	5	400	1	80
C–L	60	2	120	5	300
D–E	120	1	120	1	120
E–I	40	2	80	2	80
E–K	90	3	270	1	90
F–G	120	4	480	1	120
G–H	40	4	160	1	40
G–I	50	3	150	2	100
H–I	80	1	80	1	80
I–K	60	3	<u>180</u>	1	<u>60</u>
		$ld =$	2970	$ld =$	1730

The load-distance score decreased from 2970 to 1730, which represents a 42% reduction.

17. Electric can openers.

   a. Maximum hourly output rate.

Station	Total Time per Cycle	Station Slack
S1	1.8	0.2
S2	1.3	0.7
S3	2.0	0.0
S4	1.9	0.1
S5	1.6	0.4
S6	<u>1.5</u>	<u>0.5</u>
Total	10.1	1.9

The busiest station is S3, which takes 2.0 minutes per unit. Therefore, the maximum output of the whole line is:

$$(60 \text{ min/hr})/(2.0 \text{ min/unit}) = 30 \text{ units/hr}$$

   b. The cycle time would be 2 minutes, allowing no idle time for the "bottleneck" station S3.

   c. Idle time is 1.9 minutes per cycle. Since 30 units are made each hour, the total idle time lost over an 8-hour shift is:

$$(1.9 \text{ min/unit})(30 \text{ units/hr})(8\text{hr/shift}) = 456 \text{ min/shift, or } 7.6 \text{ hr/shift}$$

   d. Efficiency = $[(10.1)/(6)(2)]100 = 84.2\%$

18. Good Samaritan Medical Center.

a. An effective block plan.

12 Sec L	8 Acct H	4 Adm D	4 Adm D	11 Rcev K
10 Lnge J	9 Info I	1 Mgt A	6 Trng F	5 Lab E
3 Reco C	3 Reco C	3 Reco C	7 Supl G	5 Lab E
Util	2 Surg B	2 Surg B	2 Surg B	2 Surg B

b. The department pairs that contribute most to the total rating score are:

2 - Surgery	3 - Recovery	20
1 - Management	6 - Training	15
6 - Training	11 - Receiving	12
2 - Surgery	7 - Supplies	10
5 - Laboratory	7 - Supplies	10
1 - Management	9 - Information	10
5 - Laboratory	11 - Receiving	9
1 - Management	8 - Accounting	8
4 - Admissions	8 - Accounting	8
9 - Information	8 - Accounting	8

Loads

		A	B	C	D	E	F	G	H	I	J	K	L
1. Management	A	0	2	1	5	2	15	3	8	10	2	2	6
2. Surgery	B		0	20	1	6	4	10		1	3	1	3
3. Recovery	C			0		2	4	3					4
4. Admissions	D				0	2	3		8	4	3	5	
5. Laboratory	E					0	4	10	2	5	2	9	2
6. Training	F						0					12	1
7. Supplies	G							0	2				3
8. Accounting	H								0	8	2		4
9. Information	I									0	2		3
10. Lounge	J										0		2
11. Receiving	K											0	5
12. Security	L												0

Rectilinear Distances

		A	B	C	D	E	F	G	H	I	J	K	L
1. Management	A	0	2	1	1	2	1	2	2	1	2	3	3
2. Surgery	B		0	1	3	1	2	1	3	3	3	3	4
3. Recovery	C			0	2	2	2	1	2	1	1	4	2
4. Admissions	D				0	2	1	2	1	1	3	1	2
5. Laboratory	E					0	1	1	4	3	4	1	5
6. Training	F						0	1	3	2	3	2	4
7. Supplies	G							0	4	3	4	3	5
8. Accounting	H								0	1	2	3	1
9. Information	I									0	1	4	2
10. Lounge	J										0	5	1
11. Receiving	K											0	4
12. Security	L												0

ld Score*	378

* The spreadsheet calculates the total *ld* score by using an array formula {=SUM(C3:N14*C18:N29)} to multiply each load times the appropriate distance and add the products.

c. The following arrangement reduces ld score slightly.

6 Trng F	1 Mgt A	8 Acct H	4 Adm D	4 Adm D
11 Recv K	12 Secr L	9 Info I	10 Lnge J	3 Reco C
5 Lab E	5 Lab E	7 Supl G	3 Reco C	3 Reco C
Util	2 Surg B	2 Surg B	2 Surg B	2 Surg B

Loads

		A	B	C	D	E	F	G	H	I	J	K	L
1. Management	A	0	2	1	5	2	15	3	8	10	2	2	6
2. Surgery	B		0	20	1	6	4	10		1	3	1	3
3. Recovery	C			0			2	4	3				4
4. Admissions	D				0	2	3		8	4	3	5	
5. Laboratory	E					0	4	10	2	5	2	9	2
6. Training	F						0					12	1
7. Supplies	G							0	2				3
8. Accounting	H								0	8	2		4
9. Information	I									0	2		3
10. Lounge	J										0		2
11. Receiving	K											0	5
12. Security	L												0

Rectilinear Distances

		A	B	C	D	E	F	G	H	I	J	K	L
1. Management	A	0	3	4	2	2	1	3	1	2	3	2	1
2. Surgery	B		0	1	3	1	4	1	3	2	2	3	2
3. Recovery	C			0	2	2	5	1	3	2	1	4	3
4. Admissions	D				0	4	3	3	1	2	1	4	3
5. Laboratory	E					0	3	1	3	2	3	1	1
6. Training	F						0	4	2	3	4	1	2
7. Supplies	G							0	2	1	2	3	2
8. Accounting	H								0	1	2	3	2
9. Information	I									0	1	2	1
10. Lounge	J										0	3	2
11. Receiving	K											0	1
12. Security	L												0

ld Score*	**368**

d. The following shows the management department moving to the northwest corner, trading places with the training department. This increases the ld score from 368 to 401, an 8% increase.

1 Mgt A	6 Trng F	8 Acct H	4 Adm D	4 Adm D
11 Recv K	12 Secr L	9 Info I	10 Lnge J	3 Reco C
5 Lab E	5 Lab E	7 Supl G	3 Reco C	3 Reco C
Util	2 Surg B	2 Surg B	2 Surg B	2 Surg B

Loads		A	B	C	D	E	F	G	H	I	J	K	L
1. Management	A	0	2	1	5	2	15	3	8	10	2	2	6
2. Surgery	B		0	20	1	6	4	10		1	3	1	3
3. Recovery	C			0		2	4	3					4
4. Admissions	D				0	2	3		8	4	3	5	
5. Laboratory	E					0	4	10	2	5	2	9	2
6. Training	F						0					12	1
7. Supplies	G							0	2				3
8. Accounting	H								0	8	2		4
9. Information	I									0	2		3
10. Lounge	J										0		2
11. Receiving	K											0	5
12. Security	L												0

Rectilinear Distances		A	B	C	D	E	F	G	H	I	J	K	L
1. Management	A	0	4	5	3	2	1	4	2	3	4	1	2
2. Surgery	B		0	1	3	1	3	1	3	2	2	3	2
3. Recovery	C			0	2	2	4	1	3	2	1	4	3
4. Admissions	D				0	4	2	3	1	2	1	4	3
5. Laboratory	E					0	2	1	3	2	3	1	1
6. Training	F						0	3	1	2	3	2	1
7. Supplies	G							0	2	1	2	3	2
8. Accounting	H								0	1	2	3	2
9. Information	I									0	1	2	1
10. Lounge	J										0	3	2
11. Receiving	K											0	1
12. Security	L												0
ld Score*	**401**												

19. Sanders Manufacturing

The solution shown below was developed using the ALDEP computer model. Other good solutions are also possible.

Department 5 entered first, followed by 2 (A between 5 and 2), 3 (E between 2 and 3), 4 (random), 8 (E between 4 and 8), and 7 (only one left). A strip width of 2 columns was used.

1	1	2	2	2	2	4	4	4	8	7	7
1	1	5	5	2	82	4	4	8	8	7	7
1	1	99	99	99	99	99	99	99	99	7	7
1	1	99	5	3	3	3	4	8	99	6	6
1	1	99	5	3	3	3	3	8	99	6	6
1	1	99	5	3	3	3	83	83	99	6	6
1	5	99	99	99	99	99	99	99	99	6	6
5	5	5	5	84	84	84	84	8	8	6	6
5	5	5	5	84	84	84	84	7	7	6	6

20. ALDEP scores for Sanders Manufacturing

Shared Boundaries	Score
1–2	3
1–5	5
2–3	5
2–4	2
2–5	6
3–4	4
3–5	3
3–8	2
4–8	5
6–7	4
6–8	3
7–8	4
Total	46

21. Tastegood Pizza Parlor.

   a. Precedence Diagram for Tastegood Pizza Parlor

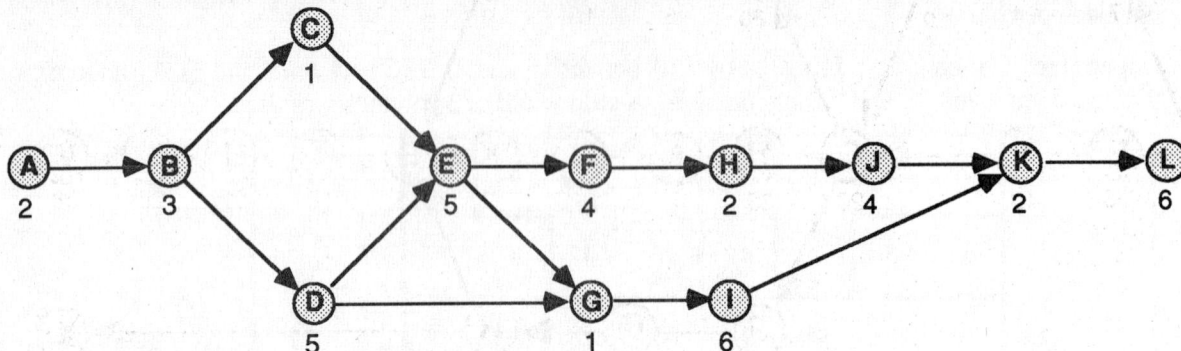

Nodes (with times below): A 2, B 3, C 1, D 5, E 5, F 4, G 1, H 2, I 6, J 4, K 2, L 6

   b. Cycle time:

$$r = 10 \text{ pizzas per hour}$$

$$c = \frac{1}{r} = \frac{1 \text{ hour} \times 60 \text{ min/hour}}{10 \text{ pizzas}} = 6 \text{ min/pizza}$$

   c. First calculate the theoretical minimum number of stations, to get a benchmark on what might be achievable. $TM = \left(\frac{\Sigma t}{c}\right) = \frac{41}{6} = 6.83$ or 7 stations

Using the longest work element rule, we get the following work element assignments.

Station	Candidates	Choice	Cumulative Time	Idle Time (c = 6)
S1	A	A	2	4
	B	B	5	1
	C	C	6	0
S2	D	D	5	1
S3	E	E	5	1
	G	G	6	0
S4	F, I	I	6	0
S5	F	F	4	2
	H	H	6	0
S6	J	J	4	2
	K	K	6	0
S7	L	L	6	0

This 7-station solution has the minimum number of stations possible because *TM* is also 7.

   d. If the time of work element F increases to 6 minutes, then

$$TM = \left(\frac{\Sigma t}{c}\right) = \frac{43}{6} = 7.17 \text{ or 8 stations}$$

The best possible solution will require one more work station.

If the time of work element F decreases to just 2 minutes, the number of stations cannot be decreased to 6 stations because:

$$TM = \left(\frac{\Sigma t}{c}\right) = \frac{39}{6} = 6.5 \text{ or 7 stations}$$

22. Green Grass, Inc.

a.

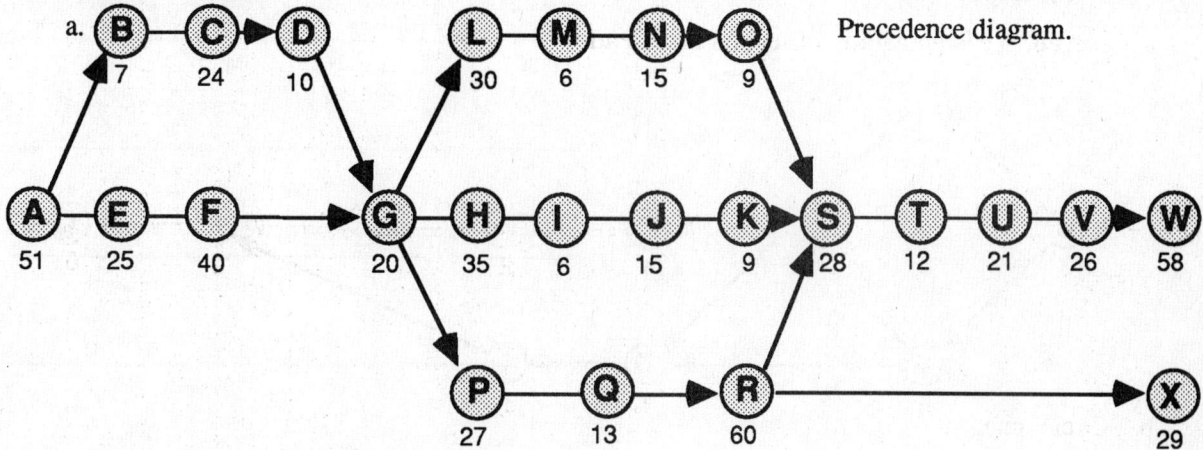

Precedence diagram.

b. Line balance using longest work element rule.

$$c = \frac{1}{r} = \frac{40 \text{ hr} \times 3600 \text{ sec / hr}}{2400 \text{ broadcasters}}$$
$$= 60 \text{ sec / broadcaster}$$

Station	Candidates	Assignment	Cumulative Time	Idle Time ($c = 60$)
S1	A	A	51	9
	B	B	58	2
S2	C, E	E	25	35
	C	C	49	11
	D	D	59	1
S3	F	F	40	20
	G	G	60	0
S4	H, L, P	H	35	25
	I	I	41	19
	J	J	56	4
S5	K, L, P	L	30	30
	K, M, P	P	57	3
S6	K, M, Q	Q	13	47
	K, M	K	22	38
	M	M	28	32
	N	N	43	17
	O	O	52	8
S7	R	R	60	0
S8	S, X	X	29	31
	S	S	57	3
S9	T	T	12	48
	U	U	33	27
	V	V	59	1
S10	W	W	58	2

c. Efficiency, (%)

$$= \left(\frac{\sum t}{nc}\right)(100\%)$$

$$= \frac{576}{(10)60}(100\%) = 96\%$$

Balance delay, (%)

= 100% − Efficiency (%)

= 100% − 96%

= 4%

23. Big Broadcaster.
    a. Completion of Table 9.7.

Work Element	Number of Followers	Work Element	Number of Followers
A	23	M	7
B	20	N	6
C	19	O	5
D	18	P	8
E	19	Q	6
F	18	R	6
G	17	S	4
H	8	T	3
I	7	U	2
J	6	V	1
K	5	W	0
L	8	X	0

b. Line balancing using largest number of followers rule.

Station	Candidates	Choice	Cumulative Time	Idle Time ($c = 60$)
S1	A	A	51	9
	B	B	58	2
S2	C, E (tie)	E	25	35
	C	C	49	11
	D	D	59	1
S3	F	F	40	20
	G	G	60	0
S4	H, L, P (tie)	H	35	25
	I	I	41	19
	J	J	56	4
S5	L, P (tie), K	L	30	30
	K, M, P	P	57	3
S6	M, Q , K	M	6	53
	N, Q (tie), K	N	21	39
	Q, O, K	Q	34	26
	K, O (tie)	K	43	17
	O	O	52	8
S7	R	R	60	0
S8	S, X	S	28	32
	T, X	T	12	20
S9	U, X	U	21	39
	V, X	V	47	13
S10	W,X	W	58	2
S11	X	X	29	31

c. Efficiency, (%)

$$= \left(\frac{\sum t}{nc}\right)(100\%)$$

$$= \frac{576}{(11)60}(100\%) = 87.3\%$$

Balance delay, (%)

= 100% − Efficiency (%)

= 100% − 87.3%

= 12.7%

24. Green Grass forever.

a. Output rates of 50 and 55 have a higher theoretical maximum efficiency. Since a solution has already been found that achieves 96% efficiency, only the output rates between 50 units/hr and 60 units/hr offer a potential gain in efficiency.

Output Rate	Cycle Time	TM	Theoretical Max. Efficiency
30	120	4.8 or 5	96.0%
35	102.9	5.6 or 6	93.3
40	90	6.4 or 7	91.4
45	80	7.2 or 8	90.0
50	72	8	100.0
55	65.5	8.8 or 9	97.7
60	60	9.6 or 10	96.0

b. Here we explore solutions with output rates between 50 and 59 in hopes of finding a more efficient solution.

Output Rate	Cycle Time	Number of Stations	Efficiency
50	72	10	80.0
51	70.6	10	81.6
52	69.2	10	83.2
53	67.9	10	84.8
54	66.7	10	86.4
55	65.5	10	88.0
56	64.3	10	89.6
57	63.2	10	91.2
58	62.1	10	92.8
59	61.0	10	94.4

Unfortunately, changing output rate does not offer any gain in efficiency in this case although such gain is theoretically possible.

25. Mohan Assemblies, Inc.

a. Given Solution   Improved Solution.

Given Solution

4	4	2	2	99	99
4	4	2	2	3	3
4	4	2	2	3	3
5	1	1	1	3	3
5	1	1	1	10	10
5	6	6	6	10	10
5	7	7	11	10	10
5	9	9	9	10	10
5	8	8	8	10	10
12	12	12	99	99	99
13	14	12	99	99	99
13	14	15	99	99	99
13	14	15	99	99	99
13	14	15	99	99	99
16	16	16	99	99	99

Improved Solution

1	1	2	2	99	99
1	1	2	2	3	3
1	1	2	2	3	3
5	4	4	4	3	3
5	4	4	4	10	11
5	6	6	6	10	8
5	10	10	10	10	8
5	10	10	10	10	8
5	15	15	15	7	7
14	14	14	99	99	99
14	13	12	99	99	99
9	13	12	99	99	99
9	13	12	99	99	99
9	13	12	99	99	99
16	16	16	99	99	99

b. The following table identifies for all nonzero closeness ratings whether or not the departments share a common boundary. The scores that do are included in the score total for each layout.

Scores if Share

Departments with Non-Zero Closeness Ratings	Closeness Rating	Common Boundary	
		Current	**Improved**
1–2	1	1	1
1–4	8	8	8
1–5	4	4	4
1–7	4		
2–3	1	1	1
2–10	2		
3–4	8		8
3–6	5		
4–5	11	11	11
4–6	16		16
4–8	1		
5–6	18	18	18
5–7	5	5	
5–10	6		
5–13	3		
5–14	5		5
5–15	5		5
6–7	2	2	
7–8	2		2
7–10	6		6
7–13	1		
7–14	1		
7–15	1		1
8–10	3	3	3
10–13	3		
10–14	2		
10–15	3		3
12–13	2	2	2
12–14	2	2	2
12–15	1	1	
13–14	2	2	2
13–15	2		
14–15	1	1	1
Totals		61	99

26. Getwell Hospital. This solution was prepared with computer assistance, using a procedure similar to the CRAFT logic mentioned in the textbook. Otherwise the calculations would be too tedious.

a. The *ld* of the current layout (shown below) is 755.

4	6	5	7
2	8	3	1

Department Pair	Closeness Rating (l_{ij})	Distance (d_{ij})	$l_{ij}d_{ij}$
1–2	25	3	75
1–3	35	1	35
1–4	5	4	20
1–5	10	2	20
1–6	15	3	45
1–7	0	1	0
1–8	20	2	40
2–3	5	2	10
2–4	10	1	10
2–5	15	3	45
2–6	0	2	0
2–7	0	4	0
2–8	15	1	15
3–4	20	3	60
3–5	30	1	30
3–6	20	2	40
3–7	0	2	0
3–8	·10	1	10
4–5	25	2	50
4–6	15	1	15
4–7	0	3	0
4–8	20	2	40
5–6	20	1	20
5–7	0	1	0
5–8	25	2	50
6–7	40	2	80
6–8	0	1	0
7–8	15	3	45

$$ld = 755$$

b. The following layout, and the rotations and mirror images of it, was found to have an *ld* score of only 595.

6	3	5	4
7	1	8	2

c. When department 1 is fixed at its current location, the best layout found is shown below. Its *ld* score increased somewhat, to 605.

7	4	8	2
6	5	3	1

d. Assuming throughout the rest of the analysis that department 1 must be fixed at its current location, the 50 percent increase in the flow between the examining room and x-ray (from 20 to 30) causes the *ld* score of the solution (*c*) to increase to 625. The best revised layout found in response to the change is shown below. Its *ld* score is slightly less, at 620.

7	4	8	2
6	3	5	1

If the flow between the examining room and x-ray is instead decreased by 50 percent (from 20 to 10), the *ld* score of the solution to (*c*) drops to 585. No improvements could be found over the layout in (*c*) to capitalize of the data change.

Chapter 10

Forecasting

Study Questions

1. Colleges of Business typically serve juniors, seniors, and graduate (MBA, MS) students.

External factors	— Business economy (graduate student demand varies inversely) — Population — Local demographics
Internal factors	— Tuition and scholarships — Evening class schedules — Class size policy
Leading indicators	— Number of sophomores — Local and national economy
Demand management	— enrollment qualifications — tuition and scholarships — limit credit hours enrolled per semester
Level of aggregation	— by major (accounting, marketing, operations) and — by grade level (junior, senior, graduate)

2. Czajkow (pronounced psycho), could look to the following causal factors to predict demand for hot water at the Bates Motel:

   — number of guests registered
   — weather
   — amount of tar embedded in the sand (pollution)

   Demand management options would include:

   — limit the number of guests per room
   — install flow restrictors on shower heads
   — somewhat self-limiting, cold showers reduce demand
   —make a scary movie about taking showers at the Bates Motel ☺

3. Although causal and qualitative approaches can be used for short-term forecasting, the least expensive approach for forecasting thousands of items on a weekly basis would be time series. Adjustments would be necessary to account for advertised specials. The accuracy of the forecasts and the costs of poor forecasts should also be considered.

4. One way to smooth the load on Saturday is to offer Saturday afternoon price reductions. To smooth the load during the week, price reductions for weeknight showings of the horror film could draw the usual weekend crowd to other nights. Finally, the manager could study the process used for choosing the other movies shown so that more popular films are scheduled for the weekdays.

5. The simple moving average and weighted moving average methods require the storage and updating of more data than does the single exponential smoothing method. Consequently, the single exponential smoothing model would be easier to use and less costly.

6. An example of an electronic spreadsheet set up for calculating exponential smoothing forecasts is shown below. The model can be extended by copying the formulas down the forecast column, or modified by changing the value for alpha in cell B2.

	A	B	C
1	Initial Forecast	100	
2	Alpha	0.2	
3			
4		Actual	
5	Time Period	Demand	Forecast
6	January	100	=B1+((B2)*(B6-B1))
7	February	120	=C6+((B2)*(B7-C6))
8	March	110	=C7+((B2)*(B8-C7))
9	April	90	=C8+((B2)*(B9-C8))
10	May	100	=C9+((B2)*(B10-C9))
11	June		
12	July		

7. Sushi bubble gum. The fatal flaw in this market survey is that the persons surveyed are not representative of the target market. Financial district upwardly mobile persons willing to say/do anything for $50 (even eat sushi) probably have different tastes than do bubble gum aged children.

8. Naive forecasting methods, even when applied to data exhibiting a trend, use only *actual* demand (or differences between *actual* demands) in determining the forecast. Exponential smoothing is not a naive forecasting method because it uses the previous forecast in addition to previous actual demand in making the calculation.

9. A single exponential smoothing model with a low value for alpha would be most appropriate for a demand pattern for which there is no trend or seasonality and the underlying average demand is stable. Low values of alpha place greater weights on old demands than do high values of alpha. In a stable time series, old demands are very relevant for estimating the average of the series. Production managers prefer stable production rates to level work force and equipment requirements. Marketing managers want to provide good customer service and react to new market opportunities. A high alpha would make the forecasts more responsive to changes in the level of demand.

10. Because the actual *MAD* doubled in value, it should raise some concern—at least enough to watch the model performance closely. It suggests that the data of the past week did not come from the same population as the data used to construct the model. However, more than one week's experiences should be collected before taking drastic measures such as constructing a new model.

11. Using historical data, a regression model can be constructed where the dependent variable is demand and the independent variable is the time period (i.e., $X = 1, 2, $). Using the linear equation derived from the model, a straight-line is extended to represent the trend of future demand. That extrapolation is then multiplied by the seasonal factor to attain the modified forecast values.

12. Cumulative forecast errors measure forecast bias only, not the variability of forecast errors. An error of -1000 is counterbalanced by an error of $+1000$, giving a *CFE* of zero. What is also needed is a measure of forecast variability, such as *MAD*. Then *MAD* and a tracking signal with pre-specified control limits can be used to judge forecasting performance.

13. In the area of technological forecasting, qualitative methods of forecasting are best. One such approach is the Delphi method, whereby the consensus of a panel of experts is sought.

14. There typically is a trade-off between bias and *MAD*. Random errors, having no assignable cause, tend to occur symmetrically around the mean. Therefore, random errors eventually cancel out and result in little or no bias. However the magnitude of random errors do contribute to *MAD*. This is important when the forecasts are used for inventory control. Larger *MAD*'s imply greater needs for safety stocks. When the actual demand is consistently lower relative to the forecast, bias (actual – forecast) is negative. Production driven by the forecast will cause a very large inventory to accumulate. This will eventually consume all cash (causing bankruptcy). On the other hand, when the actual demand is consistently higher than forecasted, all inventory, including safety stock, will eventually be consumed. No amount of safety stock can provide long-term protection from biased forecasts. Customer service will be poor.

15. The forecast that says that the demand next month will be between 400 and 600 units conveys more information than does the single-estimate forecast. The only thing the manager knows about a single-estimate forecast is that it will be wrong. There is no indication of the range of possible demands.

Discussion Questions

1a. There is no trend in the data. Single exponential smoothing or moving average would be appropriate for estimating the average.

b. The primary external factors that can be forecasted three days in advance and can appreciably affect air quality is wind velocity and temperature inversions.

c. Weather conditions can not be forecast two summers in advance. Medium-term causal factors affecting air quality are population, regulations and policies affecting wood burning, mass transit, use of sand and salt on roads, relocation of the airport, and scheduling of major tourism events such as parades, car races, and stock shows.

d. This is similar to Study Question 13. In the area of technological forecasting, qualitative methods of forecasting are best. One such approach is the Delphi method, whereby the consensus of a panel of experts is sought. Here we would survey experts in the fields of electric powered vehicles, coal-fired combustion for electric utilities, and development of alternatives to sand and salt on roads. We hope to determine whether to expect any technological breakthroughs sufficient to affect air quality within the next ten years.

2. *What's Happening?* My objective in writing this discussion question is to ensure students recognize the difference between sales and demand. Demand forecasting techniques require demand data. Michael is making the common mistake of using sales data as the basis for demand forecasts. Sales are generally equal to the *lesser* of demand or inventory. Say that inventory matches average demand at a particular location and is 100 newspapers. However, for the current edition, demand is less than average, say 90. Michael enters *sales* (which happens to be equal to demand in this period) into the forecasting system resulting in an inventory reduction at that location for the next edition. Now suppose that demand for the next edition is 110. But since inventory has been reduced to 90, only 90 newspapers will be sold. Michael would then enter *sales* (which happens to be equal to *inventory*, not demand) into the forecasting system. This approach rachets downward and tends to starve the distribution system. Since the publication is not reliably available, some customers eventually stop looking for *What's Happening?*, and demand truly declines. It is important that data used for demand forecasting is *demand* data, not sales data.

Problems

1. Printer rentals.
   a. The forecast for week 11 is 23 rentals.

Week Forecast Calculated	A_t		Forecast for Following Week (F_{t+1})
5	$\dfrac{25 + 28 + 30 + 26 + 27}{5}$	=	27.2 or 27
6	$\dfrac{28 + 30 + 26 + 27 + 22}{5}$	=	26.6 or 27
7	$\dfrac{30 + 26 + 27 + 22 + 26}{5}$	=	26.2 or 26
8	$\dfrac{26 + 27 + 22 + 26 + 24}{5}$	=	25.0 or 25
9	$\dfrac{27 + 22 + 26 + 24 + 20}{5}$	=	23.8 or 24
10	$\dfrac{22 + 26 + 24 + 20 + 23}{5}$	=	23.0 or 23

   b. The Mean Absolute Deviation is 2.8 rentals.

Week	Actual	Forecast	Absolute Error
6	22	27	5
7	26	27	1
8	24	26	2
9	20	25	5
10	23	24	1
		Total	14

$$MAD = 14 / 5 = 2.8$$

2. Midwest Telephone Company.
   a. Four-week moving average

Week	A_t		Forecast for Following Week (F_{t+1})
6	$\dfrac{12 + 27 + 23 + 19}{4}$	=	20.25 or 20
7	$\dfrac{27 + 23 + 19 + 20}{4}$	=	22.25 or 22
8	$\dfrac{23 + 19 + 20 + 26}{4}$	=	22.00 or 22
9	$\dfrac{19 + 20 + 26 + 29}{4}$	=	23.50 or 24
10	$\dfrac{20 + 26 + 29 + 32}{4}$	=	26.75 or 27

b. Six-week moving average

Week	A_t		Forecast for Following Week (F_{t+1})
6	$\dfrac{15 + 18 + 12 + 27 + 23 + 19}{6}$	=	19.00 or 19
7	$\dfrac{18 + 12 + 27 + 23 + 19 + 20}{6}$	=	19.83 or 20
8	$\dfrac{12 + 27 + 23 + 19 + 20 + 26}{6}$	=	21.17 or 21
9	$\dfrac{27 + 23 + 19 + 20 + 26 + 29}{6}$	=	24.00 or 24
10	$\dfrac{23 + 19 + 20 + 26 + 29 + 32}{6}$	=	24.83 or 25

c. Performance comparison.

Week	Actual Demand	Forecast 4-wk	Forecast 6-wk	Error 4-wk	Error 6-wk
7	20	20	19	0	1
8	26	22	20	4	6
9	29	22	21	7	8
10	32	24	24	8	8
			MAD	= 4.75	=5.75

An upward trend develops in the last few weeks of the data. Moving averages with smaller n react more quickly to changes in the level of demand. This is shown here in that the 4-week moving average appears to give slightly better results.

3. Karl's Copiers.

$$A_t = \alpha D_t + (1 - \alpha)A_{t-1}$$

Week Forecast Calculated	A_t		F_{t+1}
7/3	0.25(27) + 0.75(23)	=	24
7/10	0.25(36) + 0.75(24)	=	27
7/17	0.25(31) + 0.75(27)	=	28
7/24	0.25(24) + 0.75(28)	=	27
7/31	0.25(23) + 0.75(27)	=	26

The forecast for the week of August 7 is 26 calls.

4. K & R Camera Shop.

a. Weighted Moving Average

Month Forecast Calculated	A_t		F_{t+1}
3	0.5(15) + 0.3(17) + 0.2(12)	=	15
4	0.5(20) + 0.3(15) + 0.2(17)	=	17.9 or 18
5	0.5(18) + 0.3(20) + 0.2(15)	=	18

b. Exponential Smoothing $\qquad A_t = \alpha D_t + (1-\alpha)A_{t-1}$

Month Forecast

Calculated	A_t		F_{t+1}
3	0.2(15) + 0.8(15)	=	15
4	0.2(20) + 0.8(15)	=	16
5	0.2(18) + 0.8(16)	=	16.4

c. Forecasts for month 7 are:

Weighted Moving Average:

$F_t = 0.5(23) + 0.3(18) + 0.2(20) = 20.9$ or 21

Exponential Smoothing:

$F_t = 0.2(23) + 0.8(16.4) = 17.72$ or 18

	Weighted Moving Average			Exponential Smoothing	
Month	E_t	CFE_t		E_t	CFE_t
4	(20 − 15) = 4	5		(20 − 15) = 5	5
5	(18 − 18) = 0	5		(18 − 16) = 2	7
6	(23 − 18) = 5	10		(23 − 16.4) = 6.6	13.6

Based on these data, the weighted moving average method provides a more accurate forecast. However there may be a trend in the data that would result in both of these forecasts being biased.

5. Vending machines.

$$A_t = 0.2D_t + 0.8(A_{t-1} + T_{t-1})$$
$$CT_t = A_t - A_{t-1}$$
$$T_t = 0.1CT_t + 0.9T_{t-1}$$
$$F_{t+1} = A_t + T_t$$

May

$A_{\text{May}} = 0.2(760) + 0.8(700 + 50) = 752$
$CT_{\text{May}} = 752 - 700 = 52$
$T_{\text{May}} = 0.1(52) + 0.9(50) = 50.2$
Forecast for June = 752 + 50.2 = 802.2 or 802

June

$A_{\text{June}} = 0.2(800) + 0.8(752 + 50.2) = 801.76$ or 802
$CT_{\text{June}} = 801.76 - 752 = 49.76$
$T_{\text{June}} = 0.1(49.76) + 0.9(50.2) = 50.15$ or 50
Forecast for July = 801.76 + 50.15 = 851.91 or 852

July

$A_{\text{July}} = 0.2(820) + 0.8(801.76 + 50.15) = 845.52$ or 846
$CT_{\text{July}} = 845.52 - 801.76 = 43.76$
$T_{\text{July}} = 0.1(43.76) + 0.9(50.15) = 49.15$
Forecast for August = 845.52 + 49.15 = 895.03 or 895

6. Sunnyvale Bank.

$$A_t = 0.3D_t + 0.7(A_{t-1} + T_{t-1})$$
$$CT_t = A_t - A_{t-1}$$
$$T_t = 0.2CT_t + 0.8T_{t-1}$$
$$F_{t+1} = A_t + T_t$$

April

$A_{Apr} = 0.3(680) + 0.7(600 + 60) = 666.0$
$CT_{Apr} = 666 - 600 = 66.0$
$T_{Apr} = 0.2(66) + 0.8(60) = 61.2$
Forecast for May = $666.0 + 61.2 = 727.2$ or 727

May

$A_{May} = 0.3(710) + 0.7(666.0 + 61.2) = 722.04$
$CT_{May} = 722.04 - 666.0 = 56.04$
$T_{May} = 0.2(56.04) + 0.8(61.2) = 60.17$
Forecast for June = $722.04 + 60.17 = 782.21$ or 782

June

$A_{June} = 0.3(790) + 0.7(722.04 + 60.17) = 784.55$
$CT_{June} = 784.55 - 722.04 = 62.51$
$T_{June} = 0.2(62.51) + 0.8(60.17) = 60.64$
Forecast for July = $784.55 + 60.64 = 845.19$ or 845

7. A particular product.

a. $A_t = 0.7D_t + 0.3A_{t-1}$ and $F_{t+1} = A_t$

Week Forecast Calculated	A_t		Forecast for Following Week (F_{t+1})
1	$0.7(29) + 0.3(30.0)$	=	29.3 or 29
2	$0.7(35) + 0.3(29.3)$	=	33.3 or 33
3	$0.7(32) + 0.3(33.3)$	=	32.4 or 32
4	$0.7(40) + 0.3(32.4)$	=	37.7 or 38

b. $A_t = 0.1D_t + 0.9(A_{t-1} + T_{t-1})$
$CT_t = A_t - A_{t-1}$
$T_t = 0.1CT_t + 0.9T_{t-1}$
$F_{t+1} = A_t + T_t$

Week 1

$A_1 = 0.1(29) + 0.9(30 + 3) = 32.6$
$CT_1 = 32.6 - 30 = 2.6$
$T_1 = 0.1(2.6) + 0.9(3) = 3.0$
$F_2 = 32.6 + 3.0 = 35.6$ or 36

Week 2

$A_2 = 0.1(35) + 0.9(32.6 + 3) = 35.5$
$CT_2 = 35.5 - 32.6 = 2.9$
$T_2 = 0.1(2.9) + 0.9(3) = 3.0$
$F_3 = 35.5 + 3.0 = 38.5$ or 39

Week 3

$$A_3 = 0.1(32) + 0.9(35.5 + 3.0) = 37.9$$
$$CT_3 = 37.9 - 35.5 = 2.4$$
$$T_3 = 0.1(2.4) + 0.9(3.0) = 2.9$$
$$F_4 = 37.9 + 2.9 = 40.8 \text{ or } 41$$

$$? \quad CT_t = A_t - A_{t-1} ?$$

Week 4

$$A_4 = 0.1(40) + 0.9(37.9 + 2.9) = 40.7$$
$$CT_4 = 40.7 - 37.9 = 2.8$$
$$T_4 = 0.1(2.8) + 0.9(2.9) = 2.9$$
$$F_5 = 40.7 + 2.9 = 43.6 \text{ or } 44$$

c. Compare performance

Week	Actual Demand (D_t)	Exp Smoothing Forecast (F_t)	Absolute Error (E_t)	Trend-Adjusted Exp Smoothing Forecast (F_t)	Absolute Error (E_t)
2	35	29	6	36	1
3	32	33	1	39	7
4	40	32	8	41	1
Total			15		9
MAD			15 / 3 = 5	9 / 3 = 3	

The trend-adjusted exponential smoothing model did better but was always higher than the actual. Perhaps when it settles down it will be better. The exponential smoothing model lags the actual and misses the direction because it does not have a mechanism to reflect the trend in the data.

8. Calculator sales

$$A_1 = 0.2(46) + 0.8(45 + 2) = 46.8$$
$$CT_1 = 46.8 - 45 = 1.8$$
$$T_1 = .2(1.8) + 0.8(2) = 1.96$$
$$F_2 = 46.8 + 1.96 = 48.76 \text{ or } 48.8$$

$$A_2 = 0.2(49) + 0.8(46.8 + 1.96) = 48.81$$
$$CT_2 = 48.81 - 46.8 = 2.01$$
$$T_2 = 0.2(2.01) + 0.8(1.96) = 1.97$$
$$F_3 = 48.81 + 1.97 = 50.78 \text{ or } 51$$

$$A_3 = 0.2(43) + 0.8(48.81 + 1.97) = 49.224$$
$$CT_3 = 49.224 - 48.81 = 0.414$$
$$T_3 = 0.2(0.414) + .08(1.97) = 1.659$$
$$F_4 = 49.22 + 1.66 = 50.88 \text{ or } 51$$

$$A_4 = 0.2(50) + 0.8(49.22 + 1.66) = 50.7$$
$$CT_4 = 50.7 - 49.22 = 1.48$$
$$T_4 = 0.2(1.48) + 0.8(1.66) = 1.624$$
$$F_5 = 50.7 + 1.62 = 52.32 \text{ or } 52$$

$$A_5 = 0.2(53) + 0.8(50.7 + 1.62) = 52.456$$
$$CT_5 = 52.46 - 50.7 = 1.76$$
$$T_5 = 0.2(1.76) + 0.8(1.62) = 1.648$$
$$F_6 = 52.46 + 1.65 = 54.11 \text{ or } 54$$

9. Forrest's boxes of chocolates.

a. Estimated forecast for Year 4;

Quarter	Forecast
1	3,700
2	2,700
3	1,900
4	6,500
	14,800

b. Multiplicative seasonal method.

Quarter	Year 1	Seasonal Factor	Year 2	Seasonal Factor	Year 3	Seasonal Factor	Average Seasonal Factor
1	3,000	1.20	3,300	1.1	3502	1.03	1.11
2	1,700	0.68	2,100	0.7	2448	0.72	0.70
3	900	0.36	1,500	0.5	1768	0.52	0.46
4	4,400	1.76	5,100	1.7	5882	1.73	1.73
Total	10,000		12,000		13,600		
Average	2,500		3,000		3,400		

Forecast for Year 4, 14,800. Average = 3700

Quarter	Average	Factor	Forecast
1	3,700	1.11	4,107
2	3,700	0.70	2,590
3	3,700	0.46	1,702
4	3,700	1.73	6,401
			14,800

This technique forecasts the third quarter sales will *decrease* compared to sales for the third quarter of the third year. Betcha thought it would increase. Mamma always said: "Life is full of surprises!"

10. Snyder's Garden Center

Quarter	Year 1	Seasonal Factor	Year 2	Seasonal Factor	Average Seasonal Factor
1	30	0.138	50	0.198	0.168
2	370	1.701	420	1.663	1.682
3	290	1.333	330	1.307	1.320
4	180	0.828	210	0.832	0.830
Total	870		1010		
Average	217.50		252.50		

Average quarterly sales in 1993 are expected to be 287.50 (1150 / 4). Using the average seasonal factors, the 1993 forecasts are:

Quarter		Forecast
1	0.168(287.50)	48
2	1.682(287.50)	484
3	1.320(287.50)	380
4	0.830(287.50)	239

11. North American Auto.

Month	Year 1	Seasonal Factor	Year 2	Seasonal Factor	Average	Year 3 Forecast
Jan.	25	0.398	28	0.403	0.401	31
Feb.	29	0.462	33	0.475	0.469	36
Mar.	35	0.558	41	0.590	0.574	44
Apr.	47	0.749	55	0.791	0.770	59
May	75	1.195	79	1.137	1.166	89
June	98	1.562	104	1.496	1.529	116
July	120	1.912	142	2.043	1.978	151
Aug.	144	2.295	153	2.201	2.248	171
Sep.	60	0.956	62	0.892	0.924	70
Oct.	49	0.781	54	0.777	0.779	59
Nov.	41	0.653	47	0.676	0.665	51
Dec.	30	0.478	36	0.518	0.498	38
Total	753		834			915
Average	62.75		69.5			76.25

12. Tony's Garage.

a.

Month	Forecast	Month	XY	X^2
January	31	1	31	1
February	36	2	72	4
March	47	3	141	9
April	42	4	168	16
May	49	5	245	25
June	41	6	246	36
July	50	7	350	49
August	52	8	416	64
Total	348	36	1669	204

The regression equation is $Y_R = 32.464 + 2.45X$

b. Forecasts

$Y(\text{Sep}) = 32.464 + 2.45(9) = 54.514$ or 55

$Y(\text{Oct}) = 32.464 + 2.45(10) = 56.964$ or 57

$Y(\text{Nov}) = 32.464 + 2.45(11) = 59.414$ or 59

13. Elemental Standard Data.

Cutting Time (min) (Y)	Teeth (X)	XY	X^2
115	23	2645	529
84	17	1428	289
52	10	520	100
138	28	3864	784
67	14	938	196
Totals 456	92	9395	1898

$$\bar{X} = \frac{92}{5} = 18.4$$

$$\bar{Y} = \frac{456}{5} = 91.2$$

$$b = \frac{\sum XY - n\overline{X}\,\overline{Y}}{\sum X^2 - n\overline{X}^2} = \frac{9395 - 5(18.4)(91.2)}{1898 - 5(18.4)^2} = \frac{1004.6}{205.2} = 4.896$$

$$a = \overline{Y} - b\overline{X} = 91.2 - 4.896(18.4) = 1.1136$$

Regression Equation:

$$Y_R = 1.1136 + 4.896X$$

Because the next job has 20 teeth, the estimated time required to cut the gear is:

$$Y = 1.1136 + 4.896(20) = 99.034 \text{ or } 99 \text{ minutes}$$

14. Ohio Swiss Milk.

a. Regression equation.

$\sum X$	$\sum Y$	$\sum XY$	$\sum X^2$	$\sum Y^2$	$\overline{X}$	$\overline{Y}$
3654.4	10,182	3,686,637	1,457,049.08	10,378,192	365.44	1018.2

$$b = \frac{3,686,637 - 10(365.44)(1018.2)}{1,457,049.08 - 10(365.44)^2} = \frac{-34,273.08}{121,585.144} = -0.2819$$

$$a = 1018.2 - (-0.2819)(365.44) = 1121.22$$

$$Y_R = 1121.22 - 0.2819X$$

b. Correlation coefficient.

$$r^2 = \frac{a\sum Y + b\sum XY - n\overline{Y}^2}{\sum Y^2 - n\overline{Y}^2}$$

$$r^2 = \frac{1121.22(10182) + (-0.2819)(3,686,637) - 10(1018.2)^2}{10,378,192 - 10(1018.2)^2}$$

$$= \frac{9686.67}{10,879.6} = 0.8904$$

$$r = 0.944$$

Standard error of the estimate.

$$s_{YX} = \sqrt{\frac{\sum Y^2 - a\sum Y - b\sum XY}{n-2}}$$

$$= \sqrt{\frac{10,378,192 - 1121.22(10,182) - (-0.2819)(3,686,637)}{10-2}}$$

$$= \sqrt{149.11}$$

$$= 12.21$$

c. Estimated cost per gallon at volume = 325,000 gallons

$$Y = 1121.22 - 0.2819(325) = 1029.60$$

Advanced Problems

15. Large Public Library
    Simple Moving Average:

Period	Forecast	MAD	Bias
1	2451	282	604
2	**2299**	**267**	**-68**
3	2221	257	-291
4	2127	242	-524
5	2037	242	-846
12	2203	223	-632

In general, as *n* increases, MAD decreases and Bias increases. The 2-month moving average appears to be the best because of its relatively low *MAD* and bias.

16. Large Public Library, (continued, using 1847 as initial average)
    Exponential Smoothing

α	Forecast	MAD	Bias
0.30	2186	256	1132
0.50	2259	258	823
0.65	**2325**	**255**	**736**
0.70	2346	256	713
0.80	2385	262	673
1.00	2451	282	604

As alpha increases, Bias generally decreases and MAD generally increases. When alpha = 0.65 there seems to be a good combination of low Bias and low MAD.

17. Large Public Library, (continued, using 1847 as initial average and 0 as initial trend)
    Trend-Adjusted Exponential Smoothing

α	β	Forecast	MAD	Bias	MSE
0.2	0.2	2101	263	-329	105,879
0.3	0.1	2150	261	-171	100,186
0.35	0.1	2166	264	-78	100,823
0.4	**0.1**	**2189**	**266**	**2**	**101,782**
0.45	0.1	2216	267	69	102,905

18. Large Public Library, continued.   When alpha = 0.4 and beta = 0.1, MSE = 101,782. Since MSE is approximately the square of the standard deviation, standard deviation = $\sqrt{101,782} \approx 319$.
    A 95% confidence interval is at $\pm 1.96 (319) = \pm 625$. We can be 95% confident that the actual number of checkouts will be somewhere in the range 2189 ± 625, or between 1564 and 2814.

19. College Bookstore. Since there are trend and seasonal components, simple moving average (SMA) and exponential smoothing (ES) produce biased results. Note that as the number of period in SMA increase and as alpha in ES decreases, bias increases. One way these methods can deal with a trend is to become naive (next forecast = last forecast). In other words, in SMA, $n = 1$ or in ES, alpha =1. Notice that SMA also gives good results when $n = 12$, the number of periods in a year.

Simple Moving Average

(# periods)	Forecast	*MAD*	*Bias*
1	**2669**	**327**	**1005**
2	2544	277	682
3	2507	265	1070
4	2547	284	1618
5	2462	287	1315
12	**2219**	**254**	**681**

Exponential Smoothing	Forecast	*MAD*	*Bias*
$\alpha = 0.6$	2572	280	1513
$\alpha = 1.0$	**2669**	**327**	**1005**

Below is the multiplicative seasonal method to forecast inbound shipments for the fourth year:

Month	Year 1 Shipments	Seasonal Index	Year 2 Shipments	Seasonal Index	Year 3 Shipments	Seasonal Index
January	1,664	0.06527	1,882	0.07511	1983	0.07151
February	2,365	0.09277	1,922	0.07671	2291	0.08261
March	1,891	0.07417	1,928	0.07695	2162	0.07796
April	1,731	0.06790	1,594	0.06362	2969	0.10706
May	2,441	0.09575	2,020	0.08062	1845	0.06653
June	1,478	0.05797	1,445	0.05767	1968	0.07096
July	2,215	0.08688	2,054	0.08198	2205	0.07951
August	2,373	0.09308	2,662	0.10624	2122	0.07652
September	2,460	0.09649	2,200	0.08780	2667	0.09617
October	2,088	0.08190	2,150	0.08581	2432	0.08770
November	2,467	0.09677	2,635	0.10516	2419	0.08723
December	2,321	0.09104	2,564	0.10233	2669	0.09624
Total	25,494		25,056		27,732	

Month	Year 4 Shipments	Average Index				
January	2001	0.07063				
February	2381	0.08403				
March	2163	0.07636				
April	2253	0.07953				
May	2294	0.08097				
June	1762	0.06220				
July	2346	0.08279				
August	2605	0.09195				
September	2649	0.09349				
October	2412	0.08514				
November	2731	0.09639				
December	2735	0.09654	Linear Regression, Y = 23,856 + 1,119 X			
Total	28,332		When X = 4, Y = 28,332			

20. Midwest Computer Company
   a. Trend-adjusted exponential smoothing

	MAD	Bias
$\alpha = .35, \beta = 0.15$	65.17*	– 18.67
$\alpha = .70, \beta = 1.0$	90.67	– 1.22*

   The trend-adjusted exponential smoothing model provides the lowest bias with a reasonable *MAD* value when $\alpha = 0.7$ and $\beta = 1.0$. The forecasts for weeks 51–53 using this method are

Month	Forecast
51	2452
52	2493
53	2535

   b. The linear regression model is
   $$Y_R = -28.69 + 4.98X$$
   or
   $$\text{Sales} = -28.69 + 4.98 \text{ (number of leases)}$$

   The forecast for months 51–53 can be based on actual lease information for months 48–50.

Month	Forecast Sales
51	2441
52	2506
53	2571

   c. The linear regression model has (based on the 47 data points used to develop the model) a *MAD* of 65.88 and a bias of 18.01. Therefore the trend-adjusted exponential smoothing model of part (a) will still provide the best forecasts.
   The actual data are

Month	Actual Sales
51	2450
52	2497
53	2526

21. Wise Owl Supermakets. Numerous methods could be used.

Moving Average

Number of Periods	MAD	Bias	Forecast
2	7.09	5.00	39.50
3	6.87	13.67	41.33
4	6.21	12.75	41.50
5	4.52*	1.00*	**44.80**
6	4.80	7.00	44.17
7	4.94	7.43	43.43
12	5.15	3.08	43.08

Exponential Smoothing

Use α = 0.20 for the lowest MAD.

	MAD	Bias	Forecast
α = 0.20	5.34	47.62	42.53
α = 1.00	7.52	5.00	38

Use α = 1.00 for the lowest bias.

Exponential Smoothing with Trend

Best MAD	MAD	Bias	Forecast
α = 0.20	5.34	47.64	42.53
β = 0.00			

Best Bias	MAD	Bias	Forecast
α = 0.63	6.72	– 0.03	39.81
β = 0.05			

A graphic plot of the data reveals a spike every fifth data point. The best of the above methods would appear to be the moving average with 5 periods, due to its relatively low MAD and bias. But none of these methods reasonably account for the fifth-period spike. Another way to deal with this cyclical data is to use the multiplicative seasonal method with 5 periods in a cycle. With this method, the forecast for the 25th month would be 60.

Period	Cycle 1	Seasonal Index	Cycle 2	Seasonal Index	Cycle 3	Seasonal Index	Cycle 4	Seasonal Index
1	33	0.1701	38	0.1767	43	0.1972	41	0.1907
2	37	0.1907	42	0.1953	39	0.1789	36	0.1674
3	31	0.1598	40	0.1860	37	0.1697	39	0.1814
4	39	0.2010	41	0.1907	43	0.1972	41	0.1907
5	54	0.2784	54	0.2512	56	0.2569	58	0.2698
	194		215		218		215	

Month	Actual Cycle 5	Average Seasonal Index	Fcast Cycle 5
21	42	0.1837	42
22	45	0.1831	42
23	41	0.1742	40
24	38	0.1949	44
25	??	0.2640	**60**
			227

Linear Regression, $Y = 194 + 6.6 X$
When X = 5, Y 227

22. Air visibility.
    a. This data contiains no detectable trend component over the two-summer history. Either the simple moving average, or exponential smoothing should give unbiased results. As long as forecast parameters are chosen for stability (high n in simple moving average, or low alpha in exponential smoothing) the forecast for August 31 will be about 120.5. Because the data is stable, linear regression will yield a nearly zero slope with a forecast of about 120.5 as well.

    b. There is no historical data to support expectations for air quality in the third year to be any different than that of the first two years. It will average about 120.5 unless public policy affects transportation, population growth, or utilities burning natural gas rather than coal. That might make a detectable difference in air quality. However, the effects of public policy are not recorded in the data base, so qualitative forecasting methods are needed.

23. Flatlands Public Power District. The historical data shows both trend and seasonal components. We will use the multiplicative seasonal method to forecast demand for the next year, then look for a low-demand period of two weeks during which the Comstock plant can be serviced. Weeks 7 and 8 look like the best two-week period to schedule maintenance.

Week	Demand Year 1	Seasonal Index	Demand Year 2	Seasonal Index	Demand Year 3	Seasonal Index	Demand Year 4	Seasonal Index	Demand Year 5	Seasonal Index
1	2050	0.1017	2000	0.0959	1950	0.0922	2100	0.1010	2275	0.1064
2	1925	0.0955	2075	0.0995	1800	0.0851	2400	0.1154	2300	0.1076
3	1825	0.0906	2225	0.1067	2150	0.1017	1975	0.0950	2150	0.1006
4	1525	0.0757	1800	0.0863	1725	0.0816	1675	0.0805	1525	0.0713
5	1050	0.0521	1175	0.0564	1575	0.0745	1350	0.0649	1350	0.0632
6	1300	0.0645	1050	0.0504	1275	0.0603	1525	0.0733	1475	0.0690
7	1200	0.0596	1250	0.0600	1325	0.0626	1500	0.0721	1475	0.0690
8	1175	0.0583	1025	0.0492	1100	0.0520	1150	0.0553	1175	0.0550
9	1350	0.0670	1300	0.0624	1500	0.0709	1350	0.0649	1375	0.0643
10	1525	0.0757	1425	0.0683	1550	0.0733	1225	0.0589	1400	0.0655
11	1725	0.0856	1625	0.0779	1375	0.0650	1225	0.0589	1425	0.0667
12	1575	0.0782	1950	0.0935	1825	0.0863	1475	0.0709	1550	0.0725
13	1925	0.0955	1950	0.0935	2000	0.0946	1850	0.0889	1900	0.0889
Total	20150		20850		21150		20800		21375	

Week	Demand Year 6	Average Seasonal Index
1	2147	0.0995
2	2172	0.1006
3	2135	0.0989
4	1707	0.0791
5	1343	0.0622
6	1371	0.0635
7	1396	0.0647
8	1164	0.0539
9	1422	0.0659
10	1475	0.0683
11	1529	0.0708
12	1733	0.0803
13	1992	0.0923
Total	21585	

Linear Regression Y = 20145 + 240(X)
When X = 6, Y = 21585

24. Comnet Communications.

    a. Moving Average, n = 3:   Forecast = 51.22   MAD = 3.707

        Exponential Smoothing, alpha = 0.75:   Forecast = 54.16   MAD = 3.232

        Trend Adj. Exp. Sm., alpha = 0.395, beta = 0.01 (36) Forecast = 53.91   MAD = 3.039

                                                  (37) Forecast = 54.80

                                                  (38) Forecast = 55.70

    b. Linear Regression Y = 19.50 + 0.94 X   (36) Forecast = 53.34   MAD = 2.850

                                                  (37) Forecast = 54.28

                                                  (38) Forecast = 55.22

    c. The forecasts are all very close, but since there is a trend in the data, linear regression will give better results.

25. Getsmart Computers.

Using exponsntial smoothing with trend and seasonal factoring the quarterly forecast for year 10 is:

1699, 2122, 2489, 1486.

Using the multiplicative seasonal method the quarterly forecast for year 10 is:

1861, 2177, 2710, 1608.

Quarter	Year 1	Seasonal Index	Year 2	Seasonal Index	Year 3	Seasonal Index	Year 4	Seasonal Index	Year 5	Seasonal Index
1	1,115	0.1975	1,320	0.2484	1,390	0.2258	1,405	0.2213	1,490	0.2346
2	1,450	0.2569	1,375	0.2588	1,615	0.2624	1,595	0.2512	1,690	0.2661
3	1,845	0.3268	1,678	0.3158	2,005	0.3258	2,125	0.3346	2,225	0.3504
4	1,235	0.2188	940	0.1769	1,145	0.1860	1,225	0.1929	1,280	0.2016
Total	5,645		5,313		6,155		6,350		6,685	

Quarter	Year 6	Seasonal Index	Year 7	Seasonal Index	Year 8	Seasonal Index	Year 9	Seasonal Index	Year 10	Average Seasonal Index
1	1,450	0.2569	1,560	0.2936	1,590	0.2583	1,605	0.2528	1861	0.2433
2	1,630	0.2888	1,810	0.3407	1,970	0.3201	2,010	0.3165	2177	0.2846
3	2,100	0.3720	2,250	0.4235	2,265	0.3680	2,360	0.3717	2710	0.3543
4	1,220	0.2161	1,335	0.2513	1,390	0.2258	1,410	0.2220	1608	0.2102
Total	6,400		6,955		7,215		7,385		7649	

Linear Regression, Y = 5,262.9 + 238.6(X)
When X = 10, Y = 7,648.9 or 7,649

Chapter 11

Materials Management

Study Questions

1. Large investments in inventory can mask many inefficient practices. For example, excessive work-in-process inventories can hide problems such as unnecessarily long setup times, frequent machine failures, and poor yields. Consequently, not only does inventory cost a lot of money, it also hides these problems. Carrying inventory hampers efforts to improve efficiency.

2. Materials management concepts apply to service organizations in the same way as to manufacturing organizations. The materials management decisions such as staffing plan, work-force schedule, inventory control (44 percent of the economy's inventory is held by wholesalers and retailers alone), operations scheduling, and purchasing are as important for the efficient management of service organizations as they are for manufacturing organizations.

3. Centralizing all materials management functions under one key executive facilitates coordination of the various activities and elevates the materials management function in the organization. The key executive might be able to better allocate the work of his or her subordinates but will have to handle the increased work load that the position will require. In some cases, centralized coordination may be so demanding that a more decentralized arrangement may be more realistic.

4. As a manufacturing firm begins to participate in international business, purchasing activity increases. U.S. manufacturers tend to specialize in final assembly and distribution of their own product designs from components fabricated in other countries. Sometimes a U. S. firm designs and markets products, but does almost no manufacturing. In those firms, the proportion of purchased materials and services becomes very high, and the materials management function may revert to the segmented structure. Purchasing takes on a leading role, while production control is insignificant. International business causes supplier relations to become more cooperative. Strategic alliances, collaborative efforts, joint ventures, and licensing agreements are formed. The trend toward production and purchasing of parts from all over the globe favors more centralization, because of the specialized knowledge and skills such as understanding of foreign languages and cultures.

5. The supplier selection process must be centered on an assessment of the supplier's capability to supply high-quality parts at the time needed at the lowest cost. Care should be taken not to focus on low price alone to the exclusion of quality and delivery performance. Lead time and on-time delivery performance should be given high priority to ensure a smooth assembly operation. Once a specific supplier is selected, a long-term supply contract is preferred so that both the buyer's purchasing function and the supplier's manufacturing function can be improved through the enhanced repeatability.

6. Supplier relations can become more cooperative by building long-term relationships with suppliers, emphasizing trust, and creating interest in mutual growth. This can be facilitated by negotiating long-term contracts, providing technical assistance, and profit-sharing so that suppliers have an incentive to improve performance of the supplier-customer partnership. Sharing information on future buying decisions can also promote supplier relations. The cooperative orientation may not be desirable for one-time purchases, when suppliers operate in an uncertain environment, or when suppliers are subject to strikes or material shortages. In such an environment having multiple sources of supply may be better and safer.

7. In which situations would you favor...

   a. Long-term purchase contracts are favored when the demand for the part is high and repetitive. Suppliers can be preselected, and negotiated contracts can cover one year or more with delivery dates, quantities, and often prices left open. This option is advantageous to the buyer because complex paperwork can be avoided, supplier capacity can be reserved, and price concessions are possible. Suppliers like long-term contracts because they make future demand more certain. Increased certainty fosters better supplier relations.

   b. Centralized buying is preferred when specialized expertise is justified by requirements for the best quality, delivery or price. Opportunities for centralization occur when two or more local facilities use the same standardized items. It can increase purchasing clout, benefiting the buyer through better service, lower prices, long-term supply availability, or new supplier capability.

8. Data on each type of inventory (cycle, safety stock, anticipation, and pipeline) can help identify problems, particularly when compared over time from an internal perspective or to industry averages from an external perspective. Reducing the production-distribution lead time, forward positioning of inventory, and careful selection of carriers can reduce pipeline inventory **and** reduce the total lead time of the product to the customer. Information is a good substitute for inventory. Improved forecasting provides advanced information for scheduling shipping quantities and dates and reduces the need for safety stock. Better scheduling improves delivery date performance and reduces transportation costs.

9. The purpose of anticipation inventory is to level demand on the factory. Potential advantages of anticipation inventory include (i) better customer service due to the fewer risks of stockout, (ii) lower costs of overtime, and (iii) reduced transportation and purchasing costs.

10. Part commonality, centralized buying, and supplier consolidation may increase volumes to the point where transportation costs and quantity discounts no longer prevent small lot sizes. Lot size reductions mean smaller cycle inventories. The higher volumes give the buyer more clout, which can result in more favorable contract terms, better quality, and more reliable deliveries. Improved supplier reliability means less need for safety stock. Quicker deliveries reduce pipeline inventory. Finally, streamlining the purchasing function with better organization and information systems can help reduce the cost of buying and holding materials.

11. ABC analysis groups the items into three classes (A, B, and C) based on their relative importance represented by dollar usage. This classification allows management to apply different levels of attention to each category. Although the typical organization keeps thousands of items in inventory, not all of them justify the expense of close attention and tight control. It is typical to find the top 20 percent of the items representing about 80 percent of the dollar usage. Therefore, it is natural to pay close attention to Class A items while looser control is applied to Class C items.

12. Examples of how competitive priorities can affect choices made in materials management are:

    • Firms with a product focus have less tolerance for capacity cushions, extra workers, and high inventories because they are likely to be competing on the basis of price (or cost). However there is less complexity and uncertainty to buffer against, so these cushions can be decreased.

    • Firms with a process focus tend to derive more benefits from an integrated materials management organizational structure because their uncertain environments require more coordination among purchasing, production and inventory control, and distribution.

    • Firms with a product focus use longer planning horizons for developing production plans and schedules. Forward scheduling, used to maximize facility and equipment utilization, is feasible due to less uncertainty, and standardized products. High capital intensity requires high utilization.

Discussion Questions

1. The self-policing element of the Defense Industry Initiatives calls for contractors to investigate suspected wrongdoing internally and to voluntarily report fraud and waste to the Pentagon. They also are to conduct ethics training sessions and establish company hotlines for employees to report problems. The right choice is for you to report the friend to the Pentagon and give the information back. Many managers might have second thoughts about turning in a friend of 20 years, but the core purpose of an ethics program is to expose the truth, however unpleasant it is, so that the firm takes a fair and honest approach to business.

   The Defense Industry Initiatives have had mixed reviews. The 46 contractors have turned over 96 cases to the Pentagon and returned $43 million of government money. At the same time, 39 of them were investigated for alleged abuses that weren't reported. It would seem that Pentagon oversight is still needed in addition to self-governance. For more information on the ethics programs of various contractors, see "Defense Contractors' Ethics Programs Get Scrutinized," *The Wall Street Journal*, July 21, 1988.

2. USX

   a. Supplier proximity reduces ordering and transportation costs, which allows Q (and therefore cycle inventory) to be reduced. It also avoids long delivery times and the likelihood of uncertain deliveries, which reduces the need for excessive safety stock. Finally, supplier proximity cuts the lead time, which by definition reduces the amount of inventory in transit from the supplier; pipeline inventory drops.

   b. Inviting suppliers to a two-day seminar can be defended in several ways. Attracting businesses to Gary, a down-and-out Rust Belt city, can help the local economy. The advantages of lower inventory and quicker responses to changing customer demand can help USX stay competitive in spite of softening demand and growing competition from minimills. Keeping a competitive edge enables the firm to retain its work force and met its responsibilities to stockholders.

   At the same time, USX spared little expense in its extravagant seminar. Gifts such as this are generally perceived to create ethical problems for both the firm and its suppliers. A sense of obligation to repay the gift can be created. In this case the suppliers may relocate their plants. Often the direction of the obligation is reversed. Suppliers make gifts to buyers, which can lead to larger purchase orders than would otherwise be justified. Recent estimates of business gift expenditures put them over $1.5 billion per year. Almost all organizational buyers (97 percent) accept gifts or favors from their suppliers, be they lunches, tickets to entertainment events, or faster delivery times. For more background on the topic, see:

   "Looking to Lure Suppliers, USX Plays Up a Town," *Wall Street Journal,* August 17, 1989.

   Kelley, Scott W., and Michael J. Dorsch, "Ethical Climate, Organizational Commitment, and Indebtedness Among Purchasing Executives," *Journal of Personal Selling & Sales Management*, vol. 11, no. 4 (Fall 1991), pp. 55–66.

Problems

1. A company

    a. Cost of Materials   =   0.60($500 million)

                                = $300 million

    Percentage change
    in cost of material   =   (($20 million / $300 million))(100%)

                                =   6.67%

    b. Let S be the increase in sales dollars that would add $20 million to gross profits. With a 15 percent gross profit margin, we get:

             $0.15S$ = $20 million

                 S = $133.3 million

    Percentage change
    in sales   = $133.3 / $500 million

                     =   26.67%

    The calculations show that the company could achieve the same increase in profits either by reducing the material cost by 6.67 percent or by increasing sales by 26.67 percent.

2. Money Enterprises. Average aggregate inventory value can be calculated as:

    Average aggregate
    inventory value   =   Raw materials + WIP + Finished goods

                     = $2,845,000 + $5,670,000 + $2,985,000

                     = $11,500,000

    a. Sales per week   =   Cost of goods sold/52 weeks per year

                       = $29,900,000 / 52

                       = $575,000

    Weeks of supply   =   Average aggregate inventory value/Weekly sales

                       = $11,500,000 / $575,000

                       =   20 wk

    b. Inventory turnover   =   (Annual sales)/(Average aggregate inventory value)

                         = $29,900,000 / $11,500,000

                         =   2.6 turns/year

3. One product line.

    Inventory turnover   =   Annual sales/Average aggregate inventory value

    After substituting in the information available and solving, we get:

             8.0   = $775,000/Average aggregate inventory value

    Average aggregate
    inventory value   = $775,000 / 8 = $96,875

4. Henderson Corporation. Average aggregate inventory value can be calculated as:

Average aggregate inventory value	=	Raw materials + WIP + Finished goods
	=	$2,725,000 + $1,152,000 + $3,225,000
	=	$7,102,000

a.
Sales per week	=	Cost of goods sold/52 weeks per year
	=	$24,000,000 / 52
	=	$461,538
Weeks of supply	=	Average aggregate inventory value/Weekly sales
	=	$7,102,000 / $461,538
	=	15.4 wk

b.
Inventory turnover	=	(Annual sales)/(Average aggregate inventory value)
	=	$24,000,000 / $7,102,000
	=	3.4 turns/year

5. A firm.

a.
Sales per week	=	Cost of goods sold/52 weeks per year
	=	$3,500,000 / 52
	=	$67,308
Weeks of supply	=	Average aggregate inventory value/Weekly sales
	=	$1,200,000 / $67,308
	=	17.8 wk

b.
Inventory turnover	=	(Annual sales)/(Average aggregate inventory value)
	=	$3,500,000 / $1,200,000
	=	2.9 turns/year

6. A part.

a.
Average cycle inventory	=	$Q/2$
	=	(500 units) / 2
	=	250 units
Value of cycle inventory	=	(250 units)($50 + $45)
	=	$23,750

b.
Pipeline inventory	=	[(1976 units/yr)/(52 wk/yr)](5 wk)
	=	190 units
Value of pipeline inventory	=	(190 units)$72.50
	=	$13,775

7. Sterling Inc.

a. Pipeline inventory

$$= (75 \text{ units/wk})(2 \text{ wk})$$
$$= 150 \text{ units}$$

Value of pipeline inventory $= (150 \text{ units})(\$500)$
$$= \$75,000$$

b. Total inventory

$$= \text{cycle} + \text{safety stock} + \text{pipeline}$$
$$= 5[400 / 2 + 2(75) + 150]$$
$$= 2,500 \text{ units for all 5 DCs}$$

Value of total inventory $= (2,500 \text{ units})(\$500/\text{unit})$
$$= \$1,250,000$$

8. McKenzie Industries. First we rank the items from top to bottom on the basis of their dollar usage. Then we partition them into classes.

Item	Usage ($)	Class
13	$70,800	
15	57,900	A: These 4 items (20% of 20) have a
7	44,000	combined dollar usage of $206,100.
3	33,400	This is 71% of the total.
19	19,000	
20	15,500	B: These 6 items (30% of 20) have a
12	10,400	combined dollar usage of $69,000.
1	9,200	This is 24% of the total.
4	8,100	
14	6,800	
18	4,800	
16	3,900	
5	1,100	C: These 10 items (50% of 20) have a
8	900	combined dollar usage of $13,500,
17	700	which is 5% of the total.
10	700	
6	600	
2	400	
11	300	
9	100	

The dollar usage percentages don't exactly match the predictions of ABC analysis. For example, Class A items account for only 71 percent of the total, rather than 80 percent. Nonetheless, the important finding is that ABC analysis did find the "significant few." For the items sampled, particularly close control is needed for items 3, 7, 13, and 15.

9. Ben Dare.

   a.   Average cycle inventory   = $Q/2$

                                            =   150 / 2

                                            =   75 units

       Value of cycle inventory   =   (75 units)($500)

                                            = $37,500

       Pipeline inventory   =   [(2000 units/yr)/(50 wk/yr)](4 wk)

                                            =   160 units

       Value of pipeline inventory   =   (160 units)($300 + $200 / 2)

                                            = $64,000

10. Dunnet.

   a.   Each supplier's performance can be calculated as:

Performance Criterion	Weight	Supplier A	Weighted Rating Supplier B	Supplier C
1. Price	0.2	0.4(0.2) = 0.08	0.7(0.2) = 0.14	0.6(0.2) = 0.12
2. Quality	0.2	0.3(0.2) = 0.06	0.5(0.2) = 0.10	0.8(0.2) = 0.16
3. Delivery	0.2	0.4(0.2) = 0.08	0.5(0.2) = 0.10	0.7(0.2) = 0.14
4. Production facilities & capacity	0.1	0.6(0.1)= 0.06	0.9(0.1) = 0.09	0.6(0.1) = 0.06
5. Warranties & claim policies	0.2	0.7(0.2) = 0.14	0.6(0.2) = 0.12	0.7(0.2) = 0.14
6. Financial position	0.1	0.8(0.1) = <u>0.08</u>	0.9(0.1)= <u>0.09</u>	0.7(0.1) = <u>0.07</u>
Total weighted score		0.50	0.64	0.69

   b.   Suppliers B and C survived the hurdle. Supplier B would receive 48% of the orders and Supplier C would receive 52% of the orders.

   c.   Ben's system provides some assurance that orders are placed with qualified suppliers. The orders are divided among two suppliers, so there is a ready alternative if a strike, fire or other problem prevents one supplier from performing. The system also rewards suppliers with more orders if they improve performance.

11. Acme Bicycle Company.

Part No.	Item	Quantity	Price		Usage	Cumulative	
7	Crank sets	2400	157.55		378120	378120	Class A
8	Derailer Asm.	2400	82.45		197880	576000	
9	Fork Asm.	2400	39.36		94464	670464	
22	Tubing, large	10000	9.25	meters	92500	762964	
11	Head sets	2400	30.85		74040	837004	
14	Paint	800	42.00	gallons	33600	870604	Class B
21	Tires	4800	6.68		32064	902668	
25	Wheel rims	4800	5.25		25200	927868	
19	Sprockets	2400	8.18		19632	947500	
23	Tubing, small	8000	2.15	meters	17216	964716	
16	Seats	2400	5.26		12624	977340	
12	Inner tubes	4800	2.49		11952	989292	
3	Brake Asm.	4800	2.17		10416	999708	
5	Chains	2400	3.70		8880	1008588	Class C
10	Handlebar Asm.	2400	3.49		8376	1016964	
4	Brake levers	4800	1.65		7920	1024884	
17	Shift levers	4800	1.50		7200	1032084	
1	Axles	2400	2.85		6840	1038924	
18	Spokes	200000	0.02		4200	1043124	
6	Control cable	8000	0.25	meters	2000	1045124	
2	Bolts	50000	0.04		1900	1047024	
24	Welding rod	1000	1.25	feet	1251	1048275	
13	Nuts	40000	0.02		760	1049035	
20	Tape	5000	0.12	meters	605	1049640	
15	Rivets	20000	0.00		60	1049700	
					1049700		

12. Suppose that a product.

a. Number of orders
$$= \text{(Annual demand)/(Lot size)}$$
$$= \text{(390 units/yr)/(130 units/lot)}$$
$$= \text{3 lots/yr}$$

b. Pipeline inventory
$$= \text{(3 lots/yr)(130 units/lot)(4 wk)}$$
$$= \text{1560 unit-weeks/yr}$$

c. Average pipeline inventory
$$= \text{(1560 unit-weeks/yr)/(52 weeks/yr)}$$
$$= \text{30 units/wk}$$

d. Average pipeline inventory
$$= \frac{(D/Q)(Q)(L)}{52}$$
$$= (D/52)(L)$$
$$= \text{(Demand per week)(Lead time in weeks)}$$

Therefore, we can estimate the average pipeline inventory by dL.

13. Finished Goods Item A

    a. The bill of materials is shown below.

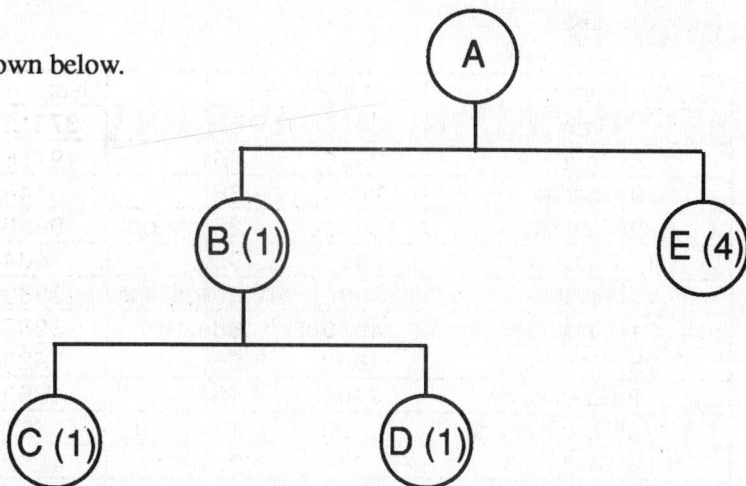

    b. The value of one unit of A upon completion:

        $140 + 4($25) + $20 = $260

        The value of one unit of A as WIP:

        $140 + 4($25) + $20/2 = $250

    c.

Average Inventory (Units)

Item	Cycle	Safety	Anticipation	Pipeline	Total
A	10/2 = 5	10	0	1(10) = 10	25
B	40/2 = 20	0	10	11(10) =110	140
C	40/2 = 20	10	0	1(10) = 10	40
D	80/2 = 40	0	0	5(10) = 50	90
E	160/2= 80	80	0	2(40) = 80	240
ALL	165	100	10	260	535

Average Inventory (Dollars)

Item	Cycle	Safety	Anticipation	Pipeline	Total
A	1,300	2,600	0	2,500	6,400
B	2,800	0	1,400	11,550	15,750
C	600	300	0	300	1,200
D	1,600	0	0	2,000	3,600
E	2,000	2,000	0	2,000	6,000
ALL	8,300	4,900	1,400	18,350	32,950

    d. Aggregate average inventory value = $32,950

$$\frac{\$32,950}{(10 \text{ units/wk})(\$260/\text{unit})} = 12.7 \text{ weeks}$$

$$\text{Inventory turnover} = \frac{(10 \text{ units/week})(\$260/\text{unit})(52 \text{ weeks/year})}{\$32,950}$$

$$= 4.1 \text{ turns / year}$$

    e. The pipeline inventory for item B stands out at $11,550, and the primary target for improvement is reducing its lead time.

Chapter 12

Independent-Demand Inventory

Study Questions

1. An item's lot size has an inverse relationship with the frequency of placing orders for it. If a larger lot size is used, the frequency of orders is decreased.

2. $$EOQ = \sqrt{\frac{2DS}{H}} \qquad R = dL + z\sigma_L$$

    a. As demand, D, increases, the lot size also increases, but it increases in proportion to the square root of the increase in demand. The reorder point should also be increased to satisfy the higher demand during lead time, dL.

    b. When setup costs, S, decrease, the best lot size also decreases, again in proportion to the square root of the decrease in setup costs. However, the reorder point will not be affected by the change in setup costs.

    c. An increase in interest rates in turn increases the cost of holding inventory, H. Therefore, if interest rates increase, the lot size will decrease. Also, safety stock is determined by a trade-off between the costs of holding inventory and the cost of stocking out. If the cost to hold inventory becomes large relative to the cost of stocking out, the safety stock, $z\sigma_L$, and hence the reorder point will decrease.

    d. Forecast errors in H and S may offset each other and cause only small changes in Q. On the other hand, they might make a considerable change in Q if they are moving in the "right" directions. For example, a high forecast for H coupled with a low forecast for S combine to make Q smaller. Errors in D can cause Q to be larger or smaller, depending on the direction of the error. Forecast errors also affect the safety stock needed and thus affect R. Fortunately, the effect of all such forecast errors on Q are dampened, since D, H, and S are under the square root sign in the EOQ formula.

3. It is true that very few actual situations are simple and well behaved enough to comply with the EOQ assumptions. Nevertheless, EOQ is often a reasonable first estimate of average lot size. Also, by adjusting the EOQ model to reflect the various changes in the basic assumptions, a planner can make more realistic decisions in managing inventories. Most of all, the EOQ concept provides valuable information about the structural relationships among the related variables. It provides a means to estimate the directions in which inventories will change in response to various changes in the cost and demand parameters.

4. Setting a service level policy is often a difficult task, and is usually managerially set after consideration of certain factors. The important factors are the probability of not running out of stock in any one inventory cycle, the expected number of stockouts per year, the proportion of annual demand filled from stock, and the proportion of days not out-of-stock. These considerations must be traded off against inventory holding costs.

5. Having accurate inventory records pays off through better customer service and lower inventory costs. Inaccurate records result in faulty replenishment decisions. Inventory record accuracy can be increased by assigning responsibility to specific people for issuing and receiving material, using closed stores, cycle counting, and making logic error checks.

6. Many factors need to be considered before selecting a particular inventory system. A Q system is preferable when quantity discounts and capacity limitations are important factors and less safety stock is desired. A P system is preferable when a continuous review policy is unreasonably expensive and an amalgamation of orders is desirable. A base-stock system is appropriate when very expensive or bulky items are being stocked, and any withdrawal warrants an immediate replenishment. A visual system is appropriate for very low cost items where the holding cost is almost negligible and the demand for the items is steady.

Discussion Question

The short answer is that higher inventories do not provide an advantage in <u>any</u> of the eight competitive priority categories.

The only relevant costs considered in this chapter are ordering costs, holding costs, and stockout costs. In the economic order quantity (EOQ) model, costs of placing replenishment orders trade-off against the costs of holding inventory. Under the assumptions of the EOQ, average inventory is one-half of the order quantity. The number of orders placed per year varies inversely with order quantity. When we consider stockout costs, an additional inventory (safety stock), is held to trade-off costs of poor customer service.

In the Just-in-time (JIT) chapter, we see order quantities (lot sizes) which are much smaller than the "ideal" suggested by the EOQ model. As a result, JIT average inventory is also much lower. Are there some other relevant costs of holding inventory which we have not considered in the EOQ model? If there are, a firm that ignores these costs will make the wrong inventory decisions. These wrong decisions will make the firm less competitive.

Let's examine the relationships between inventory and the eight competitive priorities discussed in Chapter Two. We compare competitors H and L. They are similar in all respects except H maintains much higher inventory than does L.

1) Low cost operations. Costs include materials, scrap, labor and equipment capacity which are wasted when products are defective. When a process drifts out of control, competitor H's large lot sizes tend to result in large quantities of defectives. The EOQ does not consider the cost of defectives, and erroneously assumes that setup costs are constant. Small lots cause frequent setups, but the cost per setup decreases due to the learning curve. Competitor L will enjoy competitive advantages with lower setup, materials, labor, equipment, and inventory holding costs.

2) High-performance design. Superior features, durability, safety and convenience result from improved designs. High inventories force competitor H to choose between scrapping obsolete designs or delaying introduction of product improvements until the old inventory is consumed. In either case, L gains a competitive advantage.

3) Consistent quality. Consistency in conforming to design specifications requires consistency in supplied materials, setups, and processes. Small lots made frequently tend to increase consistency. Again, advantage goes to L.

4) Fast delivery time. Large lots take longer to produce than small lots. A customer will wait less time for competitor L to setup and produce orders made in small batches.

5) On-time delivery. Contrary to expectations, large inventories do not equate to on-time delivery. It's more like, lots of inventory equals lots of chaos. Big lots make big scheduling problems. Big lots get dropped, mishandled, pilfered. Most JIT companies experience dramatic improvement in on-time delivery.

6) Development speed. This response is similar to that given for to high-performance design. Low inventories result in getting new designs to the market more quickly.

7) Customization. JIT companies usually don't claim an advantage in customization. However, large inventories provide no advantage with regard to customization either. It remains unlikely that a customized product will be found in inventory, no matter how large.

8) Volume. JIT (low inventory) companies tend to produce the same quantity of every product every day, but they claim considerable volume flexibility from month to month. On the other hand, a large finished goods inventory can be used to absorb volume fluctuations. We will have to leave further discussion to the JIT chapter, but for our purposes here, JIT is claimed to be a more efficient method of dealing with volume flexibility.

In summary, a case can be made that several competitive priorities are not considered in the EOQ model. It is sometimes difficult to place a dollar value on these competitive advantages, but the advantages invariably goes to the low inventory, small lot-size firm. So if the EQO is too large, what is the "ideal" lot-size? According to JIT philosophy, the "ideal" lot size is one.

Problems

1. Full Court Press, Inc.
   a. Economic order quantity

   $D = 1920 \text{ rolls}$

   $\text{Price} = \$1000 / \text{roll}$

   $H = 30\%(\$1000) = \$300 / \text{roll-year}$

   $S = \$500$

   $$EOQ = \sqrt{\frac{2DS}{H}} = \sqrt{\frac{2(1920 \text{ rolls} / \text{year})(\$500)}{\$300 / \text{roll-year}}}$$

   $$= \sqrt{6400 \text{ square rolls}} = 80 \text{ rolls}$$

   b. Time between orders

   $$\frac{Q}{D} = \frac{80}{1920} = 0.04167 \text{ years or } 0.5 \text{ months}$$

2. Es Oh Si Que Es?
   a.

   $d = 200 \text{ tapes} / \text{month}$

   $D = 2400 \text{ tapes} / \text{year}$

   $H = \$0.24$

   $S = \$50$

   $$EOQ = \sqrt{\frac{2DS}{H}} = \sqrt{\frac{2(2400)(\$50)}{\$0.24}}$$

   $$= \sqrt{1,000,000} = 1000 \text{ tapes}$$

   b. Time between orders

   $$\frac{Q}{D} = \frac{1000}{2400} = 0.4167 \text{ years or } 5 \text{ months}$$

3. Dandy Doughnuts. Both the demand and holding costs are stated on the basis of one week. Therefore the units of time will cancel in the EOQ equation. It is not necessary to convert demand and holding costs to an annual basis. The same answer will result if both numerator and denominator are multiplied by 52 weeks/year.

$$demand = 28 \text{ dozen doughnuts / week}$$
$$S = \$1.75$$
$$H = \$0.20 \text{ / dozen doughnuts / week}$$
$$EOQ = \sqrt{\frac{2DS}{H}} = \sqrt{\frac{2(28 \text{ dozen doughnuts / week})(\$1.75)}{\$0.20 \text{ / dozen doughnuts / week}}}$$
$$= \sqrt{490 \text{ dozen}^2 \text{ doughnuts}^2}$$
$$= 22.136 \text{ or about 22 dozen doughnuts per order}$$

4. Lou Zephyr, Purgatory Schools.
   a. Economic order quantity.

   $$d = 225 \text{ cakes / month}$$
   $$D = 2700 \text{ cakes / year}$$
   $$H = \$1.50$$
   $$S = \$123.21$$
   $$EOQ = \sqrt{\frac{2DS}{H}} = \sqrt{\frac{2(2700)(\$123.21)}{\$1.50}}$$
   $$= \sqrt{443,556}$$
   $$= 666 \text{ devil's food cakes } \ominus$$

   b. Reorder point

   R = demand during protection interval + safety stock

   Demand during protection interval = $d\,L$ = 225 * 2 = 450 cakes

   Safety stock = $z\sigma_L$

   When the desired cycle-service level is 90%, $z = 1.28$.

   $$\sigma_L = \sigma_t \sqrt{L}$$
   $$= 35.36\sqrt{2}$$
   $$= 50$$

   Safety stock = 1.28 * 50 = 64

   R = 450 + 64 = 514

   c. Inventory Position $\quad = OH + SR - BO$
   $$= 100 + 666 - 112 = 654$$

   Even though back orders exceed on-hand inventory, inventory position is above the reorder point. Therefore Lou should do nothing. He could "pray" that the replenishment order from B. Elsie Bubba Co. arrives quickly. But it is doubtful whether such prayers would be answered.

5. Ophthalmologist's office. The problem statement ignores the fairly important notion that contacts have different specifications for different prescriptions. This could be worked around by stating that the demand for + 4.00 (diopter?) contacts is 90 per week.

a. Economic order quantity

$$d = 90 / \text{week}$$

$$D = 4{,}680$$

$$S = \$54$$

$$\text{Price} = \$11.70$$

$$H = 27\%(\$11.70) = \$3.159$$

$$EOQ = \sqrt{\frac{2DS}{H}} = \sqrt{\frac{2(4680)(54)}{3.159}}$$

$$= \sqrt{160{,}000} = 400 \text{ pairs}$$

Time between orders, in weeks

$$\frac{Q}{D} = \frac{400}{4680} = 0.08547 \text{ years} = 4.44 \text{ weeks}$$

b. Reorder point, R

R = demand during protection interval + safety stock

Demand during protection interval = $d\,L$ = 90 * 3 = 270 pairs

Safety stock = $z\sigma_L$

When the desired cycle-service level is 80%, $z = 0.84$.

$$\sigma_L = \sigma_t \sqrt{L}$$

$$= 15\sqrt{3} = 26$$

Safety stock = 0.84 * 26 = 21.82 or about 22 pairs

R = 270 + 22 = 292

c. Initial Inventory Position = $OH + SR - BO$ = 320 + 0 − 0

320 − 10 = 310.

Since inventory position remains above 292, it is not yet time to place an order.

d. Annual holding cost   Annual ordering cost

$$\frac{Q}{2}H = \frac{500}{2}(27\%)(\$11.70) \qquad \frac{D}{Q}S = \frac{4680}{500}\$54$$

$$= \$789.75 \qquad\qquad\qquad\qquad = \$505.44$$

At the EOQ, these two costs are equal. When Q = 500, the annual holding cost is larger than the ordering cost, therefore Q is too large. Total costs are $789.75 + $505.44 = $1,295.19

e. Annual holding cost   Annual ordering cost

$$\frac{Q}{2}H = \frac{400}{2}(27\%)(\$11.70) \qquad \frac{D}{Q}S = \frac{4680}{400}\$54$$

$$= \$631.80 \qquad\qquad\qquad\qquad = \$631.80$$

Total costs at EOQ: = $1,263.60, which is $31.59 less than when order quantity is 500 pairs.

6. Ophthalmologist's office, revisited.
   a. If the demand is only 60 pairs per week, the correct *EOQ* is:

   $D = (60 \text{ units/wk})(52 \text{ wk/yr}) = 3{,}120 \text{ pairs}$

   $$EOQ = \sqrt{\frac{2DS}{H}} = \sqrt{\frac{2(3120)(54)}{3.159}} = 326.6 \text{ or } 327 \text{ pairs}$$

   If the demand is incorrectly estimated at 90 pairs, the *EOQ* would be incorrectly calculated (from problem 5) as 400 pairs:

   The total cost, working with the actual demand, is:

   $$C = \frac{Q}{2}H + \frac{D}{Q}S$$

   $$C_{327} = \frac{327}{2}3.159 + \frac{3120}{327}54$$

   $$C_{327} = \$516.50 + \$515.23$$

   $$C_{327} = \$1031.73$$

   $$C_{400} = \frac{400}{2}3.159 + \frac{3120}{400}54$$

   $$C_{400} = \$631.80 + \$421.20$$

   $$C_{400} = \$1053$$

   We can see clearly now that the cost penalty of the ophthalmologist's difficulty in foreseeing demand for contacts is $21.27 ($1053.00 − $1031.73).

   b. If $S = \$6$, and $D = 60 \times 52 = 3120$ the correct *EOQ* is:

   $$EOQ = \sqrt{\frac{2DS}{H}} = \sqrt{\frac{2(3120)(6)}{3.159}} = 108.9 \text{ or } 109 \text{ pairs}$$

   The total cost, working with the actual ordering cost, is

   $$C = \frac{Q}{2}H + \frac{D}{Q}S$$

   $$C_{109} = \frac{109}{2}3.159 + \frac{3120}{109}6$$

   $$C_{109} = \$172.17 + \$171.74$$

   $$C_{109} = \$343.91$$

   $$C_{327} = \frac{327}{2}3.159 + \frac{3120}{327}6$$

   $$C_{327} = \$516.50 + \$57.25$$

   $$C_{327} = \$573.74$$

   · If the reduced ordering cost continues to be unseen, the cost penalty for not updating the *EOQ* is (573.74 − 343.91) = $229.83.

7. A Q system (also known as a reorder point system).

$$d = 200 \ \frac{\text{gizmos}}{\text{week}}$$

$$\sigma_t = 15 \text{ gizmos}$$

  a. Standard deviation of demand during the protection interval:

$$\sigma_L = \sigma_t \sqrt{L}$$

$$\sigma_L = 15\sqrt{4} = 30 \text{ gizmos}$$

  b. Average demand during the protection interval:

$$dL = 200 \frac{\text{gizmos}}{\text{week}} (4 \text{ weeks}) = 800 \text{ gizmos}$$

  c. Reorder point

R = demand during protection interval + safety stock

Safety stock = $z\sigma_L$

When the desired cycle-service level is 99%, $z = 2.33$.

Safety stock = 2.33 * 30 = 69.9 or about 70 gizmos

$R = 800 + 70 = 870$

8. A continuous review system (also known as a reorder point system). Find cycle-service level, given:

$$L = 3 \text{ weeks}$$

$$dL = 450 \text{ widgets}$$

$$\sigma_t = 15 \text{ widgets}$$

$$R = 489 \text{ widgets}$$

Safety stock = $R - dL = 489 - 450 = 39$ widgets

Safety stock = $z\sigma_L = 39$ widgets

$$\sigma_L = \sigma_t \sqrt{L} = 15\sqrt{3} = 26 \text{ widgets}$$

$$z(26 \text{ widgets}) = 39 \text{ widgets}$$

$$z = \frac{39 \text{ widgets}}{26 \text{ widgets}} = 1.50$$

When $z = 1.5$, cycle-service level is 93.32%.

9. A perpetual system (also known as a reorder point system). Find the safety stock reduction when lead time is reduced from 5 weeks to 1 week, given:

Standard deviation of demand during the (5 week) protection interval is 85 dohickies. Desired cycle service level is 99% (therefore $z = 2.33$).

Safety stock required for five-week protection interval

Safety stock = $z\sigma_L = 2.33(85) = 198$ dohickies

Safety stock required for one-week protection interval

$$\sigma_L = \sigma_t \sqrt{L} = 85 \text{ dohickies}$$

$$\sigma_t = \frac{85}{\sqrt{5}} = 38 \text{ dohickies}$$

Safety stock = $z\sigma_1 = 2.33(38) = 88.54$ or 89 dohickies

10. A two-bin system.

> "The two-bin system is really a Q system, with the normal level in the second bin being the reorder point R."

Find cycle-service level, given:

$L = 2$ weeks

$d = 53$ whatchamacallits / week

$\sigma_t = 5$ whatchamacallits

$R = 120$ whatchamacallits

Safety stock $= R - dL = 120 - 106 = 14$ whatchamacallits

Safety stock $= z\sigma_L = 14$ whatchamacallits

$\sigma_L = \sigma_t\sqrt{L} = 5\sqrt{2} = 7.07$ or 7 whatchamacallits

$z(7) = 14$

$z = 2$

When $z = 2$, the cycle-service level is 97.72%.

11. A periodic review system (P system).
    $L = 3$ weeks
    $P = 2$ weeks
    $d = 216.4$ doodads/week
    $\sigma_t = 68$ doodads

    a. Find standard deviation of demand during the protection interval $(P + L)$.

    $$\sigma_{P+L} = \sigma_t\sqrt{P+L}$$
    $$\sigma_{P+L} = 68\sqrt{2+3} = 152 \text{ doodads}$$

    b. Find average demand during the protection interval.
       $d(P + L) = 216.4$ doodads/week(5 weeks) $= 1082$ doodads

    c. Find target inventory T resulting in 95% cycle-service level.
       T = average demand during the protection interval (part b) + Safety stock
       $T = 1082 +$ Safety stock
       For a cycle-service level of 95%, $z = 1.645$.

       Safety stock $= z\sigma_{P+L} = 1.645(152) = 250$ doodads
       $T = 1082 + 250 = 1,332$ doodads

12. A P system (also known as a periodic review system). Find cycle-service level, given"

    $L = 2$ weeks

    $P = 1$ week

    $d(P + L) = 218$ gadgets

    $\sigma_{P+L} = 40$ gadgets

    $T = 300$ gadgets

    T = Average demand during protection interval + Safety stock
    $T = 218 + z(40) = 300$
    $z = (300 - 218)/40 = 2.05$
    When $z = 2.05$, cycle-service level is 97.98 or about 98%.

13. Potpourri. Optional replenishment system (much like a P system).

   $P = 2$ weeks

   $L = 1$ week

   If Potpourri reduces the review period to 1 week, then the protection interval decreases from 3 weeks to 2 weeks. Safety stock is proportional to the square root of the protection interval.

   $$\text{Percent change} = \frac{\sqrt{3} - \sqrt{2}}{\sqrt{3}}(100\%) = 18.35034\%$$

   If the current safety stock investment is $100,000, reducing the review period by one week will result in a savings of $100,000 (18.35034%) = $18,350.34.

14. Ophthalmologist's office with a P system.

   a. Referring to Reveiw Problem 5, the EOQ is 400 pairs. When the demand rate is 15 per day, the average time between orders is (400/15) = 26.67 or about 27 days. The lead time is 3 weeks x 6 days per week = 18 days. If the review period is set equal to the EOQ's average time between orders (27 days) then the protection interval $(P + L) = (27 + 18) = 45$ days.

   For an 80% cycle-service level

   $$z = 0.84$$
   $$\sigma_{P+L} = \sigma_t \sqrt{P + L}$$
   $$\sigma_{P+L} = 6.124\sqrt{45} = 41.08$$
   $$\text{Safety stock} = z\sigma_{P+L} = 0.84(41.08) = 34.51 \text{ or } 35 \text{ pairs}$$

   T = Average demand during the protection interval + Safety stock

   T = (15*45) + 35 = 710

   b. In problem 5, the Q system required a safety stock of 22 pairs to achieve an 80% cycle-service level. Therefore, the P system requires a safety stock which is larger by (35 – 22) = 13 pairs.

   c. From Review Problem 5, inventory position, $IP = 310$.

   The amount to reorder is $T - IP = 710 - 310 = 400$.

15. Continuous review system.

   a. Economic order quantity.

   $$EOQ = \sqrt{\frac{2DS}{H}} = \sqrt{\frac{2(20000)(40)}{2}} = 894.4 \text{ or } 894 \text{ units}$$

   Time between orders (TBO) = Q/D = 894/20000 = 0.0447 years = 2.32 weeks

   b. Weekly demand = 20,000 / 52 = 385 units

   For a 95 percent cycle-service level, $z = 1.645$

   $$\text{Safety stock} = z\sigma_L = z\sigma_t\sqrt{L}$$
   $$= 1.645(100)\sqrt{2}$$
   $$= 232.6 \text{ or } 233 \text{ units}$$

   Now solve for R, as

   $R = dL + \text{Safety stock} = 385(2) + 233 = 1003$ units

c. i. Annual holding cost of cycle inventory

$$\frac{Q}{2}H = \frac{894}{2}(2) = \$894$$

ii. Annual ordering cost

$$\frac{D}{Q}S = \frac{20,000}{894}\$40 = \$894.85$$

d. With the 15-unit withdrawal, *IP* drops from 1040 to 1025 units. Because this level is above the reorder point (1025 > 1003), a new order is not placed.

16. Periodic review system.

a. From problem 15,

$$EOQ = \sqrt{\frac{2DS}{H}} = \sqrt{\frac{2(20000)(40)}{2}} = 894.4 \text{ or } 894 \text{ units}$$

Number of orders per year = *D/Q* = 20,000/894 = 22.4 orders per year.

$$P = \frac{EOQ}{D} = \frac{894}{20,000} = .0447 \text{ years} \times 52 \text{ weeks / year } = 2.3244 \text{ weeks}$$

P is rounded to two weeks.

b. For a 95% cycle-service level, *z* = 1.645. Therefore
Safety stock = $z\sigma_{P+L}$

$$\sigma_{P+L} = \sigma_t\sqrt{P+L}$$

$$\sigma_{P+L} = 100\sqrt{2+2} = 200 \text{ units}$$

Safety stock = 1.645(200) = 329 units
T = Average demand during the protection interval + Safety stock

T = (385 * 4) + 329 = 1869 units

c. In Problem 15, with a *Q* system the safety stock is 233 units.
Therefore, (329 − 233) = 96 more units of safety stock are needed.

17. Continuous review system.

a. Economic order quantity.

$$EOQ = \sqrt{\frac{2DS}{H}} = \sqrt{\frac{2(64)(52)(50)}{13}} = 160 \text{ units}$$

b. Safety stock. When cycle-service level is 88%, *z* = 1.175.

$$\sigma_L = \sigma_t\sqrt{L} = 12\sqrt{2} = 17 \text{ units}$$

Safety stock $= z\sigma_L = 1.175(17) = 20 \text{ units}$

c. Reorder point

$$R = dL + \text{Safety stock}$$

$$= 64(2) + 20$$

$$= 148 \text{ units}$$

d. If *Q* = 200 and *R* = 180, average inventory investment is higher than necessary to achieve an 88% cycle-service level. The larger order quantity increases average cycle stock by 20 units, and the higher reorder point increases safety stock by 32 units.

18. Periodic review system.

    a. From problem 17, EOQ = 160

$$P = \frac{EOQ}{d} = \frac{160}{64 \text{ / week}} = 2.5 \text{ weeks}$$

        P is rounded to three weeks.

    b. For a 88% cycle-service level, $z = 1.175$. Therefore

        Safety stock $= z\sigma_{P+L}$

        $\sigma_{P+L} = \sigma_t \sqrt{P+L}$

        $\sigma_{P+L} = 12\sqrt{3+2} = 26.8$ or 27 units

        Safety stock $= 1.175(27) = 32$ units

19. Wood County Hostpital

    a. $D = (500 \text{ boxes/wk})(52 \text{ wk/yr}) = 26{,}000 \text{ boxes}$

        $H = (0.15)(\$70/\text{box}) = \$10.50/\text{box}$

$$EOQ = \sqrt{\frac{2DS}{H}} = \sqrt{\frac{2(26{,}000)(60)}{10.50}} = 545.1 \text{ or } 545 \text{ boxes}$$

$$C = \frac{Q}{2}H + \frac{D}{Q}S$$

$$C_{900} = \frac{900}{2}\$10.50 + \frac{26{,}000}{900}\$60.00 = \$6{,}458.33$$

$$C_{545} = \frac{545}{2}\$10.50 + \frac{26{,}000}{545}\$60.00 = \$5{,}723.64$$

        The savings would be ($6,458.33 – $5,723.64) = $734.69.

    b. When the cycle-service level is 97%, $z = 1.88$. Therefore,

        $\sigma_L = \sigma_t \sqrt{L}$

        $\sigma_L = 100\sqrt{0.5} = 70.7$ or 71 boxes

        Safety stock $= z\sigma_L = 1.88(70.7) = 132.9$ or 133 boxes

        $R = dL +$ Safety stock $= 500(0.5) + 133 = 383$ boxes

    c. In a periodic review system, find target inventory T, given:

        $P = 2$ weeks

        $L = 0.5$ weeks

        Safety stock $= z\sigma_{P+L}$

        $\sigma_{P+L} = \sigma_t \sqrt{P+L}$

        $\sigma_{P+L} = 100\sqrt{2+0.5} = 158.1$ units

        Safety stock $= 1.88(158.1) = 297$ units

        $T =$ Average demand during the protection interval + Safety stock

        $T = 500(2.5) + 297$

        $T = 1547$ units

20. Golf specialty wholesaler.

  a. Periodic Review System.

$$EOQ = \sqrt{\frac{2DS}{H}} = \sqrt{\frac{2(1000)(20)}{2}} = 141.4 \text{ or about 142 1-irons}$$

$$P = \frac{EOQ}{D} = \frac{142}{1000} = 0.142 \text{ years} = 7.1 \text{ or 7 weeks}$$

When cycle-service level is 85%, $z = 1.04$.

Weekly demand is (1,000 units/yr)/(50 wk/yr) = 20 units/wk

$L = 3$ weeks

$$R = d(P+L) + z\sigma_{P+L}\sqrt{P+L}$$
$$= 20(10) + 1.04(3)\sqrt{10}$$
$$= 209.9 \text{ or about 210 1-irons}$$

  b. Continuous Review System

$$dL = 20 \times 3 = 60$$
$$SS = z\sigma_L = (1.04)(3)\sqrt{3} = 5.4$$
$$R = 60 + 5.4 = 65.4 \text{ or about 65 1-irons}$$

21. Clone Computer Mart

  a. R should be 60 because the probability that it is enough to avoid a stockout is
      0.80 (0.20 + 0.40 + 0.20).

  b. The (expected) average demand during the protection interval is computed first as:
      = 20(0.20) + 40(0.40) + 60(0.20) + 80(0.10) + 100(0.10)
      = 50 units

      Now compute safety stock:

      R = Average demand during the protection interval + Safety stock

      60 = 50 + Safety stock

      Safety stock = 10 units

22. Club hardware.

  a. R should be 100 because a stockout occurs only if the demand during lead time is 125 units,
      which has a probability of 0.10.

  b. The (expected) average demand during the protection interval is computed first as:
      = 0(0.20) + 25(0.20) + 50(0.20) + 75(0.20) + 100(0.10) + 125(0.10)
      = 52.5 units

      Now compute safety stock:

      R = Average demand during the protection interval + Safety stock

      100 = 52.5 + Safety stock

      Safety stock = 47.5 units

23. The simulation results with $Q = 40$ and $R = 15$ are:

Day	Beginning Inventory	Open Orders Received	Daily Demand	Ending Inventory	Inventory Position	Amount Ordered
1	19	-	5	14	14	40
2	14	-	3	11	51	-
3	11	-	4	7	47	-
4	7	40	1	46	46	-
5	46	-	10	36	36	-
6	36	-	9	27	27	-
7	27	-	7	20	20	-
8	20	-	4	16	16	-
9	16	-	2	14	14	40
10	14	-	7	7	47	-
11	7	-	3	4	44	-
12	4	40	6	38	38	-
13	38	-	10	28	28	-
14	28	-	0	28	28	-
15	28	-	5	23	23	-
16	23	-	10	13	13	40
17	13	-	4	9	49	-
18	9	-	7	2	42	-
	TOTAL			343		

a. The average ending inventory is:

$$\frac{343}{18} = 19.05 \text{ or } 19 \text{ units}$$

b. No stockouts occurred during any of the three cycles.

24. The simulation results with $P = 8$ days and $T = 55$ units are:[a]

Day	Beginning Inventory	Open Orders Received	Daily Demand	Ending Inventory	Inventory Position	Amount Ordered
1	19	-	5	14	14	41
2	14	-	3	11	52	-
3	11	-	4	7	48	-
4	7	41	1	47	47	-
5	47	-	10	37	37	-
6	37	-	9	28	28	-
7	28	-	7	21	21	-
8	21	-	4	17	17	-
9	17	-	2	15	15	40
10	15	-	7	8	48	-
11	8	-	3	5	45	-
12	5	40	6	39	39	-
13	39	-	10	29	29	-
14	29	-	0	29	29	-
15	29	-	5	24	24	-
16	24	-	10	14	14	-
17	14	-	4	10	10	45
18	10	-	7	3	48	-
	TOTAL			358		

a. The average ending inventory is:

$$\frac{358}{18} = 19.88 \text{ or } 20 \text{ units}$$

b. No stockouts occurred yet, although there is a good chance that it will happen on day 19.

25. Simulation of Q system for hand drills ($Q = 440$ drills and $R = 373$ drills)

Day	Beginning Inventory	Open Orders Received	Daily Demand	Ending Inventory	Inventory Position	Amount Ordered
Monday	40	440	143	337	337	440
Tuesday	337	—	82	255	695	—
Wednesday	255	—	103	152	592	—
Thursday	152	—	127	25	465	—
Friday	25	440	85	380	380	—
Monday	380	—	60	320	320	440
Tuesday	320	—	94	226	666	—
Wednesday	226	—	87	139	579	—
Thursday	139	—	102	37	459	—
Friday	37	440	42	435	435	—
Monday	435	—	123	312	312	440
Tuesday	312	—	140	172	612	—
Wednesday	172	—	85	87	527	—
Thursday	87	—	67	20	460	—
Friday	20	440	83	377	377	—
Monday	377	—	123	254	254	440
Tuesday	254	—	108	146	586	—
Wednesday	146	—	88	58	498	—
Thursday	58	—	120	(62)	378	—
Friday	–60	440	138	442	240	440
Monday	240	—	74	166	606	—

Total = 4,278

a. The average ending inventory is:

$$\frac{4278}{21} = 203.7 \text{ or } 204 \text{ drills}$$

b. Five new orders are placed. One stockout occurs (on Thursday of the fourth week). This short simulation indicates a service level of about 80% instead of the 92% expected from the solution to Solved Problem 3. However, a more lengthy similulation ought to approximate the theoretical service level.

26. P = 4. T = 811

Day	Beginning Inventory	Open Orders Received	Daily Demand	Ending Inventory	Inventory Position	Amount Ordered
Monday	40	440	143	337	337	474
Tuesday	337	—	82	255	729	—
Wednesday	255	—	103	152	626	—
Thursday	152	—	127	25	526	—
Friday	25	474	85	414	414	397
Monday	414	—	60	354	751	—
Tuesday	354	—	94	260	657	—
Wednesday	260	—	87	173	570	—
Thursday	173	397	102	468	468	343
Friday	468	—	42	426	769	—
Monday	426	—	123	303	646	—
Tuesday	303	—	140	163	506	—
Wednesday	163	343	85	421	421	390
Thursday	421	—	67	354	744	—
Friday	354	—	83	271	661	—
Monday	271	—	123	148	538	—
Tuesday	148	390	108	430	430	381
Wednesday	430	—	88	342	723	—
Thursday	342	—	120	222	603	—
Friday	222	—	138	84	465	—
Monday	84	381	74	391	391	420

Total = 5,993

a. The average ending inventory is:

$$\frac{5993}{21} = 285.4 \text{ or } 285 \text{ drills}$$

b. Six new orders are placed. Average inventory is higher. No stockouts occurred.

27. Lisa Rankin.

Let   A = fraction of material A used in a gallon of finished product
      B = fraction of material B used in a gallon of finished product
      C = fraction of material C used in a gallon of finished product

The linear programming model is formulated as:

Minimize: $0.6A + 0.4B + 0.5C$

Subject to:
$$200A + 180B + 280C \geq 220$$
$$4A + 3B + 10C \leq 6$$
$$20A + 10B + 8C \geq 12$$
$$A + B + C = 1$$
$$A, B, C \geq 0$$

The optimal solution is:
$A = 0.269$ $B = 0.385$ $C = 0.346$

Supplement H

Special Inventory Models

Study Questions

1. Looking at the second square root term in the ELS equation:

$$ELS = \sqrt{\frac{2DS}{H}} \sqrt{\frac{p}{p-d}}$$

we see that as demand rate d approaches production rate p, the denominator approaches zero. Dividing by zero results in an infinite lot size. This is rational. If the demand rate matches or exceeds the production rate, we would make one setup, then run that product continuously.

2. The maximum amount in inventory is:

$$I_{MAX} = Q\left(\frac{p-d}{p}\right) \text{ or } Q\left(1-\frac{d}{p}\right)$$

For example, say we set out to make a lot size of 12 units ($Q = 12$), the production rate is 3 units ($p = 3$), and the demand rate is one unit per day ($d = 1$).

Then the production run time would be (12/3) = 4 days. After the first day, we would have produced three units and consumed one, leaving two inventory. After the second, third, and fourth days, the inventory would be four, six, and eight units, respectively. The maximum inventory when the production run ends is not twelve units, but instead is eight units.

$$Q\left(\frac{p-d}{p}\right) = 12\left(\frac{3-1}{3}\right) = 8$$

After that, during the fifth through twelfth days, inventory decreases at the demand rate of one unit per day, until after the twelfth day, inventory is zero. A new production run begins, and the cycle is repeated.

What is the average inventory for the cycle?
$$\frac{2+4+6+8+7+6+5+4+3+2+1+0}{12} = 4$$

In other words, average inventory is equal to one-half of maximum inventory.

$$I_{AVG} = \frac{I_{MAX}}{2} = \frac{Q}{2}\left(\frac{p}{p-d}\right)$$

3. Quantity discounts can lead to the simultaneous reduction of all three relevant costs. Price reductions directly reduce the cost of purchased materials. In order to obtain the discount, one must buy a quantity, which by coincidence or not, is usually larger than the EOQ. Orders are placed less frequently, which reduces annual order costs. Finally if holding costs are expressed as a percentage of price, and the discount reduces unit price substantially, then annual holding costs could decrease even though more units are held in inventory on the average.

4. Big Six Corporation. If purchasing agents are evaluated on the basis of purchase price variance, agents will always buy larger quantities in order to obtain price discounts. That reduces the price per unit, and generates favorable performance evaluations. While this practice makes the purchasing department look good, there is a good chance the larger purchases will consume cash and lead to bankruptcy. Larger purchases increase cycle inventory, and will probably increase holding costs. As we will see in the Just-in-Time (JIT) chapter, larger lots usually retard quality improvement. As long as there is plenty of material to work with (large lots), and some of it is okay, then we tend not to be concerned about the root cause of defects. Since this performance measure rewards purchasing decisions that consume cash, increase costs, and decrease quality, Big Six will be at a competitive disadvantage.

5. Textbooks, since they depend on professor's adoption decisions and regularly become obsolete, are good candidates for one-period inventory decisions. There is a high risk that inventory left over after the first round of midterm exams will become obsolete. Most food items sold at sporting events are stocked on a one-period basis. But just to be sure, never buy a hot dog during the first quarter of the homecoming game. Items that do not require one-period decisions have long-term demand, moderate to high price, low risk of obsolescence and low storage costs. One example is the game ball. Others include team clothing, pennants, and autographed paraphernalia. But even here the "period" may simply be measured in seasons rather than in games. The team or school logo or mascot could change from season to season. One year a Bull's jersey with the number 23 may be very popular. Another year it might be number 45.

Problems

1. Big Blue (laser toner) Inc.

$$ELS = \sqrt{\frac{2DS}{H}} \sqrt{\frac{p}{p-d}}$$

$$= \sqrt{\frac{2(625)(52)(150)}{.3(130)}} \sqrt{\frac{1736}{1736-625}}$$

$$= \sqrt{250,000} \sqrt{1.5626} = (500)(1.25)$$

$$= 625 \text{ toner cartridges}$$

2. Monitor Lizards.

$$ELS = \sqrt{\frac{2DS}{H}} \sqrt{\frac{p}{p-d}}$$

$$= \sqrt{\frac{2(3,000)(12)(8,000)}{.25(1,200)}} \sqrt{\frac{23,275}{23,275-3,000}}$$

$$= \sqrt{1,920,000} \sqrt{1.148} = (1,385.6)(1.071)$$

$$= 1,484.6 \text{ or } 1485 \text{ lizards}$$

3. Sud's Bottling Company.

$$ELS = \sqrt{\frac{2DS}{H}} \sqrt{\frac{p}{p-d}}$$

$$= \sqrt{\frac{2(400)(52)(1000)}{.45(10.40)}} \sqrt{\frac{2000}{2000-400}}$$

$$= \sqrt{8,888,888.9} \sqrt{1.25} = (2,981.4)(1.118)$$

$$= 3333 \text{ cases}$$

4. Bucks Grande major-league baseball.

Step 1: Calculate the *EOQ* at the lowest price ($48.50):

$$EOQ = \sqrt{\frac{2DS}{H}} = \sqrt{\frac{2(4)(52)(70)}{.38(48.50)}} = 39.75 \text{ or } 40 \text{ bats}$$

This solution is infeasible. We can not buy 40 bats at a price of $48.50 each. Therefore we calculate the *EOQ* at the next lowest price ($51.00):

$$EOQ = \sqrt{\frac{2DS}{H}} = \sqrt{\frac{2(4)(52)(70)}{.38(51.00)}} = 38.76 \text{ or } 39 \text{ bats}$$

This solution is feasible.

Step 2: Calculate total costs at the feasible *EOQ* and at higher discount quantities:

$$C = \frac{Q}{2}H + \frac{D}{Q}S + PD$$

$$C_{39} = \frac{39}{2}\left[.38(\$51.00)\right] + \frac{(4)(52)}{39}\$70 + \$51.00(4)(52)$$

$$C_{39} = \$377.91 + \$373.33 + \$10,608$$

$$C_{39} = \$11,359.24$$

$$C_{144} = \frac{144}{2}\left[.38(\$48.50)\right] + \frac{(4)(52)}{144}\$70 + \$48.50(4)(52)$$

$$C_{144} = \$1,326.96 + \$101.11 + \$10,088$$

$$C_{144} = \$11,516.07$$

a. Is is less costly on an annual basis to buy 39 bats at a time.

b. The total annual costs associated with buying 39 bats at a time is $11,359.24.

c. Yes, if the price is reduced to $45 at an order quantity of 180 bats:

$$C_{180} = \frac{180}{2}\left[.38(\$45.00)\right] + \frac{(4)(52)}{180}(\$70) + \$45.00(4)(52)$$

$$C_{180} = \$1,539 + \$80.88 + \$9,360$$

$$C_{180} = \$10,979.88$$

Therefore, Bucks Grande should purchase 180 bats at a time.

5. Pfisher. The *EOQ* at the lowest price ($49.00) remains infeasible and the *EOQ* at the next lowest price ($50.25) remains at 79 packages. The total annual cost of buying disposable surgical packages also remains at $25,416.44 per year. Now we calculate the annual cost associated with ordering 500 at a time:

$$C_{500} = \frac{500}{2}(.2 \times \$47.80) + \frac{490}{500}\$64 + \$47.80(490)$$

$$C_{500} = \$2,390 + \$62.72 + \$23,422$$

$$C_{500} = \$25,874.72$$

The quantity discount is still not sufficient to cause Pfisher to buy the larger order quantity.

6. Plumbing supply.

Step 1: Calculate the *EOQ* at the lowest price ($1.20):

$$EOQ = \sqrt{\frac{2DS}{H}} = \sqrt{\frac{2(6,000)(10)}{.2(1.20)}} = 707.1 \text{ or } 707$$

This solution is feasible. We should buy 707 valves at a price of $1.20 each.

7. Mac-In-The Box, Inc.

Step 1: Calculate the *EOQ* at the lowest price ($594):

$$EOQ = \sqrt{\frac{2DS}{H}} = \sqrt{\frac{2(1,200)(400)}{.16(594)}} = 100.5 \text{ or } 101 \text{ scanners}$$

This solution is infeasible. We can not buy 101 scanners at a price of $594 each. Therefore we calculate the *EOQ* at the next lowest price ($600):

$$EOQ = \sqrt{\frac{2DS}{H}} = \sqrt{\frac{2(1,200)(400)}{.16(600)}} = 100 \text{ scanners}$$

This solution is feasible.

Step 2: Calculate total costs at the feasible *EOQ* and at higher discount quantities:

$$C = \frac{Q}{2}H + \frac{D}{Q}S + PD$$

$$C_{100} = \frac{100}{2}\left[.16(\$600)\right] + \frac{(1200)}{100}\$400 + \$600(1200)$$

$$C_{100} = \$4,800 + \$4,800 + \$720,000$$

$$C_{100} = \$729,600$$

$$C_{144} = \frac{144}{2}\left[.16(\$594)\right] + \frac{(1,200)}{144}\$400 + \$594(1,200)$$

$$C_{144} = \$6,842.88 + \$3,333.33 + \$712,800$$

$$C_{144} = \$722,976.21$$

The order quantity should be 144 scanners.

8. Order quantity for "an item".

Step 1: Calculate the *EOQ* at the lowest price ($2.00):

$$EOQ = \sqrt{\frac{2DS}{H}} = \sqrt{\frac{2(2,000)(20)}{.2(2.00)}} = 447.2 \text{ or } 447 \text{ units}$$

This solution is infeasible. We can not buy 447 units at a price of $2.00 each. Therefore we calculate the *EOQ* at the next lowest price ($2.25):

$$EOQ = \sqrt{\frac{2DS}{H}} = \sqrt{\frac{2(2,000)(20)}{.2(2.25)}} = 421.6 \text{ or } 422 \text{ units}$$

This solution is feasible.

Step 2: Calculate total costs at the feasible *EOQ* and at higher discount quantities:

$$C = \frac{Q}{2}H + \frac{D}{Q}S + PD$$

$$C_{422} = \frac{422}{2}\left[.2(\$2.25)\right] + \frac{(2,000)}{422}\$20 + \$2.25(2,000)$$

$$C_{422} = \$94.95 + \$94.79 + \$4,500.00$$

$$C_{422} = \$4,689.74$$

$$C_{1000} = \frac{1,000}{2}\left[.2(\$2.00)\right] + \frac{(2,000)}{1,000}\$20 + \$2.00(2,000)$$

$$C_{1000} = \$200.00 + \$40.00 + \$4,000$$

$$C_{1000} = \$4,240.00$$

The order quantity should be 1,000 units.

9. Investment Clothiers.

The following payoff matrix was constructed, where

$$\text{Payoff} = \begin{cases} 40Q & \text{if } Q \leq D \\ 40D - 10(Q-D) & \text{if } Q > D \end{cases}$$

Order Quantity Q	Demand, D			
	100	200	300	400
100	$4,000	$4,000	$4,000	$4,000
200	$3,000	$8,000	$8,000	$8,000
300	$2,000	$7,000	$12,000	$12,000
400	$1,000	$6,000	$11,000	$16,000

Now we can compute the expected payoff for each row:

Order Quantity	Expected Payoff		
100	0.1(4,000) + 0.4(4,000) + 0.4(4,000) + 0.1 (4,000)	=	$4,000
200	0.1(3,000) + 0.4(8,000) + 0.4(8,000) + 0.1 (8,000)	=	$7,500
300	0.1(2,000) + 0.4(7,000) + 0.4(12,000) + 0.1 (12,000)	=	$9,000
400	0.1(1,000) + 0.4(6,000) + 0.4(11,000) + 0.1 (16,000)	=	$8,500

The best solution is to order 300 overcoats.

10. Kay's Pastries.

The following payoff matrix was constructed, where

$$\text{Payoff} = \begin{cases} 0.40Q & \text{if } Q \leq D \\ 0.40D - 0.30(Q-D) & \text{if } Q > D \end{cases}$$

Order Quantity Q	Demand, D		
	100	200	300
100	$40	$40	$40
200	$10	$80	$80
300	($20)	$50	$120

Now we can compute the expected payoff for each baking quantity Q.

Order Quantity	Expected Payoff				
100	0.30(40)	+ 0.40(40)	+ 0.30(40)	=	$40
200	0.30(10)	+ 0.40(80)	+ 0.30(80)	=	$59
300	0.30(− 20)	+ 0.40(50)	+ 0.30(120)	=	$50

Therefore, 200 pastries should be baked each day.

11. Aggies versus Tech.

The following payoff matrix was constructed, where

$$\text{Payoff} = \begin{cases} 1.75Q & \text{if } Q \leq D \\ 1.75D - 0.75(Q-D) & \text{if } Q > D \end{cases}$$

Order Quantity Q	Demand, D				
	2000	3000	4000	5000	6000
2000	$3,500	$3,500	$3,500	$3,500	$3,500
3000	$2,750	$5,250	$5,250	$5,250	$5,250
4000	$2,000	$4,500	$7,000	$7,000	$7,000
5000	$1,250	$3,750	$6,250	$8,750	$8,750
6000	$500	$3,000	$5,500	$8,000	$10,500

Now we can compute the expected payoff for each baking quantity Q.

Order Quantity	Expected Payoff						
2000	0.15(3500)	+ 0.30(3500)	+ 0.25(3500)	+ 0.20(3500)	+ 0.10(3500)	=	$3500
3000	0.15(2750)	+ 0.30(5250)	+ 0.25(5250)	+ 0.20(5250)	+ 0.10(5250)	=	$4875
4000	0.15(2000)	+ 0.30(4500)	+ 0.25(7000)	+ 0.20(7000)	+ 0.10(7000)	=	$5500
5000	0.15(1250)	+ 0.30(3750)	+ 0.25(6250)	+ 0.20(8750)	+ 0.10(8750)	=	$5500
6000	0.15(500)	+ 0.30(3000)	+ 0.25(5500)	+ 0.20(8000)	+ 0.10(10500)	=	$5000

There is a tie between ordering 4000 or 5000 hot dogs. The tie-breaking decison would probably depend on whether the manager is risk averse. There is greater potential risk and reward associated with ordering 5000 hot dogs.

12. Akaga Corporation.

Step 1: Calculate the *EOQ* at the lowest price (0.97 x $7500) = $7,275:

$$EOQ = \sqrt{\frac{2DS}{H}} = \sqrt{\frac{2(60,000)(2,000)}{.15(7,275)}} = 468.97 \text{ or } 469 \text{ units}$$

This solution is infeasible. We can not buy 469 units at a price of $7,275 each. Therefore we calculate the *EOQ* at the next lowest price (0.98 x $7,500) = $7,350:

$$EOQ = \sqrt{\frac{2DS}{H}} = \sqrt{\frac{2(60,000)(2,000)}{.15(7,350)}} = 466.57 \text{ or } 467 \text{ units}$$

This solution is infeasible. We can not buy 467 units at a price of $7,350 each. Therefore we calculate the *EOQ* at the next lowest price (0.99 x $7,500) = $7,425:

$$EOQ = \sqrt{\frac{2DS}{H}} = \sqrt{\frac{2(60,000)(2,000)}{.15(7,425)}} = 464.21 \text{ or } 464 \text{ units}$$

This solution is infeasible. We can not buy 464 units at a price of $7,425 each. Therefore we calculate the *EOQ* at the next lowest price, $7,500:

$$EOQ = \sqrt{\frac{2DS}{H}} = \sqrt{\frac{2(60,000)(2,000)}{.15(7,500)}} = 461.88 \text{ or } 462 \text{ units}$$

It is feasible to buy 462 units at a price of $7,500 each.

Step 2: Calculate total costs at the feasible *EOQ* and at higher discount quantities:

$$C = \frac{Q}{2}H + \frac{D}{Q}S + PD$$

$$C_{462} = \frac{462}{2}\left[.15(\$7,500)\right] + \frac{(60,000)}{462}\$2,000 + \$7,500(60,000)$$

$$C_{422} = \$259,875 + \$259,740 + \$4,500,000,000$$

$$C_{422} = \$4,500,519,615$$

$$C_{5000} = \frac{5,000}{2}\left[.15(\$7,425)\right] + \frac{(60,000)}{5,000}\$2,000 + \$7,425(60,000)$$

$$C_{5000} = \$2,784,375 + \$24,000 + \$445,500,000$$

$$C_{5000} = \$448,308,375$$

$$\boxed{\begin{array}{l}C_{10000} = \frac{10,000}{2}\left[.15(\$7,350)\right] + \frac{(60,000)}{10,000}\$2,000 + \$7,350(60,000) \\[6pt] C_{10000} = \boxed{\$5,512,500} + \$12,000 + \$441,400,000 \\[6pt] C_{10000} = \$446,524,500\end{array}}$$

$$C_{30000} = \frac{30,000}{2}\left[.15(\$7,275)\right] + \frac{(60,000)}{30,000}\$2,000 + \$7,275(60,000)$$

$$C_{30000} = \$16,368,750 + \$4,000 + \$436,500,000$$

$$C_{30000} = \$452,872,750$$

a. The optimal order quantity is 10,000 units.

The lead time is one month or 1/12th year.

The average demand during the lead time is 5,000 units.

The standard deviation of demand *for one year* is given at 12,000 units.

The standard deviation of demand during the one-month lead time is *NOT* 1000 units:

$$\sigma_L = \sigma_t \sqrt{L}$$

$$\sigma_L = 12,000\sqrt{1/12}$$

$$\sigma_L = 12,000(0.40825)$$

$$\sigma_L = 3,464.1 \text{ or } 3,464$$

Safety stock $z\sigma_L = 1.645(3,464.1) = 5,698.4$ or $\boxed{5,698}$

Reorder point is Average demand during the lead time *plus* Safety stock

$R = 5,000 + 5,698 = 10,698$ units

b. The safety stock level (5,698) is calculated in part a.

The total annual inventory holding costs are:

$5,512,500 for cycle stock (shown on previous page) plus $0.15(5,698)(\$7,350) =$
$\underline{\$\ 6,282,045}$ for safety stock
$11,794,545 in total

c. Yes, Akaga should purchase 10,000 units at a time to obtain the 2% discount.

Total costs are:

$441,400,000	Purchase price costs
$ 11,794,545	Holding costs (cycle plus safety stock)
$\underline{\$\qquad 12,000}$	Ordering costs
$453,206,545	Total

Holding costs as a proportion of total costs = ($11,794,545/453,206,545) = 0.026025 or 2.6%

d. If the stockout probability in increase to 10 percent, service level decreases to 90% and z decreases from 1.645 to 1.282. The effect is to multiply safety stock by the factor:

$$\frac{1.645 - 1.282}{1.645} = 0.597135$$

Safety stock holding costs would drop from $6,282,045 to $3,751,229. This reduces total costs by $2,530,816 down to $450,675,729 or about 0.5%.

Chapter 13

Aggregate Planning

Study Questions

1. An aggregate plan is a <u>managerial</u> statement of time-phased production rates, work-force levels, and inventory investment that takes into consideration customer requirements and capacity limitations. It balances conflicting objectives of maximizing customer service, minimizing inventory investment, maintaining a stable work force, minimizing production cost, and maximizing profit. The aggregate plan is useful because it states a general course of action, consistent strategic goals and objectives. Large corporations aggregate the plan into product families because linking strategic goals and objectives to detailed plans for each product would be prohibitive from a time and effort perspective. It would also hide the forest (big picture) behind a dense stand of trees (details).

2. Aggregate plans provide the direction and objectives that more detailed plans must achieve in order to comply with the overall strategies of the organization. Aggregate plans play a key role in translating the strategies of the business plan or annual plan into operational plans.

3. Production planning coordinates manufacturing, marketing, and finance with respect to the conflicting objectives of these areas. When it becomes the responsibility of only one area the production plan no longer adequately reflects the needs of the other areas and a lack of coordination between the areas will result. If left solely to manufacturing, there is a temptation to create a production plan using the level strategy, which optimizes manufacturing efficiency, but may at times provide poor customer service and at other times consume too much cash in the form of inventory. Even though manufacturing deals directly with the production resources of the firm, those resources must be used to achieve the goals of the firm, not only manufacturing.

4. Executive interest in aggregate planning.
   a. Marketing: Provides inputs in the way of forecasts, economic conditions, and competitor behavior and is interested in maintaining or improving customer service, which often implies more finished goods inventory.
   b. Manufacturing: Provides inputs such as capacities, productivities, and equipment plans and is typically interested in maintaining stable production rates or enough capacity to achieve volume flexibility, as the case may be.
   c. Materials: Provides inputs such as inventory levels, subcontractor capabilities, storage capacity, and raw materials availability and is interested in maintaining the proper levels of inventory.
   d. Finance: Provides cost data and the financial condition of the firm and is interested in keeping the cash-flow needs and inventory investment within acceptable levels.
   e. Human resources: Provides labor market conditions and training capacities and is interested in the hiring and firing plans and human resource implications of the production plan.
   f. Engineering: Provides information on new product development, major product changes, and labor and machine standards.

5. The typical objectives of aggregate planning are:
   - Minimize costs/maximize profits
   - Maximize customer service
   - Minimize inventory investment
   - Minimize changes in production rates
   - Minimize changes in work-force levels
   - Maximize utilization of plant and equipment

   Examples of their conflicting nature include (1) minimizing costs may not be consistent with maximizing customer service, particularly if larger inventories or capacities are needed for the latter; (2) minimizing inventory investment may cause work-force levels to change in order to meet demand; and (3) maximizing the utilization of plant and equipment may conflict with cost minimization if it means building unnecessary inventories or overtime in some areas.

6. Reactive alternatives in aggregate planning are actions taken to cope with demand requirements. The alternatives react to demand is taken as a "given" that must be entirely fulfilled. Examples include building seasonal inventories, using overtime, and changing the production rate and/or work-force level. Aggressive alternatives are actions taken to adjust the demand pattern in order to achieve operations efficiency and reduce costs. Examples are complementary products, promotional campaigns, and creative pricing.

7. A chase strategy adjusts production rates or staff levels to match the demand requirements over the planning horizon. This strategy is useful in environments where the cost to hold inventories is high relative to the cost to change the production rate and when back orders are to be avoided. A level strategy maintains a constant production rate or staff level over the planning horizon. This strategy is useful in environments where the cost of adjusting the production rate is high relative to the costs of holding inventories and/or allowing back orders.

8. The planning process consists of determining demand requirements; identifying the appropriate alternatives, constraints, and costs; developing a prospective plan and testing it for feasibility regarding constraints and acceptability regarding objectives; and finally implementing and updating the plan. Often this process takes place with a committee of high-level managers from each of the functional areas.

9. Both plans could have similar objectives as shown in the answer to Study Question 5, except that a staffing plan for a service organization would not have an inventory objective. Also, staffing plans would not use anticipation inventory as a planning alternative for service organizations. The planning process itself for production plans is basically the same as that for staffing plans, even though the nature of the data, constraints, and alternatives may be different.

10. Hometown Bank.
    a. Alternatives to consider would include: (i) adjusting work-force levels or using part-time employees for the peak periods and stabilizing the work force; (ii) using overtime for the peak periods and undertime for the other periods; and (iii) using vacation schedules in such a way as to allow the most regular-time workers on duty at peak hours.
    b. Data requirements would include: (i) demand forecasts or customer arrival distributions; (ii) productivities; (iii) costs of hiring, firing, and regular-time and overtime wages; and (iv) constraints.
    c. Objectives to consider would include: (i) maximizing customer service; (ii) minimizing costs or maximizing profits; and (iii) minimizing changes in the regular-time work force.

Discussion Questions

1. Over the past several years, many corporations have experienced reductions in the work force of sufficient size to receive attention in the media. Restructuring charges reflected in the annual reports to stockholders are often in the order of magnitude of $100,000 per employee. If business is expected to recover within a year, the company would usually be better off to keep these employees on the payroll, perhaps shifting some of them to sales, or loan others for community volunteer work. It is difficult to estimate the monetary value of the following costs associated with layoffs:
   - decreased morale and loyalty of employees not fired
   - fired employee stress, mortgage defaults, failed marriages, suicides
   - customers may question the ability to perform, creating a chilling effect on sales
   - suppliers may become suspicious of firm's financial strength, demand cash
   - loss of experience
   - loss of goodwill in community, future cooperation in zoning, loss of redevelopment incentives
   - loss of reputation as an employer, future difficulty in hiring qualified work force

2. Responses will vary depending on which firms are used as examples. Some industries, such as the U. S. auto industry have a long history and tradition of work force furlough and recall to match production with demand. Generations of employees are accustomed to this cycle, and fairly smoothly transition between working in the plant during good times and finding other temporary careers when business is slow. Other industries, such as utilities, have a history of stable employment, but are now faced with competition, restructuring, and dealing with employees who hired on for life, and now feel betrayed. Stable employment requires stable markets, management loyalty to the work force, long product life-cycles, financial strength, skilled work forces, and competition that also needs stable work forces.

3. As automobile sales increased, management was reluctant to recall furloughed workers. Instead, the existing work force was required to work more and more overtime on assembly lines running at a faster and faster pace. Recalled workers might have been less skilled, or it might have been more profitable to work a small force long hours than to work a large force short hours. However, overtime is not an effective long-term technique for increasing output. Workers become too tired. Work force size and overtime are controllable variables in production planning. GM workers went on strike because of stress associated with the production planning strategy calling for long-term use of overtime. They preferred to recall furloughed workers even though it meant they would take home less pay as individuals.

Problems

1. Barberton Municipal Division of Road Maintenance.

   a. The peak demand is 19,000 hours in quarter 3. As each employee can work 624 hours per quarter (520 on regular time and 104, or 0.20 * 520, on overtime). The level work force that allows no delay and minimizes undertime is 19,000 / 624 = 30.45 or 31 employees.

Cost	Calculation	Amount
Regular wages	($6240 per quarter)(31)(4 quarters)	$773,760
Overtime wages*	(2880 hr in Quarter 3)($18 per hr)	51,840
Hire costs	($3000 per hire)(20 hires)	60,000
	TOTAL	$885,600

   * The 31 workers can produce (31)(520) = 16,120 hours of regular time in any quarter. The 19,000-hour requirement in quarter 3 exceeds this amount by 2880 hours.

   The total undertime hours can be calculated as:

Quarter 1	31(520) – 6,000	=	10,120 hours
Quarter 2	31(520) – 12,000	=	4,120
Quarter 4	31(520) – 9,000	=	7,120
			21,360 hours

   b. The chase strategy:

Quarter	Demand (hr)	Work Force	Hires	Fires
1	6,000	12	1	—
2	12,000	24	12	—
3	19,000	37	13	—
4	9,000	18	=	19
TOTAL		91	26	19

Cost	Calculation	Amount
Regular wages	($6240 per quarter)(91)	$567,840
Hire costs	($3000 per hire)(26 hires)	78,000
Layoff costs	($2000 per hire)(19 fires)	38,000
	TOTAL	$683,840

   c. Proposed plan

Quarter	Demand (hr)	Work Force	Hires	Fires	Overtime (hr)
1	6,000	12	1	—	—
2	12,000	24	12	—	—
3	19,000	31	7	—	2,880
4	9,000	18	=	13	=
TOTAL		85	20	13	2,800

Cost	Calculation	Amount
Regular wages	($6240 per quarter)(85)	$530,400
Hire costs	($3000 per hire)(20 hires)	60,000
Fire costs	($2000 per hire)(13 fires)	26,000
Overtime	($18 per hour)(2880 hours)	51,840
	TOTAL	$668,240

2. Jill B. Nimble.

   a. The peak demand is 6,400 hours in quarter 2. As each employee can work 600 hours per quarter (480 on regular time and 120 on overtime). The level work force that covers requirements and minimizes undertime is 6,400 / 600 = 10.67 or 11 employees.

Cost	Calculation	Amount
Regular wages	($7200 per quarter)(11)(8 quarters)	$633,600
Overtime wages*	(1,120 hr in Quarter 2)($20 per hr)	22,400
	(960 hr in Quarter 6)($20 per hr)	19,200
Hire costs	($10,000 per hire)(3 hires)	30,000
	TOTAL	$705,200

    *   The 11 workers can produce (11)(480) = 5,280 hours of regular time in any quarter. The 6,400-hour requirement in quarter 2 exceeds this amount by 1,120 hours. The 6,240-hour requirement in quarter 6 exceeds this amount by 960 hours.

The total undertime hours can be calculated as:

Quarter 1	11(480) – 4,200	=	1,080 hours
Quarter 3	11(480) – 3,000	=	2,280
Quarter 4	11(480) – 4,800	=	480
Quarter 5	11(480) – 4,400	=	880
Quarter 7	11(480) – 3,600	=	1,680
Quarter 8	11(480) – 4,800	=	480
			6,880 hours

   b. The chase strategy:

Quarter	Demand (hr)	Work Force	Hires	Fires
1	4,200	9	1	—
2	6,400	14	5	—
3	3,000	7	—	7
4	4,800	10	3	—
5	4,400	10	—	—
6	6,240	13	3	—
7	3,600	8	—	5
8	4,800	10	2	—
TOTAL		81	14	12

Cost	Calculation	Amount
Regular wages	($7,200 per quarter)(81)	$583,200
Hire costs	($10,000 per hire)(14 hires)	140,000
Layoff costs	($4,000 per hire)(12 fires)	48,000
	TOTAL	$771,200

   c. Proposed plan

Quarter	Demand (hr)	Work Force	Hires	Fires	Overtime (hr)
1	4,200	9	1	—	—
2	6,400	11	2	—	1,120
3	3,000	9	—	2	—
4	4,800	9	—	—	480
5	4,400	9	—	—	80
6	6,240	11	2	—	960
7	3,600	9	—	2	—
8	4,800	9	—	—	480
TOTAL		76	5	4	3,120

Cost	Calculation	Amount
Regular wages	($7,200 per quarter)(76)	$547,200
Hire costs	($10,000 per hire)(5 hires)	50,000
Fire costs	($4,000 per hire)(4 fires)	16,000
Overtime	($20 per hour)(3,120 hours)	62,400
	TOTAL	$675,600

3. Jill B. Nimble with part-time instructors.

   a. One of many plans that take advantage of flexibility provided by part-time instructors. this plan reduces hiring and firing of certified instructors, reduces overtime, and reduces total costs.

Qtr	Demand (hr)	Certified Work Force	Cert Hires	Cert Fires	PT Work Hours	PT Hires	PT Fires	Overtime (hr)
1	4,200	9	1	—	—	—	—	—
2	6,400	10	1	—	720	3	—	880
3	3,000	8	—	2	—	—	3	—
4	4,800	8	—	—	720	3	—	240
5	4,400	8	—	—	560	—	—	—
6	6,240	10	2	—	720	—	—	720
7	3,600	8	—	2	—	—	3	—
8	4,800	8	—	—	720	3	—	240
	TOTAL	69	4	4	3,440	9	6	2,080

Cost	Calculation	Amount
Regular wages	($7,200 per quarter)(69)	$496,800
Cert. Hire costs	($10,000 per hire)(4 hires)	40,000
Cert. Fire costs	($4,000 per hire)(4 fires)	16,000
PT. Hire costs	($2,000 per hire)(9 hires)	18,000
PT. Labor costs	($12/hr) (3,440 hrs)	41,280
Overtime	($20 per hour)(2,080 hours)	41,600
	TOTAL	$653,680

4. Crop Chemical Company.

   a. The total cumulative demand is 340,000 gallons for the year. The average quarterly production rate is 340,000 / 4 = 85,000 gallons per quarter. Part (b) shows that this production rate has no stockouts or back orders.

   b.

Quarter	Cum. Production Rate (gallons)	Cumulative Demand (gallons)	Anticipation Inventory (gallons)
1	85,000	80,000	5,000
2	170,000	130,000	40,000
3	255,000	210,000	45,000
4	340,000	340,000	0

   c.

Quarter	Cumulative Demand (gal.)	Average Demand Rate per Qtr(gal.)
1	80,000	80,000
2	210,000	105,000
3	260,000	86,667
4	340,000	85,000

The average production rate per quarter is that rate needed to avoid stockouts or back orders. To avoid stockouts in the second quarter, we need to produce at the rate of 105,000 gallons per quarter. Because this rate is the largest one needed and a level plan is desired, that is the rate we must use.

5. Ross Corporation

a. The peak demand is 3000 units in month 11. The total demand up to month 12 is 16,300 units, requiring 1630 employees. 1630 ÷ 11 = 148.2 or 149 employees are required for the level strategy. Therefore 9 employees will be hired in month 1.

Level Strategy

Month	Demand	Work Force	Ending Inv
1	500	149	990
2	800	149	1680
3	1000	149	2170
4	1400	149	2260
5	2000	149	1750
6	1600	149	1640
7	1400	149	1730
8	1200	149	2020
9	1000	149	2510
10	2400	149	1600
11	3000	149	90
12	1000	149	580
			19,020

b. **Chase Strategy**

Month	Demand (units)	Work Force	Hires	Fires
1	500	50	–	90
2	800	80	30	–
3	1000	100	20	–
4	1400	140	40	–
5	2000	200	60	–
6	1600	160	–	40
7	1400	140	–	20
8	1200	120	–	20
9	1000	100	–	20
10	2400	240	140	–
11	3000	300	60	–
12	1000	100	=	200
		1730	350	390

c. **Costs**

Level Strategy		**Amount**
Wages	($2,000 per quarter)(149 workers)(12 months)	$3,576,000
Hire costs	($2,000 per hire)(9 hires)	18,000
Inventory costs	($32/unit)(19,020 units)	608,640
	TOTAL	$4,202,640

Chase Strategy		**Amount**
Regular wages	($2,000 / month)(1,730)	$3,460,000
Hire costs	($2,000 / hire)(350 hires)	700,000
Fire costs	($500 / fire)(390 fires)	195,000
	TOTAL	$4,355,000

d. **Proposed Mixed Strategy**

Month	Demand	Work Force	Ending Inv.	Hires	Fires
1	500	100	500	–	40
2	800	100	700	–	–
3	1000	100	700	–	–
4	1400	100	300	–	–
5	2000	170	–	70	–
6	1600	170	100	–	–
7	1400	170	400	–	–
8	1200	170	900	–	–
9	1000	170	1600	–	–
10	2400	170	900	–	–
11	3000	210	–	40	–
12	1000	100	=	=	110
		1,730	6,100	110	150

Total costs	Calculation	Amount
Wages	($2000/month)(1730)	$3,460,000
Hire costs	($2000/hire)(110 hires)	220,000
Fire costs	($500/fire)(150 fires)	75,000
Inventory costs	($32/unit)(6100)	195,200
		$3,950,200

This strategy makes use of extra capacity—inventory—to level off higher demand without spending too much money on hiring and firing costs.

6. Flying Frisbee Company.

a. **Level Strategy**

The most overtime we can use is 25 percent of regular-time capacity (W), so we have

$$1.25W = 20 \text{ employees (maximum need in any period)}$$
$$W = 20 / 1.25 = 16 \text{ employees}$$

This staff size mimimizes the resulting amount of undertime. As there are already 10 employees, Flying Frisbee should hire 6 more. Plan 1 shows the resulting hires and overtime.

Plan 1: Level Strategy for Flying Frisbee Company

	Jan	Feb	Mar	Apr	May	Jun	Jul	Aug	Sep	Oct	Nov	Dec	Total
Requirement	2	2	4	6	18	20	12	18	7	3	2	1	95
Staff level	16	16	16	16	16	16	16	16	16	16	16	16	192
Hires	6	—	—	—	—	—	—	—	—	—	—	—	6
Layoffs	—	—	—	—	—	—	—	—	—	—	—	—	0
Overtime	—	—	—	—	2	4	—	2	—	—	—	—	8

b. **Chase Strategy**

This strategy simply involves adjusting the work force as needed to meet demand. Plan 2 shows the effect of changing the staff level with hires and layoffs. Note that the maximum number of hires per period is 10, so that Flying Frisbee can hire only 10 workers in May and must use 2 worker months of overtime to fulfill labor requirements for that month.

Plan 2: Chase Strategy for Flying Frisbee Company

	Jan	Feb	Mar	Apr	May	Jun	Jul	Aug	Sep	Oct	Nov	Dec	Total
Requirement	2	2	4	6	18	20	12	18	7	3	2	1	95
Staff level	2	2	4	6	16	20	12	18	7	3	2	1	93
Hires	—	—	2	2	10	4	—	6	—	—	—	—	24
Layoffs	8	—	—	—	—	—	8	—	11	4	1	1	33
Overtime	—	—	—	—	2	—	—	—	—	—	—	—	2

c. **Plan3: Mixed Strategy for Flying Frisbee Company**

	Jan	Feb	Mar	Apr	May	Jun	Jul	Aug	Sep	Oct	Nov	Dec	Total
Requirement	2	2	4	6	18	20	12	18	7	3	2	1	95
Staff level	4	4	4	6	16	16	14	14	7	3	2	1	91
Hires	—	—	—	2	10	—	—	—	—	—	—	—	12
Layoffs	6	—	—	—	—	—	2	—	7	4	1	1	21
Overtime	—	—	—	—	—	4	—	4	—	—	—	—	8

d. **Cost Comparisons for the Flying Frisbee Company Staffing Plans**

Cost	Plan 1: Level Strategy		Plan 2: Chase Strategy		Plan 3: Mixed Strategy	
RT @ $1500	192 wrk-mo.	= $288,000	93 worker-mo.	= $139,500	91 worker-mo.	= $136,500
OT@$2,250	8 worker-mo.	= $ 18,000	2 worker-mo.	= $ 4,500	8 worker-mo.	= $ 18,000
Hire@$2,500	6 workers	= $ 15,000	24 workers	= $ 60,000	12 workers	= $ 30,000
Layoff@$2,000	0 workers	= $ 0	33 workers	= $ 66,000	21 workers	= $ 66,000
	Total	$321,000		$270,000		$250,500

The mixed strategy is most cost effective and requires less hiring and firing than does the chase strategy. The advantages of the level plan include a stable work force and excess capacity to meet increases in demand. The disadvantage of a level plan is greater cost than for a mixed strategy. The disadvantage of a chase strategy is the frequent changes in staff level.

7. Little Shoe Company.

   a. The plan is infeasible because of the stockout in period 6.

	1	2	3	4	5	6
Requirements	25,000	6,500	15,000	19,000	32,000	29,000
Regular Production	16,000	16,000	16,000	16,000	16,000	16,000
Overtime (units)	3,200	–	–	–	3,200	3,200
Inventory (12,000)	6,200	15,700	16,700	13,700	900	**– 8,900**
Work force	8	8	8	8	8	8

   *Production equals (8 employees)(2,000 pairs per period) + 20%overtime in periods 1, 5 & 6.

   b. The solution to this part depends upon the plans submitted by the students. It is anticipated that the plans would have a varying work-force level or more use of overtime in periods 2 thru 4.

8. Bull Grin. The production plan is shown in tabular format on the next page. Note the fourth quarter demand is inflated to create the required ending inventory (470 demand + 40 inventory) = 510.

Summary of Bull Grin production plan.

Quarter	Regular-Time Production	Overtime Production	Subcontracting	Anticipation Inventory
1	390,000	20,000	0	320,000
2	400,000	20,000	30,000	370,000
3	460,000	20,000	30,000	80,000
4	380,000	20,000	30,000	40,000

The cost of this plan is $1,592,700.

Bull Grin Production Plan

	Source of Product	Demand				Unused Capacity	Capacity (barrels)
		First Quarter	Second Quarter	Third Quarter	Fourth Quarter		
	Initial Inventory	$0 40	$100	$200	$300	$400	40
1	First Quarter Regular Time	$830 90	$930	$1030 270	$1130 30	$0	390
	First Quarter Overtime	$910	$1010	$1110	$1210 20	$0	20
	First Quarter Subcontract	$1000	$1100	$1200	$1300	$0 30	30
2	Second Quarter Regular Time	$9999	$830 400	$930	$1030	$0	400
	Second Quarter Overtime	$9999	$910	$1010 20	$1110	$0	20
	Second Quarter Subcontract	$9999	$1000	$1100	$1200 30	$0	30
3	Third Quarter Regular Time	$9999	$9999	$830 460	$930	$0	460
	Third Quarter Overtime	$9999	$9999	$910 20	$1010	$0	20
	Third Quarter Subcontract	$9999	$9999	$1000 30	$1100	$0	30
4	Fourth Quarter Regular Time	$9999	$9999	$9999	$830 380	$0	380
	Fourth Quarter Overtime	$9999	$9999	$9999	$910 20	$0	20
	Fourth Quarter Subcontract	$9999	$9999	$9999	$1000 30	$0	30
	Demand (barrels)	130	400	800	510	30	1870

9. Waverly Scale Company.

   a. **Plan 1:**

Total production and inventory costs	$446,610,000
Hires [200($3,000)]	600,000
Fires [200($2,000)]	400,000
Total	$447,610,000

Source of Product	Demand				Unused Capacity	Capacity (barrels)
	First Quarter	Second Quarter	Third Quarter	Fourth Quarter		
Initial Inventory	$0 4	$300	$600	$900	$900	4
First Quarter Regular Time	$2430 6	$2730 2	$3030 28	$3330	$270	36
First Quarter Overtime	$2700	$3000	$3300	$3600 3	$0	3
First Quarter Subcontract	$3300	$3600	$3900	$4200	$0 1	1
Second Quarter Regular Time	$9999	$2430 39	$2730	$3030	$270	39
Second Quarter Overtime	$9999	$2700	$3000	$3300 3	$0	3
Second Quarter Subcontract	$9999	$3300	$3600	$3900 1	$0	1
Third Quarter Regular Time	$9999	$9999	$2430 46	$2730	$270	46
Third Quarter Overtime	$9999	$9999	$2700 3	$3000	$0	3
Third Quarter Subcontract	$9999	$9999	$3300	$3600 1	$0	1
Fourth Quarter Regular Time	$9999	$9999	$9999	$2430 36	$270	36
Fourth Quarter Overtime	$9999	$9999	$9999	$2700 3	$0	3
Fourth Quarter Subcontract	$9999	$9999	$9999	$3300 1	$0	1
Demand (barrels)	10	41	77	48	1	177

Waverly Scale Company. (continued)

Plan 2:

Total production and inventory costs		$441,000,000
Hires	[140($3,000)]	<u>420,000</u>
Total		$441,420,000

Source of Product	Demand				Unused Capacity	Capacity (barrels)
	First Quarter	Second Quarter	Third Quarter	Fourth Quarter		
Initial Inventory	$0 4	$300	$600	$900	$900	4
First Quarter Regular Time	$2430 6	$2730	$3030 29	$3330 2	$270 6	43
First Quarter Overtime	$2700	$3000	$3300	$3600	$0 3	3
First Quarter Subcontract	$3300	$3600	$3900	$4200	$0 1	1
Second Quarter Regular Time	$9999	$2430 41	$2730 2	$3030	$270	43
Second Quarter Overtime	$9999	$2700	$3000	$3300	$0 3	3
Second Quarter Subcontract	$9999	$3300	$3600	$3900	$0 1	1
Third Quarter Regular Time	$9999	$9999	$2430 43	$2730	$270	43
Third Quarter Overtime	$9999	$9999	$2700 3	$3000	$0	3
Third Quarter Subcontract	$9999	$9999	$3300	$3600	$0 1	1
Fourth Quarter Regular Time	$9999	$9999	$9999	$2430 43	$270	43
Fourth Quarter Overtime	$9999	$9999	$9999	$2700 3	$0	3
Fourth Quarter Subcontract	$9999	$9999	$9999	$3300 1	$0	1
Demand (barrels)	10	41	77	48	16	192

Plan 2 has the lower costs and it has a stable work-force plan, which should contribute to overall productivity. However, it also has more unused capacity. If that capacity is charged to the plan, Plan 2 may be more costly.

b. Waverly with creative pricing.

Plan 1:

Total production and inventory costs $436,710,000
Hire and fire costs   1,000,000
Total $437,710,000

Source of Product	Demand				Unused Capacity	Capacity (barrels)
	First Quarter	Second Quarter	Third Quarter	Fourth Quarter		
Initial Inventory	$0 — 4	$300	$600	$900	$900	4
First Quarter Regular Time	$2430 — 16	$2730 — 15	$3030 — 5	$3330	$270	36
First Quarter Overtime	$2700	$3000	$3300	$3600 — 3	$0	3
First Quarter Subcontract	$3300	$3600	$3900	$4200	$0 — 1	1
Second Quarter Regular Time	$9999	$2430 — 39	$2730	$3030	$270	39
Second Quarter Overtime	$9999	$2700	$3000	$3300 — 3	$0	3
Second Quarter Subcontract	$9999	$3300	$3600	$3900 — 1	$0	1
Third Quarter Regular Time	$9999	$9999	$2430 — 46	$2730	$270	46
Third Quarter Overtime	$9999	$9999	$2700 — 3	$3000	$0	3
Third Quarter Subcontract	$9999	$9999	$3300	$3600 — 1	$0	1
Fourth Quarter Regular Time	$9999	$9999	$9999	$2430 — 36	$270	36
Fourth Quarter Overtime	$9999	$9999	$9999	$2700 — 3	$0	3
Fourth Quarter Subcontract	$9999	$9999	$9999	$3300 — 1	$0	1
Demand (barrels)	20	54	54	48	1	177

b. Waverly with creative pricing.
   Plan 2:

Total production and inventory costs	$431,100,000
Hire costs	420,000
Total	$431,520,000

Source of Product	Demand				Unused Capacity	Capacity (barrels)
	First Quarter	Second Quarter	Third Quarter	Fourth Quarter		
Initial Inventory	$0 — 4	$300	$600	$900	$900	4
First Quarter Regular Time	$2430 — 16	$2730 — 11	$3030 — 8	$3330 — 2	$270 — 6	43
First Quarter Overtime	$2700	$3000	$3300	$3600	$0 — 3	3
First Quarter Subcontract	$3300	$3600	$3900	$4200	$0 — 1	1
Second Quarter Regular Time	$9999	$2430 — 43	$2730	$3030	$270	43
Second Quarter Overtime	$9999	$2700	$3000	$3300	$0 — 3	3
Second Quarter Subcontract	$9999	$3300	$3600	$3900	$0 — 1	1
Third Quarter Regular Time	$9999	$9999	$2430 — 43	$2730	$270	43
Third Quarter Overtime	$9999	$9999	$2700 — 3	$3000	$0	3
Third Quarter Subcontract	$9999	$9999	$3300	$3600	$0 — 1	1
Fourth Quarter Regular Time	$9999	$9999	$9999	$2430 — 43	$270	43
Fourth Quarter Overtime	$9999	$9999	$9999	$2700 — 3	$0	3
Fourth Quarter Subcontract	$9999	$9999	$9999	$3300 — 1	$0	1
Demand (barrels)	20	54	54	48	16	192

If creative pricing is used, Plan 2 should still be used because it has the lower costs (compared to Plan 1). The savings between the original demand schedule and the creative pricing demand schedule is $6,190,000. If the cost of implementing the price incentives is less than $36/unit ($6,190,000 / 172,000), then creative pricing should be used.

10. Gretchen's Kitchen.

   a. Each hamburger requires 4 minutes, each pint of chili requires 3 minutes, each drink/shake requires 2 minutes, and each bag of french fries requires 2 minutes. Since the average customer buys 2.1 hamburgers, 0.2 pint of chili, 1 drink, and 1 bag of french fries, th average time required per customer is:

$$2.1(4) + 0.2(3) + 1.0(2) + 1.0(2) = 13 \text{ minutes}$$

   The service requirements, given in hours, are:

Month

	J	F	M	A	M	J	J	A	S	O	N	D	Total
Cust.	3200	2600	3300	3900	3600	4200	4800	4200	3800	3600	3500	3000	43,700
Hrs.*	693.3	563.3	715	845	780	910	1040.0	910.0	823.3	780.0	758.3	650.0	9468.2

*In any month, the hours of requirements are the estimated number of customers times 13 minutes divided by 60 minutes.

   b. **Level Work-Force Strategy with Overtime**

   The maximum requirement in any month is 1040 hours. The maximum number of hours an employee can work is 96 hours: 80 on regular time and 16 on overtime. Consequently, to avoid lost demand we need 1040 / 96 = 10.83 or 11 employees. This gives us a monthly capacity of 11(80) = 880 hours on regular time. With this work force we would need the following overtime: 30 hours in June, 160 hours in July, and 30 hours in August, for a total of 220 hours.

   Total cost = Regular-time wages + Overtime wages + Hire costs
   = 11($400)(12 months) + 220($7.50) + 1($250)
   = $54,700

   Chase Strategy with a Base Work Force

   With 10 employees the regular-time capacity is 800 hours per month. Hiring and laying off to avoid overtime and undertime results in the following plan:

Month

	J	F	M	A	M	J	J	A	S	O	N	D
Requirements	693.3	563.3	715.0	845.0	780.0	910.0	1040.0	910.0	823.3	780.0	758.3	650.0
Work force	10	10	10	11	10	12	13	12	11	10	10	10
Capacity	800	800	800	880	800	960	1040	960	880	800	800	800
Hires	–	–	–	1	–	2	1	–	–	–	–	–
Layoffs	–	–	–	–	1	–	–	1	1	1	–	–

   Total cost = Wages + Hire costs + Layoff costs
   = (129 employee-months)($400) + 4($250) + 4($50)
   = $52,800

Pure Chase Strategy

With this plan, hiring and laying off is used to match the requirements without the need for overtime.

Month	J	F	M	A	M	J	J	A	S	O	N	D
Requirements	693.3	563.3	715	845	780	910	1040.0	910.0	823.3	780.0	758.3	650.0
Work force	9	8	9	11	10	12	13	12	11	10	10	9
Capacity	720	640	720	880	800	960	1040	960	880	800	800	720
Hires	–	–	1	2	–	2	1	–	–	–	–	–
Layoffs	1	1	–	–	1	–	–	1	1	1	–	1

Total cost = Wages + Hire costs + Layoff costs
= (124 employee-months)($400) + 6(250) + 7($50)
= $51,450

The best plan is the pure chase strategy.

c.   If the cost of hiring were only $50, the total costs of the plans would be:

Level work-force strategy: $54,500
Chase strategy with base work force: $52,000
Pure chase strategy: $50,250

The strategy would not change in this case. The best is still a pure chase strategy. However, the manager should consider the morale of the work force. Hiring and laying off employees may cause a reduction in productivity. Eventually, it may be difficult to find employees willing to work if they think they may be laid off after a few months.

Supplement I

Linear Programming

Study Questions

1. A **parameter,** also known as a coefficient or given constant, is a value that the decision maker cannot control. **Decision variables** represent choices under the control of the decision maker.

2. Graphic analysis uses one axis to portray each decision variable. This approach limits graphic representation to two, or at best three decision variables, assuming skill in representing three-dimensional objects on paper. Since nearly all practical linear programming problems involve a large number of decision variables, graphic analysis can not be used to model realistic situations.

3. Overtime would relax the labor constraint, but the additional labor resource comes at a cost. Would additional labor hours improve the solution at a rate sufficient to pay for overtime? If so, how many additional hours would be of value? Which of the other resources would then bind the solution? In what way would the decision change if additional labor is made available? Storage space is not a binding constraint in the optimal solution. The linear programming model would show that the shadow price for storage is zero. No amount of rent to obtain additional storage can be justified.

4. For a ≤ constraint, the amount that the left side falls short of the right-hand side is called slack. A slack variable is added to the left side to represent the shortfall, so that the ≤ constraint becomes an equality. Each slack variable is associated with a constraint. When the optimal solution contains a slack variable, it is known how much of that resource is not used.

5. An iso-profit line connects the points representing solutions that result in equal profit. "Iso" meaning same or equal. Iso bars connect geographic points having equal barometric pressure. Isotherms are similar with respect to temperature. One difference between iso-profit lines and isobars and isotherms is that iso-profit lines in linear programming are always linear, while the others may be curves.

Problems

1. Really Big Shoe.

   Definition of decision variables:

   X_1 = number of basketball teams sponsored

   X_2 = number of football teams sponsored

   a. Objective function and constraints

   Maximize: $1X_1 + 1X_2$

   Subject to:

   1) money: $\$1,000,000X_1 + \$300,000X_2 \le \$30,000,000$

   2) flubber: $3(32)X_1 + 1(120)X_2 \le 4,000$

b. Graphical analysis. The optimal solution occurs at point B.

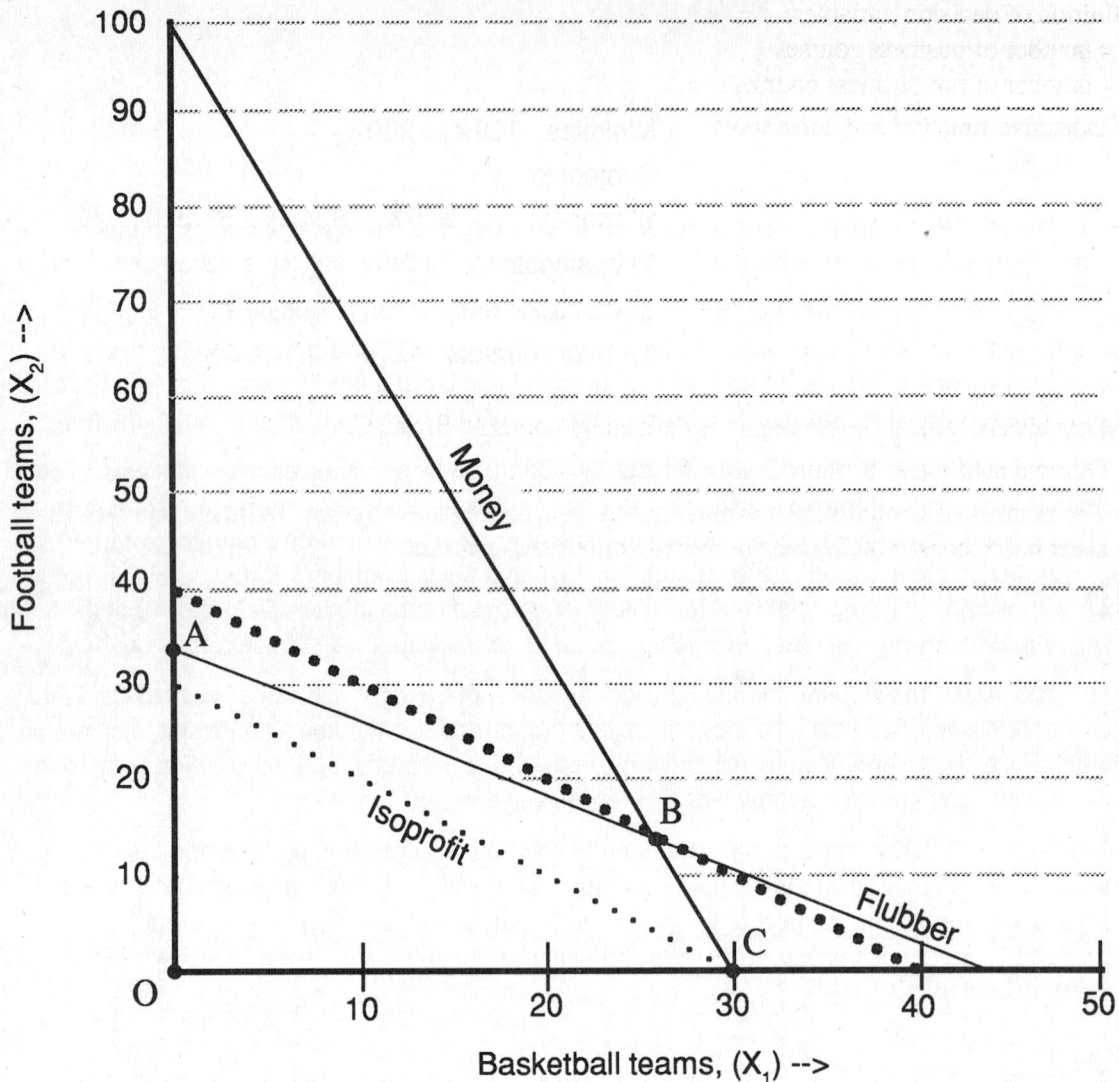

c. The optimal solution at point B occurs at the intersection of the money and flubber constraints. This appears to be at coordinates (26, 14).

To algebraically find the intersection of the money and flubber constraints, we multiply the money constraint by 0.0004, then subtract the flubber constraint from the money constraint.

$$400X_1 + 120X_2 = 12,000$$
$$\underline{-96X_1 - 120X_2 = -4,000}$$
$$304X_1 \qquad\quad = 8,000$$

$X_1 = 26.3$ or 26 basketball teams

$400(26) + 120X_2 = 12,000$

$120X_2 = 1,600$

$X_2 = 13.33$ or 13 football teams

2. Nowledge College. (minimize hours of study)

Definition of decision variables:
X_1 = number of business courses
X_2 = number of nonbusiness courses

a. Objective function and constraints

Minimize: $120X_1 + 200X_2$
Subject to:
1) money: $\$60X_1 + \$24X_2 \leq \$3,000$
2) business: $1X_1 \geq 23$
3) non business: $1X_2 \geq 20$
4) total courses: $1X_1 + 1X_2 \geq 65$

b. Graphic analysis. Feasible region is defined by points A, B, and C.

c. Optimal solution is at point C, $X_1 = 40$ and $X_2 = 25$.

d. The number of nonbusiness classes is not binding the optimal solution. There are 5 units of slack in the constraint for the number of nonbusiness courses.

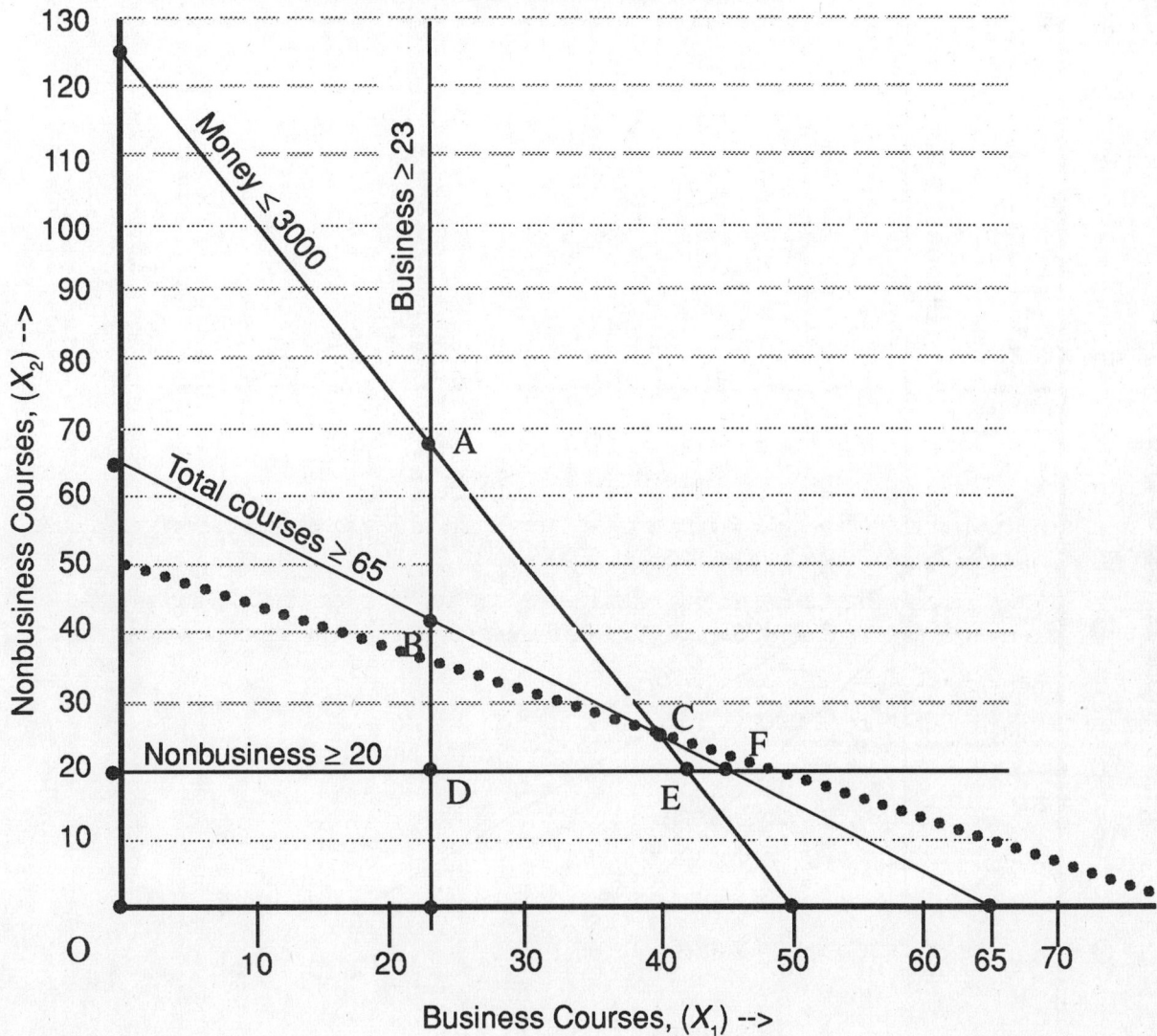

3. Nowledge College. (minimize cost of books)

Definition of decision variables:
X_1 = number of business courses
X_2 = number of nonbusiness courses

a.   Objective function and constraints

Minimize: $60X_1 + 24X_2$
Subject to:
1) time: $120X_1 + 200X_2 \leq 12{,}600$
2) business: $1X_1 \qquad \geq 23$
3) non business: $1X_2 \geq 20$
4) total courses: $1X_1 + \quad 1X_2 \geq 65$

b.   Graphic analysis is shown below.

c.   Optimal solution is at point B, $X_1 = 23$ and $X_2 = 42$.

d.   The number of nonbusiness classes is not binding the optimal solution. There is slack in the constraint for the number of nonbusiness courses and in the study time constraint.

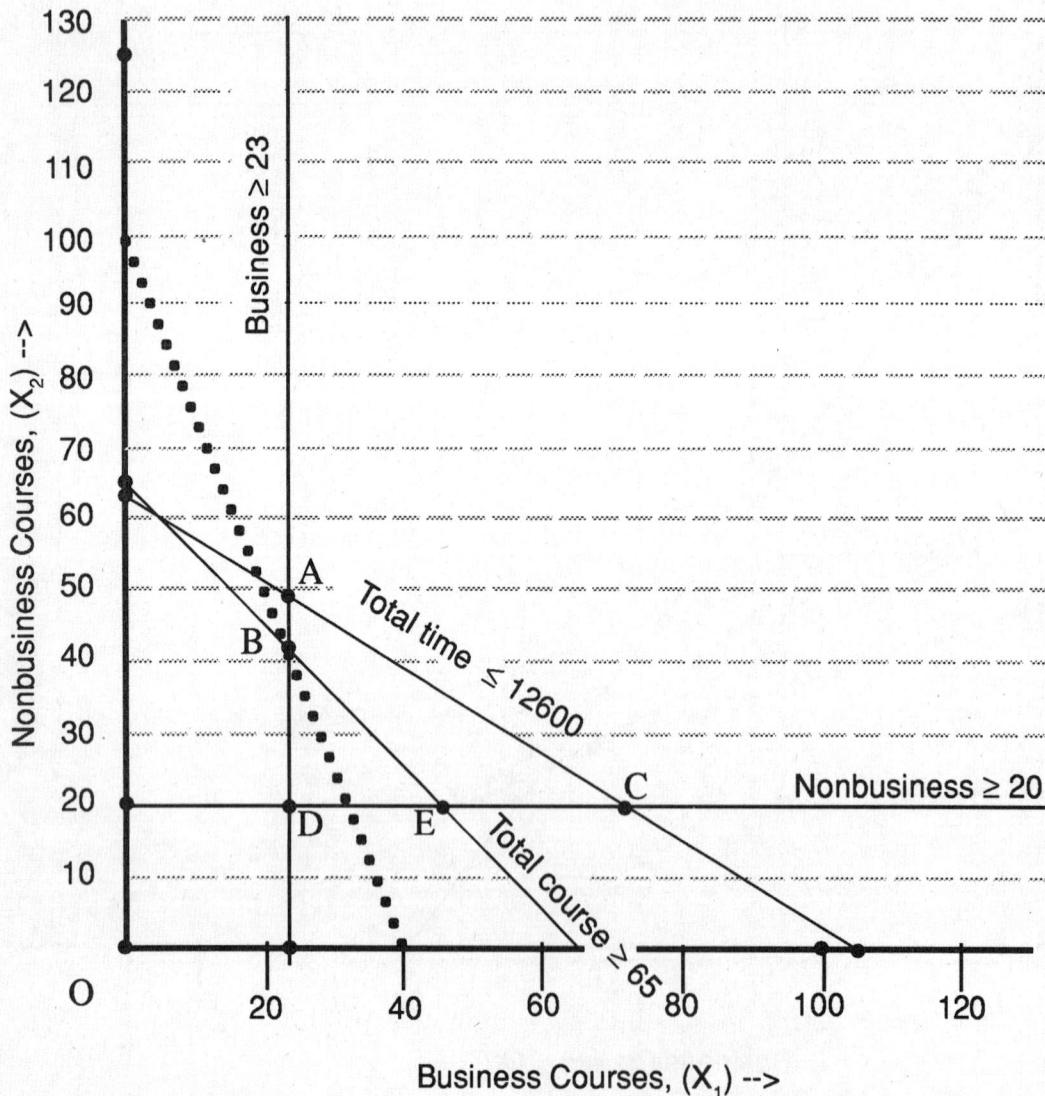

4. Mile-High Microbrewery.

Definition of decision variables:
X_1 = bottles of light beer
X_2 = bottles of dark beer

a. Graphical method

Maximize: $\$0.20X_1 + \$0.50X_2$

Subject to:

1) barley: $0.1X_1 + 0.6X_2 \leq 2,000$
2) bottling: $1.0X_1 + 1.0X_2 \geq 6,000$
3) market: $1.0X_1 \leq 4,000$

Feasible region is defined by O-A-B-C-D-O. The optimal solution is at point B, the intersection between the barley constraint and the bottling constraint.

1) barley (×10): $1.0X_1 + 6.0X_2 = 20,000$
2) bottling(× − 1): $-1.0X_1 - 1.0X_2 = -6,000$
$$5.0X_2 = 14,000$$
$$X_2 = 2,800$$
$$X_1 + 2,800 = 6,000$$
$$X_1 = 3,200$$

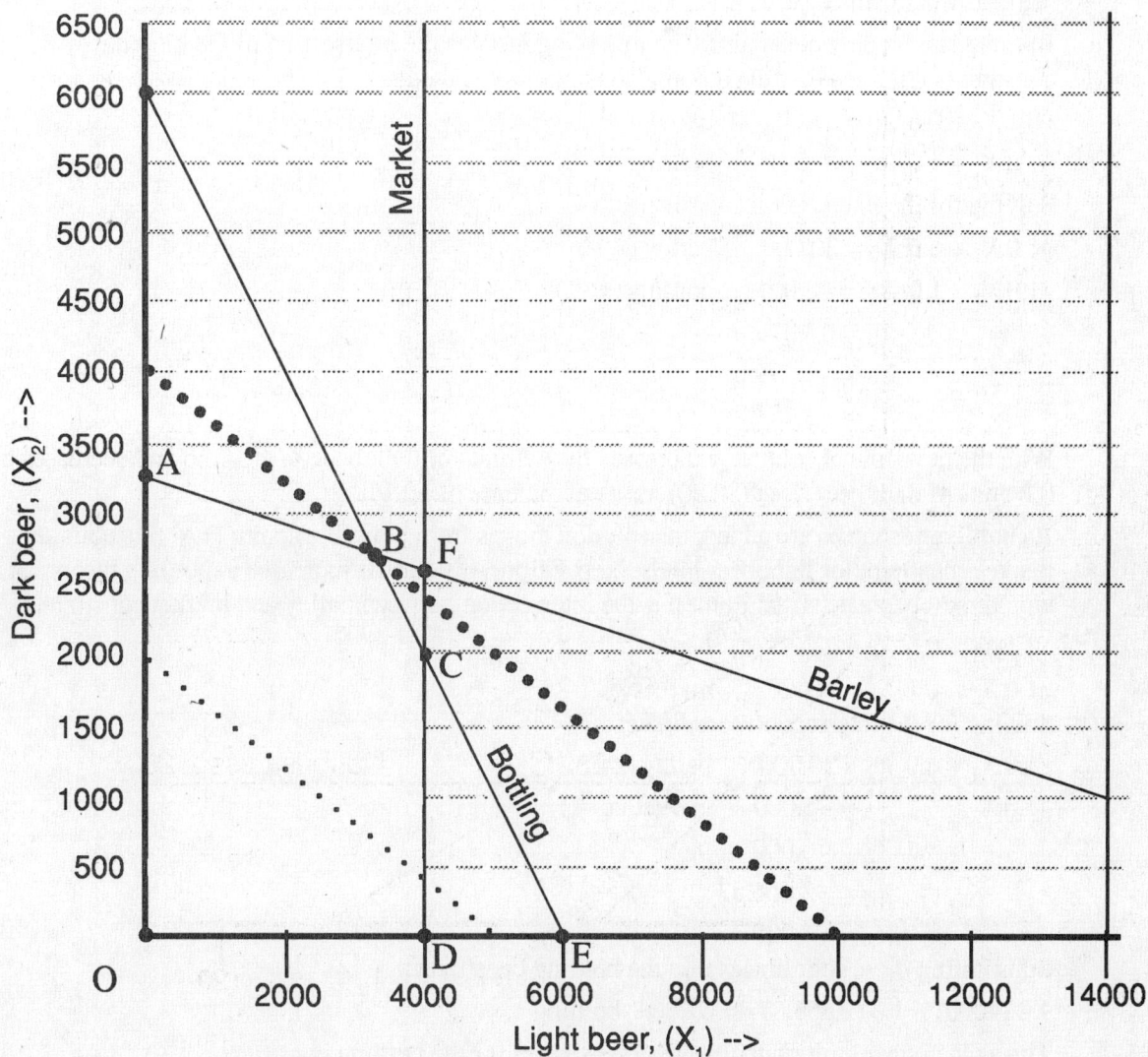

b. There is 800 bottles of slack in the market constraint for light beer.

$X_1 + S_3 = 4{,}000$

$3{,}200 + S_3 = 4{,}000$

$S_3 = 800$

c. Point B remains optimal as long as the objective function slope $(-c_1/c_2)$ is between $-1/6$, the slope of the barley constraint, and -1.00, the slope of the bottling constraint.

$$-\tfrac{1}{6} \le -c_1/c_2 \le -1$$

Holding c_2 constant at 0.5

$$-\tfrac{1}{6} \le -c_1/0.5 \le -1$$

multiply by -2

$$\tfrac{1}{3} \le c_1 \le 2$$

d. Since there is slack in the market constraint for light beer, the optimal solution will not improve if the market is increased. More demand for light beer would simply increase slack. Increased demand would not be served.

e. Bottling is a binding constraint. The following restates the intersection of the binding constraints after relaxing the bottling constraint by one unit.

$0.1\,X_1 + 0.6\,X_2 = 2{,}000$ barley

$1.0\,X_1 + 1.0\,X_2 = 6{,}001$ bottling

Solving for the intersection coordinates:

$1.0\,X_1 + 6.0\,X_2 = 20{,}000$ barley (x 10)

$-1.0\,X_1 - 1.0\,X_2 = -6{,}001$ bottling (x -1)

$\qquad\quad 5.0\,X_2 = 13{,}999$

$\qquad\qquad X_2 = 2{,}799.8$

$\qquad\qquad X_1 = 3{,}201.2$

With the new opimal soluion, z increases by 1.2 units of light beer X_1 @ \$0.20 and decreases by 0.2 units of dark beer X_2 @ (\$0.50) for a net increase of \$0.14.

f. As bottling resources are added, the solution moves from point B to point F. At this point the market constraint for light beer binds the solution. Any further increases in bottling resources would merely create slack. Point F is the intersection between barley and market constraints.

$0.1\,X_1 + 0.6\,X_2 = 2{,}000$ barley

$1.0\,X_1 \qquad\quad = 4{,}000$ market

Solving for the intersection coordinates:

$1.0\,X_1 + 6.0\,X_2 = 20{,}000$ barley (x 10)

$-1.0\,X_1 \qquad\quad = -4{,}000$ market (x -1)

$\qquad\quad 6.0\,X_2 = 16{,}000$

$\qquad\qquad X_2 = 2{,}666.67$

$\qquad\qquad X_1 = 4{,}000$

Substituting these coordinates into the bottling constraint:

$1.0\,(4000) + 1.0\,(2{,}666.67) = 6{,}666.7$ bottling

This is the upper limit on the range of feasibility for the bottling constraint.

5. Plastic pipe.

Definition of decision variables:
X_1 = hundreds of feet of pipe, routing 1
X_2 = hundreds of feet of pipe, routing 2

a. Objective function and constraints

b. Graphical analysis. For purposes of drawing the graph to a large scale, the extruder B constraint is not shown. It does not bind the solution. The optimal solution occurs at point D: $X_1 = 0$, $X_2 = 45$.

c. Max $z = \$80(45) = \$3,600$

d. If the objective function slope $(-c_1/c_2)$ changed to match the slope of the melting constraint, we could bring X_1 into the solution without penalty. The coefficient sensitivity equals the difference between this value and the current value of c_1. ($\$80 - \$60) = \$20$. If we forced one unit of X_1 into the solution without changing the objective function, there would be a \$20 penalty.

Maximize: $\$60X_1 + \$80X_2 = z$

Subject to:

1) melting: $1X_1 + 1X_2 \le 45$
2) extruder A: $3X_1 \le 90$
3) extruder B: $1X_2 \le 160$
4) raw material: $5X_1 + 4X_2 \le 200$

$-c_1/c_2 = -1.00$

$-c_1/\$80 = -1.00$

$c_1 = \$80$

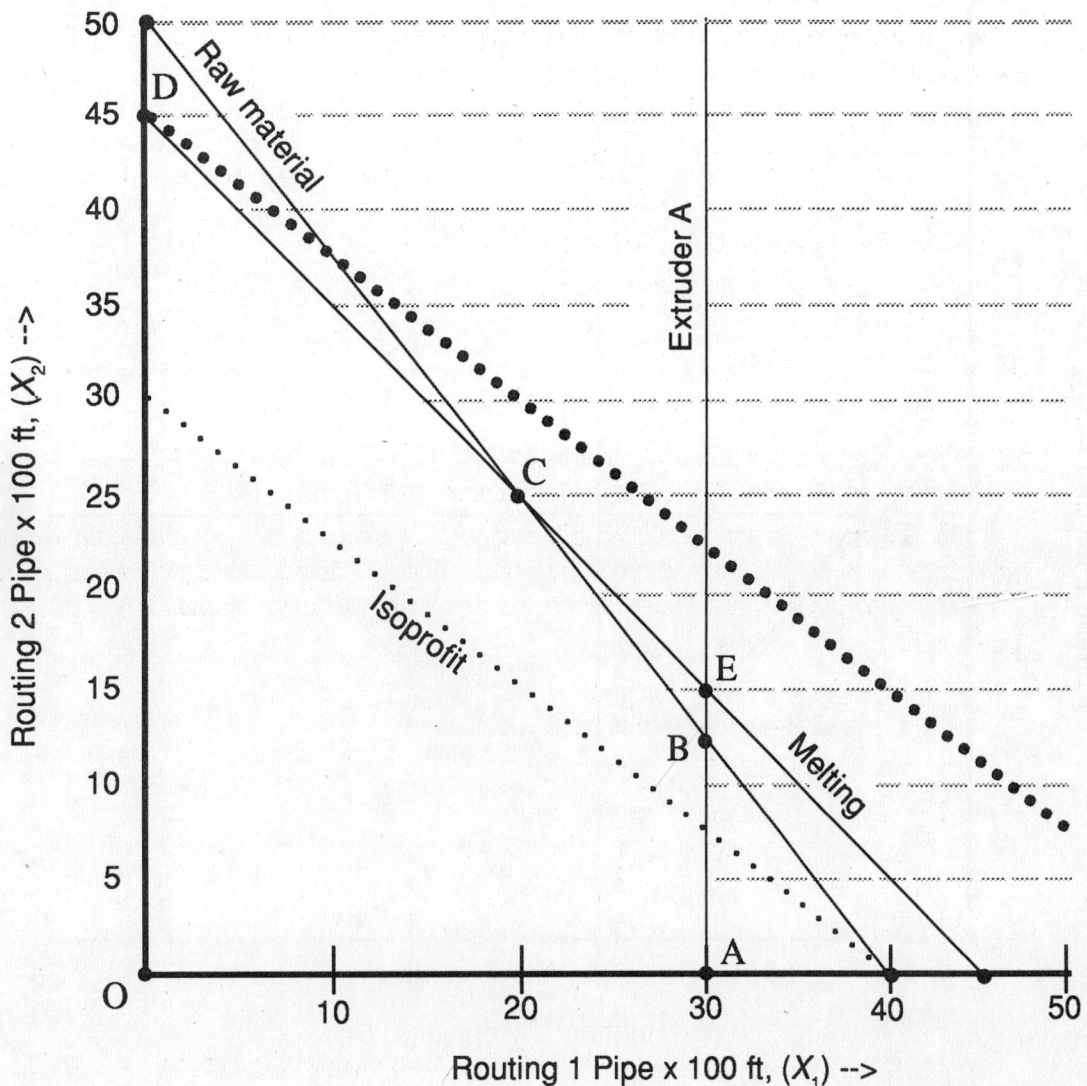

Routing 1 Pipe x 100 ft, (X_1) -->

Routing 2 Pipe x 100 ft, (X_2) -->

6. Manufacturer of textile dyes.

   a. Let X_1 = amount of dye produced on routing 1, measured in kilograms;

      X_2 = amount of dye produced on routing 2, measured in kilograms.

   Maximize: $\$50X_1 + \$65X_2$

   Subject to:
   $$2X_1 + \ 2X_2 \le 54 \quad \text{(mixing)}$$
   $$6X_1 \qquad\quad \le 120 \quad \text{(dryer A)}$$
   $$8X_2 \le 180 \quad \text{(dryer B)}$$
   $$20X_1 + \ 15X_2 \le 450 \quad \text{(chemicals)}$$
   $$X_1, X_2 \ \ge 0$$

   b. Graphical analysis. The optimal solution at point D is to produce 4.5 kilograms on routing 1 and 22.5 kilograms on routing 2. The total profit is \$1,687.50 [\$50(4.5) + \$65(22.5)].

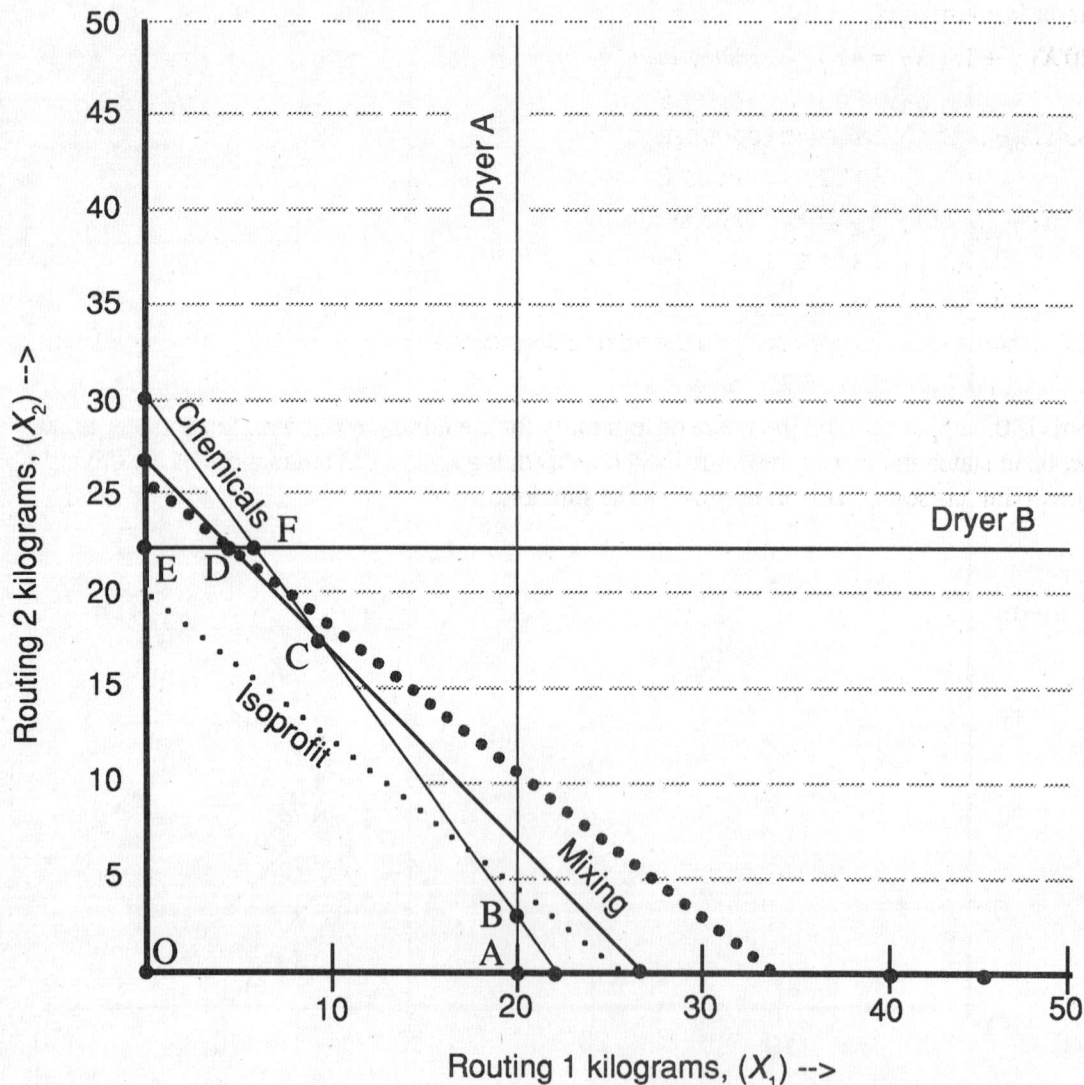

c. Point D is the intersection of the Dryer B and the Mixing constraint. There is slack in the DryerA and the Chemicals constraints.

d. Mixing is a binding constraint. The following restates the intersection of the binding constraints after relaxing the mixing constraint by one unit.

$$2\,X_1 \quad + 2\,X_2 = 55 \qquad\qquad \text{mixing}$$
$$8\,X_2 \; = 180 \qquad\qquad \text{dryer B}$$

Solving for the intersection coordinates:

$$X_2 = 22.5 \qquad\qquad \text{dryer B}$$
$$2\,X_1 \quad + 2\,X_2 = 55 \qquad\qquad \text{mixing}$$
$$2\,X_1 \; + 2(22.5) = 55$$
$$X_1 = \;\; 5.0$$

With the new opimal soluion, z increases by 0.5 units of X_1 @$50 with no change to units of X_2 for a net increase of $25. As mixing resources are added, the solution moves from point D to point F. At this point the chemicals constraint binds the solution. Any further increases in bottling resources would merely create slack. Point F is the intersection between chemicals and dryer B constraints.

$$20\,X_1 \quad + 15 \;\; X_2 = 450 \qquad\qquad \text{chemicals}$$
$$8 \;\; X_2 \; = 180 \qquad\qquad \text{dryer B}$$

Solving for the intersection coordinates:

$$X_2 = \;\; 22.5 \qquad\qquad \text{dryer B}$$
$$20\,X_1 + 15(22.5) = 450 \qquad\qquad \text{chemicals}$$
$$20 \;\; X_1 \; = 112.5$$
$$X_1 = \;\;\; 5.625$$

Substituting these coordinates into the mixing constraint:

$$2\,(5.625) + 2\,(22.5) = 56.25 \quad \text{mixing}$$

This is the upper limit on the range of feasibility for the mixing constraint. Since the original problem stated the mixing resource is 54 hours, adding up to 2.25 hours more of the mixing constraint has some value in improving the solution.

CMOM computer output for Textile Dye Problem.

CMOM — Linear Programming
Maximization

Data Entered

Number of Variables   : 2
Number of <= Constraints : 4
Number of = Constraints : 0
Number of >= Constraints : 0

Model

	X_1	X_2		RHS
Max-Z	50	65		
Mix	2	2	<=	54
A	6	0	<=	120
B	0	8	<=	180
Chem	20	15	<=	450

CMOM — Linear Programming
Maximization

Solution

Variable Label	Variable Value	Original Coefficient	Coefficient Sensitivity
X_1	4.5000	50	0
X_2	22.5000	65	0

Constraint Label	Original RHV	Slack or Surplus	Shadow Price
Mix	54	0	25
A	120	93	0
B	180	0	1.8750
Chem	450	22.5000	0

Objective Function Value: 1687.5000

7. Trim-Look Company.

    a. Let X_1 = number of skirts produced

        X_2 = number of dresses produced

        X_3 = number of sport coats produced

      Maximize: $\$5X_1 + \$17X_2 + \$30X_3$

      Subject to : $X_1 + \quad 3X_2 + \quad 4X_3 \quad \leq 100$ (cutting)

                  $X_1 + \quad 4X_2 + \quad 6X_3 \quad \leq 180$ (sewing)

                  $X_1 + \quad \quad X_2 + \quad 4X_3 \quad \leq \ 60$ (material)

                       $X_1, X_2,$ and $X_3 \quad \geq \quad 0$

    b. CMOM output is shown on below.

      The optimal solution is :

$X_1 =$	0 skirts	$s_1 = $	0	(no slack in cutting)
$X_2 =$	20 dresses	$s_2 = $	40	(slack in sewing)
$X_3 =$	10 sport coats	$s_3 = $	0	(no extra material)

      The total profit is \$640.

CMOM computer output for Trim-Look Company Problem.

CMOM — Linear Programming

Maximization

Data Entered

Number of Variables   : 3

Number of <= Constraints : 3

Number of = Constraints : 0

Number of >= Constraints : 0

Model

	X_1	X_2	X_3	RHS
Max-Z	5	17	30	
Cutting	1	3	4	<= 100
Sewing	1	4	6	<= 180
Material	1	1	4	<= 60

CMOM — Linear Programming

Maximization

Solution

Variable Label	Variable Value	Original Coefficient	Coefficient Sensitivity
X_1	0	5	2.5000
X_2	20	17	0
X_3	10	30	0

Constraint Label	Original RHV	Slack or Surplus	Shadow Price
CUT	100	0	4.7500
SEW	180	40	0
MTL	60	0	2.7500

Objective Function Value: 640

CMOM computer output for Trim-Look Company Problem. (continued)

Sensitivity Analysis

Objective Function Coefficients

Variable Label	Lower Limit	Original Coefficient	Upper Limit
X_1	no limit	5	7.5000
X_2	20	17	22.5000
X_3	10	30	68

Right-Hand-Side Values

Constraint Label	Lower Limit	Original Value	Upper Limit
CUT	60	100	132
SEW	140	180	no limit
MTL	33.3333	60	100

8. Refer to the CMOM sensitivity analysis output in Problem 7.

   a. The shadow price on <u>cutting time</u> is $4.75. This means that an additional hour of cutting time, (if it could be obtained for free) will generate an additional $4.75 in profits. We would be willing to add an extra hour of cutting time if the cost were less than $4.75 per hour.

   We already have slack in the <u>sewing department</u>. Adding extra hours here is not necessary.

   The shadow price on <u>material</u> is $2.75. We would be willing to add an extra yard of material if its cost were less than $2.75.

   b. RHS ranges.

   i. The cutting department currently has 100 hours of capacity. The lower end of the range is 60 hours (100 – 40). The upper end of the range is 132 hours.

   ii. The shadow price for material is valid over the range of 33.33 to 100 yards.

9. Polly Astaire

   a. Let X_1 = number of shirts produced

   X_2 = number of shorts produced

   X_3 = number of pants produced

   Maximize: $\$10X_1 + \$10X_2 + \$23X_3$

   Subject to : $2X_1 + 2X_2 + 3X_3 \leq 120$ (department A)

   $X_1 + 3X_2 + 4X_3 \leq 160$ (department B)

   $2X_1 + X_2 + 4X_3 \leq 90$ (material)

   $X_1, X_2, \text{ and } X_3 \geq 0$

CMOM computer output for Polly Astaire.

CMOM — Linear Programming
Maximization
Data Entered

Number of	Variables	:	3
Number of	<= Constraints	:	3
Number of	= Constraints	:	0
Number of	>= Constraints	:	0

Model

	X_1	X_2	X_3	RHS
Max-Z	10	10	23	
Cutting	2	2	3	<= 120
Sewing	1	3	4	<= 160
Material	2	1	4	<= 90

CMOM — Linear Programming
Maximization
Solution

Variable Label	Variable Value	Original Coefficient	Coefficient Sensitivity
X_1	7.78	10	0
X_2	38.89	10	0
X_3	8.89	23	0

Constraint Label	Original RHV	Slack or Surplus	Shadow Price
DeptA	120	0	0.55
DeptB	160	40	1.7778
MTL	90	0	3.5556

Objective Function Value: 671.111

b. The optimal solution is :

$X_1 =$ 7.78 shirts $s_1 =$ 0 (no slack in department A)

$X_2 =$ 38.89 shorts $s_2 =$ 40 (slack in department B)

$X_3 =$ 8.89 pants $s_3 =$ 0 (no extra material)

Total profits = 7.78($10) + 38.89($10) + 8.89($23)

$$= \$77.80 + \$388.90 + \$204.47$$

$$= \$671.17$$

c. Referring to the computer output columns for shadow prices, Polly Astaire would pay

i. $0.55 for an additional hour of capacity in department A.

ii. $1.78 for an additional hour of capacity in department B.

iii. The shadow prices for department A are valid for right-hand values from 111.25 hours to 136 hours. For department B, they range from 120 hours to 174 hours.

10. Butterfield

    a. Maximize: $\$10X_1 + \$10.5X_2 + \$9C + \$11D + \$9E$

        Subject to:

$0.05X_1 + 0.15X_2 + 0.20X_3 + 0.15X_4 + 0.05X_5$	$\leq$	1,500	(machine 1)
$0.10X_1 + 0.10X_2 + 0.05X_3 + 0.10X_4 + 0.10X_5$	$\leq$	1,400	(machine 2)
$0.15X_1 + 0.05X_2 + 0.10X_3 + 0.10X_4 + 0.10X_5$	$\leq$	1,600	(machine 3)
$0.05X_1 + 0.05X_2 + 0.20X_3 + 0.10X_4 + 0.05X_5$	$\leq$	1,500	(machine 4)
$4X_1 + 6X_2 + 1X_3 + 2X_4 + 6X_5$	$\leq$	75,000	(material 1)
$2X_1 + 8X_2 + 3X_3 + 5X_4 + 10X_5$	$\leq$	100,000	(material 2)
X_1, X_2, X_3, X_4, X_5	$\geq$	0	

    b. The optimal solution is :

            $X_1 = $ 7,875 units

            $X_2 = $ 5,375 units

            $X_3 = $ 1,500 units

        Total profit is $148,687.50.

11. Nutmeg Corporation

    a. Linear programming formulation, where the first letter in a variable name indicates the type of nut (A for almond, W for walnut, and P for peanut) and the second letter indicates the type of pack (A for almond, W for walnut, G for gourmet, F for fancy, and T for thrifty).

Maximize:

$\$0.80AA + \$0.80AG + \$0.80AF + \$0.80AT + \$0.60WW + \$0.60WG + \$0.60WF + \$0.60WT + \$0.35PG + \$0.35PF + \$0.35PT$

Subject to:

(1) limit on almonds

    $AA + AG + AF + AT \leq 3000$

(2) limit on walnuts

    $WW + WG + WF + WT \leq 2000$

(3) almond pack demand

    $AA = 1250$

(4) walnut pack demand

    $WW = 750$

(5) gourmet pack demand

    $AG + WG + PG = 1000$

(6) fancy pack demand

    $AF + WF + PF = 500$

(7) thrifty pack demand

    $AT + WT + PT = 1500$

(8) almonds in gourmet pack

    $AG \geq 450$

(9) walnuts in gourmet pack

    $WG \geq 450$

(10) almonds in fancy pack

    $AF \geq 150$

(11) walnuts in fancy pack

    $WF \geq 150$

(12) almonds in thrifty pack

    $AT \geq 300$

(13) walnuts in thrifty pack

    $WT \geq 300$

(nonnegative constraints)

    $AA, AG, AF, AT, WW, WG, WF, WT, PG, PF, PT \geq 0$

CMOM Solution to Nutmeg Corporation

The CMOM input data for the Nutmeg problem is shown below. The demand for each type of pack is met for a total cost of $3,130. A total of 2150 pounds of almonds (1250 + 450 + 150 + 300) = 1650 pounds of walnuts (750 + 450 + 150 + 300), and 1200 pounds of peanuts are in the optimal mix.

CMOM — Linear Programming
Minimization

Data Entered

Number of Variables	:	11	
Number of <= Constraints	:	2	
Number of = Constraints	:	5	
Number of >= Constraints	:	6	

Model

	AA	AG	AF	AT	WW	WG	WF
Min-Z	0.80	0.80	0.80	0.80	0.60	0.60	0.60
C1	1	1	1	1	0	0	0
C2	0	0	0	0	1	1	1
C3	1	0	0	0	0	0	0
C4	0	0	0	0	1	0	0
C5	0	1	0	0	0	1	0
C6	0	0	1	0	0	0	1
C7	0	0	0	1	0	0	0
C8	0	1	0	0	0	0	0
C9	0	0	0	0	0	1	0
C10	0	0	1	0	0	0	0
C11	0	0	0	0	0	0	1
C12	0	0	0	1	0	0	0
C13	0	0	0	0	0	0	0

	WT	PG	PF	PT	RHV
Min-Z	0.60	0.35	0.35	0.35	
C1	0	0	0	0	<=3000
C2	1	0	0	0	<=2000
C3	0	0	0	0	= 1250
C4	0	0	0	0	= 750
C5	0	1	0	0	= 1000
C6	0	0	1	0	= 500
C7	1	0	0	1	= 1500
C8	0	0	0	0	>= 450
C9	0	0	0	0	>= 450
C10	0	0	0	0	>= 150
C11	0	0	0	0	>= 150
C12	0	0	0	0	>= 300
C13	1	0	0	0	>= 300

CMOM Solution to Nutmeg Corporation

CMOM — Linear Programming
Minimization

Solution

Variable Label	Variable Value	Original Coefficient	Coefficient Sensitivity
AA	1250	0.8000	0
AG	450	0.8000	0
AF	150	0.8000	0
AT	300	0.8000	0
WW	750	0.6000	0
WG	450	0.6000	0
WF	150	0.6000	0
WT	300	0.6000	0
PG	100	0.3500	0
PF	200	0.3500	0
PT	900	0.3500	0

Constraint Label	Original RHV	Slack or Surplus	Shadow Price
C1	3000	850	0
C2	2000	350	0
C3	1250	0	0.8000
C4	750	0	0.6000
C5	1000	0	0.3500
C6	500	0	0.3500
C7	1500	0	0.3500
C8	450	0	0.4500
C9	450	0	0.2500
C10	150	0	0.4500
C11	150	0	0.2500
C12	300	0	0.4500
C13	300	0	0.2500

Objective Function Value: 3130

b. There is no impact of a 2000-pound limit because this amount exceeds the 1200 pounds now used in the optimal solution. There will be an impact when the limit is less than 1200 pounds.

c. The right-hand sides become 500 pounds for constraints 8 and 9. The solution to the revised problem is shown on the next page. The total cost increases to \$3,165 because the amount of peanuts (a relatively inexpensive resource) must be less. A total of 2200 pounds of almonds (1250 + 500 + 150 + 300), 1700 pounds of walnuts (750 + 500 + 150 + 300), and 1100 pounds of peanuts (0 + 200 + 900) are in the optimal mix.

CMOM Solution to Nutmeg Corporation, Part c.

CMOM — Linear Programming
Minimization

Solution

Variable Label	Variable Value	Original Coefficient	Coefficient Sensitivity
AA	1250	0.8000	0
AG	500	0.8000	0
AF	150	0.8000	0
AT	300	0.8000	0
WW	750	0.6000	0
WG	500	0.6000	0
WF	150	0.6000	0
WT	300	0.6000	0
PG	0	0.3500	no limit
PF	200	0.3500	0
PT	900	0.3500	0

Constraint Label	Original RHV	Slack or Surplus	Shadow Price
C1	3000	800	0
C2	2000	300	0
C3	1250	0	0.8000
C4	750	0	0.6000
C5	1000	0	no limit
C6	500	0	0.3500
C7	1500	0	0.3500
C8	500	0	no limit
C9	500	0	no limit
C10	150	0	0.4500
C11	150	0	0.2500
C12	300	0	0.4500
C13	300	0	0.2500

Objective Function Value: 3165

d. Three right-hand sides in the original formulation must be changed: 1000 pounds for constraint 6, 300 pounds for constraint 10, and 300 pounds for constraint 11. The CMOM output for this revised formulation is shown on the next page. The objective function increases to $3,410, because of the additional production. A total of 2300 pounds of almonds (1250 + 450 + 300 + 300), 1800 pounds of walnuts (750 + 450 + 300 + 300), and 1400 pounds of peanuts (100 + 400 + 900) are in the new solution.

CMOM — Linear Programming
Minimization

Solution

Variable Label	Variable Value	Original Coefficient	Coefficient Sensitivity
AA	1250	0.8000	0
AG	450	0.8000	0
AF	300	0.8000	0
AT	300	0.8000	0
WW	750	0.6000	0
WG	450	0.6000	0
WF	300	0.6000	0
WT	300	0.6000	0
PG	100	0.3500	0
PF	400	0.3500	0
PT	900	0.3500	0

Constraint Label	Original RHV	Slack or Surplus	Shadow Price
C1	3000	700	0
C2	2000	200	0
C3	1250	0	0.8000
C4	750	0	0.6000
C5	1000	0	0.3500
C6	1000	0	0.3500
C7	1500	0	0.3500
C8	450	0	0.4500
C9	450	0	0.2500
C10	300	0	0.4500
C11	300	0	0.2500
C12	300	0	0.4500
C13	300	0	0.2500

Objective Function Value: 3410

12. Lisa Rankin.

Let A = fraction of material A used in a gallon of finished product

B = fraction of material B used in a gallon of finished product

C = fraction of material C used in a gallon of finished product

The linear programming model is formulated as:

$$
\begin{array}{lrcrcrclcl}
\text{Minimize:} & 0.6A & + & 0.4B & + & 0.5C & & & & \\
\text{Subject to:} & 4A & + & 3B & + & 10C & \leq & 6 & & \text{(1) Gamma content} \\
& A & + & B & + & C & = & 1 & & \text{(2) Fractions sum to one} \\
& 200A & + & 180B & + & 280C & \geq & 220 & & \text{(3) Combustion point} \\
& 20A & + & 10B & + & 8C & \geq & 12 & & \text{(4) Zeta content} \\
& & & & & A, B, C & \geq & 0 & &
\end{array}
$$

The optimal solution is:

$$A = 0.269 \qquad B = 0.385 \qquad C = 0.346$$

CMOM computer output for Lisa Rankin.

CMOM — Linear Programming

Maximization

Data Entered

Number of	Variables	: 3
Number of	<= Constraints	: 1
Number of	= Constraints	: 1
Number of	>= Constraints	: 2

Model

	A	B	C		RHS
Min-Z	0.6	0.4	0.5		
GAMMA	4	3	10	<=	6
FRACT	1	1	1	=	1
CMBPT	200	180	280	>=	220
ZETA	20	10	8	>=	12

CMOM — Linear Programming

Maximization

Solution

Variable Label	Variable Value	Original Coefficient	Coefficient Sensitivity
A	0.2692	0.6	0
B	0.3846	0.4	0
C	0.3462	0.5	0

Constraint Label	Original RHV	Slack or Surplus	Shadow Price
GAMMA	6	0.3077	0
FRACT	1	0	0.0154
COMB	220	0	0.0013
ZETA	12	0	0.0173

Objective Function Value: 0.4885

13. Small fabrication firm

a. First, determine the contribution margin of each blade type by subtracting the material costs from the selling price.

Component A

32 oz. @ $0.20 per oz.	= $ 6.40	(material 1)
12 oz. @ $0.35 per oz.	= 4.20	(material 2)
Cost	= $10.60	

Contribution margin = $40.00 − $10.60 = $29.40

Component B

26 oz. @ $0.20 per oz.	= $ 5.20	(material 1)
16 oz. @ $0.35 per oz.	= 5.60	(material 2)
Cost	= $10.80	

Contribution margin = $28.00 − $10.80 = $17.20

Component C

19 oz. @ $0.20 per oz.	= $3.80	(material 1)
9 oz. @ $0.35 per oz.	= 3.15	(material 2)
Cost	= $6.95	

Contribution margin = $24.00 − $6.95 = $17.05.

The objective function and constraints are as follows:

Maximize : $29.40A + 17.20B + 17.05C$

Subject to :

$$0.25A + 0.20B + 0.10C \leq 1,600 \quad \text{(machine 1)}$$
$$0.10A + 0.15B + 0.05C \leq 1,400 \quad \text{(machine 2)}$$
$$0.05A + 0.10B + 0.15C \leq 1,500 \quad \text{(machine 3)}$$
$$32A + 26B + 19C \leq 200,000 \quad \text{(material 1)}$$
$$12A + 16B + 9C \leq 85,000 \quad \text{(material 2)}$$
$$B \geq 1,200 \quad \text{(minimum for product B)}$$
$$A, B, C \geq 0$$

b. The optimal solution is :

A = 5,275 units
B = 1,200 units
C = 0 unit

Total Profit	= $29.40(5,275) + $17.20(1,200)
	= $155,085 + $20,640
	= $175,725

CMOM computer output for Small Fabrication Firm.

CMOM — Linear Programming
Maximization
Data Entered

Number of	Variables	: 3
Number of	<= Constraints	: 5
Number of	= Constraints	: 0
Number of	>= Constraints	: 1

Model

	A	B	C		RHS
Max-Z	29.40	17.20	17.05		
MCHN1	0.25	0.20	0.10	<=	1600
MCHN2	0.10	0.15	0.05	<=	1400
MCHN3	0.05	0.10	0.15	<=	1500
MATL1	32	26	19	<=	200000
MATL2	12	16	9	<=	85000
MINB	0	1	0	<=	1200

CMOM — Linear Programming
Maximization
Solution

Variable Label	Variable Value	Original Coefficient	Coefficient Sensitivity
A	5275	29.4000	0
B	1200	17.2000	0
C	0	17.0500	0.4063

Constraint Label	Original RHV	Slack or Surplus	Shadow Price
MCHN1	1600	41.2500	0
MCHN2	1400	692.5000	0
MCHN3	1500	1116.2500	0
MATL1	200000	0	0.9187
MATL2	85000	2500	0
MINB	1200	0	6.6875

Objective Function Value: 175725

Sensitivity Analysis
Objective Function Coefficients

Variable Label	Lower Limit	Original Coefficient	Upper Limit
A	28.7158	29.4000	no limit
B	no limit	17.2000	23.8875
C	no limit	17.0500	17.4562

Right-Hand-Side Values

Constraint Label	Lower Limit	Original Value	Upper Limit
MCHN1	1.5588	1.6000	no limit
MCHN2	0.7075	1.4000	no limit
MCHN3	0.3837	1.5000	no limit
MATL1	31.2000	200	205.2800
MATL2	82.5000	85	no limit
MINB	0	1.2000	1.600

14. Maxine's hat Company.

   a. False. The coefficient sensitivity of variable x_3 is \$0.75, which means the price of hat 3 must increase by 75 cents in order to warrant the production of hat 3 and maximize profits. A selling price of \$2.50 would not be high enough.

   b. True. The lower limit for machine C is 59.375 hours, and the current solution has a slack of 100.625 hours. Therefore, if the new capacity is reduced from 95 hours to 65 hours, the production schedule will remain unchanged and yield the same profits.

   c. False. Each extra hour of machine A's time has a shadow price of \$0.25, which continues until the capacity expands from 150 hours to 166.7 hours. The amount of production and profits over that range is changing.

15. Washington Chemical Company.

   Let X_1 = annual production quantity of product 1
   X_2 = annual production quantity of product 2
   X_3 = annual production quantity of product 3
   X_4 = annual production quantity of product 4
   X_5 = annual production quantity of product 5

Maximize:

$$4X_1 + 7X_2 + 3.5X_3 + 4X_4 + 5.7X_5$$

Subject to:

$$0.05X_1 + 0.10X_2 + 0.80X_3 + 0.57X_4 + 0.15X_5 \leq 7{,}500$$
$$0.20X_1 + 0.02X_2 + 0.20X_3 + 0.09X_4 + 0.30X_5 \leq 7{,}500$$
$$0.20X_1 + 0.50X_2 + 0.10X_3 + 0.40X_4 + 0.18X_5 \leq 10{,}000$$
$$0.70X_2 + 0.50X_4 \leq 6{,}000$$
$$0.10X_1 + 0.20X_2 + 0.40X_3 \leq 7{,}000$$
$$X_3 \geq 3{,}000$$
$$X_4 \geq 3{,}000$$

CMOM computer output for Washington Chemical Company problem.

CMOM — Linear Programming

Maximization

Data Entered

Number of Variables   : 5
Number of <= Constraints   : 5
Number of = Constraints   : 0
Number of >= Constraints   : 2

Model

	X_1	X_2	X_3	X_4	X_5	RHS
Max-Z	4	7	3.50	4	5.70	
REACT	0.05	0.10	0.80	0.57	0.15	<= 7500
SEPR	0.20	0.02	0.20	0.09	0.30	<= 7500
RMTL1	0.20	0.50	0.10	0.40	0.18	<=10000
RMTL2	0	0.70	0	0.50	0	<= 6000
RMTL3	0.10	0.20	0.40	0	0	<= 7000
MINX3	0	0	1	0	0	>= 3000
MINX4	0	0	0	1	0	>= 3000

CMOM — Linear Programming
Maximization
Solution

Variable Label	Variable Value	Original Coefficient	Coefficient Sensitivity
X_1	17310.7051	4	0
X_2	6428.5718	7	0
X_3	3000	3.5	0
X_4	3000	4	0
X_5	10130.9590	5.7	0

Constraint Label	Original RHV	Slack or Surplus	Shadow Price
REACT	7500	361.9636	0
SEPR	7500	0	17.500
RMTL1	10000	0	2.500
RMTL2	6000	0	7.7143
RMTL3	7000	2783.2153	0
MINX3	3000	0	0.2500
MINX4	3000	0	2.4321

Objective Function Value: 194489.2810

The optimal solution is:

$$X_1 = 17{,}311, X_2 = 6429, X_3 = 3000, X_4 = 3000, X_5 = 10{,}131$$

Sensitivity Analysis
Objective Function Coefficients

Variable Label	Lower Limit	Original Coefficient	Upper Limit
X_1	3.8000	4	4.8852
X_2	3.5950	7	no limit
X_3	no limit	3.5000	3.7500
X_4	no limit	4	6.4321
X_5	5.4000	5.7000	6

Right-Hand-Side Values

Constraint Label	Lower Limit	Original Value	Upper Limit
REACT	7.1380	7.5000	no limit
SEPR	6.2843	7.5000	7.9137
RMTL1	9.4209	10	11.2157
RMTL2	4.2271	6	6.6415
RMTL3	4.2168	7	no limit
MINX3	0	3	3.5265
MINX4	0	3	3.7884

16. Warwick Manufacturing Company.

Let I_t = number of shovels to be left over as inventory in period t
W_t = number of workers in period t
H_t = number of workers hired in period t
F_t = number of workers fired in period t
O_t = number of shovels produced by overtime
S_t = number of shovels produced by subcontracting
D_t = forecasted demand in period t

Objective and Constraints

Minimize $\$280\,I_t + 14{,}000W_t + 3700O_t + 4200\,S_t + 1000H_t + 600F_t$

Subject to:

$$
\begin{aligned}
4W_1 + O_1 + S_1 + I_0 - I_1 &= 70 \\
4W_2 + O_2 + S_2 + I_1 - I_2 &= 150 \\
4W_3 + O_3 + S_3 + I_2 - I_3 &= 320 \\
4W_4 + O_4 + S_4 + I_3 - I_4 &= 100 \\
W_1 - W_0 - H_1 + F_1 &= 0 \\
W_2 - W_1 - H_2 + F_2 &= 0 \\
W_3 - W_2 - H_3 + F_3 &= 0 \\
W_4 - W_3 - H_4 + F_4 &= 0
\end{aligned}
$$

$$
\begin{aligned}
O_t &\le 15 & t &= 1, 2, 3, 4 \\
S_t &\le 5 & t &= 1, 2, 3, 4 \\
W_0 &= 30 \\
W_4 &= 30 \\
I_0 &= 30 \\
I_4 &= 30
\end{aligned}
$$

Optimal Solution

$I_0 = 30$	$W_0 = 30$		
$W_1 = 30$	$W_2 = 46.875$	$W_3 = 46.875$	$W_4 = 30$
$O_1 = 0$	$O_2 = 0$	$O_3 = 15$	$O_4 = 10$
$S_1 = 0$	$S_2 = 0$	$S_3 = 0$	$S_4 = 0$
$I_1 = 80$	$I_2 = 117.5$	$I_3 = 0$	$I_4 = 30$
$H_1 = 0$	$H_2 = 16.875$	$H_3 = 0$	$H_4 = 0$
$F_1 = 0$	$F_2 = 0$	$F_3 = 0$	$F_4 = 16.875$

Production Plan

Quarter	Regular Time	Overtime	Subcontracting	Anticipated Inventory
1	30	0	0	80
2	46.875	0	0	117.5
3	46.875	15	0	0
4	30	10	0	30

Total cost = $2,335,700

17. Warwick, continued. The model is the same as for Problem 16, except for the demand constraints:

$$4W_1 + O_1 + S_1 + I_0 - I_1 = 120$$
$$4W_2 + O_2 + S_2 + I_1 - I_2 = 180$$
$$4W_3 + O_3 + S_3 + I_2 - I_3 = 180$$
$$4W_4 + O_4 + S_4 + I_3 - I_4 = 160$$

Optimal Solution

$$I_0 = 30 \qquad\qquad W_0 = 30$$

$W_1 = 30$	$W_2 = 46.25$	$W_3 = 46.25$	$W_4 = 30$
$O_1 = 0$	$O_2 = 0$	$O_3 = 15$	$O_4 = 15$
$S_1 = 0$	$S_2 = 0$	$S_3 = 0$	$S_4 = 0$
$I_1 = 30$	$I_2 = 35$	$I_3 = 55$	$I_4 = 30$
$H_1 = 0$	$H_2 = 16.25$	$H_3 = 0$	$H_4 = 0$
$F_1 = 0$	$F_2 = 0$	$F_3 = 0$	$F_4 = 16.25$

Production Plan

Quarter	Regular Time	Overtime	Subcontracting	Anticipated Inventory
1	30	0	0	30
2	46.25	0	0	35
3	46.25	15	0	55
4	30	15	0	30

Total cost = $2,314,000

The cost of this plan is $21,700 lower than for the original demand structure plan in Problem 18.

Demand management can reduce the costs of production, primarily through reduced inventory costs in this problem.

18. Briley Cosmetics.

Definition of decision variables

X_1 = Cartons of face cream produced during first shift

X_2 = Cartons of face cream produced during second shift

X_3 = Cartons of face cream imported

X_4 = Cartons of body cream produced during first shift

X_5 = Cartons of body cream produced during second shift

X_6 = Cartons of body cream imported

X_7 = Cartons of shampoo produced during first shift

X_8 = Cartons of shampoo produced during second shift

Per carton cost of $X_1 = \$8.50(1.5) + \$9.25(0.8) + \$1.00(5) + \$1.50(7) = \$35.65$

Per carton cost of $X_2 = \$9.35(1.5) + \$10.175(0.8) + \$1.00(5) + \$1.50(7) = \$37.665$

Per carton cost of $X_3 = \qquad\qquad = \$40.00$

Per carton cost of $X_4 = \$8.50(1.8) + \$9.25(1.0) + \$1.00(8) + \$1.50(4) = \$38.55$

Per carton cost of $X_5 = \$9.35(1.8) + \$10.175(1.0) + \$1.00(8) + \$1.50(4) = \$41.005$

Per carton cost of $X_6 = \qquad\qquad = \$55.00$

Per carton cost of $X_7 = \$8.50(1.0) + \$9.25(0.5) + \$1.00(3) + \$1.50(9) = \$29.625$

Per carton cost of $X_8 = \$9.35(1.0) + \$10.175(0.5) + \$1.00(3) + \$1.50(9) = \$30.9375$

Minimize:

$\$35.65X_1 + \$37.665X_2 + \$40X_3 + \$38.55X_4 + \$41.005X_5 + \$55X_6 + \$29.625X_7 + \$30.9375X_8 = z$ (objective function)

Subject to:

$$1.5X_1 \qquad\qquad +1.8X_4 \qquad\qquad +1.0X_7 \qquad \le 15,000 \text{ (1) 1st shift, stage 1 labor}$$

$$1.5X_2 \qquad\qquad +1.8X_5 \qquad\qquad +1.0X_8 \le 13,500 \text{ (2) 2nd shift, stage 1 labor}$$

$$0.8X_1 \qquad\qquad +1.0X_4 \qquad\qquad +0.5X_7 \qquad \le 10,000 \text{ (3) 1st shift, stage 2 labor}$$

$$0.8X_2 \qquad\qquad +1.0X_5 \qquad\qquad +0.5X_8 \le 9,000 \text{ (4) 2nd shift, stage 2 labor}$$

$$5.0X_1 +5.0X_2 \quad +8.0X_4 +8.0X_5 \quad +3.0X_7 +3.0X_8 \le 200,000 \text{ (5) raw material A}$$

$$7.0X_1 +7.0X_2 \quad +4.0X_4 +4.0X_5 \quad +9.0X_7 +9.0X_8 \le 150,000 \text{ (6) raw material B}$$

$$X_1 + X_2 + X_3 \qquad\qquad\qquad \ge 10,000 \text{ (7) face cream demand}$$

$$X_4 + X_5 + X_6 \qquad\qquad \ge 5,000 \text{ (8) body cream demand}$$

$$X_7 + X_8 \ge 15,000 \text{ (9) shampoo demand}$$

$$X_1, X_2, X_3, X_4, X_5, X_6, X_7, X_8 \ge 0 \text{ (non-negativity)}$$

a. Optimal production schedule.

First shift:			Second shift		
X_1 = Face Cream,	0	cartons	X_2 = Face Cream,	0	cartons
X_4 = Body Cream,	3,750	cartons	X_5 = Body Cream,		cartons
X_7 = Shampoo,	8,250	cartons	X_8 = Shampoo,	6,750	cartons

Import:

X_3 = Face Cream, 10,000 cartons

X_6 = Body Cream, 1,250 cartons

b. Minimum cost of production schedule = $\$1,066,550$

c. Shadow price of stage 1 labor = $\$1.313$ (first shift)

   Shadow price of stage 2 labor = $\$0$

d. Shadow price of raw material A = $\$0$ /lb

   Shadow price of raw material B = $\$3.5216$ /lb

e. RHS ranging for raw material B. Shadow price is valid from 135,000 lb/mo to 155,000 lb/mo.

f. Re-solve for constraints 7, 8, and 9 decreased by 10%:

First shift:			Second shift		
X_1 = Face Cream,	1,500	cartons	X_2 = Face Cream,	0	cartons
X_4 = Body Cream,	4,500	cartons	X_5 = Body Cream,	0	cartons
X_7 = Shampoo,	4,650	cartons	X_8 = Shampoo,	8,850	cartons

Import:

X_3 = Face Cream,   7,500   cartons
X_6 = Body Cream,   0   cartons

Minimum cost of production schedule = \$938,507.50

g. Imported body cream would enter the solution if the cost is \$42.2737 per carton (or less).
See sensitivity analysis objective function coefficient lower limit for X_6.

19. Westlake Electronics.

Definition of decision variables

P_1 = portable televisions produced in facility 1

P_2 = portable televisions produced in facility 2

P_3 = portable televisions produced in facility 3

R_1 = regular televisions produced in facility 1

R_2 = regular televisions produced in facility 2

R_3 = regular televisions produced in facility 3

H_1 = home theater televisions produced in facility 1

H_2 = home theater televisions produced in facility 2

H_3 = home theater televisions produced in facility 3

Maximize:

$\$75P_1 + \$75P_2 + \$75P_3 + \$125R_1 + \$125R_2 + \$125R_3 + \$200H_1 + \$200H_2 + \$200H_3 = z$ (objective function)

Subject to:

$3P_1 \qquad\qquad + 4R_1 \qquad\qquad + 7H_1 \qquad\qquad \leq 10,000$ (1) fabrication facility 1

$3P_2 \qquad\qquad + 4R_2 \qquad\qquad + 7H_2 \qquad \leq 15,000$ (2) fabrication facility 2

$3P_3 \qquad\qquad + 4R_3 \qquad\qquad + 7H_3 \leq 5,000$ (3) fabrication facility 3

$9P_1 \qquad\qquad + 12R_1 \qquad\qquad + 16H_1 \qquad\qquad \leq 50,000$ (4) assembly facility 1

$9P_2 \qquad\qquad + 12R_2 \qquad\qquad + 16H_2 \qquad \leq 60,000$ (5) assembly facility 2

$9P_3 \qquad\qquad + 12R_3 \qquad\qquad + 16H_3 \leq 35,000$ (6) assembly facility 3

$P_1, P_2, P_3, R_4, R_5, R_6, H_7, H_8, H_9 \geq 0$ (non-negativity)

a. Optimal production schedule.

Facility #1:			Facility #2		
R_1 = Regular TV,	2,500	units	R_2 = Regular TV,	3,750	units

Facility #3:

R_3 = Regular TV,   1,250   units

b. Maximum value of production schedule = \$937,500

c. Shadow price of facility 1 fabrication time = \$31.25/hour
d. Additional constraints

$$P_1 + P_2 + P_3 \geq 1{,}500 \quad \text{(7) portable TV production}$$
$$H_1 + H_2 + H_3 \geq 500 \quad \text{(8) home theater TV production}$$

Revised production schedule.

Facility #1:

P_1 = Portable TV, 1,500 units
R_1 = Regular TV, 1,375 units

Facility #2

R_2 = Regular TV, 3,750 units

Facility #3:

R_3 = Regular TV, 375 units
H_3 = Regular TV, 500 units

Maximum value of production schedule = \$900,000

e. Increased RHS of constraints 1 - 6 by 10% (if part d portable and home theater production requirements are included).

Revised production schedule.

Facility #1:

P_1 = Regular TV, 1,500 units
R_1 = Regular TV, 1,625 units

Facility #2

R_2 = Regular TV, 4,125 units

Facility #3:

R_3 = Regular TV, 500 units
H_3 = Regular TV, 500 units

Maximum value of production schedule = \$993,750

(If part d requirements are not included, the solution is simply part a times 1.1.)

f. Constraints for equal utilization (in addition to constraints of part a only).

$$U_1 = \frac{12P_1 + 16R_1 + 23H_1}{60{,}000} \qquad \text{Utilization of facility 1}$$

$$U_2 = \frac{12P_2 + 16R_2 + 23H_2}{75{,}000} \qquad \text{Utilization of facility 2}$$

$$\frac{12P_1 + 16R_1 + 23H_1}{60{,}000} = \frac{12P_2 + 16R_2 + 23H_2}{75{,}000} \qquad \text{Utilization required to be equal}$$

$$60P_1 + 80R_1 + 115H_1 = 48P_2 + 64R_2 + 92H_2 \qquad \text{multiplied by 300,000}$$

$$60P_1 - 48P_2 + 80R_1 - 64R_2 + 115H_1 - 92H_2 = 0 \qquad \text{New constraint (#7)}$$

$$U_1 = \frac{12P_1 + 16R_1 + 23H_1}{60{,}000} \qquad \text{Utilization of facility 1}$$

$$U_3 = \frac{12P_2 + 16R_2 + 23H_2}{75{,}000} \qquad \text{Utilization of facility 3}$$

$$\frac{12P_1 + 16R_1 + 23H_1}{60{,}000} = \frac{12P_3 + 16R_3 + 23H_3}{40{,}000} \qquad \text{Utilization required to be equal}$$

$$24P_1 + 32R_1 + 46H_1 = 36P_3 + 48R_3 + 69H_3 \qquad \text{multiplied by 120,000}$$

$$24P_1 - 36P_3 + 32R_1 - 48R_3 + 46H_1 - 69H_3 = 0 \qquad \text{Constraint (#8)}$$

Constraint #7 sets utilization of facility 1 equal to utilization of facility 2. Constraint #8 sets utilization of facility 1 equal to utilization of facility 3. Therefore utilization of facility 2 must be equal to utilization of facility 3, since they are both equal to utilization of facility 1.

Revised production schedule.

Facility #1:   Facility #2

H_1 = Home theater,   1,304   units H_2 = Home theater,   1,630   units

Facility #3:

R_3 = Regular TV,   1,250   units

Maximum value of production schedule = $743206.56

Check:

Utilization of facility #1 = (1,304 x 23)/60,000 = 50%

Utilization of facility #2 = (1,630 x 23)/75,000 = 50%

Utilization of facility #3 = (1,250 x 16)/40,000 = 50%

20. Bull Grin.

Definition of decision variables:

D_t = thousands of pounds of supplement forecasted as demand for quarter t

I_t = thousands of pounds of supplement in inventory in quarter t

O_t = thousands of pounds of supplement produced on overtime in quarter t

S_t = thousands of pounds of supplement produced by subcontractor in quarter t

W_t = number of workers in quarter t

H_t = number of workers hired in quarter t

F_t = number of workers fired in quarter t

Minimize:

$$\sum_{t=1}^{4} 110I_t + 1620W_t + 1800O_t + 1000H_t + 600F_t 1100S_t = z$$

Subject to:

$$2W_t + O_t + S_t + I_{t-1} - I_t = D_t \quad (t = 1, 2, 3, 4)$$

$$W_t - W_{t-1} - H_t + F_t = 0 \quad (t = 1, 2, 3, 4)$$

$$O_t \le 30 \quad (t = 1, 2, 3, 4)$$

$$S_t \le 10 \quad (t = 1, 2, 3, 4)$$

$$I_4 = 40$$

$$W_4 = 180$$

$$I_0 = 40$$

$$W_0 = 180$$

$$I_t, O_t, S_t, W_t \ge 0 \quad (t = 1, 2, 3, 4)$$

21. Inside traders.

Definition of decision variables:

X_{CB} = millions of dollars invested in corporate bonds
X_{CS} = millions of dollars invested in common stock
X_{GC} = millions of dollars invested in gold certificates
X_{RE} = millions of dollars invested in real estate

Maximize:

$$8.5X_{CB} + 9X_{CS} + 10X_{GC} + 13X_{RE}$$

Subject to:

$$X_{CB} + X_{CS} + X_{GC} + X_{RE} \leq 5 \quad \text{(total)}$$
$$X_{CB} + X_{CS} \geq 2 \quad \text{(40\%)}$$
$$X_{RE} \leq 1 \quad \text{(20\%)}$$
$$X_{CB}, X_{CS}, X_{GC}, X_{RE} \geq 0 \quad \text{(non-negativity)}$$

22. NYNEX

Definition of decision variables

X_j = Number of operators beginning work in time period j.

Minimize:

$$X_1 + X_2 + X_3 + X_4 + X_5 + X_6 = z$$

Subject to:

$$X_1 + X_6 \geq 4$$
$$X_1 + X_2 \geq 6$$
$$X_2 + X_3 \geq 90$$
$$X_3 + X_4 \geq 85$$
$$X_4 + X_5 \geq 55$$
$$X_5 + X_6 \geq 20$$

$$X_1, X_2, X_3, X_4, X_5, X_6 \geq 0$$

Chapter 14

Material Requirements Planning

Study Questions

1. Independent and dependent demands are distinguished by the **source** of the demand. Those items demanded by customers **external** to the inventory system are said to experience **indepen:dent** demand. Dependent demand is derived from those entities, be they items or echelons, that experience independent demand. Most commonly the source of derived demand is the production plans of parent items.

   For the manufacturing firm selling products directly to customers, the items ordered by customers (finished goods and spare parts) experience independent demand. The component parts and raw materials used to produce the finished goods and spare parts experience dependent demand. Because the spare part items are usually components of an end item, they experience both independent and dependent demand.

   For the forwardly integrated distribution firm, the source of independent demand depends on where the inventory analyst draws the boundaries of the inventory system. If retail store inventories are centrally controlled, the demand for finished goods by customers in the store is independent demand. Demand for these same finished goods at a regional warehouse is dependent demand. If the inventory system boundary is drawn between the retail stores and the regional warehouses, orders placed by retail stores to the warehouse are considered to be dependent demand. The line is drawn where control over replenishment orders ends, and uncertainty begins.

   Independent demand is, at best, somewhat uncertain as to the quantity and timing of the demand. Generally the firm will attempt to forecast the level of independent demand. Forecasting levels of dependent demand does not make sense because, given a forecast for independent demand items, the firm can **compute** the timing and quantity of the dependent demand items.

2. The purposes of the MPS are to:
   - determine the production quantity of each end item in each planning period. Once the production lot sizes for the end items are determined, the requirements for the intermediate and purchased items can be determined using the bills of materials.
   - determine the due dates for the completion of production orders. It is the main source of information for marketing to establish delivery dates for specific customer orders.
   - provide the basis for determining the resources required to support the production plan.

3. The production plan is specified in terms of aggregate products, resources, and time. Its primary intent is to balance various objectives such as minimal costs, maximum customer service, and stable work-force levels, and consequently, to provide the system with production, shipping, work-force level, and inventory targets. The master production schedule (MPS) differs from the production plan in that it specifies the schedule for individual end items using smaller time periods. The MPS operationalizes the production plan and uses it as a goal or target.

4. Linking the production plan to the master production schedule has the advantage of taking into consideration the trade-offs associated with level work forces or increased anticipation inventories. It also has the advantage of including the goals and objectives of a variety of managers, including marketing and finance.

5. The master production scheduling process begins with an authorized production plan. With this plan as a guideline, a prospective (or trial) MPS is developed and checked to determine whether it is feasible with respect to available resources (or those authorized by the production plan). If the MPS satisfies the production plan and the resources provided, it becomes authorized. If insufficient resources are available, either the MPS must be changed (better timing of production quantities) or the production plan must be changed (more resources). The MPS is "prospective" until all constraints are checked and it becomes authorized.

6. Rough-cut capacity planning takes a prospective master production schedule and checks it for feasibility with respect to the firm's critical resources. Although it is only a crude estimate of the resource implications of a prospective MPS, it allows a quick evaluation of the schedule and helps to avoid authorizing schedules that will overload or otherwise inefficiently utilize the plant.

7. With an assemble-to-order strategy the MPS usually is prepared for major assemblies or modules rather than individual end items. In this environment a large number of end items are produced from a much smaller number of intermediate items. It is very difficult (if not impossible) to forecast demands for specific end items in this environment. It is easier to produce the major assemblies or modules and then wait for the specific customer order before assembling the desired product.

8. The procedures used in master production scheduling depend on the firm's competitive priorities and the approach it utilizes to create its competitive niche in the marketplace. If the firm uses a make-to-stock strategy, the MPS deals primarily with end items. With an assemble-to-order strategy, the MPS usually deals with major assemblies and coordinates with a final assembly schedule. A make-to-order strategy requires a master schedule of raw materials or critical resources such as labor or machine hours.

9. Production plans define what will be produced and how much capital is required to execute the plans. Unless marketing considers the production plan in developing its own plans, it may target quantities that production may not be able to produce, which may lead to unfilled orders and dissatisfied customers. Thus a realistic marketing plan must be based on a realistic production plan.

   Financial plans project resources required to support the production plan. In addition to requiring accurate estimates of the variable costs of production, estimating inventory levels is also needed to determine working capital needs. So realistic financial plans can be developed only by considering realistic and feasible production plans.

10. The available-to-promise information can be used by marketing or sales to set shipping dates for customers in a make-to-stock environment. The net effect is to help marketing or sales specify the lead time to the customers. When all delivery promises are made from the ATP information, and when production performs according to the MPS, customer service approaches 100%.

11. The on-hand balance is a time-phased projection of the actual physical quantity on hand plus any planned MPS receipts minus the larger of 1) actual requirements or 2) forecast requirements. This row is used in preparing the prospective MPS. Prospective MPS receipts are positioned in time periods as necessary to prevent the on-hand balance from dropping below the safety stock level (or zero if there is no safety stock). The available-to-promise quantity displays the net difference between a given MPS receipt quantity and the total of actual requirements until the next receipt of an MPS order. More simply put, the ATP shows the amount of each MPS order that is unsold, uncommitted, and therefore literally "available to promise." Whenever the ATP drops below zero, a promise has been made to a customer that will not be kept. Negative ATP's are an indication of poor customer service. The on-hand and the available-to-promise quantities could be the same in the first period if there are no requirements in any time period between the first period and the time period of the first MPS receipt.

12. The gross requirements for a component is the time-phased sum resulting from multiplying the planned order releases for each parent times the BOM usage quantities. The records of all of this component's parent items must be processed first, before the sum can be determined. Since the parents' records are located higher in the product structure than the component's records, a top-down processing of records is necessary.

13. Scheduled receipts are open orders, either within the company or to outside suppliers, that are expected to be received at the time expressed by the due date. Scheduled receipts are added to the projected-on-hand inventory balance in the week they are due. Planned order receipts are new orders not yet released. Planning for the receipt of these new orders will keep the projected on-hand balance from dropping below the safety stock. Planned order releases are simply the planned order receipts, offset by the item's lead time. They show when new orders will be released, rather than received, if everything goes according to plan. When a planned order release is actually released, the associated "planned" receipt becomes a "scheduled" receipt.

14. When safety stock is desired, planned order receipts are timed to prevent the projected on-hand inventory from dropping below the safety stock quantity. The MRP system will never *plan* to use safety stock, since safety stock is positioned to cover *unplanned* use. Since safety stock is intended to protect against uncertainty in lead time, demand, or supply, the proper amount and positioning of safety stock depends on the degree and location of uncertainty. With high uncertainty in end-item demand, it is better to maintain safety stock at the master production schedule (end-item) level. Safety stocks of components provide no protection for uncertainty in end-item demand. If unexpected demand occurs, there is no guarantee that safety stocks at the component level will exist in the matched sets required to produce additional end-items. On the other hand, if suppliers or production processes are unreliable, it is better to maintain safety stock at the component level. This will provide protection in the event of higher than expected defects or yield losses. Safety stocks are costly. They should be viewed as a *temporary* concession to practicality while searching for and eliminating the root causes of lead time variations, defects, and process yield losses.

15. The notion of a fundamental trade-off applies only when the firm already enjoys high levels of performance in inventory, customer service, and productivity. If the firm is not doing a good job in production and inventory control, it can suffer from:

    • high levels of inventory in items not currently needed;

    • low levels of customer service by not meeting customer orders within the prescribed lead time;

    • poor productivity due to frequent setups to produce urgently needed parts and frequent work interruptions due to component shortages.

    MRP systems simply substitute information for inventory. All three of these dimensions can show simultaneous improvement if the MRP adopter is able to utilize the MRP information to provide just the right parts, in just the right quantity, at just the right time, (just-in-time) to meet the production schedule. If we could have perfect information, it would theoretically be possible to have 100% customer service with zero inventory.

16. Safety stock and the previous week's projected on-hand balance can be ignored because they are equal and cancel each other out. The POQ rule aims to eliminate remnants. Thus the projected on-hand inventory is equal to the safety stock in the week prior to the receipt of a new planned order.

17. To realize measurable improvements from MRP, the firm must have the capability to utilize the MRP information to manage a complex set of activities. Thus a company will fail to achieve improvements if the MRP information is bad or its ability to execute the MRP plans is weak.

Bad MRP information can be generated by inaccurate inventory records, incorrect bills of materials, and unstable master production schedules. Poor execution can be caused by inadequate user education (users don't know how to use the MRP reports), lack of user support (they don't want to use MRP or don't believe the reports), and lack of top management support to create an environment conducive to successful execution of MRP schedules. Top management support is of primary importance because it has direct control over resources that must be expended to make MRP successful.

Of course, some manufacturing environments are more suited to the concept of MRP than others. The advantages of MRP are diminished when (i) there are few levels in the bills of materials; (ii) the lot sizes used in the MPS are small; (iii) there is great volatility in the manufacturing environment; and (iv) when the manufacturing process tends to be continuous and capital intensive.

18. Sharing planned order release information with suppliers can be advantageous to both the manufacturer and the supplier. Lead times for preparing and processing a purchase order can be reduced, thereby reducing the overall lead time of the manufactured product. Knowing the manufacturer's production requirements, the suppliers can plan their production better and thus reduce costs to themselves—and perhaps also to the buyer. There could be disadvantages in sharing information also. If plans and schedules are changed, the suppliers may also have to adjust their plans. This can be a problem if the manufacturer changes plans often. Linking the planned order releases of the manufacturer to the master schedule of the supplier could actually increase costs if the supplier reacts to every change.

19. MRP logic assumes that the time-phased gross requirements are accurate and reliable. For example the gross requirement projected for three weeks from now is expected to remain as projected next week. The types of changes and disruptions mentioned reduce the accuracy of such projections. For example:

- Last-minute changes in the master production schedule make the actual gross requirements of components different from what was previously projected. A master schedule change means in turn a change in component gross requirements.

- Unexpected scrap means an item's actual scheduled receipts will be different from those projected earlier. This discrepancy ultimately affects the item's planned order releases and therefore the gross requirements of the item's components.

- Late supplier shipments or capacity bottlenecks can mean a component is not available when needed. This shortage delays the parent's actual production which in turn delays the actual gross requirements for co-components.

- Once inventory record inaccuracies are discovered, an item's planned order releases can change. The result in turn is a change in the gross requirements of its components.

Problems

1. Bill of materials Fig. 14.28
   a. Item I has only one parent (item E). However, item E has two parents (items B and C).
   b. Item A has ten unique components (items B, C, D, E, F, G, H, I, J, and K).
   c. Item A has five purchased items (I, F, G, H, and K). These are the items without components.
   d. Item A has five intermediate items (B, C, D, E, and J). These items have both parents and components.
   e. The longest path is I-E-C-A at 11 weeks.

2. Item A. The bill of materials for item A is shown below.

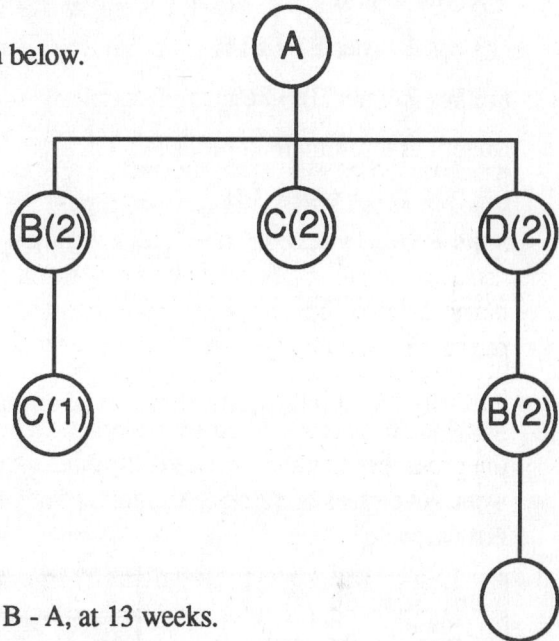

3. Lead time is determined by the longest path, C - B - A, at 13 weeks.

4. The bill of materials for item A with lead times is shown below.
   a. Lead time is determined by the longest path
      A - C - F = 10 weeks.
   b. If purchased items D, F, G and H are already in inventory, the lead time is reduced to: A - B - E = 6 weeks.

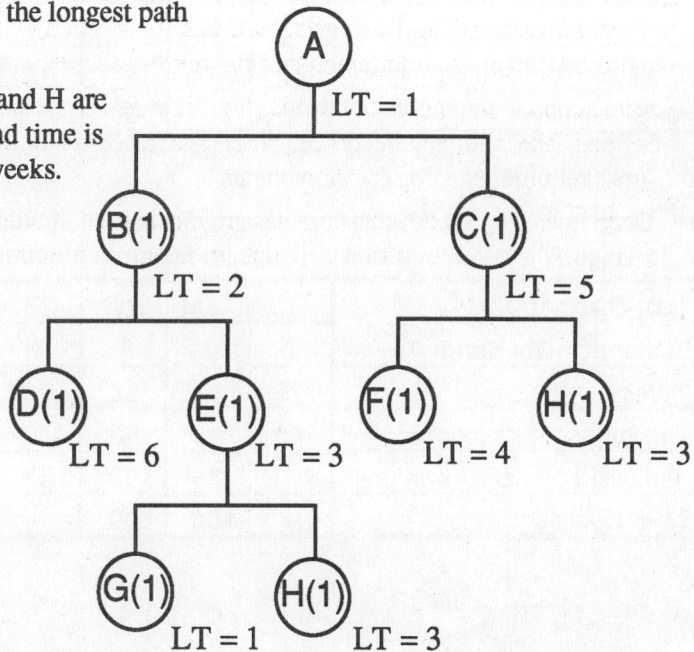

5. Refer to Figure 14.22 and Solved Problem 1.

FIGURE 14.22

Material requirement to produce 5 units of end-item A:

(5 A x 3 B per A) = 15 B – 2 B on hand = 13 B

(5 A x 1) = 5 C

Material requirement to produce 13 B:

(13 B x 1 D per B) = **13 D**

(13 B x 2 E per B) = **26 E**

Material requirement to produce 5 C:

(5 C x 1 D per C) = **5 D**

(5 Cx 1 F per C) = 5 F – 1 F on hand = 4 F

Material requirement to produce 4 F:

(4 F x 1 G) = **4 G**

Purchased material requirements net of on-hand inventory: 13 + 5 = 18 D, 26 E and 4G.

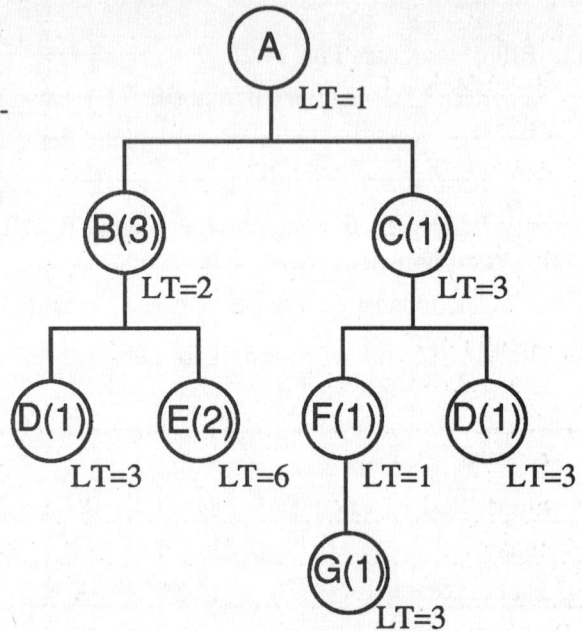

[Figure 14.22: Bill of materials tree. A (LT=1) branches to B(3) (LT=2) and C(1) (LT=3). B(3) branches to D(1) (LT=3) and E(2) (LT=6). C(1) branches to F(1) (LT=1) and D(1) (LT=3). F(1) branches to G(1) (LT=3).]

6. MPS record in Fig. 14.30.

Lot Size: 60	Week							
Quantity On Hand: 35	1	2	3	4	5	6	7	8
Forecast	17	15	25	25	20	27	30	35
Customer orders (booked)	15	16	5	11	9	0	5	0
Projected on-hand inventory	18	2	37	12	52	25	55	20
MPS Quantity			60		60		60	

7. MPS record in Fig. 14.31.

Lot Size: 100	January				February			
Quantity On Hand: 75	1	2	3	4	5	6	7	8
Forecast	75	65	50	45	65	65	75	75
Customer orders (booked)	40	10	55	0	35	70	0	0
Projected on-hand inventory	0	35	80	35	70	0	25	50
MPS Quantity		100	100		100		100	100

8. An end-item.

Lot Size: 75	Week									
Quantity On Hand: 70	1	2	3	4	5	6	7	8	9	10
Forecast	30	20	35	50	25	25	0	40	0	50
Customer orders (booked)	22	30	15	9	0	0	5	3	7	0
Projected on-hand inventory	40	10	50	0	50	25	20	55	48	73
MPS Quantity			75		75			75		75

9. At present.

   a. Prospective MPS

Lot Size: 125	Week									
Quantity On Hand: 50	1	2	3	4	5	6	7	8	9	10
Forecast	10	15	20	30	40	60	80	120	120	120
Customer orders (booked)	12	9	11	5	2	0	4	0	0	0
Projected on-hand inventory	38	23	3	98	58	123	43	48	53	58
MPS Quantity				125		125		125	125	125

   b. Revised MPS

Lot Size: 125	Week									
Quantity On Hand: 50	1	2	3	4	5	6	7	8	9	10
Forecast	10	15	20	30	40	60	80	120	120	120
Customer orders (booked)	12	9	11	5	2	0	4	0	0	0
Projected on-hand inventory	38	148	128	223	183	248	168	173	53	58
MPS Quantity		125		125		125		125		125

Advantage: production requirements are leveled.

Disadvantages: increased average inventory, linear-term increase in production for week 2.

10. Orange Peelers.

Prospective MPS.

Lot Size: 500	Week									
Quantity On Hand: 400	1	2	3	4	5	6	7	8	9	10
Forecast	550	300	400	450	300	350	200	300	450	400
Customer orders (booked)	300	350	250	250	200	150	100	100	100	100
Projected on-hand inventory	350	0	100	150	350	0	300	0	50	150
MPS Quantity	500		500	500	500		500		500	500

i. The first order for 500 (in week 4) should be accepted. Through week 4, on hand (400) plus three MPS quantities of 500 each = 1900. Of those, (300 + 350 + 250 + 250) = 1150 have been sold, leaving 750 available (250 after this commitment).

ii. The second order for 100 (in week 5) should be accepted. Through week 5, the 250 remaining after the first order plus one more MPS quantity of 500 = 750. Of those, 200 have been sold in the 5th week and 150 in the sixth week. Therefore, (250 + 500 – 200 – 150) = 400 are still available. There will be 300 remaining for sale even after accepting this order.

iii. The third order for 300 units (in week 1) should <u>not</u> be accepted. At that time, of the 400 on hand, plus 500 MPS quantity to arrive in the first week , a total of 300 plus 350 have been sold. Note that since no MPS is scheduled for the second week, the 350 ordered for the second week must come from those on hand or those arriving in the first week.

In total [(400 + 500) – (300 + 350)] = 250 remaining, which will not cover the order for 300.

iv. The fourth order for 350 units (in week 7) should be accepted. After accepting the second order (part ii), 300 units remained available. In the seventh week 500 more arrive. 300 + 500 = 800. Of those, demands of 100 in each of weeks 7 and 8 have been promised, leaving (800 – 200) = 600. This order of 350 units would reduce the quantity available to promise to 250 units.

11. Morrison Electronics.

a. Prospective MPS.

Quantity on hand: 100	1	2	3	4	5	6	7	8
Forecast	70	70	65	60	55	85	75	85
Customer orders (booked)	50	60	55	40	35	0	0	0
Projected on-hand inventory	30	110	45	135	80	145	70	135
MPS quantity		150		150		150		150

b. Revised forecast.

Quantity on hand: 100	1	2	3	4	5	6	7	8
Forecast	70	70	75	70	70	100	100	110
Customer orders (booked)	50	60	55	40	35	0	0	0
Projected on-hand inventory	30	110	35	115	45	95	–5	35
MPS quantity		150		150		150		150

Although the projected on-hand row indicates a negative balance, this difficulty will occur only if the actual orders meet the new forecast. If the new forecasts are "solid," we should consider revising the master production schedule or shifting demand to avoid stockouts in week 7.

12. Conestoga Wagon Company.

    a. Direct-labor requirements at frome building work station.

			Week				
	1	**2**	**3**	**4**	**5**	**6**	**Total**
Units	50	50	40	30	30	50	250
Direct labor hours	150	150	120	90	90	150	750

    b. Revised MPS.

			Week				
	1	**2**	**3**	**4**	**5**	**6**	**Total**
Forecast	50	50	40	30	30	50	250
Projected inventory	0	0	0	0	10	0	10
Revised MPS quantity	50	50	40	30	**40**	**40**	250
Direct labor hours	150	150	120	90	120	120	750

13. Marshall Fans.

				Month			
	Jan	**Feb**	**Mar**	**Apr**	**May**	**June**	**Total**
Desktop fans, units	300	400	200	400	500	750	2550
Total critical hours *	600	800	400	800	1000	1500	5100
Total noncritical hours †	900	1200	600	1200	1500	2250	7650
Total labor hours	1500	2000	1000	2000	2500	3750	12,750
Critical Work Stations							
401A (80% of critical hrs)	480	640	320	640	800	1200	4080
401B (20% of critical hrs)	120	160	80	160	200	300	1020
	600	800	400	800	1000	1500	5100

---

* fan units x 2 hours per unit
† fan units x 3 hours per unit

14. Karry Kart Comapny

    a. Load Profile, method of overall factors

			Week				
	1	**2**	**3**	**4**	**5**	**6**	**Total**
Deluxe Kart (DK), units	50	50	30	30	30	30	220
Standard Kart (SK), units	60	—	60	—	60	—	180
Total critical hours *	910	550	690	330	690	330	3500
Total noncritical hours †	440	200	360	120	360	120	1600
Total labor hours	1350	750	1050	450	1050	450	5100
Critical Work Stations							
Z101 (40%)	364	220	276	132	276	132	1400
Z105 (30%)	273	165	207	99	207	99	1050
Z107 (30%)	273	165	207	99	207	99	1050
	910	550	690	330	690	330	3500

---

* (DK x 11) + (SK x 6)
† (DK x 4) + (SK x 4)

b. The proposed schedule results in an uneven load in the factory. Total capacity is exceeded in week 1. Critical labor hour capacity is exceeded in week 1. By altering the MPS of SK such that 30 units are produced per week, the following load profile results.

	Week						
	1	**2**	**3**	**4**	**5**	**6**	**Total**
Deluxe Kart (DK), units	50	50	30	30	30	30	220
Standard Kart (SK), units	30	30	30	30	30	30	180
Total critical hours	730	730	510	510	510	510	3500
Total noncritical hours	320	320	240	240	240	240	1600
Total labor hours	1050	1050	750	750	750	750	5100
Critical Work Stations							
Z101 (40%)	292	292	204	204	204	204	1400
Z105 (30%)	219	219	153	153	153	153	1050
Z107 (30%)	219	219	153	153	153	153	1050
	730	730	510	510	510	510	3500

15. Inventory record

a. Fixed Order Quantity = 110.

Item:	M405—X			Lot Size:			FOQ: 110	
Description:	Table top assembly			Lead Time:			2 weeks	
				Safety Stock:			0 units	

Week		1	2	3	4	5	6	7	8
Gross requirements		90		85		80		45	90
Scheduled receipts		110							
Projected on hand	40	60	60	85	85	5	5	70	90
Planned receipts				110				110	110
Planned order releases		110				110	110		

b. L4L.

Item:	M405—X			Lot Size:			L4L	
Description:	Table top assembly			Lead Time:			2 weeks	
				Safety Stock:			0 units	

Week		1	2	3	4	5	6	7	8
Gross requirements		90		85		80		45	90
Scheduled receipts		110							
Projected on hand	40	60	60	0	0	0	0	0	0
Planned receipts				25		80		45	90
Planned order releases		25		80		45	90		

c. POQ, $P = 2$.

Item:	M405—X			Lot Size:			POQ, P = 2	
Description:	Table top assembly			Lead Time:			2 weeks	
				Safety Stock:			0 units	

Week		1	2	3	4	5	6	7	8
Gross requirements		90		85		80		45	90
Scheduled receipts		110							
Projected on hand	40	60	60	0	0	0	0	90	0
Planned receipts				25		80		135	
Planned order releases		25		80		135			

16. Rear wheel assembly, Fig. 14.35.

   a. Fixed Order Quantity = 220

Item:	MQ—09					Lot Size:		FOQ: 220	
Description:	Rear wheel assembly					Lead Time:		1 week	
						Safety Stock:		50 units	
Week		**1**	**2**	**3**	**4**	**5**	**6**	**7**	**8**
Gross requirements		205		130	85		70	60	95
Scheduled receipts		220							
Projected on hand	100	115	115	205	120	120	50	210	115
Planned receipts				220				220	
Planned order releases			220				220		

   b. Lot-for-lot.

Item:	MQ—09					Lot Size:		L4L	
Description:	Rear wheel assembly					Lead Time:		1 week	
						Safety Stock:		50 units	
Week		**1**	**2**	**3**	**4**	**5**	**6**	**7**	**8**
Gross requirements		205		130	85		70	60	95
Scheduled receipts		220							
Projected on hand	100	115	115	50	50	50	50	50	50
Planned receipts				65	85		70	60	95
Planned order releases			65	85		70	60	95	

   c. Period Order Quantity, $P = 3$.

Item:	MQ—09					Lot Size:		POQ = 3	
Description:	Rear wheel assembly					Lead Time:		1 week	
						Safety Stock:		50 units	
Week		**1**	**2**	**3**	**4**	**5**	**6**	**7**	**8**
Gross requirements		205		130	85		70	60	95
Scheduled receipts		220							
Projected on hand	100	115	115	135	50	50	205	145	50
Planned receipts				150			225		
Planned order releases			150			225			

17. Rear wheel assembly, Fig. 14.36.

    a. Fixed Order Quantity = 60

Item: GF—4								Lot Size:		FOQ: 60		
Description: Motor assembly								Lead Time:		3 weeks		
								Safety Stock:		30 units		
Week	1	2	3	4	5	6	7	8	9	10	11	12
Gross requirements		50		35		55		30		10		25
Scheduled receipts			60									
Projected on hand 40	40	−10	50	75	75	80	80	50	50	40	40	75
Planned receipts				60		60						60
Planned order releases	60		60						60			

The negative projected on hand in the second period would trigger an action notice, probably suggesting that the open order for the third week should be expedited to the second week.

    b. Lot-for-lot.

Item: GF—4								Lot Size:		L4L		
Description: Motor assembly								Lead Time:		3 weeks		
								Safety Stock:		30 units		
Week	1	2	3	4	5	6	7	8	9	10	11	12
Gross requirements		50		35		55		30		10		25
Scheduled receipts			60									
Projected on hand 40	40	−10	50	30	30	30	30	30	30	30	30	30
Planned receipts				15		55		30		10		25
Planned order releases	15		55		30		10		25			

    c. Period Order Quantity.

       $P = 60/15 = 4$.

Item: GF—4								Lot Size:		POQ, P=4		
Description: Motor assembly								Lead Time:		3 weeks		
								Safety Stock:		30 units		
Week	1	2	3	4	5	6	7	8	9	10	11	12
Gross requirements		50		35		55		30		10		25
Scheduled receipts			60									
Projected on hand 40	40	−10	50	85	85	30	30	40	40	30	30	30
Planned receipts				70				40				25
Planned order releases	70				40				25			

18. BOM for product A shown in Fig. 14.37.

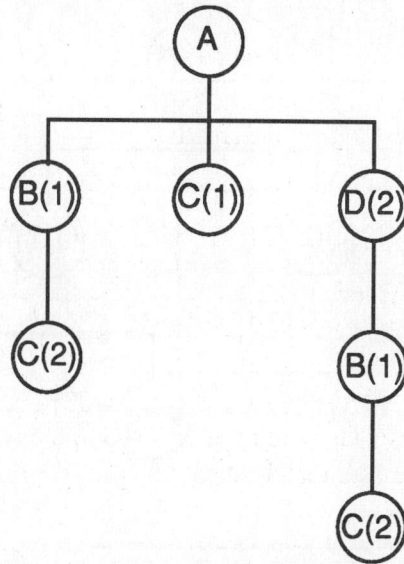

Item: D						Lot Size:		L4L
Description:						Lead Time:		3 weeks
						Safety Stock:		0 units

Week		1	2	3	4	5	6	7	8
Gross requirements							500		
Scheduled receipts									
Projected on hand	0	0	0	0	0	0	0		
Planned receipts							500		
Planned order releases				500					

Item: B						Lot Size:		L4L
Description:						Lead Time:		2weeks
						Safety Stock:		0 units

Week		1	2	3	4	5	6	7	8
Gross requirements				500			250		
Scheduled receipts									
Projected on hand	0	0	0	0	0	0	0		
Planned receipts				500			250		
Planned order releases		500			250				

Item: C						Lot Size:		FOQ 1000
Description:						Lead Time:		1 week
						Safety Stock:		100 units

Week		1	2	3	4	5	6	7	8
Gross requirements		1000			500		250		
Scheduled receipts		1000							
Projected on hand	200	200	200	200	700	700	450		
Planned receipts					1000				
Planned order releases				1000					

The only action required is to order 500 units of item B

19. MRP for Fig. 14.38.

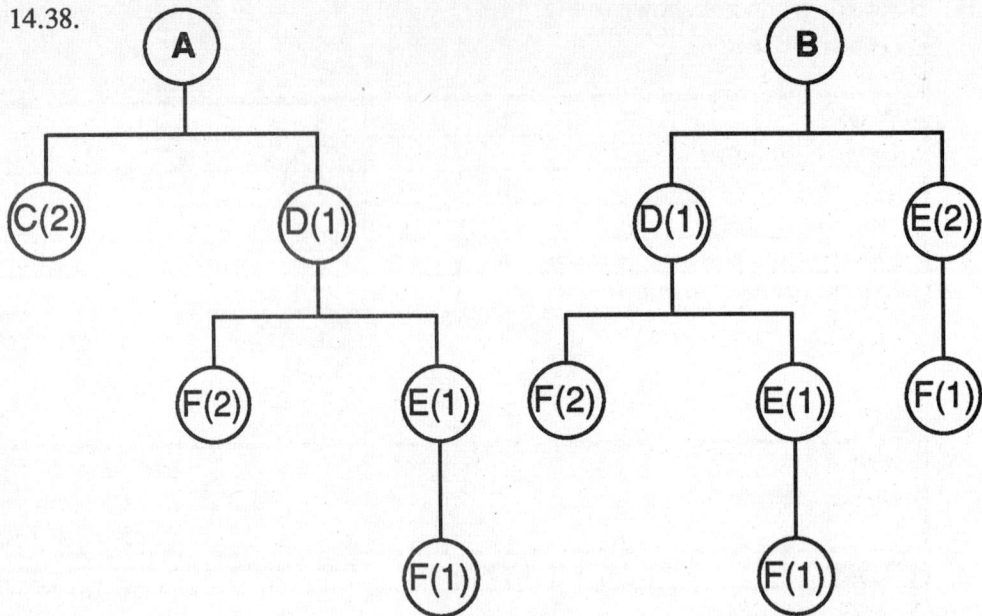

A
- C(2)
- D(1)
  - F(2)
  - E(1)
    - F(1)

B
- D(1)
  - F(2)
  - E(1)
    - F(1)
- E(2)
  - F(1)

Data Category	Item			
	C	D	E	F
Lot-size rule	FOQ = 220	L4L	FOQ = 300	POQ = (P=2)
Lead time	3 weeks	2 weeks	3 weeks	2 weeks
Safety stock	20	0	0	80
Scheduled receipts	280 (week 1)	None	300 (week 3)	None
On-hand inventory	25	0	150	600

Item: A	Week	1	2	3	4	5	6	7	8
MPS Quantity (due)					85			100	
MPS Quantity (release)				85			100		

Item: B	Week	1	2	3	4	5	6	7	8
MPS Quantity (due)								180	
MPS Quantity (release)						180			

Item: C   **Lot Size:** FOQ = 220
Description: **Lead Time:** 3 weeks
     Safety Stock: 20 units

Week		1	2	3	4	5	6	7	8
Gross requirements				170			200		
Scheduled receipts		280							
Projected on hand	25	305	305	135	135	135	155	155	155
Planned receipts							220		
Planned order releases				220					

Item: D   **Lot Size:** L4L
Description: **Lead Time:** 2 weeks
     Safety Stock: 0 units

Week		1	2	3	4	5	6	7	8
Gross requirements				85		180	100		
Scheduled receipts									
Projected on hand	0	0	0	0	0	0	0	0	0
Planned receipts				85		180	100		
Planned order releases		85		180	100				

Item: E   **Lot Size:** FOQ = 300
Description: **Lead Time:** 3 weeks
     Safety Stock: 0 units

Week		1	2	3	4	5	6	7	8
Gross requirements		85		180	100	360			
Scheduled receipts				300					
Projected on hand	150	65	65	185	85	25	25	25	25
Planned receipts						300			
Planned order releases			300						

Item: F   **Lot Size:** POQ = 2
Description: **Lead Time:** 2 weeks
     Safety Stock: 80 units

Week		1	2	3	4	5	6	7	8
Gross requirements		170	300	360	200				
Scheduled receipts									
Projected on hand	600	430	130	280	80	80	80	80	80
Planned receipts				510					
Planned order releases		510							

20. MRP for Fig. 14.39.

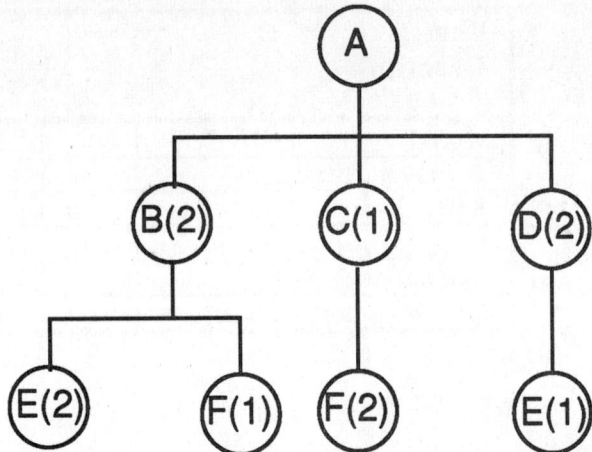

Item: A	Week	1	2	3	4	5	6	7	8	9	10
MPS Quantity (due)					50			65			80
MPS Quantity (release)			50			65			80		

Item: B				Lot Size:	L4L
Description:				Lead Time:	2 weeks
				Safety Stock:	0 units

Week		1	2	3	4	5	6	7	8
Gross requirements			100			130			160
Scheduled receipts			50						
Projected on hand	50	50	0	0	0	0	0	0	0
Planned receipts						130			160
Planned order releases				130			160		

Item: C				Lot Size:	POQ = 3
Description:				Lead Time:	1 weeks
				Safety Stock:	30 units

Week		1	2	3	4	5	6	7	8
Gross requirements		20	70	20	20	85	20	20	100
Scheduled receipts									
Projected on hand	50	30	70	50	30	70	50	30	30
Planned receipts			110			125			100
Planned order releases		(110)			125			100	

Item: D				Lot Size:	FOQ = 250
Description:				Lead Time:	2 weeks
				Safety Stock:	0 units

Week		1	2	3	4	5	6	7	8
Gross requirements			100			130			160
Scheduled receipts									
Projected on hand	120	120	20	20	20	140	140	140	230
Planned receipts						250			250
Planned order releases				250			250		

Item:		E				Lot Size:		FOQ = 600
Description:						Lead Time:		2 weeks
						Safety Stock:		0 units

Week		1	2	3	4	5	6	7	8
Gross requirements				510			570		
Scheduled receipts									
Projected on hand	70	70	70	160	160	160	190	190	190
Planned receipts				600			600		
Planned order releases		(600)			600				

Item:		F				Lot Size:		L4L
Description:						Lead Time:		1 week
						Safety Stock:		0 units

Week		1	2	3	4	5	6	7	8
Gross requirements		220		130	250		160	200	
Scheduled receipts									
Projected on hand	250	30	30	0	0	0	0	0	0
Planned receipts				100	250		160	200	
Planned order releases			100	250		160	200		

Action notices signal the need to place orders for 110 Cs and 600 Es.

21. MRP for products A, B, and C in Fig. 14.40.

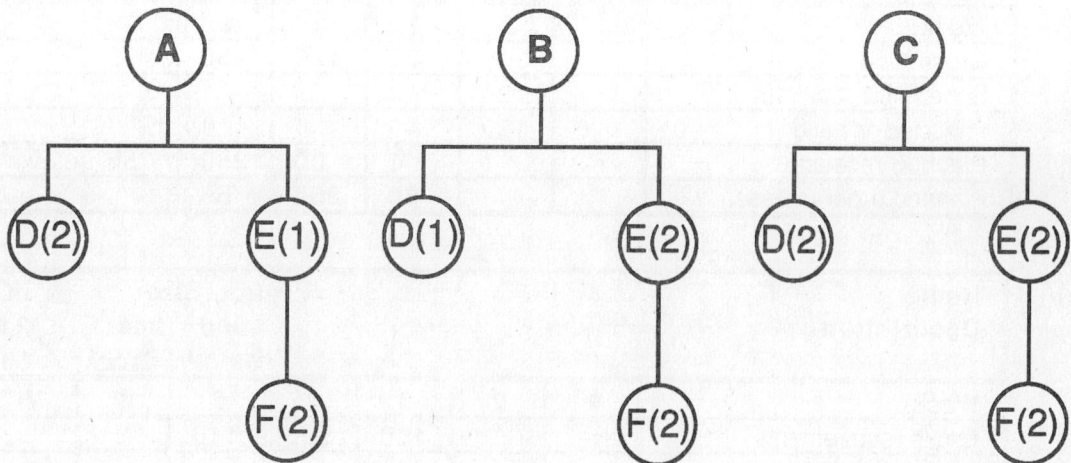

Item: A	Week	1	2	3	4	5	6	7	8	9	10
MPS Quantity (due)					80			55			
MPS Quantity (release)				80			55				

Item: B	Week	1	2	3	4	5	6	7	8	9	10
MPS Quantity (due)								125			
MPS Quantity (release)						125					

Item: C	Week	1	2	3	4	5	6	7	8	9	10
MPS Quantity (due)								60			
MPS Quantity (release)					60						

Item: D   **Lot Size:** FOQ = 150
Description: **Lead Time:** 3 weeks
     Safety Stock: 40 units

Week	1	2	3	4	5	6	7	8
Gross requirements			160	120	125	110		
Scheduled receipts	250							
Projected on hand | 150	400	400	240	120	145	185	185	185
Planned receipts					150	150		
Planned order releases		150	150					

Item: E   **Lot Size:** L4L
Description: **Lead Time:** 1 week
     Safety Stock: 0 units

Week	1	2	3	4	5	6	7	8
Gross requirements			80	120	250	55		
Scheduled receipts		120						
Projected on hand | 0	0	120	40	0	0	0	0	0
Planned receipts				80	250	55		
Planned order releases			80	250	55			

Item: F   **Lot Size:** POQ = 2
Description: **Lead Time:** 2 weeks
     Safety Stock: 30 units

Week	1	2	3	4	5	6	7	8
Gross requirements			160	500	110			
Scheduled receipts								
Projected on hand | 100	100	100	530	30	30	30	30	30
Planned receipts			590		110			
Planned order releases	590		110					

22. Input - Output Control, Fig. 14.41.

Work Station: Chair Assembly Tolerance: ± 50 hours					Week 49
Week	45	46	47	48	49
Inputs					
Planned	310	310	310	310	320
Actual	305	285	295	270	
Cumulative deviation	−5	−30	−45	−85	
Outputs					
Planned	320	320	320	320	320
Actual	320	305	300	290	
Cumulative deviation	0	−15	−35	−65	

Planned Ending Backlog		50 hours	40 hours	30 hours	20 hours	20 hours
Actual Backlog	60 hours	45 hours	25 hours	20 hours	0 hours	

a. The cumulative deviation exceeded the tolerance of ± 50 hours in week 48.

b. Chair assembly backlog has decreased to zero. This center is starved for work because the actual amount of work authorized (inputs) is far less than planned. Notice also that as the backlog declined, these workers slowed their output in a futile attempt to rebuild inventory (and job security). When management intends to reduce inventory, they should advise and consult with workers so that they don't react to dwindling inventory by slowing their work.

c. We should look to preceding work centers and production control departments to determine why inputs are declining.

Advanced Problems

23.

a.

Item: A Description:						Lot Size: 90 units Lead Time: 1 week Safety Stock: 0 units		
Week	1	2	3	4	5	6	7
Gross requirements		85		50			110	60
Scheduled receipts								
Projected on-hand	65	−20	70	20	20	20	0	30
Planned receipts			90				90	90
Planned order releases		90				90	90	

Item: B Description:						Lot Size: L4L Lead Time: 3 weeks Safety Stock: 0 units		
Week	1	2	3	4	5	6	7
Gross requirements		270				270	270	
Scheduled receipts			270					
Projected on-hand	0	−270	0	0	0	0	0	0
Planned receipts						270	270	
Planned order releases			270	270				

b. The action notices would be to expedite the scheduled receipt for item B from week 2 to this week. There is a slight chance that 60 Bs could be obtained in less time than the full order of 270. If it looks like item B can be obtained, then we release an order for 90 units (or at least 20 units) of item A. We would consume the expedited item B to try to finish at least 20 As yet this week. Most likely the parent for A will have to be delayed unless item B can be expedited and the new order for item A is given very high priority.

24. MRP for Fig. 14.43.

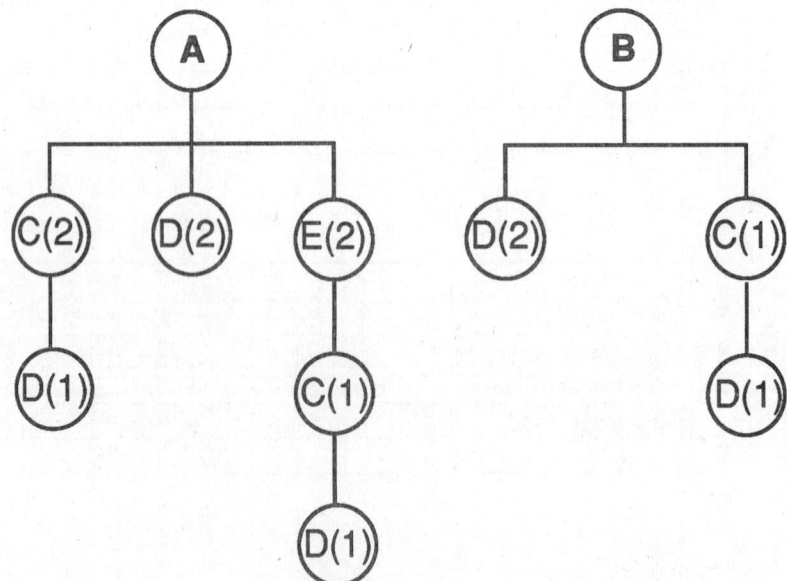

					Date			
Product	1	2	3	4	5	6	7	8
A		125		95		150		130
B			80			70		

	Item		
Data Category	C	D	E
Lot-size rule	POQ ($P = 3$)	FOQ = 800	L4L
Lead time	2 weeks	1 week	3 weeks
Safety stock	75	120	0
Scheduled receipts	None	800 (week 1)	200 (week 2)
On-hand inventory	625	350	85

Item: E
Description:
Lot Size: L4L
Lead Time: 3 weeks
Safety Stock: 0 units

Week		1	2	3	4	5	6	7	8
Gross requirements			250		190		300		260
Scheduled receipts			200						
Projected on hand	85	85	35	35	0	0	0	0	0
Planned receipts					155		300		260
Planned order releases		155		300		260			

Item: C
Description:
Lot Size: POQ = 3
Lead Time: 2 weeks
Safety Stock: 75 units

Week		1	2	3	4	5	6	7	8
Gross requirements		155	250	380	190	260	370		260
Scheduled receipts									
Projected on hand	625	470	220	525	335	75	335	335	75
Planned receipts				685			630		
Planned order releases		685			630				

Item: D
Description:
Lot Size: FOQ = 800
Lead Time: 1 week
Safety Stock: 120 units

Week		1	2	3	4	5	6	7	8
Gross requirements		685	250	160	820		440		260
Scheduled receipts		800							
Projected on hand	350	465	215	855	835	835	395	395	135
Planned receipts				800	800				
Planned order releases			800	800					

b. New orders should be opened for 155 Es, and 685 Cs.

25. MRP for Fig. 14.44.

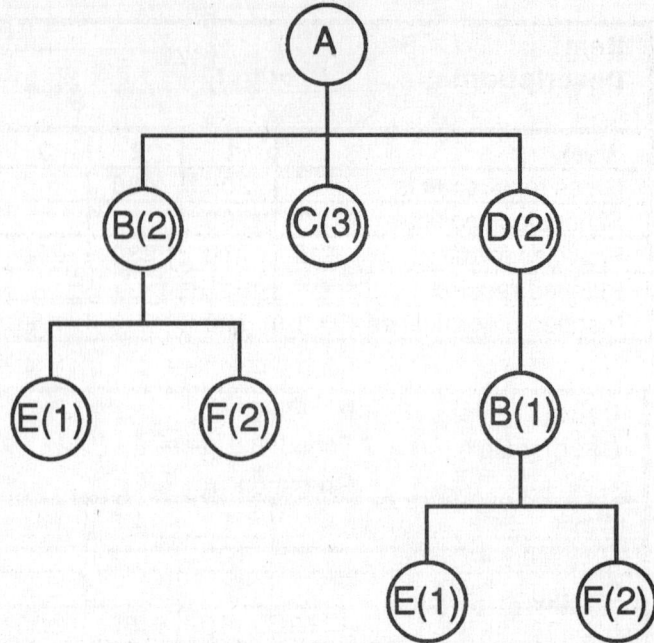

Data Category	Item				
	B	C	D	E	F
Lot-size rule	FOQ = 700	FOQ = 700	L4L	L4L	L4L
Lead time	4 weeks	3 weeks	3 weeks	2 weeks	1 week
Safety stock	50	100	0	100	0
Scheduled receipts	700 (week 1)	450 (week 2)	150 (week 2)	None	1400 (week 1)
Beginning (on-hand) inventory	215	105	125	750	0

Item: C					Lot Size:	FOQ = 700		
Description:					Lead Time:	3 weeks		
					Safety Stock:	100 units		

Week	1	2	3	4	5	6	7	8
Gross requirements		360		360	360			360
Scheduled receipts		450						
Projected on hand | 105	105	195	195	535	175	175	175	515
Planned receipts				700				700
Planned order releases	700				700			

Item: D					Lot Size:	L4L		
Description:					Lead Time:	3 weeks		
					Safety Stock:	0 units		

Week	1	2	3	4	5	6	7	8
Gross requirements		240		240	240			240
Scheduled receipts		150						
Projected on hand | 125	125	35	35	0	0	0	0	0
Planned receipts				205	240			240
Planned order releases	205	240			240			

Item: B						Lot Size:	FOQ = 700	
Description:						Lead Time:	4 weeks	
						Safety Stock:	50 units	

Week	1	2	3	4	5	6	7	8
Gross requirements	205	480		240	480			240
Scheduled receipts	700							
Projected on hand | 215	710	230	230	-10	210	210	210	670
Planned receipts					700			700
Planned order releases	700			700				

Item: E						Lot Size:	L4L	
Description:						Lead Time:	2 weeks	
						Safety Stock:	100 units	

Week	1	2	3	4	5	6	7	8
Gross requirements	700			700				
Scheduled receipts								
Projected on hand | 750	50	50	100	100	100	100	100	100
Planned receipts			50	700				
Planned order releases	50	700						

Item: F						Lot Size:	L4L	
Description:						Lead Time:	1 week	
						Safety Stock:	0 units	

Week	1	2	3	4	5	6	7	8
Gross requirements	1400			1400				
Scheduled receipts	1400							
Projected on hand | 0	0	0	0	0	0	0	0	0
Planned receipts				1400				
Planned order releases			1400					

Action notices are to open orders for 700 Cs and 205 Ds. An expedited order for 700 Bs to arrive in three weeks (less than the usual four-week) lead time should also be opened. It is debatable whether the order for 50 Es should be ordered, since it serves no purpose other than to replenish safety stock.

26. MRP for Fig. 14.22.

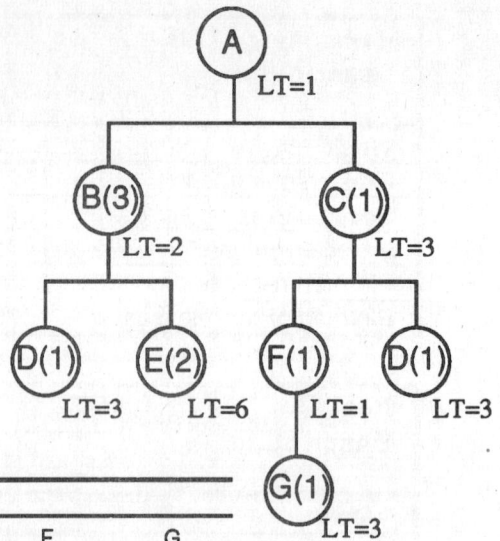

Data Category	Item					
	B	C	D	E	F	G
Lot-size rule	L4L	L4L	POQ ($P=2$)	L4L	L4L	FOQ = 100
Lead time	2 weeks	3 weeks	3 weeks	6 weeks	1 week	3 weeks
Safety stock	30	10	0	0	0	0
Scheduled receipts	150 (wk 2)	50 (wk 2)	None	400 (wk 6)	40 (wk 3)	None
On-hand inventory	30	20	60	400	0	0

Item: A
Lot Size: 50
Final Asm. Lead Time: 1 wk
Quantity On Hand: 5

	Week									
	1	2	3	4	5	6	7	8	9	10
MPS start		50				50		50	50	

Item: B	Lot Size:	L4L
Description:	Lead Time:	2 weeks
	Safety Stock:	30 units

Week	1	2	3	4	5	6	7	8	9	10
Gross requirements		150				150		150	150	
Scheduled receipts		150								
Projected on hand 30	30	30	30	30	30	30	30	30	30	30
Planned receipts						150		150	150	
Planned order releases				150		150	150			

Item: C	Lot Size:	L4L
Description:	Lead Time:	3 weeks
	Safety Stock:	10 units

Week	1	2	3	4	5	6	7	8	9	10
Gross requirements		50				50		50	50	
Scheduled receipts		50								
Projected on hand 20	20	20	20	20	20	10	10	10	10	10
Planned receipts						40		50	50	
Planned order releases			40		50	50				

Item: D						Lot Size:		POQ = 2		
Description:						Lead Time:		3 weeks		
						Safety Stock:		0 units		

Week	1	2	3	4	5	6	7	8	9	10
Gross requirements			40	150	50	200	150			
Scheduled receipts										
Projected on hand | 60	60	60	20	50	0	150	0	0	0	0
Planned receipts				180		350				
Planned order releases	180		350							

Item: E						Lot Size:		L4L		
Description:						Lead Time:		6 weeks		
						Safety Stock:		0 units		

Week	1	2	3	4	5	6	7	8	9	10
Gross requirements				300		300	300			
Scheduled receipts						400				
Projected on hand | 400	400	400	400	100	100	200	0	0	0	0
Planned receipts							100			
Planned order releases	100									

Item: F						Lot Size:		L4L		
Description:						Lead Time:		1 week		
						Safety Stock:		0 units		

Week	1	2	3	4	5	6	7	8	9	10
Gross requirements			40		50	50				
Scheduled receipts			40							
Projected on hand | 0	0	0	0	0	0	0	0	0	0	0
Planned receipts					50	50				
Planned order releases				50	50					

Item: G						Lot Size:		FOQ = 100		
Description:						Lead Time:		3 weeks		
						Safety Stock:		0 units		

Week	1	2	3	4	5	6	7	8	9	10
Gross requirements				50	50					
Scheduled receipts										
Projected on hand | 0	0	0	0	50	0	0	0	0	0	0
Planned receipts				100						
Planned order releases	100									

27.

Item: A
Description:

Lot Size: 90 units
Lead Time: 2 weeks
Safety Stock: 10 units

Week	1	2	3	4	5	6	7	8	9	10
Gross requirements	120			70			85	90		70
Scheduled receipts	90									
Projected on-hand 110	80	80	80	10	10	10	15	15	15	35
Planned receipts							90	90		90
Planned order releases					90	90		90		

Item: B
Description:

Lot Size: L4L
Lead Time: 4 weeks
Safety Stock: 0 units

Week	1	2	3	4	5	6	7	8	9	10
Gross requirements					360	360		360		
Scheduled receipts		360								
Projected on-hand 0	0	360	360	360	0	0	0	0	0	0
Planned receipts						360		360		
Planned order releases		360		360						

The only action noticed would be to delay the scheduled receipt of B until week 5.

Chapter 15

Just-in-Time Systems

Study Questions

1. Traditionally the source of materials, in order to maximize its own output and rewards for individual performance, *pushes* material upon the destinations, whether the material is needed at those destinations or not. The source's work schedule is determined according to convenience, capability, efficiency, and utilization of the source. Just-in-time systems are intended to provide materials and components for production just in time to meet needs at the destination, and not intended to stockpile inventories in anticipation of a need.

   JIT is considered a *pull* system because the signal to get more materials is driven by the need to produce a product at the materials' destination. Making the product consumes the materials. When the worker needs more material, she pulls it from its source to her work area according to her needs. She has the best possible information about what materials she needs, how many materials she needs, and when she needs the materials. In the pull system, the source's work schedule is determined by the need to replace whatever has been taken (pulled) away to meet the destinations' needs. The signal for the source to produce more is given by a withdrawal from inventory.

   Competitive advantages of pull systems include lower cost operations, more consistent quality, faster and more reliable delivery, faster product development, and greater volume flexibility.

   A related note: In the *pull* system, the source's output is determined entirely by demand from destination work centers. The source can no longer produce according to its own initiative, and is powerless to increase its own output in isolation from destination work center considerations. Therefore it would be unfair to evaluate the source's work efforts based upon its individual output. Performance measures such as manufacturing efficiency are obsolete. JIT performance measures must take a larger view to encourage improvement of the group as a set of coordinated source-destination, or supplier-customer partnerships.

2. Push systems are theory X. Example: "I have to push homework on students and design a reward system that forces them to complete it, because they would never learn the material on their own." Theory X is a low-risk, low-reward approach. Theory Y says that students want to learn. Example: "As an the instructor, I just need to provide a conducive environment, and the students will seek out (pull) homework and learning opportunities." (Ha!) Theory Y is a high-risk, high-reward approach.

3. The two cards are the production-ordering kanban and the withdrawal kanban. The production-ordering kanban is the card that authorizes the production of the part described on the card itself. It is detached from a full container of parts when those parts are pulled by a succeeding process, then posted to visibly signal the need to replenish whatever has been taken. The production-authorization card is then attached to a new full container as the part is replenished. At the same time the production-ordering card was detached from the first full container, a withdrawal card would have been attached. The withdrawal card is authorization to pull the full container from the source and move them to where they are needed. Instructions are on the withdrawal card itself. When workers at the succeeding process start to use the parts stored in the container, the withdrawal card is detached and visibly posted. The withdrawal card then signals the need to go get (pull) another full container from the preceding process.

The maximum amount of inventory in the system is limited by the total number of production-authorization plus withdrawal cards. If the preceding process continues work while the succeeding process has stopped, it is theoretically possible to have one full container for each production-authorization card to be stored at the preceding process and for one full container for each withdrawal card to be stored at the succeeding process. The flow of cards and materials is shown in Fig. 15.3.

4. In an inefficient process, $\overline{w}$ and α would be larger than desirable. The average waiting time, $\overline{w}$, could be larger because of inefficient materials handling or scheduling practices. The policy variable, α, would be larger to allow more inventory to buffer inefficiencies such as machine failures, quality, or worker ability. To increase safety stock, the supervisor would increase the policy variable, α.

5. In the kanban system, the lead time is the sum of the waiting (transportation) time plus the process time, $(\overline{w} + \overline{p})$. The demand during the lead time is $d(\overline{w} + \overline{p})$ and safety stock is determined by the size of the policy variable, α. Kanban safety stock is proportional to the <u>magnitude</u> of demand during the lead time, $d(\overline{w} + \overline{p})(\alpha)$. This contrasts with the reorder point system, where the safety stock is proportional to the <u>variability</u> of demand during the lead time, σ_L.

6. The process of continuous improvement is tied to inventory reduction. Areas for improvement are identified by reducing the amount of inventory in the system and looking for disruptions. The root cause of the disruption is sought out and permanently solved. Then inventory is reduced again. The process continues until there is "zero inventory" remaining in the system.

7. The master production schedule is critical to the JIT system because it determines the daily requirements for the entire system. A stable schedule, to produce the same amount of every product every day, results in a uniform flow of materials that is within the capacity limits of the various work centers or group cells. Usually once each month, there is an opportunity to implement engineering product design changes and to rebalance assembly lines to change production rates. Then the supplier-customer system produces to that daily quota for the next month.

8. The production line can not continue because all of the material has been consumed in producing the daily quota. There is no extra inventory in the system. The workers are not sent home for several reasons. First, if worker are sent home without pay, the next day the workers would slow down so that they would receive a full days pay. If they are sent home with pay, resources are being wasted. The JIT system emphasizes worker involvement in decisions and improvement efforts. Most of that involvement occurs after the daily quota has been produced. If we send the workers home we also send this message: "The physical work is done now. Since you can't contribute to mental work, you might as well go on home."

9. The just-in-time system actually addresses more of the total manufacturing environment than does the kanban system. A kanban system is just a part of the just-in-time concept. JIT concerns itself with work-force, capacity, automation, behavioral, as well as inventory and scheduling issues. A kanban system deals only with the inventory and scheduling issues.

10. Many factors should be considered before implementing a JIT system (in its entirety, including a pull inventory system), including: (i) Can the workers and first line supervisors be given responsibility for shop floor production control? (ii) Can management trust the workers and vice versa? (iii) Can daily production schedules be identical for extended periods? (iv) Do product mix, product designs, or demands change frequently? (v) Can setup times be reduced to make small-lot production viable? and (vi) Are there many irregularly used or specially ordered parts?

11. JIT applications in service firms are similar to JIT applications in manufacturing firms in that both aim to reduce inefficiencies and unproductive time by considering the basic elements of JIT systems. However, continuous improvement is approached differently in manufacturing and in services. In manufacturing, problems are identified by a reduction in inventory rather than a reduction in staff level. In addition, JIT in services is generally applicable only to services that have "manufacturing-like" operations. For example, it would be difficult to implement JIT in the emergency room of a hospital, whereas it may be feasible to implement JIT in the billing department of the same hospital.

12. The sources of stress in JIT systems comes from repetitive work, which may be addressed by cross-training and job rotation, and from peer pressure. JIT system rewards are based on group performance. If one worker is having difficulty in doing her share, she is affecting the income of the group. The other workers should not just criticize, because they do share responsibility for team member's difficulties. They are empowered to go over and help out.

    Workers in the push system are paid as individuals. The group suffers only indirectly, as employees of the firm, when one worker has difficulties. Although there is less peer pressure, push systems are still stressful. In push systems the worker feels stress to keep up with work pushed upon them by others. They are also held responsible to perform work over which they have little or no control. Responsibility without authority is very stressful.

13. The choice of a production/inventory system has implications for the firm as a whole because it can affect inventory levels and customer service performance. High inventories drain cash-flow reserves, and poor customer service puts pressure on retaining market share.

Discussion Questions

1. Many students buy in to JIT as a philosophy until they are faced with the prospect of having their own work evaluated on the basis of performance of a group rather than as an individual. This discussion will probably uncover conflicts between our culture and JIT philosophy. The discussion might be turned to look for compromises or ways JIT could be modified to work with our culture.

2. Aspects of JIT that have proved troublesome for some U.S. users are realignment of managerial reward systems, restrictive labor contracts, plant layouts, and adversarial supplier relationships. Our culture focuses on individuals rather than groups, and our legal system contains hurdles to forming partnerships which restrict competition. Many firms have already overcome these obstacles.

Problems

1. Hama motorcycles.

   a. What is the cycle time for the assembly line?

   $$c = \frac{1}{r} = \frac{7 \text{ hours}}{126 \text{ motorcyles}} = 0.0555 \frac{\text{hours}}{\text{motorcycle}}$$

   $$= 3.33 \frac{\text{minutes}}{\text{motorcycle}}$$

   b. If Hama uses small-lot production, what is the batch size of each model?

   Mama Hama = 9
   Yoka Hama = 7
   Llama Hama = 5

   Repeat the sequence six times per shift, for a total of (6 x 3) = 18 setups.

   c. <u>M Y M YL MY ML</u> <u>M Y M YL M Y M L</u> <u>M Y L</u>

   d. Mama Hama = 4
   Yoka Hama = 3
   Llama Hama = 2
   Hemn Hama = 1

   Repeat the sequence thirteen times per shift, for a total of (13 x 3) = 39 setups. Unless the setup time is reduced, there may be too much loss of capacity in performing 39 setups per day.

2. Spradley's Sprockets.

   $$k = \frac{d(\bar{w} + \bar{p})(1 + \alpha)}{c}$$

   $$k = \frac{500[0.20 + 1.80](1 + 0.05)}{20}$$

   $$k = 52.5$$

3. Le Jit.

   a. Implied policy variable

   $$k = \frac{d(\bar{w} + \bar{p})(1 + \alpha)}{c}$$

   $$11 = \frac{2000[1.10 + 0.001(270)](1 + \alpha)}{270}$$

   $$(1 + \alpha) = \frac{11(270)}{2000[1.10 + 0.001(270)]} = 1.0839$$

   $$\alpha = 1.0839 - 1 = 0.0839$$

   b. Reduction in waiting time

   $$10 = \frac{2000(\bar{w} + 0.27)(1.0839)}{270} = \frac{2168\bar{w} + 585.3}{270}$$

   $$2168\bar{w} = 2700 - 585.3$$

   $$\bar{w} = 0.975 \text{ days}$$

   The reduction in waiting time is:

   $$\frac{(1.10 - 0.975)}{1.10} = 11.4\%$$

4. Gadjits and Widjits.

   a. Kanban card sets for gadjits.

$$k = \frac{d(\overline{w} + \overline{p})(1 + \alpha)}{c}$$

$$k = \frac{800(3)\left[0.09 + (80)0.06\right](1 + 0.09)}{80} = 159.9$$

$$k = 160$$

   b. Kanban card sets for widjits.

$$k = \frac{d(\overline{w} + \overline{p})(1 + \alpha)}{c}$$

$$k = \frac{800(2)\left[0.14 + (50)0.20\right](1 + 0.08)}{50} = 350.4$$

$$k = 351$$

5. Gestalt, Inc.

$$\overline{p} = \frac{150(20)}{8(60)(60)} = 0.10417 \text{ days}$$

$$\overline{w} = \frac{2.4}{8} = 0.30 \text{ days}$$

$$k = \frac{d(\overline{w} + \overline{p})(1 + \alpha)}{c}$$

$$10 = \frac{d(0.30 + 0.10417)(1.1)}{20}$$

$$d = \frac{200}{(0.40417)(1.1)} = 449.86 \text{ or } 450$$

6. Jittery USPS.

$$\overline{p} = \frac{480(1\text{sec})}{8(60)(60)} = 0.01667 \text{ days}$$

$$\overline{w} = \frac{40\text{min}}{8(60)} = 0.08333 \text{ days}$$

$$k = \frac{d(\overline{w} + \overline{p})(1 + \alpha)}{c}$$

$$k = \frac{120,000(0.08333 + 0.01667)(1.20)}{480}$$

$$k = 30$$

Chapter 16

Scheduling

Study Questions

1. A schedule tends to be more detailed than a plan. Schedules attach specific dates or dates and times to planned events. Scheduling duties are usually assigned to frontline managers. However in some JIT systems, production workers schedule their own work. Specific scheduled events usually do not have long lasting or strategic impact. The firm can generally recover from a poor scheduling decision in a reasonably short time by simply "rescheduling." However continued poor scheduling decisions over time have a cumulative effect. For example, the crunch of term projects students attempt to complete during the final week of the semester.

   There is also a psychological difference between the two terms. There is some doubt as to whether a "plan" will become a reality. It is often difficult to determine who is taking responsibility for making a plan happen. When an event is "scheduled," there is a greater sense of assigned responsibility and commitment. Referring to the terms in Chapter 14. A "planned receipt" becomes a "scheduled receipt" when a contractual commitment (purchase order or work order) is issued.

2. First, work-force scheduling involves the specification of on-duty and off-duty time periods for each employee over a certain time horizon, whereas operations scheduling assigns people to jobs or assigns jobs to machines over some time period. Second, work-force scheduling actually determines the capacity available each time period, whereas operations scheduling begins with a known capacity and decides how best to use it. Finally, the nature of the constraints is typically different. Work-force scheduling often involves legal, behavioral, and psychological factors, while operations scheduling typically involves more technical considerations.

3. Job flow time is the difference between the time a job is finished and the time it was available for initial processing. Makespan is a similar measure but deals with a group of jobs. It is the difference between the time the *last* job of a group of jobs is finished and the time the *group* was available for initial processing. Makespan becomes relevant when scheduling involves two or more processes.

4. Most students sequence homework according to earliest due date (EDD). Some will use shortest processing time rule (SPT). Students having much greater homework capacity than homework assignments will complete the work in the order assigned (FCFS). As the work load approaches capacity, students quickly learn that FCFS and SPT rules cause some homework to be completed too late for credit and result in decreased performance evaluations (grades). When the amount of homework exceeds the time remaining, no priority rule will save them. Scheduling and capacity are two different concepts. Schedule sequences do not create capacity.

5. Multiple-dimension priority rules outperform single-dimension priority rules when we are concerned with global operation of a system of work centers, rather than optimizing performance for just one work center.

6. One simple modification to the SPT rule to avoid having some jobs wait in queue for a long time is to add the stipulation that we use the shortest processing time to select jobs from the queue, but if a job has been waiting longer than n hours, select it next regardless of its processing time.

7. The cash only line uses a combination of the SPT rule and the FCFS rule. It sorts out the short tasks and reduces average customer waiting time. New clerks are assigned to the cash only checkout lane because the transactions are theoretically more simple. Unfortunately, many uncooperative customers ignore the signs and request lengthy and complex transactions beyond the training of the new clerk. This irritates other customers who chose that line specifically because they were in a hurry. In practice, it can be argued whether cash only lanes improve customer satisfaction.

8. One possibility is to take the absolute value of the slack. In that way |-2|/10 would be less than |-1|/1. However, the ratio would get confused with a job that has, for example, 10 more operations but a slack of +2. Another approach would be to divide the jobs into two classes: those that have negative slack (past due) and those that have positive slack. The ones with positive slack can be scheduled with S/RO, but will have a lower priority than any job with negative slack. The jobs with negative slack could be scheduled with earliest due date, breaking ties by choosing the job with the most operations remaining, or by multiplying the negative slack by the number of operations remaining (as a weight) and choosing the job with the most negative score.

9. Work-force schedules (i) translate the staffing plan into periods of duty for the employees; (ii) satisfy the expected daily work-force requirements; and (iii) provide the basis for day-to-day reallocation of employees. Take the police department as an example. A staff plan determines the number of officers to have on hand in each precinct. However, the work-force schedule must determine their on-duty days per week, their shift schedule, and may even specify their "beat," which depends on the requirements for police protection.

Discussion Questions

1. The optimizing approach, of course, would give the optimal schedule for a group of jobs. However, implementing the model would be difficult. For example, significant amounts of data would need to be maintained and updated each time the model was used. There would also likely be circumstances when the schedule would have to be manually adjusted to account for unexpected happenings. Of course, the model's assumptions (linearity or nonlinearity, deterministic or stochastic, and so forth) could come into serious question.

   The dispatching approach does not claim to provide an optimal solution, but it is much easier to implement and "adjusts" to unexpected happenings as they occur. The optimizing approach might prove to be the better choice in environments where there are few new job arrivals during the week (or they can be held until the next scheduling session) and there are few unexpected disruptions to the process. The dispatching approach is likely to be the better choice in dynamic environments where control of the schedule is difficult without making changes periodically.

   Technology and software advances for real-time scheduling may offer the best of both approaches.

2. Priority systems affect operations performance and aid management in making operational decisions. They facilitate prioritizing of work in the organization since all the work to be performed in the organization cannot be done at the same time. The choice of priority system also helps management to focus and consciously decide on the scheduling system that will emphasize the performance criteria it considers to be important. By providing guidance for the numerous routine decisions associated with determining the sequence in which jobs are to be processed, priority systems allow managers to spend more time with strategic issues.

Problems

1. Studywell Company.

    a. SPT

Schedule	Start Time	Finish Time	Flow Time	Due Date	Past Due
PC088	0	3	3	18	0
DM246	3	11	11	20	0
SX435	11	21	21	6	15
AZ135	21	35	35	14	21
			70		

    EDD

Schedule	Start Time	Finish Time	Flow Time	Due Date	Past Due
SX435	0	10	10	6	4
AZ135	10	24	24	14	10
PC088	24	27	27	18	9
DM246	27	35	35	20	15
			96		

		SPT	EDD
i.	Average flow time (hr)	70 / 4 = 17.5	96 / 4 = 24.0
ii.	Percentage of jobs past due	2 / 4 = 50%	4 / 4 = 100%

    iii. EDD minimizes the maximum past due (15 hours versus 21 hours).

    b.

		SPT	EDD
i.	Average WIP (orders)	70 / 35 = 2.0	96 / 35 = 2.7

    ii. Average total inventory (orders)

    $(18 + 20 + 21 + 35) / 35 \qquad = 2.69$ (SPT)

    $(10 + 24 + 27 + 35) / 35 \qquad\qquad\qquad = 2.74$ (EDD)

    c. EDD minimizes the maximum past due but has a greater flow time and (with this particular set of data) causes more jobs to be past due. SPT minimizes the average work-in-process and the average inventory.

2. Drill press

a. i. SPT:

Priority	Start Time	Finish Time (Flow Time)
EE	0	2
AA	2	6
DD	6	12
BB	12	20
CC	20	33
		73

ii. EDD:

Priority	Start Time	Finish Time (Flow Time)
AA	0	4
EE	4	6
BB	6	14
CC	14	27
DD	27	33
		84

iii. S/RO:

Job	S/RO			Priority	Start Time	Finish Time (Flow Time)
AA	$(10 - 5 - 4)/3$	$= 0.33$		AA	0	4
BB	$(16 - 5 - 6)/4$	$= 1.25$		CC	4	17
CC	$(21 - 5 - 9)/10$	$= 0.70$		EE	17	19
DD	$(23 - 5 - 12)/3$	$= 2.00$		BB	19	27
EE	$(12 - 5 - 3)/5$	$= 0.80$		DD	27	33
						100

iv. CR:

Job	CR			Priority	Start Time	Finish Time (Flow Time)
AA	$(10 - 5)/4$	$= 1.25$		AA	0	4
BB	$(16 - 5)/6$	$= 1.83$		DD	4	10
CC	$(21 - 5)/9$	$= 1.78$		CC	10	23
DD	$(23 - 5)/12$	$= 1.50$		BB	23	31
EE	$(12 - 5)/3$	$= 2.33$		EE	31	33
						101

b.

	SPT	EDD	S/RO	CR
Average flow time	$73/5 = 14.6$	$84/5 = 16.8$	$100/5 = 20.0$	$101/5 = 20.2$

c. Priority planning with an MRP system relies on proper timing of materials. Planners manipulate scheduled due dates to match material need dates with order due dates. Consequently, priority rules incorporating due dates would be most useful in communicating these changes to the shop floor. Of those listed in this problem, EDD, S/RO, and CR would work best.

3. Blackwell Industries

Job	Total Processing Time (hours)
1	$80(0.10) + 1 = 9.0$
2	$100(0.05) + 2 = 7.0$
3	$160(0.08) + 3 = 15.8$
4	$300(0.02) + 4 = 10.0$

a. Using SPT:

Job	Arrival	Start	Finish	Flow (hr)	Past Due (hr)
1	8:00 a.m. (T)	8:00 a.m. (T)	5:00 p.m. (T)	9.00	0.00
2	8:45 a.m. (T)	5:00 p.m. (T)	12:00 mdn (W)	15.25	1.00
4	9:15 a.m. (T)	12:00 mdn (W)	10:00 a.m. (W)	24.75	16.00
3	9:00 a.m. (T)	10:00 a.m. (W)	1:48 a.m. (Th)	40.80	27.80
				89.80	44.80

Tuesday				Wednesday						Thursday		
8-12	12-4	4-8	8-12	12-4	4-8	8-12	12-4	4-8	8-12	12-4	4-8	8-12
Job 1 9 hours			Job 2 7 hours			Job 4 10 hours			Job 3 15.8 hours			

Using EDD:

Job	Arrival	Start	Finish	Flow (hr)	Past Due (hr)
1	8:00 a.m. (T)	8:00 a.m. (T)	5:00 p.m. (T)	9.00	0.00
4	9:15 a.m. (T)	5:00 p.m. (T)	3:00 a.m. (W)	17.75	9.00
3	9:00 a.m. (T)	3:00 a.m. (W)	6:48 p.m. (W)	33.80	20.80
2	8:45 a.m. (T)	6:48 p.m. (W)	1:48 a.m. (Th)	41.05	26.80
				101.60	56.60

Tuesday				Wednesday						Thursday		
8-12	12-4	4-8	8-12	12-4	4-8	8-12	12-4	4-8	8-12	12-4	4-8	8-12
Job 1 9 hours			Job 4 10 hours			Job 3 15.8 hours				Job 2 7 hours		

b.

	SPT	EDD
Average flow time (hours)	22.45	25.40
Average hours past due	11.20	14.15

c. EDD minimizes the maximum number of past-due hours and the variance of the past due hours; however, EDD does worse with regard to average flow times and average hours past due. Consequently, in this example EDD does better with respect to some customer service measures but does worse with respect to inventory. SPT processes some jobs and gets them out of inventory quickly, assuming jobs can be shipped upon completion whether or not they are due. Typical trade-offs involve customer service and inventory investment.

4. Refer to Gantt chart Fig. 16.4.

FIGURE 16.4

Machine

A	Job 1	Job 2	Job 3	Idle

B	Idle	Job 1	Job 2	Job 3

```
0   1   2   3   4   5   6   7   8   9
```

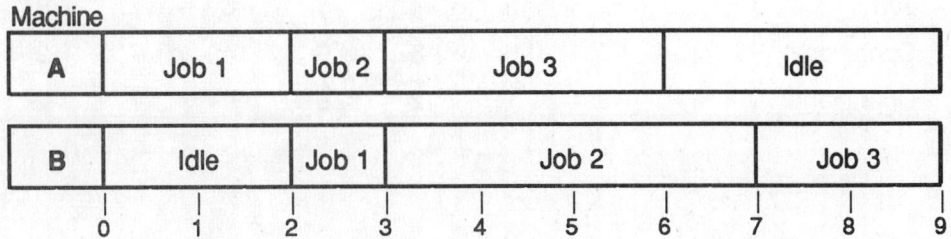

a. To minimize the makespan if each job must be processed on machine A first, we can use Johnson's rule:

Job	Process Time (hr) Machine A	Machine B
1	2	1
2	1	4
	3	2

The optimal sequence would be 2-3-1. The revised Gantt chart is:

FIGURE 16.4

Machine

A	Job 2	Job 3	Job 1	Idle

B	Idle	Job 2	Job 3	Job 1

```
0   1   2   3   4   5   6   7   8   9
```

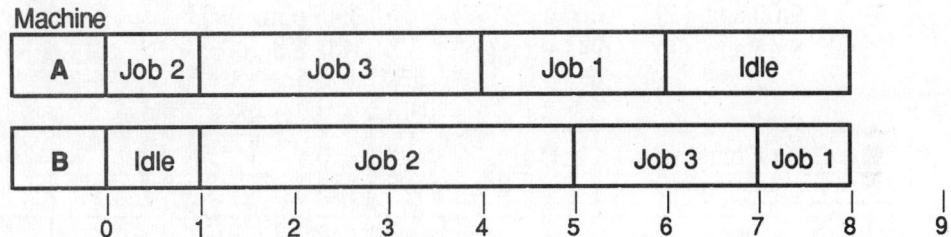

The makespan is now 8 hours, which is an improvement of 1 hour.

b. Now suppose that the only restriction is that no job may be processed on different machines at the same time. One of several schedules that yield a makespan of 7 hours is given below:

FIGURE 16.4

Machine

A	Job 2	Job 3	Job 1	Idle

B	Job 1	Job 2	Job 3

```
0   1   2   3   4   5   6   7   8   9
```

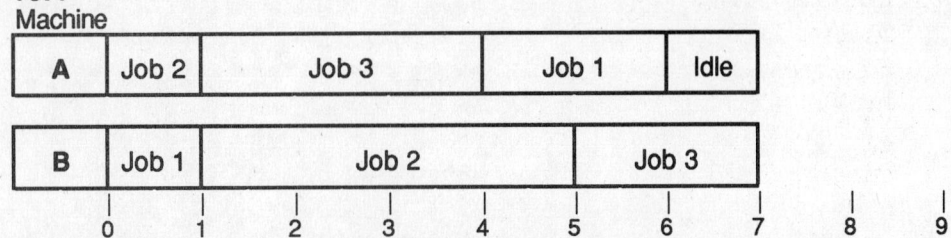

With the restriction of flow from machine A to machine B removed, we are able to utilize the first hour on machine B. This is why we could beat the schedule in part (a).

5. Manufacturer of small-boat sails.

Job	1	2	3	4	5	6	7	8	9	10
Operation 1	1	5	8	3	9	4	7	2	4	9
Operation 2	8	3	1	2	8	6	7	2	4	1

a. One possible sequence is
   1-8-6-7-5-9-2-4-10-3

b.

	Machine 1		**Machine 2**	
Job	**Start**	**Finish**	**Start**	**Finish**
1	0	1	1	9
8	1	3	9	11
6	3	7	11	17
7	7	14	17	24
5	14	23	24	32
9	23	27	32	36
2	27	32	36	39
4	32	35	39	41
10	35	44	44	45
3	44	52	52	53

The Gantt Chart is shown below.

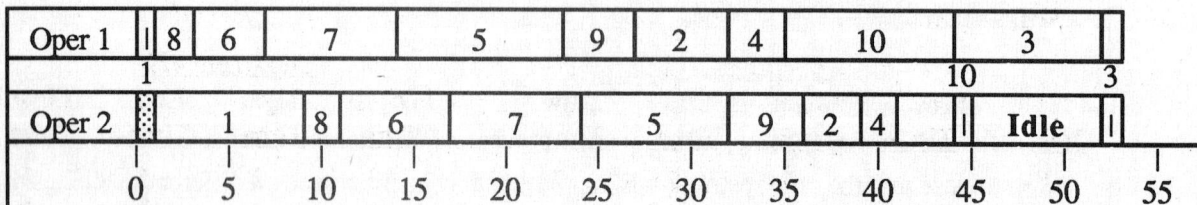

6. Mighty Metal Company.

To minimize the makespan if each job must be deburred prior to heat treatment we can use Johnson's rule:

Processing Time (days)

Job	Debur	Heat Treat
1	2	3
2	3	4
3	6	1
4	3	6
5	1	3
6	3	2

One optimal sequence would be 5-1-4-2-6-3. The Gantt chart is shown below. The orders can be shipped in 20 working days.

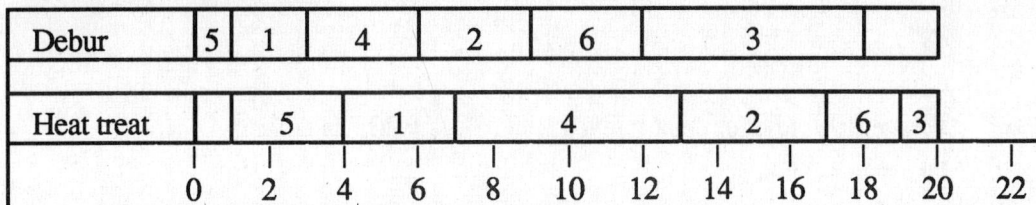

Debur	5	1	4	2	6	3	

Heat treat		5	1	4	2	6	3

```
 |   |   |   |   |   |   |   |   |   |   |   |
 0   2   4   6   8  10  12  14  16  18  20  22
```

7. Universal Manufacturing.

Job	1	2	3	4	5	6	7	8
Department 12	2	4	7	5	4	10	8	2
Department 22	3	6	3	8	2	6	6	5

a. SPT, Department #12.

	Department #12				Depament #22			
Job	Process Time	Begin Time	End Time	Flow Time	Process Time	Begin Time	End Time	Flow Time
1	2	0	2	2	3	2	5	5
8	2	2	4	4	5	5	10	10
5	4	4	8	8	2	10	12	12
2	4	8	12	12	6	12	18	18
4	5	12	17	17	8	18	26	26
3	7	17	24	24	3	26	29	29
7	8	24	32	32	6	32	38	38
6	10	32	42	42	6	42	48	48
				141				186

i. Average flow time in department 12 = (141/8) = 17.625 days

ii. Makespan = 48 days

iii. Sum of job-days [(1 job * 48 days)+(2*38)+(3*29)+(4*26)+(5*18)+(6*12)+(7*10)+(8*5) = 587 job-days

b. **Johnson's rule** minimizes makespan time when scheduling two facilities. First we establish the sequence of jobs based on Johnson's rule:

Department #12	1	8	2	4	6	7	3	5
Department #22	1	8	2	4	6	7	3	5

| | Department #1 | | | | Depament #22 | | | |
Job	Process Time	Begin Time	End Time	Flow Time	Process Time	Begin Time	End Time	Flow Time
1	2	0	2	2	3	2	5	5
8	2	2	4	4	5	5	10	10
2	4	4	8	8	6	10	16	16
4	5	8	13	13	8	16	24	24
6	10	13	23	23	6	24	30	30
7	8	23	31	31	6	31	37	37
3	7	31	38	38	3	38	41	41
5	4	38	42	42	2	41	43	43
				161				206

i. Average flow time for department 12 = (161/8) = 20.125 days.

ii. Makespan = 43 days.

iii. Sum of job-days [(1 job * 43 days)+(2*41)+(3*37)+(4*30)+(5*24)+(6*16)+(7*10)+(8*5) = 682 job-days

c. The SPT rule results in a lower inventory of uncompleted jobs (see sum of job-days). Johnson's rule minimizes makespan for a set of jobs over a group of machines. However, to implement Johnson's rule the informational requirements increase and the cost of applying the priority rule increases. The trade-off is between improving the overall utilization of the whole facility (2 machines) versus the optimum utilization of an individual facility.

The implication of centralized priority planning is that the additional information requirement may increase the cost. However, centralized planning allows better overall performance and control by higher management.

8. Richland Distribution Center.

Day	M	T	W	Th	F	S	Su
Requirements	6	3	5	3	7	2	3

M	T	W	Th	F	S	Su	Employee
6	3	5	3	7	2	3	1
5	2	4	2	6	2	3	2
4	1	3	1	5	2	3	3
3	1	3	0	4	1	2	4
2	0	2	0	3	1	2	5
1	0	2	0	2	0	1	6
0	0	1	0	1	0	1	7
0	0	0	0	0	0	0	

The number of employees is 7. They are scheduled to take the boxed days off.

9. Arthur Tumble's ski school needs 9 instructors.

  a. Alternative 1 The heuristic does not always find the optimal solution.

M	T	W	Th	F	S	Su	Instructor
5	4	4	5	5	7	6	1
5	4	4	4	4	6	5	2
4	4	4	4	3	5	4	3
3	3	4	4	3	4	4	4
3	3	4	3	2	3	3	5
2	2	3	3	2	3	2	6
2	2	2	2	1	2	2	7
1	1	1	1	1	2	2	8
0	0	1	1	1	1	1	9
0	0	1	0	0	0	0	10

Alternative 2 (Optimal)

M	T	W	Th	F	S	Su	Instructor
5	4	4	5	5	7	6	1
5	4	4	4	4	6	5	2
4	3	4	4	4	5	4	3
4	3	3	3	3	4	4	4
3	3	3	3	2	3	3	5
2	2	2	2	2	3	3	6
2	2	2	1	1	2	2	7
1	1	1	1	1	2	1	8
1	1	0	0	0	1	1	9

  b. Instructors are scheduled to take the boxed days off.

	M	T	W	Th	F	S	Su
On-duty	5	4	4	5	5	7	6
Requirements	5	4	4	5	5	7	6
Slack	0	0	0	0	0	0	0

10. The environmentally progressive Mayor of Massilon, Ohio.

  a. We used the method in the text to arrive at the minimum number of collectors. For each employee, the box represents his or her two off-days.

M	T	W	Th	F	S	Su	Collector
12	7	9	9	5	3	6	1
11	6	8	8	5	3	5	2
10	5	7	7	4	3	5	3
9	4	6	6	4	3	4	4
8	3	5	5	3	3	4	5
7	2	4	4	3	3	3	6
6	1	3	3	2	3	3	7
5	1	3	2	1	2	2	8
4	0	2	1	1	2	1	9
3	0	1	1	1	1	0	10
2	0	0	0	0	1	0	11
1	0	0	0	0	0	0	12

The minimum number of employees is 12. However, many schedules (particular assignments of on-duty periods) are possible. This one puts a priority on Saturday-Sunday off periods.

b. The work schedule for the analysis in part (a) is to assign employees the boxed days off.

On-duty	12	10	10	11	7	3	7
Requirements	12	7	9	9	5	3	6
Slack	0	3	1	2	2	0	1

c. We can use the heuristic method again to find whether we can get by with fewer employees. One solution follows:

M	T	W	Th	F	S	Su	Employee
8	7	7	7	7	[7	7]	1
7	6	6	[6	6]	7	7	2
6	[5	5]	6	6	6	6	3
5	5	5	5	5	[5	5]	4
4	4	4	[4	4]	5	5	5
3	[3	3]	4	4	4	4	6
[2	3	3]	3	3	3	3	7
2	3	2	2	2	[2	2]	8
1	2	1	[1	1]	2	2	9
[0	1]	0	1	1	1	1	10
0	1	0	0	0	[0	0]	11

i. Only 11 employees would be needed now. Total slack generated from this work schedule is:

	M	T	W	Th	F	S	Su
On-duty	9	7	9	8	8	7	7
Requirements	8	7	7	7	7	7	7
Slack	1	0	2	1	1	0	0

ii. With preference to S-Su pairs.

M	T	W	Th	F	S	Su	Employee
8	7	7	7	7	[7	7]	1
7	6	6	[6	6]	7	7	2
6	[5	5]	6	6	6	6	3
5	5	5	5	5	[5	5]	4
4	4	4	[4	4]	5	5	5
3	[3	3]	4	4	4	4	6
[2]	3	3	3	3	3	[3]	7
2	2	2	2	[2	2]	3	8
1	1	[1	1]	2	2	2	9
[0	0]	1	1	1	1	1	10

The number of employees needed is reduced to 10, and no slack is generated from this solution.

	M	T	W	Th	F	S	Su
On-duty	8	7	7	7	7	7	7
Requirements	8	7	7	7	7	7	7
Slack	0	0	0	0	0	0	0

iii. Because each employee requires a truck, the number of trucks needed would be 8 to cover Monday, even though the actual number of employees available would be 9 in the preceding solution. Assuming that extra employees are put to work doing some support activities, the smoothing of the workload will result in a reduction of 4 trucks over the requirements schedule in part (a).

11. Universal Electronics.

Job	Work Time (days)	Due Date (days)	Shop Time Remaining (days)	Operations Remaining	Slack (days)	Slack per Remaining Operation	Critical Ratio
1	0.25	5	1.5	5	3.5	0.7	3.333
2	1.75	4	2.5	7	1.5	0.214	1.600
3	1.50	6	3.0	9	3.0	0.333	2.000
4	2.00	5	3.5	12	1.5	0.125	1.429
5	1.50	4	2.0	8	2.0	0.25	2.000
6	0.75	7	1.5	6	5.5	0.917	4.667
7	1.25	6	2.0	9	4.0	0.444	3.000
8	1.00	4	1.5	3	2.5	0.833	2.667

Rule	Sequence							
FCFS	1	2	3	4	5	6	7	8
Due date	5	4	6	5	4	7	6	4
Completion	0.25	2.00	3.50	5.50	7.00	7.75	9.00	10.00
Days late	—	—	—	0.5	3.00	0.75	3.00	6.00
SPT	1	6	8	7	3	5	2	4
Due date	5	7	4	6	6	4	4	5
Completion	0.25	1.00	2.00	3.25	4.75	6.25	8.00	10.00
Days late	—	—	—	—	—	2.25	4.00	5.00
EDD	2	5	8	1	4	3	7	6
Due date	4	4	4	5	5	6	6	7
Completion	1.75	3.25	4.25	4.50	6.50	8.00	9.25	10.00
Days late	—	—	0.25	—	1.50	2.00	3.25	3.00
S/RO	4	2	5	3	7	1	8	6
Due date	5	4	4	6	6	5	4	7
Completion	2.00	3.75	5.25	6.75	8.00	8.25	9.25	10.00
Days late	—	—	1.25	0.75	2.00	3.25	5.25	3.00
CR	4	2	3	5	8	7	1	6
Due date	5	4	6	4	4	6	5	7
Completion	2.00	3.75	5.25	6.75	7.75	9.00	9.25	10.00
Days late	—	—	—	2.75	3.75	3.00	4.25	3.00

a. Relative performance. The table below shows that SPT results in the lowest proportion of jobs completed late. Earliest due date results in the lowest average lateness and maximum lateness.

Rule	Percent of jobs late	Average lateness	Maximum lateness
FCFS	62.5%	1.656 days	6.00 days
SPT	**37.5%**	1.406 days	5.00 days
EDD	62.5%	**1.250 days**	**3.25 days**
S/RO	62.5%	1.938 days	5.25 days
CR	62.5%	2.094 days	4.25 days

b. All of these rules result in some jobs being late. If customers can tolerate a small amount of lateness but would be very upset and likely to move their business elsewhere if jobs are very late, then EDD would be a good rule to use.

12. Penultimate Support Systems.

Model	A	B	C	D
Fabrication	12	24	6	18
Assembly	8	30	12	15

Using Johnson's rule, the sequence of Models is C - B - D - A.

Fabrication	C	B		D	A	Idle	

Assembly		C	Idle	B		D	A

```
0   10   20   30   40   50   60   70   80
```

	Fabrication		Assembly	
Job	Start	Finish	Start	Finish
C	0	6	6	18
B	6	30	30	60
D	30	48	60	75
A	48	60	75	83

The duration of this schedule (83 hours) is longer than can be completed within two 40-hour shifts.

13. Little 6, Inc.

	Time	M	T	W	Th	F	S	Su
Personal Tax Returns	1.5	24	14	18	18	10	28	16
Corporate Tax Returns	4.0	18	10	12	15	24	12	4
Total Hours Required		108	61	75	87	111	90	40
Accountants	10	11	7	8	9	12	9	4

a. We used the method in the text to schedule accountants. Tie-breaking preference was given to S-Su pairs of days off. For each employee, the box represents his or her two off-days.

M	T	W	Th	F	S	Su	Accountant
11	7	8	9	12	[9	4]	1
10	6	7	8	11	[9	4]	2
9	[5	6]	7	10	9	4	3
8	5	6	6	9	[8	3]	4
7	[4	5]	5	8	8	3	5
[6]	4	5	4	7	7	[2]	6
6	[3	4]	3	6	6	2	7
5	3	4	2	5	[5	1]	8
4	2	[3	1]	4	5	1	9
[3]	1	3	1	3	4	[0]	10
3	0	2	[0	2]	3	0	11
2	[0	1]	0	2	2	0	12
1	0	1	0	1	[1	0]	13
0	0	0	0	0	1	0	14

This schedule calls for 14 accountants.

b. Three part-time accountants working on the "X" days as shown below could be effectively used to replace the three full time accountants numbered 12 through 14.

M	T	W	Th	F	S	Su	Accountant
X	off	off	off	X	X	off	PT1
X	off	X	off	X	off	off	PT2
off	off	off	off	off	X	off	PT3

14. Eight jobs processed on three machines.

Job	1	2	3	4	5	6	7	8
Machine 1	2	5	2	3	1	2	4	2
Machine 2	4	1	3	5	5	6	2	1
Machine 3	6	4	5	2	3	2	6	2

a. Using SPT for M2, the makespan for the eight jobs is 38 hours.
   Sequence 2 - 8 - 7 - 3 - 1 - 4 - 5 - 6

```
M1 |   2   | 8 | 7 | 3 | 1 | 4 |5| 6 |          Idle            |

M2 |   Idle    |2| 8 |   7 | 3 |  1  |    4    |    5    |    6    |
    |          |
   2 A.M.    7 A.M.

M3 |    Idle    |   2  | 8 |    7    |    3    |    1    | 4 | 5 |  6  |
   0    3    6    9   12   15   18   21   24   27   30   33   36   39
```

b. We can use Johnson's rule with some modifications. For example, we sum the processing times of M1 and M2 and then sum the processing times of M2 and M3 as follows:

Job	M1 + M2	M2 + M3
1	6	10
2	6	5
3	5	8
4	8	7
5	6	8
6	8	8
7	6	8
8	3	3

By Johnson's rule, the revised schedule is 8-3-1-5-7-6-4-2. TheGantt chart is shown below. If we start the M2 schedule at 7:00 a.m., M1 begins at 5:00 a.m. The result is a makespan of 35 hours. Note that Johnson's rule utilizes M2 better than when SPT was used for scheduling.

```
M1 | 8 | 3 | 1 |5| 7 | 6 | 4 |   2   |            Idle            |

M2 |   | 8 |  3  |    1    |   5   | 7 |    6    |  4  |2|    Idle    |
    |       |
   2 A.M.  7 A.M.

M3 | Idle | 8 |     3     |    1    |   5   |    7    | 6 | 4 |   2   | Idle |
   0    3    6    9   12   15   18   21   24   27   30   33   36   39
```

15. Two operations scheduled through three machines

   a. Job schedules using four rules:

     i. SPT:

M1 Schedule

Job	Start Time	Finish Time
2	0	2
6	2	5
3	5	9
4	9	14
1	14	20
5	20	27

M2 Schedule

Job	Start Time	Finish Time
8	0	2
7	2	6
9	6	12
10	12	20

M3 Schedule

Job	Arrival Time	Process Time	Job Sequence	Start Time	Finish Time	Hours Early	Past Due
2	2	1	2	2	3	15	–
8	2	10	8	3	13	18	–
6	5	1	6	13	14	15	–
7	6	6	4	14	17	–	1
3	9	7	7	17	23	19	–
9	12	9	10	23	25	15	–
4	14	3	1	25	29	–	16
10	20	2	5	29	33	–	3
1	20	4	3	33	40	–	18
5	27	4	9	40	49	=	1
				Total		82	39
				Average		8.2	3.9

     ii. EDD:

M1 Schedule

Job	Start Time	Finish Time
1	0	6
4	6	11
2	11	13
3	13	17
6	17	20
5	20	27

M2 Schedule

Job	Start Time	Finish Time
8	0	2
10	2	10
7	10	14
9	14	20

M3 Schedule

Job	Arrival Time	Due Date	Job Sequence	Start Time	Finish Time	Hours Early	Past Due
8	2	31	8	2	12	19	–
1	6	13	1	12	16	–	3
10	10	40	4	16	19	–	3
4	11	16	2	19	20	–	2
2	13	18	3	20	27	–	5
7	14	42	6	27	28	1	–
3	17	22	5	28	32	2	–
6	20	29	10	32	34	–	6
9	20	48	7	34	40	2	–
5	27	30	9	40	49	=	1
					Total	24	20
					Average	2.4	2.0

iii. S/RO:

M1 Schedule

Job	S/RO	Job	Start Time	Finish Time
1	1.5	1	0	6
2	7.5	4	6	11
3	5.5	3	11	15
4	4.0	2	15	17
5	9.5	5	17	24
6	12.5	6	24	27

M2 Schedule

Job	S/RO	Job	Start Time	Finish Time
7	16	8	0	2
8	9.5	10	2	10
9	16.5	7	10	14
10	15	9	14	20

M3 Schedule

Job	Arrival Time	S/RO	Job Sequence	Start Time	Finish Time	Hours Early	Past Due
8	2	19	8	2	12	19	–
1	6	– 3	1	12	16	–	3
10	10	0	4	16	19	–	3
4	11	– 3	3	19	26	–	4
7	14	4	2	26	27	–	9
3	15	– 4	5	27	31	–	1
2	17	– 9	6	31	32	–	3
9	20	– 1	7	32	38	4	–
5	24	– 1	10	38	40	0	–
6	27	– 3	9	40	49	=	1
					Total	23	24
					Average	2.3	2.4

iv. CR:

M1 Schedule

Job	CR	Job	Start Time	Finish Time
1	1.3	1	0	6
2	6	3	6	10
3	2	4	10	15
4	2	5	15	22
5	2.7	2	22	24
6	7.3	6	24	27

M2 Schedule

Job	CR	Job	Start Time	Finish Time
7	4.2	8	0	2
8	2.6	9	2	8
9	3.2	10	8	16
10	4.0	7	16	20

M3 Schedule

Job	Arrival Time	CR	Job Sequence	Start Time	Finish Time	Hours Early	Past Due
8	2	2.9	8	2	12	19	–
1	6	.25	1	12	16	–	3
9	8	.89	4	16	19	–	3
3	10	.43	3	19	26	–	4
4	15	0	2	26	27	–	9
10	16	1	5	27	31	–	1
7	20	1.67	6	31	32	–	3
5	22	.75	7	32	38	4	–
2	24	– 8	10	38	40	0	–
6	27	– 2	9	40	49	=	1
					Total	23	24
					Average	2.3	2.4

b. EDD minimizes the past due but results in producing product early. If the product will have to be held in inventory and has a high inventory carrying cost, S/RO or CR minimizes early production.

16. Return to Problem 8. 16. We still use the same method except now the requirement is to have four consecutive days off.

Employee	M	T	W	Th	F	S	Su
1	8	3	5	3	9	2	3
2	8	3	4	2	8	2	3
3	7	2	3	2	8	2	3
4	7	2	2	1	7	2	3
5	7	2	2	1	6	1	2
6	6	1	1	1	6	1	2
7	5	0	1	1	6	1	1
8	5	0	0	0	5	1	1
9	5	0	0	0	4	0	0
10	4	0	0	0	4	0	0
11	3	0	0	0	4	0	0
12	3	0	0	0	3	0	0
13	2	0	0	0	3	0	0
14	2	0	0	0	2	0	0
15	1	0	0	0	2	0	0
16	1	0	0	0	1	0	0
17	0	0	0	0	1	0	0

The minimum number of employees required is 17. The work schedule is determined by assigning the boxed days off.

	M	T	W	Th	F	S	Su
On-duty employees	8	8	14	7	9	2	3
Requirements	8	3	5	3	9	2	3
Slack	0	5	9	4	0	0	0

Chapter 17

Managing Complex Projects

Study Questions

1. The basic steps in effective project management are as follows: describe the project; diagram a network model; determine time estimates; analyze the model; develop the project plan; and periodically assess the progress of the project and replan as needed.

2. To construct a network diagram for a project, (i) all the activities, including a clear specification of the starting and finishing points of the project, must be identified; (ii) activity times, or the most pessimistic, most likely, of most optimistic times if uncertainty is involved, must be identified; and (iii) the precedence relationships between activities must be specified.

   Most projects can be diagrammed as networks. However, PERT/CPM network diagrams do not accurately model situations where one activity must start and end before another, but the two activities can be overlapped and worked on simultaneously. Also, in some situations the actual precedence relationships cannot be specified beforehand because the sequencing of some activities is contingent on the result of certain other activities.

3. A frequent root cause of major project delays and cost overruns is changed scope or design.

4. Experienced advertising professionals would be polled to acquired three time estimates for each activity: (i) most optimistic time (a); (ii) most likely time (m); and (iii) most pessimistic time (c). It may be difficult to obtain the needed participation and cooperation from these experienced professionals. They may be impatient, feel their time is better spent elsewhere, or hold inconsistent definitions of "pessimistic." Once the three estimates are obtained for each activity, and assuming the beta distribution reasonably describes the distribution of these times, the expected time (t_e) is calculated. Expected times are used when analyzing the diagram to identify the critical path. Based on the expected duration of the critical path and its variation, we can use the normal probability distribution to estimate the probability of completing the project by the desired date.

5. The distribution of activity times can take on a variety of shapes. The only restriction required is that the most likely time (m) should locate between the most optimistic time (a) and the most pessimistic time (b). Other distributions—for example the normal distribution—require that m should locate equidistant from a and b, which is too restrictive. The beta distribution allows a variety of shapes, thereby better matching the estimates of the actual probability distributions.

6. The critical path is important because it determines project duration. Delays in the activities along the critical path extend the project duration. Such delays are often costly due to penalty costs and other indirect costs. The critical path can change during the course of the project if noncritical activities are delayed by more than the amount of their slack times.

7. We assume that each activity along the critical path is independent of the other activities with respect to the probability distribution of its time duration. We then assume that the central limit theorem applies, and we can use a normal distribution to estimate the probability of the time duration of the project, which is the sum of the activity times along the critical path.

   The variances of other paths play a role in that these other paths could become the critical path, even if their length is a little shorter than the critical path. There is a possibility that the actual duration of near-critical paths might increase, causing the critical path to change.

8. For a cost analysis the following data are required: (i) normal time and normal cost for each activity; (ii) crash time and crash cost for each activity; and (iii) the CPM diagram, which shows all precedence relationships.

   To determine a minimum-cost schedule, the following steps are taken: (i) Determine the critical path; (ii) Find the activity on the critical path that is the cheapest to crash per week; (iii) Reduce the time for this activity until (a) it cannot be further reduced, (b) another path becomes critical, or (c) the increase in direct cost exceeds the savings from indirect cost and penalty cost; (iv) Repeat steps (i) through (iii) as necessary.

   In this process it is usually assumed that there is a linear increase in costs as the activity time is reduced from the normal time.

9. The slack-sorted report is useful for allocating resources from one activity to another in a project. When all slacks are positive, the report indicates that either the project could be completed earlier than expected or excess resources could be shifted to another project.

10.
   a. PERT/CPM are tools useful for managing large projects. As such, if the full potential of these methods is to be realized, management must not delegate the PERT/CPM analysis to technicians who do not have the expertise to manage a project. If the technicians are the only ones using them, it is usually due to one of two reasons: (i) management does not fully understand the methods and therefore does not completely trust their results or (ii) PERT/CPM are not appropriate tools for a given situation because of the assumptions that must be made.

   b. It is true that managers of activities on the critical path are in the spotlight, but this may not be bad from an organizational perspective. Bad performers can be identified, and good performers rewarded. However, here is where total slack must be clearly understood. Consuming total slack will affect everyone else on the noncritical paths.

   c. It is true that PERT/CPM requires comprehensive information systems to be effective. Any new system (MRP for example) requires the same sort of change from current practices. How much of a change depends on the nature of the current practice. Management should weigh the costs and expected benefits carefully before implementing these systems.

Problems

1. a. AON Network diagram.

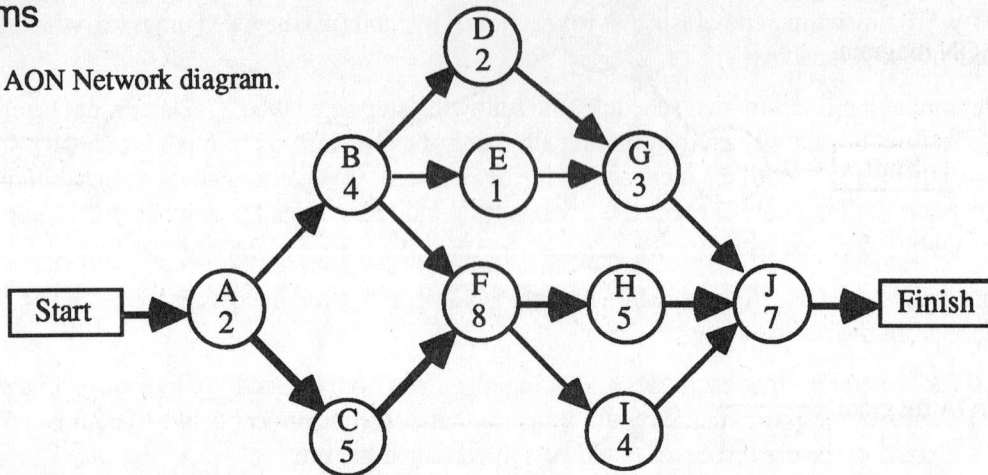

a. AOA Network diagram.

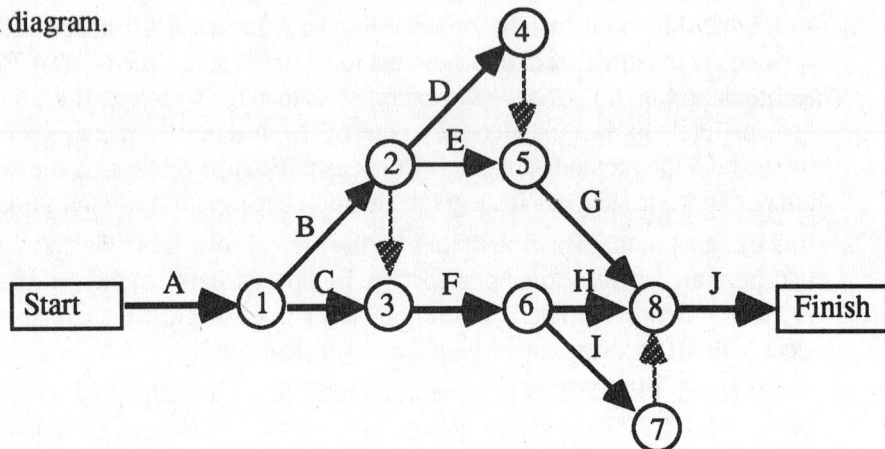

b. The critical path is A-C-F-H-J with a completion time of 27 days.

c.

Activity	Duration	Earliest Start	Latest Start	Earliest Finish	Latest Finish	Slack	On Critical Path?
A	2	0	0	2	2	0	Yes
B	4	2	3	6	7	1	No
C	5	2	2	7	7	0	Yes
D	2	6	15	8	17	9	No
E	1	6	16	7	17	10	No
F	8	7	7	15	15	0	Yes
G	3	8	17	11	20	9	No
H	5	15	15	20	20	0	Yes
I	4	15	16	19	20	1	No
J	7	20	10	27	27	0	Yes

2.

a. AON diagram.

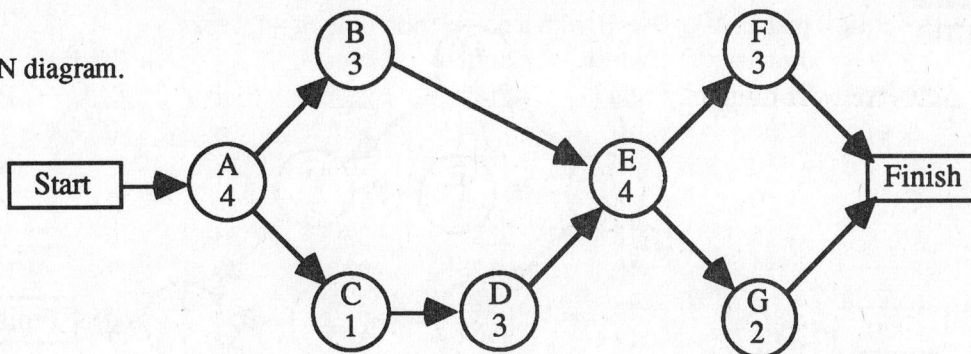

AOA diagram.

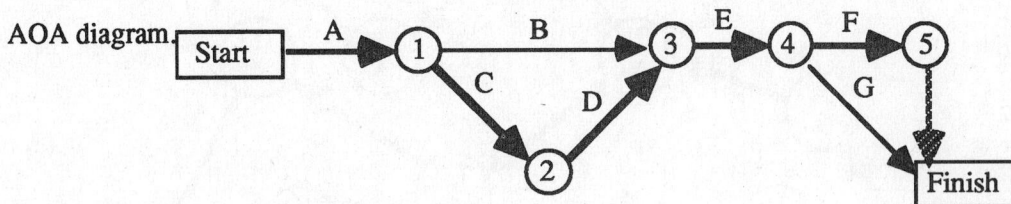

The critical path is A-C-D-E-F with a completion time of 15 days.

b.

Activity	Duration	Earliest Start	Latest Start	Earliest Finish	Latest Finish	Slack	On Critical Path?
A	4	0	0	4	4	0	Yes
B	3	4	5	7	8		No
C	1	4	4	5	5	0	Yes
D	3	5	5	8	8	0	Yes
E	4	8	8	12	12	0	Yes
F	3	12	12	15	15	0	Yes
G	2	12	13	14	15	1	No

3. a. AON diagram

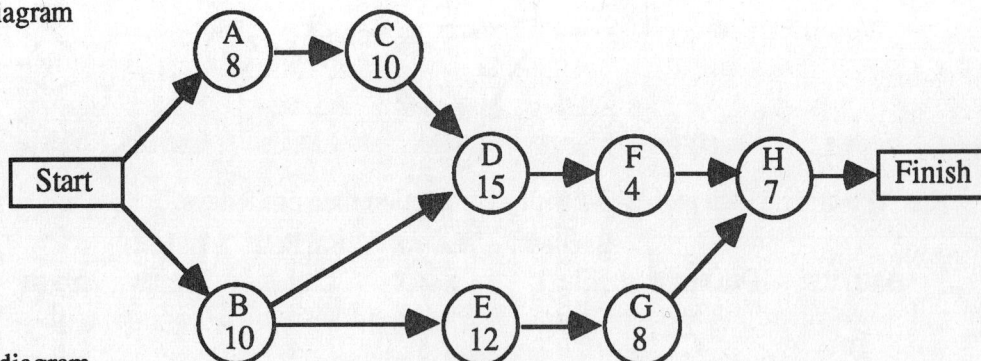

AOA diagram

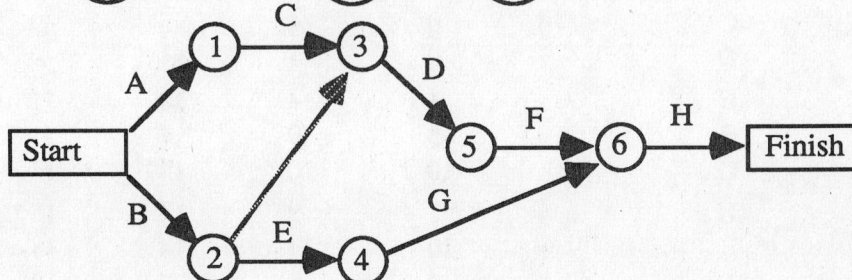

b. The critical path is A-C-D-F-H with a completion time of 44 weeks.

Activity	Earliest Duration	Latest Start	Earliest Start	Latest Finish	Finish	On Critical Slack	Path?
A	8	0	0	8	8	0	Yes
B	10	0	7	10	17	7	No
C	10	8	8	18	18	0	Yes
D	15	18	18	33	33	0	Yes
E	12	10	17	22	29	7	No
F	4	33	33	37	37	0	Yes
G	8	22	29	30	37	7	No
H	7	37	37	44	44	0	Yes

4. AON

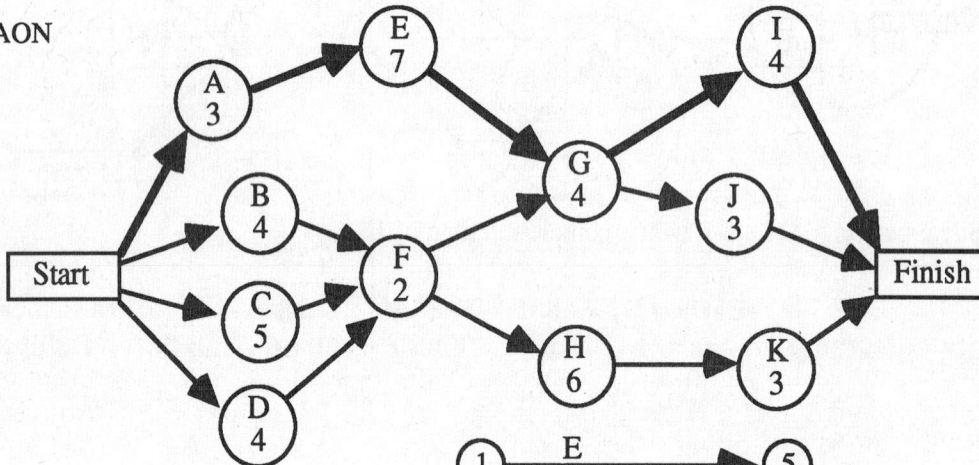

AOA

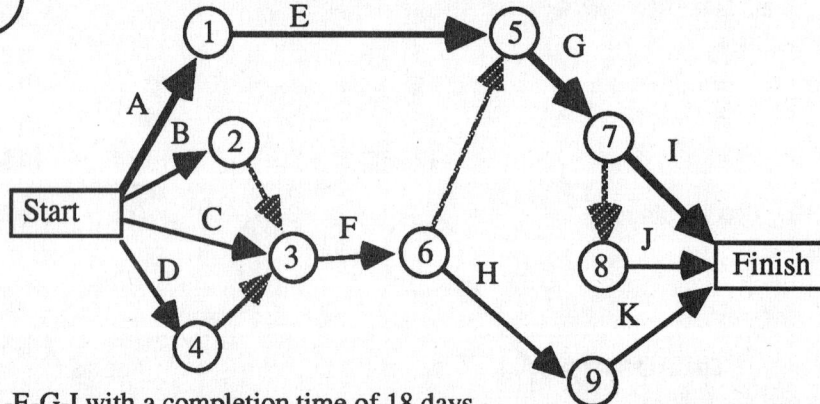

b. The critical path is A-E-G-I with a completion time of 18 days.

Activity	Duration	Earliest Start	Latest Start	Earliest Finish	Latest Finish	Slack	On Critical Path?
A	3	0	0	3	3	0	Yes
B	4	0	5	4	9	5	No
C	5	0	4	5	9	4	No
D	4	0	5	4	9	5	No
E	7	3	4	10	11	0	Yes
F	2	5	9	7	11	4	No
G	4	10	10	14	14	0	Yes
H	6	7	9	13	15	2	No
I	4	10	14	14	18	0	Yes
J	3	14	15	17	18	1	No
K	3	13	15	16	18	2	No

5.

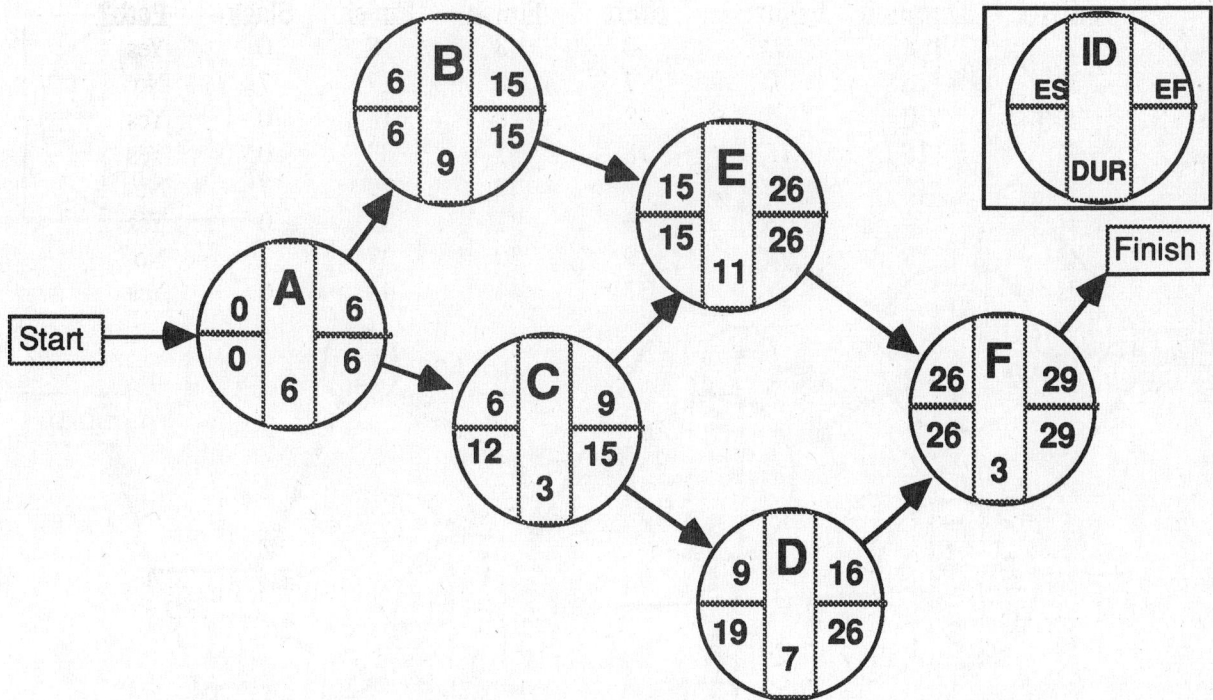

a. The AON network is:

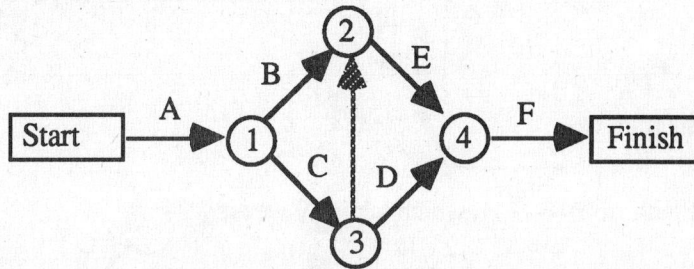

The AOA network is:

b. Activity slacks for the project:

	Start		Finish		Activity	Critical
Activity	Earliest	Latest	Earliest	Latest	Slack	Path
A	0	0	6	6	0	Yes
B	6	6	15	15	0	Yes
C	6	12	9	15	6	No
D	9	19	16	26	10	No
E	15	15	26	26	0	Yes
F	26	26	29	29	0	Yes

Critical path is A-B-E-F, and the project completion date is week 29.

6.

   a. The AON diagram is:

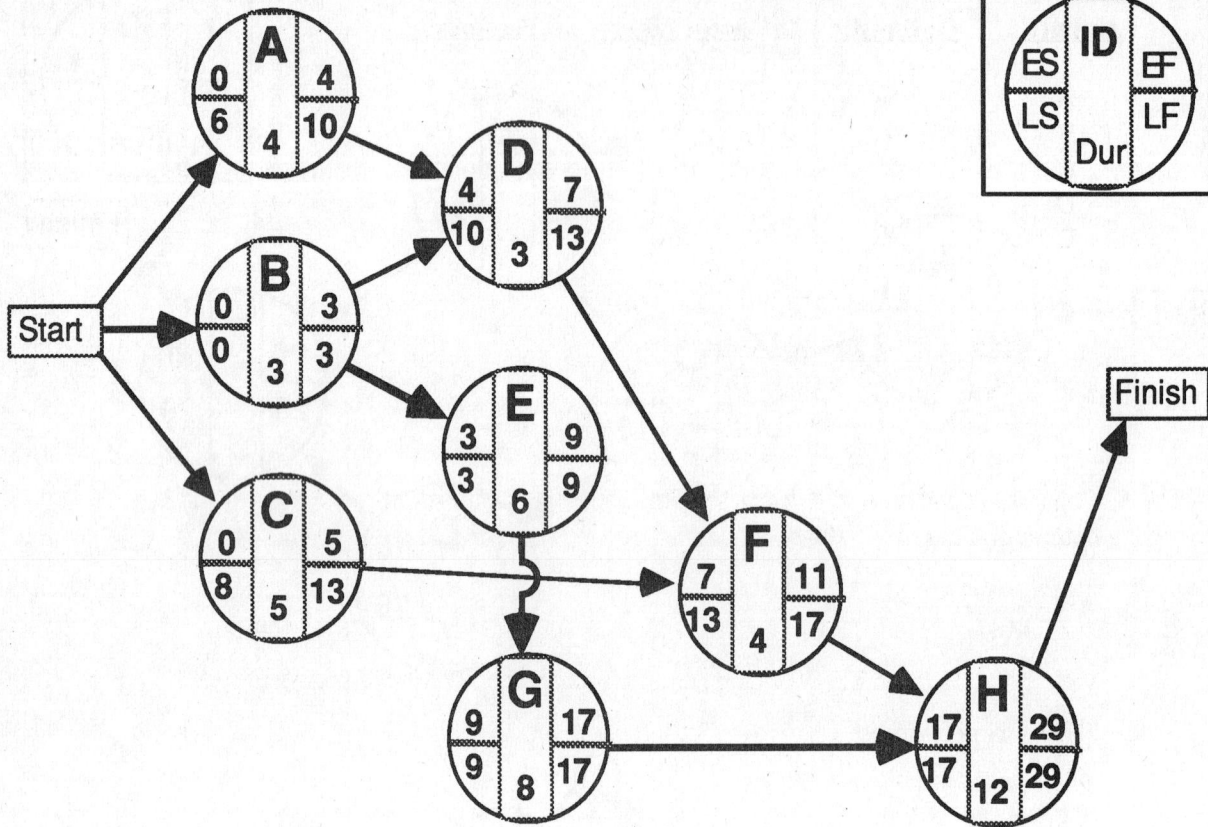

      The AOA diagram is:

   b. The critical path is: B-E-G-H, which takes 29 weeks.

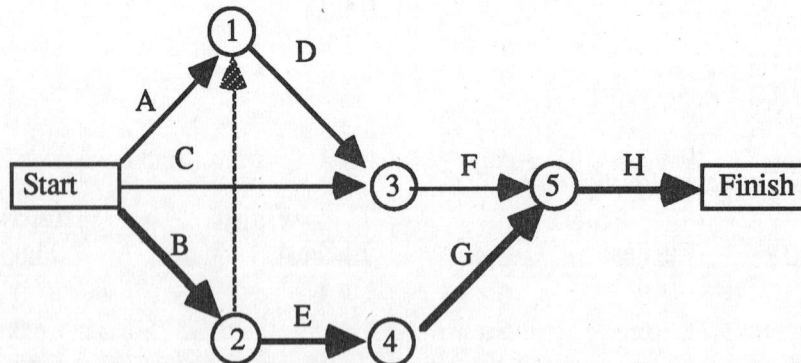

   c. The total slack for activity A = 10 − 4 = 6 weeks.
       The total slack for activity D = 13 − 7 = 6 weeks.

   d. If A takes 5 weeks, then D will have 10 − 5 = 5 weeks' slack.

7.

  a. The expected activity times (in days) are:

Activity	Optimistic	Most Likely	Pessimistic	t_e	σ^2
A	5	8	11	8	1.00
B	4	8	11	7.83	1.36
C	5	6	7	6	0.11
D	2	4	6	4	0.44
E	4	7	10	7	1.00

Path	Total Expected Time
A-C	$8 + 6 = 14.00$
A-D-E	$8 + 4 + 7 = 19.00$
B-E	$7.83 + 7 = 14.83$

The critical path is A-D-E because it has the longest time duration. The expected completion time is 19 days.

  b. $$z = \frac{T - TE}{\sqrt{\sigma^2}}$$

Where T = 21 days, TE = 19 days, and the sum of the variances for critical path A-D-E is $(1.00 + 0.44 + 1.00) = 2.44$.

$$z = \frac{21 - 19}{\sqrt{2.44}} = \frac{2}{1.562} = 1.28$$

Assuming the normal distribution applies (which is questionable for a sample of 3 activities) we use the table for the normal probability distribution. Given z = 1.28, the probability that the project can be completed in 21 days is 0.8997, or about 90%.

  c. Since the normal distribution is symetrical, the probability the project can be completed in 17 days is $(1 - 0.8997) = 0.1003$, or about 10%.

8. $$z = \frac{T - TE}{\sqrt{\sigma^2}}$$

Where T = 20 weeks, TE = $(5.5 + 9.0 + 4.5) = 19$ weeks, and the sum of the variances for critical path B-F-G is $(0.69 + 2.78 + 0.69) = 4.16$.

$$z = \frac{20 - 19}{\sqrt{4.16}} = \frac{1}{2.0396} = 0.4903$$

Assuming the normal distribution applies we use the table for the normal probability distribution. Given z = 0.49, the probability that activities B-F-G is $(1-0.6879)$, or 31.21%.

9.

a. The AON diagram is:

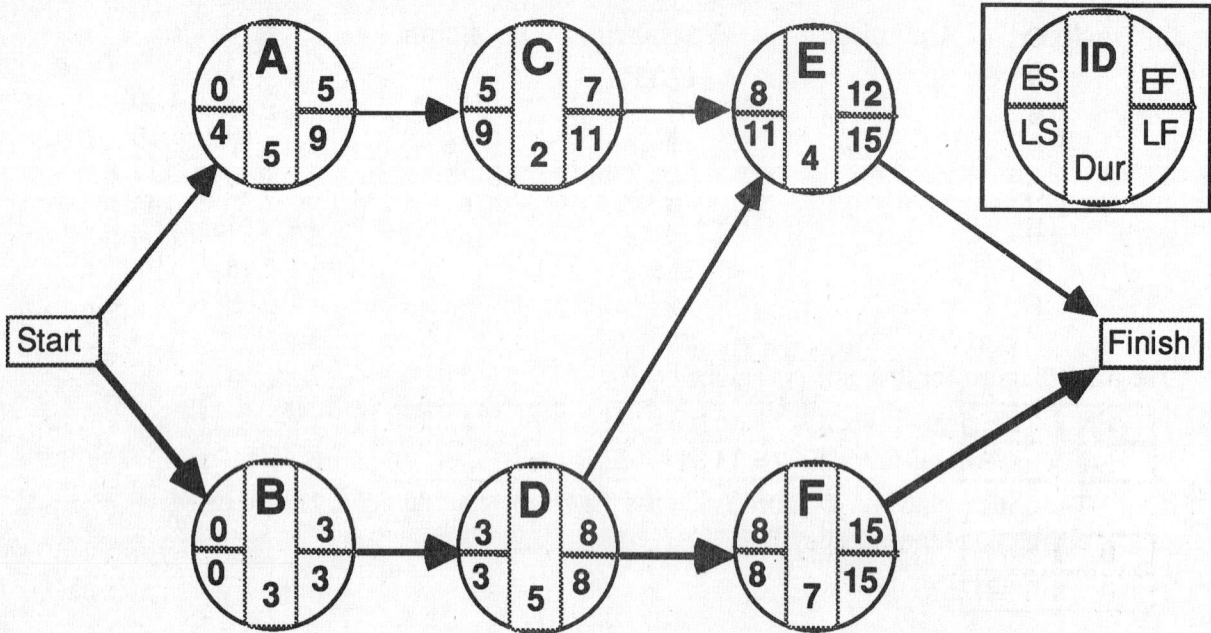

The AOA diagram is:

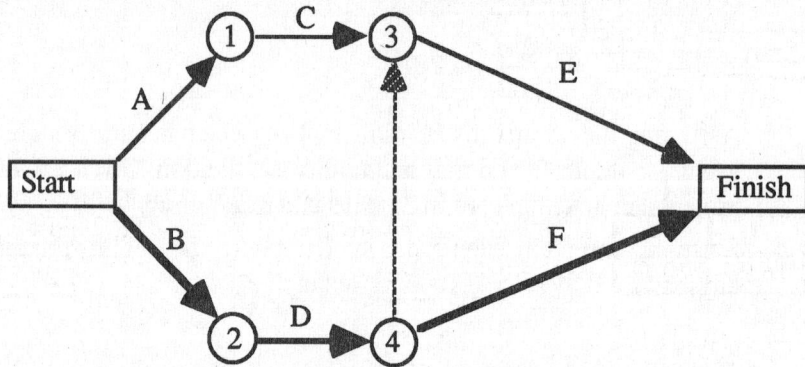

b. Critical path is B-D-F. Expected duration of the project is 15 weeks.

c. Activity slacks for the project are:

Activity	Start Earliest	Latest	Finish Earliest	Latest	Activity Slack	Critical Path
A	0	4	5	9	4	No
B	0	0	3	3	0	Yes
C	5	9	7	11	4	No
D	3	3	8	8	0	Yes
E	8	11	12	15	3	No
F	8	8	15	15	0	Yes

10. **Bluebird University.** Calculation of activity statistics (in days):

Activity	Expected Time	Variance
A	**6.83**	**0.25**
B	8.33	1.00
C	4	0.11
D	**17.33**	**5.44**
E	10	0.44
F	4	0.11
G	**7.5**	**0.69**
H	7	0.44
I	**11.5**	**2.25**
J	4	0.00

The AOA diagram for this project is given below.

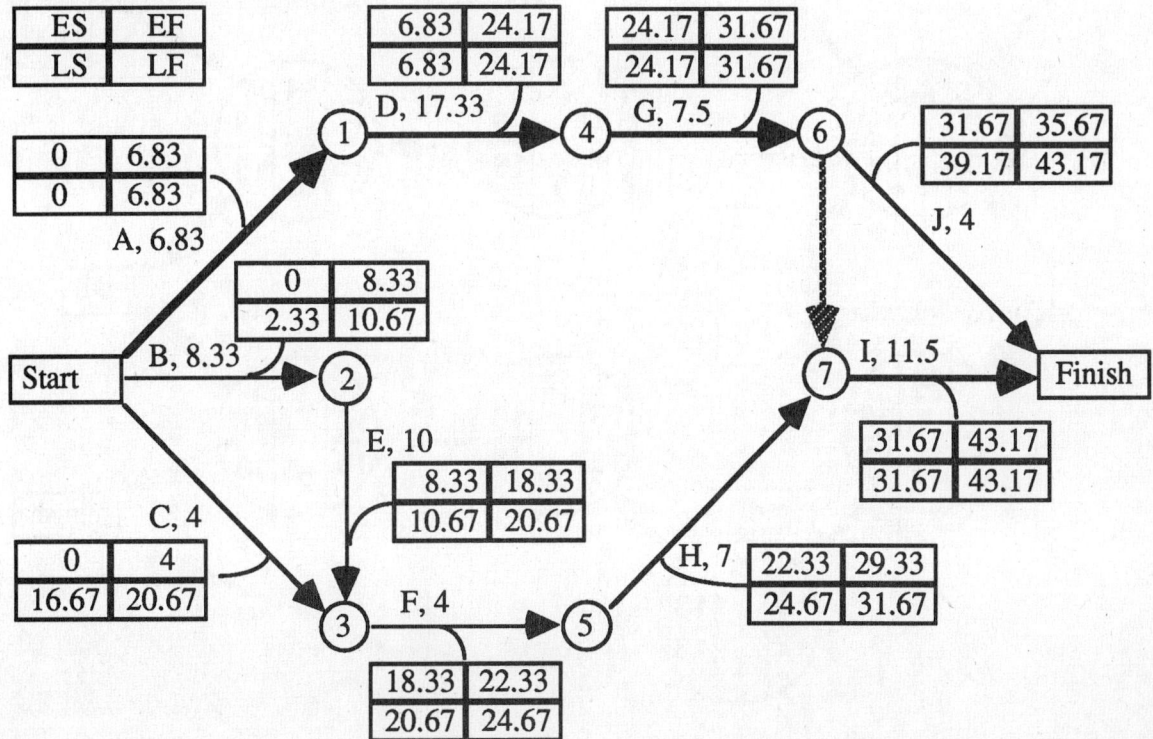

The AON diagram is:

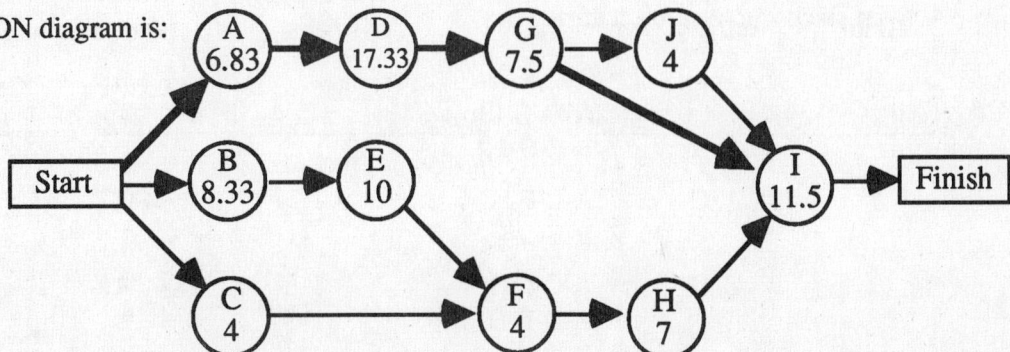

The critical path is A-D-G-I and the expected completion time is 43.17 days.

T = 47days, TE = 43.17 days, and the sum of the variances for the critical activities is: $(0.25 + 5.44 + 0.69 + 2.25) = 8.63$.

$$z = \frac{T - TE}{\sqrt{\sigma^2}} = \frac{47 - 43.17}{\sqrt{8.63}} = \frac{3.83}{2.94} = 1.30$$

Assuming the normal distribution applies we use the table for the normal probability distribution. Given z = 1.30, the probability activities A-D-G-I can be completed in 47 days or less is 0.9032.

11.

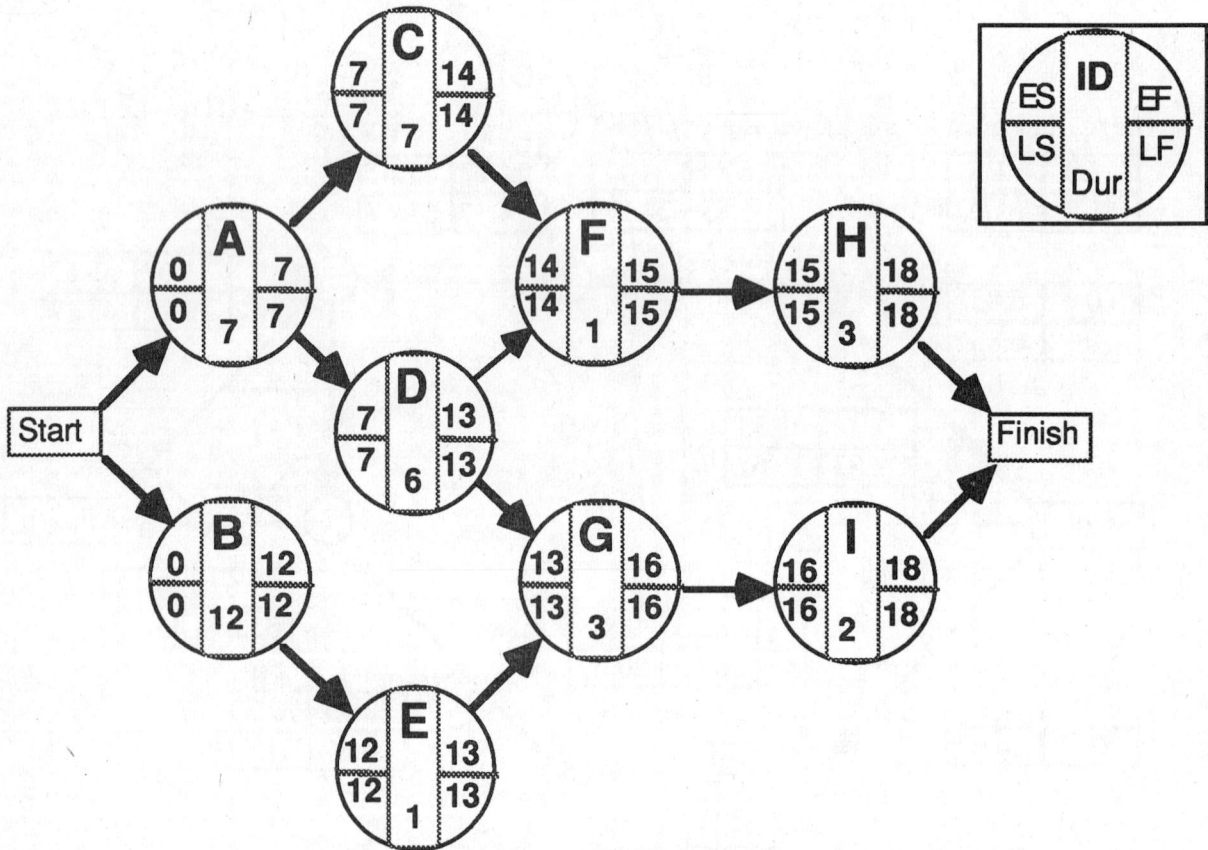

Trial	Crash Activity	Resulting Critical Path	Time Reduction (weeks)	Project Duration (weeks)	Crash Cost
0	–	A-C-F-H A-D-G-I B-E-G-I	–	18	0
1	A, G	A-C-F-H B-E-G-I	1	17	$400
2	C, G	A-C-F-H A-D-F-H B-E-G-I	1	16	$450

12.

a. The AON diagram is:

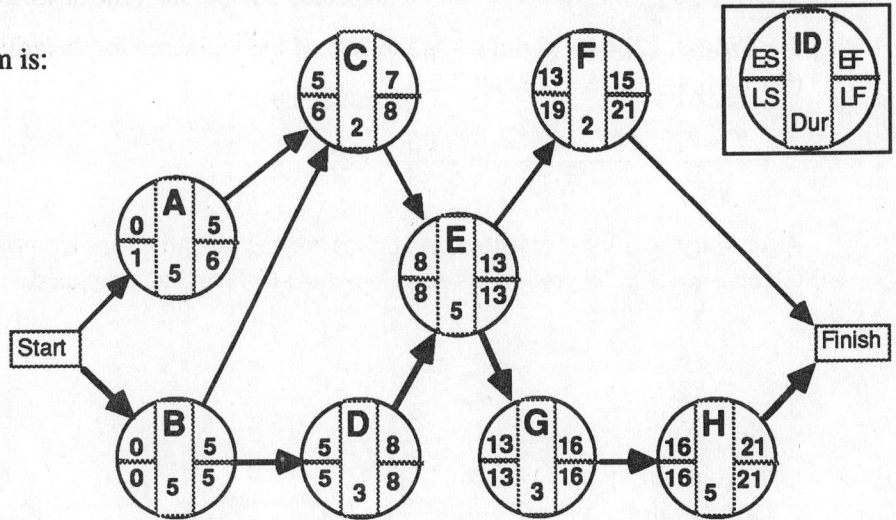

The AOA diagram is:

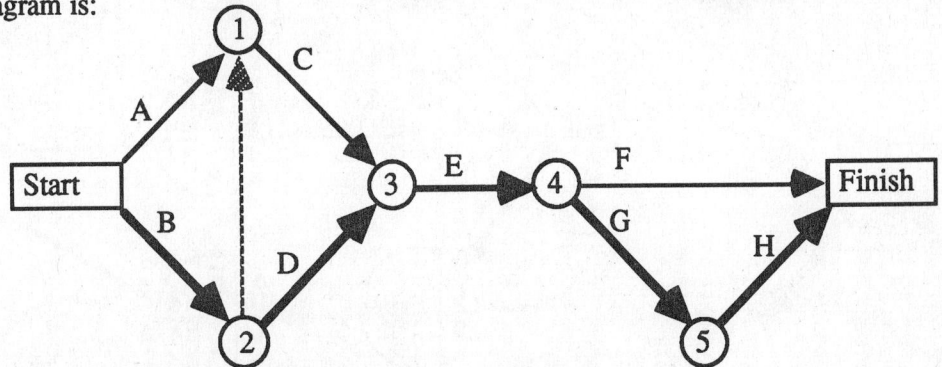

The critical path is B-D-E-G-H, and the project duration is 21 days.

b. Direct cost and time data for the activities:

Activity	Crash Cost/Day	Maximum Crash Time (days)
A	200	1
B	600	2
C	300	1
D	500	1
E	150	2
F	100	1
G	0	0
H	200	2

A summary of the cost analysis is given below. The recommended completion date is day 17 by crashing activity E by 2 days and activity H by 2 days.

Trial	Crash Activity	Resulting Critical Paths	Time Reduction (days)	Project Duration (days)	Direct Costs Last Trial	Crash Cost Added	Total Indirect Costs	Total Penalty Costs	Total Project Costs
0	–	B-D-E-G-H	–	21	$7,500	–	$5,250	$700	$13,450
1	E	B-D-E-G-H	2	19	$7,500	$300	$4,750	$500	$13,050
2	H	B-D-E-G-H	2	17	$7,800	$400	$4,250	$300	$12,750

c. The critical path is B-D-E-G-H.

13. Hamilton Berger.

a. Calculation of the activity statistics:

Activity	Expected Time	Variance
A	4	0.44
B	8	1.00
C	**10**	**2.77**
D	2	0.11
E	5	2.77
F	4	**0.00**
G	1	0.00
H	2	**0.00**

The AON diagram for the hiring project is shown is:

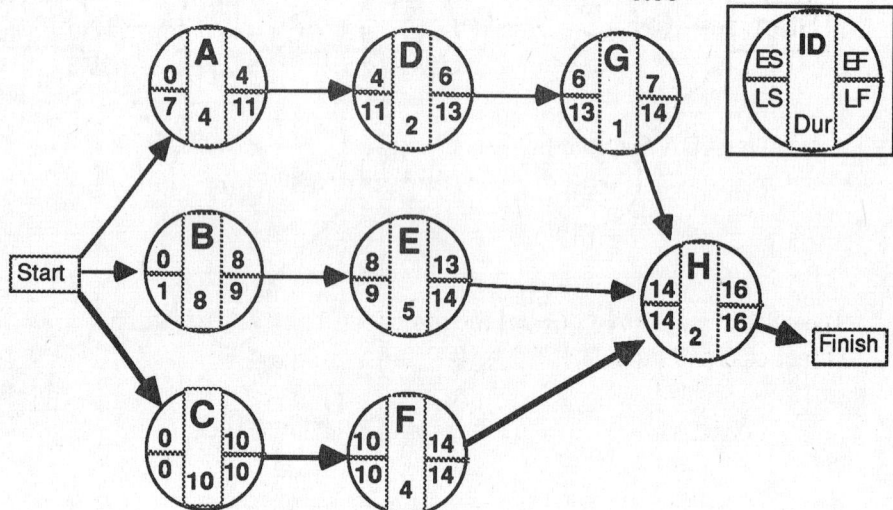

The AOA diagram for the hiring project is shown is:

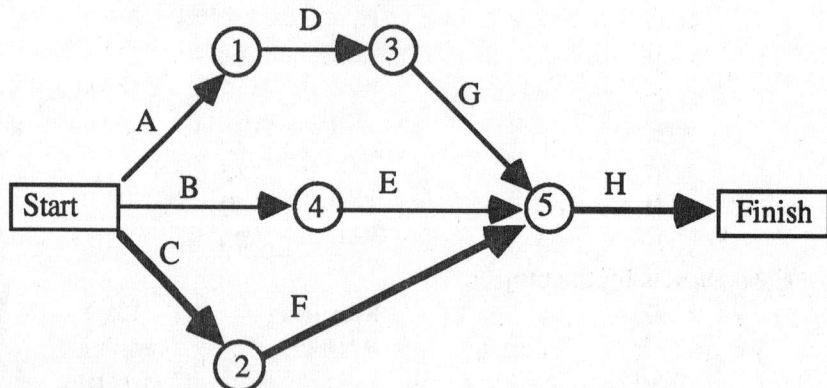

The critical path is C-F-H and the project is expected to take 16 weeks.

b.

$$z = \frac{T - TE}{\sqrt{\sigma^2}} = \frac{14 - 16}{\sqrt{2.77}} = -\frac{2}{1.66} = -1.20$$

Using the normal distribution table, the probability that the project can be completed in only 14 weeks is $(1 - 0.8849)$ or 0.1151.

c. No additional expenditures are recommended. Reducing activity A would not help since it is not on the critical path. Reducing activity B would shorten the entire project by two weeks, but it would cost more than the lease costs for two weeks. In addition, activity B is not on the critical path.

14. An AON diagram using the normal times follows.

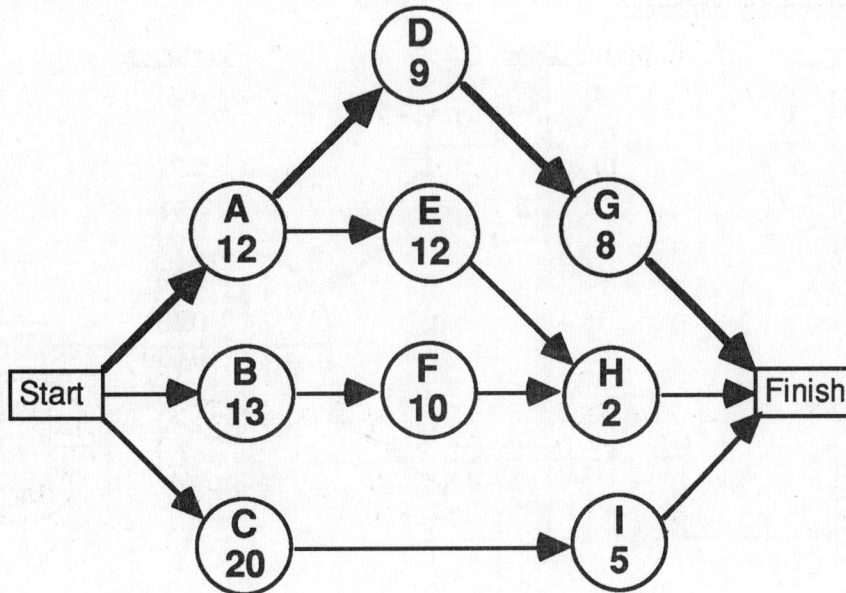

The critical path is A-D-G and the project duration is 29 days.
Direct cost and time data:

Activity	Crash Cost/Day	Maximum Crash Time (days)
A	$400	1
B	116.67	3
C	750	2
D	250	4
E	116.67	3
F	175	2
G	125	2
H	350	1
I	500	3

Cost analysis for the project:

Trial	Crash Activity	Resulting Critical Path	Time Reduction (weeks)	Project Duration (weeks)	Crash Cost
0	–	A-D-G	–	29	–
1	G	A-D-G	2	27	250
2	D	A-D-G	2	25	500

The total cost for this project is:
$13,200 + $250 + $500 = $13,950

The activity times are:

A: 12   B: 13   C: 20   D: 7   E: 12

F: 10   G: 6   H: 1   I: 5

15. Johnson Homebuilders.

a. The AON diagram for this project is:

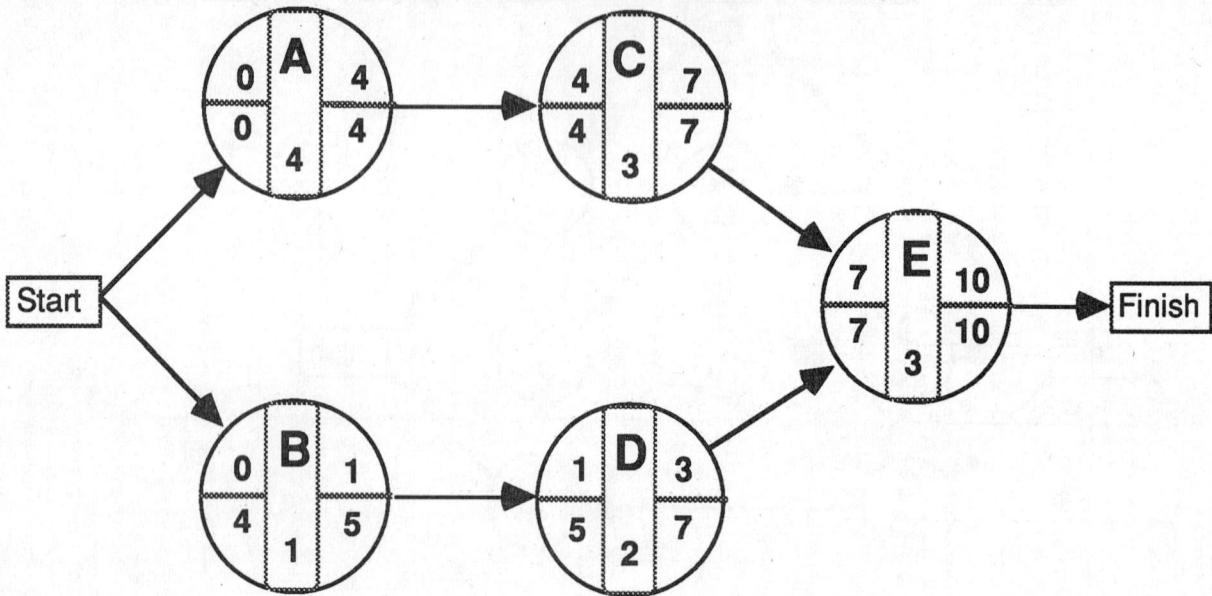

b. The critical path is A-C-E, and the project duration is 10 days.

c.
Activity	Activity Slack
A	0
B	5 – 1 = 4
C	0
D	7 – 3 = 4
E	0

d. We start off by scheduling activity A because it has no slack. Activity B must be scheduled next. C and D are scheduled next so that E can be scheduled. The Gantt chart is shown below:

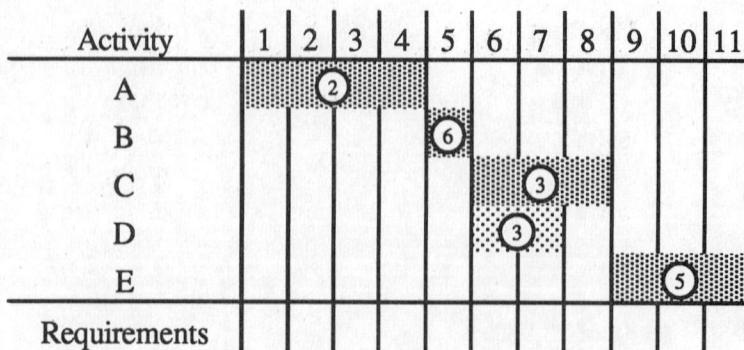

   i. The critical path is A-B-C-E. Activity D has one day's slack.

   ii. The project will now take 11 days.

16. The slack for each activity is shown below:

Activity	Start Earliest	Start Latest	Finish Earliest	Finish Latest	Activity Slack
A	0	0	5	5	0
B	5	5	9	9	0
C	5	6	8	9	1
D	9	9	11	11	0
E	8	12	10	14	4
F	11	11	14	14	0
G	10	15	13	18	5
H	14	14	18	18	0

The Gantt chart is shown below:

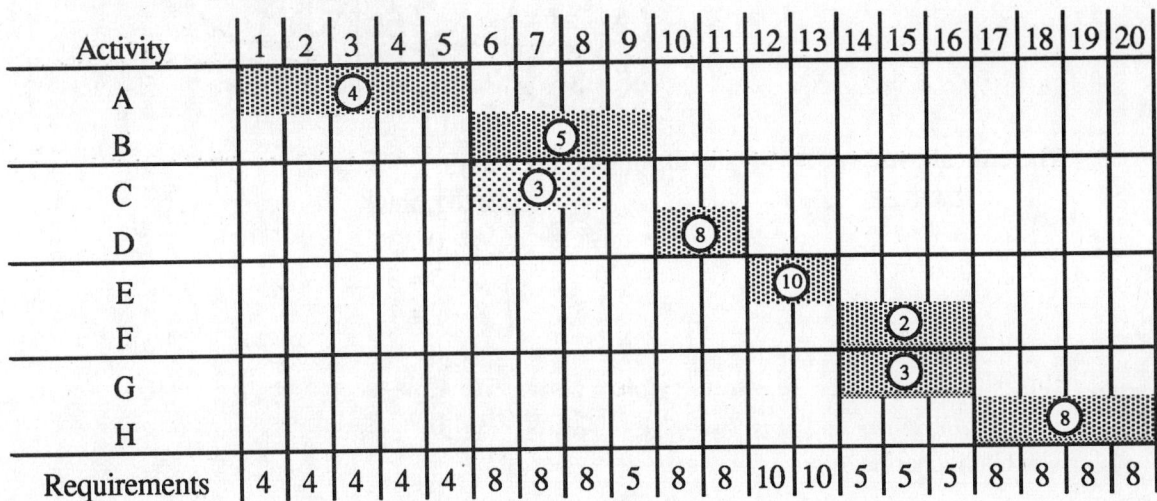

Activity	1	2	3	4	5	6	7	8	9	10	11	12	13	14	15	16	17	18	19	20
A			④																	
B								⑤												
C							③													
D										⑧										
E													⑩							
F															②					
G															③					
H																		⑧		
Requirements	4	4	4	4	4	8	8	8	5	8	8	10	10	5	5	5	8	8	8	8

a. Although in Fig. 17.19, the critical path is A-B-D-F-H, with a length of 18 days, when we impose a ten-worker limit, the project will take 20 days.

b. The critical path is A-B-D-E-F-H, recognizing the ten-worker limitation. Activity E is also critical. Attempting to work on activity E in parallel with other activities would violate the capacity limitation.

17.

a. The AON diagram is:

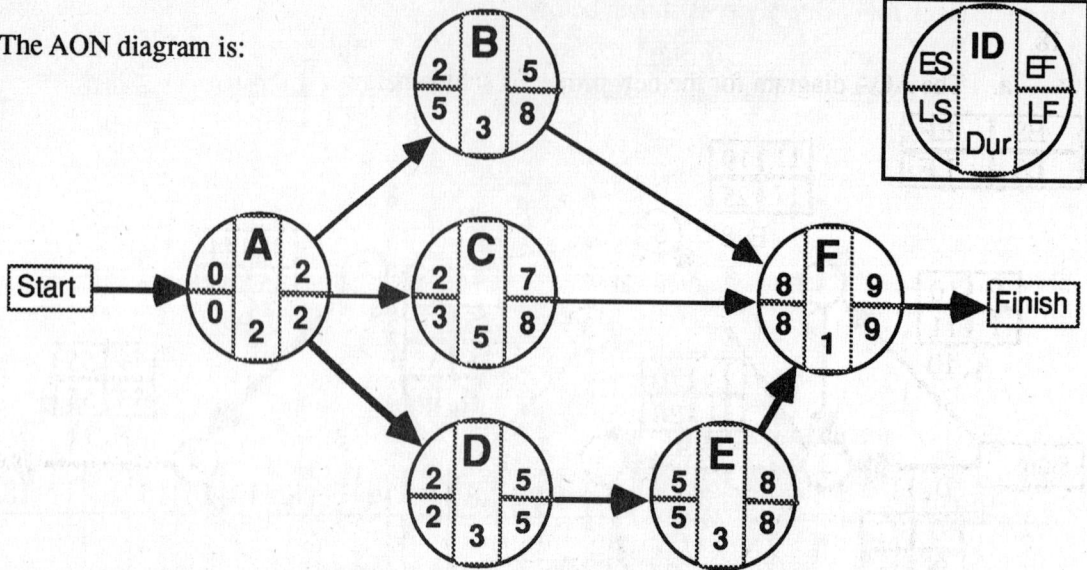

Legend box:
| ES | **ID** | EF |
| LS | Dur | LF |

Start → A → B, C, D

A: ES 0, LS 0, ID A, EF 2, LF 2, Dur 2
B: ES 2, LS 5, ID B, EF 5, LF 8, Dur 3
C: ES 2, LS 3, ID C, EF 7, LF 8, Dur 5
D: ES 2, LS 2, ID D, EF 5, LF 5, Dur 3
E: ES 5, LS 5, ID E, EF 8, LF 8, Dur 3
F: ES 8, LS 8, ID F, EF 9, LF 9, Dur 1

B → F, C → F, D → E, E → F, F → Finish

The critical path is A-D-E-F and the duration is 9 days.

Activity	Activity Slack
A	0
B	8 − 5 = 3
C	8 − 7 = 1
D	0
E	0
F	0

The Gantt chart is:

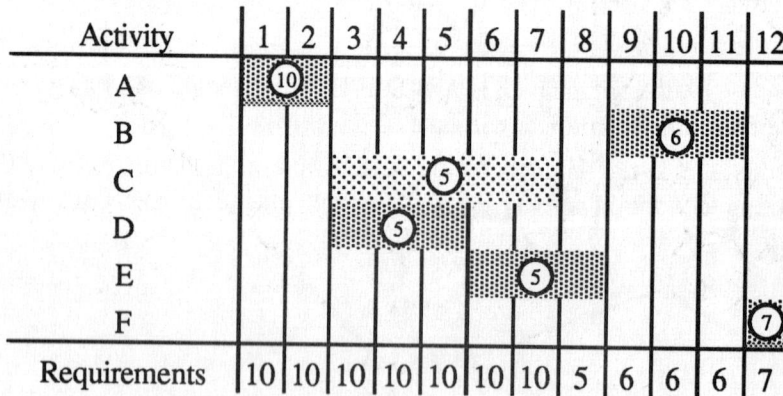

Activity	1	2	3	4	5	6	7	8	9	10	11	12
A	⑩											
B										⑥		
C					⑤							
D				⑤								
E							⑤					
F												⑦
Requirements	10	10	10	10	10	10	10	5	6	6	6	7

b. i. The critical path is A-D-E-B-F.

ii.
Activity	Activity Slack
A	0
B	0
C	4
D	0
E	0
F	0

iii. The project will now take 12 days.

18.

a. The AOA diagram for the new project is shown below.

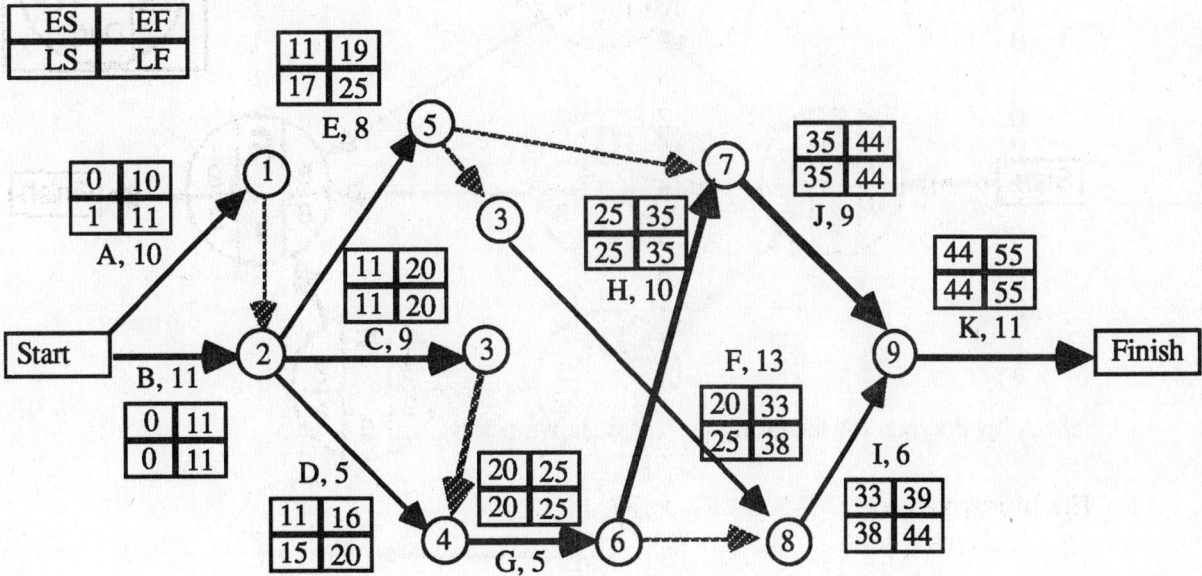

ES	EF
LS	LF

E, 8

11	19
17	25

0	10
1	11

A, 10

35	44
35	44

J, 9

25	35
25	35

H, 10

11	20
11	20

C, 9

44	55
44	55

K, 11

Start

B, 11

0	11
0	11

F, 13

20	33
25	38

I, 6

D, 5

20	25
20	25

11	16
15	20

G, 5

33	39
38	44

Finish

The AOA diagram for the hiring project is shown below.

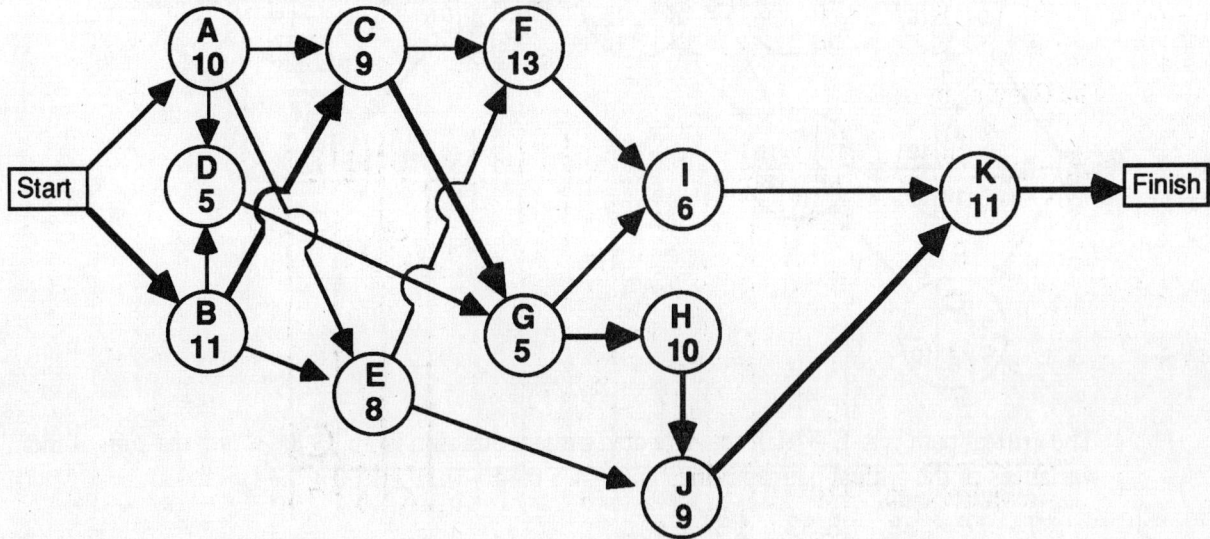

A 10 C 9 F 13 D 5 Start I 6 K 11 Finish B 11 G 5 H 10 E 8 J 9

b. The critical path is B-C-G-H-J-K, and the expected project duration is 55 days.

19. a. Calculation of the activity statistics:

Activity	Expected Time	Variance
A	**10**	**0.44**
B	9	4
C	8	0.11
D	2	0.11
E	**10**	**0.44**
F	**6**	**0.11**
G	3	0.44
H	**5**	**1.0**
I	4	0.44
J	**5.33**	**0.44**
K	2	0

The AON diagram for the hiring project is shown below.

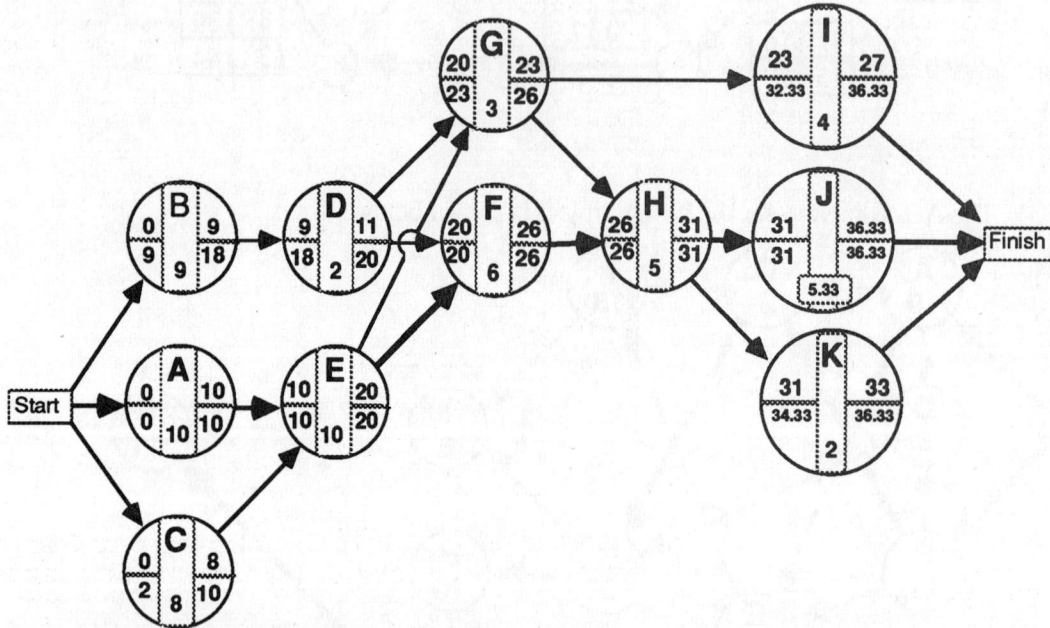

The critical path is A-E-F-H-J, the expected project duration is 36.33 days, and the sum of the variances of the critical path activities is $(0.44 + 0.44 + 0.11 + 1.00 + 0.44) = 2.43$.

b.
$$z = \frac{T - TE}{\sqrt{\sigma^2}} = \frac{38 - 36.33}{\sqrt{2.43}} = \frac{1.67}{1.56} = 1.07$$

The probability that the project will take more than 38 days is

$1 - 0.8577$ or 0.1423

c. The path A-E-G-H-J has a duration of 33.33 weeks with variance of 2.76.
Therefore,

$$z = \frac{T - TE}{\sqrt{\sigma^2}} = \frac{36.33 - 33.33}{\sqrt{2.76}} = 1.81$$

The probability that the path A-E-G-H-J exceeds 36.33 weeks is $1 - 0.9649$, or 0.0351.

20. Webb Enterprises.

Calculation of activity statistics:

Activity	Start Earliest	Latest	Finish Earliest	Latest	Slack	Expected Time	Variance
A	0	31.83	7.17	39.00	31.83	7.17	0.69
B	0	0	18.17	18.17	0	18.17	4.69
C	18.17	18.17	27.17	27.17	0	9.00	1.00
D	27.17	27.17	39.00	39.00	0	11.83	1.36
E	27.17	43.17	30.17	46.17	16	3.00	0.112
F	39	41	44.17	46.17	2	5.17	0.69
G	39	39	43.17	43.17	0	4.17	0.69
H	43.17	43.17	46.17	46.17	0	3.00	0.11
I	39	47.34	41	49.34	8.34	2.00	0.11
J	46.17	46.17	49.34	49.34	0	3.17	0.03
K	30.17	47.34	32.17	49.34	17.17	2.00	0
L	18.17	46.51	21	49.34	28.34	2.83	0.25
M	7.17	50.34	9.17	52.34	43.17	2.00	0
N	49.34	49.34	52.34	52.34	0	3.00	0
O	52.34	52.34	54.34	54.34	0	2.00	0.11

The AOA diagram for Webb is shown below.

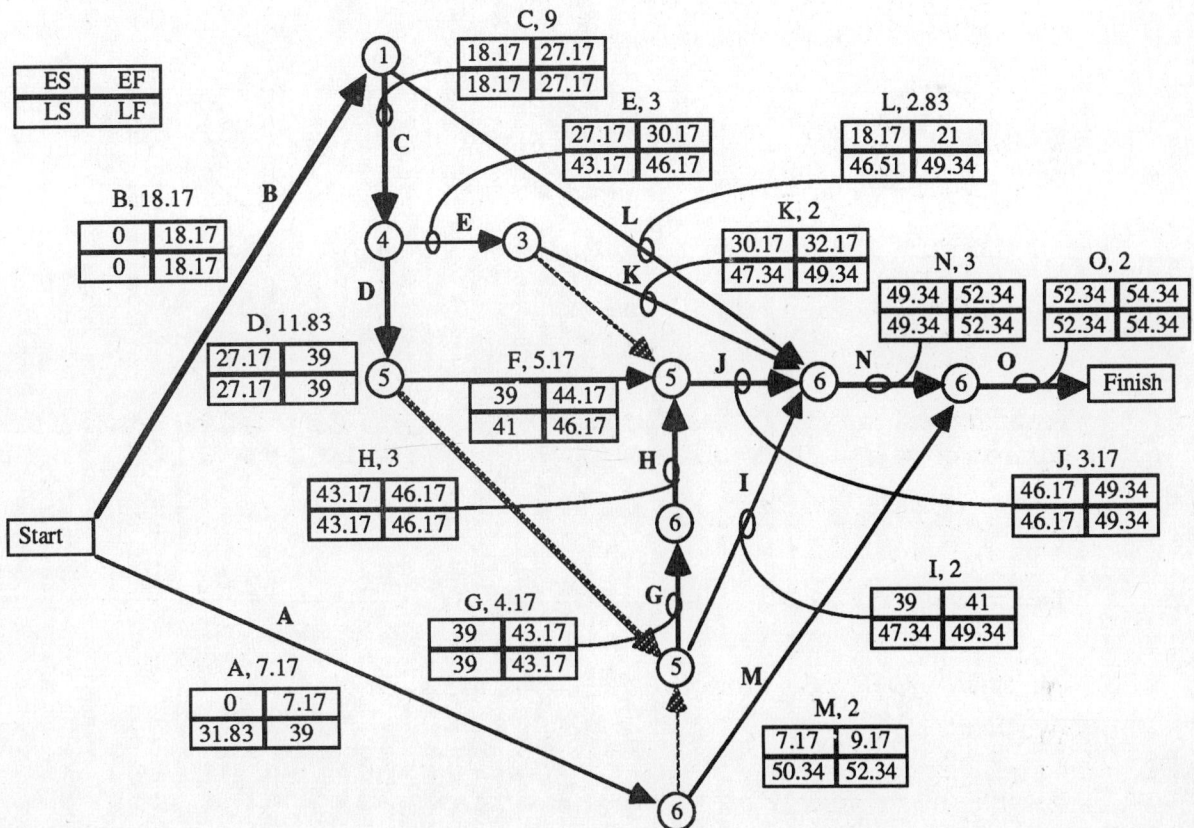

a. The expected project duration is $(18.17 + 9.00 + 11.83 + 4.17 + 3.00 + 3.17 + 3.00 + 2.00) = 54.34$ weeks. The sum of the variances of the critical activities is $(4.69 + 1.00 + 1.36 + 0.69 + 0.11 + 0.03 + 0.00 + 0.11) = 7.99$. The standard deviation is the square root of 7.99 or 2.83 weeks.

b. The critical path is B-C-D-G-H-J-N-O.

c. The probability of completing the project in 55 weeks.

$$z = \frac{T - TE}{\sqrt{\sigma^2}} = \frac{55 - 54.34}{\sqrt{7.99}} = \frac{0.66}{2.83} = 0.23$$

The probability that the project will be completed within 55 weeks is .5910.

The probability of completing the project in 60 weeks.

$$z = \frac{T - TE}{\sqrt{\sigma^2}} = \frac{60 - 54.34}{\sqrt{7.99}} = \frac{5.66}{2.83} = 2.00$$

The probability that the project will be completed within 60 weeks is .9772.

d. Since activity F has two weeks of slack, there is no effect on project completion if the project is delayed by one week. On the other hand, a three-week delay would cause the critical path to shift from B-C-D-G-H-J-N-O (length 54.34 weeks), to B-C-D-F-J-N-O (length 55.34 weeks).

21. Los Angeles Transit Authority. (All activities are critical.)

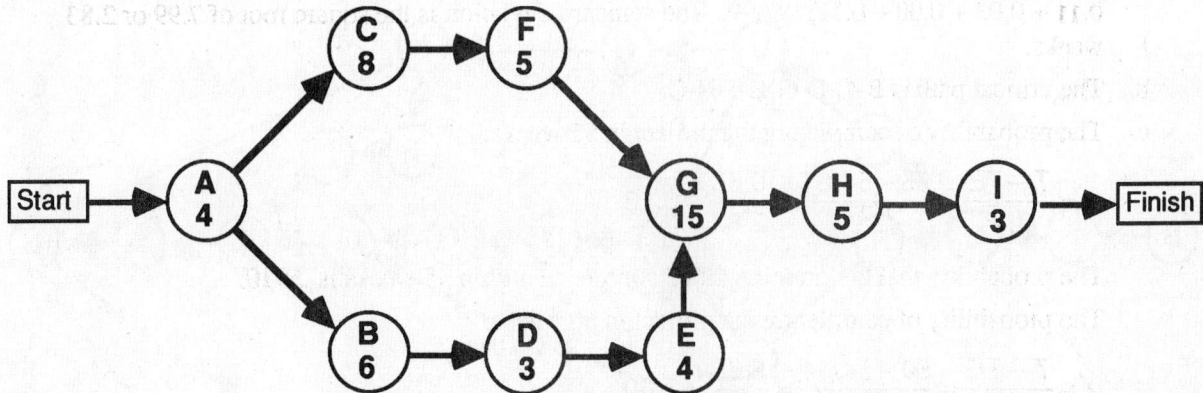

Task	Normal Time (mo)	Crash Time (mo)	Normal Cost ($000)	Crash Cost ($000)	Cost per day ($000)
A. Finalize Plan	4	3	200	250	50
B. Obtain Permits	6	4	500	800	150
C. Design Tunnel	8	6	800	1200	200
D. Specify Equipment	3	3	100	100	—
E. Order Equipment	4	3	200	350	150
F. Prepare Route	5	3	400	800	200
G. Evacuate Tunnel	15	10	1000	3500	500
H. Test System	5	4	600	800	200
I. Certify System	3	2	300	400	100

Cost analysis for the project:

Trial	Crash Activity	Time Reduction (months)	Project Duration (months)	Cum Crash Costs	Cum Crash Penalty/Savings	Total Penalty/ Savings
0	–	–	40	–	(4000)	(4000)
1	A	1	39	(50)	(3000)	(3050)
2	I	1	38	(150)	(2000)	(2150)
3	H	1	37	(350)	(1000)	(1350)
4	B+C	1	36	(700)	0	(700)
5	B+C	1	35	(1050)	250	(800)
6	G	5	30	(3550)	1500	(2050)

The activity times for the minimum cost plan for for this project is:

A: 3   B: 5   C: 7   D: 3   E: 4
F: 5   G: 15   H: 4   I: 2

b. The penalty is large enough to give the contractor an incentive to complete the project on time (in 36 months). However, as seen when comparing trials number 4 and 5, the $250,000 bonus is not sufficient to cover the cost of expediting activities B and C ($350,000). If the bonus is increased to at least $350,000 per month, the contractor would have an incentive to make further reductions in the project duration.

22. **Bentonite Homes.** One of many possible arrangements for the project activities is shown below:

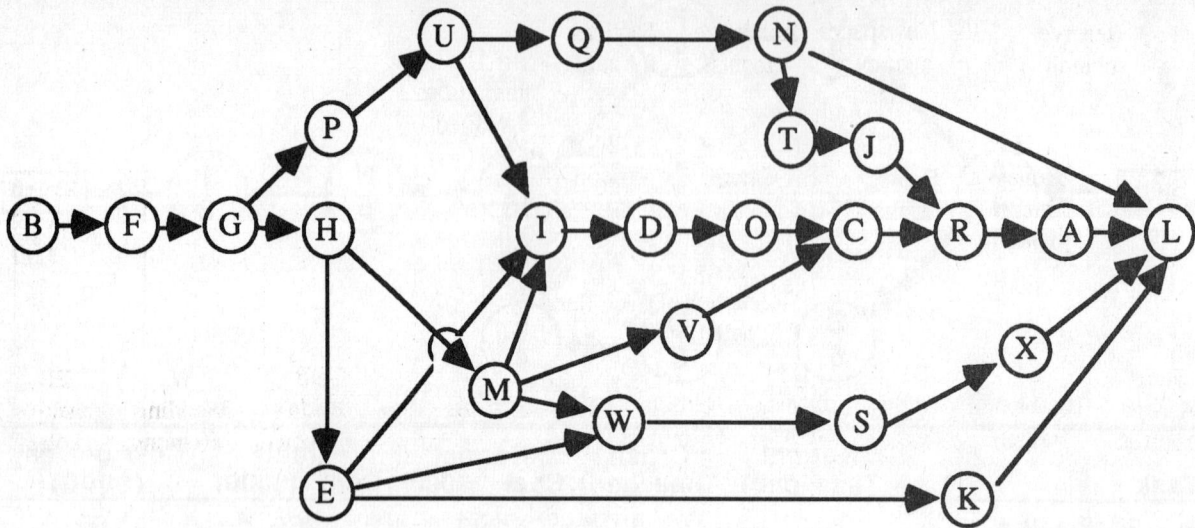

U	Q	N
Windows	Siding	Outside painting

	T	J
P		
Roof	Doors	Kitchen Cabinets

B	G	H	I	D	O	C	R	A
Building Permit	Framing	HVAC	Insulation	Dry wall	Interior Painting	Carpets and flooring	Final trim	Appliance installation

F
Foundation

M	V		X
Rough-in plumbing	Bath Fixtures		Landscaping

W	S
Lawn sprinkler	Sidewalks

E
Electrical wiring

K
Lighting Fixtures

23. Will, Bea Wright-Bach Wedding.

V Reserve church   **N** Newspaper announcement   **A** Announcements   **CC** Register for china   **I** Invitations mailed

H Honeymoon planning   **P** Photographer   **K** Caterer   **M** Menu

J Guest List   **Q** Reception hall   **DD** Dance Band

Start Accept Proposal   **E** Establish budget   **D1** Wedding dress   **D3** Bride's Mother's dress   **D4** Groom's Mother's dress   **Z** Rehearsal   **S** Bachelor party   **BB** Bride's nervous breakdown   **W** Wedding ceremony   **EE** thankyou notes

R Rings

C Colors   **F** Flowers   **O** Order Cake, Mints

Y Select bridesmaids   **D2** Bridesmaids' dresses   **G** Gifts for Wedding party

X Select groomsmen   **U** Ushers   **T** Tuxedos

B Blood tests   **L** License   **AA** Pre-nuptial agreement

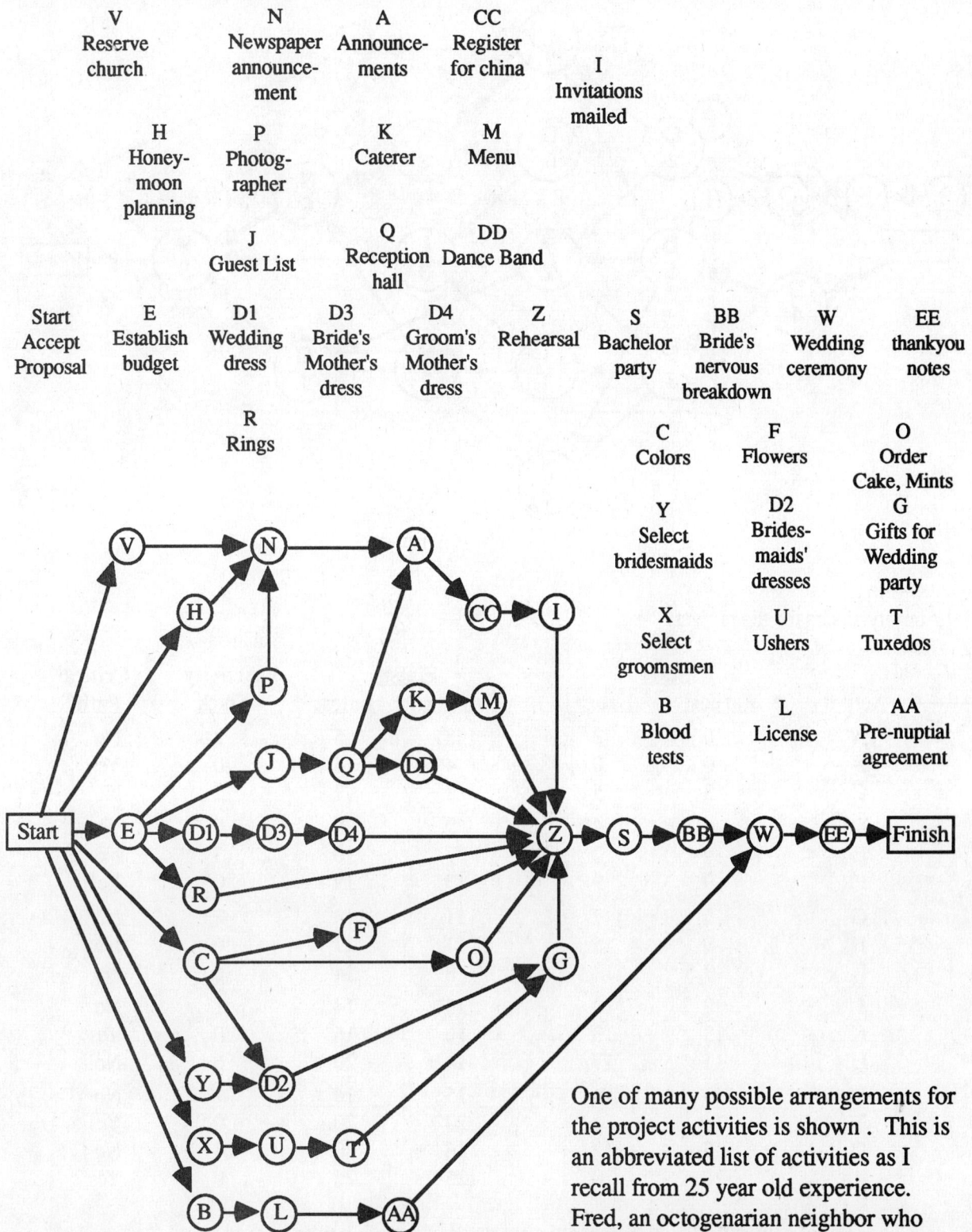

One of many possible arrangements for the project activities is shown . This is an abbreviated list of activities as I recall from 25 year old experience. Fred, an octogenarian neighbor who eloped with his lifelong spouse, says that simple ceremonies seem to "stick" at least as well as elaborate ones.

24. AON diagram.

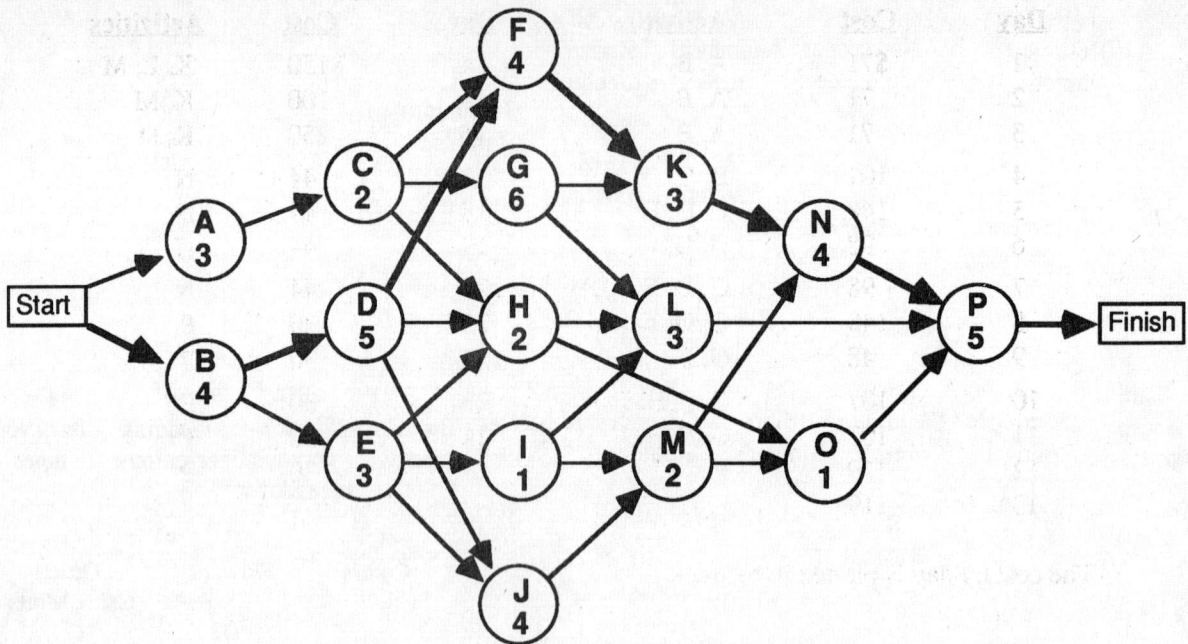

Activity slacks for the project:

Activity	Start Earliest	Start Latest	Finish Earliest	Finish Latest	Activity Slack	Critical Path?
A	0	2	3	5	2	No
B	0	0	4	4	0	Yes
C	3	5	5	7	2	No
D	4	4	9	9	0	Yes
E	4	7	7	10	3	No
F	9	9	13	13	0	Yes
G	5	7	11	13	2	No
H	9	15	11	17	6	No
I	7	13	8	14	6	No
J	9	10	13	14	1	No
K	13	13	16	16	0	Yes
L	11	17	14	20	6	No
M	13	14	15	16	1	No
N	16	16	20	20	0	Yes
O	15	19	16	20	4	No
P	20	20	25	25	0	Yes

The critical path is B-D-F-K-N-P and the expected completion time is 25 days.

Project cost with the earliest start time for each activity:

Day	Cost	Activities	Day	Cost	Activities
1	$71	A, B	14	$150	K, L, M
2	71	A, B	15	100	K, M
3	71	A, B	16	250	K, O
4	101	B, C	17	44	N
5	148	C, D, E	18	44	N
6	98	G, D, E	19	44	N
7	98	G, D, E	20	44	N
8	148	G, D, I	21	30	P
9	48	G, D	22	30	P
10	107	G, F, H, J	23	30	P
11	107	G, F, H, J	24	30	P
12	119	F, J, L	25	30	P
13	119	F, J, L			

The cost by day is plotted in below.

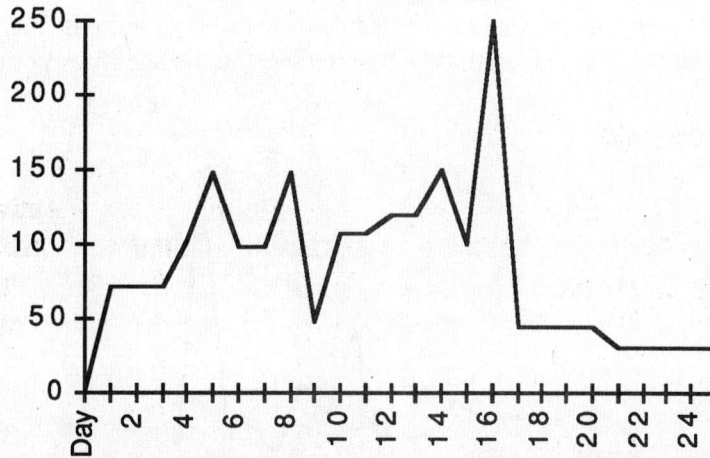

Project cost with the latest start times for each activities:

Day	Cost	Activities	Day	Cost	Activities
1	$38	B	14	$169	I, J, K
2	38	B	15	100	K, M
3	71	A, B	16	125	H, K, M
4	71	A, B	17	69	H, N
5	68	A, D	18	94	L, N
6	98	C, D	19	94	L, N
7	98	C, D	20	294	L, N, O
8	98	G, D, E	21	30	P
9	98	G, D, E	22	30	P
10	113	G, E, F	23	30	P
11	82	G, F, J	24	30	P
12	82	G, F, J	25	30	P
13	82	G, F, J			

b. Cost by day is plotted below.

These two plots indicate the patterns of cash flow associated with the two different project schedules. Management can select the schedule that fits better with its financial status. Notice that the latest start dates delay cash flow requirements to the later time periods of the project.

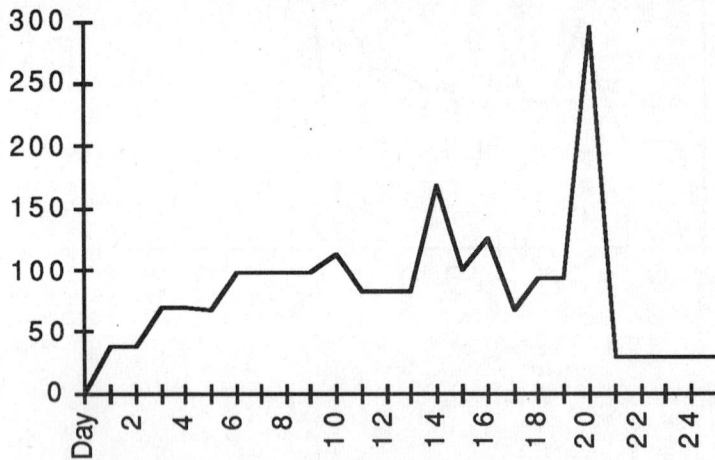

Preface to the Appendix

Dr. Jack Yurkiewicz, Professor of Management Science, Lubin School of Business, Pace University, New York, contributed the Appendix containing solutions to selected exercises from the text. Jack used <u>Computer Models for Operations Management</u> software to get the results. Having taught operations management, management science, and statistics to MBA students for more than twelve years, Jack believes that texts and instructors should use the computer to teach these traditional quantitative method courses.

Supplement C- Selected Solutions

Problem 13.

AQL = 0.5%, LTPD = 2%, producer's risk = 5%, consumer's risk = 6%, N = 1000.

CMOM gives us, for these parameters:

CMOM - Quality Control
Acceptance Sampling Plan

Data Entered

Acceptable Quality Level (AQL)	:	0.0050
Producer's Risk (Alpha)	:	0.0500
Lot Tolerance Percent Defective (LTPD)	:	0.0200
Consumer's Risk (Beta)	:	0.0600
Lot Size (N)	:	1000

CMOM - Quality Control
Acceptance Sampling Plan

Solution

Acceptable Level(c) = 5   Sample Size(n) = 510

Acceptance Number	AQL BASED Expected Defectives	Sample Size	LTPD BASED Expected Defectives	Sample Size
0	0.0513	10	2.8135	141
1	0.3553	71	4.5222	226
2	0.8176	164	6.0449	302
3	1.3663	273	7.4780	374
4	1.9702	394	8.8564	443
5 *	2.6130	523	10.1968	510
6	3.2854	657	11.5083	575
7	3.9810	796	12.7974	640
8	4.6953	939	14.0684	703
9	5.4253	1085	15.3242	766
10	6.1689	1234	16.5674	828

p	Pac	AOQ
0.0100	0.5983	0.0029
0.0200	0.0581	0.0006
0.0300	0.0020	0.0000
0.0400	0.0000	0.0000
0.0500	0.0000	0.0000
0.0600	0.0000	0.0000
0.0700	0	0
0.0800	0	0
0.0900	0	0
0.1000	0	0

```
 0.5983 |   |*
        | A |
 0.5354 | C |
        | C |
 0.4724 | E |
        | P |
 0.4094 | T |
        |   |
 0.3464 | P |
        | R |
 0.2834 | O |
        | B |
 0.2204 | A |
        | B |
 0.1575 | I |
        | L |
 0.0945 | I |
        | T |         *
 0.0315 | Y |       *   *   *   *   *   *   *   *   *   *   *   *   *   *
        |   |
        |   |------------------------------------------------------------
        |       P R O P O R T I O N   D E F E C T I V E
        |   |------------------------------------------------------------
c =   5         .01 .02 .03 .04 .05 .06 .07 .08 .09 .10 .11 .12 .13 .14 .15

Sample Size(n) =   510
 0.2932 |   |*
        | O |
 0.2623 | U |                              AOQL = 0.0029
        | T |
 0.2315 | G |
        | O |
 0.2006 | I |
        | N |
 0.1697 | G |
        |   |
 0.1389 | F |
        | R |
 0.1080 | A |
        | C |
 0.0772 | T |
        | I |        *
 0.0463 | O |
        | N |
 0.0154 |   |       *   *   *   *   *   *   *   *   *   *   *   *   *   *
  1     |   |------------------------------------------------------------
 ---    |       I N C O M I N G   F R A C T I O N   D E F E C T I V E
 100    |   |------------------------------------------------------------
c =   5         .01 .02 .03 .04 .05 .06 .07 .08 .09 .10 .11 .12 .13 .14 .15
Sample Size(n) =   510
```

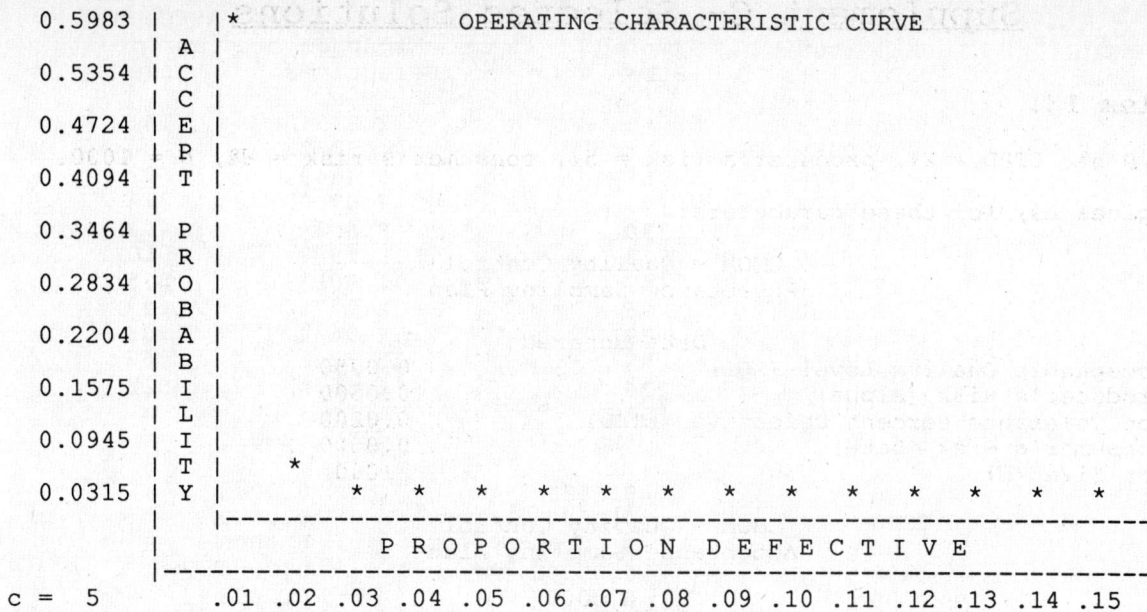

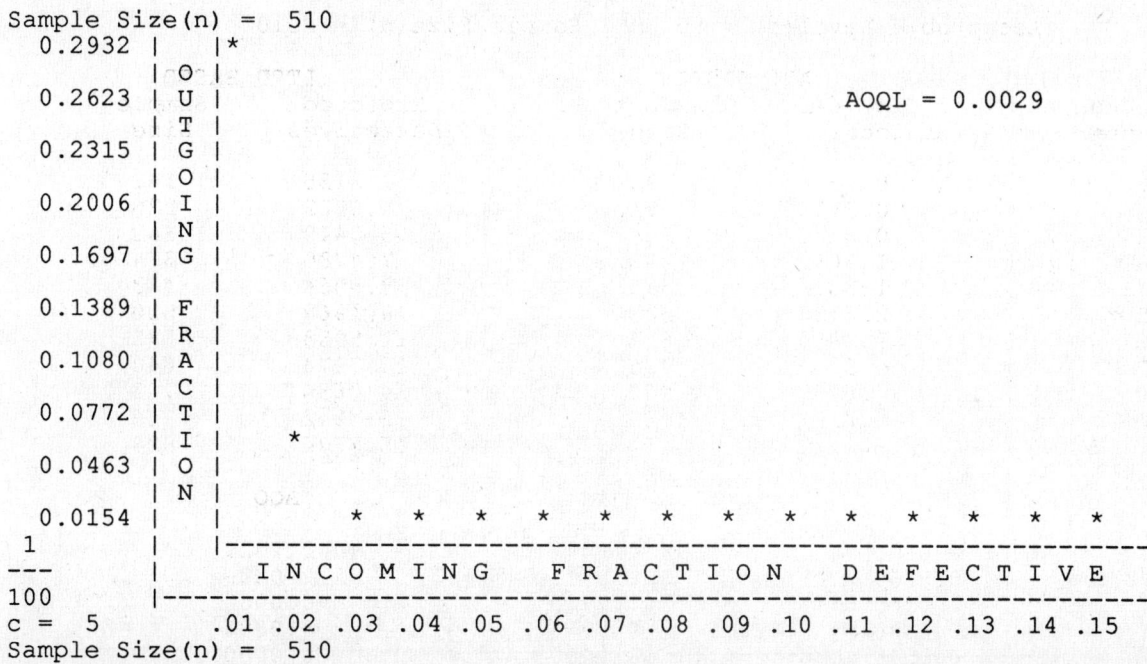

a) The single sampling plan is: sample 510, with an acceptance number 5. With recitifying inspection we see that the AOQL is 0.0029.

b) i) Now N = 2000

Solution

Acceptable Level(c) =   5   Sample Size(n) =   510

```
                     AQL BASED                        LTPD BASED
 Acceptance      Expected      Sample           Expected       Sample
  Number        Defectives      Size           Defectives       Size

    0             0.0513         10               2.8135         141
    1             0.3553         71               4.5222         226
    2             0.8176        164               6.0449         302
    3             1.3663        273               7.4780         374
    4             1.9702        394               8.8564         443
    5  *          2.6130        523              10.1968         510
    6             3.2854        657              11.5083         575
    7             3.9810        796              12.7974         640
    8             4.6953        939              14.0684         703
    9             5.4253       1085              15.3242         766
   10             6.1689       1234              16.5674         828

                 p                     Pac                AOQ

              0.0100                  0.5983            0.0045
              0.0200                  0.0581            0.0009
              0.0300                  0.0020            0.0000
              0.0400                  0.0000            0.0000
              0.0500                  0.0000            0.0000
              0.0600                  0.0000            0.0000
              0.0700                  0                 0
```

```
Sample Size(n) =    510
  0.4458 |   |*
         | O |
  0.3988 | U |                              AOQL = 0.0044
         | T |
  0.3519 | G |
         | O |
  0.3050 | I |
         | N |
  0.2581 | G |
         |   |
  0.2111 | F |
         | R |
  0.1642 | A |
         | C |
  0.1173 | T |
         | I |       *
  0.0704 | O |
         | N |
  0.0235 |   |     *   *   *   *   *   *   *   *   *   *   *   *   *
       1 |   |------------------------------------------------------
  ---    |   |   I N C O M I N G   F R A C T I O N   D E F E C T I V E
  100    |-----------------------------------------------------------
  c =  5         .01 .02 .03 .04 .05 .06 .07 .08 .09 .10 .11 .12 .13 .14 .15
Sample Size(n) =    510
```

ii) AQL = 0.8%

                              Solution

        Acceptable Level(c) =   10   Sample Size(n) =   942

| | AQL BASED | | LTPD BASED | |
Acceptance Number	Expected Defectives	Sample Size	Expected Defectives	Sample Size
0	0.0513	6	3.9121	196
1	0.3553	44	5.8340	292
2	0.8176	102	7.5166	376
3	1.3663	171	9.0840	454
4	1.9702	246	10.5801	529
5	2.6130	327	12.0273	601
6	3.2854	411	13.4355	672
7	3.9810	498	14.8164	741
8	4.6953	587	16.1738	809
9	5.4253	678	17.5098	875
10	6.1689	771	18.8301	942

p	Pac	AOQ
0.0100	0.6555	0.0004
0.0200	0.0190	0.0000
0.0300	0.0001	0.0000
0.0400	0.0000	0.0000
0.0500	0	0

```
0.3802 |   |*
       | O |
0.3402 | U |                            AOQL = 0.0003
       | T |
0.3002 | G |
       | O |
0.2601 | I |
       | N |
0.2201 | G |
       |   |
0.1801 | F |
       | R |
0.1401 | A |
       | C |
0.1001 | T |
       | I |
0.0600 | O |
       | N |
0.0200 |   |   *   *   *   *   *   *   *   *   *   *   *   *   *   *   *
  1    |   |-----------------------------------------------------------
----   |   INCOMING   FRACTION   DEFECTIVE
1000   |-----------------------------------------------------------
c = 10      .01 .02 .03 .04 .05 .06 .07 .08 .09 .10 .11 .12 .13 .14 .15
Sample Size(n) =  942
```

iii) LTPD = 6%

Solution

Acceptable Level(c) = 2   Sample Size(n) = 125

| | AQL BASED | | LTPD BASED | |
Acceptance Number	Expected Defectives	Sample Size	Expected Defectives	Sample Size
0	0.0513	10	3.9121	65
1	0.3553	71	5.8340	97
2 *	0.8176	164	7.5166	125
3	1.3663	273	9.0840	151
4	1.9702	394	10.5801	176
5	2.6130	523	12.0273	200
6	3.2854	657	13.4355	224
7	3.9810	796	14.8164	247
8	4.6953	939	16.1738	270
9	5.4253	1085	17.5098	292
10	6.1689	1234	18.8301	314

p	Pac	AOQ
0.0100	0.8693	0.0076
0.0200	0.5425	0.0095
0.0300	0.2727	0.0072
0.0400	0.1196	0.0042
0.0500	0.0477	0.0021
0.0600	0.0177	0.0009
0.0700	0.0062	0.0004
0.0800	0.0021	0.0001
0.0900	0.0007	0.0001
0.1000	0.0002	0.0000
0.1100	0.0001	0.0000

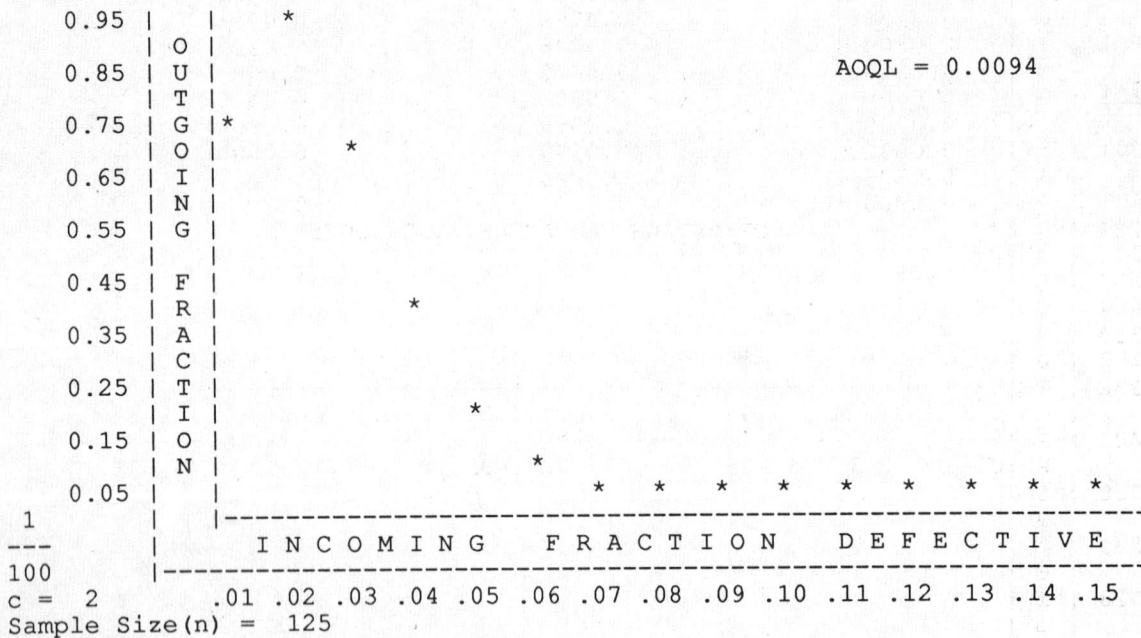

```
 0.95 |   |      *
      | O |                                    AOQL = 0.0094
 0.85 | U |
      | T |
 0.75 | G |*
      | O |       *
 0.65 | I |
      | N |
 0.55 | G |
      |   |
 0.45 | F |
      | R |          *
 0.35 | A |
      | C |
 0.25 | T |
      | I |             *
 0.15 | O |
      | N |                *
 0.05 |   |                    *   *   *   *   *   *   *   *   *   *
  1   |   |-----------------------------------------------------------
 ---  |   |  I N C O M I N G   F R A C T I O N   D E F E C T I V E
 100  |   |-----------------------------------------------------------
c = 2      .01 .02 .03 .04 .05 .06 .07 .08 .09 .10 .11 .12 .13 .14 .15
Sample Size(n) = 125
```

Problem 14.

AQL = 0.2%, LTPD = 2.5%, producer's risk = 2%, consumer's risk = 1%, N = 1000.

CMOM gives us, for these parameters:

360

```
                      CMOM - Quality Control
                     Acceptance Sampling Plan
                          Data Entered
       Acceptable Quality Level (AQL)            :      0.0020
       Producer's Risk (Alpha)                   :      0.0200
       Lot Tolerance Percent Defective (LTPD) :      0.0250
       Consumer's Risk (Beta)                    :      0.0100
       Lot Size (N)                              :      1000

                      Acceptance Sampling Plan
                            Solution

         Acceptable Level(c) =  3      Sample Size(n) =   402
```

	AQL BASED		LTPD BASED	
Acceptance	Expected	Sample	Expected	Sample
Number	Defectives	Size	Defectives	Size
0	0.0202	10	4.6055	184
1	0.2147	107	6.6387	266
2	0.5671	284	8.4063	336
3 *	1.0161	508	10.0449	402
4	1.5295	765	11.6055	464
5	2.0894	1045	13.1094	524
6	2.6841	1342	14.5703	583
7	3.3071	1654	16	640
8	3.9531	1977	17.4023	696
9	4.6182	2309	18.7832	751
10	5.2998	2650	20.1445	806

p	Pac	AOQ
0.0100	0.4286	0.0026
0.0200	0.0398	0.0005
0.0300	0.0020	0.0000
0.0400	0.0001	0.0000
0.0500	0.0000	0.0000
0.0600	0.0000	0.0000
0.0700	0.0000	0
0.0800	0	0

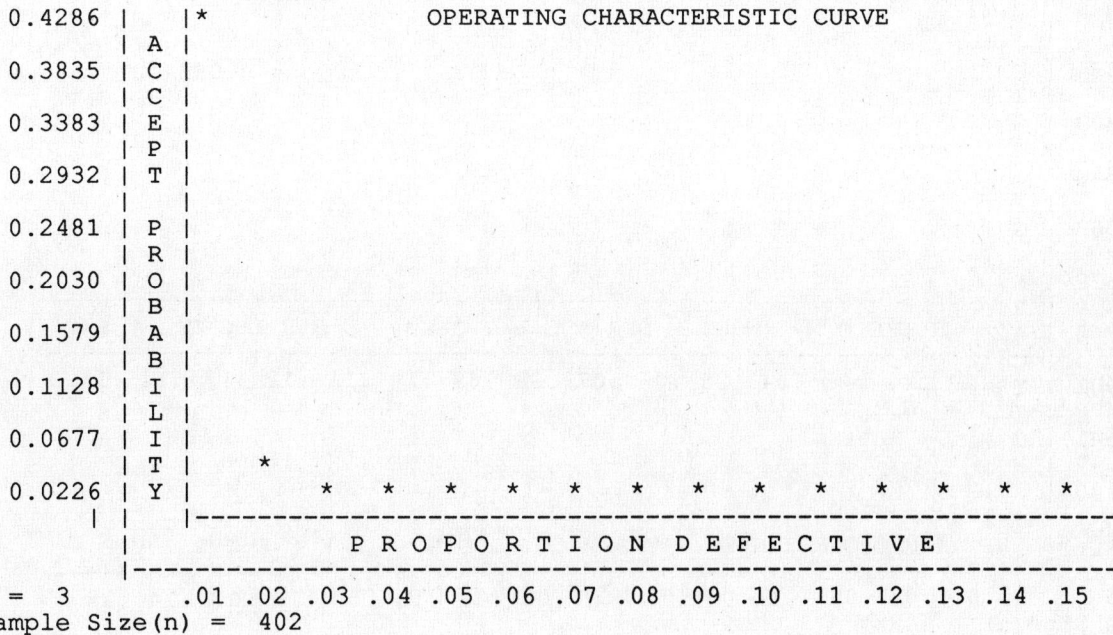

```
0.4286 |   |*              OPERATING CHARACTERISTIC CURVE
       |  A|
0.3835 |  C|
       |  C|
0.3383 |  E|
       |  P|
0.2932 |  T|
       |   |
0.2481 |  P|
       |  R|
0.2030 |  O|
       |  B|
0.1579 |  A|
       |  B|
0.1128 |  I|
       |  L|
0.0677 |  I|
       |  T|       *
0.0226 |  Y|       *   *   *   *   *   *   *   *   *   *   *   *   *
       |  |  |-------------------------------------------------------
       |     P R O P O R T I O N   D E F E C T I V E
       |-----------------------------------------------------------
 c =  3        .01 .02 .03 .04 .05 .06 .07 .08 .09 .10 .11 .12 .13 .14 .15
Sample Size(n) =   402
```

```
0.2563 |   |*                                      AOQL = 0.0025
       | O |
0.2293 | U |
       | T |
0.2023 | G |
       | O |
0.1754 | I |
       | N |
0.1484 | G |
       |   |
0.1214 | F |
       | R |
0.0944 | A |
       | C |
0.0674 | T |
       | I |          *
0.0405 | O |
       | N |
0.0135 |   |       *   *   *   *   *   *   *   *   *   *   *   *   *
  1    |   |   |---------------------------------------------------------------
 ---   |   |     I N C O M I N G    F R A C T I O N    D E F E C T I V E
 100   |       |---------------------------------------------------------------
c =  3            .01 .02 .03 .04 .05 .06 .07 .08 .09 .10 .11 .12 .13 .14 .15
Sample Size(n) =  402
```

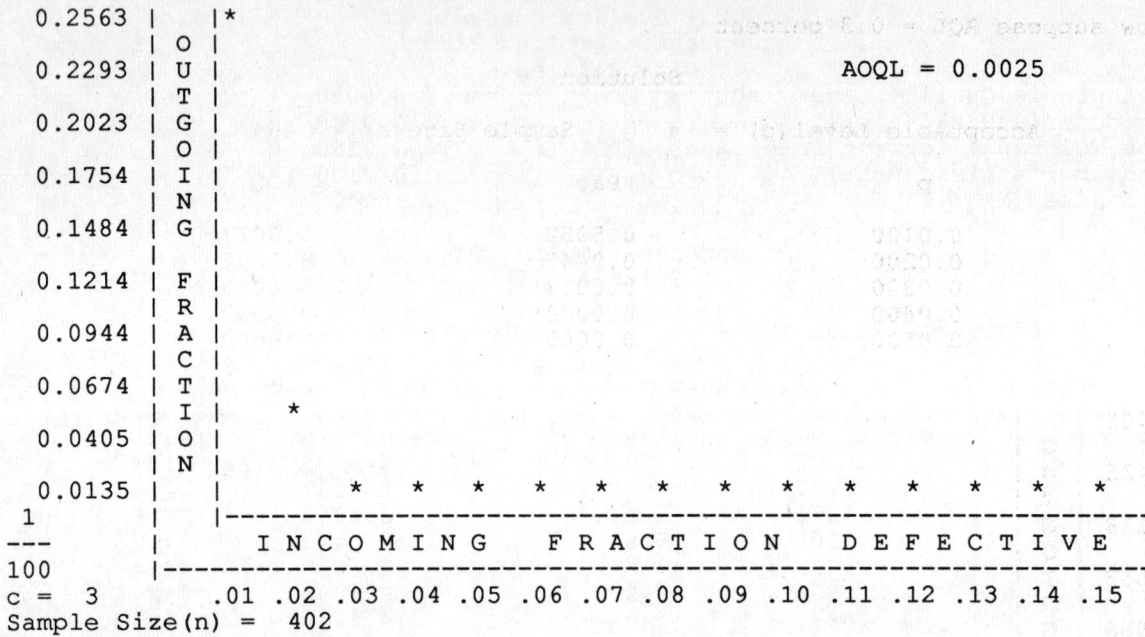

b) I) If we now let N = 2000

Solution

Acceptable Level(c) = 3   Sample Size(n) = 402

p	Pac	AOQ
0.0100	0.4286	0.0034
0.0200	0.0398	0.0006
0.0300	0.0020	0.0000
0.0400	0.0001	0.0000
0.0500	0.0000	0.0000

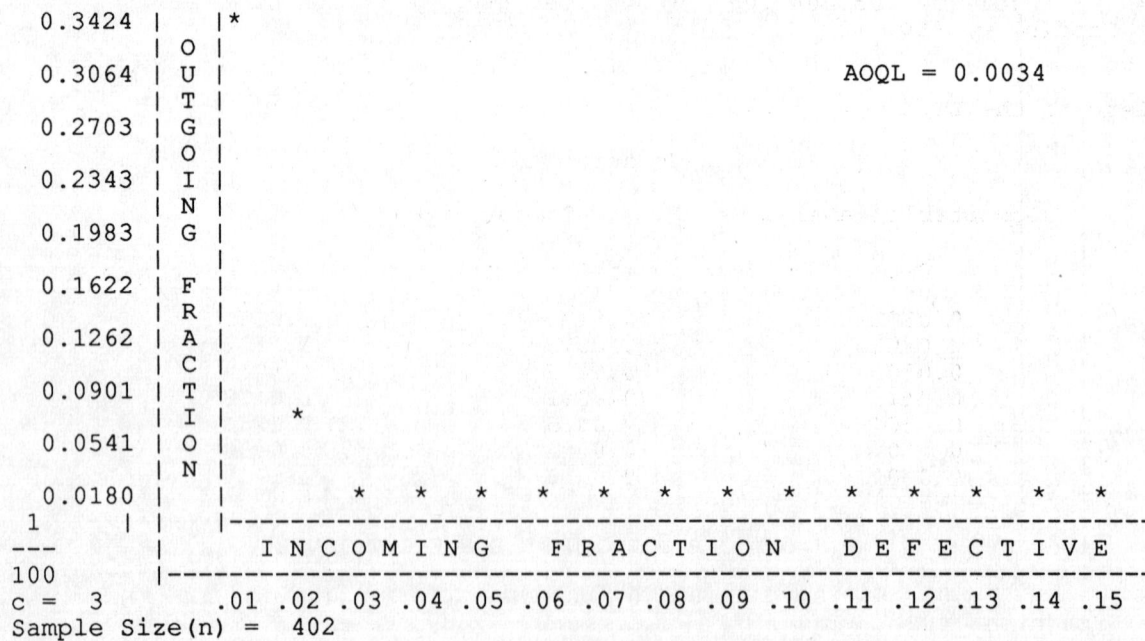

```
0.3424 |   |*
       | O |
0.3064 | U |                                      AOQL = 0.0034
       | T |
0.2703 | G |
       | O |
0.2343 | I |
       | N |
0.1983 | G |
       |   |
0.1622 | F |
       | R |
0.1262 | A |
       | C |
0.0901 | T |
       | I |          *
0.0541 | O |
       | N |
0.0180 |   |       *   *   *   *   *   *   *   *   *   *   *   *   *
  1    | | |   |---------------------------------------------------------------
 ---   |       I N C O M I N G    F R A C T I O N    D E F E C T I V E
 100   |       |---------------------------------------------------------------
c =  3            .01 .02 .03 .04 .05 .06 .07 .08 .09 .10 .11 .12 .13 .14 .15
Sample Size(n) =  402
```

362

ii) Now suppose AQL = 0.3 percent

```
                        Solution

         Acceptable Level(c) =  4      Sample Size(n) =   464

              p                    Pac               AOQ

            0.0100               0.5052            0.0027
            0.0200               0.0447            0.0005
            0.0300               0.0017            0.0000
            0.0400               0.0000            0.0000
            0.0500               0.0000            0.0000


  0.2708 |    |*
         | O  |
  0.2423 | U  |                                    AOQL = 0.0027
         | T  |
  0.2138 | G  |
         | O  |
  0.1853 | I  |
         | N  |
  0.1568 | G  |
         |    |
  0.1283 | F  |
         | R  |
  0.0998 | A  |
         | C  |
  0.0713 | T  |
         | I  |
  0.0428 | O  |     *
         | N  |
  0.0143 |    |       *    *    *    *    *    *    *    *    *    *    *    *    *
  1      |    |
 ---     |    |-------------------------------------------------------------------
 100     |    | I N C O M I N G   F R A C T I O N   D E F E C T I V E
         |    |-------------------------------------------------------------------
 c =  4          .01 .02 .03 .04 .05 .06 .07 .08 .09 .10 .11 .12 .13 .14 .15
 Sample Size(n) =   464
```

iii) Letting the LTPD = 4%

```
                        Solution

         Acceptable Level(c) =  2      Sample Size(n) =   210

              p                    Pac               AOQ

            0.0100               0.6495            0.0051
            0.0200               0.2073            0.0033
            0.0300               0.0475            0.0011
            0.0400               0.0091            0.0003
            0.0500               0.0015            0.0001
            0.0600               0.0002            0.0000
            0.0700               0.0000            0.0000
```

363

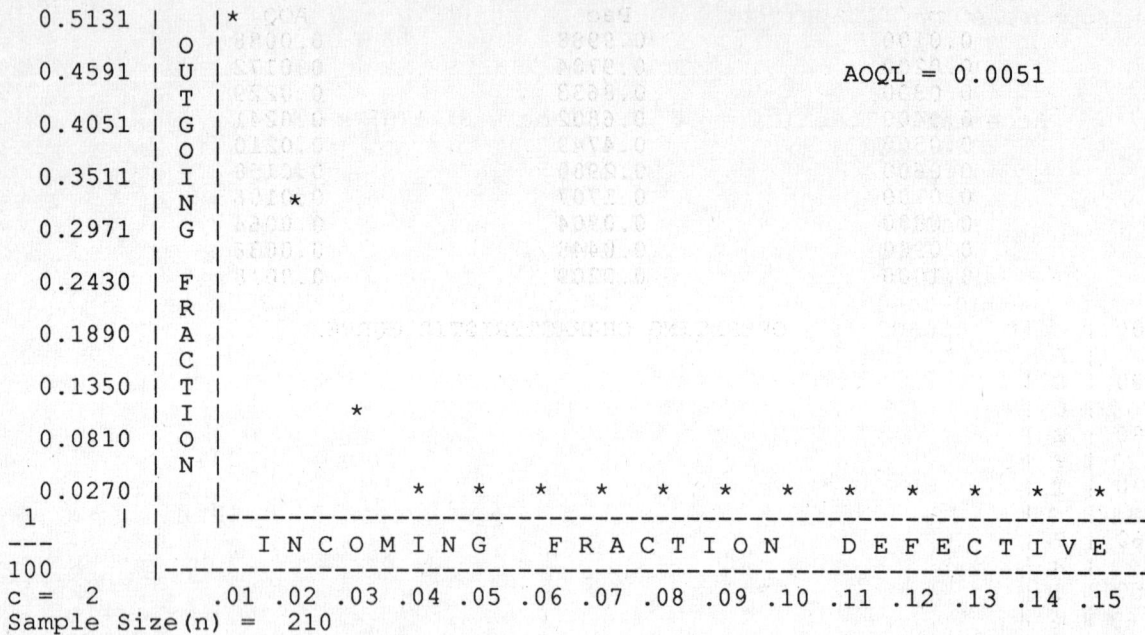

```
0.5131  |    |*
        | O  |
0.4591  | U  |                                           AOQL = 0.0051
        | T  |
0.4051  | G  |
        | O  |
0.3511  | I  | *
        | N  |
0.2971  | G  |
        |    |
0.2430  | F  |
        | R  |
0.1890  | A  |
        | C  |
0.1350  | T  |
        | I  |      *
0.0810  | O  |
        | N  |
0.0270  |    |       *   *   *   *   *   *   *   *   *   *   *   *   *
   1    |  | |------------------------------------------------------------
  ---   |    |    I N C O M I N G   F R A C T I O N   D E F E C T I V E
  100   |------------------------------------------------------------
c =  2         .01 .02 .03 .04 .05 .06 .07 .08 .09 .10 .11 .12 .13 .14 .15
Sample Size(n) =  210
```

Problem 15.

The parameters of the problem are: AQL = 0.02, LTPD = 0.08, producer's risk =
5%, consumer's risk = 10%, N = 1000.

a and b)

CMOM - Quality Control
Acceptance Sampling Plan

Data Entered

Acceptable Quality Level (AQL)	:	0.0200
Producer's Risk (Alpha)	:	0.0500
Lot Tolerance Percent Defective (LTPD)	:	0.0800
Consumer's Risk (Beta)	:	0.1000
Lot Size (N)	:	1000

CMOM - Quality Control
Solution

Acceptable Level(c) = 5   Sample Size(n) =   116

	AQL BASED			LTPD BASED	
Acceptance Number	Expected Defectives	Sample Size		Expected Defectives	Sample Size
0	0.0513	3		2.3025	29
1	0.3553	18		3.8896	49
2	0.8176	41		5.3223	67
3	1.3663	68		6.6807	84
4	1.9702	99		7.9937	100
5 *	2.6130	131		9.2747	116
6	3.2854	164		10.5322	132
7	3.9810	199		11.7710	147
8	4.6953	235		12.9946	162

```
              p                    Pac                   AOQ
           0.0100                 0.9988                0.0088
           0.0200                 0.9704                0.0172
           0.0300                 0.8633                0.0229
           0.0400                 0.6802                0.0241
           0.0500                 0.4749                0.0210
           0.0600                 0.2980                0.0158
           0.0700                 0.1707                0.0106
           0.0800                 0.0904                0.0064
           0.0900                 0.0448                0.0036
           0.1000                 0.0209                0.0018

   1.00  |   | *              OPERATING CHARACTERISTIC CURVE
         | A |      *
   0.90  | C |
         | C |         *
   0.80  | E |
         | P |
   0.70  | T |            *
         |   |
   0.60  | P |
         | R |
   0.50  | O |               *
         | B |
   0.40  | A |
         | B |
   0.30  | I |                  *
         | L |
   0.20  | I |
         | T |                     *
   0.10  | Y |                        *    *    *    *    *    *    *    *
         |   |  |---------------------------------------------------------
         |         P R O P O R T I O N   D E F E C T I V E
         |---------------------------------------------------------------
  c =  5           .01 .02 .03 .04 .05 .06 .07 .08 .09 .10 .11 .12 .13 .14 .15
  Sample Size(n) =  116


   0.2405 |   |           *
          | O |      *
   0.2152 | U |              *                    AOQL = 0.0240
          | T |
   0.1899 | G |
          | O |   *
   0.1647 | I |
          | N |         *
   0.1394 | G |
          |   |
   0.1141 | F |
          | R |            *
   0.0888 | A | *
          | C |
   0.0635 | T |               *
          | I |
   0.0382 | O |                  *
          | N |
   0.0130 |   |                     *    *    *    *    *    *
  1       |   |  |---------------------------------------------------------
  --      |         I N C O M I N G   F R A C T I O N   D E F E C T I V E
  10      |---------------------------------------------------------------
  c =  5           .01 .02 .03 .04 .05 .06 .07 .08 .09 .10 .11 .12 .13 .14 .15
  Sample Size(n) =  116
```

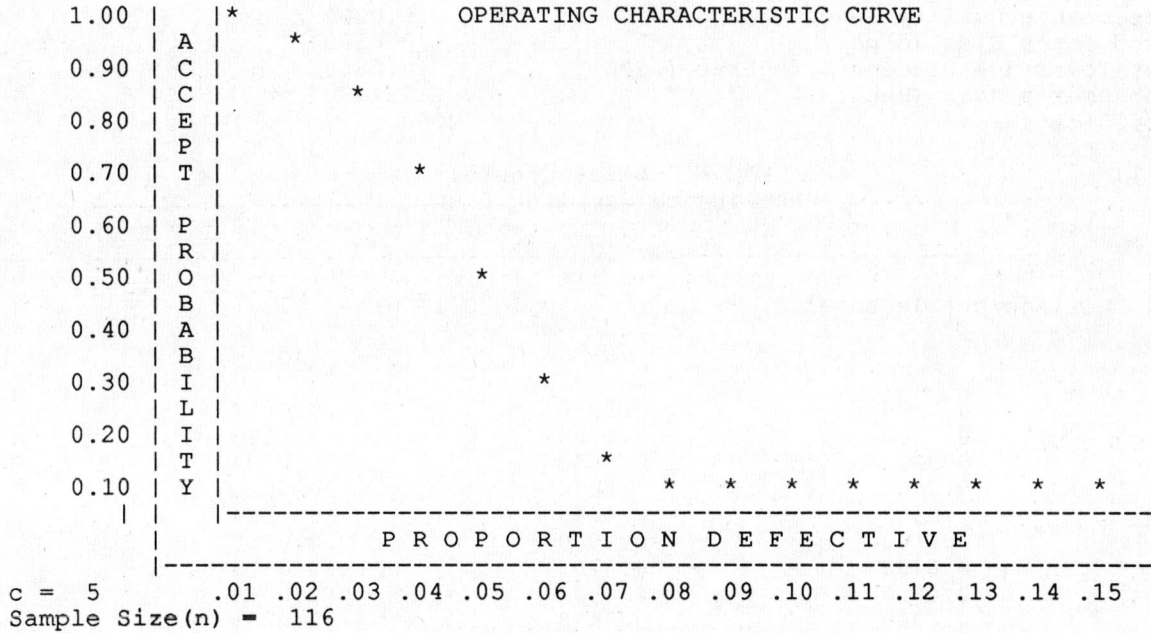

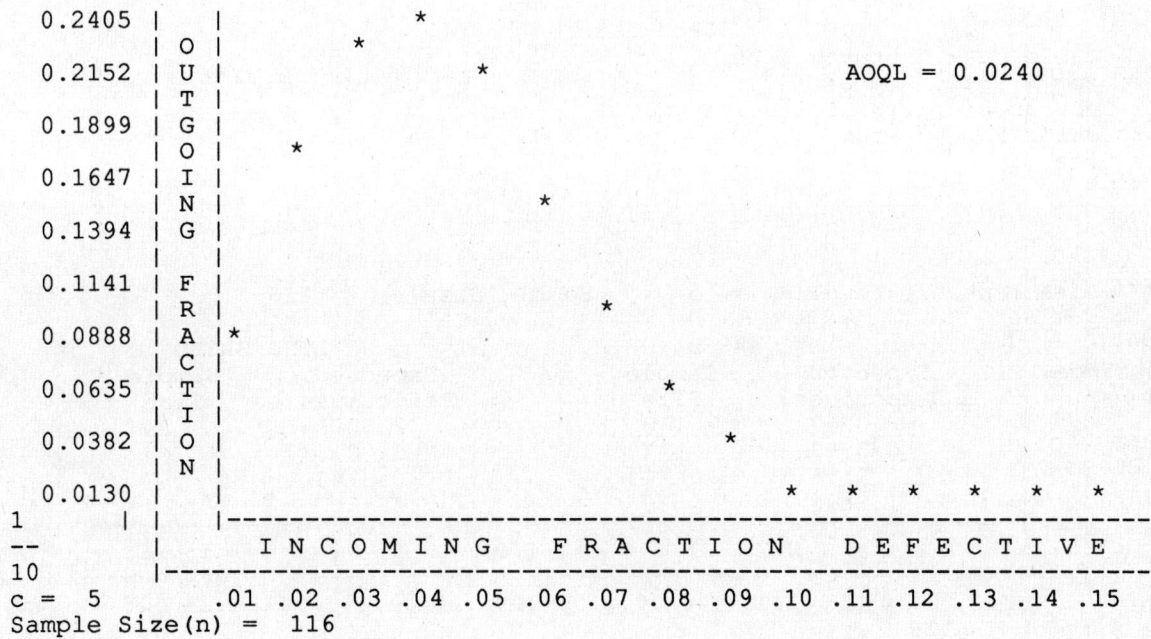

15c) If the fraction nonconforming is 4%, based on our sample plan, the probability that we will accept the lot is 68.02%. If the fraction nonconforming were 6%, the probability of accepting the lot is 29.8%.

d) We see from the above output that the AOQL is 0.0024. If the lot size is increased to 2000, then CMOM gives an AOQL = 0.0256, as the output below shows.

CMOM - Quality Control
Acceptance Sampling Plan
Data Entered

Acceptable Quality Level (AQL)	:	0.0200
Producer's Risk (Alpha)	:	0.0500
Lot Tolerance Percent Defective (LTPD)	:	0.0800
Consumer's Risk (Beta)	:	0.1000
Lot Size (N)	:	2000

CMOM - Quality Control
Acceptance Sampling Plan

Solution

Acceptable Level(c) = 5   Sample Size(n) = 116

p	Pac	AOQ
0.0100	0.9988	0.0094
0.0200	0.9704	0.0183
0.0300	0.8633	0.0244
0.0400	0.6802	0.0256
0.0500	0.4749	0.0224
0.0600	0.2980	0.0168
0.0700	0.1707	0.0113
0.0800	0.0904	0.0068
0.0900	0.0448	0.0038
0.1000	0.0209	0.0020

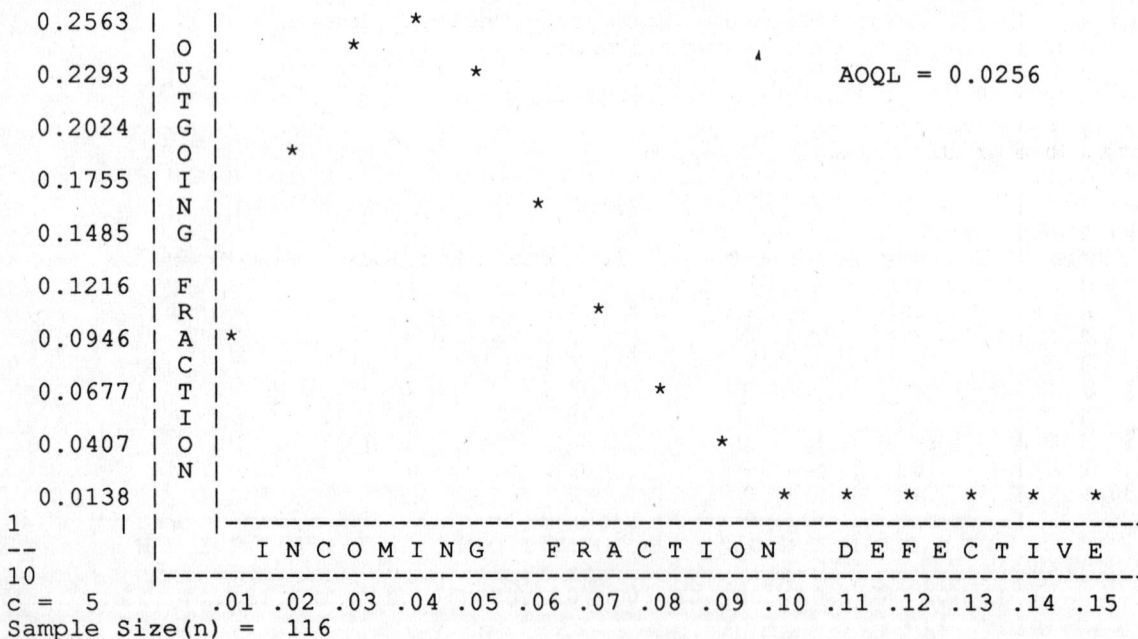

```
0.2563 |   |           *
       | O |         *
0.2293 | U |            *                      ▲   AOQL = 0.0256
       | T |
0.2024 | G |     *
       | O |
0.1755 | I |
       | N |              *
0.1485 | G |
       |   |
0.1216 | F |
       | R |             *
0.0946 | A |*
       | C |
0.0677 | T |           *
       | I |
0.0407 | O |               *
       | N |
0.0138 |   |                  *   *   *   *   *   *
1      |   | ------------------------------------------------------
--     |   INCOMING   FRACTION   DEFECTIVE
10     |   ------------------------------------------------------
c =  5         .01 .02 .03 .04 .05 .06 .07 .08 .09 .10 .11 .12 .13 .14 .15
Sample Size(n) =  116
```

Problem 11.
The decision tree for the Dintell Corporation is:

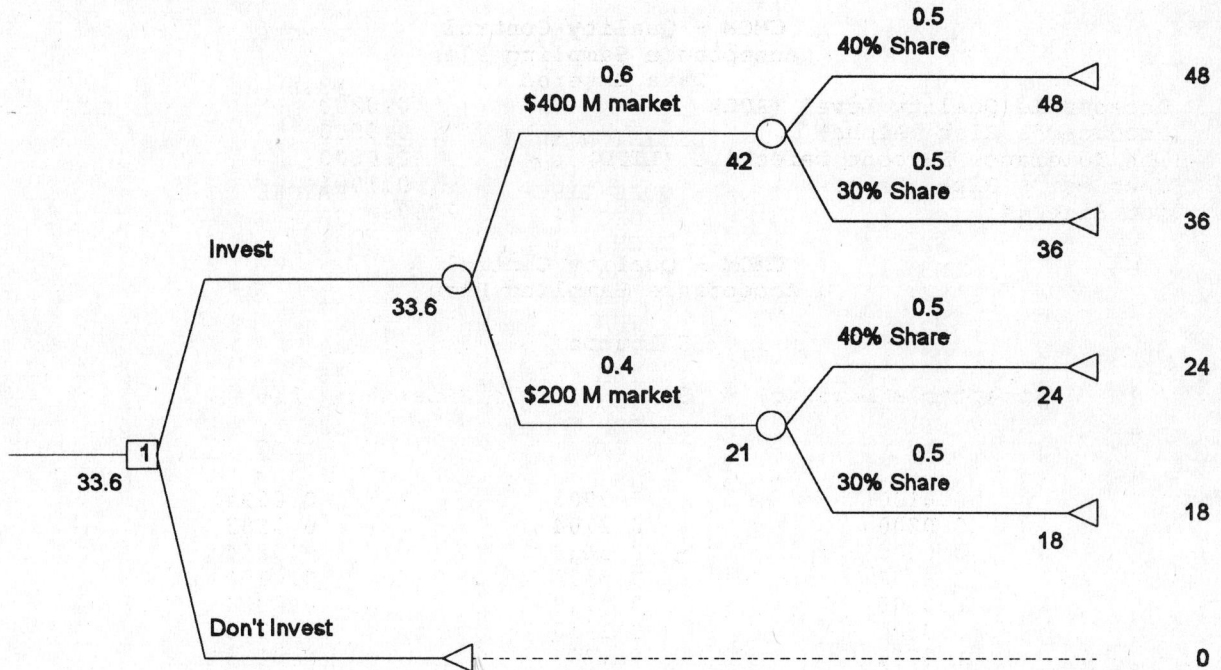

The output from CMOM for this problem is:

CMOM – Capacity Planning – Decision Trees
Maximization

Data Entered

Total Number of Nodes :   9

Model

	Type	No./Payoff	End Node	Alt/Prob	End Node	Alt/Prob
N1	1	2	2	1	5	2
N2	2	2	3	0.6	4	0.4
N3	2	2	6	0.5	7	0.5
N4	2	2	8	0.5	9	0.5
N5	3	0	0	0	0	0
N6	3	48	0	0	0	0
N7	3	36	0	0	0	0
N8	3	24	0	0	0	0
N9	3	18	0	0	0	0

367

CMOM - Capacity Planning - Decision Trees
Maximization

Solution

TOTAL PAYOFF = 33.6

DECISION SEQUENCE

NODE	ALTERNATIVE	PAYOFF
N1	1	33.6

DECISION TREE

NODE	NODE TYPE	PAYOFF
N1	DEC	33.6
N2	CHA	33.6
N3	CHA	42
N4	CHA	21
N5	TER	0
N6	TER	48
N7	TER	36
N8	TER	24
N9	TER	18

Selected Solutions--Chapter 8

Problem 25.

CMOM solves the transportation problem readily. The solution is:

CMOM - Location Analysis - Transportation Model
Minimization

Data Entered

Number of Columns :   4

Number of Rows   :   3

Model

	A	B	C	D	Rows
1	1.7	1.6	1.6	1.6	60000
2	1.5	1.8	1.6	1.7	80000
3	1.8	1.5	1.8	1.6	50000
Cols	50000	40000	60000	40000	190000

CMOM - Location Analysis - Transportation Model
Minimization

Solution

	A	B	C	D	Rows
1	0	0	30000	30000	60000
2	50000	0	30000	0	80000
3	0	40000	0	10000	50000
Cols	50000	40000	60000	40000	190000

Total Payoff :   295000

Problem 26.

CMOM - Location Analysis - Transportation Model
Minimization

Data Entered

Number of Columns :   5

Number of Rows   :   4

Model

	W1	W2	W3	W4	W5	Rows
F1	1	3	4	5	6	80000
F2	2	2	1	4	5	60000
F3	1	5	1	3	1	60000
F4	5	2	4	5	4	50000
Cols	60000	70000	50000	30000	40000	250000

Solution

```
(000)   W1   W2   W3   W4   W5  Rows

F1      60   10    0   10    0    80
F2       0   10   50    0    0    60
F3       0    0    0   20   40    60
F4       0   50    0    0    0    50
Cols    60   70   50   30   40   250
```

Total Payoff :   410000

Problem 27.

CMOM – Location Analysis – Transportation Model
Minimization

Data Entered

Number of Columns :   5

Number of Rows   :   3

Model

```
        R1      R2      R3      R4      R5     Rows

W1       4       3       1       5       6    60000
W2       2       2       3       4       5    30000
W3       1       5       1       3       2    50000
Cols 20000   30000   40000   10000   40000  140000
```

CMOM – Location Analysis – Transportation Model
Minimization

Solution

```
        R1      R2      R3      R4      R5     Rows

W1       0   20000   40000       0       0    60000
W2   20000   10000       0       0       0    30000
W3       0       0       0   10000   40000    50000
Cols 20000   30000   40000   10000   40000  140000
```

Total Payoff :   270000

Problem 28.

CMOM – Location Analysis – Transportation Model
Minimization

Data Entered

Number of Columns :   6

Number of Rows   :   2

370

Model

	OUT1	OUT2	OUT3	OUT4	OUT5	DUM	Rows
PLNT1	0.50	0.75	0.90	1.10	1.25	0	2000
PLNT2	0.80	0.45	1.15	0.80	1	0	4000
Cols	1500	750	2000	500	750	500	6000

CMOM - Location Analysis - Transportation Model
Minimization

Solution

	OUT1	OUT2	OUT3	OUT4	OUT5	DUM	Rows
PLNT1	1500	0	500	0	0	0	2000
PLNT2	0	750	1500	500	750	500	4000
Cols	1500	750	2000	500	750	500	6000

Total Payoff :   4412.5000

b) With the new plant and the corresponding transportation costs, CMOM gives:

CMOM - Location Analysis - Transportation Model
Minimization

Data Entered

Number of Columns :   6

Number of Rows   :   3

Model

	OUT1	OUT2	OUT3	OUT4	OUT5	DUM	Rows
PLNT1	0.50	0.75	0.90	1.10	1.25	0	2000
PLNT2	0.80	0.45	1.15	0.80	1	0	4000
PLNT3	1.10	0.75	0.90	0.55	0.65	0	5000
Cols	1500	750	2000	500	750	5500	11000

CMOM - Location Analysis - Transportation Model
Minimization

Solution

	OUT1	OUT2	OUT3	OUT4	OUT5	DUM	Rows
PLNT1	1500	0	500	0	0	0	2000
PLNT2	0	750	0	0	0	3250	4000
PLNT3	0	0	1500	500	750	2250	5000
Cols	1500	750	2000	500	750	5500	11000

Total Payoff :   3650

d) If outlets 2 and 4 each increase their demands by 1 million pounds, the new transportation problem and solution is:

Data Entered

Number of Columns :   6
Number of Rows   :   3

371

Model

	OUT1	OUT2	OUT3	OUT4	OUT5	DUM	Rows
PLNT1	0.50	0.75	0.90	1.10	1.25	0	2000
PLNT2	0.80	0.45	1.15	0.80	1	0	4000
DUM	0	0	0	0	0	0	2000
Cols	1500	1750	2000	1500	750	500	8000

CMOM - Location Analysis - Transportation Model
Minimization

Solution

	OUT1	OUT2	OUT3	OUT4	OUT5	DUM	Rows
PLNT1	1500	0	500	0	0	0	2000
PLNT2	0	1750	0	1500	250	500	4000
DUM	0	0	1500	0	500	0	2000
Cols	1500	1750	2000	1500	750	500	8000

Total Payoff :   3437.50

372

Problem 21.

b) The cycle time is (10 hour day)*(60 minutes per hour)/100 pizzas = 6 minutes per pizza.

c)

```
                              CMOM - Layout Design
                                 Data Entered
```

activity			# pred	-predecessor activity numbers----	
1-WE1	Time	2	0		
2-WE2	Time	3	1	1-WE1	
3-WE3	Time	1	1	2-WE2	
4-WE4	Time	5	1	2-WE2	
5-WE5	Time	5	2	3-WE3	4-WE4
6-WE6	Time	4	1	5-WE5	
7-WE7	Time	1	2	4-WE4	5-WE5
8-WE8	Time	2	1	6-WE6	
9-WE9	Time	6	1	7-WE7	
10-WE10	Time	4	1	8-WE8	
11-WE11	Time	2	2	9-WE9	10-WE10
12-WE12	Time	6	1	11-WE11	

```
                              CMOM - Layout Design
                                    Solution
```

station		# tasks	-----task activity numbers-------		
1	Total Time: Station Slack:	6 0	3	1-WE1	2-WE2	3-WE3
2	Total Time: Station Slack:	5 1	1	4-WE4		
3	Total Time: Station Slack:	6 0	2	5-WE5	7-WE7	
4	Total Time: Station Slack:	6 0	1	9-WE9		
5	Total Time: Station Slack:	6 0	2	6-WE6	8-WE8	
6	Total Time: Station Slack:	6 0	2	10-WE10	11-WE11	
7	Total Time: Station Slack:	6 0	1	12-WE12		

```
Number of Work Elements          :  12
Desired Production Rate          :  100
Total Operating Time             :  600

Cycle Time                       :  6

Minimum Number of Stations       :  7
Optimal Number of Stations       :  7

Sum of the Work-Elements         :  41

Production Cycle Efficiency(%)   :  97.61

Shortest Station Time            :  5
Longest Station Time             :  6

Maximum Production Rate          :  100
Max Production Cycle Efficiency(%) : 97.61
```

d) The time for work element F or 6 increased by 50%. It is now 6 min. CMOM gives us:

```
Number of Work Elements          :  12
Desired Production Rate          :  100
Total Operating Time             :  600

Cycle Time                       :  6

Minimum Number of Stations       :  8
Optimal Number of Stations       :  8

Sum of the Work-Elements         :  43

Production Cycle Efficiency(%)   :  89.58

Shortest Station Time            :  2
Longest Station Time             :  6

Maximum Production Rate          :  100
Max Production Cycle Efficiency(%) : 89.58
```

If the time for work element F is 2 minutes, CMOM gives:

```
Number of Work Elements          :  12
Desired Production Rate          :  100
Total Operating Time             :  600

Cycle Time                       :  6

Minimum Number of Stations       :  7
Optimal Number of Stations       :  7

Sum of the Work-Elements         :  39

Production Cycle Efficiency(%)   :  92.85

Shortest Station Time            :  4
Longest Station Time             :  6

Maximum Production Rate          :  100
Max Production Cycle Efficiency(%) : 92.85
```

374

Problem 22.

b and c) The line must produce 2400 Big Broadcasters in a 40 hour shift. The
cycle time is thus 60 Broadcaster per hour.

CMOM - Layout Design
Data Entered

activity			# pred	--predecessor activity numbers----		
1-A	Time	51	0			
2-B	Time	7	1	1-A		
3-C	Time	24	1	2-B		
4-D	Time	10	1	3-C		
5-E	Time	25	1	1-A		
6-F	Time	40	1	5-E		
7-G	Time	20	2	4-D	6-F	
8-H	Time	35	1	7-G		
9-I	Time	6	1	8-H		
10-J	Time	15	1	9-I		
11-K	Time	9	1	10-J		
12-L	Time	30	1	7-G		
13-M	Time	6	1	12-L		
14-N	Time	15	1	13-M		
15-O	Time	9	1	14-N		
16-P	Time	27	1	7-G		
17-Q	Time	13	1	16-P		
18-R	Time	60	1	17-Q		
19-S	Time	28	3	11-K	15-O	18-R
20-T	Time	12	1	19-S		
21-U	Time	21	1	20-T		
22-V	Time	26	1	21-U		
23-W	Time	58	1	22-V		
24-X	Time	29	1	18-R		

```
station                              # tasks ----task activity numbers-------

    1    Total Time:        58        2      1-A       2-B
         Station Slack:      2

    2    Total Time:        59        3      5-E       3-C      4-D
         Station Slack:      1

    3    Total Time:        60        2      6-F       7-G
         Station Slack:      0

    4    Total Time:        56        3      8-H       9-I     10-J
         Station Slack:      4

    5    Total Time:        57        2     12-L      16-P
         Station Slack:      3

    6    Total Time:        52        5     17-Q      11-K     13-M     14-N
         Station Slack:      8            15-O

    7    Total Time:        60        1     18-R
         Station Slack:      0

    8    Total Time:        57        2     24-X      19-S
         Station Slack:      3

    9    Total Time:        59        3     20-T      21-U     22-V
         Station Slack:      1

   10    Total Time:        58        1     23-W
         Station Slack:      2
```

```
         Number of Work Elements           :  24
         Desired Production Rate           :  2400
         Total Operating Time              :  144000

         Cycle Time                        :  60

         Minimum Number of Stations        :  10
         Optimal Number of Stations        :  10

         Sum of the Work-Elements          :  576

         Production Cycle Efficiency(%)    :  96

         Shortest Station Time             :  52
         Longest Station Time              :  60

         Maximum Production Rate           :  2400
         Max Production Cycle Efficiency(%) :  96
```

376

Problem 26.

CMOM – Layout Design – Block Planning
Rectilinear

Solution

Block Plan   Total LD Score

D F E G   765
B H C A

G H C A   635
F D E B

a) The initial ld score is 765.

b) CMOM gives the best layout, with an ld score of 635.

Selected Solutions–Chapter 10

<u>NOTE</u>: CMOM, when trying to find the best parameters for a model, gives the user the choice of either minimizing MAD (mean absolute deviation) or MSE (mean squared error) as the optimization criterion. We have used, unless the problem specially calls for MAD, the MSE criterion in these answers. Many forecasters and texts prefer to minimize MSE, and we have followed that convention. Also, we are showing only selected output from CMOM in the solutions. CMOM, in its output, gives the data and a table showing the actual values, fitted values from the model, and residuals. In the interest of conserving space, we will generally not include that output here.

Problem 15.
The problem calls for the moving average approach. CMOM gives, after mini-mizing the MSE, the following:

```
                              Solution

                  CMOM - Forecasting - Moving Averages
        Average Y1                    :      2247.2778
        Mean Square Error             :     24317.7090
        Mean Absolute Deviation       :       147.5883
        Forecast Value                :      2246.6470


   26.69 |   | h                 h                 h
         |   |                            h
   25.70 | Y |                            h
         |   |
   24.71 | 1 |   h h                             h
         |   |     h   h  h   h      h
   23.72 |   |       h                   h
         |   |            h
   22.73 |   |         h           h              e
         |   |           h      h          h    e f
   21.74 |   |                 h   h
         |   |            h              h
   20.74 |   |         h              h  h
         |   |           h
   19.75 |   |               h
         |   |      h
   18.76 |   |     h        h
         |   |h                           h
   17.77 |   |
         |   |                        h
     |   |   |------------------------------------------------------
   (00)|         M O V I N G      A V E R A G E S
         |------------------------------------------------------
            1 3 5 7 9 11 14 17 20 23 26 29 32 35
```

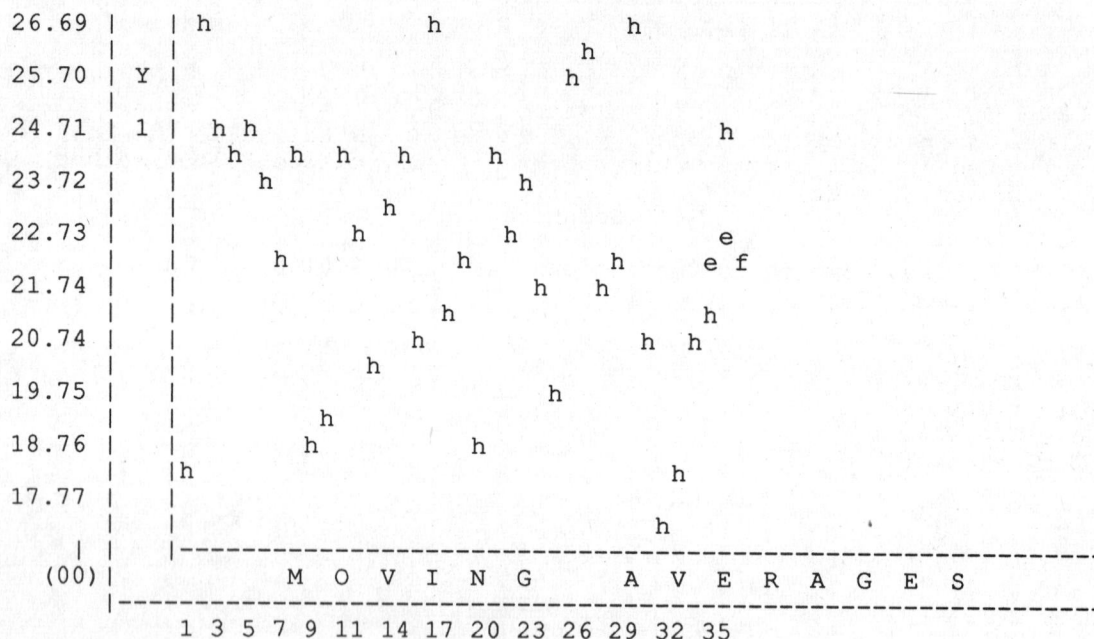

Problem 16.
The same data from problem 15 is used, except that CMOM is now asked to find the optimal parameters using simple exponential smoothing.

Solution
```
Optimized Data Smoothing Coefficient :            1
Average Y1                           :         2247.2778
Mean Square Error                    :       214130.5313
Mean Absolute Deviation              :          325.4167
Forecast Value                       :         2451
```

```
2669. |  |  he              he          he he
      |  |                               he
2402. | Y|  hsssehe he  he      hehe            hf
      |  |      he   hehe   he he
2135. | 1|         hehe      he  hse    he
      |  |           he         he    he he
1868. |  |he     hse        he          he
      |  |                              he
1601. |  |
      |  |
1335. |  |
      |  |
1068. |  |
      |  |
 801. |  |
      |  |
 534. |  |
      |  |
 267. |  |
      |  |e
  |  |  |---------------------------------------------------------
  |  |     S I M P L E    S M O O T H I N G
  |------------------------------------------------------------------
         1 3 5 7 9 11 14 17 20 23 26 29 32 35
```

Problem 17.
Once again the same data from problem 15 is used, and this time the best
trend-adjusted exponential smoothing model (usually called Holt's method) is
used to make the forecast.
Solution

```
Optimized Trend Smoothing Coefficient :          0.0100
Optimized Data Smoothing Coefficient  :          1
Average Y1                             :       2247.2778
Mean Square Error                      :     215031.5625
Mean Absolute Deviation                :        325.8044
Forecast Value(36)                     :       2468.8809
Forecast Value(37)                     :       2486.7617
Forecast Value(38)                     :       2504.6426
```

```
2695.51 |  |  he              he          he he
        |  |                               he
2425.95 | Y|  hsssehe he  he      hehe            hf
        |  |       e   hehe        he
2156.40 | 1|       h         ehse    he  hse    he
        |  |                 he h       he    he he
1886.85 |  |he     hse        he          he
        |  |                               e
1617.30 |  |  |                            h
        |  |e
   |  |  |---------------------------------------------------------
   |     S M O O T H I N G    W I T H    T R E N D   F A C T O R I N G
   |------------------------------------------------------------------
          1 3 5 7 9 11 14 17 20 23 26 29 32 35
```

379

Problem 19.

The monthy shipments of books for the past three years are the data. The problem says to "arrive at the best forecasting method." Thus, it is up to the user to decided the methodology. If the data has no apparent trend and no seasonality, then Brown's simple exponential smoothing would the appropriate mdoel. If there were trend, then Holt's method should be used. Since the data is monthly, perhaps there is some seasonality, and so Winters' method should be employed. A time-series plot is usually found first to give a clue about behavior of the data. We try the three methods and compare the results.

```
              CMOM - Forecasting - Simple Exponential Smoothing
                              Solution
                   Smoothing Coefficient Optimized for MSE

         Optimized Data Smoothing Coeff(a) :          0.3442
         Average Y1                         :       2171.7222
         Mean Square Error                  :     109243.3281
         Mean Absolute Deviation            :        269.0593
         Forecast Value                     :       2468.5144

    26.69 |   |                    a              a  a
          |   |                             a
    25.50 | Y |                            a
          |   |             a                          f
    24.31 | 1 |    a    a         a         e         aa
          |   | a        a                  e          e
    23.12 |   |            ae        e     a        ee
          |   |          e  e            e    eee
    21.93 |   |       a   e         a e          a
          |   |        e    e     e    a      a e   a
    20.74 |   |      e    a    e    ae           ee
          |   |             ea                 e
    19.54 |   |      e      a  e         a  a  e
          |   |   se        aa  e              a
    18.35 |   |     e  e                  a
          |   |
    17.16 |   |    a
          |   |se
    15.97 |   |             a
          |   |     a                              S. Coeff =   .3442
      |   |   |----------------------------------------------------------
    (00)|     a = actual,  e = estimate,  s = shared,  f = forecast
          |----------------------------------------------------------------
            1 3 5 7 9 11 14 17 20 23 26 29 32 35
```

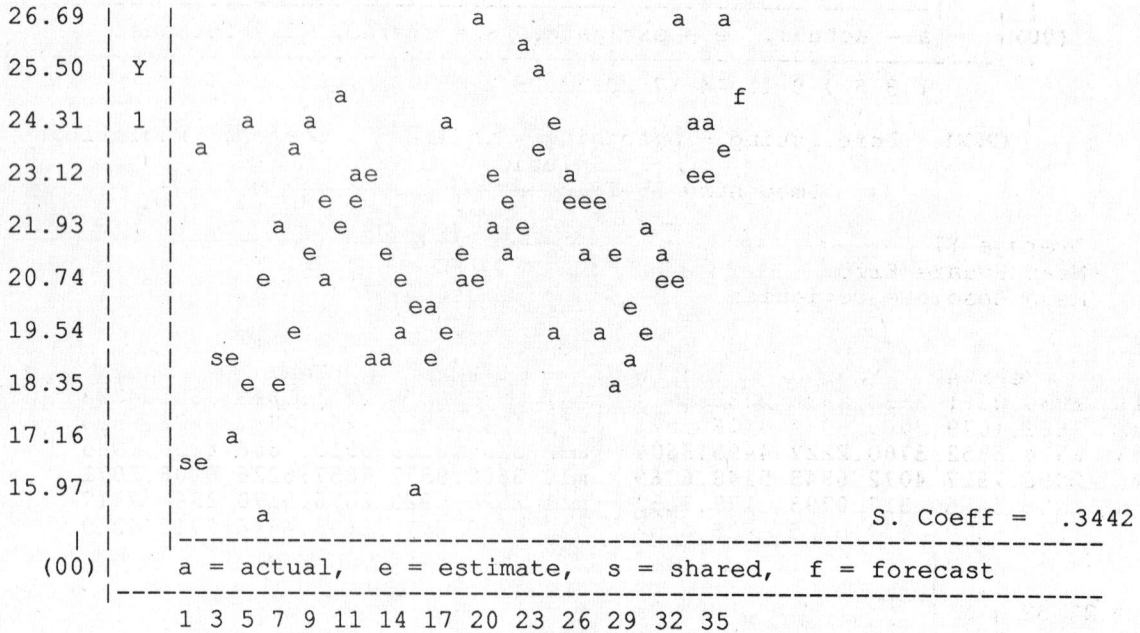

```
              CMOM - Forecasting - Smoothing with Trend Factoring
                              Solution
                   Smoothing Coefficients Optimized for MSE

         Optimized Trend Smoothing Coeff(b) :          0.0100
         Optimized Data Smoothing Coeff(a)  :          0.3248
         Average Y1                         :       2171.7222
         Mean Square Error                  :     109077.6953
         Mean Absolute Deviation            :        268.8643
         Forecast Value(37)                 :       2473.2981
         Forecast Value(38)                 :       2479.9302
         Forecast Value(39)                 :       2486.5623
```

380

```
26.69 |   |                    a              a  a
      |   |                  a
25.50 | Y |                  a
      |   |                              f
24.31 | 1 |      a    a        a        e      aa
      |   | a        a              e          e
23.12 |   |            se      e     se      ee
      |   |          e              ee      e
21.93 |   |      a    e   e      a        e  a
      |   |          e      e  a      a      a
20.74 |   |      a    e    ae      e  ee
      |   | e          ea              a
19.54 |   |    e      a    ae      a    a
      |   |    se        aa  e          a
18.35 |   |    e  e                  a
      |   |
17.16 |   |  a
      |  se
15.97 |   |          a
      |   |                                      S. Coeff =   .3248
  |  |   |----------------------------------------------------------
(00)|   |   a = actual,  e = estimate,  s = shared,  f = forecast
    |   |----------------------------------------------------------
        1 3 5 7 9 11 14 17 20 23 26 29 32 35
```

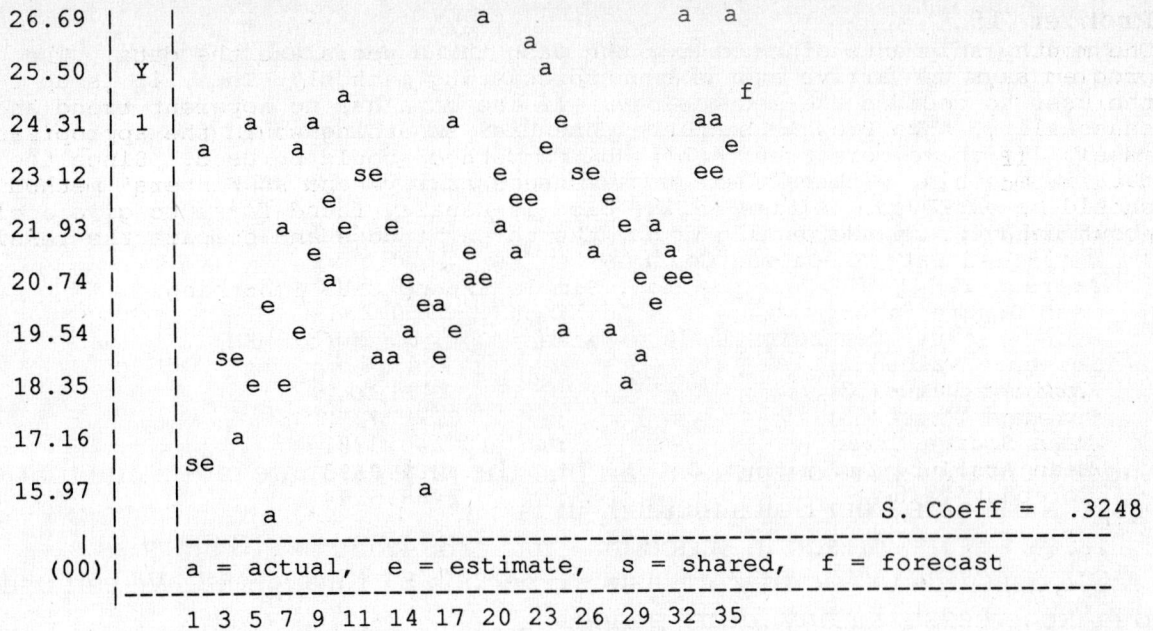

CMOM - Forecasting - Smoothing with Trend & Seasonal Factoring
Solution
Smoothing Coefficient Optimized for MSE

Average Y1   :   2171.7222
Mean Square Error   :   189162
Mean Absolute Deviation   :   340.5963

                          Forecast
      Year 4   Year 5   Year 6   Year 4   Year 5   Year 6
m1 2030.0961 2131.8838 2233.6714   m7 1911.8575 1711.1699 1510.4823
m2 2662.1079 3069.3074 3476.5071   m8 1237.5559   255.2877 -726.9805
m3 2904.5852 3700.2227 4495.8604   m9 3187.3853 3918.7688 4650.1523
m4 2996.7617 4072.6843 5148.6069   m10 3608.9377 4857.6226 6106.3071
m5 1456.4456   817.0793   177.7132   m11 2590.0923 2576.9170 2563.7417
m6 1037.6510   174.5226 -688.6058   m12 2680.4470 2695.4646 2710.4819

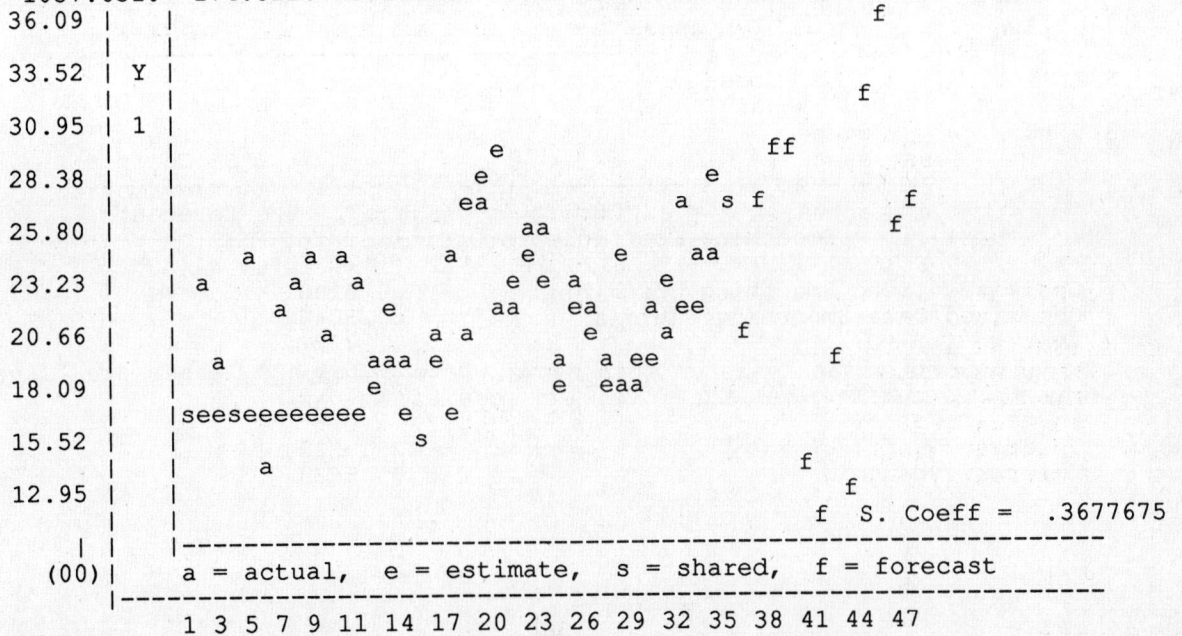

```
36.09 |   |                                      f
      |   |
33.52 | Y |                                        f
      |   |
30.95 | 1 |                                      ff
      |   |                  e                e
28.38 |   |                  e              e
      |   |                ea            a  s f        f
25.80 |   |                  aa                    f
      |   |      a  a  a      a    e    e    aa
23.23 |   | a      a    a      e e a      e
      |   |    a      e      aa  ea  a ee
20.66 |   |      a      a  a      e      a  f
      |   |    a      aaa e      a  a ee        f
18.09 |   |      e          e  eaa
      |   |seeseeeeeeee  e  e
15.52 |   |            s
      |   |    a                          f
12.95 |   |                              f
      |   |                            f  S. Coeff =   .3677675
  |  |   |----------------------------------------------------------
(00)|   |   a = actual,  e = estimate,  s = shared,  f = forecast
    |   |----------------------------------------------------------
        1 3 5 7 9 11 14 17 20 23 26 29 32 35 38 41 44 47
```

381

Problem 20.

a) The optimal trend-adjusted exponentially smoothed model is shown, as well as the forecasts for periods 51 through 53.

```
          CMOM - Forecasting - Smoothing with Trend Factoring
                            Solution
              Smoothing Coefficients Optimized for MSE

     Optimized Trend Smoothing Coeff(b)  :        0.0100
     Optimized Data Smoothing Coeff(a)   :        0.3099
     Average Y1                          :     1188.5400
     Mean Square Error                   :     5750.2549
     Mean Absolute Deviation             :       61.9087
     Forecast Value(51)                  :     2441.6282
     Forecast Value(52)                  :     2488.5176
     Forecast Value(53)                  :     2535.4070
```

Notice from the above output, we can find the final estimate of the line that best fits the data from Holt's method. It is

$$\text{Trend in period } t = 2394.739 + 46.889*t$$

CMOM uses this to find the forecasts for periods 51 through 53. We can use it to make forecasts for any future period.

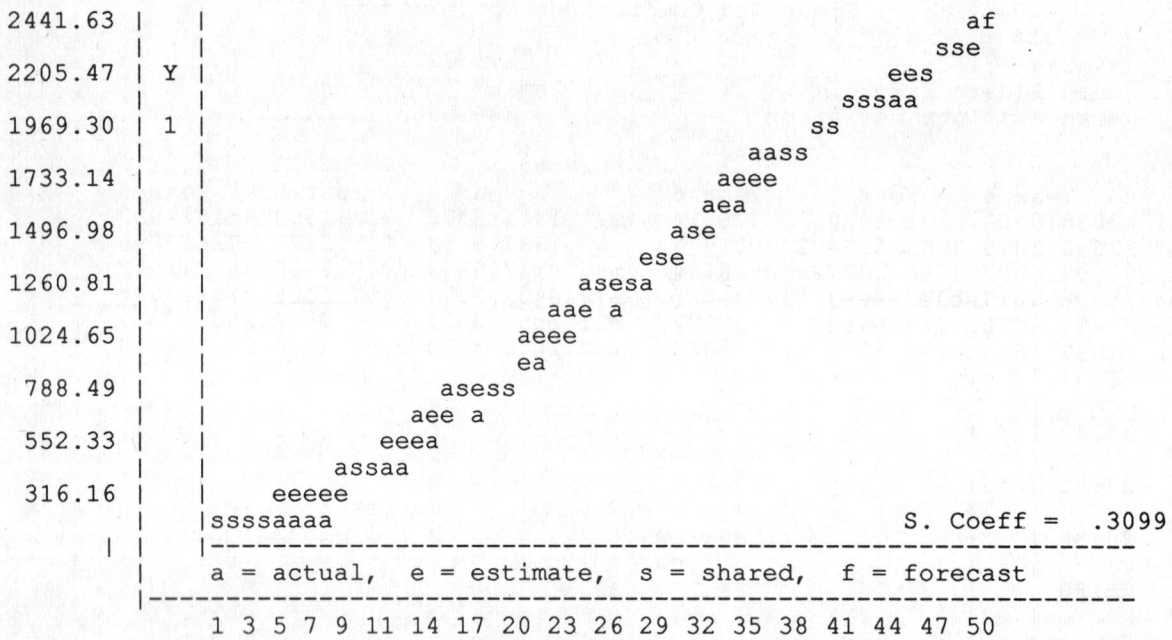

```
2441.63 |   |                                        af
        |   |                                      sse
2205.47 | Y |                                    ees
        |   |                                  sssaa
1969.30 | 1 |                                 ss
        |   |                               aass
1733.14 |   |                              aeee
        |   |                              aea
1496.98 |   |                            ase
        |   |                           ese
1260.81 |   |                        asesa
        |   |                      aae a
1024.65 |   |                     aeee
        |   |                      ea
 788.49 |   |                 asess
        |   |               aee a
 552.33 |   |             eeea
        |   |            assaa
 316.16 |   |      eeeee
        |   |ssssaaaa                          S. Coeff =  .3099
    |   |   |-------------------------------------------------------
        |   | a = actual,  e = estimate,  s = shared,  f = forecast
        |   |-------------------------------------------------------
            1 3 5 7 9 11 14 17 20 23 26 29 32 35 38 41 44 47 50
```

b) Using regression analysis on this data, where sales and leases are "lagged" by four months, CMOM gives the following results:

```
                CMOM - Forecasting - Linear Regression
                             Solution

        Variable            B-Coeff           Beta              T-Value
        X2                  4.9815            0.9927            55.1629

     B0 Intercept                        :      -28.6935
     Mean Square Regression              :      21983918
     Mean Square Residual                :      7224.5449
     Coefficient of Determination        :         0.9854
     Adjusted C.O.D.                     :         0.9851
     Multiple Correlation Coefficient    :         0.9927
     Standard Error Estimate             :        84.9973
     Degrees of Freedom - Regression     :         1
     Degrees of Freedom - Error          :        45
     Computed F                          :      3042.9485
     Average X1                          :      1256.8511
     Mean Square Error                   :      6917.2847
     Mean Absolute Deviation             :        65.8369

                       Correlation Coefficients
        X2      X1

 X2  1        0.9927
 X1  0.9927  1

        Mean Value    Standard Deviation
 X2     258.0638          138.7758
 X1    1256.8511          696.4042

                F O R E C A S T I N G
     |---- Variable ----|    |-- B-coefficient -|    |------ Value -----|
     |      X2          |    |      4.98        |    |      490         |
     |------------------|    |------------------|    |------------------|

                     X1 = 2412.241

                F O R E C A S T I N G
     |---- Variable ----|    |-- B-coefficient -|    |------ Value -----|
     |      X2          |    |      4.98        |    |      496         |
     |------------------|    |------------------|    |------------------|

                     X1 = 2442.13

                F O R E C A S T I N G
     |---- Variable ----|    |-- B-coefficient -|    |------ Value -----|
     |      X2          |    |      4.98        |    |      509         |
     |------------------|    |------------------|    |------------------|

                     X1 = 2506.889
```

From the output, we see that the estimated regression model is:
Sales in period t = -28.6935 + 4.9815*(Contracts in period t-3)

```
C)Comparing MSE's, the trend-adjusted exponential smoothing model is
   Mean Square Error                    :      5750.2549
while the regression model shows
   Mean Square Error                    :      6917.2847
Both are low. While getting a good fit for the historical data is no guarantee
that the future forecasts will be accurate, all else equal, the model with the
better fit of that data is preferred.  Thus, we choose the time series model.
```

Problem 21.

The problem asks for the "best" forecast for month 25. If we make a line plot of the data, we see that there does not seem to be any trend, so Holt's method will not be considered. There is a pronounced "jump" every fifth month, so this data shows seasonality. Winters' method willl probably give the lowest MSE here. Unfortunately, many statistical programs, CMOM included, do not allow periodicity other than quarters (4), or months (12). Thus, we will use the simple exponential smoothing model here.

```
               CMOM - Forecasting - Simple Exponential Smoothing

                                    Solution
                       Smoothing Coefficient Optimized for MSE

          Optimized Data Smoothing Coeff(a) :        0.2274
          Average Y1                         :        42
          Mean Square Error                 :        55.2923
          Mean Absolute Deviation           :         5.1283
          Forecast Value                    :        42.4279


    58. |   |                                          a
        |   |                                   a
    55. | Y |                    a        a
        |   |
    53. | 1 |
        |   |
    50. |   |
        |   |
    47. |   |
        |   |
    45. |   |                              e e       e s e
        |   |                 s e  a                     e
    42. |   |           a          e  e      e e e a       f
        |   |            a a e      e    a      a       a
    39. |   |       a  e e e e        a          a
        |   |         a                              a
    36. |   | a                      a      a
        |   |      e
    34. |   |   e e
        |   |s e a                                  S. Coeff =   .2274
      | |   |-----------------------------------------------------
      | |   | a = actual,  e = estimate,  s = shared,  f = forecast
        |------------------------------------------------------------
          1 2 3 4 5 6 7 8 9 10  12  14  16  18  20  22  24
```

The forecasted demand for month 25 is 42.4. However, considering the obvious "jumps" the data takes every fifth month, we should have little faith that this demand for month 25 will actually occur. A more reasonal guess would be a number in the upper fifties.

Problem 24.

The problem calls for forecasts for January through March of the fourth year. Different methodologies, moving averages, simple exponential smoothing, and trend-adjusted exponential smoothing are required, all minimizing MAD.

```
                  CMOM - Forecasting - Moving Averages
                                  Solution
          Average Y1                  :        36.8889
          Mean Square Error          :        17.1953
          Mean Absolute Deviation    :         3.7071
          Forecast Value             :        51.3333
```

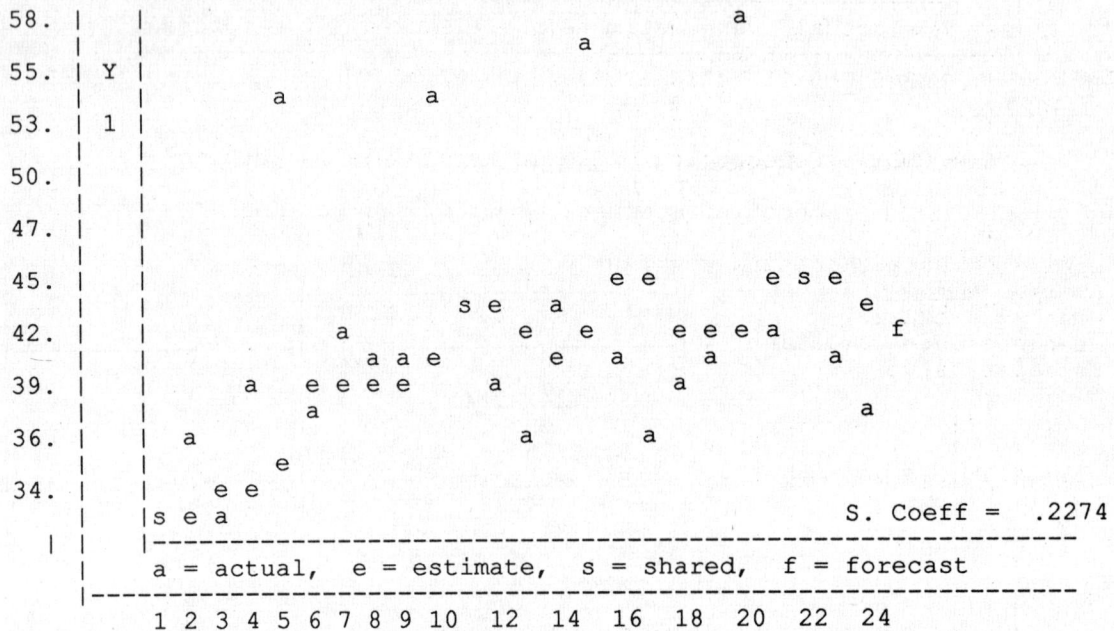

384

```
56. |    |                                    a
    |    |                               a
53. | Y  |                        a              a
    |    |                                    aeef
49. | 1  |                     a ee         e
    |    |                    a e    a a
46. |    |                  a e a    ae
    |    |                  a e  aae e
42. |    |                a e          e
    |    |               a e        a
39. |    |            a   a
    |    |              a e
35. |    |          ee e
    |    |            a   e
32. |    |        a a eaa
    |    |         a  ee
28. |    |           s
    |    |      a a ae
25. |    |    a eeseaeee                              No. Periods = 3
    |    |aa ea   a
  | |  |-----------------------------------------------------------------
    |    | a = actual,  e = estimate,  s = shared,  f = forecast
    |-------------------------------------------------------------------
       1 3 5 7 9 11 14 17 20 23 26 29 32 35
```

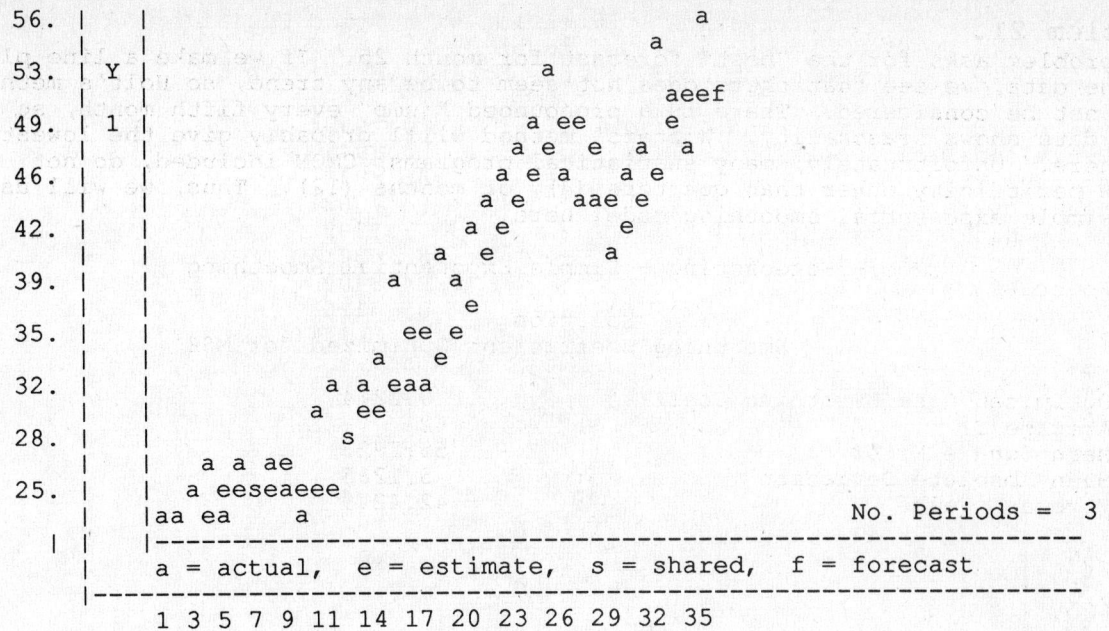

```
              CMOM - Forecasting - Simple Exponential Smoothing
                                    Solution
                    Smoothing Coefficient Optimized for MAD
```

Optimized Data Smoothing Coeff(a) :   0.7500
Average Y1   :   36.8889
Mean Square Error   :   14.2350
Mean Absolute Deviation   :   3.2323
Forecast Value   :   54.1609

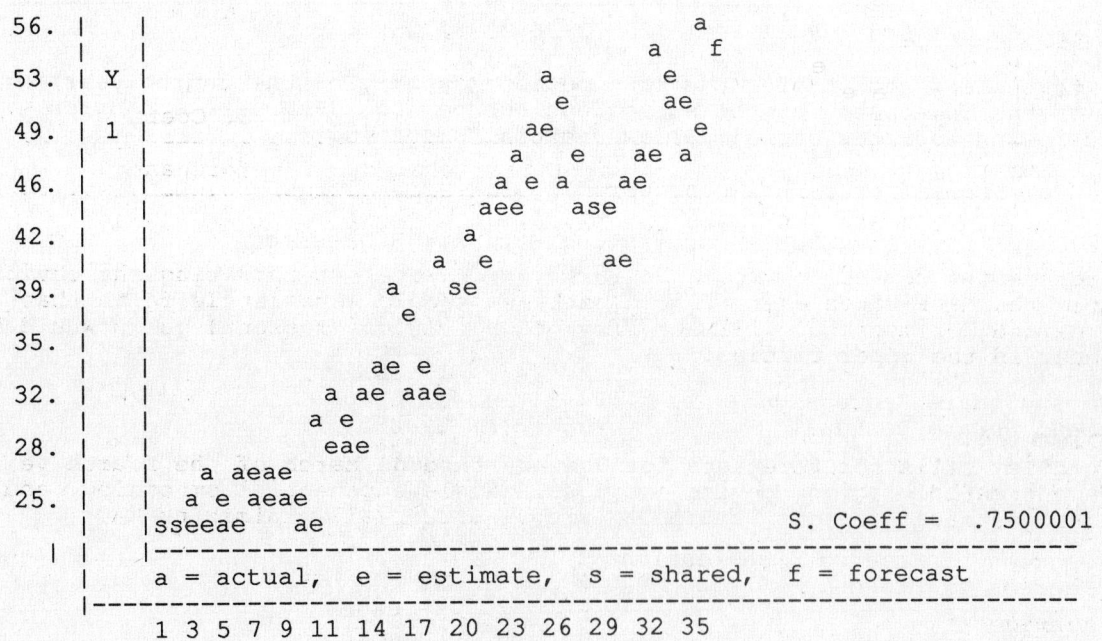

```
56. |    |                                    a
    |    |                                a  f
53. | Y  |                      a         e
    |    |                       e       ae
49. | 1  |                    ae         e
    |    |                     a  e   ae a
46. |    |                   a e a   ae
    |    |                   aee   ase
42. |    |                 a
    |    |                 a  e     ae
39. |    |            a    se
    |    |                 e
35. |    |
    |    |             ae e
32. |    |          a ae aae
    |    |           a e
28. |    |            eae
    |    |       a aeae
25. |    |    a e aeae
    |    |sseeae   ae                            S. Coeff =  .7500001
  | |  |-----------------------------------------------------------------
    |    | a = actual,  e = estimate,  s = shared,  f = forecast
    |-------------------------------------------------------------------
       1 3 5 7 9 11 14 17 20 23 26 29 32 35
```

```
Optimized Trend Smoothing Coeff(b)  :       0.1999
Optimized Data Smoothing Coeff(a)   :       0.3948
Average Y1                          :      36.8889
Mean Square Error                   :      14.7062
Mean Absolute Deviation             :       3.1399
Forecast Value(37)                  :      53.5301
Forecast Value(38)                  :      54.5409
Forecast Value(39)                  :      55.5516
```

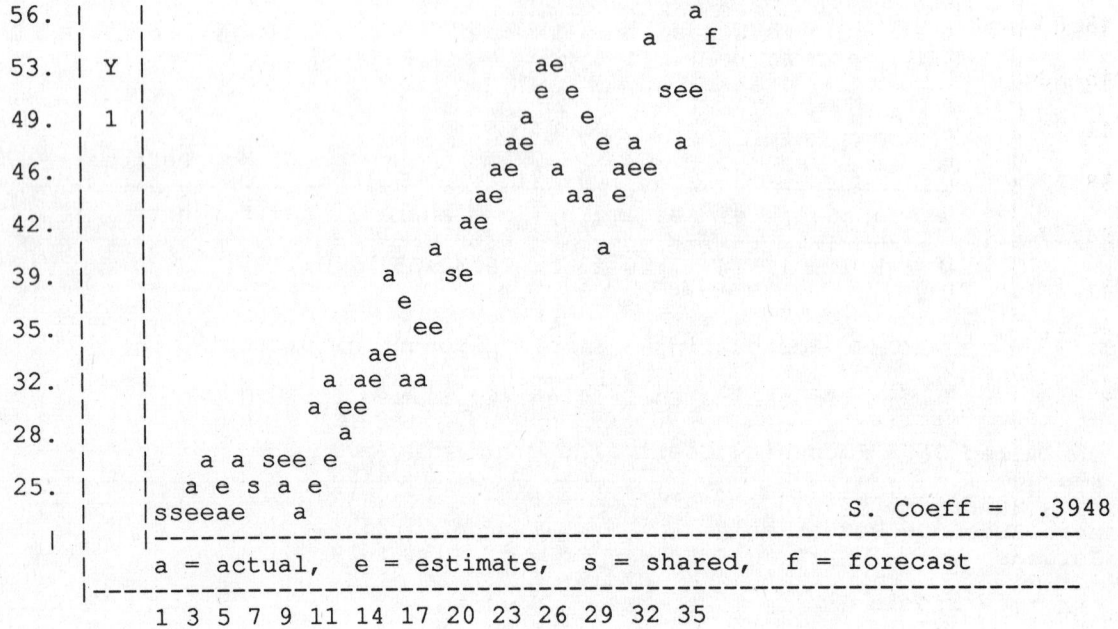

```
56. |   |                                          a
    |   |                                    a      f
53. | Y |                          ae
    |   |                          e  e       see
49. | 1 |                       a     e
    |   |                     ae    e a  a
46. |   |                  ae   a   aee
    |   |                  ae      aa e
42. |   |                ae
    |   |              a               a
39. |   |            a    se
    |   |                 e
35. |   |              ee
    |   |              ae
32. |   |         a ae aa
    |   |          a ee
28. |   |          a
    |   |       a a see e
25. |   |     a e s a e
    |          |sseeae   a                    S. Coeff =  .3948
  | |      |--------------------------------------------------------
    |    a = actual,  e = estimate,  s = shared,  f = forecast
    |--------------------------------------------------------------
        1 3 5 7 9 11 14 17 20 23 26 29 32 35
```

Note that the forecasts for the next period (January of the fourth year) will also be the forecasts for the subsequent two periods (February and March) under moving averages and simple exponential smoothing.

b) Linear regression is now considered.

CMOM – Forecasting – Linear Regression
Solution

Variable	B-Coeff	Beta	T-Value
X1	0.9398	0.9416	16.3114

```
B0 Intercept                        :      19.5032
Mean Square Regression              :    3431.0940
Mean Square Residual                :      12.8959
Coefficient of Determination        :       0.8867
Adjusted C.O.D.                     :       0.8834
Multiple Correlation Coefficient    :       0.9416
Standard Error Estimate             :       3.5911
Degrees of Freedom – Regression     :       1
Degrees of Freedom – Error          :      34
Computed F                          :     266.0602
Average X2                          :      36.8889
Mean Square Error                   :      12.1795
Mean Absolute Deviation             :       2.8499
```

386

Correlation Coefficients

```
        X1       X2
X1   1         0.9416
X2   0.9416  1
```

```
           Mean Value    Standard Deviation
X1         18.5000          10.5357
X2         36.8889          10.5147
```

```
   56.00 |   |                                          a
         |   |                                     a
   52.44 | X |                           a              rr
         |   |                                      rr
   48.89 | 2 |                         a       rr
         |   |                       a       rr a   a
   45.33 |   |                      a    rr    a
         |   |                      a   rr aa
   41.78 |   |                     a rr
         |   |                    a rr            a
   38.22 |   |                  a   rr
         |   |                     r
   34.67 |   |                 arr
         |   |                 rr
   31.11 |   |              rra  aa
         |   |             rr
   27.55 |   |          a rr   a
         |   |         a rr
   24.00 |   |        arr    a
         |   | rrr a       a X2 =   19.50318 + .9397683 * X1
    |    |   |------------------------------------------------------
         |   a = actual           X1            r = regression
         |-----------------------------------------------------------
          1 3 5 7 9 11 14 17 20 23 26 29 32 35
```

```
                    F O R E C A S T I N G
|---- Variable ----|      |-- B-coefficient -|      |------ Value -----|
|       X1         |      |      0.94         |      |       37         |
|------------------|      |------------------|      |------------------|
```

$$X2 = 54.2746$$

```
                    F O R E C A S T I N G
|---- Variable ----|      |-- B-coefficient -|      |------ Value -----|
|       X1         |      |      0.94         |      |       38         |
|------------------|      |------------------|      |------------------|
```

$$X2 = 55.21437$$

```
                    F O R E C A S T I N G
|---- Variable ----|      |-- B-coefficient -|      |------ Value -----|
|       X1         |      |      0.94         |      |       39         |
|------------------|      |------------------|      |------------------|
```

$$X2 = 56.15414$$

c) Comparing the MAD's of each method shows that the MAD using regression is marginally the lowest. While getting a good fit of the historical data is no guarantee that the future forecasts will be accurate, all else equal, we would choose that method that gives the best fit. We would thus choose the forecasts made with regression over the forecasts made with the others.

Problem 25.

A line plot of the time series shows a clear seasonal pattern. Hence Winters' method, or, as CMOM calls it, "Smoothing with Trend & Seasonal Factoring" is the preferred method on this data set. Letting CMOM find the appropriate parameters that will minimize the MAD, we get:

```
      CMOM - Forecasting - Smoothing with Trend & Seasonal Factoring
                              Solution
                Smoothing Coefficient Optimized for MAD


        Average Y1                    :        1613.9722
        Mean Square Error             :       35458.2461
        Mean Absolute Deviation       :         127.7310


                              Forecast


           Year 10      Year 11      Year 12

    q1     1698.698     1789.309     1879.920
    q2     2121.658     2233.169     2344.680
    q3     2489.126     2618.247     2747.367
    q4     1485.875     1560.430     1634.985


    248.913 |   |                                            f
            |   |                                  e
    233.421 | Y |                          e           s
            |   |                    s  e      a     a
    217.930 | 1 |                                        f
            |   |             a           a
  / 202.439 |   |      e   a      e                  s
            |   |             e                  a
    186.948 |   |   a                          e
            |   |           e   e    a
    171.456 |   |    ea      e    a       e      e  f
            |   |         a e      a      e    a
    155.965 |   |         a   e   e   a    a
            |   | a       a      a     e       e   f
    140.474 |   |   ea  ae  a             s     a
            |   |      a          e      s
    124.983 |   |    a    e      a    a   s
            |   |      e   s    e
    109.491 |   |seee                          S. Coeff = .3284304
            |   |    a              ---------------------------------------
     | |    |----------------------------------------------------------
    (0)|    |  a = actual,  e = estimate,  s = shared,  f = forecast
            |----------------------------------------------------------
            1 3 5 7 9 11 14 17 20 23 26 29 32 35 38
```

388

Selected CMOM Solutions

Supplement I

Problem 7.

The linear program for this problem is:
maximize 5skirt + 17dress+ 30coat
st

$$skirt + 3dress + 4coat \leq 100 \text{ (cutting)}$$
$$skirt + 4dress + 6coat \leq 180 \text{ (sewing)}$$
$$skirt + dress + 4coat \leq 60 \text{ (material)}$$
$$\text{All variables} \geq 0$$

CMOM gave the following results:

6-24-1995 input file: KRSUP47.LPD   output file: krsi7.LPO   23:53:53

CMOM - Linear Programming
Maximization

Data Entered

Number of Variables :	3
Number of <= Constraints :	3
Number of = Constraints :	0
Number of => Constraints :	0

Model

	skirt	dress	sport	RHV
Max-Z	5	17	30	
cut	1	3	4	<=100
sew	1	4	6	<=180
mat	1	1	4	<= 60

CMOM - Linear Programming
Maximization

Solution

Variable Label	Variable Value	Original Coefficient	Coefficient Sensitivity
skirt	0	5	2.50
dress	20	17	0
sport	10	30	0

Constraint Label	Original RHV	Slack or Surplus	Shadow Price
cut	100	0	4.7500
sew	180	40	0
mat	60	0	2.7500

Objective Function Value: 640

Objective Function Coefficients

Variable Label	Lower Limit	Original Coefficient	Upper Limit
skirt	0	5	7.5000
dress	7.5000	17	22.5000
sport	22.6667	30	68

Right-Hand-Side Values

Constraint Label	Lower Limit	Original Value	Upper Limit
cut	60	100	132
sew	140	180	no limit
mat	33.3333	60	100

Problem 8.

Referring to problem 7 above, we use the sensitivity analysis to answer the questions posed.

a) An extra hour of cutting time is worth $4.75 above what Trim-Look ordinarily pays for an hour of cutting time, while they would not pay anything for an extra hour of sewing. An extra yard of material is worth $2.75 above and beyond what they ordinarily pay. The shadow prices gives us these values. The reason the shadow price for sewing is zero is because we only used 140 hours of the 180 hours available (40 hours slack) and so we would not pay for any additional hours of sewing.

b) We can have as little as 60 hours of cutting or as many as 132 hours and still be assured that the shadow price for cutting is $4.75. The corresponding range for material is: as little as 33.33 yards to as many as 100 yards and still have the shadow price of material be $2.75.

Problem 9.

a) The linear program formulation is:

```
maximize   10shirt + 10short + 23pants
st
          2shirt +  2short +  3pants ≤ 120 (dept.  A)
           shirt +  3short +  4pants ≤ 160 (dept.  B)
          2shirt +   short +  4pants ≤ 90 (material)
                All variables ≥ 0
```

b) CMOM gave the following output:

06-24-1995 input file: KRSUP9.LPD   output file: krsi9.LPO   23:54:54

CMOM - Linear Programming
Maximization

Number of Variables   :   3

Number of <= Constraints :   3

Number of = Constraints :   0

Number of => Constraints :   0

Model

	shirt	short	pants	RHV
Max-Z	10	10	23	
deptA	2	2	3	<=120
deptB	1	3	4	<=160
mat	2	1	4	<= 90

CMOM - Linear Programming
Maximization

Solution

Variable Label	Variable Value	Original Coefficient	Coefficient Sensitivity
shirt	7.78	10	0
short	38.89	10	0
pants	8.89	23	0

Constraint Label	Original RHV	Slack or Surplus	Shadow Price
deptA	120	0	0.5556
deptB	160	0	1.7778
mat	90	0	3.5556

Objective Function Value: 671.1111

Sensitivity Analysis & Ranging

Objective Function Coefficients

Variable Label	Lower Limit	Original Coefficient	Upper Limit
shirt	9.3750	10	13.2000
short	8.7500	10	16.4000
pants	15	23	24

Right-Hand-Side Values

Constraint Label	Lower Limit	Original Value	Upper Limit
deptA	111.2500	120	136
deptB	120	160	174
mat	70	90	160

c) Astaire should be willing to pay: $.56 above what they ordinarily pay for an extra hour of department A capacity, $1.78 above what they regularly pay for an extra hour of department B capacity. These shadow prices are valid so long as we have somewhere between 111.25 and 136 hours of department A capacity, and somewhere between 120 and 174 hours of department B capacity.

Problem 10.
Letting A, B, C, D, and E represent the number of knives of each type to make, we get the following linear program:

```
MAX       10 A + 10.5 B + 9 C + 11 D + 9 E
SUBJECT TO
              0.05 A + 0.15 B + 0.2 C + 0.15 D + 0.05 E <=   1500 (machine1)
              0.1 A + 0.1 B + 0.05 C + 0.1 D + 0.1 E <=    1400 (machine 2)
              0.15 A + 0.05 B + 0.1 C + 0.1 D + 0.1 E <=   1600 (machine 3)
              0.05 A + 0.05 B + 0.2 C + 0.1 D + 0.05 E <=   1500 (machine 4)
              4 A + 6 B + C + 2 D + 6 E <=   75000 (raw material 1)
              2 A + 8 B + 3 C + 5 D + 10 E <=   100000 (raw material 2)
                  All variables >= 0
```

CMOM gives the following output:

06-24-1995 input file: KRSUPI10.LPD   output file: krsi10.LPO   23:57:12

CMOM - Linear Programming
Maximization

Data Entered

Number of Variables   :   5

Number of <= Constraints :   6

Number of = Constraints   :   0

Number of => Constraints :   0

Model

	A	B	C	D	E		RHV
Max-Z	10	10.50	9	11	9		
MACH1	0.05	0.15	0.20	0.15	0.05	<=	1500
MACH2	0.10	0.10	0.05	0.10	0.10	<=	1400
MACH3	0.15	0.05	0.10	0.10	0.10	<=	1600
MACH4	0.05	0.05	0.20	0.10	0.05	<=	1500
RAW1	4	6	1	2	6	<=	75000
RAW2	2	8	3	5	10	<=	100000

CMOM - Linear Programming
Maximization

Solution

Variable Label	Variable Value	Original Coefficient	Coefficient Sensitivity
A	7875	10	0
B	5375	10.50	0
C	1500	9	0
D	0	11	0.28
E	0	9	0.22

Constraint Label	Original RHV	Slack or Surplus	Shadow Price
MACH1	1500	0	20.6250
MACH2	1400	0	66.2500

392

MACH3	1600	0	15.6250
MACH4	1500	537.5000	0
RAW1	75000	9750.0068	0
RAW2	100000	36750.0039	0

Objective Function Value: 148687.4844

Problem 11

The linear program for this problem follows the following convention: the first two letters in a variable name indicate the type of nut (AL for almond, WA for walnut, and PE for peanut) and the second two letters indicate the type of pack (AL for almond, WA for walnut, GR for gourmet, FN for fancy, and TH for thrifty. The linear program is thus:

```
MIN     0.8 ALAL + 0.8 ALGR + 0.8 ALFN + 0.8 ALTH + 0.6 WAWA + 0.6 WAGR
     + 0.6 WAFN + 0.6 WATH + 0.35 PEGR + 0.35 PEFN + 0.35 PETH
SUBJECT TO
          ALAL + ALGR + ALFN + ALTH <=   3000 (limit on almonds)
          WAWA + WAGR + WAFN + WATH <=   2000 (limit on walnuts)
          0.7 ALFN - 0.3 WAFN - 0.3 PEFN >=   0 (almonds in fancy pack)
       - 0.3 ALFN + 0.7 WAFN - 0.3 PEFN >=   0 (walnuts in fancy pack)
          0.55 ALGR - 0.45 WAGR - 0.45 PEGR >=  0 (almonds in gourmet pack)
       - 0.45 ALGR + 0.55 WAGR - 0.45 PEGR >=  0 (walnuts in gourmet pack)
          0.8 ALTH - 0.2 WATH - 0.2 PETH >=   0 (almonds in thrifty pack)
       - 0.2 ALTH + 0.8 WATH - 0.2 PETH >=   0 (walnuts in gourmet pack)
       ALAL >=   1250 (almond pack demand)
       WAWA >=    750 (walnut pack demand)
       ALGR + WAGR + PEGR >=   1000 (gourmet pack demand)
       ALFN + WAFN + PEFN >=    500 (fancy pack demand)
       ALTH + WATH + PETH >=   1500 (thrifty pack demand)
             All variables >= 0
```

CMOM gives the following output:

07-04-1995 input file: KRSUPI11.LPD   output file: krsi11.LPO   12:45:45

CMOM - Linear Programming
Minimization

Data Entered

Number of Variables   :   11

Number of <= Constraints :   2

Number of = Constraints :   0

Number of => Constraints :   11

Model

	AL_AL	AL_GR	AL_FN	AL_TH	WA_WA	WA_GR	WA_FN
Min-Z	0.80	0.80	0.80	0.80	0.60	0.60	0.60
ALMON	1	1	1	1	0	0	0
WALNT	0	0	0	0	1	1	1
ALFAN	0	0	0.70	0	0	0	-0.30
WAFAN	0	0	-0.30	0	0	0	0.70

393

ALGOR	0	0.55	0	0	0	-0.45	0
WAGOR	0	-0.45	0	0	0	0.55	0
ALTHR	0	0	0	0.80	0	0	0
WATHR	0	0	0	-0.20	0	0	0
ALCAN	1	0	0	0	0	0	0
WACAN	0	0	0	0	1	0	0
GRCAN	0	1	0	0	0	1	0
FACAN	0	0	1	0	0	0	1
THCAN	0	0	0	1	0	0	0

	WA_TH	PE_GR	PE_FN	PE_TH	RHV	
Min-Z	0.60	0.35	0.35	0.35		
ALMON	0	0	0	0	<=	3000
WALNT	1	0	0	0	<=	2000

	WA_TH	PE_GR	PE_FN	PE_TH	RHV	
ALFAN	0	0	-0.30	0	>=	0
WAFAN	0	0	-0.30	0	>=	0
ALGOR	0	-0.45	0	0	>=	0
WAGOR	0	-0.45	0	0	>=	0
ALTHR	-0.20	0	0	-0.20	>=	0
WATHR	0.80	0	0	-0.20	>=	0
ALCAN	0	0	0	0	>=	1250
WACAN	0	0	0	0	>=	750
GRCAN	0	1	0	0	>=	1000
FACAN	0	0	1	0	>=	500
THCAN	1	0	0	1	>=	1500

CMOM - Linear Programming
Minimization

Solution

Variable Label	Variable Value	Original Coefficient	Coefficient Sensitivity
AL_AL	1250	0	0
AL_GR	450	0	0
AL_FN	150	0	0
AL_TH	300	0	0
WA_WA	750	0	0
WA_GR	450	0	0
WA_FN	150	0	C
WA_TH	300	0	0
PE_GR	100	0	0
PE_FN	200	0	0
PE_TH	900	0	0

Constraint Label	Original RHV	Slack or Surplus	Shadow Price
ALMON	3000	850	0
WALNT	2000	350.0000	0
ALFAN	0	0	0
WAFAN	0	0	0
ALGOR	0	0	0
WAGOR	0	0	0
ALTHR	0	0	0
WATHR	0	0	0
ALCAN	1250	0	0
WACAN	750	0	0
GRCAN	1000	0	0
FACAN	500	0	0
THCAN	1500	0	0

394

Objective Function Value: 3130
Sensitivity Analysis & Ranging
Objective Function Coefficients

Variable Label	Lower Limit	Original Coefficient	Upper Limit
AL_AL	0	0	no limit
AL_GR	0	0	no limit
AL_FN	0	0	no limit
AL_TH	0	0	no limit
WA_WA	0	0	no limit
WA_GR	0	0	no limit
WA_FN	0	0	no limit
WA_TH	0	0	no limit
PE_GR	0	0	0
PE_FN	0	0	0
PE_TH	0	0	0

Right-Hand-Side Values

Constraint Label	Lower Limit	Original Value	Upper Limit
ALMON	2150	3000	no limit
WALNT	1650	2000	no limit
ALFAN	0	0	200.0000
WAFAN	0	0	200.0000
ALGOR	0	0	100.0000
WAGOR	0	0	100.0000
ALTHR	0	0	850
WATHR	0	0	350.0000
ALCAN	0	1250	2100
WACAN	0	750	1100
GRCAN	0	1000	1777.7776
FACAN	0	500	1666.6664
THCAN	0	1500	3249.9993

b) From the optimal solution we see that PE_FN + PE_GR + PE_TH = 1200 pounds. Thus there is no impact of a 2000 pound limit on peanuts since we only use 1200 pounds in the optimal solution.

c) We now must change the constraints for the almonds in the gourmet packs and also for the walnuts in the gourmet packs.   The new model is:

```
MIN     0.8 ALAL + 0.8 ALGR + 0.8 ALFN + 0.8 ALTH + 0.6 WAWA + 0.6 WAGR
      + 0.6 WAFN + 0.6 WATH + 0.35 PEGR + 0.35 PEFN + 0.35 PETH
SUBJECT TO
          ALAL + ALGR + ALFN + ALTH <=   3000
          WAWA + WAGR + WAFN + WATH <=   2000
          0.7 ALFN - 0.3 WAFN - 0.3 PEFN >=    0
        - 0.3 ALFN + 0.7 WAFN - 0.3 PEFN >=    0
          0.5 ALGR - 0.5 WAGR - 0.5 PEGR >=    0
        - 0.5 ALGR + 0.5 WAGR - 0.5 PEGR >=    0
          0.8 ALTH - 0.2 WATH - 0.2 PETH >=    0
        - 0.2 ALTH + 0.8 WATH - 0.2 PETH >=    0
       ALAL >=    1250
       WAWA >=    750
       ALGR + WAGR + PEGR >=    1000
       ALFN + WAFN + PEFN >=    500
       ALTH + WATH + PETH >=    1500
            All variables >= 0
```

395

CMOM gives us the following solution:

Solution

Variable Label	Variable Value	Original Coefficient	Coefficient Sensitivity
AL_AL	1250	0.80	0
AL_GR	500	0.80	0
AL_FN	150	0.80	0
AL_TH	300	0.80	0
WA_WA	750	0.60	0
WA_GR	500	0.60	0
WA_FN	150	0.60	0
WA_TH	300	0.60	0
PE_GR	0	0.35	no limit
PE_FN	200	0.35	0
PE_TH	900	0.35	0

Constraint Label	Original RHV	Slack or Surplus	Shadow Price
ALMON	3000	800	0
WALNT	2000	300.0000	0
ALFAN	0	0	0.4500
WAFAN	0	0	0.2500
ALGOR	0	0	no limit
WAGOR	0	0	no limit
ALTHR	0	0	0.4500
WATHR	0	0	0.2500
ALCAN	1250	0	0.8000
WACAN	750	0	0.6000
GRCAN	1000	0	0.7000
FACAN	500	0	0.5600
THCAN	1500	0	0.4900

Objective Function Value: 3165

d) If the demand for the fancy pack doubles, from 500 to 1000 cans, CMOM gives us, after we change the righthandside of that constraint:

Solution

Variable Label	Variable Value	Original Coefficient	Coefficient Sensitivity
AL_AL	1250	0.80	0
AL_GR	450	0.80	0
AL_FN	300	0.80	0
AL_TH	300	0.80	0
WA_WA	750	0.60	0
WA_GR	450	0.60	0
WA_FN	300	0.60	0
WA_TH	300	0.60	0
PE_GR	100	0.35	0
PE_FN	400	0.35	0
PE_TH	900	0.35	0

396

Constraint Label	Original RHV	Slack or Surplus	Shadow Price
ALMON	3000	700	0
WALNT	2000	200.0000	0
ALFAN	0	0	0.4500
WAFAN	0	0	0.2500
ALGOR	0	0	0.4500
WAGOR	0	0	0.2500
ALTHR	0	0	0.4500
WATHR	0	0	0.2500
ALCAN	1250	0	0.8000
WACAN	750	0	0.6000
GRCAN	1000	0	0.6650
FACAN	1000	0	0.5600
THCAN	1500	0	0.4900

Objective Function Value: 3410

Problem 12.

Let A=fraction of material A used in a gallon of the finished product
    B=fraction of material B used in a gallon of the finished product
    C=fraction of material C used in a gallon of the finished product

The linear program is thus:

```
MIN     0.6 A + 0.4 B + 0.5 C
SUBJECT TO
        4 A + 3 B + 10 C <=   6
        A + B + C =   1
        200 A + 180 B + 280 C >=   220
        20 A + 10 B + 8 C >=   12
            All variables >= 0
```

CMOM gives us:

07-04-1995 input file: KRSUPI12.LPD   output file: krsi12.LPO   12:46:33

CMOM - Linear Programming
Minimization

Data Entered

Number of Variables   :   3

Number of <= Constraints :   1

Number of = Constraints :   1

Number of => Constraints :   2

Model

	A	B	C		RHV
Min-Z	0.6000	0.4000	0.5000		
GAMMA	4	3	10	−	6
FRACT	1	1	1	=	1
CMBPT	200	180	280	−	220
ZETA	20	10	8	−	12

397

CMOM - Linear Programming
Minimization

Solution

Variable Label	Variable Value	Original Coefficient	Coefficient Sensitivity
A	0	0	0
B	0	0	0
C	0	0	0

Constraint Label	Original RHV	Slack or Surplus	Shadow Price
GAMMA	6	0	0
FRACT	1	0	0
CMBPT	220	0	0
ZETA	12	0	0

Objective Function Value: 0.4885

Sensitivity Analysis & Ranging

Objective Function Coefficients

Variable Label	Lower Limit	Original Coefficient	Upper Limit
A	0	0	no limit
B	0	0	0
C	0	0	1.4000

Right-Hand-Side Values

Constraint Label	Lower Limit	Original Value	Upper Limit
GAMMA	5.6923	6	no limit
FRACT	0	1	1.2059
CMBPT	184	220	224.4444
ZETA	9.2000	12	17.0000

Problem 13.

In order to formulate this problem, we must find the profit margin of each blade type by subtracting the material costs from the selling price.

Component A:
32 oz. @ $0.20 per oz. = $6.40   (Material 1)
12 oz. @ $0.35 per oz. = $4.20   (Material 2)
              Cost $10.60

Profit margin = $40.00 - 10.60 = $29.40

Component B:
26 oz. @ $0.20 per oz. = $5.20   (Material 1)
16 oz. @ $0.35 per oz. = $5.60   (Material 2)
              Cost $10.80

Profit margin = $28.00 - 10.80 = $17.20

398

Component C:
19 oz. @ $0.20 per oz. = $3.80   (Material 1)
9oz. @ $0.35 per oz. = $3.15   (Material 2)
                Cost $6.95

Profit margin = $24.00 - 6.95 = $17.05

The linear program for this problem is thus:

   MAX   29.4 A + 17.2 B + 17.05 C
   SUBJECT TO
            0.25 A + 0.2 B + 0.1 C <=   1600 (machine 1)
            0.1 A + 0.15 B + 0.05 C <=   1400 (machine 2)
            0.05 A + 0.1 B + 0.15 C <=   1500 (machine 3)
            32 A + 26 B + 19 C <=   200000 (material 1)
            12 A + 16 B + 9 C <=   85000 (material 2)
               B >=   1200   (Minimum for product B)
           All variables >= 0

The CMOM output is:

06-25-1995 input file: KRSUPI13.LPD   output file: krsi13.LPO   16:00:56

CMOM - Linear Programming
Maximization

Data Entered

Number of Variables   :   3

Number of <= Constraints :   5

Number of = Constraints :   0

Number of => Constraints :   1

Model

	A	B	C		RHV
Max-Z	29.40	17.20	17.05		
MACH1	0.25	0.20	0.10	<=	1600
MACH2	0.10	0.15	0.05	<=	1400
MACH3	0.05	0.10	0.15	<=	1500
MAT1	32	26	19	<=	200000
MAT2	12	16	9	<=	85000
MINB	0	1	0	>=	1200

CMOM - Linear Programming
Maximization

Solution

Variable Label	Variable Value	Original Coefficient	Coefficient Sensitivity
A	5275	29.40	0
B	1200	17.20	0
C	0	17.05	0

Constraint Label	Original RHV	Slack or Surplus	Shadow Price
MACH1	1600	41.2500	0
MACH2	1400	692.5000	0
MACH3	1500	1116.2500	0
MAT1	200000	0	0
MAT2	85000	2500	0
MINB	1200	0	6.6875

Objective Function Value: 175725

Sensitivity Analysis & Ranging

Objective Function Coefficients

Variable Label	Lower Limit	Original Coefficient	Upper Limit
A	28.7158	29.4000	no limit
B	0	17.2000	23.8875
C	0	17.0500	17.4562

Right-Hand-Side Values (000)

Constraint Label	Lower Limit	Original Value	Upper Limit
MACH1	1.5588	1.6000	no limit
MACH2	0	1.4000	no limit
MACH3	0	1.5000	no limit
MAT1	31.2000	200	205.2800
MAT2	82.5000	85	no limit
MINB	0	1.2000	1.6000

Problem 14.

06-25-1995 input file: KRSUPI14.LPD   output file: krsi14.LPO
16:01:31

CMOM - Linear Programming
Maximization

Data Entered

Number of Variables   :   3

Number of <= Constraints :   3

Number of = Constraints   :   0

Number of => Constraints :   0

Model

	X1	X2	X3		RHV
Max-Z	7	5	2		
C1	3	5	1	<=	150
C2	5	3	2	<=	100
C3	1	2	1	<=	160

CMOM - Linear Programming
Maximization

Solution

Variable Label	Variable Value	Original Coefficient	Coefficient Sensitivity
X1	3.12	7	0
X2	28.13	5	0
X3	0	2	0

Constraint Label	Original RHV	Slack or Surplus	Shadow Price
C1	150	0	0
C2	100	0	1.2500
C3	160	100.6250	0

Objective Function Value: 162.5000

Sensitivity Analysis & Ranging

Objective Function Coefficients

Variable Label	Lower Limit	Original Coefficient	Upper Limit
X1	5.2857	7	8.3333
X2	4.2000	5	11.6667
X3	0	2	2.7500

Right-Hand-Side Values

Constraint Label	Lower Limit	Original Value	Upper Limit
C1	60	150	166.6667
C2	90	100	250.0000
C3	59.3750	160	no limit

a) False. Since the upper limit for the price of hat 3 is $2.75, the product mix stays the same if the price of hat 3 were increased to $2.50.

b) True. The lower limit for machine C's capacity is 59.375 hours, and the current solution has a slack of 100.625 hours there. Thus, if the new capacity is reduced from 160 hours to 65 hours, the product mix remains the same, the profit stays the same, but the slack in machine C's capacity is now 5.625 hours.

c) False. Since the upper limit of machine A's capacity is 166.67 hours, the optimal solution will change at 170 hours of capacity. When we change the righthandside of a constraint (even if we stay within the allowable range), the shadow prices stay the same, but the optimal solution generally changes. We do not know what the new optimal solution would be then, and we would have to re-run the problem to get the new solution.

Problem 15.
Letting Xi=the annual production quantity of product i, where i = 1,2,3,4,5 the linear program model is:

401

```
MAX      4 X1 + 7 X2 + 3.5 X3 + 4 X4 + 5.7 X5
SUBJECT TO
            0.05 X1 + 0.1 X2 + 0.8 X3 + 0.57 X4 + 0.15 X5 <=    7500
            0.2 X1 + 0.02 X2 + 0.2 X3 + 0.09 X4 + 0.3 X5 <=    7500
            0.2 X1 + 0.5 X2 + 0.1 X3 + 0.4 X4 + 0.18 X5 <=    10000
            0.7 X2 + 0.5 X4 <=    6000
            0.1 X1 + 0.2 X2 + 0.4 X3 <=    7000
                    X3 >=    3000
                    X4 >=    3000
            All variables >= 0
```

CMOM gives us:

CMOM - Linear Programming
Maximization

Data Entered

Number of Variables   :   5

Number of <= Constraints :   5

Number of = Constraints   :   0

Number of => Constraints :   2

Model

	X1	X2	X3	X4	X5		RHV
Max-Z	4	7	3.50	4	5.70		
C1	0.05	0.10	0.80	0.57	0.15	<=	7500
C2	0.20	0.02	0.20	0.09	0.30	<=	7500
C3	0.20	0.50	0.10	0.40	0.18	<=	10000
C4	0	0.70	0	0.50	0	<=	6000
C5	0.10	0.20	0.40	0	0	<=	7000
C6	0	0	1	0	0	>=	3000
C7	0	0	0	1	0	>=	3000

CMOM - Linear Programming
Maximization

Solution

Variable Label	Variable Value	Original Coefficient	Coefficient Sensitivity
X1	17310.71	4	0
X2	6428.57	7	0
X3	3000	3.50	0
X4	3000	4	0
X5	10130.96	5.70	0

Constraint Label	Original RHV	Slack or Surplus	Shadow Price
C1	7500	361.9638	0
C2	7500	0	17.5000
C3	10000	0	2.5000
C4	6000	0	7.7143
C5	7000	2783.2148	0
C6	3000	0	0
C7	3000	0	2.4321

Objective Function Value: 194489.2813
Sensitivity Analysis & Ranging

Objective Function Coefficients

Variable Label	Lower Limit	Original Coefficient	Upper Limit
X1	3.8000	4	4.8852
X2	3.5950	7	no limit
X3	0	3.5000	3.7500
X4	0	4	6.4321
X5	5.4000	5.7000	6

Right-Hand-Side Values (000)

Constraint Label	Lower Limit	Original Value	Upper Limit
C1	7.1380	7.5000	no limit
C2	6.2843	7.5000	7.9137
C3	9.4209	10	11.2157
C4	4.2271	6	6.6415
C5	4.2168	7	no limit
C6	0	3	3.5265
C7	0	3	3.7884

Problem 16.

Let I_t = the number of shovels left over in inventory at the end of period t
W_t = the number of workers in period t
H_t = the number of workers hired in period t
F_t = the number of workers fired in period t
O_t = the number of shovels produced in overtime in period t
S_t = the number of shovels made by subcontracting in period t
D_t = the forecasted demand in period t

The linear program is:

```
MIN    280 I1 + 280 I2 + 280 I3 + 280 I4 + 14000 W1 + 14000 W2
     + 14000 W3 + 14000 W4 + 3700 O1 + 3700 O2 + 3700 O3 + 3700 O4
     + 4200 S1 + 4200 S2 + 4200 S3 + 4200 S4 + 1000 H1 + 1000 H2 + 1000 H3
     + 1000 H4 + 600 F1 + 600 F2 + 600 F3 + 600 F4
SUBJECT TO
          - I1 + 4 W1 + O1 + S1 + I0 =     70
            I1 - I2 + 4 W2 + S2 =      150
            I2 - I3 + 4 W3 + O3 + S3 =    320
            I3 - I4 + 4 W4 + O4 + S4 =    100
            W1 - H1 + F1 - W0 =      0
          - W1 + W2 - H2 + F2 =      0
          - W2 + W3 - H3 + F3 =      0
          - W3 + W4 - H4 + F4 =      0
            O1 <=    15
            O2 <=    15
            O3 <=    15
            O4 <=    15
            S1 <=     5
            S2 <=     5
            S3 <=     5
            S4 <=     5
            W0 =     30
            W4 =     30
            I0 =     30
            I4 =     30
```

403

The CMOM output is:

Solution

Variable Label	Variable Value	Original Coefficient	Coefficient Sensitivity
I0	30	0	0
I1	80	280	0
I2	117.50	280	0
I3	0	280	420
I4	30	280	0
W0	30	0	0
W1	30	14000	0
W2	46.88	14000	0
W3	46.88	14000	0
W4	30	14000	0
O1	0	3700	420
O2	0	3700	140
O3	15	3700	0
O4	10	3700	0
S1	0	4200	920
S2	0	4200	640
S3	0	4200	360
S4	0	4200	500
H1	0	1000	880
H2	16.88	1000	0
H3	0	1000	240
H4	0	1000	1600
F1	0	600	720
F2	0	600	1600
F3	0	600	1360
F4	16.88	600	0

Constraint Label	Original RHV	Slack or Surplus	Shadow Price
C1	15	15	0
C2	15	15	0
C3	15	0	140
C4	15	5	0
C5	5	5	0
C6	5	5	0
C7	5	5	0
C8	5	5	0
C9	70	0	3280
C10	150	0	3560
C11	320	0	3840
C12	100	0	3700
C13	30	0	120
C14	30	0	1400
C15	30	0	3280
C16	30	0	3980
C17	0	0	120
C18	0	0	1000
C19	0	0	760
C20	0	0	600

Objective Function Value: 2335700

Sensitivity Analysis & Ranging

Objective Function Coefficients

Variable Label	Lower Limit	Original Coefficient	Upper Limit
I0	0	0	no limit
I1	60	280	460
I2	0	280	400
I3	0	280	no limit
I4	0	280	no limit
W0	0	0	no limit
W1	13120	14000	14720
W2	12880	14000	14480
W3	13520	14000	15120
W4	0	14000	no limit
O1	3280	3700	no limit
O2	3560	3700	no limit
O3	0	3700	3840
O4	0	3700	4120
S1	3280	4200	no limit
S2	3560	4200	no limit
S3	3840	4200	no limit
S4	3700	4200	no limit
H1	120	1000	no limit
H2	520	1000	1480
H3	760	1000	no limit
H4	0	1000	no limit
F1	0	600	no limit
F2	0	600	no limit
F3	0	600	no limit
F4	120	600	1720

Right-Hand-Side Values

Constraint Label	Lower Limit	Original Value	Upper Limit
C1	0	15	no limit
C2	0	15	no limit
C3	0	15	150
C4	10	15	no limit
C5	0	5	no limit
C6	0	5	no limit
C7	0	5	no limit
C8	0	5	no limit
C9	0	70	150
C10	15	150	385
C11	185	320	no limit
C12	90	100	105
C13	10	30	41.2500
C14	28.7500	30	32.5000
C15	0	30	165
C16	20	30	35
C17	0	0	11.2500
C18	0	0	16.8750
C19	0	0	33.7500
C20	0	0	no limit

Problem 17.
The model is the same as that for problem 16, except for the demand constraints:

$$- I1 + 4 \ W1 + O1 + S1 + I0 = 120$$
$$I1 - I2 + 4 \ W2 + S2 = 180$$
$$I2 - I3 + 4 \ W3 + O3 + S3 = 180$$
$$I3 - I4 + 4 \ W4 + O4 + S4 = 160$$

CMOM now gives us:

Solution

Variable Label	Variable Value	Original Coefficient	Coefficient Sensitivity
I0	30	0	0
I1	30	280	0
I2	35	280	0
I3	55	280	0
I4	30	280	0
W0	30	0	0
W1	30	14000	0
W2	46.25	14000	0
W3	46.25	14000	0
W4	30	14000	0
O1	0	3700	420
O2	0	3700	140
O3	15	3700	0
O4	15	3700	0
S1	0	4200	920
S2	0	4200	640
S3	0	4200	360
S4	0	4200	80
H1	0	1000	880
H2	16.25	1000	0
H3	0	1000	240
H4	0	1000	1600
F1	0	600	720
F2	0	600	1600
F3	0	600	1360
F4	16.25	600	0

Objective Function Value: 2314000

Problem 18.

Let X1 = cartons of face cream produced during the first shift
X2 = cartosn of face cream produced during the second shift
X3 = cartons of face cream imported
X4 = cartons of body cream produced during the first shift
X5 = cartons of body cream produced during the second shift
X6 = cartons of body cream imported
X7 = cartons of shampoo produced during the first shift
X8 = cartons of shampoo produced during the second shift

Cost per carton of X1 = 8.50(1.5) + 9.25(0.8) + 1.00(5) +1.5(7) = $35.65
Cost per carton of X2 = 9.35(1.5) + 10.175(0.8) + 1.00(5) +1.5(7) = $37.665
Cost per carton of X3 = $40.00
Cost per carton of X4 = 8.50(1.8) + 9.25(1.00) + 1.00(8) +1.5(4) = $38.55
Cost per carton of X5 = 9.35(1.8) + 10.175(1.00) + 1.00(8) +1.5(4) = $41.005
Cost per carton of X6 = $55.00
Cost per carton of X7 = 8.50(1.0) + 9.25(0.5) + 1.00(3) +1.5(9) = $29.625
Cost per carton of X8 = 9.35(1.0) + 10.175(0.5) + 1.00(3) +1.5(9) = $30.9375

```
MIN     35.65 X1 + 37.665 X2 + 40 X3 + 38.55 X4 + 41.005 X5 + 55 X6
    + 29.625 X7 + 30.9375 X8
SUBJECT TO
        1.5 X1 + 1.8 X4 + X7 <=      15000 (stage 1 labor, first shift)
        1.5 X2 + 1.8 X5 + X8 <=      13500 (stage 1 labor, second shift)
        0.8 X1 + X4 + 0.5 X7 <=      10000 (stage 2 labor, first shift)
        0.8 X2 + X5 + 0.5 X8 <=       9000 (stage 2 labor, second shift)
        5 X1 + 5 X2 + 8 X4 + 8 X5 + 3 X7 + 3 X8 <=    200000 (material A)
        7 X1 + 7 X2 + 4 X4 + 4 X5 + 9 X7 + 9 X8 <=    150000 (material B)
        X1 + X2 + X3 >=    10000   (face cream demand)
        X4 + X5 + X6 >=     5000   (body cream demand)
        X7 + X8 >=    15000   (shampoo demand)
        All variables >= 0
```

The CMOM output is:

06-25-1995 input file: KRSUPI18.LPD   output file: krsi18.LPO   16:04:07

Solution

Variable Label	Variable Value	Original Coefficient	Coefficient Sensitivity
X1	0	35.65	22.27
X2	0	37.67	22.32
X3	10000	40	0
X4	3750	38.55	0
X5	0	41.01	0
X6	1250	55	0
X7	8250	29.63	0
X8	6750	30.94	0

Constraint Label	Original RHV	Slack or Surplus	Shadow Price
C1	15000	0	1.3130
C2	13500	6750.0005	0
C3	10000	2125.0007	0
C4	9000	5625.0005	0
C5	200000	125000.0078	0
C6	150000	0	3.5216
C7	10000	0	40
C8	5000	0	55.0000
C9	15000	0	62.6329

Objective Function Value: 1066550.2500

Sensitivity Analysis & Ranging

Objective Function Coefficients

Variable Label	Lower Limit	Original Coefficient	Upper Limit
X1	13.3790	35.6500	no limit
X2	15.3485	37.6650	no limit
X3	0	40	62.2710
X4	0	38.5500	38.6416
X5	40.9134	41.0050	no limit
X6	42.2737	55	no limit
X7	29.5741	29.6250	30.9380
X8	29.6250	30.9380	30.9889

407

Right-Hand-Side Values (000)

Constraint Label	Lower Limit	Original Value	Upper Limit
C1	8.2500	15	19.2500
C2	6.7500	13.5000	no limit
C3	7.8750	10	no limit
C4	3.3750	9	no limit
C5	75.0000	200	no limit
C6	135	150	155
C7	0	10	0
C8	3.7500	5	0
C9	14.4444	15	16.6667

c) One additional hour of stage 1 labor is worth $1.31 (first shift). One additional hour of stage 2 labor is worth $0.

d) The value of one additional pound of material A is worth $0 while the value of one additional pound of material B is $3.52.

e) The shadow prices will remain valid if the number of pounds of material B is between 135 thousand and 155 thousand.

f) We would stop importing body cream if its price would drop to $42.27 or less.

g) The new linear program is:

```
MIN     35.65 X1 + 37.665 X2 + 40 X3 + 38.55 X4 + 41.005 X5 + 55 X6
        + 29.625 X7 + 30.9375 X8
SUBJECT TO
            1.5 X1 + 1.8 X4 + X7 <=     15000
            1.5 X2 + 1.8 X5 + X8 <=     13500
            0.8 X1 + X4 + 0.5 X7 <=     10000
            0.8 X2 + X5 + 0.5 X8 <=     9000
            5 X1 + 5 X2 + 8 X4 + 8 X5 + 3 X7 + 3 X8 <=    200000
            7 X1 + 7 X2 + 4 X4 + 4 X5 + 9 X7 + 9 X8 <=    150000
            X1 + X2 + X3 >=    9000
            X4 + X5 + X6 >=    4500
            X7 + X8 >=    13500
            All variables >= 0
```

Problem 19.

Let Pi = portable televisions produced in facility i, where i = 1,2,3
    Ri = regular televisions produced in facility i, where i = 1,2,3
    Hi = home theater televisions produced in facility i, where i = 1,2,3

The linear program is:

```
MAX     75 P1 + 75 P2 + 75 P3 + 125 R1 + 125 R2 + 125 R3 + 200 H1
        + 200 H2 + 200 H3
SUBJECT TO
            3 P1 + 4 R1 + 7 H1 <=    10000 (fabrication facility 1)
            3 P2 + 4 R2 + 7 H2 <=    15000 (fabrication facility 2)
            3 P3 + 4 R3 + 7 H3 <=    5000   (fabrication facility 3)
            9 P1 + 12 R1 + 16 H1 <=    50000 (assembly facility 1)
            9 P2 + 12 R2 + 16 H2 <=    60000 (assembly facility 2)
            9 P3 + 12 R3 + 16 H3 <=    35000 (assembly facility 3)
            All variables >=0
```

CMOM gives us:

Solution

Variable Label	Variable Value	Original Coefficient	Coefficient Sensitivity
P1	0	75	18.75
P2	0	75	18.75
P3	0	75	18.75
R1	2500	125	0
R2	3750	125	0
R3	1250	125	0
H1	0	200	18.75
H2	0	200	18.75
H3	0	200	18.75

Constraint Label	Original RHV	Slack or Surplus	Shadow Price
C1	10000	0	31.2500
C2	15000	0	31.2500
C3	5000	0	31.2500
C4	50000	20000	0
C5	60000	15000.0020	0
C6	35000	20000	0

Objective Function Value: 937500

Sensitivity Analysis & Ranging

Objective Function Coefficients

Variable Label	Lower Limit	Original Coefficient	Upper Limit
P1	0	75	93.7500
P2	0	75	93.7500
P3	0	75	93.7500
R1	114.2857	125	no limit
R2	114.2857	125	no limit
R3	114.2857	125	no limit
H1	0	200	218.7500
H2	0	200	218.7500
H3	0	200	218.7500

Right-Hand-Side Values

Constraint Label	Lower Limit	Original Value	Upper Limit
C1	0	10000	16666.6660
C2	0	15000	20000
C3	0	5000	11666.6660
C4	30000	50000	no limit
C5	45000	60000	no limit
C6	15000	35000	no limit

c) The shadow price of facility 1 fabrication time is $31.25 per hour.

d) Adding the constraints:
    P1 + P2 + P3 >= 1500 (portable TV production)
    H1 + H2 + H3 >= 500   (home theater TV production)
to the original model, CMOM gives us:

409

Solution

Variable Label	Variable Value	Original Coefficient	Coefficient Sensitivity
P1	0	75	0
P2	1500	75	0
P3	0	75	0
R1	2500	125	0
R2	1750	125	0
R3	1250	125	0
H1	0	200	0
H2	500	200	0
H3	0	200	0

Constraint Label	Original RHV	Slack or Surplus	Shadow Price
C1	10000	0	31.2500
C2	15000	0	31.2500
C3	5000	0	31.2500
C4	50000	20000	0
C5	60000	17500.0039	0
C6	35000	20000	0
C7	1500	0	18.7500
C8	500	0	18.7500

Objective Function Value: 900000

e) We will assume here that the constraints in part (d), concerning portable and home theater production, are not included. That is, we will increase production capacities of all three plants by 10% of the original model.

The new model is thus:

```
MAX     75 P1 + 75 P2 + 75 P3 + 125 R1 + 125 R2 + 125 R3 + 200 H1
    + 200 H2 + 200 H3
SUBJECT TO
        3 P1 + 4 R1 + 7 H1 <=   11000 (fabrication facility 1)
        3 P2 + 4 R2 + 7 H2 <=   16500 (fabrication facility 2)
        3 P3 + 4 R3 + 7 H3 <=   5500  (fabrication facility 3)
        9 P1 + 12 R1 + 16 H1 <=   55000 (assembly facility 1)
        9 P2 + 12 R2 + 16 H2 <=   66000 (assembly facility 2)
        9 P3 + 12 R3 + 16 H3 <=   38500 (assembly facility 3)
        All variables >=0
```

CMOM gives:

Solution

Variable Label	Variable Value	Original Coefficient	Coefficient Sensitivity
P1	0	75	18.75
P2	0	75	18.75
P3	0	75	18.75
R1	2750	125	0
R2	4125	125	0
R3	1375	125	0
H1	0	200	18.75
H2	0	200	18.75
H3	0	200	18.75

410

Constraint Label	Original RHV	Slack or Surplus	Shadow Price
C1	11000	0	31.2500
C2	16500	0	31.2500
C3	5500	0	31.2500
C4	55000	22000.0020	0
C5	66000	16499.9980	0
C6	38500	22000	0

Objective Function Value: 1031250

f) Once again, we will consider the original problem in part (a) and add the new utilization constraints. The first one, which says that utitilization at facility 1 must equal the utilization at facility 2.

$$\frac{12P1 + 16R1 + 23H1}{60000} = \frac{12P2 + 16R2 + 23H2}{75000}$$

After we perform the algebra, we get:

$$60P1 - 48P2 + 80R1 - 64R2 + 115H1 - 92H2 = 0$$

as our first additional constraint.

We also need that the utilization at facility 1 equals the utilization at facility 3.

$$\frac{12P1 + 16R1 + 23H1}{60000} = \frac{12P3 + 16R3 + 23H3}{40000}$$

After the algebra, we get:

$$24P1 - 36P3 + 32R1 - 48R3 + 46H1 - 69H3 = 0$$

The new linear program, with the additional constraints, is:

```
MAX     75 P1 + 75 P2 + 75 P3 + 125 R1 + 125 R2 + 125 R3 + 200 H1
    + 200 H2 + 200 H3
SUBJECT TO
        3 P1 + 4 R1 + 7 H1 <=   10000
        3 P2 + 4 R2 + 7 H2 <=   15000
        3 P3 + 4 R3 + 7 H3 <=    5000
        9 P1 + 12 R1 + 16 H1 <=   50000
        9 P2 + 12 R2 + 16 H2 <=   60000
        9 P3 + 12 R3 + 16 H3 <=   35000
        60 P1 - 48 P2 + 80 R1 - 64 R2 + 115 H1 - 92 H2 =    0
        24 P1 - 36 P3 + 32 R1 - 48 R3 + 46 H1 - 69 H3 =    0
                All variables >= 0
```

CMOM gives us:

Variable Label	Variable Value	Original Coefficient	Coefficient Sensitivity
P1	0	75	29.35
P2	0	75	29.35
P3	0	75	18.75
R1	0	125	14.13
R2	0	125	14.13
R3	1250	125	0
H1	1304.35	200	0
H2	1630.43	200	0
H3	0	200	165.49

Constraint Label	Original RHV	Slack or Surplus	Shadow Price
C1	10000	869.5654	0
C2	15000	3586.9558	0
C3	5000	0	148.6413
C4	50000	29130.4336	0
C5	60000	33913.0430	0
C6	35000	20000	0
C7	0	0	2.1739
C8	0	0	9.7826

Objective Function Value: 743206.5625

Selected Solutions - Chapter 17

Problem 19.

a) The input to and output from CMOM for this problem are shown below.
We get the expected duration of the project is 36.33 days.

Data Entered

activity	times		# pred	--predecessor activity numbers--	
1-A	Optimistic	8	0		
	Modal	10			
	Pessimistic	12			
2-B	Optimistic	5	0		
	Modal	8			
	Pessimistic	17			
3-C	Optimistic	7	0		
	Modal	8			
	Pessimistic	9			
4-D	Optimistic	1	1	2-B	
	Modal	2			
	Pessimistic	3			
5-E	Optimistic	8	2	1-A	3-C
	Modal	10			
	Pessimistic	12			
6-F	Optimistic	5	2	4-D	5-E
	Modal	6			
	Pessimistic	7			
7-G	Optimistic	1	2	4-D	5-E
	Modal	3			
	Pessimistic	5			
8-H	Optimistic	2	2	6-F	7-G
	Modal	5			
	Pessimistic	8			
9-I	Optimistic	2	1	7-G	
	Modal	4			
	Pessimistic	6			
10-J	Optimistic	4	1	8-H	
	Modal	5			
	Pessimistic	8			
11-K	Optimistic	2	1	8-H	
	Modal	2			
	Pessimistic	2			

Solution

Activity		Start	Finish	Expected Time	Slack	Critical Path
1-A	Earliest: Latest:	0 0	10 10.000	10	0	yes
2-B	Earliest: Latest:	0 9.000	9 18.000	9	9.000	no
3-C	Earliest: Latest:	0 2.000	8 10.000	8	2.000	no
4-D	Earliest: Latest:	9 18.000	11 20.000	2	9.000	no
5-E	Earliest: Latest:	10 10.000	20 20.000	10	0	yes
6-F	Earliest: Latest:	20 20.000	26 26.000	6	0	yes
7-G	Earliest: Latest:	20 23.000	23 26.000	3	3.000	no
8-H	Earliest: Latest:	26 26.000	31 31.000	5	0	yes
9-I	Earliest: Latest:	23 32.333	27 36.333	4	9.333	no
10-J	Earliest: Latest:	31 31.000	36.333 36.333	5.333	0	yes
11-K	Earliest: Latest:	31 34.333	33 36.333	2	3.333	no

Project Summary

Expected Completion Time :   36.333
Variance on Critical Path: 2.444
Standard Deviation   :   1.563

Critical Path =   1-A   5-E   6-F   8-H   10-J

P R O B A B I L I T Y   A N A L Y S I S

T'	=	Project Due Date	:	38
TE	=	Expected Completion Time	:	36.333
E||	=	Variance on Critical Path	:	2.444
$\overline{\text{E} \| \|}$	=	Standard Deviation	:	1.563
Z	=	(T' - TE) / $\overline{\| \text{E} \| \|}$	:	1.066

Probability of Completion by Due Date   :   0.857

Estimated Project Due Date =   38

414

b) The probability that the project will take more than 38 weeks is 1 - 0.857 or 14.3%.

c) Path A-E-G-H-J has an expected duration of 10+10+3+5+5.33 = 33.33 days. The standard deviation of the duration of this path is found by adding the standard deviations of the durations of these activities. The standard deviation of the duration of a task is given by

$$\frac{\text{pessimistic time - optimistic time}}{6}$$

For path A-E-G-H-J we get

$$\frac{12-8}{6} + \frac{12-8}{6} + \frac{5-1}{6} + \frac{8-2}{6} + \frac{8-4}{6} = \frac{22}{6} = 2.2 \text{ days}$$

The probability that this path will exceed the expected project duration of 38 days is

$$1 - Pr(X \leq 38) = 1 - Pr(Z \leq \frac{38-33.33}{2.2}) = 0.017$$

Problem 20.
CMOM gives the following output for this problem.

Solution

Activity		Start	Finish	Expected Time	Slack	Critical Path
1-A	Earliest:	0	7.167	7.167	31.833	no
	Latest:	31.833	39			
2-B	Earliest:	0	18.167	18.167	0	yes
	Latest:	0	18.167			
3-C	Earliest:	18.167	27.167	9	0	yes
	Latest:	18.167	27.167			
4-D	Earliest:	27.167	39	11.833	0	yes
	Latest:	27.167	39			
5-E	Earliest:	27.167	30.167	3	16	no
	Latest:	43.167	46.167			
6-F	Earliest:	39	44.167	5.167	2	no
	Latest:	41	46.167			
7-G	Earliest:	39	43.167	4.167	0	yes
	Latest:	39	43.167			
8-H	Earliest:	43.167	46.167	3	0	yes
	Latest:	43.167	46.167			
9-I	Earliest:	39	41	2	8.333	no
	Latest:	47.333	49.333			
10-J	Earliest:	46.167	49.333	3.167	0	yes
	Latest:	46.167	49.333			

415

11-K	Earliest:	30.167	32.167	2	17.167	no
	Latest:	47.333	49.333			
12-L	Earliest:	18.167	21	2.833	28.333	no
	Latest:	46.500	49.333			
13-M	Earliest:	7.167	9.167	2	43.167	no
	Latest:	50.333	52.333			
14-N	Earliest:	49.333	52.333	3	0	yes
	Latest:	49.333	52.333			
15-O	Earliest:	52.333	54.333	2	0	yes
	Latest:	52.333	54.333			

a)

Project Summary

Expected Completion Time :   54.333
Variance on Critical Path: 8
Standard Deviation   :   2.828

b) Critical Path =   2-B   3-C   4-D   7-G   8-H   10-J
                                 14-N   15-O

c)   P R O B A B I L I T Y   A N A L Y S I S

T' =   Project Due Date   :   55
T_E =   Expected Completion Time   :   54.333
$E||$ =   Variance on Critical Path   :   8

$|\overline{E||}|$ =   Standard Deviation   :   2.828

Z = $(T' - T_E) / |\overline{E||}|$:   0.236

Probability of Completion by Due Date   :   0.594
Estimated Project Due Date =   55

         P R O B A B I L I T Y   A N A L Y S I S

T' =   Project Due Date   :   60
T_E =   Expected Completion Time   :   54.333
$E||$ =   Variance on Critical Path   :   8

$|\overline{E||}|$ =   Standard Deviation   :   2.828

Z = $(T' - T_E) / |\overline{E||}|$:   2.003

Probability of Completion by Due Date   :   0.594
Estimated Project Due Date =   60

d) If task F is delayed by 1 week, the critical path is not delayed at all because task F has 2 weeks of slack. If it is delayed by three weeks, then the critical path is affected.

416

Problem 21.

a)

CMOM - Project Planning & Control
Crashing

Data Entered

activity			# pred	--predecessor activity numbers--	
1-A	Normal Time	4	0		
	Normal Cost	200			
	Crash Time	3			
	Crash Cost	300			
2-B	Normal Time	6	1	1-A	
	Normal Cost	500			
	Crash Time	4			
	Crash Cost	1300			
3-C	Normal Time	8	1	1-A	
	Normal Cost	800			
	Crash Time	6			
	Crash Cost	2000			
4-D	Normal Time	3	1	2-B	
	Normal Cost	100			
	Crash Time	3			
	Crash Cost	200			
5-E	Normal Time	4	1	4-D	
	Normal Cost	200			
	Crash Time	3			
	Crash Cost	550			
6-F	Normal Time	5	1	3-C	
	Normal Cost	400			
	Crash Time	3			
	Crash Cost	1200			
7-G	Normal Time	15	2	5-E	6-F
	Normal Cost	1000			
	Crash Time	10			
	Crash Cost	4500			
8-H	Normal Time	5	1	7-G	
	Normal Cost	600			
	Crash Time	4			
	Crash Cost	1400			
9-I	Normal Time	3	1	8-H	
	Normal Cost	300			
	Crash Time	2			
	Crash Cost	700			

Solution

Activity		Start	Finish	Expected Time	Slack	Critical Path
1-A	Earliest:	0	4	4	0	yes
	Latest:	0	4			

417

Activity		Start	Finish	Expected Time	Slack	Critical Path
2-B	Earliest:	4	10	6	0	yes
	Latest:	4	10			
3-C	Earliest:	4	12	8	0	yes
	Latest:	4	12			
4-D	Earliest:	10	13	3	0	yes
	Latest:	10	13			
5-E	Earliest:	13	17	4	0	yes
	Latest:	13	17			
6-F	Earliest:	12	17	5	0	yes
	Latest:	12	17			
7-G	Earliest:	17	32	15	0	yes
	Latest:	17	32			
8-H	Earliest:	32	37	5	0	yes
	Latest:	32	37			
9-I	Earliest:	37	40	3	0	yes
	Latest:	37	40			

Project Summary

```
Expected Completion Time :      40
Total Project Cost       :    4100
Cost on Critical Path    :    4100
```

Critical Path =	1-A	2-B	3-C	4-D	5-E	6-F
	7-G	8-H	9-I			

C R A S H I N G   A N A L Y S I S

```
Project Completion Time (Normal)        :   40
Project Completion Time (Minimum)       :   29
Project Due Date (Crash)                :   39
Project Cost (Normal)                   : 4100
Added Cost for Crash Due Date           :  100
Penalty for exceeding 36 month mark     : 3000
Estimated Project Due Date =   39       : 7200

Total Cost
```

C R A S H I N G   A N A L Y S I S

```
Project Completion Time (Normal)        :   40
Project Completion Time (Minimum)       :   29
Project Due Date (Crash)                :   38
Project Cost (Normal)                   :4100
Added Cost for Crash Due Date           :  500
Penalty for exceeding 36 month mark     : 2000
Estimated Project Due Date =   38

Total Cost                                6600
```

```
               C R A S H I N G    A N A L Y S I S

Project Completion Time (Normal)       :   40
Project Completion Time (Minimum)      :   29
Project Due Date (Crash)               :   37
Project Cost (Normal)                  : 4100
Added Cost for Crash Due Date          : 1200
Penalty for exceeding 36 month mark    : 1000
Estimated Project Due Date =    37

Total Cost                             : 6300


               C R A S H I N G    A N A L Y S I S

Project Completion Time (Normal)       :   40
Project Completion Time (Minimum)      :   29
Project Due Date (Crash)               :   36
Project Cost (Normal)                  :4100
Added Cost for Crash Due Date          : 1900
Penalty for exceeding 36 month mark    :    0
Estimated Project Due Date =    36

Total Cost                             : 6000


               C R A S H I N G    A N A L Y S I S

Project Completion Time (Normal)       :   40
Project Completion Time (Minimum)      :   29
Project Due Date (Crash)               :   35
Project Cost (Normal)                  :4100
Added Cost for Crash Due Date          : 2600
Bonus for Early Completion             :  250
Estimated Project Due Date =    35

Total Cost                             : 6450


               C R A S H I N G    A N A L Y S I S

Project Completion Time (Normal)       :   40
Project Completion Time (Minimum)      :   29
Project Due Date (Crash)               :   34
Project Cost (Normal)                  :4100
Added Cost for Crash Due Date          : 3300
Bonus for Early Completion             :  500
Estimated Project Due Date =    34

Total Cost                             : 6900


               C R A S H I N G    A N A L Y S I S

Project Completion Time (Normal)       :   40
Project Completion Time (Minimum)      :   29
Project Due Date (Crash)               :   33
Project Cost (Normal)                  :4100
Added Cost for Crash Due Date          : 4000
Bonus for Early Completion             :  750
Estimated Project Due Date =    33

Total Cost                             : 7350
```

```
                C R A S H I N G      A N A L Y S I S

        Project Completion Time (Normal)         :   40
        Project Completion Time (Minimum)        :   29
        Project Due Date (Crash)                 :   32
        Project Cost (Normal)                    :4100
        Added Cost for Crash Due Date            :  4750
        Bonus for Early Completion               :  1000
        Estimated Project Due Date =      32

        Total Cost                               :  7750


                C R A S H I N G      A N A L Y S I S

        Project Completion Time (Normal)         :   40
        Project Completion Time (Minimum)        :   29
        Project Due Date (Crash)                 :   31
        Project Cost (Normal)                    :4100
        Added Cost for Crash Due Date            :  5550
        Bonus for Early Completion               :  1250
        Estimated Project Due Date =      31

        Total Cost                               :  8400


                C R A S H I N G      A N A L Y S I S

        Project Completion Time (Normal)         :   40
        Project Completion Time (Minimum)        :   29
        Project Due Date (Crash)                 :   30
        Project Cost (Normal)                    :4100
        Added Cost for Crash Due Date            :  6350
        Bonus for Early Completion               :  1500
        Estimated Project Due Date =      30

        Total Cost                               :  8950


                C R A S H I N G      A N A L Y S I S

        Project Completion Time (Normal)         :   40
        Project Completion Time (Minimum)        :   29
        Project Due Date (Crash)                 :   29
        Project Cost (Normal)                    :4100
        Added Cost for Crash Due Date            :  7350
        Bonus for Early Completion               :  1750
        Estimated Project Due Date =      29

        Total Cost                               :  9700
```

a) From the above crashing analysis, we see that the best plan that minimizes total cost ($6 million) is to get the project done on time, by the 36th month.